FUNDAMENTALS OF PSYCHOLOGY

Audrey Haber
University of California, Los Angeles

Richard P. Runyon
C. W. Post College of Long Island University

Addison-Wesley Publishing Company

Reading, Massachusetts
Menlo Park, California • London • Don Mills, Ontario

Photo research and special features by Joan Labby.

ISBN 0-201-02674-0
ABCDEFGHIJ-DO-7987654

PREFACE

We are living during one of the most critical and challenging periods in the history of mankind. Mushrooming population combined with almost insatiable demands for higher and higher material living standards are threatening to exhaust many of our vital natural resources—energy, minerals, food, and water are on the verge of becoming luxuries. It is increasingly apparent that all men cannot hope to achieve the standard of living that now prevails in the United States. Yet there is unrest even among those who enjoy the comforts of life. We see around us an ever growing disenchantment with technology, an awareness that deep psychological satisfactions do not come with the material gains that technology has wrought. What is the answer? The next great frontier is not going to be the outer space of distant stars and planets, but rather the inner space of man himself. We must turn increasingly to the insights of the behavioral sciences—particularly to psychology—in our efforts to cope with the rapid, almost chaotic change that appears to be the order of the day.

Psychology is a vibrant science, living, breathing, and ever growing. Although its roots are in the distant past, it has flourished in the twentieth century. In short, psychology is the science of today, concerned with and dealing with the problems of today.

Recognizing the key role that psychology is playing in the contemporary affairs of man, more and more students are attracted to the study of psychology. Some will become psychology majors. For the majority, however, this course will be their only formal exposure to the scientific principles of behavior. It is in this light that we have written this text. We have attempted to present the most recent and exciting work of psychologists without ignoring the classics, drawing many of our examples from everyday real-life experiences. We have avoided some of the abstract and esoteric subjects that the psychology major will eventually be exposed to as he pursues his study of psychology. In short, we have attempted to communicate the flavor of the field in a light, straightforward manner which we hope will make the material easy to digest. On the other hand, we have sought to lay a foundation for the more advanced study of behavior by those wishing to pursue a major in the field. Thus, we have attempted to produce an interesting, highly readable introduction to psychology while maintaining the integrity of the underlying scientific principles.

We have tried to make the student's task a bit easier by supplying him with some tools to assist in the learning process. For example, at the end of each chapter is a "mini-glossary" in which important terms to remember are defined. For the student wishing to pursue more detailed study of a given area, we have provided an annotated list of recommended readings. Interspersed throughout the book are essays that relate psychological principles to important contemporary issues. In addition, many students will find the accompanying workbook an invaluable aid to learning through its programmed reviews, practice quizzes, and active participation sections. The workbook also contains a comprehensive glossary and an appendix on statistical analysis. We hope that the students who use this book will enjoy reading it as much as we enjoyed writing it.

A textbook is always a collaborative effort by many people, from the researchers and professionals who provide the basic input of scientific information, to the members of the production staff who assemble the bits and pieces into an organic whole.

Specifically, we should like to give special thanks to our many colleagues who, at various points along the way, read the manuscript and provided many useful insights and criticisms. Although our manuscript has been immeasurably enriched by their thoughtful and conscientious comments, we take full responsibility for the final version: Isabel H. Beck, Santa Barbara City College; Richard Brislin, Western Washington State College; Sheldon S. Brown, North Shore Community College; John H. Doolittle, California State University, Sacramento; Jonathan C. Finkelstein, University of Maryland, Baltimore County; Irene M. Hulicka, State University of New York College at Buffalo; Wendell Jeffrey, University of California, Los Angeles; Richard M. Lerner, Eastern Michigan University; Jon E. Roeckelein, Mesa Community College; George C. Rogers, Jr., Massachusetts Bay

Community College; Jerry S. Wiggins, University of British Columbia.

Any book of this sort requires a prodigious amount of library research. We are greatly indebted to Pamela Reese for her indefatigable work in this area.

Many people have provided creative input to this book. We should like to express our appreciation to Liz Muller for much of the photography. In addition, a host of people at Addison-Wesley made enormous contributions to the project.

Working frequently from a hodgepodge of scrawled notes, various typists accomplished the herculean feat of transcribing them into a readable manuscript. Among these were Sally Brenner, Rosemary Kopzynski, and Mabel Perham.

Finally, without the constant encouragement and support of our spouses, Jerry Jassenoff and Lois Runyon, this book would still be in the "talking stage."

Los Angeles, California   A. H.
Greenvale, L. I., New York   R. P. R.
November 1973

CONTENTS

Psychology Issues/B. Ethical Implications of Psychological Knowledge

Bay State Inmates Fear Brain Surgery, Chemical Mind-Control, by Jean Dietz, from *The Boston Globe*

Ethical Considerations: Electrical Manipulation of the Psyche, by José M. R. Delgado

The Real and Urgent Problems of Science and Ethics, an interview by Ira Mothner, with Willard Gaylin

Dedicated to
Laurie Beth Jassenoff,
Maribeth, Tommy, Nancy, and Richie Runyon,
and Amy Gaiennie

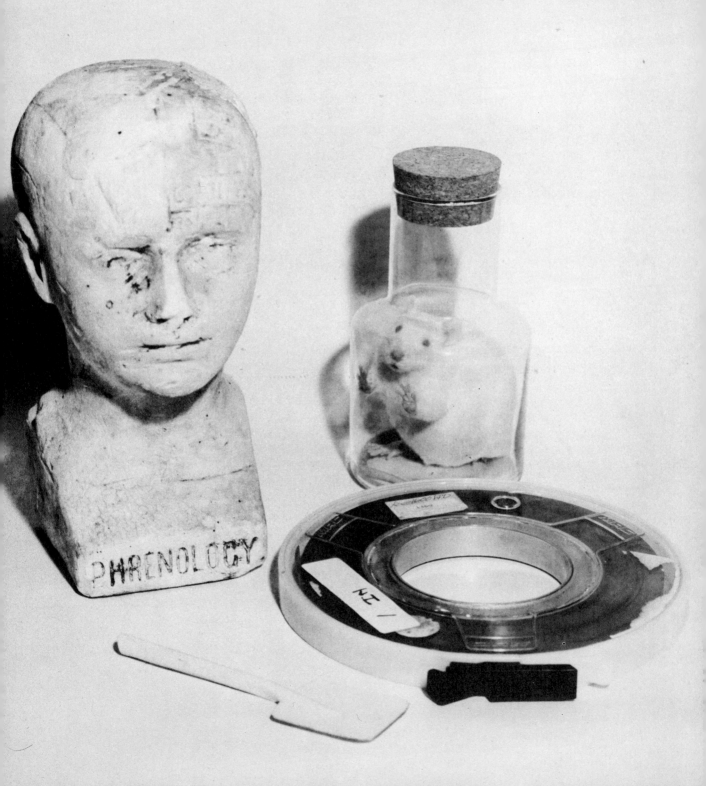

1
WHAT IS PSYCHOLOGY?

What is psychology?

Objectivity — Systematic observation

Psychology: a long past, but a short history

The many faces of psychology

Clinical and counseling psychologists
Developmental and social psychologists
Experimental psychologists

Methods of psychology

Naturalistic observation — Case history method
Survey method — Experimental method

An application of the methods of psychology

Naturalistic observation — Case history method
Survey method — Experimental method

What Is Psychology?

How often have you heard someone claim that he is a "good psychologist"? Have you ever made this claim? Have you ever "used psychology" or "psyched someone out"? Perhaps you have described someone's problems as "psychological"?

It is virtually impossible to pick up a newspaper or magazine nowadays without coming across some claim to psychological insight, or some reference to an individual who is a "good psychologist," as demonstrated by his sales ability, acumen in human relations, insight into personal problems, and so forth. In addition, newspapers and magazines frequently carry articles that deal with psychological phenomena such as personality, emotional problems, drug use and abuse, racism, violence, and sexuality.

Many people feel that they have some special knowledge of psychology, whether they have studied it or not. It is interesting that this claim is rarely, if ever, made about other scientific fields. How often have you heard anybody who has not studied extensively in the field claim to be a "good biologist," or to "use" chemistry or physics? It is quite natural for people to feel that they have a certain degree of expertise in psychology. After all, everybody has had to grow and interact with other people. In the course of everyday living, we all make observations of ourselves and of other people, frequently allowing these observations to flavor our relationships. For example, we may recognize that a certain acquaintance has a "short fuse" and temper our relationship with him accordingly. Or we may become so sensitive to a friend's pressing problems that we willingly spend hours of our time quietly listening to him "bare his chest." Examples of this sort could be cited almost without limit. The truth of the matter is that we are constantly making decisions based on our expectations and suppositions about other people. Is this psychology?

What is psychology? Psychology is defined as the science of behavior. Let us pause for a moment and reflect on the implications of this definition. What do we mean by behavior?

Is sleeping behavior? Is reading this book behavior? What about thinking, daydreaming, going to the movies, driving a car, attending a lecture, smoking a "joint," "shooting speed"? The answer to all of these questions is "Yes"; these things are all

a) b)

c) d)

examples of behavior. And, as you can see, not only is behavior a very comprehensive term, but it is impossible for a living organism not to be "behaving" (Fig 1.1). Even when asleep, an organism is behaving. As you read this textbook, you are behaving. We, as authors, are especially interested in this last behavior. Our textbook presents the fundamental principles of behavior, and we are concerned with one specific aspect of your behavior as you read the book: your achieving an understanding of these fundamentals.

Fig. 1.1
Awake or asleep, we are always behaving. (a, Jeff Albertson—Stock, Boston. b, Ellis Herwig—Stock, Boston. c, Dan O'Neill—Editorial Photocolor Archives. d, Lucinda Fleeson—Stock, Boston.)

What Is Psychology?

Clearly, the basic subject matter of psychology, behavior, is of vital concern to all of us. It is perhaps because of this that psychology has become a household word. But the mere fact that we attach the word psychology to what we do, does not confer any special significance upon our actions, nor does it make us psychologists. Many of us are quite competent to drive a car and maneuver it through heavy traffic, snow, sleet, and rain. Does this mean that we understand the car? The true depth of our understanding may be revealed with shocking suddenness the moment the car breaks down and we are forced to call a serviceman. Likewise, we may become aware of our own limitations as "psychologists" only when our lives, or the lives of others, suddenly become disordered. This does not mean that psychologists are concerned only with "breakdowns"; indeed, much of their interest is directed toward understanding the smooth, integrated functioning of the intact organism.

Two characteristics of the professional psychologist's approach to the study of behavior distinguish it from the casual observations of the layman. The psychologist's method of inquiry is both *objective* and *systematic.*

Objectivity

When the layman observes behavior, he tends to inject his own personal biases into any observations he makes. He sees the world through eyes that are colored by his likes and dislikes, and by the beliefs, attitudes, and motivations that he has developed through a lifetime of experiences. What is more, he tends to make value judgments about the things he observes. Thus, if he sees a child pull the tail of a cat, he is likely to describe the child's behavior with such terms as bad, cruel, sadistic, or brutal. A psychologist, outside his professional role, might be tempted to apply the same descriptive labels. In the role of a scientist, however, his foremost objective is to *understand* the child's behavior. He realizes that prejudgments are likely to blind him to other possible explanations. For example, the child may merely have been trying to pick the cat up, and the cat's tail may have provided the most accessible, or convenient, "handle." Or the child may simply not have developed the rather advanced concept of "inflicting pain." The tail-pulling episode may represent nothing more than the child's indomitable curiosity about the world.

The psychologist recognizes the need to stand back from the behavior he studies, to make carefully planned observations calmly and dispassionately, and to consider various alternatives. We speak of these characteristics as objectivity. Objectivity does not imply that the psychologist lacks interest in or concern about the subject matter of his science. Rather, objectivity assures him that his findings may be repeated, and thus verified, by other scientists at other times and places.

Systematic Observation

Perhaps the characteristic that most clearly distinguishes the observations of the scientist from those of the layman is the *way* in which the scientist makes his observations. Whereas the nonscientist is typically casual about his observations, the professional investigator is systematic—he plans and prepares his investigations well in advance of carrying them out, and he strives to control the conditions under which he makes his observations. Let's look at an example.

Suppose we are interested in determining both the extent of marijuana use and the way it affects ongoing behavior. The chances are that the layman's approach to this problem would be significantly different from the trained observer's. For example, if the nonscientist happened to note that most of his friends smoke marijuana on occasion, he might conclude that "Practically everybody smokes it." Moreover, in attempting to ascertain the effects of marijuana, he might ask several of his friends to describe their "high": "What does it feel like when you are stoned?" "Do you notice any changes in your behavior?" "Do you find you have difficulty concentrating?"

On the other hand, the scientist who wishes to obtain information about the extent and effect of marijuana use might begin by carefully delineating the behaviors he is interested in observing, and then working out systematic ways of collecting relevant information. He might sit in on groups of people who are smoking marijuana and make carefully recorded observations of such things as changes in verbal behavior and alterations in social interactions. He might study, in depth, the backgrounds of a number of marijuana users to see if there are any factors in their histories that might account for their use of marijuana or that would explain certain behavioral effects. He might interview large numbers of individuals and ask them the same questions, in order to determine such things as the incidence and frequency of use. When conducting studies of this sort, the scientist usually assures the anonymity of the respondents so that the responses are more likely to be honest.

The most precise method the scientist has evolved for making observations is the experiment. If he wants to know the effect that marijuana has on certain psychological processes, he might study an individual's behavior in a prearranged experimental setting. For example, if he is interested in the effects of marijuana on driving, he might observe how his subjects drive before and after smoking.

Later in this chapter we shall take a closer look at the various methods used by psychologists in their quest for a scientific understanding of behavior. First, let's take a glimpse into the past and see how psychology evolved into the science it is today, and look at the many faces of psychology as it appears on the present scene.

Psychology: A Long Past, But a Short History

Psychology has been described as a science with a long past, but a short history. This means that ever since man became a separate species, he has been concerned with problems that are psychological in nature; but the systematic study of behavior and the controlled laboratory observations characteristic of the other sciences, developed only in the late nineteenth century. Prior to that time, psychology was largely in the domain of philosophy. Behavior was viewed only in the context of some philosophical position, usually one derived from a religious point of view that included certain assumptions about the goodness or evil of human nature. It did not matter if these conclusions were inconsistent with everyday observations. The philosophers asked, "What is the fundamental nature of man?" They did not ask how individual people behave and why they do what they do, except from the lofty and detached heights of philosophical speculation.

The physical sciences have a somewhat similar past: philosophical assumptions about the basic nature of the universe determined the way earlier scientists characterized physical reality. However, during the Renaissance, a period of great advances in art and science, scientists began to develop striking theories about the world based, not on philosophical tradition but, rather, on systematic observations of the world and of the interactions among events in physical reality. This was when the physical sciences threw off the shackles of philosophical speculation. The contrast between the old philosophical approach and the new scientific approach is well illustrated in the following excerpt from the writings of Sir Francis Bacon (1561–1626):

> In the year of our Lord 1432, there arose a grievous quarrel among the brethren over the number of teeth in the mouth of a horse. For 13 days the disputation raged without ceasing. All the ancient books and chronicles were fetched out, and wonderful and ponderous erudition, such as was never before heard of in this region, was made manifest. At the beginning of the 14th day, a youthful friar of goodly bearing asked his learned superiors for permission to add a word, and straightway, to the wonderment of the disputants, whose deep wisdom he sore vexed, he beseeched them to unbend in a manner coarse and unheard-of, and to look in the open mouth of a horse and find answer to their questionings. At this, their dignity being grievously hurt, they waxed exceedingly wroth; and, joining in a mighty uproar, they flew upon him and smote him hip and thigh, and cast him out forthwith. For, said they, surely Satan hath tempted this bold neophyte to declare unholy and unheard-of ways of finding truth contrary to all the teachings of the fathers. After many days more of grievous strife the dove of peace sat on the assembly, and they as one man, declaring the problem to be an everlasting mystery because of a grievous dearth of historical and theological evidence thereof, so ordered the same writ down.

With the liberation of physical science from philosophical restraints, many philosophers began to question their own approach to the understanding of man. Philosophers were greatly impressed with the tremendous insights provided by looking at experience. As a result, a new school of philosophy called *empiricism* (meaning based on experience), emerged. The empirical philosophers maintained that man might best be understood by *observing* man and his behavior. One of the great philosophers of that period, John Locke (1632–1704), suggested that there is no basic human nature, that our minds at birth are a *tabula rasa,* a "blank slate," and that all that is written on it will be written by experience. Thus, if you know the individual's experiences, you understand the individual. This position did not lead, however, to any truly systematic observations of man under controlled conditions. It led, by and large, to a great deal of armchair speculation, mostly based on casual observations.

In the mid-1800's a number of investigators were working in areas closely related to, and later integrated into, psychology. These investigators studied the way we see and hear the world, providing us with empirically obtained descriptions of the relationship between sights and sounds and our reception of them.

The year 1879 is generally accepted as the birthdate of modern psychology. This was the year Wilhem Wundt (1832–1920) established the first laboratory for the scientific study of psychology (in Leipzig, Germany). Wundt was trained in physiology, physics, and philosophy. His definition of psychology —as the science of conscious experience—was quite different from the one we use today. His idea was that you could take some object in the physical world, present it to a trained observer, and have him describe the basic fundamental elements of his conscious experience. For example, if you presented a red ball, he could say, "I see redness, I feel weight, I see roundness." This method of looking within one's conscious experience is known as *introspection.* Once you are able to analyze the conscious compound (in this case a red ball) into its basic elements (redness, weight, roundness), you can investigate the laws that bind these elements together into complex conscious experiences. Wundt maintained that developing a science of conscious experience is no different from formulating a science of physical reality. Once you have found the basic building blocks of which the world is made, and have discovered the laws that hold them together, you have constructed a science of physics or chemistry. Likewise, once you have discovered the basic building blocks of conscious experience and the laws that bind them together, you will have constructed a science of conscious experience. Because of the

Fig. 1.2
Wilhelm Wundt.
(Culver Pictures.)

*What Is
Psychology?*

emphasis on structure, Wundt's position became known as *structuralism*.

One of Wundt's American students, William James (1842–1910), expanded psychology well beyond Wundt's original conceptions. James wrote an extremely influential two-volume treatise entitled *The Principles of Psychology* (1890) in which he extended the study of psychology to include more than just conscious experience. He delved into such phenomena as learning, motivation, emotions, as well as many other areas that interest psychologists today. His work was the beginning of a departure from the narrow structuralist point of view.

By the early twentieth century the scope of psychology had been radically altered to include the study of lower animals, learning, motivation, and abnormal behavior. As long as psychology was defined as the science of conscious experience, it had remained relatively static. But after it had been redefined as the science of behavior, it dramatically expanded its scope to become the dynamic science it is today.

The redefinition of psychology as the science of behavior is usually associated with J. B. Watson (1878–1958). Noting that only the individual himself is able to observe his own conscious experiences, Watson concluded that there cannot be a science based on conscious experience, since it is *private* in nature; the science of psychology must be based on *publicly observable* events, i.e., behavior. Watson emphasized that one could expose individuals to various kinds of physical events (stimuli); one could observe the behavior of these individuals under these conditions; and one could construct a complete science of behavior without any reference to conscious experience. It is interesting that contemporary psychology, although greatly influenced by the behaviorist movement, has now found objective ways of investigating the very thing that Watson had repudiated —the mental life of the individual.

Behaviorism was not the only movement to reject Wundt's position. At the very time behaviorism was making its debut on the psychological stage, other acts were clamoring for attention. A predominantly German movement, known as the *Gestalt* school, also rejected structuralism, but for very different reasons. The Gestaltists maintained that a science of behavior cannot be developed by analyzing complex behaviors into simple parts, and

Fig. 1.5
Sigmund Freud and
his daughter Anna, 1912.
(Pictorial Parade,
Editorial Photocolor
Archives.)

then combining these parts to produce a whole. They believed, on the contrary, that behavior should be studied as organized entities rather than as discrete, independent parts. Hence the word Gestalt which, in German, means something complete, a whole, a total configuration. The Gestalt movement, as we will see (Chapter 9), has greatly influenced the study of perception.

Quite independent from the movements that were taking place in academic settings—structuralism, behaviorism, Gestalt psychology—was a theoretical school primarily concerned with understanding abnormal human behavior. Sigmund Freud (1856–1939) is regarded as the father of psychoanalysis, a movement which is at once a theory of personality, a philosophical view of human nature, and a method for treating disturbed individuals. In broad terms, psychoanalytic theory stresses unconscious determinants of behavior. Later chapters will discuss many aspects of psychoanalysis, both as a theory of personality (Chapter 13) and as a psychotherapeutic method (Chapter 14).

Present-day psychology is exceedingly complex, and is tending more and more to include many different areas of specialization. In a sense, this entire book is a description of the contemporary scene in psychology.

The Many Faces of Psychology

In order to answer the question, "What is psychology?" it will be helpful to look at what psychologists do. We have already indicated that, awake or asleep, behavior is always taking place. Wherever there is behavior, it is appropriate that a psychologist be there studying it. Different psychologists have concentrated their attention on widely varying aspects of behavior. Few people outside the field of psychology are aware of the psychologist's pervasive role in virtually every aspect of our lives.

When you brush your teeth or wash your face in the morning, the chances are that psychologists have influenced your choice of toothpaste and soap through their participation in both marketing and advertising. The design of the car you drive may very well have the imprint of a psychologist on it; for example, psychologists have thoroughly studied the arrangement of the

*What Is
Psychology?*

Fig. 1.6
Fields of specialization within psychology. (Data from Judith Cates, "Psychology's Manpower: Report on the 1968 National Register of Scientific and Technical Personnel," *American Psychologist, 25,* 1970, pp. 254–263.)

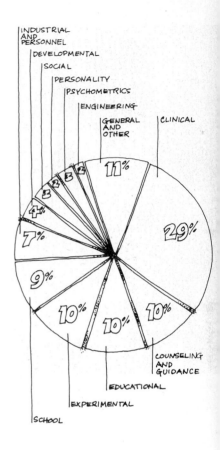

instrument panel in order to maximize driving efficiency and safety. Your admission into college as well as your choice of a major may have been based, at least in part, on tests designed by psychologists. Psychological research has influenced many aspects of educational instruction. Indeed, the very books you use, the instructional materials, and even the way the course is taught probably reflect, to some degree, the research and insights of psychologists. Occasionally, the problems and pressures of everyday life can so overwhelm us that we seek the professional assistance of a psychologist. Finally, psychology keeps its fingers on the pulse of the nation, engaging in vital research on such crucial contemporary issues as drug use and abuse, alcoholism, divorce, and violence, to name but a few.

With such a broad spectrum of interest and concern, it is not surprising that there has been a proliferation of subfields within psychology too numerous and complex to classify adequately. In Fig. 1.6 we see one effort to classify psychologists according to their own reports of their primary fields of specialization. In reading this figure, remember that only fields of specialization are shown and not places of employment. A large percentage of psychologists (approximately 56 percent) are employed full-time in educational institutions and practice their specialities within academic settings. Psychologists are also found in such disparate settings as business, industry, the military, hospitals, and private practice. Let's look at several major areas of specialization in psychology. Remember that although we discuss them separately, there is much overlap within and between fields.

Clinical and Counseling Psychologists

Clinical and counseling psychologists make up almost 50 percent of the specialists in the field. Although a number are in private practice exclusively, most clinical psychologists work in an institutional setting and are involved in the diagnosis, assessment, and treatment of emotionally disturbed individuals. In this connection they work closely with such allied health and social professions as medicine and social work.

Although it is impossible to draw a fine line between clinical and counseling psychology, counseling psychologists typically work with normal people, focusing on minor adjustment problems

The Many Faces of Psychology

or on vocational and educational guidance. Counseling psychologists must be able to recognize individuals with deep-seated emotional problems and to refer them to the appropriate clinical agencies.

People outside the field frequently confuse clinical psychologists, psychiatrists, and psychoanalysts. Although all three types of specialists are involved in the treatment and assessment of human emotional problems, they differ in a number of ways. The clinical psychologist usually has a Ph.D. degree and has had specialized training in psychology and in research methodology. Since he is not a medical doctor, he cannot prescribe medicines or practice surgery. He can, however, refer patients for medical diagnosis.

The psychiatrist first obtains his M.D. degree and then pursues specialized training in psychiatry. He may, or may not, be well grounded in psychology and research methodology. Since he is a medical doctor, he may prescribe medicines and practice surgery or refer patients for surgery.

The psychoanalyst bases his approach to treatment of the emotionally disturbed on psychoanalytic theories. In the past, a psychoanalyst has had to have a medical degree; however, many clinical psychologists have received extensive training in psychoanalysis and are regarded as psychoanalysts, even without the M.D. degree.

Developmental and Social Psychologists

Developmental psychologists study the behavior and behavioral changes of the individual from the prenatal period through maturity and old age. The developmental psychologist is interested in describing the ways in which the child gradually develops adult ways of thinking, feeling, and interacting with both the physical and the social environment. He tries to formulate general principles of intellectual, emotional, motivational, and perceptual growth, and to relate these general principles to an understanding of the individual child. It is only through the study of developmental psychology that we can fully comprehend the subtleties and complexities of adult behavior.

Social psychologists are concerned with the individual's interactions with groups, and the ways in which groups influence his feelings, attitudes, and beliefs. They seek to understand the dynamics of many of our current social problems, such as prejudice and mob behavior.

Both developmental and social psychology are burgeoning fields of endeavor and they are contributing many valuable insights that are having a great impact on the broader field of psychology.

Experimental Psychologists

Experimental psychologists usually work in an academic setting, where they conduct laboratory research in addition to teaching. Their activities include a broad range of phenomena, in both animal and human subjects. Many of the basic principles of behavior appearing in this text have been formulated in the laboratories of the experimental psychologist. Some experimental psychologists focus on the learning process (learning theorists); others on the relationship between organic processes and behavior (physiological psychologists); and yet others have directed their attention to comparing the behaviors of a variety of organisms (comparative psychologists).

Methods of Psychology

Regardless of the area of specialization, all psychologists have one thing in common: they all strive to understand behavior. Their methods for studying behavior have evolved over a long period of time in response to man's almost insatiable desire to predict and control those forces that shape his destiny.

The first attempts to understand behavior were speculative and abstract. The idea of using scientific methods involving controlled observation stemmed largely from the successes enjoyed by the physical and biological sciences. However, it is not always easy to apply these methods to psychological phenomena, since it is difficult to be objective about ourselves and about others. This problem, perhaps more than any other, has delayed the emergence and acceptance of psychology as a bona fide science. Nevertheless, psychology has developed a number of techniques for studying behavior. Let's examine a few of these methods.

Naturalistic Observation

Naturalistic or field studies involve careful observations of behavior in a natural setting. Although there is usually no attempt to systematically manipulate the situation, this form of observation is by no means casual. Much prior thought must be devoted to such questions as: What behaviors shall I study? How shall I record the observations? What are the characteristics or features of the situation in which I shall do the observing? Naturalistic observation has been employed in the study of both animal and human behavior. Since the subject is usually unaware of the observer (or the observer is made as unobtrusive as possible), we may assume that his behavior is not affected by the presence of the observer.

Notable success has been achieved with this method in the study of animals and insects in their natural environments. The results of these observations have often contradicted popular beliefs. For example, do you believe that the gorilla is a hostile, aggressive, combative animal? This commonly held conception is contrary to evidence compiled from observations of the mountain gorilla in its natural habitat:

> My technique of habituating the gorillas was simple but essential, for I could only obtain unbiased data on their behavior if they remained relatively unaffected by my presence. I usually attempted to approach the group undetected to within about 150 feet before climbing slowly and in full view of the animals onto a stump or the low branch of a tree where I settled myself as comfortably as possible without paying obvious attention to them. By choosing a prominent observation post not only was I able to see the gorillas over the screen of herbs, but, reciprocally, they could inspect me clearly, which was the most important single factor in habituating the animals. Under such circumstances they usually remained in the vicinity to watch me, and even approached me to within 5 feet. I found it remarkably easy to establish rapport with the gorillas. This process was greatly facilitated by the placid temperament of the animals, and by certain conditions which I imposed on myself: (a) I carried no firearms which might inbue my actions with unconscious aggressiveness; (b) I moved slowly, and used binoculars and cameras sparingly at the beginning to eliminate gestures which could be interpreted as threat;

(c) I nearly always approached them alone, leaving any companions behind and out of sight at the point where the animals were first noted; (d) I wore the same drab olive-green clothes every day; and (e) I almost never tracked the gorillas after they had voluntarily moved out of range. This last point was, I believe, of special value, for at no time were they subjected to pursuit, an action which could easily frighten them as well as increase the chance of attacks. By adhering to my conditions I not only habituated six groups to my presence quite well but also was never attacked, even though I inadvertently stumbled into the middle of a group or nearly collided with animals several times.

(Schaller, 1963, pp. 22–23)

One of the outstanding examples of the use of this method with humans is found in the work of Arnold Gesell (1940). Utilizing one-way vision screens, Gesell and his associates observed preschool children in various naturally occurring

Fig. 1.7
Jane van Lawick-Goodall has been observing chimpanzees "at home" in the Gombe Stream Chimpanzee Reserve in Tanzania since 1960. She and her staff have been careful not to disrupt the chimps' lives, nor their habitat. Her husband Hugo van Lawick is keeping a careful photographic record. (From Jane van Lawick-Goodall, *In the Shadow of Man*, Houghton Mifflin Company, 1971. By permission of the publishers.)

Methods of Psychology

activities (for example, play). On the basis of these observations, they outlined schedules of development, specifying the ages at which various functions and activities (grasping, sitting up, walking, and so on) normally occur.

Naturalistic observation is a valuable tool through which we gain information and insights about the behavior of organisms in their natural settings. Moreover, in the course of these observations the investigator develops hunches as to which factors are of critical importance and which may largely be ignored. Indeed, he may develop certain hypotheses, or informed guesses, that he will later subject to systematic investigation in the laboratory.

Case History Method

Often situations arise that require knowledge of the past history of an individual or groups of individuals in order to understand present behavior. This method is commonly employed by clinical psychologists to gain insight into a patient's present problems. The following excerpt illustrates the use of the case history method in clinical practice:

> The patient was the oldest of seven children. For the first five years of her life she had been the only child, indulged and overprotected by her mother. Then came the second child, a girl, and the patient was abruptly cut off from the fondling, petting, praise and attention which had formerly been hers. Later in childhood, the younger sister consistently excelled her in school and made friends more easily than she. In adolescence the sister enjoyed pretty clothes, dancing and the company of boys, which the patient herself characterized as "having a good time in a wicked way." Throughout her life, the patient compared herself unfavorably with her sister, calling herself "dumb," shy and "old-maidish." She had few boy friends, went to college dances alone, and was always critical of any young man who came to call on her. Her fantasies and dreams, however, centered around love affairs, marriage and child-bearing. Her younger sister became engaged and then married six months before the patient came to the clinic—the time at which . . . the patient began her voracious eating.
>
> (Cameron and Magaret, 1951, p. 39)

Survey Method

The survey method is commonly employed when the investigators wish to obtain information from a large number of people in a relatively short period of time. Typically, a set of questions is prepared and attitudes, feelings, or opinions on some issue are obtained through the use of mail, telephone, or direct interview. These questions are constructed with great care so as not to bias the outcome of the survey. For example, there is a great deal of difference between these two questions: "Are you in agreement with the political philosophy of John Doe?" and "Do you agree with the radical left-wing stance of John Doe?" A good survey will avoid questions like the latter.

We are all familiar with public opinion surveys such as those conducted by Gallup and by Harris. The results of these polls are regularly reported in newspapers and popular magazines. They provide valuable insights into how segments of the public feel about various current issues, and inform us of the extent to which the public engages in certain practices. By repeating surveys at different times, it is possible to see how attitudes, opinions, beliefs, and practices change over time. For example, a Gallup poll taken in 1971 reported that 42 percent of college students polled had used marijuana. If we contrast this finding with the results of a survey taken four years earlier, reporting that only 5 percent of college students had used marijuana, we see evidence of a marked increase in marijuana use, at least among college students. Some typical survey questions, and the results obtained, are shown in Box 1.1 on the following page.

Experimental Method

Many of you have undoubtedly seen various devices advertised in the newspaper or in your favorite magazine that promise to teach, while you sleep, a foreign language, the principles of economics, or some other subject. Since the learning process is so frequently laborious and there are many times when you would rather spend your afternoon and evening hours at activities other than study, the temptation to invest in a "sleep-learning machine" can become quite great. But before committing a substantial sum of money to this enterprise, you would like to know if there is any

Society— Institutions and Restraints	YOUTH			PARENTS		
	Total Youth	College Youth	Non-college Youth	Total Parents	Parents College Youth	Parents Noncollege Youth
21. A. Which of the following activities do you feel are *morally wrong* from your personal point of view, and which do you feel are *not a moral issue?*	**Having an abortion**					
	Morally wrong 58%	36%	64%	62%	50%	66%
	Not a moral issue 40	63	35	36	48	33
	Relations between consenting homosexuals					
	Morally wrong 66	42	72	75	63	79
	Not a moral issue 33	57	27	22	35	19
	Pre-marital sexual relations					
	Morally wrong 53	34	57	85	74	88
	Not a moral issue 46	64	41	14	25	11
	Extra-marital sexual relations					
	Morally wrong 77	77	77	91	90	92
	Not a moral issue 21	22	21	7	9	7
B. Which of these activities do you think your parent (of same sex) would feel are *morally wrong*, and which do you think he would feel are *not a moral issue?*	**Having an abortion**			NOT ASKED OF PARENTS		
	Morally wrong 75	65	78			
	Not a moral issue 19	32	16			
	Relations between consenting homosexuals					
	Morally wrong 84	74	87			
	Not a moral issue 11	23	8			
	Pre-marital sexual relations					
	Morally wrong 85	80	86			
	Not a moral issue 10	17	8			
	Extra-marital sexual relations					
	Morally wrong 88	91	88			
	Not a moral issue 7	6	7			
C. Under which of the following conditions would you approve of abortion:				NOT ASKED OF PARENTS		
	Recommended by a physician 77	83	76			
	Pregnancy as the result of rape 64	79	60			
	Failure of birth control practices in marriage 14	30	10			
	Pre-marital pregnancy 21	42	16			
	Under no conditions 13	8	15			

Box 1.1
Part of a lengthy survey on the generation gap prepared and conducted for CBS News in March and April, 1969. (Reprinted from *Public Opinion,* R. R. Bowker, New York, 1972, by permission of the Columbia Broadcasting System, Inc. Copyright © 1972 by Columbia Broadcasting System, Inc.)

truth to the advertising claim: "Now you can learn while you sleep." If it is possible to learn during sleep and if the gains are substantial, you might reason, "A few hundred dollars spent on a sleep-learning device would be a worthwhile investment which, if spread over a lifetime of learning, would amount to less than the proverbial few pennies a day."

The question whether or not learning occurs during sleep seems easy enough to answer by conducting a simple experiment: present unfamiliar learning materials to a subject while he is asleep and then test him, after he is awake, to see whether he has learned anything.

This is precisely what was done in early investigations of sleep-learning. The results of these studies supported the view that learning can, in fact, occur during sleep. However, two investigators (Simon and Emmons, 1956) regarded these findings with a healthy, scientific skepticism. They raised such penetrating questions as: How can we be certain that the subjects were asleep? Is it possible that the subjects were awake at least part of the time and that the learning observed in prior studies had actually occurred during periods of wakefulness?

Questions such as these go directly to the heart of psychology as a science. As we shall see throughout this text, much of what we study in psychology is not directly observed, but must be inferred from various sources of evidence. We study motivation, but motivation is not directly observed. We do not see hunger, thirst, or a "desire to learn." Rather, we infer these states from several lines of evidence, including the behavior of the organism. Similarly, we do not directly observe learning; we infer it from changes in behavior.

But what about sleep? Surely sleep is directly observed and unambiguous. A person is either asleep or not asleep. If you are lying quietly in bed, with your eyes closed and your breathing rhythmic and even, it seems reasonable to assume that you are asleep. But think for a moment. When you retire at night, isn't there a period of time when you lie quietly with your eyes closed but still remain alert, responsive to external sounds and smells? You may even have noted a brief interval during which you are in the transition period between wakefulness and sleep. If someone asks you a question during this period, you will still be able to respond, albeit drowsily. A few moments later, the question may go unanswered.

Because of an inability to define sleep unambiguously, the early sleep studies were inconclusive. To obtain a definitive answer to the question, "Are we able to learn during sleep?" we must first be able to state clearly what we mean by sleep and then show how its presence or absence can be ascertained. Fortunately, as is often the case in science, a seemingly unrelated development in another field came to the rescue by providing a tool that enabled us to define sleep and ascertain whether or not a person is asleep. Engineering advances in electronic circuitry made it possible to amplify the minute electrical impulses, or "brain waves," that are constantly produced by the brain, whether we are awake or asleep. We shall have more to say about these brain waves in Chapter 2. For the moment, it is sufficient to note that they allow us to determine whether a person is really asleep and also how deeply a person is sleeping. A device called an electroencephalograph (or EEG) can measure these brain waves, and enables us to define the stages of sleep in terms of the types of brain waves produced. Such a definition is known as an *operational definition*: the term or concept is defined by the way it is measured. Thus, sleep is defined in terms of certain types of brain waves observed on the EEG. You are already familiar with some common measurements which are operationally defined; an inch and an ounce, for example, are operationally defined in terms of a platinum rod and a weight housed in the National Bureau of Standards.

Having arrived at a satisfactory basis for confirming that someone is asleep, it is now necessary to define and measure learning. In the Simon and Emmons sleep study, the subjects were given 96 questions at the outset of the study. These questions were then repeated on a tape recorder, with answers, while the subjects were supposedly asleep. If subsequent testing showed improved scores, the researchers assumed that learning had occurred.

The results of the study were quite conclusive. Analysis of the EEG records revealed that the subjects did not sleep uninterruptedly throughout the night. There were occasional periods of wakefulness. What is of particular interest is the fact that the subjects learned about 80 percent of the material that was presented during the waking periods. In contrast, there was no evidence that learning took place when the EEG records indicated sleep. It appears safe to conclude from this study that learning does not take place during sleep; it occurs only during the waking portions of the sleep cycle. The advertisement which promises to teach you while you sleep may be right for the wrong reason: it may, indeed, teach you, but only if it succeeds in disturbing your sleep sufficiently to keep you awake!

We have gone to some pains to present this case history illustrating the use of the experimental method. Unlike the other methods we have discussed, the experimental method permits us to control the variables that affect behavior. A *variable* is a characteristic or phenomenon that may take on different values. For example, in the experiment discussed above, both the level of sleep and the scores on the learning task are variables, since both may take on different values. Many variables affect behavior at any given time. The experimental method permits us to systematically study a single variable at a time (in this case, level of sleep) to determine what effect it has on observed behavior (learning scores).

The variable that is examined to determine its effects on behavior is called the *independent variable.* The behavior that is being observed and measured is known as the *dependent variable.* In the example cited above, the level of sleep is the independent variable, and learning score is the dependent variable.

The independent variable is usually some aspect of the environment that can be manipulated, such as intensity of light, number of practice trials in a learning task, or dosage level of a drug. The independent variable can also be a naturally occurring characteristic of the organism, such as sleep levels, sex, or age. We refer to these naturally occurring characteristics as *organismic variables.* The dependent variable, however, is always some measurable aspect of behavior.

Clearly, variables other than the independent variable under investigation may also affect behavior (the dependent variable). For example, prior experience, external noises, motivation, and level of intelligence are all *extraneous variables* that might affect the dependent measure (learning scores in the sleep study). Since we are interested in the effects of only one variable (level of sleep), it is vital that we control the effects of these extraneous variables. This is often accomplished by using at least two groups of subjects that are comparable with respect to the extraneous

Box 1.2
(From *Psychological Research: An Introduction*, 2nd ed., by Arthur J. Bachrach. Copyright © 1962 by Random House, Inc. Reprinted by permission of the publisher.)

People don't usually do research the way people who write books about research say that people do research. . . . In short, books about research (to mix a metaphor) are white tie and tails, research itself is a pair of blue jeans . . .

Let me give you a personal example. . . . In research some of my associates and I were doing on verbal behavior in human subjects, we were looking for some sort of reinforcer to use as a reward for speaking. Our subjects were equipped with individual microphones and we were studying the verbal patterns of individuals and of these same individuals in group interaction. They were paid by the hour for this. But it seemed to us, as we were sitting around talking about the experiment, that this was not an adequate reward for our purposes inasmuch as it did not matter how much or how loud the subject spoke during

the session. He received the same amount no matter how much he talked. So we wondered what would happen if we tried to get him to speak louder or faster by rewarding him for such verbalization. Recognizing that money is a very good reward in our culture, we decided that it would be a fine idea to see what would happen if we paid the subject in money as he was speaking, so that each impulse spoken into the microphone would be rewarded. What would happen if we paid him by the spoken impulse? We thought that a coin dropping into a chute each time he spoke above a certain amplitude would be a good reinforcer to produce and maintain such behavior.

But then we started counting up the number of such impulses during an hour session and found that there would be several hundred. It would be

variable, and by conducting the experiment under the same laboratory conditions for all subjects. Only this way can we attribute any observed changes in learning scores to the stage of sleep at which the learning material was presented.

An Application of the Methods of Psychology

Now that we have discussed some of the methods employed in studying behavior, let's look at a concrete application of these methods to a specific problem.

financially impossible to use coins unless we were to use pennies. In the course of this informal discussion, it was decided that pennies are not really very good rewards in our culture because of an informal test which everyone has experienced. Even a $25,000-a-year executive is likely to stoop down and pick up a nickel if he sees it, but is likely to pass a penny by. There seems to be more than five times the rewarding value of a penny on a nickel. So the minimum successful financial reward in the form of a coin would probably be a nickel. This would become so expensive as a reward in such an experiment that if we did use the nickel the chances are the experimenters would try to change places with the subject!

Someone suggested that we might try using poker chips which the subjects could exchange for money at the end of the session. In this way they would be working for a symbolic monetary reward, which is very strongly reinforced in our culture. We talked about the meaning of poker chips and the images that poker chips conjured up in the minds of various people in a group. Stacks of poker chips in front of a gambler in a smoke-filled room and the various dramatic associations of poker chips in the folklore of our culture were discussed. Of course there was a lot of joking about this and someone wanted to know if we would have to wear green eyeshades and roll up our sleeves and put garters on them, whether we would have to use a round table for the experiment with a green felt cloth over it and so on, invoking the humor of the gambling situation. We finally decided to use chips.

The above account is merely a capsule record of the many hours of discussion on an informal level which went on during this particular part of the experiment. When the paper was finally written up for publication in professional journals, it merely reported that "because of the generalized reinforcing nature of poker chips, they were used as a reinforcement for verbal behavior as a substitute for monetary reward (but symbolic of such secondary monetary reinforcement) and to be exchanged for money." Nothing about the green eyeshade, the green felt cloth, the sleeve-garters, the smoke-filled room—remarks which would be inappropriate for a scientfic paper.

Imagine that you are a director of rehabilitation at a large medical facility. Each year you receive several patients who have been blinded as a result of industrial accidents. Rehabilitating such individuals is exceedingly difficult, particularly because of the pervasive sense of helplessness they feel after being deprived of sight. You think, "If there were only some way to remove that feeling of helplessness, the process of rehabilitation might be advanced." You have heard that people born blind frequently show an extraordinary ability to move about in their dark world and somehow avoid obstacles that lie in their path. You begin to

An Application of the Methods of Psychology

wonder how they accomplish this feat, and ask yourself whether their techniques might be taught to people who lost their sight as a result of an accident. Put your book down for a few moments and consider how you would go about determining how blind people are able to avoid obstacles in their paths. Then, continue reading the text and compare your approach to the one scientists take.

Naturalistic Observation

The scientist does not accept common belief at face value. A necessary and desirable skepticism underlies his approach to all problems. A scientist would not ask, "How are blind people able to avoid obstacles in their paths?" Instead he would eliminate the word "how" from the question, and ask, "Are blind people able to avoid obstacles in their paths?"

The scientist's first approach to this problem might involve careful observation of blind people in their natural settings. On the basis of these observations, he would note that blind people do consistently avoid obstacles in their paths. Even in naturalistic observations, the investigator may occasionally modify some aspect of the environment in order to test a hunch or hypothesis. For example, he might place unfamiliar obstacles in the paths of blind people. After repeated observations of their success in avoiding even these obstacles, he would probably be ready to conclude that they do, in fact, possess this ability. Note that the investigator has not explained *how* blind people are able to avoid obstacles, but merely *that* they are able to do so.

ontological rather than teleological

Case History Method

The scientist might have approached this problem by studying case histories of people who were blind at birth as well as those blinded later in life. If these studies consistently revealed that the ability to avoid obstacles improved with experience, he might begin to suspect that learning is involved. The following is an excerpt from a case history of a young man who was blind throughout his life and was suddenly thrust into an unfamiliar situation:

When John J. first came to the university, he was completely dependent on others for support and guidance. He literally had to be led from place to place. One day his friends decided to withdraw this constant support and supervision— they were determined that John "stand on his own two feet." They walked John around various parts of the campus, urging him to memorize the directions and numbers of steps between points. In time, John became extremely proficient in moving unaided throughout the entire campus. The remarkable thing about John's accomplishment was that, once he achieved a degree of independence, he was able to successfully avoid collisions even when unfamiliar obstacles appeared in his path.

Survey Method

The investigator might possibly gain some insight into the way blind people avoid obstacles by interviewing them. Such a survey was, in fact, conducted in 1923. Soldiers blinded in the war were asked about the ways in which they avoided obstacles. The results were as follows: 25 percent of them thought that they detected obstacles by the ear; 25 percent by the sense of touch; and 50 percent by a combination of the two senses

Although the survey method does not establish cause-and-effect relationships, it may generate fruitful ideas for more systematic investigation. The results obtained from this survey revealed that blind people felt that they were avoiding obstacles by using their other senses. These results provided the hypotheses for the experimental studies summarized below.

Experimental Method

The experimental method permits us to systematically evaluate the effects of selected variables on some dependent measure. The question, "How are blind people able to avoid obstacles in their paths?" was, in fact, answered through an experimental approach (Supa et al., 1944).

In a series of experiments, blind people were systematically deprived of the use of touch, smell, taste, and hearing, and were then tested for their ability to avoid obstacles. Hearing, for example, was blocked by having the subjects wear earplugs. The

An Application
of the Methods
of Psychology

deprivation of each sense separately and in succession constituted the independent variable, and the measure of obstacle avoidance was the dependent variable. The results of the study were illuminating. Only when the subjects were deprived of the sense of hearing were they unable to avoid obstacles.

Further experimentation established the precise mechanism. When blind subjects walked on a carpeted floor in their stocking feet so that no sounds were created by their walking movements, their ability to avoid obstacles was seriously impaired. Thus, it was concluded that blind people avoid obstacles on the basis of echoes from their own footsteps.

Although this method of avoiding obstacles in a dark world could not be considered normal behavior in sighted humans, research has established that a number of animal species use echoes as a primary means of avoiding obstacles or locating food. The bat, for example, emits a steady stream of high pitched tones which echo off solid surfaces. The reception of these echoes permits the bat to avoid large objects. Using a similar mechanism, porpoises are able to go directly to food even though the water may be too cloudy to permit direct sighting.

These studies on the avoidance of obstacles by both human subjects and lower animals illustrate how psychologists, through the use of scientific methods, were able to reach very meaningful conclusions (with significant practical consequences) about this one aspect of behavior. These conclusions did not necessarily correspond to "common sense."

Summary

1. Psychology is defined as the science of behavior. Behavior refers to everything we do.

2. The psychologist's method of inquiry is both objective and systematic.

3. Psychology emerged as a science relatively recently in the history of man. Prior to that time, psychology was largely in the domain of philosophy. In the mid-1800's, studies concerned largely with man's sensory capabilities paved the way for the scientific study of man.

4. In 1879, Wilhelm Wundt established the first laboratory for the scientific study of psychology. Wundt's position, called structuralism, defined psychology as the science of conscious experience. Employing the method of introspection, Wundt tried to discover the basic building blocks of conscious experiences and the laws that bind these elements together into complex experiences.

5. William James expanded the definition of psychology to include more than conscious experience; he delved into such phenomena as learning, motivation, and emotions.

6. J. B. Watson objected to the private nature of conscious experiences and contended that psychology must deal with publicly observable events. He therefore redefined psychology as the science of behavior. The school Watson founded is known as behaviorism.

7. The Gestalt school of psychology objected to both structuralism and behaviorism, maintaining that complex behavior cannot be analyzed into simple parts and recombined to produce a meaningful whole.

8. Sigmund Freud developed psychoanalysis, which was at once a theory of personality, a philosophical view of human nature, and a method for treating disturbed individuals. Psychoanalytic theory stresses unconscious determinants of behavior.

9. Many fields and subfields of specialization have developed in psychology. There are three main areas of specialization: (1)

clinical and counseling psychology, (2) developmental and social psychology, and (3) experimental psychology.

10. The methods of psychology include naturalistic observation, the case history method, the survey method, and the experimental method.

11. Since most of what psychologists study cannot be directly observed, it must be inferred from what can be measured. In the typical experimental study, an independent variable is manipulated in order to see how it affects behavior. The independent variable is often some aspect of the environment.

12. Many variables other than the independent variable may affect behavior. The effects of these extraneous variables are usually controlled by dividing the subjects into at least two groups that are comparable with respect to the extraneous variables and that differ only with respect to the independent variable.

Terms to Remember

Behavior   In the most general sense, anything an organism does.

Behaviorism   A school of psychology (associated with Watson) which maintains that psychologists should study only what is observable—behavior, not conscious experience.

Case History Method   Data assembled about the past history of an individual or group in order to understand present behavior.

Clinical Psychologist   A psychologist who is involved in diagnosis, assessment, and treatment of emotionally disturbed individuals.

Counseling Psychologist   A psychologist who focuses on minor adjustment problems or assists in vocational and educational guidance. Counseling psychologists typically work with people whose problems are less serious and less deep-rooted than those treated by clinical psychologists.

Dependent Variable   Behavior that is being observed and measured and that depends on changes in the independent variable.

Developmental Psychologist   A psychologist who studies the behavior and behavioral changes of the individual from the prenatal period through maturity and old age.

Empiricists   Theorists who maintain that behavior is determined by experience and that man can best be understood by *observing* him and his behavior.

Experiment   A scientific method in which the experimenter systematically studies a single variable at a time (the independent variable) so that he may attribute the observed changes in behavior (the dependent variable) to that independent variable.

Experimental Psychologist   A psychologist involved in the experimental investigation of psychological phenomena.

Extraneous variables   Variables other than the independent variable under investigation that may affect behavior (the dependent variable).

Gestalt Psychology   A school of psychology that emphasizes studying behavior as organized wholes rather than as discrete, independent parts.

Independent Variable   A variable that is examined in order to determine its effects on behavior (the dependent variable).

Introspection   Method of looking within and describing one's conscious experience.

Naturalistic Observation   A scientific method which involves careful observations of behavior in a natural setting.

Objectivity   One of the characteristics of the professional psychologist's approach to the study of behavior; studying behavior without allowing personal prejudices and opinions to affect one's judgment.

Operational Definition   A definition of terms or concepts by the way in which they are measured.

Organismic Variable   Some naturally occurring characteristic of the organism, such as sleep levels, age, or sex.

Psychiatrist   A medical doctor who has received specialized training in treating emotional disturbances.

Terms to Remember

Psychoanalysis   A school of psychology (associated with Sigmund Freud) primarily concerned with the study of abnormal behavior. Psychoanalytic theory stresses unconscious determinants of behavior.

Psychoanalyst   A psychologist or psychiatrist who bases his approach to treatment of the emotionally disturbed on psychoanalytic theories.

Psychology   The science of behavior.

Social Psychologist   A psychologist who studies the individual's interactions with groups, and the ways in which groups influence his feelings, attitudes, and beliefs.

Structuralism   A school of psychology (associated with Wilhelm Wundt) that emphasized the structure of conscious experience.

Survey Method   A method of collecting data through the use of interviews and questionnaires.

Systematic Observation   Planning and preparing well in advance and controlling the conditions under which observations are made.

Tabula Rasa   A "blank slate"; a term used to describe the theory which maintains that the baby's mind at birth is blank and all that appears upon it is written by experience.

Variable   A characteristic or phenomenon that may take on different values.

Recommended Readings

American Psychological Association, *A Career in Psychology*, Washington, D.C.: American Psychological Association, 1970.

A pamphlet which describes the major basic and applied fields of psychology plus information about requirements for becoming a psychologist.

Boring, E., *A History of Experimental Psychology* (2nd ed.), New York.: Appleton-Century-Crofts, 1950.

Comprehensive description of the early history of experimental psychology.

Clark, K. E., and Miller, G. A. (Eds.), *Psychology: Behavioral and Social Science Survey*, Englewood Cliffs, N.J.: Prentice-Hall, Inc., 1970.

A short and authoritative guide to the field of psychology, its present facilities, and its prospects for future growth.

Deese, J., *Psychology as Science and Art*, New York: Harcourt Brace Jovanovich, Inc., 1972.

A brief overview of the attitudes, methods, and approaches of contemporary psychology.

Doherty, M. W., and Shemberg, K. M., *Asking Questions About Behavior: An Introduction to What Psychologists Do*, Glenview, Illinois: Scott, Foresman and Co., 1970.

This short paperback introduces the requirements of scientific research by dealing with questions that concern the student.

Murphy, G., and Kovach, J. K., *Historical Introduction to Modern Psychology* (3rd ed.), New York: Harcourt Brace Jovanovich, Inc., 1972.

Up-to-date presentation of the development of modern psychology; the evolution of research and theory and important figures and schools.

Scott, W., and Wertheimer, M., *Introduction to Psychological Research*, New York: John Wiley & Sons, Inc., 1962.

Chapters 1 and 2 contain good discussions of the process involved in the development of research ideas.

Watson, R. I., *The Great Psychologists: From Aristotle to Freud* (3rd ed.), Philadelphia: J. B. Lippincott Co., 1971.

Comprehensive description of the leading figures in the development of psychology as a science.

2
PHYSIOLOGICAL FOUNDATIONS OF BEHAVIOR

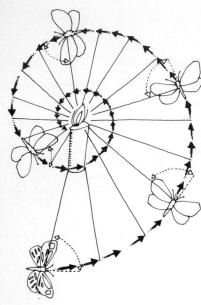

Fig. 2.1
The moth and the flame

The so-called suicidal tendency of a moth to fly directly into a light source has a simple scientific explanation. Under normal circumstances, the moth uses light from the sun or the moon to guide its flight. It is able to maintain a straight course by flying so that the light of these distant sources always strikes its eye at the same angle. The moth only encounters difficulty when it attempts to use a nearby light source as its guide. In the illustration above, the moth pursues a course in which the light of the candle always strikes its eye at a given angle. However, because the light source is so close, the moth flies in a decreasing spiral to its death.

Physiological Foundations of Behavior

Have you ever attempted to read out-of-doors on a summer night only to find your peace of mind disturbed by an endless array of uninvited guests bombarding your light source? You might have wondered why these winged creatures are so inexorably drawn to the light. The behavior of moths, for example, appears to be senseless and almost suicidal—they constantly batter their frail bodies against light bulbs or fly directly into candle flames. Why?

Let's speculate for a moment on some possible explanations for this apparently meaningless behavior. We might hypothesize that light attracts moths, and accept this as an adequate explanation. But, if you think about this "explanation" for a moment, you will realize that it is really not very satisfactory. All that we have done is describe their behavior. In effect we are saying that they behave that way *because* they behave that way.

If a physiological psychologist were to become interested in this problem, he would attempt to relate the observed behavior to the way in which the organism is put together. In other words, the physiological psychologist would look for some correspondence between the structure of the moth and the way it behaves. If he could determine how the moth is constructed, he might find a clue to its behavior.

Scientists have studied the structure of the moth, and they now understand why the moth flies toward light. They found that a moth automatically orients itself toward the light so that the illumination always strikes its eye at a given angle (see Fig. 2.1).

Success in understanding such relatively simple behaviors has encouraged physiological psychologists to probe ever more deeply into the mysteries of behavior. What are the physiological mechanisms by which learning occurs? Why does forgetting take place? To what extent do abnormal behaviors result from imbalances in body chemistry? These are but a few of the questions that physiological psychologists are now exploring. Even though there is much we do not yet know about the physiological mechanisms underlying behavior, scientists in this field have already made some exciting and significant breakthroughs.

We have defined psychology as the science of behavior. Most of this text will be concerned with the fundamental principles of observable behavior. However, the organism has a structure, and this structure is intimately related to how it responds to its environment, both external and internal. In order to understand many aspects of behavior, it is important to know something about the physiological processes that go on inside our bodies.

The Nervous System

A woman is driving her car. She is deeply engrossed in conversation with a friend. Her favorite song is playing softly over the car radio. She checks traffic moving in both directions, and then passes a slow-moving vehicle. Suddenly a dog runs in front of the car. Although the woman is being assailed by an almost endless variety of stimuli, she somehow manages instantly to depress the brake, swerve into another lane, avoid the dog, and escape a collision with other vehicles. It is almost miraculous, if you stop to think about it, that the woman was able to integrate information coming from so many different sources and translate this information into a coordinated series of responses. Minor miracles of this sort occur every moment of our lives. At this very moment you are looking at black marks against a white background and deriving coherent meaning from them (we hope). This is, in itself, an awesome accomplishment.

How is it possible to perform these data-processing feats with such apparent ease? The clues to this mystery are found in the remarkably complex organization of the billions of elements that make up the nervous system.

There are two major subdivisions of the nervous system, the central nervous system and the peripheral nervous system. The central nervous system includes the brain and spinal cord; the peripheral nervous system consists of the afferent nerves, the efferent nerves, and the autonomic system. The autonomic system controls the smooth muscles (such as we find in the stomach and intestines) and the glands.

To understand the nervous system and its role in behavior, we must look at some of its basic units.

Basic Units of Reception, Neural Conduction, and Action

Receptors and Effectors

Imagine that you are an engineer and are given the assignment of designing a robot. Before you can undertake the many details of mechanical design, you must first decide upon the various functions you want this "organism" to perform. Since physiology is concerned with function, you might say that your first job is concerned with the "physiology" of the robot. At the outset, you decide to keep the robot very simple. Its sole task will be to move away from light. What would be required to enable the robot to perform this task?

First, you would need to develop a specialized surface that would be sensitive to the amount of incoming light: the sensory receptor. In the living organism there are many types of sensory receptors; some are sensitive to light (for example, the eyes), others to sound (for example, the ears), and still others to a wide variety of stimuli such as pressure, temperature, and odor. Chapter 9 presents a more detailed discussion of sensory processes. For the time being, it is sufficient to note that receptors usually initiate a sequence of behavior. When receptors are acted upon by stimuli to which they are "tuned," they provide information about the world external to them.

Once you have made the robot capable of light reception, you need a primitive nervous system that will carry messages from the receptor to the "muscles," and thereby permit the robot to move away from the light. The muscles and glands in living organisms are referred to as effectors. In man there are three types of muscles. The striped, or skeletal muscles are involved in voluntary motor activities such as walking, standing, and swimming. The smooth muscles control such internal organs as the stomach and the intestines. The heart muscles are unlike muscles found in any other part of the body, and control the action of that organ alone. The response of effectors permits the organism to make some sort of adjustment to its environment, either internal or external.

In this simplified example we see the three essentials of a behaving organism: a receptor that is "tuned" to some particular source of stimulation, electrical circuits to carry messages to the

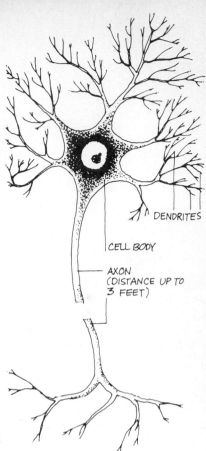

DENDRITES

CELL BODY

AXON
(DISTANCE UP TO
3 FEET)

muscles, and a motor system to move the robot away from light sources. The basic units for the transmission of these messages in animals are the individual nerve cells, or neurons.

The Neuron

The neuron itself, were it a human invention, would be a remarkable engineering accomplishment. Each of our 10 billion neurons is a miniature information-processing center, capable of receiving thousands of messages and, in a fraction of a second, sorting and acting upon them.

Neurons vary greatly in size and appearance. Some are fairly long; others are but a fraction of an inch in length. The neuron is a living cell consisting of a cell body and two types of nerve fibers, an axon and dendrites. *Dendrites* are hairlike structures which function as the "receivers." They receive messages and carry them toward their own cell body. The *axon* is a long fiber which extends from the cell body and functions as the "transmitter." It carries messages away from the cell body toward other elements of the nervous system. Thus, neurons are *directional* in their operation, and as we will see, so is the entire nervous system.

The main parts of a neuron are depicted in Fig. 2.2.

The three classes of neurons

Although neurons may be classified in many ways, a convenient and useful distinction is the following:

1. Afferent neurons. These are sometimes called sensory neurons because they transmit messages from the sense organs (eyes, ears, skin) *toward* the central nervous system (spinal cord and brain).

2. Efferent neurons. These are sometimes called motor neurons because they transmit messages *from* the central nervous system to the motor organs (effectors).

3. Association neurons. These neurons are generally within the central nervous system. They may transmit messages to other association neurons, but they also serve as connectors between afferent and efferent neurons; hence the term association.

Basic Units

The Neural Impulse

The "message" we have been referring to is actually electrochemical in nature. Each neuron can generate and hold small electrochemical charges. When stimulated, it releases or, just as important, does not release this charge. A popular misconception is that neural impulses travel at the same speed as electrical current. As a matter of fact, the maximum rate of conduction of the neural impulse is about 125 meters per second whereas electric current may travel as rapidly as 300 million meters per second.

Not all stimulation that comes to the dendrites causes an electrochemical reaction within the neuron. There is a certain intensity of stimulation below which the neuron will not fire. This minimum intensity necessary to activate a neuron is known as the *threshold of excitability.* Whenever this threshold is reached or exceeded, the neuron will transmit an electrochemical impulse. Surprisingly, the neuron fires at full charge no matter how intense the stimulation, so long as it is above the threshold. An analogous situation is a fuse in a firecracker. The fuse requires a certain intensity of fire to start it burning. As long as the fire is hot enough the fuse will burn exactly the same, whether it is ignited by a match or by an acetylene torch. This characteristic of neural condition is known as the *all-or-none law.*

Given the all-or-none law, how can we explain the fact that a single neuron can distinguish between stimuli of different intensities? The answer is provided by the number of impulses the neuron will transmit in a given time period. Let's see how this works. After the neuron fires, there is a short period of time—known as the *absolute refractory period*—during which it will not fire again, regardless of the intensity of the stimulation. Following this, there is another brief interval—the *relative refractory period*—during which the neuron will fire, but only if the stimulation is more intense than is usually required. The more frequent occurrence of impulses under strong stimulation is illustrated in Fig. 2.3.

The Synapse

How does an impulse get from one neuron to another? There are no direct connections, electrical or otherwise, between neurons. The axon of one neuron is separated from the dendrites of an

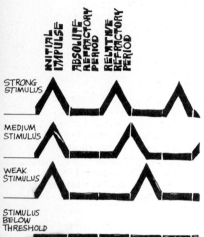

Fig. 2.3
The characteristics of neural impulses in a single neuron under four different levels of stimulation

Note that the neuron fires at full charge as long as the stimulation is above the threshold. No discharge occurs during the absolute refractory period. However, firing can occur during the relative refractory period if the stimulus is sufficiently strong. The strong stimulation causes the neuron to fire more often in a given period of time.

Physiological Foundations of Behavior

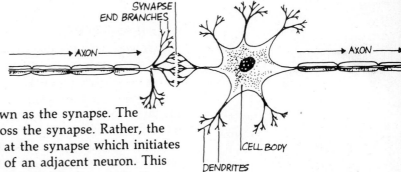

Fig. 2.4
The synapse

When one neuron is activated, an electrical impulse moves along the axon. A transmitter chemical is released at the end branches which, in turn, initiates an electrical impulse in the dendrites of an adjacent neuron. The arrows show the direction of the impulse.

adjacent neuron by a small gap known as the synapse. The electrical impulse does not jump across the synapse. Rather, the axon releases a transmitter chemical at the synapse which initiates an electrical impulse in the dendrite of an adjacent neuron. This means that the nervous impulse can travel only from axon to dendrite, and not in the reverse direction. Figure 2.4 shows the synaptic connection between two neurons.

It is interesting that the transmitter chemical at the synapse is very similar in composition to the well-known psychedelic drug LSD. Some scientists have speculated that LSD produces its bizarre visual and auditory experiences by connecting axons to dendrites in a more or less random fashion rather than by the normal pathways.

Not all synaptic connections are excitatory; some inhibit the transmission of impulses. Inhibitory synapses are as important as excitatory ones; without them our higher brain centers would be virtually inundated with useless information.

The activity of the neural elements of the nervous system is not as simple as we have depicted in this brief outline. Hundreds of axons may converge upon the dendrites of a single neuron at any given time, resulting in complex interconnections and interactions. Indeed, it is estimated that there are as many as 500 trillion synaptic connections in the nervous system of a person. However, there are a number of relatively simple responses that occur automatically in the presence of certain types of stimulation. These *reflexes,* as they are called, occur when the nervous system functions much as a switchboard, connecting receptors and effectors.

The Reflex Arc

Imagine that you are at a cocktail party and, in the course of conversation, you accidentally touch the lit end of a cigarette. Your response is immediate. Without thinking about what you are doing, you automatically pull your hand away. Only after you

Basic Units

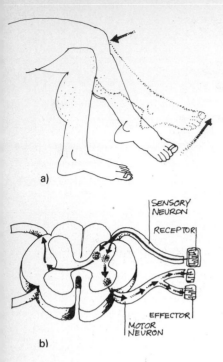

a)

b)

Fig. 2.5
Reflex arc

Many reflexes such as the knee jerk reflex shown in (a) involve association neurons in the spinal cord as links between sensory and motor neurons. Thus, the reflex occurs automatically and does not involve higher brain centers. In (b) we see the typical neural pathways involved in a reflex arc. When the receptor is activated, an impulse travels along a sensory neuron to the spinal cord. In the spinal cord a synaptic connection is made between the sensory and association neurons. The impulse is then transmitted to the motor neuron, which causes the muscle to contract. Synaptic connections may also be made between sensory neurons and association neurons which carry the impulse to brain centers.

Physiological
Foundations
of Behavior

make the response do you become aware of the cause for your withdrawal. This example illustrates the simplest form of integrated response, the reflex arc. Figure 2.5 shows the neural pathways involved in a typical reflex arc.

Reflex responses are inborn, automatic, and do not involve the intervention of higher brain centers. Little of our behavior is reflexive. When we read an assignment, engage in conversation, listen to the radio, or participate in an athletic event, the higher centers of the nervous system are called into play to orchestrate the incredibly complex interplay of sensory information, motor responses, and emotional reactions that comprise ongoing behavior.

Most of our reflexes are protective in nature. They shield us from the damaging effects of potentially dangerous stimulation. For example, our eyelids close automatically whenever a foreign object threatens our eyes. In popular usage, the term reflex is often erroneously applied to any behavior that appears to occur automatically, but may actually involve prior learning. Thus, when a driver instantaneously applies his brakes in an emergency, we might be tempted to classify this response as a reflex. In fact, it is not innate, and occurs "automatically" only after a great deal of prior experience.

The Central Nervous System

The Brain

Have you ever paused during the course of your daily activities to marvel over the capabilities and complexities of human behavior? Take conversation as an example. It is so much a part of our daily lives that we take it for granted. Yet, when you analyze all the activities that are required to produce conversation, you must stand in awe at the remarkable engineering feat it represents. A person speaks a sentence. Physically his words are nothing more than pulsating sound waves, which are received by the ear. Here they are transformed into electrical impulses and sent to the brain. In the brain these impulses are processed and somehow translated into coherent and

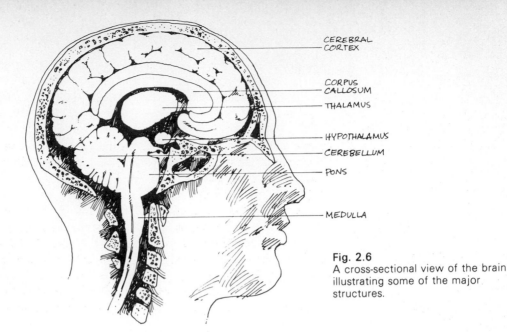

CEREBRAL CORTEX

CORPUS CALLOSUM

THALAMUS

HYPOTHALAMUS

CEREBELLUM

PONS

MEDULLA

Fig. 2.6
A cross-sectional view of the brain illustrating some of the major structures.

meaningful speech. Meanwhile, the brain is simultaneously sorting other information coming to it through the various sensory channels, suppressing some information that interferes with efficient functioning, and integrating this new information with memories stored in the brain over a lifetime.

The body may be awake or asleep, but the brain never sleeps. In addition to sorting information, it constantly regulates the many bodily functions necessary to sustain life—breathing, eating, drinking, and sleeping, to name but a few.

The human brain may be conveniently subdivided into three major divisions: the cerebral cortex, the subcortical structures, and the cerebellum. The subcortical structures include the hypothalamus, thalamus, medulla, pons, reticular activating system, and the limbic system. A cross-sectional view of the brain is shown in Fig. 2.6. Neither the reticular activating system (RAS) nor the limbic system is shown, since they are vertically oriented systems widely dispersed among the subcortical structures.

The Cerebral Cortex

A mass of convoluted, waxy-appearing nervous tissue lies atop the human brain and supervises the many activities that so clearly differentiate man from lower animals. Indeed, the cerebral cortex is almost nonexistent in lower animals, whereas it occupies 80 percent of the total volume of the human brain. Imagine folding a sheet of gray matter three feet long and two feet wide into intricate valleys and ridges. Were it not for these many convolutions, the cerebral cortex could not be contained within

The Central Nervous System

Fig. 2.8
Interhemispheric memory transfer

This spontaneous mirror writing is the work of a five-year-old girl in a New Zealand school. The lighter, correctly oriented script is the teacher's; the word order in the pupil's copy is consistently right-to-left, although some words and letters are in the normal left-to-right form. Mirror writing is evidence in favor of the hypothesis that interhemispheric memory transfers involve reversals. (Courtesy of Dr. Ivan Beale.)

Fig. 2.7
Top view of the brain

The cerebral cortex is divided into two hemispheres. Note the many convolutions and the valleys and ridges formed by these convolutions.

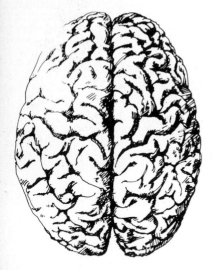

*Physiological
Foundations
of Behavior*

the skull. As we shall see, we are able to identify the various areas of the cortex by referring to the usual locations of the valleys and ridges.

The cerebral cortex is divided into two hemispheres, the *cerebral hemispheres.* These are similar in size and appearance, as you can see in the top view of the human brain shown in Fig. 2.7. The two hemispheres exchange information through connective fiber bridges known as the *corpus callosum* (see Fig. 2.6). Indeed, there is evidence that when information is transferred from one hemisphere to the other, a mirror image is produced in the other hemisphere. For example, "b" received in one hemisphere is recorded as "d" in the other. Children who tend to write and draw in mirror images (see Fig. 2.8) may suffer from interhemispheric interference (Corballis and Beale, 1971).

The split brain

Some of the most illuminating recent research in both animals and humans has involved severing the corpus callosum and other interconnecting structures. This surgical procedure, called the "split-brain" technique, eliminates communication between the left and right cerebral hemispheres. The procedure was initially introduced in the treatment of epileptics when all other medical techniques had failed. Epilepsy is characterized by a massive electrical discharge in one of the cerebral hemispheres which then spreads to the other hemispheres through the corpus callosum, resulting in a severe convulsive state. It was hoped that preventing the spread of the electrical discharge over both hemispheres of the brain would reduce the frequency and intensity of these convulsions. Following this operation many of the patients showed marked improvements. For example, one man who had been having severe convulsions for more than ten years did not have a single major convulsion during a five-year observation period subsequent to the operation (Sperry, 1968).

What is surprising is that these patients appeared to suffer no behavioral impairment as a result of the operation. Their speech, personality, and intellectual functioning apparently remained unchanged. It was only when special testing procedures were devised that subtle but dramatic effects were uncovered. The most incredible finding was that the operation had produced an individual with two independent thinking centers, almost as if there were two brains in one person.

Fig. 2.9
Apparatus employed in split-brain studies
The apparatus is employed to present visual and tactual stimuli to subjects whose cerebral hemispheres have been surgically separated. See text for an explanation.

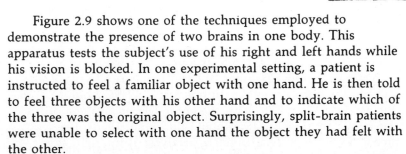

Figure 2.9 shows one of the techniques employed to demonstrate the presence of two brains in one body. This apparatus tests the subject's use of his right and left hands while his vision is blocked. In one experimental setting, a patient is instructed to feel a familiar object with one hand. He is then told to feel three objects with his other hand and to indicate which of the three was the original object. Surprisingly, split-brain patients were unable to select with one hand the object they had felt with the other.

In normal as well as split-brain subjects, stimuli presented to the left side of the body are transmitted to the right cerebral hemisphere, and vice versa. Therefore, when connections between the hemispheres are severed, the left hand literally does not know what the right hand is doing.

The Central Nervous System

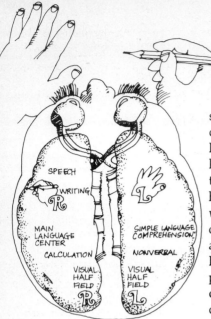

Fig. 2.10
Schematic diagram of the division of activities between the two hemispheres of the brain. Note that the dominant left hemisphere is responsible for speech, writing, and the comprehension and organization of language.

There is yet another fascinating aspect to the split-brain studies. The same apparatus shown in Fig. 2.9 can also be used to direct a visual stimulus to either the right or the left hemisphere. In right-handed people the brain center for speech and writing is located in the left hemisphere. If a picture or an object is seen to the right of center with either eye, it is transmitted to the left hemisphere, and the patient can describe, orally or in writing, what he saw. However, if a picture or object is seen to the left of center with either eye, it is transmitted to the right hemisphere, and, surprisingly, the individual cannot describe what he saw. Indeed, he will deny that he saw anything, even though he can point with his left hand to a picture or object that matches the one he was shown. Thus, although a split-brain patient cannot describe what he saw in his left visual field, he can correctly point to the object. When questioned about this apparent contradiction, he replies with comments like: "I was just guessing," or "Well, I must have done it unconsciously."

Throughout the years, many scientists have speculated about the functions of each of the cerebral hemispheres. From studies based largely on patients suffering cerebral accidents (strokes and tumors, for example), they concluded that there is a major and a minor hemisphere. The split-brain studies permitted a more precise determination of the functions of each hemisphere. In right-handed people, the left hemisphere is dominant with respect to speech and writing. As we have seen in the split-brain studies, this major, or dominant, hemisphere permits the verbal communication of experiences. The right, or minor, hemisphere is mute with respect to language; it can, however, communicate through nonverbal responses (such as pointing). Figure 2.10 outlines the division of activities between the two hemispheres.

A person can lose portions of brain tissue as a result of an accident, a tumor, or a stroke. In one case a 47-year-old right-handed man had to have the entire left hemisphere of his brain surgically removed (Smith and Burklund, 1966). The immediate results were a complete paralysis of the right side, severe impairment of speech, and loss of vision in the right half of the visual field. Follow-up studies indicated that, despite this massive loss of brain tissue, the patient showed gradual improvement in speech, reading, and writing. This case illustrates a remarkable property of the brain. When areas serving one

Physiological Foundations of Behavior

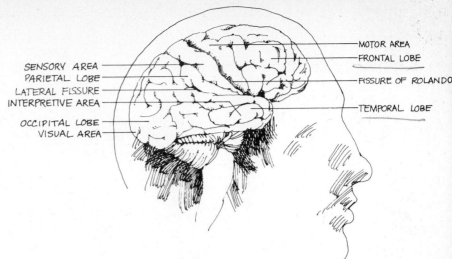

SENSORY AREA
PARIETAL LOBE
LATERAL FISSURE
INTERPRETIVE AREA
OCCIPITAL LOBE
VISUAL AREA
MOTOR AREA
FRONTAL LOBE
FISSURE OF ROLANDO
TEMPORAL LOBE

Fig. 2.11
Diagram of the areas in the cerebral hemisphere. Shown are the four lobes in each cerebral hemisphere with the various functions associated with each area.

function are destroyed, other areas of the brain can often take over the lost function.

The lobes of the brain

We have seen that the cerebral cortex is divided into two hemispheres. Each hemisphere is, in turn, divided into four lobes: *frontal, parietal, occipital,* and *temporal.* The frontal lobes, occupying the anterior portions of the brain, are separated from the parietal lobes by the *central fissure,* or *fissure of Rolando.* The temporal lobes lying below and somewhat posterior to the frontal lobes, are separated from the frontal lobes by the *lateral fissure.* The occipital lobes occupy the extreme posterior portions of the brain. There is no distinctive fissure separating the occipital lobes from the parietal and temporal lobes. Figure 2.11 is a diagram of the right cerebral hemisphere of the human brain.

Motor functions. Many scientists believe that man's precise control of his motor functions accounts partly for his superiority over other animals. Threading a needle, for instance, requires an enormous degree of motor control. So does speaking, which requires innumerable precision adjustments of facial muscles, the tongue, and the oral cavity. It is interesting that a thin strip of tissue, at the posterior portion of the frontal lobes and adjacent to the fissure of Rolando, regulates fine voluntary movements. Damage to this area, called the *motor area,* leads to the uncoordinated movements found in people with cerebral palsy.

Sensory functions. Three of our most important sensory functions are vision, hearing, and body feeling. Each of these is represented in a different lobe of the cerebral cortex (see Fig. 2.11).

The *visual area* is located in the rear portion of the occipital lobes. Our ability to discriminate fine detail is dependent on the

The Central Nervous System

capacity of the visual cortex to integrate the electrical impulses which originate in the visual receptors (the retinas of our eyes). Damage to this area impairs a person's ability to perceive visual patterns. Injuries to portions of the occipital lobe may lead to partial blindness—partial in the sense that only part of the visual field is affected. In the course of performing brain surgery, surgeons frequently introduce mild electrical stimulations in order to assess damage resulting from cerebral accidents, and to determine which functions may be impaired if certain brain tissue is surgically removed. Such stimulation of the visual area leads to a variety of visual experiences, such as flashing lights and colors.

The primary area for auditory experiences is located in the temporal lobes. Mild electrical stimulation of this area, the *auditory area,* produces an assortment of auditory experiences, such as buzzing and humming sounds.

An area devoted to body feelings is located just posterior to the fissure of Rolando, at the front portion of the parietal lobe. Stimulation of this area produces sensory experiences in which the person feels that a part of his body is being touched or moved. Persons undergoing these experiences make such comments as "My hand feels warm," or "I can feel my leg moving," even though these limbs are not being stimulated (Penfield, 1958).

Apparently other sensory systems are not so clearly represented in the cerebral cortex. For example, no area for pain has been identified. For this reason, most brain surgery is performed without a general anesthetic. Local anesthetics are used only to deaden the pain caused by penetration of the tissues outside the brain.

Associative functions. We have seen that many sensory and motor functions are well localized in the human brain. However, the identified centers account for only a small portion of the total area of the cerebral cortex. At least 75 percent of the cortex has nothing to do with sensory or motor functions (Luria, 1971). This 75 percent is referred to as the *associative cortex.* Presumably, these parts of the brain are involved in the more complex behavioral processes. For example, a young woman at a party gives her boyfriend a slight nudge just as he is about to accept a cigarette from a friend. The nudge initiates impulses which reach the body feeling area in the cortex of the boyfriend's brain. It may also

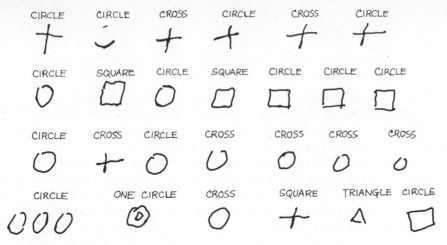

CIRCLE CIRCLE CROSS CIRCLE CROSS CIRCLE

CIRCLE SQUARE CIRCLE SQUARE CIRCLE CIRCLE CIRCLE

CIRCLE CROSS CIRCLE CROSS CROSS CROSS CROSS

CIRCLE ONE CIRCLE CROSS SQUARE TRIANGLE CIRCLE

Fig. 2.12
Lesions of frontal lobes interfere with the programming of actions and cause errors such as repetition. On each line of the illustration are drawings made by patients; printed words show what they were asked to draw. The first, second, and fourth patient had tumors of the left frontal lobe; the third patient had an abscess of the right frontal lobe. (After A. R. Luria, *The Functional Organization of the Brain.* Copyright © 1970 by Scientific American, Inc. All rights reserved.)

stimulate associations such as "Stop" or "Remember, you promised to give up smoking entirely!" because he has previous experience with his girlfriend's nudges. Memory thus adds further meaning to the initial stimulation.

The associative functions are not localized in particular areas of the brain. Rather, they seem to involve complex combinations and interconnections among various parts of the brain. Nevertheless, certain broad functions have been ascribed to associative areas in the various lobes. The frontal lobes, for example, have been of particular interest, primarily because of their relatively large size in humans and the higher vertebrates. There is evidence that the frontal lobes are involved in almost every complex behavioral process (Luria, 1971). Their major function seems to be to activate the brain and to regulate attention and concentration. Many patients who have sustained damage to the frontal lobes have difficulty expressing thoughts either orally or in writing (see Fig. 2.12).

The temporal lobes have also attracted much interest in recent years. Mild electrical stimulation of the part of the temporal lobes called the *interpretive area* (see Fig. 2.11) sometimes produces vivid experiences of past events (Penfield, 1959). These responses have occurred during brain surgery while the patient was fully conscious. There are two fascinating aspects to this behavior: the experiences are recalled in great detail, and they are abruptly terminated when the electric stimulation is turned off. Moreover, when the stimulation is reapplied to precisely the same point, the patient recounts the same experience from the beginning.

Here are some examples of patients' responses to electrical stimulation of the interpretive area: "There was a piano over

The Central Nervous System

there and someone playing. I could hear the song, you know."
"Something brings back a memory. I can see Seven-Up Bottling
Company—Harrison Bakery." "My mother is telling my brother
he has got his coat on backwards. I can just hear them."

These observations have led many scientists to suggest that
memory may be centered in the temporal lobes. However, when
this area is destroyed, some people lose their memory, but others
do not. It remains for future research to ascertain the precise role
of the temporal lobes in memory.

The Subcortical Structures

The cerebral cortex may be regarded as the master control system
of all integrated and coordinated voluntary behavior. It receives
incoming stimulation from many of the receptors, it processes and
refines this information, and it initiates and determines our bodily
responses. Below the cerebral cortex lie many tangled masses of
nerve fibers and clusters of cell bodies that control many of our
vital life-support functions, such as breathing, heart rate, and
blood pressure.

Before taking a more detailed look at several of the
subcortical structures and systems, let's take a quick overview.
The thalamus and hypothalamus (see Fig. 2.13) are located
beneath the cerebral cortex, and are characterized by *nuclei*
(clusters of nerve cells) which presumably are responsible for
diverse functions. The pons and the medulla are located near the
spinal cord. The *pons* serves as a bridge connecting various parts
of the brain, and the *medulla* plays a key role in such vital
functions as breathing and blood circulation. The reticular
activating system (RAS), a network of cells in the center of the
brain, serves to activate and arouse the higher brain centers. The
limbic system is a group of interrelated structures involved in
emotional and motivated behavior.

Among these systems and structures, the thalamus,
hypothalamus, RAS, and the limbic system have received the
most attention from investigators interested in establishing
relationships between brain function and behavior.

The thalamus

The thalamus functions mainly as a relay station, processing the
raw, untreated sensory messages from all parts of the body.

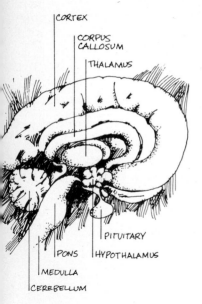

Fig. 2.13
Subcortical structures in the
human brain include the
thalamus, hypothalamus, pons,
and medulla.

*Physiological
Foundations
of Behavior*

Except for smells, nearly all sensations travel to the thalamus, where they are analyzed, sorted, and directed to appropriate areas of the cortex.

The hypothalamus

The hypothalamus, a small structure consisting of numerous nuclei, has been called the guardian of the body's well-being. When the body overheats, the hypothalamus directs blood vessels near the surface of the skin to dilate, so that more blood can pass close to the surface of the body and dissipate heat to the external environment. In this way the blood is more rapidly cooled. The hypothalamus also activates the sweat glands and controls panting behavior, both of which enable the organism to lower its body temperature. At times of stress, it initiates a series of bodily responses (including increased heart rate and augmented blood sugar) which prepare the organism for emergency reactions. The hypothalamus also plays an important role in motivated behavior such as hunger, thirst, and sex, and appears to be involved in emotional behavior. When small *lesions* (a lesion is any destruction or damage to tissue) are made in certain regions of the hypothalamus of laboratory animals, some animals are transformed into placid unemotional organisms, while others become violent and chronically savage. In humans, mild electrical stimulation of hypothalamic nuclei has produced virtually the entire spectrum of emotional reactions, from placidity to extreme terror. We shall have more to say about the functions of the hypothalamus in Chapters 7 and 8, when we consider motivation and emotion.

The reticular activating system (RAS)

The RAS is about the size of your little finger and extends vertically through several subcortical structures. It appears to control the state of alertness of the organism. The RAS receives input from the sense organs, and sends out impulses of its own to all parts of the cerebral cortex. In this way, the RAS maintains a state of arousal under conditions of sensory stimulation. When the RAS is severely damaged, the organism goes into a profound coma. Mild electric stimulation of one part of the RAS will put an animal to sleep. But the same stimulation applied to another area of the RAS will awaken the animal and immediately produce a state of arousal.

Figure 2.14 illustrates the role of the RAS in awakening a cat when external stimulation is applied.

The limbic system

The limbic system extends downward from the cerebral cortex and includes a number of subcortical structures. Three functional parts have been identified—one is involved with the sense of smell, a second is concerned with emotion and motivation, and a third has no established function.

Tiny electrodes have been implanted in certain portions of the limbic system to enable investigators to deliver mild electrical stimulation to these areas (see Fig. 2.15a, b). It may surprise you to learn that mild shock in certain parts of the limbic system is actually pleasurable. Animals will work for long periods of time to receive stimulation in these areas (Olds and Milner, 1954). In some cases, extremely hungry animals preferred to work for this stimulation than to eat (Routtenberg and Lindy, 1965). Even humans report pleasurable feelings when certain areas of the limbic system are similarly stimulated (Heath and Mickle, 1960). On the other hand, animals will work to avoid stimulation of other parts of the limbic system. In humans, stimulation of these other areas produces reactions of either rage or fear.

Fig. 2.14
Schematic representation to illustrate the role of the reticular activating system when a cat is awakened by the sound of a bell. (After J. C. French, *The Reticular Formation*. Copyright © 1957 by Scientific American, Inc. All rights reserved.)

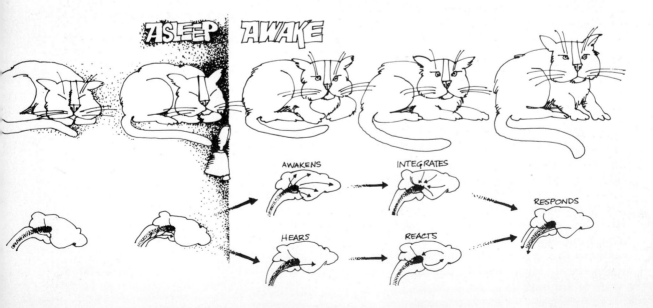

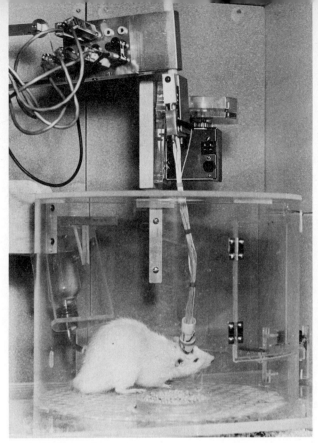

Other studies have suggested that the limbic system exerts a restraining influence on emotional behavior. Animals in which the cortex had been removed but the limbic system remained intact could be prodded and poked without arousing any apparent emotion (Bard and Mountcastle, 1947). In contrast, when lesions were made in various areas of the limbic system, some animals became extremely ferocious. More recent studies have shown that certain areas in the limbic systems serve to excite the organism, and others to calm it.

The Cerebellum

If you hold a cat several feet off the ground and drop it upside-down, it will always land on its four paws. This seemingly mysterious behavior can be attributed in part to a structure located under the rear portion of the cerebral cortex, the cerebellum (see Fig. 2.13). The cerebellum coordinates muscle movements, such as those involved in walking and swimming. When the cerebellum is damaged, an animal's ability to engage in complex coordinated movements is impaired. For example, a bird with a damaged cerebellum cannot fly, since it is unable to coordinate all the muscle systems involved in flight.

Fig. 2.15
a) In this apparatus, the rat can press a bar to deliver mild electric stimulation to its brain. So-called "pleasure" and "avoidance" areas have been identified. (Courtesy of Dr. James Olds.)
b) The man can stimulate his brain by means of a switch box at his waist. (Courtesy of Dr. Robert G. Heath.)

The Central Nervous System

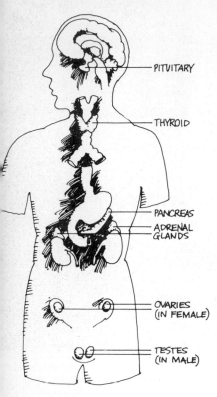

Fig. 2.16
The human endocrine system

The pituitary gland secretes hormones that regulate the functioning of the entire endocrine system. The thyroid gland regulates metabolic processes. The adrenals secrete hormones that are involved in many bodily processes, including adrenaline, which is secreted under sudden stress conditions. Blood sugar levels are controlled by the hormone insulin secreted by the pancreas. The gonads influence many aspects of sexual behavior and control the development of secondary sexual characteristics such as facial hair in males and development of breasts in females.

Physiological Foundations of Behavior

The Spinal Cord

The primary function of the spinal cord is to relay messages back and forth between the brain and other parts of the body, except for the head region. It carries data from sense organs to the brain and relays commands from the brain to the glands and muscles. The spinal cord is also involved in many of the reflex actions we have previously described (for example, the reflex arc).

Homeostasis

In general, the cerebral cortex appears to be involved in higher-order mental activity such as thinking and speaking, while the structures below the cortex regulate and maintain the organism's internal environment. This regulation of the internal environment is called homeostasis. Ordinarily, the body maintains such functions as temperature, pulse rate, breathing, and blood pressure in a more or less constant state. But in unusual environmental circumstances (such as stress), the equilibrium of the body is upset. When this happens, the homeostatic mechanisms serve to restore the equilibrium and return the body to its normal level of functioning. For example, suppose that you opened your wallet and discovered that a badly needed $10 bill was missing. For most people this would be a stress situation. You might note a quickening of your pulse rate, increased perspiration, and disturbed breathing. But your homeostatic mechanisms would be immediately set in motion to restore these processes to their normal state.

The Central Nervous System and the Endocrine Glands

The central nervous system depends on the body's life-support systems for the maintenance of its many functions. The circulatory system provides it with nutrients and carries away waste products. Any disorder that affects bodily functions may also affect the central nervous system. This is particularly true with the endocrine glands (see Fig. 2.16). The endocrine glands release chemical substances (*hormones*) directly into the bloodstream. Too much or too little of one or more of these hormones may seriously affect body functions. For example, the *thyroid gland* regulates metabolism. An insufficient amount of one

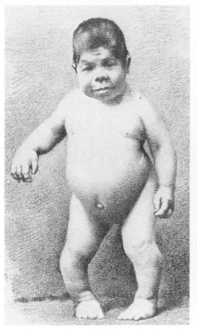

a) b)

of its hormones in infancy, if left uncorrected, will cause the child to suffer widespread bodily damage and to become incurably retarded (see Figure 2.17a and b).

The endocrine glands and the central nervous system function together. For example, there are sensors in the brain which are sensitive to specific hormones. They constantly monitor the level of the hormone to which they are "tuned," and "issue orders" based on the information they receive. Thus, the maintenance of hormonal balance involves homeostatic mechanisms. The *pituitary gland,* the so-called master gland, is one of the endocrine glands. It shares a vast network of interconnecting neural and circulatory elements with the hypothalamus. We have already seen that the hypothalamus regulates many of the life-maintaining functions. In part, it achieves this regulation through its close relationship with the pituitary gland.

The reason the pituitary is called the master gland is that the various hormones it secretes regulate the other endocrine glands. As a broad analogy, the pituitary is to the other endocrine glands as the brain is to the body. For example, under conditions of sudden stress, the pituitary secretes a hormone which causes another endocrine gland, the *adrenal gland,* to release *adrenaline.*

Fig. 2.17
a) In infancy, insufficient secretion of the thyroid gland results in cretinism. This disorder is characterized by intellectual as well as physical defects.
b) In childhood, excessive production of the growth hormone secreted by the pituitary gland results in giantism. (a, National Library of Medicine, Bethesda, Maryland. b, Editorial Photocolor Archives.)

The Central Nervous System

The adrenaline then activates various body structures and systems to prepare the individual to meet the emergency. It causes the heart to beat faster, so that it pumps more blood and oxygen to the various skeletal muscle systems that are involved in "fight or flight." Adrenaline also activates the various body mechanisms involved in temperature control (for example, perspiration), thus enabling the body to get rid of the excess heat generated by its emergency reactions.

The Peripheral Nervous System

The peripheral nervous system is outside the central nervous system. It carries input data from the sense organs to the spinal cord and brain through the afferent neurons, and transmits commands from the central nervous system to muscles and glands through the efferent neurons. The peripheral nervous system has two main subdivisions: the *somatic nervous system,* which serves the sense organs and the skeletal muscles (Fig. 2.18), and the *autonomic nervous system,* which regulates the inner organs of the body such as the heart, the stomach, and the glands (Fig. 2.19).

The Autonomic Nervous System

The autonomic system and the hypothalamus are closely interconnected. We mentioned earlier that the hypothalamus is important in regulating the organism's internal environment. This regulation is partially achieved by the hypothalamus through its connections with the autonomic system. The autonomic system has two branches: the sympathetic nervous system and the parasympathetic nervous system. The two often work in opposition to one another, and together achieve a homeostatic balance under normal conditions.

The *sympathetic* branch, which is activated under intense emotion such as anger or fear, increases heart rate and blood pressure, stimulates the sweat glands, dilates the pupils of the eyes, and directs many other functions as well.

The sympathetic branch functions in a way somewhat similar to the adrenal glands of the endocrine system. For example, under conditions of stress, adrenaline is released by the adrenal glands,

Physiological Foundations of Behavior

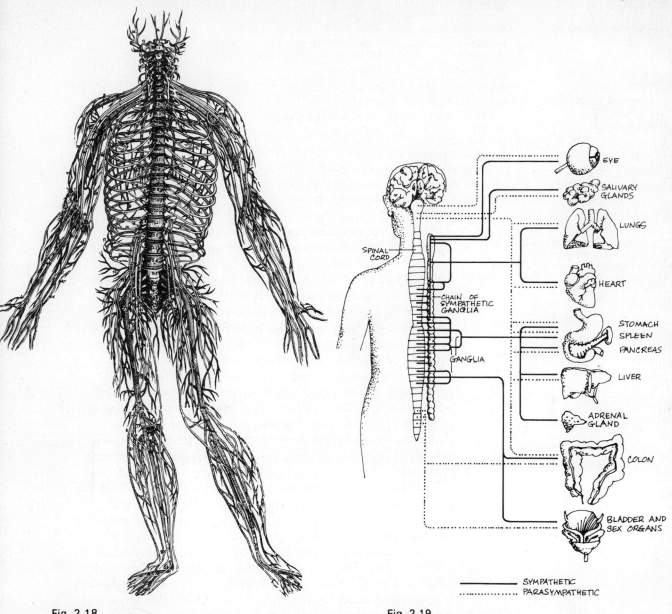

EYE

SALIVARY GLANDS

LUNGS

SPINAL CORD

HEART

CHAIN OF SYMPATHETIC GANGLIA

STOMACH
SPLEEN
PANCREAS

GANGLIA

LIVER

ADRENAL GLAND

COLON

BLADDER AND SEX ORGANS

———— SYMPATHETIC
·············· PARASYMPATHETIC

Fig. 2.18
The somatic nervous system

From the first complete textbook of human anatomy, Andreas Vesalius' *De Humani Corporis Fabrica*, which was published in 1543. (National Library of Medicine, Bethesda, Maryland.)

Fig. 2.19
The two branches of the autonomic system

The connections of the sympathetic branch are indicated by the solid lines. The connections of the parasympathetic branch are shown by dotted lines.

ORGAN	SYMPATHETIC BRANCH	PARASYMPATHETIC BRANCH
ADRENAL GLANDS	SECRETES ADRENALINE	NONE
BLADDER	INHIBITS EXCRETION OF URINE	STIMULATES EXCRETION OF URINE
BLOOD PRESSURE	INCREASES	DECREASES
BODY HAIR	GOOSEFLESH	NONE
GENITAL ORGANS (MALE)	EJACULATION	ERECTION
HEART	INCREASES HEART RATE	DECREASES HEART RATE
INTESTINES	INHIBITS TONE AND MOTILITY	INCREASES TONE AND MOTILITY
LIVER	RELEASES SUGAR	NONE
PUPILS OF EYE	DILATES	CONSTRICTS
SALIVARY GLANDS	INHIBITS SALIVATION	STIMULATES SALIVATION
SWEAT GLANDS	STIMULATES SWEATING	INHIBITS SWEATING

Table 2.1
Actions of the two branches of the autonomic system.

and adrenaline produces many of the activities described in the previous paragraph—it increases heart rate, dilates the pupils, and increases perspiration. However, whereas the adrenal glands function indirectly through the bloodstream, the sympathetic branch leads to direct neural activation.

The *parasympathetic* branch is generally dominant when the organism is placid or quiescent. It decreases the heart rate, lowers blood pressure, and allows the normal digestive processes to occur, in addition to other actions shown in Table 2.1.

The sympathetic branch has a profusion of central connections and interconnections. Therefore, when activated, it performs in a unified fashion, simultaneously sending its impulses to all the structures that it serves. On the other hand, the structures served by the parasympathetic system are activated by clusters of cells near the structures themselves. Thus, any one organ served by the parasympathetic system may be activated independently of another. For this reason, we may say that the parasympathetic branch acts in a piecemeal fashion. Figure 2.19 shows the various connections of the two branches of the autonomic system to bodily organs.

The autonomic system has usually been described as an involuntary system, primarily because it appears to function without any conscious control. Whether we are awake or asleep, it quietly and unobtrusively directs our life-support functions. And, it is always on the alert to be summoned into action in case of emergency. Because it is largely automatic, it frees us to engage in the many activities that require voluntary adjustments to our environment. Imagine trying to master the material assigned in this text, for instance, while at the same time attempting to issue all the orders necessary to digest food, regulate breathing, and control blood circulation.

Physiological Foundations of Behavior

Methods of Studying the Nervous System

We live in an age of computers—those marvelous complexes of electronic circuitry capable of awesome and sometimes exasperating feats. Yet no man-made computer even begins to approach the sophistication and capabilities of our own nervous system. We have already seen how incredibly complex the human nervous system is, with its billions of interconnecting components that somehow manage to process and sort thousands of incoming messages and, in a split second, resolve them into unified sequences of action. How remarkable is the human nervous system—at once capable of learning speech and language, remembering thousands of past experiences, recognizing a familiar face, perceiving the beauty of a rose or a great work of art, and crying for joy or sorrow. What is yet more remarkable is that the nervous system is even capable of turning inward and studying itself. Given such complexity, there are obviously many different routes that we may take in seeking to unravel the many mysteries of the nervous system. We have already touched upon several; let's now explore them in more detail.

Fig. 2.20
A chemical introduced through tubes implanted in the cat's brain causes the mother cat to ignore her kittens. (Courtesy of Dr. Kenneth E. Moyer.)

Biochemical Methods

A fairly recent technique involves the implantation of minute hollow tubes in selected areas of the brain. Through these tubes chemical substances can be introduced directly into the brain and the effects on behavior can then be studied. Figure 2.20 shows a mother cat unresponsive to her kittens because of a chemical introduced through tubes in her brain.

Destruction

Sometimes a portion of the brain is destroyed through accident or disease. When brain damage occurs under these circumstances, the investigators have exercised no control over the location or the extent of the damage. Any attempt to relate the loss of brain tissue to resulting behavioral changes is, at best, an educated guess. Even if we knew the location and extent of neurological damage, we frequently have only sketchy information about the patient's past behavior, so that any assessment of behavioral change would be difficult if not impossible. Such accidental damage can, however, provide us with clues to relationships between various parts of the nervous system and behavior. These clues can then be further explored in the laboratory, where it is possible to establish precise experimental controls.

In laboratory studies with animals, the independent variable is the location of the area from which nervous tissue is removed. The dependent variable is some well-identified and measurable aspect of behavior. Control over extraneous variables is commonly achieved by surgical removal (*ablation*) of brain tissue from other areas of the control animals' brains. This procedure allows investigators to assess the possible adverse effects of the surgical procedure itself. Such research may involve the actual removal of nervous tissue, the destruction of connections among different areas, or the production of lesions by either surgical or electrical means.

Interpreting the results of neural damage to specific areas of the nervous system is not so straightforward as it might first appear. If an animal performs a specific task prior to surgical removal of brain tissue and then is unable to perform the same task after surgery, we might be tempted to conclude that we have located the area that regulates the performance of this task. As a matter of fact, we may merely have interfered with one of the components necessary for this particular behavior. For example, we may have interfered with the reception of visual cues necessary to perform the task; we may have disturbed the arousal system; or we may have destroyed a part of the system that regulates motivation. A highly elaborate program of research is usually required before a one-to-one relationship between a certain region of the nervous system and a specific behavior can be established and frequently this research entails the use of techniques other than destruction.

*Physiological
Foundations
of Behavior*

Fig. 2.21
a) A rat with a socket implanted in the brain.
b) The plug that is inserted into the socket and
through which electrical stimulation is introduced.
(Courtesy of Dr. Neal E. Miller.)

Electrical Stimulation

In a sense, the use of destructive techniques to study the nervous
system is like firing a cannon to kill a fly. With the burgeoning
sophistication of miniature electronic circuitry, many scientists
have turned to methods involving the electrical stimulation of the
brain (ESB). This stimulation can be accomplished in one of two
ways. The scientist may explore the brain during surgery,
applying a mild electric current to selected areas, or he may
implant minute electrodes in specific areas of the brain to permit
repeated stimulation of the same area. The former method, used
primarily with human subjects in the course of surgery, has
provided information that has led to the construction of "maps"
of the brain. For example, as we have already seen, stimulation of
the sensory area of the cortex has established a one-to-one
correspondence between specific locations in the brain and
sensations arising from specific parts of the body.

Direct brain stimulation by surgical exposure of its surface
has numerous limitations. In addition to the ever present risk
involved in such surgery, the subject is, of necessity, restrained on
a surgical table, and consequently only a limited number of
different behaviors can be studied. Moreover, stimulation is
usually restricted to the readily accessible cortical structures,
leaving the depths of the brain enshrouded in mystery.

Much of this has changed recently with the development of
minute electrodes which can be precisely inserted in specific
regions of the brain and permanently anchored to the skull (see
Fig. 2.21). In the most recent developments using this technique,
any given electrode can be activated by plugging it into a
miniature receiver placed beneath the surface of the skin. This
device (which does not require connecting wires) permits
two-way communication between the brain and a remote radio
receiver and transmitter. Since the activity of the subject is
unrestricted, it is possible to study a wide variety of behaviors in
many different environmental settings.

Some of the ESB results sound like science fiction. Imagine
being able to turn rage on or off with the flick of a switch, to
control aggressiveness merely by pressing a button, or to alleviate
anxiety by turning a knob. Incredible as it may seem, scientists
have actually been able to achieve these "miracles" through the
use of ESB techniques.

In one particularly impressive study, four monkeys were
placed in a soundproofed, air-conditioned room where their social

a)

b)

*Methods of
Studying the
Nervous System*

Fig. 2.22
Elsa (on the left side of the picture) pressed the bar to stimulate Ali's brain by radio, thereby inhibiting Ali's aggressive behavior. The fact that Elsa is looking directly at Ali is significant, since looking straight at the "boss" usually provokes retaliation. (Dr. José M. R. Delgado, 1963; Courtesy Yale University News Bureau.)

Fig. 2.23
In the experimenter's left hand is a radio transmitter which can send a signal to an electrode implanted in the bull's brain. The photo on the right shows the bull being stopped in mid-charge by the radio signal. (Dr. José M. R. Delgado, 1963; Courtesy Yale University News Bureau.)

behavior could be exhaustively studied. One male, Ali, emerged as the dominant monkey. He was powerful, aggressive, and quite hostile toward the third-ranking member, a female named Elsa. Stimulation of a specific region of Ali's brain inhibited his aggressive and hostile acts. What do you suppose happened when Elsa was allowed to control the initiation of this stimulation? The results were illuminating. Elsa, not previously known as an advocate of Women's Lib, quickly learned to press the bar that "turned off" Ali's aggressive behavior. In a three-day period she pressed the bar a total of 54 times (Delgado, 1963). Figure 2.22 is a photograph of Elsa pressing the bar to inhibit Ali's aggressive behavior.

Another exciting demonstration of the effectiveness of this technique is shown in Figure 2.23. Here we see a bull stopped in mid-charge by a radio signal transmitted to an electrode implanted in his brain.

Electroencephalograph (EEG)

We have already noted that the brain never sleeps, but continuously produces rhythmic electrical discharges, the synchronized output of millions of neurons. These rhythmic electrical activities, called brain waves, can be detected by electrodes, which are usually placed on the scalp. Since the voltages produced by brain waves are extremely small, they must be amplified. Small recording pens connected to the amplifier transcribe the brain waves to paper. This apparatus is called an electroencephalograph, or EEG. Figure 2.24 shows a typical EEG in operation.

Behavioral scientists have been intrigued by the fact that a number of behavioral states of the organism have been found to be related to EEG activity. For instance, before the development of the EEG, it was difficult to arrive at a satisfactory operational definition of sleep. Analysis of EEG records taken while subjects were supposedly asleep has established that the brain waves change in a consistent fashion as the individual progresses from wakefulness through four distinct stages of sleep. When a person is awake and relaxed with his eyes closed, his brain waves are usually of high frequency (about 8 to 12 per second) and low amplitude. These waves are called *alpha waves*. As the individual

Fig. 2.24
A subject hooked up to an electroencephalograph (EEG), which records the brain waves in different parts of the brain. (Bob Henriquos—Magnum.)

Physiological Foundations of Behavior

enters the first stage of sleep, the proportion of alpha waves diminishes, to be replaced by low-frequency waves of greater amplitude. In stages two, three, and four the alpha waves are completely replaced by increasingly high-amplitude and low-frequency brain waves. Figure 2.25 shows alpha waves and the brain waves characteristic of the four stages of sleep.

The discovery of four distinct stages of sleep and of an objective criterion for measuring them have provided new impetus for probing phenomena which have hitherto been virtually inaccessible to human inquiry—sleep and dreams. While much of the research in these areas is only in its beginning stages, many long-held views about sleeping and dreaming have already been dispelled.

Many people use the expression "I slept like a log," conjuring up the image of profound and motionless sleep. As a matter of

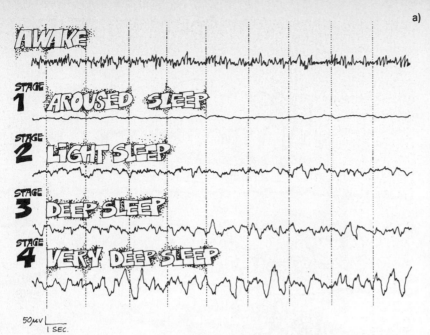

fact, a sleeping person remains still only about eleven minutes at a time, on the average (Johnson et al., 1930). Furthermore, sleep is cyclic. When an adult goes to sleep, he progresses rapidly to stage four. He remains in the very deep sleep characteristic of this stage for about an hour, and then moves back through stages three, two, and one. When he reemerges into stage one, every ninety minutes or so, his closed eyes begin to move back and forth. This period of *rapid eye movement* (REM) is referred to as stage-one REM sleep (Dement and Kleitman, 1957).

Stage-one REM sleep has interesting but paradoxical qualities. Both the physiological patterns (elevations in heart rate, irregularities in breathing pattern, increases in blood pressure, penis erection in males) and the EEG patterns closely resemble the waking state (Dement, 1965). Nevertheless, behavioral measures indicate that stage-one REM is deep sleep, similar to stage four. Individuals in stage-one REM are difficult to awaken and are less responsive to external stimuli than when they are in stage two and three. Moreover, the main muscles of the body lose their tonus, and reflexes that can be elicited during other stages of sleep are inhibited.

Research indicates that we enter the REM stage several times a night. If a person is awakened during this period, he will almost invariably report a dream in progress. In fact, dreaming is a far more common occurrence than most people think. We dream every night, and we have several dreams each night.

REM sleep appears to be vital for maintaining the well-being of the organism. If adult subjects are awakened every time they

Fig. 2.25
a) Alpha waves and the four stages of sleep as shown by EEG records. (Courtesy of Dr. Wilse B. Webb.)
b) The four stages of sleep as shown by Snoopy. (Copyright © 1956 United Feature Syndicate, Inc.)

Methods of Studying the Nervous System

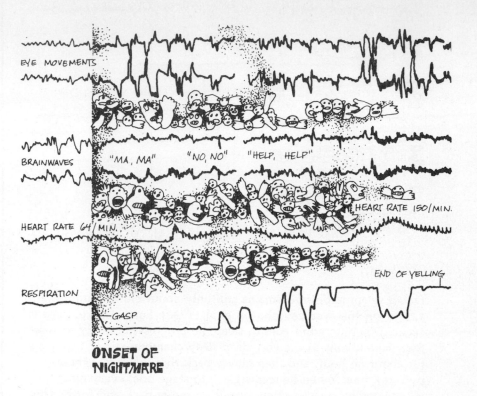

EYE MOVEMENTS

BRAINWAVES

"MA, MA"   "NO, NO"   "HELP, HELP"

HEART RATE 64/MIN.

HEART RATE 150/MIN.

RESPIRATION

END OF YELLING

GASP

ONSET OF
NIGHTMARE

Fig. 2.26
Tracings made by synchronized sleep-monitoring equipment before and during a nightmare. The patient, whose deep sleep is reflected in the subdued physical reactions recorded at the far left of the graph, suddenly enters the aroused nightmare state. Partially awake, his eyes and brain become active, his heart rate soars. The breath he uses to shout for help distorts the tracing of his respiration, which is also rising. The elapsed time shown in the graph is less than a minute. (Based on a drawing copyright © 1969 by The New York Times Company. Used by permission.)

*Physiological
Foundations
of Behavior*

go into REM, and thus are deprived of REM sleep, they may show such undesirable effects as tension and irritability during their waking hours. If they are deprived of similar amounts of non-REM sleep, these negative side effects are not observed (Dement, 1965). Even more dramatic results were obtained when specific portions of cats' brains were removed which deprived them of REM sleep but left non-REM sleep unimpaired. After several days, the cats became extremely agitated, occasionally striking at non-existent objects. Some showed heightened sexual and eating activities. In some instances, REM sleep returned and the behavioral symptoms disappeared. However, cats in which REM was permanently eliminated eventually died in a state of agitation and overactivity (Jouvet, 1962).

Although most dreams appear to occur during REM periods, the most terrifying nightmares seem to occur as the individual is coming out of deep sleep into the lighter stages of sleep (Broughton, 1968). Figure 2.26 shows the tracings made by sleep-monitoring equipment before and during a nightmare.

Most of the research we have described in this section is based on the discovery that the brain constantly produces wave patterns that can be recorded on an EEG. On the surface, it may appear that these brain waves represent a biological phenomenon which is automatic and not within the realm of conscious control. In the next section we shall look at some research that appears to contradict this assumption.

Biofeedback

It has long been claimed that Oriental mystics, such as Zen Buddhists, are able to achieve remarkable degrees of control over their bodily functions, willfully effecting changes in heart rate, blood pressure, body temperature, and other biological processes not normally considered to be subject to voluntary control. Most people have regarded these claims as the exaggerated distortions of naive and easily duped observers. Recently, however, the air of scepticism has given way to one of enthusiastic scientific inquiry. Major breakthroughs concerning the voluntary control of internal physiological processes have been made during the past decade. These have come about primarily through the use of a new and powerful tool called biofeedback.

Biofeedback may best be understood by describing its relationship to voluntary activities. With relatively simple movements, such as raising an arm or lifting a leg, we have immediate feedback; that is, we can see and feel the movement in these muscles, and we can adjust and modify subsequent movements in response to this feedback. In contrast, the organs served by the autonomic nervous system provide such imprecise sensory feedback that we cannot use this feedback to exercise effective control over these organs. For instance, you may occasionally become aware that your heart is beating more rapidly than normal, perhaps because you have been rushing to catch a bus. Or, if you have ever had high blood pressure, you know what effects it produces in you, and you can probably tell when your blood pressure goes considerably above normal. But can you do anything to get your heart rate or blood pressure back to normal? Very few people can do this with any degree of success. The autonomic system has been regarded as an involuntary system primarily because it appears to function without our conscious control. Pioneers in the area of biofeedback argue that,

Biofeedback

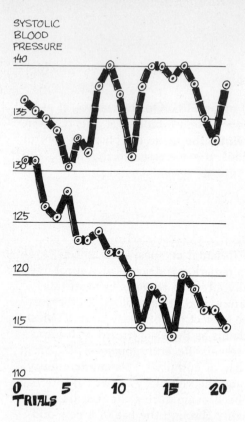

SYSTOLIC BLOOD PRESSURE

Fig. 2.27
Human subjects in the experimental group (●—●) learned to decrease their own blood pressure. The blood pressure of the control subjects (●----●) remained relatively stable (Brenner and Kleinman, 1970).

if we could receive clear-cut feedback about the actions of internal organs, we could then exercise a control similar to that which we have over our voluntary movements.

Much experimentation is now under way to test this hypothesis. In one study, five college students were placed in front of a meter which provided continuous information concerning their blood pressure, and they were told to decrease the readings on the meter. These subjects constituted the experimental group. Five other students (the control group) were placed in front of the same display but were not told to decrease the readings. The experimental subjects showed a sharp decrease in their blood pressure, while the blood pressure of the control subject remained at the same level (Brenner and Kleinman, 1970). Figure 2.27 presents the results of this experiment.

The possibility that humans may be able to learn to regulate such autonomic activities as blood pressure and heart rate has far-reaching implications (some are discussed in Chapter 3). Biofeedback techniques are now used in a variety of medical settings. For example, one investigator has reported considerable success in the treatment of people suffering from migraine

Physiological Foundations of Behavior

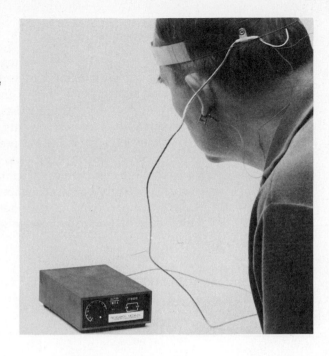

Fig. 2.28
The sound of a tone informs the subject that his brain is emitting alpha waves. He is instructed to keep the tone turned on. (Courtesy of Research Media, Hicksville, New York.)

headaches (Rorvik, 1972). It is believed that migraine attacks are caused by increased pressure within the scalp's blood vessels, presumably the result of an increased flow of blood in the head. It was thought that if this blood could be diverted from the head to other parts of the body, the pain of migraine might be alleviated. Patients suffering from migraine were given a meter to monitor temperature (and thus blood flow) in their hands. By learning to increase the temperature in their hands, many patients reported dramatic relief from migraine attacks.

In addition to regulating bodily activities not ordinarily subject to voluntary control, the autonomic system plays an important role in emotional behavior. The possibility that we can learn to control autonomic responses has important implications for the treatment of many disorders—such as high blood pressure, asthma, and hypertension—which are influenced by psychological factors.

One application of biofeedback techniques that has caught the fancy of scientists and laymen alike, involves learning conscious control over brain waves (see Fig. 2.28). We mentioned earlier that alpha brain waves are associated with the relaxed, waking state. Individuals can be trained to "turn on" alpha waves

Biofeedback

by using biofeedback techniques (Kamiya, 1969). The state of serenity and well-being achieved under alpha has been described by some subjects as a "high." Indeed, many investigators report that they have long waiting lists of volunteers wishing to participate in alpha experiments.

Some researchers have expressed the hope that, if we learn to control our brain wave patterns, we may be able to alleviate anxiety, improve memory, facilitate learning, and perhaps someday reduce our dependence on drugs, alcohol, and cigarettes. Much research remains to be done before the claims of today and the hopes of tomorrow receive scientific confirmation.

Summary

1. The physiological psychologist attempts to relate behavior to the way in which the organism is put together. His basic assumption is that behavior is intimately related to structure and that, by understanding the structure of the organism, he may better understand the "whys" and the "hows" of behavior.

2. The nervous system has two major subdivisions: the central nervous system and the peripheral nervous system.

3. There are three types of neurons in the nervous system: afferent neurons, efferent neurons, and association neurons.

4. The message carried by the neuron is electrochemical in nature. The minimum stimulation necessary to activate a neuron is called the threshold of excitability. When a stimulus, at or above the threshold, is applied to a neuron, the neuron fires at full charge. A neuron never fires at less then full charge. This characteristic is known as the all-or-none law of nervous conduction.

5. A small gap, the synapse, separates adjacent neurons from each other. The axons of one neuron release a transmitter chemical which initiates an impulse in the dendrite of the adjacent neuron.

6. The reflex arc is the simplest type of connection between sensory inputs and motor responses. Reflexes are innate, automatic, and do not involve the intervention of higher brain centers.

7. The brain may be divided into three major subdivisions: the cerebral cortex, the subcortical structures, and the cerebellum.

8. The cerebral cortex consists of two hemispheres, approximately equal in size and appearance. Each hemisphere is subdivided into four areas: the frontal, parietal, occipital, and temporal lobes. Sensory and motor functions are well localized in the cerebral cortex—patterned vision in the occipital cortex, auditory experiences in the temporal lobes, body feelings in the anterior portion of the parietal lobes, and regulation of fine voluntary movements in the posterior portion of the frontal lobes.

Summary

9. Approximately 75 percent of the cortex is involved in the more complex behavioral processes that are referred to as associative.

10. The subcortical structures are responsible for maintaining the many vital life-support functions.

11. The spinal cord is primarily responsible for carrying impulses from the sense organs to the brain and relaying messages from the brain to the effectors.

12. The maintenance of the organism's internal environment is referred to as homeostasis. Homeostatic mechanisms maintain the balance of the various body functions.

13. The endocrine glands work in close conjunction with the brain, particularly the hypothalamus, in regulating body processes.

14. The peripheral nervous system has two main subdivisions: the somatic nervous system and the autonomic nervous system. The autonomic nervous system includes the sympathetic branch, which is activated under intense emotion, and the parasympathetic branch, which is dominant when the organism is placid.

15. Four different techniques for studying the nervous system were discussed in this chapter: biochemical methods, destruction, electrical stimulation, and electrical recording of brain waves.

Terms to Remember

Ablation   Surgical removal of a part of the brain.

Absolute Refractory Period   A short period of time after a neuron discharges a nervous impulse during which it will not fire again regardless of the intensity of stimulation.

Adrenal Gland   An endocrine gland one of whose secretions is adrenaline.

Adrenaline   A hormone secreted by the adrenal glands which activates bodily structures and systems during an emergency.

Afferent Neurons   Sensory neurons that transmit nervous impulses from the sensory receptors to the brain and spinal cord.

All-or-None Law   The principle that a neuron fires at full charge or not at all, no matter how intense the stimulation, so long as it is at or above the threshold level.

Alpha Waves   Brain waves typical of a relaxed waking state.

Association Neurons   Neurons usually found in the central nervous system that connect afferent and efferent neurons.

Associative Cortex   The parts of the brain concerned with such complex behaviors as thinking, speech, and memory.

Auditory Area   An area in the temporal lobes which is responsible for auditory sensations.

Autonomic Nervous System   The part of the peripheral nervous system which regulates the inner organs of the body such as the heart, the stomach, and the glands.

Axon   A long fiber extending from the cell body of a neuron that carries nervous impulses away from the cell body.

Biofeedback   Information about a bodily response from either the senses or an outside source. On the basis of this information, the organism can adjust and modify its bodily responses.

Central Nervous System   The brain and spinal cord.

Cerebellum   A brain structure located under the rear portion of the cerebral cortex which plays a key role in muscle coordination.

Cerebral Cortex   The layer of nervous tissue beneath the skull that is the outer covering of the cerebral hemispheres and plays a major role in intellectual processes such as thought and language.

Cerebral Hemispheres   The two symmetrical halves of the cerebral cortex.

Corpus Callosum   Nerve fibers that connect the two cerebral hemispheres.

Dendrites   Hairlike structures of a neuron that receive nervous impulses from other neurons and carry them toward the cell body.

Effector   A muscle or gland.

Terms to Remember

Efferent Neurons   Motor neurons that transmit nervous impulses from the brain and spinal cord to the muscles and glands.

Electroencephalograph (EEG)   An instrument for recording the electrical activity of the brain.

Endocrine Glands   A group of glands which maintain body functioning by secreting chemical substances directly into the bloodstream.

Fissure of Rolando (Central Fissure)   The crevice or groove which separates the frontal from the parietal lobes of the brain.

Frontal Lobe   The lobe in the anterior portion of the brain, in front of the fissure of Rolando, involved in fine motor activities and possibly almost every complex behavioral process.

Homeostasis   The mechanism whereby the body maintains a state of physiological equilibrium.

Hormones   Chemical substances secreted by the endocrine glands directly into the bloodstream.

Hypothalamus   A subcortical structure that plays an important role in hunger, thirst, sex, emotion, and other physiological functions.

Interpretive Area   A portion of the temporal lobes which, when electrically stimulated, sometimes produces vivid memories of past events.

Lateral Fissure   The crevice or groove which separates the temporal and frontal lobes.

Lesion   Any destruction or damage to tissue.

Limbic System   A group of interrelated structures involved in emotional and motivated behavior.

Medulla   A subcortical structure which plays an important role in vital functions such as breathing and blood circulation.

Motor Area   The region of the brain concerned with the regulation of voluntary motor activities.

Neural Impulse   A temporary electrochemical reaction within the neuron.

Neuron   A nerve cell consisting of a cell body, an axon, and dendrites.

Nuclei   Clusters of nerve cells.

Occipital Lobe   The lobe, occupying the extreme posterior portions of the brain, primarily concerned with vision.

Parasympathetic Branch   The division of the autonomic nervous system which is dominant when the organism is placid. This system decreases heart rate and blood pressure and regulates normal digestive processes.

Parietal Lobe   One of the lobes occupying the posterior portions of the brain, located between the fissure of Rolando and the occipital lobe, concerned with sensation of body feelings.

Peripheral Nervous System   The part of the nervous system which connects the central nervous system with the receptors and effectors.

Pituitary Gland   An endocrine gland whose secretions regulate other endocrine glands; sometimes called the master gland.

Pons   Subcortical structures which serve as a bridge connecting various parts of the brain.

Rapid Eye Movement (REM)   Rapid movements of the eyes occurring during sleep. Subjects awakened during the REM stage generally report that they have been dreaming.

Reflex   An unlearned automatic bodily response to a stimulus.

Reflex Arc   The pathway from a receptor to an effector that a nervous impulse follows to produce a reflex.

Relative Refractory Period   A brief interval, following the absolute refractory period, during which the neuron will respond only to intense stimulation.

Reticular Activating System (RAS)   A network of cells in the center of the brain which is involved in activating and arousing higher brain centers.

Sensory Receptor   A specialized surface that is sensitive to a particular type of stimulus.

Terms to Remember

Somatic Nervous System   The part of the peripheral nervous system which serves the sense organs and the skeletal muscles.

Spinal Cord   The part of the central nervous system which serves primarily to relay messages back and forth between the brain and the other parts of the body.

Split-Brain Surgery   A surgical procedure whereby the structures connecting the cerebral hemispheres are severed.

Subcortical Structures   Masses of nerve fibers and clusters of cell bodies located below the cerebral cortex and responsible for such vital functions as breathing, heart rate, and blood pressure.

Sympathetic Branch   The division of the autonomic nervous system which mobilizes the body during emergencies by increasing heart rate and blood pressure, accelerating secretion of adrenaline and inhibiting digestive processes.

Synapse   The point of transmission of a nervous impulse from the axon of one neuron to the dendrites of another.

Temporal Lobe   One of the posterior lobes of the brain, located below the lateral fissure and concerned with hearing.

Thalamus   A subcortical structure which serves primarily to relay sensory impulses from all parts of the body to the cerebral cortex.

Threshold of Excitability   Minimum intensity of stimulation necessary to activate a neuron.

Thyroid Gland   An endocrine gland whose secretions regulate body metabolism.

Visual Area   The rear portion of the occipital lobes of the brain which controls visual activity.

Recommended Readings

Calder, N., *The Mind of Man*, New York: The Viking Press, Inc., 1970.

An interesting account of current research on the brain and behavior.

Eibl-Eibesfeldt, I., *Ethology: The Biology of Behavior,* New York: Holt, Rinehart and Winston, Inc., 1970.

A textbook that contains many good illustrations.

Gardner, E., *Fundamentals of Neurology* (5th ed.), Philadelphia: W. B. Saunders Co., 1968.

This is a general discussion of the basic neural structures and their functions.

Guyton, A. C., *Structure and Function of the Nervous System,* Philadelphia: W. B. Saunders Co., 1972.

Summary of the workings of the nervous system with numerous illustrations and diagrams.

Pfeiffer, John, *The Human Brain,* New York: Harper and Brothers, 1955.

A somewhat outdated popularized discussion of brain function.

Thompson, R., *Foundations of Physiological Psychology,* New York: Harper & Row, Publishers, 1967.

A textbook and reference source.

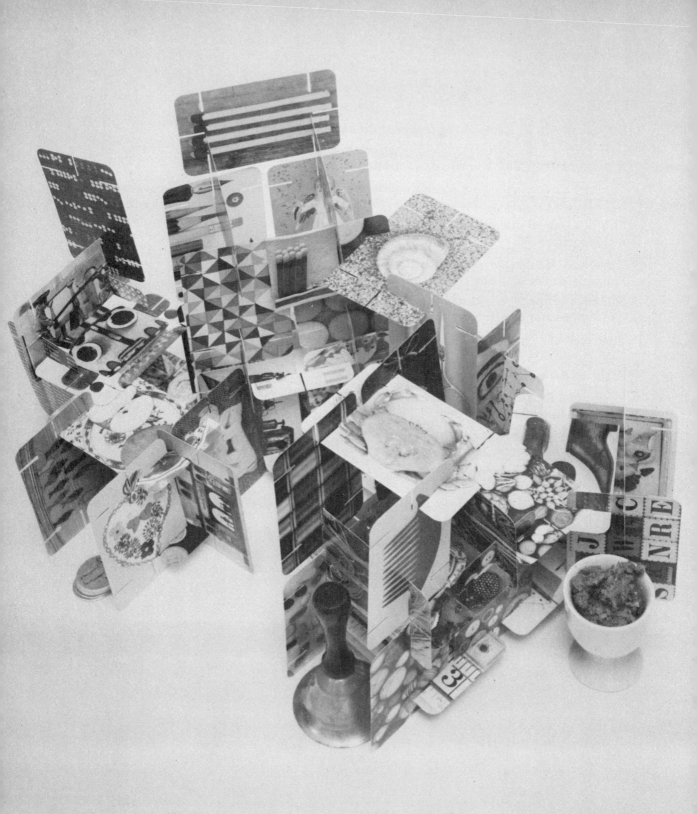

3 LEARNING

What is learning?

Classical conditioning

Conditioning procedure and acquisition
Extinction and spontaneous recovery
Stimulus generalization — Discrimination learning
Higher-order conditioning
Practical implications of classical conditioning

Operant conditioning and positive reinforcement

Shaping of operant behavior
Extinction and spontaneous recovery
Stimulus generalization — Discrimination learning
Secondary reinforcement — Partial reinforcement

Operant conditioning and negative reinforcement

Escape conditioning — Avoidance conditioning
Punishment

Practical implications of operant conditioning

Learning through imitation

a) b)

Fig. 3.1
If you've seen one gannet's nest,
you've seen them all. Why is this
not true of humans' "nests"?
a) Instinctive nest building
(Canadian gannets). (Cliff
Garboden—Stock, Boston.)
b) Learned nest building
(Boston's Government Center).
(Daniel S. Brody—Stock, Boston.)

Compare the following behavior of two very different species.
One is the stickleback, a small freshwater fish commonly found
in European rivers and streams; the other is man, found in
virtually every habitable location on the face of the earth.

During certain times of the year, the male stickleback engages
in a complicated series of responses culminating in the
construction of a nest in the riverbed. It excavates a hole in the
sand bottom, carrying the sand, mouthful by mouthful, to
another location to be dumped. When it has hollowed out a
depression of about four square inches, it collects a mass of
weeds and algae, piles this mass over the depression, coats it with
a sticky substance secreted from its own kidneys, and shapes the
mass into a mound. Finally, the stickleback bores through the
material to create a tunnel. It has constructed its nest.

When a man builds his "nest," he usually first studies a set
of blueprints. Then he selects the materials appropriate to the
home he has in mind. A wide selection is available, and he may
choose virtually any structural material or combination of
materials—bricks, brush, wood, steel, and even ice. Then, step by

Learning

78

step, and making careful measurements, he joins these materials together to conform to the requirements of the blueprints. When he has finished, the man, like the stickleback, has produced a habitable structure.

What do the activities of the stickleback and the man have in common? Both are highly complex and skilled performances. Both are directed toward the achievement of a goal—the construction of a habitat. But how do these activities differ? The stickleback's behavior represents *unlearned*, complex patterns of responses characteristic of all male members of the species. These responses vary little from member to member and are presumably inborn. Such behavior is usually described as *instinctive*. What about man? Certainly his behavior is complex but by no means can we describe it as inborn and unvarying. While lower organisms adapt to their environment largely through instinctive behaviors, higher animals, particularly humans, cope with the demands of their environment primarily through learned modes of adjustment.

What Is Learning?

We all use the word "learning" on many different occasions. Yet, if you were to ask for a definition of this word, you would probably get as many different definitions as the number of people you asked. Psychologists generally define learning as a relatively permanent change in behavior, resulting from experience or practice. Note the two qualifying parts of this definition: the behavioral change must be *relatively permanent*, and it must *result from experience or practice.* These qualifications are necessary to exclude changes in behavior that do not result from learning.

Let's consider the first qualification, that learning produces a relatively permanent change. This excludes from the definition any changes in behavior due to transient or temporary conditions resulting from motivation, fatigue, illness, or the use of drugs. We ought to point out here that learning is a construct. We can never directly observe learning; we can only infer it from some measure of performance. For example, from your performance on a test, your instructor may infer how much you have learned in his classes and through your reading over the past few weeks. The distinction between observed performance and inferred learning is extremely important, and will reappear throughout this text. Although we are completely dependent on performance measures as the basis for inferring learning, we must recognize that other factors besides learning may affect performance. We are left with an interesting paradox: performance that shows a change in behavior resulting from experience permits us to conclude that some learning has taken place; failure to perform does not necessarily mean that no learning has taken place. Many students have had the experience of "bombing" on a test for which they felt adequately prepared. Temporary factors such as lack of sleep, the influence of drugs, or an intolerably high state of anxiety may impede performance, even though learning has occurred.

The second qualification in the generally accepted definition of learning is that changes in behavior must result from *experience* or *practice*. This rules out changes due to biological growth, accident, or disease. A final point that should be made about this definition is that we do not necessarily profit from this practice or experience. Are you profiting from experience when you learn to smoke or to bite your nails? We learn poor study habits just as we learn good ones. Children may learn to cry or to throw tantrums to gain attention, just as they may learn to behave in a way the parents find more desirable. Thus, learning may lead to undesirable as well as to desirable consequences. As we shall see in later chapters, we learn to hate as well as to love; we learn distorted as well as real ways of perceiving the world; we learn prejudice as well as tolerance; and we even learn how to get "high."

Try to imagine what life would be like if you were totally incapable of learning. Without learning—and its companion, memory—every situation you encountered would be completely new and alien. You would never be able to profit from experience, but would make the same mistakes over and over again. You could never recognize places, people, or things, no matter how frequently you were exposed to them. You could accomplish nothing. Thought would be impossible, and so would language. Past and future would be meaningless terms. The beauty of the arts and the stimulation of the sciences would be beyond your reach. You could never even learn to avoid the common dangers of everyday existence. On the other hand, you

Learning

would escape the many tensions and anxieties that are the lot of civilized man.

It is no exaggeration to say that learning is so pervasive that it influences every aspect of our lives. Even turning the pages of this book, an activity we tend to take for granted, requires that we learn to coordinate and integrate a complex pattern of muscle movements.

Clearly, an understanding of some principles of learning is basic to the study of human behavior. We learn our attitudes, likes and dislikes, fears, and emotions. We learn how to perceive and react to the environment around and within us. This chapter deals with some of the basic principles of learning. We will develop a foundation for a fuller appreciation of the following chapters, which deal with such topics as emotions, personality, mental illness, and social behavior.

Classical Conditioning

In the late 1890's a Russian physiologist, Ivan Pavlov, was engaged in the most exhaustive studies of the digestive system undertaken to that date. For this work, he received the Nobel prize in physiology. During the course of his investigations he developed surgical techniques that permitted the direct observation of many digestive processes. A simple operation on a dog's cheek enabled him to expose part of the salivary gland, and to collect and measure saliva produced under varying experimental conditions. While conducting his experiments, he noted that the dogs salivated not only to the presence of food in their mouths, but to the sight of food, the sound of the food trays, and even the approach of the experimenter. This is not an unusual observation. Probably most of you have noticed that the sight of food, the rattling of dishes, or even the mere mention of food may increase your flow of saliva. What made Pavlov's observations important was his recognition that he was observing two different situations that gave rise to salivation. What, you may ask, could possibly be the significance of distinguishing between salivation that occurs when food is placed in the mouth, and salivation at the sight and sound of food trays? Salivation to food in the mouth is an inborn, unlearned response. But there is no inborn association between salivation and the sight and sound of food trays. The latter case must therefore involve some form of learning.

Let's look at another example, one you may be quite familiar with. Have you ever had an instructor with the annoying and exasperating habit of screeching the chalk as he wrote on the chalkboard? Did this screeching make you cringe and give you gooseflesh? If so, you may have found that after a while you would cringe and get gooseflesh at the mere sight of the instructor approaching the chalkboard. In this example we see several key elements of the learning process. You will recall that we defined learning as a change in behavior that results from experience. We can safely assume—we hope—that the sight of this instructor did not *initially* have you "climbing the walls." Therefore, the change in your behavior must have occurred as a result of your experience with the instructor's annoying habit.

Both of the examples discussed above involve a type of learning known as classical conditioning. Because Ivan Pavlov pioneered the investigation of this relatively simple form of learning, it is frequently referred to as Pavlovian conditioning. Let's look at a typical example of Pavlov's work, to illustrate both the techniques employed in classical conditioning and the learning principles which have emerged.

Conditioning Procedure and Acquisition

The apparatus that Pavlov used is shown in Fig. 3.2. In the typical experimental situation, a hungry dog is placed in the apparatus. If a stimulus, such as the ticking of a metronome (a device used by musicians to establish tempo), is presented to the animal, it will prick up its ears, but it will not salivate. This is not surprising, because a dog does not ordinarily salivate to the sound of a metronome. However, when meat powder is placed in the dog's mouth, its saliva flows copiously.

Pavlov systematically attempted to connect the salivary response to the sound of the metronome. First, he placed food in the dog's mouth while the metronome was beating. The dog, of course, salivated to the presence of food in its mouth. After several pairings of these two stimuli, Pavlov sounded the metronome but did not present any food. The dog salivated to

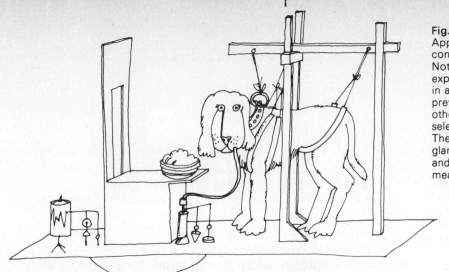

Fig. 3.2
Apparatus used by Pavlov for conditioning salivation in a dog. Note the main features of the experimental setting. The dog is in a restraining harness that prevents him from seeing events other than those specifically selected by the experimenter. The tube runs from his salivary glands into a graduated cylinder and permits a precise measurement of the saliva.

the sound of the metronome alone (Pavlov, 1927). Thus, the dog *learned* to salivate to the sound of the metronome.

Let's look at the essential elements of the classical conditioning process as it applies to the above example. Since the food naturally and automatically elicits salivation, we refer to the food as the *unconditioned stimulus* (UCS). The salivation to the meat powder, since it occurs automatically without any learning, is called the *unconditioned response* (UCR). The sound of the metronome, however, is *neutral* with respect to the salivary response, since it does not naturally elicit the UCR. We say that conditioning has occurred when the previously neutral stimulus acquires the capacity to evoke salivation. The previously neutral stimulus (the sound of the metronome) is now called the *conditioned stimulus* (CS), and the salivation which occurs to the sound of the metronome is known as the *conditioned response* (CR). Figure 3.3 is a diagram of the classical conditioning process.

Fig. 3.3
Classical conditioning

In order for classical conditioning to take place, there must be: 1) an unconditioned stimulus (UCS) that elicits an unconditioned response (UCR); 2) a neutral stimulus that does not initially elicit the unconditioned response; and 3) a pairing of the neutral stimulus and the unconditioned stimulus.
After repeated pairings of these two stimuli, the neutral stimulus gradually acquires the capacity to evoke the desired response. We now refer to the originally neutral stimulus as the conditioned stimulus (CS) and the obtained response as the conditioned response (CR).

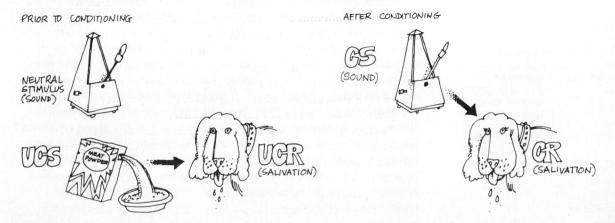

PRIOR TO CONDITIONING

AFTER CONDITIONING

NEUTRAL STIMULUS (SOUND)

UCS

UCR (SALIVATION)

CS (SOUND)

CR (SALIVATION)

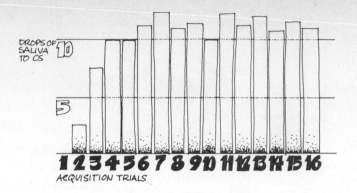

Fig. 3.4
Acquisition of a conditioned salivary response

The amount of saliva secreted to the conditioned stimulus increases rapidly during early acquisition trials (pairing of CS and UCS) and remains relatively stable thereafter (Pavlov, 1927).

The period during which the organism learns the association between the CS and the CR is called the acquisition stage of conditioning, and each pairing of the CS and the UCS is customarily called an acquisition trial. Figure 3.4 shows the acquisition of the salivary response of a dog to a conditioned stimulus (a light).

Extinction and Spontaneous Recovery

We have seen that conditioning involves the association of a response (CR) with a previously neutral stimulus (CS). One of the ways to test for the acquisition of this response is to present the CS alone (without the UCS). What do you suppose would happen if we continued to present the CS alone? Do you think the animal would continue to salivate indefinitely? Pavlov investigated this question in the following way: he took an animal that had acquired the conditioned salivary response to a conditioned stimulus (for example, a light), and repeatedly presented the light alone. Each presentation of the CS alone is called an extinction trial. Figure 3.5 shows Pavlov's results. Note that with repeated extinction trials, the conditioned response gradually decreased in strength.

If Pavlov had terminated the experiment at this point, he might have concluded that the extinction process had erased the conditioned response. But Pavlov continued, and discovered a very interesting phenomenon. If an animal that had undergone experimental extinction was brought back into the experimental situation at a later time, the presentation of the CS alone (without the UCS) elicited a greater amount of salivation than on the last extinction trial. This recovery of the previously extinguished CR following a rest period is called spontaneous recovery. The entire course of acquisition, extinction, and spontaneous recovery is illustrated in Fig. 3.6.

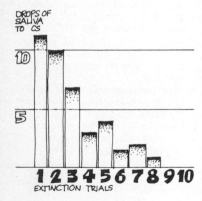

Fig. 3.5
Extinction of a conditioned salivary response

Notice what happened to the conditioned response (salivation) when the CS was no longer paired with the UCS (extinction trials). The amount of saliva secreted in response to the CS diminished rapidly during extinction (Pavlov, 1927).

Learning

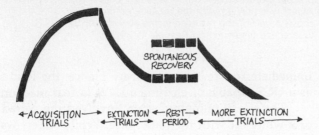

Examples of classical conditioning

The study of classical conditioning has by no means been restricted to the salivary response of a dog. Classical conditioning has been studied in an almost endless number of different organisms, and these studies have used a wide variety of conditioned stimuli and responses. Nor is classical conditioning limited to the laboratory, for we can see countless examples of classical conditioning in our everyday lives. For example, a child sees a dog and shows no fear. The dog is thus a neutral stimulus with respect to the fear response. But if the dog bites the child, this action will elicit the fear response in the child. The UCS in this situation is the dog's bite, and the UCR is the fear response. The next time the child sees the dog, he will react with fear.

A study of a child's acquisition of fear has provided an interesting laboratory example of classical conditioning. At the beginning of the study, Albert, a nine-month-old infant, was confronted with a variety of stimuli, including a white rat, a rabbit, and a dog. Albert showed no fear in the presence of any of these stimuli. In this way the investigators established that all these stimuli were neutral with respect to the fear reaction (Watson and Raynor, 1920).

Since the experimenters wanted to see if they could condition fear to these neutral stimuli, they had to find a stimulus which would naturally give rise to the fear reaction (that is, a UCS for fear). They tried a sudden, loud noise, and this produced an

*Classical
Conditioning*

85

Fig. 3.7
Conditioning the fear response in an infant
Prior to conditioning, Albert shows no fear in the presence of a rat. A loud noise was sounded while Albert was playing with the rat. Thereafter, Albert showed fear of the rat even in the absence of the loud sound (Watson and Raynor, 1920).

immediate fear reaction in Albert. Hence, the loud sound served as a UCS capable of eliciting a UCR (a fear reaction).

The conditioning procedure involved the paired presentation of a white rat with the loud noise. While Albert was playing with the white rat, a loud noise was sounded. After a few acquisition trials, the white rat was presented alone. Albert immediately showed a fear reaction (Fig. 3.7). Thus, he had become conditioned to fear the rat, which originally was a neutral stimulus.

This study demonstrates that an emotional response (such as fear) can be conditioned to previously neutral stimuli. It may well be that many of our emotional reactions have been accidentally conditioned to stimuli through a chance association of these stimuli with emotion-arousing situations. For example, recall the instructor who habitually screeched chalk on the chalkboard. Just as Albert learned to fear the rat, a student could develop a strong negative reaction to this instructor.

Not all learned emotional reactions are aversive in nature. Suppose that you enjoy the company of a particular person. It is quite possible that your positive feelings could be conditioned to a previously neutral stimulus, such as a restaurant where you ate together. Thus, even in that person's absence, the restaurant could come to evoke pleasant feelings.

Stimulus Generalization

It is difficult to trace the origin of many of our learned emotional reactions. For example, suppose that a child, seeing a horse for the very first time, begins to whimper, cry, and show other signs of acute emotional distress. How would you explain this behavior? Does the sight of a horse automatically elicit fear in young children? Not likely. The child must somehow have learned this association. Suppose you find out that this child had

Learning

previously been bitten by a dog. Does this additional information shed any light on the origin of the child's fear of the horse? A similar question was explored in the laboratory, where further aspects of Albert's behavior were examined.

Remember that before Albert was conditioned to fear the white rat, he was confronted with a rabbit, a dog, and other stimuli, and showed no fear response to these stimuli. What do you suppose happened, subsequent to the conditioning, when these stimuli were again presented to Albert? The experimenters noted:

> The rabbit was suddenly placed on the mattress in front of him. The reaction was pronounced. Negative responses began at once. He leaned as far away from the animal as possible, whimpered, then burst into tears.
>
> (Watson and Raynor, 1920)

When a dog was presented alone, Albert again showed a negative emotional reaction, though this was not as pronounced as his reaction to the rabbit. In still other tests, Albert reacted similarly to any furry object, including a man's beard. Figure 3.8 shows Albert's reactions to the rabbit and the dog.

Albert's reactions to these stimuli (rabbit, dog, furry object) illustrate the phenomenon known as stimulus generalization: once an organism has learned to associate a given behavior with a specific stimulus, it tends to show this behavior toward similar stimuli. The more similar the new stimuli were to the original conditioned stimulus, the greater was the intensity of Albert's reactions. As we noted above, the rabbit produced a more intense reaction than the dog. The fact that the intensity of the behavior generally decreases as the new stimuli become less similar to the original CS can be seen in many real-life situations. For example, suppose that a girl's father is domineering, overly strict, and generally mean to her. He is a highly competitive and successful businessman whom she views as valuing money more than anything else in life. In her teenage years, when she begins to select male companions she may show a distinct aversion to anyone who appears highly committed to materialistic goals. The less materialistic the boy, the less aversion she may feel. Therefore, she may develop a marked penchant for selecting unambitious, nonmaterialistic young men—the very antithesis of her father.

Fig. 3.8
Generalization of the fear response in an infant

After Albert was conditioned to fear a rat, he shows the fear reaction to a rabbit and a dog (Watson and Raynor, 1920).

Classical Conditioning

We can now understand why the child we mentioned earlier was frightened by an animal he had never seen before (the horse). Because he had previously been bitten by a dog, he learned (through classical conditioning) to fear that dog. Once he learned to associate a given behavior (fear) with a specific stimulus (a dog), he tended to show this behavior toward similar stimuli (such as a horse). In other words, the fear was generalized to similar stimuli. We would expect, however, that the child's fear of the dog (the original CS) would be more intense than his fear of the horse (the generalized stimulus).

Without generalization, learning would be meaningless. Since no two situations or stimuli are ever identical, we would be forced to learn a new response to every new situation. Imagine the difficulty an infant would have in learning to recognize his own mother. Without generalization, every time she appeared in a new outfit or hair style, she would be strange and unfamiliar. Clearly, the ability to generalize has adaptive value. For example, it is desirable that a child who has learned to be afraid of fire in a specific situation generalize this response to other situations. However, there are many situations which require that we inhibit the tendency to generalize. For example, it is not desirable that we respond in the same way to all persons wearing pants, to all people with long hair, or to all cards in a deck. Learning to make distinctions among similar stimuli is known as discrimination learning (see Fig. 3.9).

Discrimination Learning

It is often observed that a child who has learned to fear a *hot* stove will generalize this response to similar stimuli (*all* stoves). This generalization occurs spontaneously. The only way the child will narrow down this response to only hot stoves is through training, that is, through learning to discriminate between hot stoves and cold stoves.

This type of learning, whether it occurs in a natural setting or in a laboratory situation, involves the techniques employed in both acquisition and extinction training. The subject learns to respond (with fear, for example) to one stimulus, the *positive* stimulus (the hot stove), and to inhibit that response to a similar stimulus, the *negative* stimulus (a cold stove). In discrimination

c)

d)

Fig. 3.9
There are many divisions in contemporary American society. These often result from stimulus generalization. (a, Bruce Anspach—EPA Newsphoto. b, Harry Wilks—Stock, Boston. c, Tim Carlson—Stock, Boston. d, Daniel S. Brody—Stock, Boston.)

Fig. 3.10
Stimuli used in discrimination training
When the ellipse closely resembled the circle, the
dog could no longer discriminate. Continued
presentations led to behavior which Pavlov described
as "experimental neurosis."

learning, the UCS (pain) is associated with the positive stimulus and not with the negative stimulus. In a laboratory situation, this type of training is accomplished by pairing the positive stimulus with the UCS throughout training, and by withholding the UCS when the negative stimulus is presented. By the use of these procedures, many organisms, including humans, have been trained to discriminate between similar stimuli.

In discrimination training, the subject tends to respond to the negative stimulus as a result of stimulus generalization. Thus, the more similar the two stimuli are to each other, the more difficult is the discrimination training. When the two stimuli are extremely similar, discrimination behavior may break down, and the subject's behavior may change dramatically. Pavlov first noted this phenomenon in the course of training a dog to discriminate between a circle and an ellipse (Pavlov, 1927). When the circle and the ellipse were markedly different, the discrimination was readily acquired. Pavlov then gradually changed the shape of the ellipse to resemble the circle more closely. When the ratio of the axes was 9:8 (see Fig. 3.10), the dog could no longer discriminate; it salivated to both stimuli. Continued presentations led to further deterioration of performance, culminating in behavior which Pavlov described as "experimental neurosis." Whereas the dog had previously been compliant and placid, he now barked violently, wriggled about, and bit his restraining harness. This phenomenon has since been observed in a variety of different species, including man. For example, a father may encourage his child to come and sit on his lap. As a consequence, the child may develop positive emotional reactions to his father. However, if the child attempts to crawl onto his father's lap while his father is driving a car, he may be severely reprimanded, and the reprimand will produce fear in the child. To the father, these two situations are clearly different. The child, however, may find it difficult, if not impossible, to discriminate between these similar situations. He may become completely confused, unruly, and unmanageable every time he sees his father.

Higher-Order Conditioning

Another phenomenon of considerable significance, both practical and theoretical, is higher-order conditioning. As we have already discussed, in the typical classical conditioning experiment, a

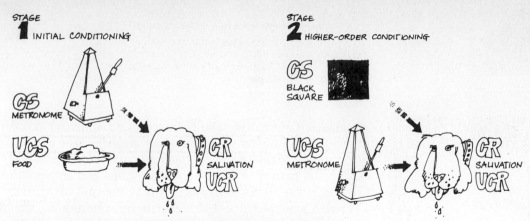

CS METRONOME

UCS FOOD

CR SALIVATION

UCR

CS BLACK SQUARE

UCS METRONOME

CR SALIVATION

UCR

response (CR) is conditioned to a previously neutral stimulus. This conditioning is accomplished by pairing the neutral stimulus with a UCS that consistently elicits the desired response. In higher-order conditioning, a previously conditioned stimulus is employed in much the same way as the UCS.

Fig. 3.11 ⑦
Higher-order conditioning
Schematic diagram of the two stages in establishing higher-order conditioning.

An experimental demonstration of this phenomenon is found in the work of Pavlov. In the first stage of the experiment, a dog was conditioned to salivate (CR) at the sound of a metronome (CS). The UCS was food. After this conditioning had been established, a black square was now paired with the sound of a metronome. The metronome, which was originally the CS, now served as the "UCS" in the second stage of this experiment. Recall that an unconditioned stimulus regularly elicits the desired response without prior training. As a result of training in the first stage, the metronome now regularly elicited salivation. Thus, in the second stage, the black square served as the CS, and the metronome as the "UCS." Figure 3.11 shows a diagram of both stages in the establishment of higher-order conditioning.

You might suppose that higher-order conditioning could be carried out _ad infinitum_. In other words, it might seem reasonable to use the black square as a "UCS" to condition another stimulus to salivation, and then use this new stimulus to condition still another stimulus, and so on. However, this is not possible. During the second stage of conditioning, the metronome's power to elicit salivation underwent experimental extinction because it was no longer being paired with the food.

Practical Implications of Classical Conditioning

You may have noticed that all of our examples of classical conditioning has involved the conditioning of some autonomic response to various stimuli.

We saw in Chapter 2 that the sympathetic branch of the autonomic system is active under conditions of stress, whereas the parasympathetic branch is generally dominant when the organism

Classical Conditioning

is placid. It should be clear that stress and nonstress reactions can both be conditioned to virtually any stimulus that precedes their occurrence. Many emotional disorders may be the result of accidental pairing of some neutral stimulus and an emotional response. We have already seen this in the case of Albert. Through generalization and higher-order conditioning, emotional disorders can become conditioned to a wide variety of different stimuli. It is believed that many unreasonable and irrational fears (phobias) arise in just this way. The following example illustrates these points:

> . . . the man who feared red skies at evening. Like most phobic persons, this patient was unable to explain why red skies had come to be anxiety-provoking for him. Only after expert behavioral analysis did he recall that as a boy he had been terrified at the red flames of a tenement fire in which he had thought at the time his mother was being burned to death.
>
> (Cameron and Magaret, 1951)

Using the principles discussed in this chapter, how can we explain the man's seemingly irrational fear of red skies? We might speculate that the thought of losing his mother acted as a "UCS" which evoked terror. This "UCS" was immediately preceded by the sight of the fire. Thus, after a single pairing, the fire (CS) acquired the capacity to elicit this strong emotional response. Finally, through generalization, the man came to fear red skies, since they resemble fire.

Operant Conditioning and Positive Reinforcement

So far, we have concerned ourselves exclusively with classically conditioned responses. But not all behavior is classically conditioned. For example, a dog learns to sit up at a signal from its master. It is then rewarded by its master with either food or praise. This is an illustration of operant conditioning. How does this situation differ from conditioning a dog to salivate at the sound of a metronome?

In classical conditioning we can specify the UCS which elicits the response, that is, salivation. When a dog learns to sit up,

Fig. 3.12
A rat in a skinner box.

what UCS elicits this response? Unlike the classical conditioning situation, we cannot specify the UCS for this response. The food or praise used as a reward is not the UCS, since it does not elicit the behavior in the first place. The food or praise *follows* the desired response, whereas in classical conditioning UCS (the food that causes the dog to salivate) both precedes and elicits the desired response.

Although operant conditioning differs in many respects from classical conditioning, many of the principles we have discussed in relation to classical conditioning apply also to operant conditioning; these include acquisition, extinction, spontaneous recovery, stimulus generalization, and discrimination.

Figure 3.12 shows a type of apparatus employed in the laboratory to study operant behavior. This apparatus is called a "Skinner box," after its developer, B. F. Skinner. When the rat presses the bar, it activates the food delivery mechanism. The food delivery mechanism is wired to a cumulative recorder which registers each response and the time at which it occurs (see Fig. 3.13).

Let's look at a typical demonstration of the acquisition of bar-pressing behavior. The animal (usually a rat) is deprived of food for a period of time preceding the experiment. We assume that the rat is now motivated by a hunger drive. The concept of drive will be discussed in Chapter 7; for the moment, it is important to know that drives increase an organism's activity.

After the rat is placed in the box, it will typically engage in a variety of different behaviors. It may move about the box, scratch itself, stand on its hind legs, and explore the cage with its paws. At some point, it may accidentally touch the bar with enough force to activate the mechanism. Food will then be delivered. The animal may or may not see the food immediately. Eventually it will see the food and eat it. Because the rat is hungry, it will then typically spend more time in the general vicinity of the food tray. After a while, it will press the bar again, and food will again be delivered. Finally, the rat will spend virtually all its time pressing the bar to obtain food (see Fig. 3.14).

What causes the rat to shift from diffuse activity to concentration upon a single behavior? To begin with, the rat is hungry, and "operates" upon its environment in various ways.

Fig. 3.13
Cumulative recorder used to register each response as it occurs in the Skinner box. The slope of the lines indicates the rate of response: a steep line indicates a high rate of response; a straight horizontal line indicates no response. (Courtesy of Ralph Gerbrands Co., Arlington, Massachusetts.)

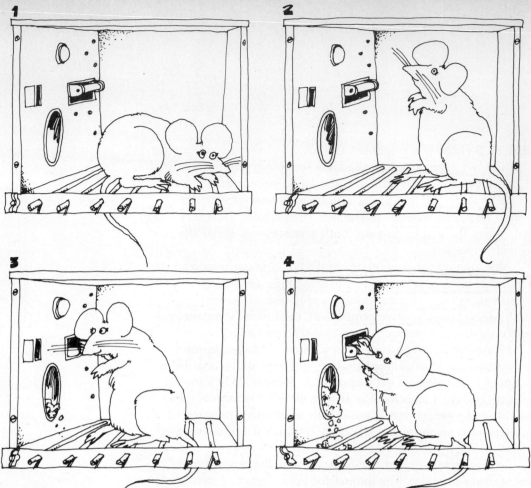

Fig. 3.14
When a hungry rat is first placed in a Skinner box, its behavior is characterized by diffuse and varied responses. When it accidentally presses the bar, food is delivered. Eventually it learns to press the bar to obtain food.

The actions by which an organism operates upon its environment are called operants. One of these operants, bar-pressing, provides food. The food in turn reinforces the rat's bar-pressing behavior—we call this positive reinforcement. A reinforcement is an event that strengthens a response that precedes it. A *positive* reinforcement strengthens the response by virtue of its *presentation*. Thus, food is a positive reinforcement because the presentation of food following a response increases the probability that the response will be repeated.

Note that, in operant conditioning, the organism's behavior is instrumental in obtaining the reinforcement. For this reason, operant conditioning is frequently referred to as instrumental learning or instrumental conditioning.

Many studies involving operant conditioning have shown that reinforcement is most effective when it immediately follows the response to be learned. The longer the delay between the response and the reinforcement, the less efficient is the learning. The principle of immediacy of reinforcement has many practical

Learning

implications. If an infant says "da-da" and we reward him several minutes later, he is less likely to learn to repeat "da-da" than if we had rewarded him immediately after his first "da-da." The importance of this principle is often overlooked in many traditional educational settings. If we assume that a good grade serves as a positive reinforcer, then a long delay between the occurrence of the desired behavior (doing well on an exam) and the attainment of the reward (getting the exam back with a good grade) runs counter to the principle of immediate reinforcement. Recent innovations in educational techniques emphasize immediate reinforcement as a means of enhancing the efficiency of the learning process. Teaching machines, programmed learning, and computer-assisted instruction are all positive examples of the application of this principle (see Chapter 5).

The example of operant conditioning that we discussed above used a rat as a subject and some elaborate equipment. Much human learning involving the conditioning of operant behavior does not require the use of laboratory equipment. Driving a car, reading, writing, speaking, and taking notes are all examples of learned operant behaviors. The key feature in all these behaviors is that the response is initiated by the organism itself instead of being elicited by the UCS. The response operates in some way upon the environment and, if followed by reinforcement, is more likely to occur again in the same situation.

Shaping of Operant Behavior

Many learned behaviors have a very low initial probability of occurrence. For example, a rat will not normally press a bar when it is first introduced into the Skinner box. As we indicated earlier, we may wait until the animal accidentally presses the bar, or we may "shape" the bar-pressing response. Shaping involves the reinforcement of a series of small steps leading to the desired response. Like the man at the beginning of this chapter who was about to build a house, we must first decide what we want the final product to look like. In other words, we must select in advance the behavior we want the organism to perform. We then place the organism in the learning situation and reward any behavior that is recognizable as an approximation of the desired performance. When the organism has learned these

Operant Conditioning and Positive Reinforcement

95

approximations, we set higher standards that are successively closer approximations to the desired behavior. Finally, we reward only the desired behavior.

Let's look at an example of how we can shape bar-pressing behavior in a rat. First, we place a hungry rat in the Skinner box and allow it to explore the box. We then deliver food when the animal is standing near the food delivery mechanism. It soon learns to go to the mechanism to obtain food. Now we begin to shape the bar-pressing response. Initially we reward the animal for merely approaching the bar. When the rat has learned this well, we reinforce it only when it touches the bar or a nearby area. Finally, we reinforce it only when it presses the bar. From this point on, reward is *contingent* only upon pressing the bar with sufficient force to activate the mechanism.

Fig. 3.15
Animals trained through operant conditioning. (Photo by Stephen Wicks, Andover, Mass.)

In addition to shaping a single response, such as bar-pressing, a whole series of responses may be shaped individually and then chained together to form a complex series of responses.

Animal trainers have obtained some dramatic results in shaping operant behavior. Figure 3.15 shows an example of a behavior that has been shaped this way. We can probably all think of examples of shaping behavior in our everyday lives—in bringing up children, in the learning of attitudes, and even in the training of our pets.

Imagine that you have an instructor who paces back and forth across the room as he lectures. Suppose that you wanted your instructor to lecture from a certain location in the room, say, in front of his desk. How would you go about shaping his behavior? First, you must decide what to use as reinforcement for the desired behavior. Many things can act as reinforcers, particularly for humans. In this situation, taking notes, paying attention, and showing interest could probably serve as effective reinforcers. Of course, you would need the cooperation of the entire class for this experiment. In the beginning, you would reinforce any activity approximating the final desired response (standing in front of the desk). At first, you would reinforce (by paying attention, or taking notes) any movement toward the selected area. Whenever the instructor moved away from the designated area you would withhold reinforcement (stop paying attention, talk, stop taking notes). Soon you should have the instructor standing close to the desk area. Now you reinforce him only when he stands in front of the desk, and you withhold reinforcement for all other movement. If your entire class has cooperated, your instructor should now be lecturing from in front of his desk. Thus, you will have succeeded in shaping his behavior.

Superstitious behavior

Sometimes behavior is shaped accidentally. Since reinforcement strengthens the response that precedes it, any response followed by reinforcement tends to be repeated. Consequently, a response may be learned simply because it happens to be followed by reinforcement, whether or not this response was instrumental in obtaining the reinforcement. Behavior learned as a result of this coincidental pairing is called superstitious behavior.

Suppose that you sit in a particular seat while taking an exam and get a high grade; and the next time you take a test, you sit in a different seat and do poorly. On the basis of these two experiences, you might come to believe that there was something "lucky" about that first seat. You are now well on the way to developing superstitious behavior. Such behavior is remarkably resistant to extinction, since failure to engage in this behavior involves a certain degree of risk. If the seat is *really* lucky, then you are taking a chance by not sitting there. Even a few poor performances in the lucky seat may not discourage you—"I'd

have completely bombed the test if it weren't for my lucky seat."
In fact, if you really believe that sitting in a particular seat is
crucial to your success, you may actually do poorly if you take a
test in another seat.

Superstitious behaviors are common in everyday life; most of
us can think of examples in our own behavior as well as in the
behavior of others. Have you ever noticed the gambler's rituals
before throwing the dice, or a ballplayer's insistence on using the
same bat or wearing the same shirt? Do you know people who
knock on wood, avoid black cats, or throw salt over their left
shoulder?

Analogous superstitious behavior has been observed in the
laboratory in experiments with lower animals. For example, a rat
may scratch itself before it presses the bar to receive
reinforcement. The animal is learning a chain of responses
(scratching and then bar-pressing) which leads to reinforcement,
even though only the final response (bar-pressing) is instrumental
in obtaining this reinforcement. The superstitious behavior
(scratching) will persist so long as reinforcement appears to be
associated with it. Superstitious behavior will disappear only if
the organism tries (and gets reinforced for) the appropriate
behavior without first making the superstitious response, that is,
if the rat presses the bar (and is reinforced) without first
scratching.

Extinction and Spontaneous Recovery

As we indicated earlier, operant conditioning follows the same
laws as classical conditioning. In classical conditioning, when the
UCS is no longer paired with the CS, the CR undergoes
experimental extinction. In operant conditioning, experimental
extinction will occur if the operant response is no longer followed
by reinforcement. For example, if the rat is no longer rewarded
for pressing the bar, it will eventually stop pressing it. If the rat
is removed from the apparatus and returned at a later time, it will
start pressing the bar again. Thus, spontaneous recovery also
occurs in operant conditioning. Figure 3.16 shows the cumulative
curves obtained during acquisition, extinction, and spontaneous
recovery of the bar-pressing response in rats.

Learning

Fig. 3.16
A useful measure of learning in the operant conditioning situation is the rate of response, which is shown in a cumulative response curve. Note that the acquisition curve is steep, indicating a high rate of response. When the line becomes horizontal, the animal is no longer responding (extinction). Notice how the rate of response picks up after a rest period (spontaneous recovery).

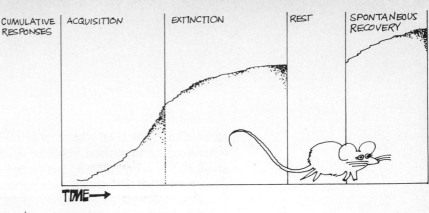

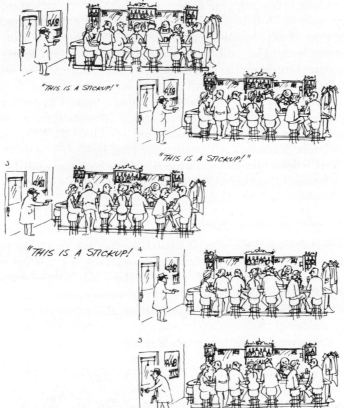

Fig. 3.17
Extinction: a cartoonist's suggestion for reducing the crime rate. (Drawing by Opie; copyright © 1961 by The New Yorker Magazine, Inc.)

Extinction procedures have many applications in real-life situations. Parents sometimes have to use extinction procedures when they find that they have inadvertently reinforced behaviors that they consider undesirable. For example, some children quickly learn that the only way to gain their parents' attention is to cry, throw temper tantrums, or engage in other forms of disruptive behavior. These behaviors are learned operants—they are instrumental in obtaining parental attention. One way to

Operant Conditioning and Positive Reinforcement

extinguish them is to withdraw reinforcement (attention) whenever the undesired behavior occurs. Optimally, extinction should be accompanied by reinforcement of the desired behaviors. That is, the parents should pay particular attention to the child when he does something constructive.

The following case illustrates an application of extinction procedures. A five-year-old girl had become a serious medical risk as a result of constantly scratching her face, neck, and other parts of her body. Her body had become a mass of open sores, suppurating wounds, and large scabs. Her mother then received training in a mental health clinic to withhold all reinforcement, including attention, whenever the child engaged in scratching behavior, and to provide liberal reinforcements (praise, gold stars, goodies, refreshments, and doll clothes) when the girl engaged in desirable behaviors while *not* scratching herself. Within a period of six weeks, the girl stopped scratching entirely, and the wounds on her body healed (Allen and Harris, 1966).

Stimulus Generalization

In our discussion of classical conditioning, we indicated that as soon as an organism has learned to associate a given behavior with a specific stimulus, it tends to show this behavior toward similar stimuli. We referred to this phenomenon as stimulus generalization. Stimulus generalization also occurs in operant conditioning. As soon as an animal has learned a response in a specific stimulus situation (such as the Skinner box), it will tend to make the same response in similar situations. Thus, if we were to slightly modify the bar, the lighting conditions, and the nature of the flooring material, the animal would continue to press the bar, though at first at a slightly lower rate. The more the new situation differs from the original, the lower will be the initial rate of responding.

In a study of stimulus generalization, pigeons were placed in a modified Skinner box and trained to peck at a panel of a specific color. After conditioning had been established, the color of the panel was varied systematically (Haber and Kalish, 1963). Figure 3.18 presents the results obtained in this study. Note that the number of responses decreases as the stimuli become increasingly different from the original stimulus.

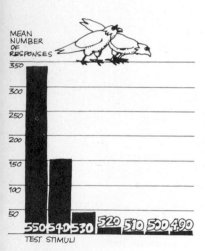

MEAN NUMBER OF RESPONSES

350
300
250
200
150
100
50

550 540 530 520 510 500 490

TEST STIMULI

Fig. 3.18
Stimulus generalization curve for six test stimuli. Pigeons were conditioned to respond to 550 mm, and then tested for stimulus generalization. (After A. Haber and I. Kalish, "Prediction of Discrimination from Generalization after Variations in Schedule of Reinforcement," *Science*, **142**, pp. 412–413, October 18, 1963. Copyright © 1963 by the American Association for the Advancement of Science.)

Discrimination Learning

The procedures for establishing discrimination in operant conditioning are similar to those we discussed in relation to classical conditioning. We reinforce the response when it occurs in the presence of the positive stimulus, and we do not reinforce the behavior in the presence of the negative stimulus.

Suppose that you wanted to determine whether a one-year-old child is color blind. Since the youngster is incapable of sophisticated language at this age, you cannot use any of the conventional color blindness tests that are available for older children and adults. However, you could set up a color discrimination task. There are many different ways you could design this task. You could, for example, use a panel displaying two geometric designs that are identical in every respect except their colors (red and green). When the child touches one color (green), you reinforce him by giving him a candy. When he touches the other color (red), you withhold this reinforcement. You must systematically vary the position of the colors, from left to right, to be sure that he is responding to color and not to location. If the child learns this discrimination, you can assume that he is not color blind (at least with respect to red and green).

Secondary Reinforcement

Let's introduce a slight modification in the bar-pressing experiment. Before placing a hungry rat in the Skinner box, we sound a buzzer, and then provide food immediately. We repeat this sequence a number of times. Then we place the animal in the Skinner box. Instead of rewarding the bar-pressing response with food, we sound the buzzer immediately following each time the rat presses the bar. We find that the animal learns the bar-pressing response.

Remember that we defined reinforcement as any event that strengthens the response that precedes it. In terms of this definition, then, the buzzer serves as a reinforcement for the bar-pressing response. How has the buzzer acquired reinforcement properties?

Food for a hungry animal and water for a thirsty animal are primary reinforcers, since their reward value depends little, if at all, on previous learning. Research has demonstrated that any event regularly associated with a primary reinforcement also comes to acquire reinforcing properties. Such events, or stimuli, are known as _secondary_ reinforcers. Because the buzzer was regularly associated with food (a primary reinforcer), it became a secondary reinforcer for the bar-pressing behavior. Secondary reinforcers do not have the permanency of primary reinforcers. They are subject to extinction if they are not at least occasionally reassociated with the primary reinforcer.

Many of the reinforcers that are so effective in controlling human behavior are secondary in nature. What was the nature of the reinforcement we used to shape the instructor's behavior in the example discussed earlier, to make him stand in front of his desk? Paying attention, taking notes, and appearing to be interested are all secondary reinforcers. An A grade on an examination certainly has a reinforcing value. In many ways, secondary reinforcers are more convenient to use than primary reinforcers. If you had to provide a primary reinforcer, such as food or candy, every time a child did something desirable, your pockets would have to be perpetually filled, and you would wreak havoc with the child's feeding schedule and nutrition. Praise is frequently used as a secondary reinforcer with children and pets.

In humans, one of the strongest secondary reinforcers is money. A somewhat similar phenomenon can be observed in lower animals. In one study, chimpanzees were trained to work for poker chips. These poker chips served as tokens which the animals could later insert into a vending machine (Cowles, 1937). Figure 3.19 shows a chimpanzee inserting a poker chip into the vending machine to obtain food, the primary reinforcer.

A relatively new therapy which has been quite successful with certain types of emotionally disturbed patients, is called behavior modification. Some forms of this therapy rely heavily on the use of tokens (secondary reinforcers) to bring about desired behavioral changes. Let's see how tokens were used in a hospital setting to condition operant behaviors.

Patients in mental hospitals typically display a wide variety of disorganized behaviors. Some are sloppy about their personal hygiene; they may not shave, bathe, or change their clothing. Often it is difficult to get them to the dining room in time for meals. Some mope listlessly around the ward and show little interest in their surroundings.

Fig. 3.19
Chimpanzee inserting token (secondary reinforcer) to obtain primary reinforcement (food). (Yerkes Regional Primate Research Center, Emory University.)

Learning

102

In one study, the experimenters wanted to condition behaviors such as getting to the dining room on time, maintaining personal hygiene, and performing simple household duties. Since the experiment was performed in a hospital setting, the experimenters had to use reinforcers that were available there. Variables such as food, sleeping and dining conditions, and privileges such as television viewing could all be controlled by the experimenters and, thus, could serve as reinforcers. Instead of rewarding desired behavior directly with these reinforcers, patients were rewarded with tokens. These tokens could then be exchanged for various special privileges that were important to individual patients (Gericke, 1965).

As a result of the introduction of the token system, many patients showed dramatic changes in behavior. Many who had been passive and inactive for years now took a sudden interest in their surroundings. One woman, who had previously refused all food except milk, eventually added other foods to her diet, including bacon and eggs for breakfast.

The use of behavior modification as a therapeutic technique is discussed in Chapter 14.

Partial Reinforcement

In the laboratory experiments that we have discussed so far, every correct response was reinforced. In real-life situations, however, reinforcement follows the conditioned operant responses only a proportion of the times that they occur.

Parents are not always available to reward their infant for saying "da-da"; gamblers do not win every time they put two dollars "on the nose"; students are not always rewarded with high grades for studying; parents are not always successful in directing their children's behavior. Yet, in spite of frequent nonreinforcements, these behaviors show considerable persistence. These situations involve partial, rather than continuous, reinforcement. In partial reinforcement the response is reinforced only a proportion of the times that it occurs.

The acquisition of operant responses usually proceeds more rapidly under continuous reinforcement than under partial reinforcement. However, when comparable levels of learning are achieved under both conditions, the extinction data are in sharp contrast to the acquisition data. Subjects successfully trained

Fig. 3.20
Resistance to extinction following continuous versus partial
reinforcement. (After W. O. Jenkins, H. McFann, and F. L.
Clayton, "A Methodological Study of Extinction Following
Aperiodic and Continuous Reinforcement," *Journal of
Comparative and Physiological Psychology*, **43**, 1950, pp.
155–167. Copyright © 1950 by the American
Psychological Association, and used by permission.)

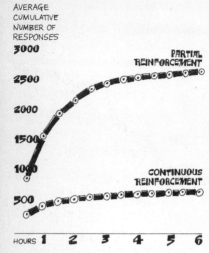

AVERAGE
CUMULATIVE
NUMBER OF
RESPONSES

under partial reinforcement typically show a greater resistance to extinction; that is, more extinction trials are required to extinguish the behavior.

Figure 3.20 compares extinction data for continuously and partially reinforced learned operant behaviors. Note the greater resistance to extinction after partial reinforcement. The number of responses required to extinguish the partially reinforced operant response was almost five times as great as the number required to extinguish the continuously reinforced operant response.

These experimental findings have many practical implications. Behaviors persist even though they are not always reinforced. The baby learns to say "da-da" despite frequent nonreinforcement; gamblers continue betting even though they may win only occasionally; most students continue to study in spite of an occasional low grade; and parents continue to direct their children's behavior despite frequent lack of success.

There are many different ways to allot partial reinforcements. When they are administered according to some plan, they are ordinarily referred to as schedules of reinforcement. At one extreme, we may reinforce each correct response (continuous reinforcement); at the other extreme, we may reinforce no responses at all (extinction).

Schedules of reinforcement

Schedules of reinforcement can be based either on the time between reinforcements, or on the number of nonreinforced responses between reinforcements. The first is called an *interval* schedule; the second is called a *ratio* schedule. The reinforcements may also be administered according to some regular, or *fixed* plan, or according to some irregular, or *variable* plan. The combination of these two dimensions yields the following four schedules:

	Interval	Ratio
Fixed plan	fixed interval	fixed ratio
Variable plan	variable interval	variable ratio

1. Fixed-interval (FI). In fixed-interval schedules, reinforcement is administered after a fixed period of time, for example, every 40 seconds. Regardless of how much the animal responds between

Learning

reinforcements, he must wait 40 seconds before the next response is reinforced.

The response rate under a fixed-interval schedule is usually less than under the other schedules. Ordinarily, the response rate drops immediately after a reinforcement, and then slowly builds up just before the next reinforcement. This results in a "scalloping" effect on the cumulative response record (Fig. 3.21). This schedule has been successful in determining how well various organisms are able to discriminate time intervals.

Many parents employ a fixed-interval feeding schedule. When parents refer to a "two o'clock feeding," they are using this schedule. Some parents will awaken a child from a deep sleep in order to keep to the schedule. Pet owners who feed their dogs on schedule will testify to the increased activity level just before feeding time.

Wage earners who receive a weekly salary are on a fixed-interval schedule. However, their response rate does not usually show the scalloping effect (with a slowdown after the weekly "reward"), since their employers will generally not permit them to decrease their work output after they get their paycheck. (It is interesting that Friday is the most common "payday." Most employees are permitted to "slow down" on weekends.)

2. Variable-interval (VI). In variable-interval schedules, reinforcement is administered after a variable interval of time. For example, reinforcement may be given 40 seconds after one reinforcement, then 5 seconds later, and then after 75 seconds, and so on. We can specify this schedule in terms of the average interval between reinforcements.

The response rate under a variable-interval schedule is generally greater than under a fixed-interval schedule. Most students spend more time studying when they know an instructor will spring a surprise quiz from time to time (variable-interval), than when regularly scheduled examinations are announced (fixed-interval). Moreover, the amount of time spent studying will be more evenly distributed when surprise quizzes are given. Many students will show a spurt of studying activity just before an announced examination, and relatively little studying between exams.

3. Fixed-ratio (FR). Fixed-ratio schedules require that the organism emit a fixed number of responses before receiving

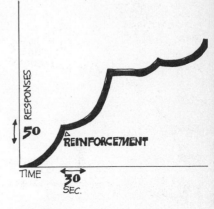

Fig. 3.21
Cumulative record under fixed-interval schedule. Note the "scalloping" effect.

Operant Conditioning and Positive Reinforcement

105

Fig. 3.22
The "one-armed" bandit puts the gambler on a variable-ratio schedule. Both the rate of response and resistance to extinction are very high under this schedule. (Reprinted by permission of The World Publishing Company from *Which Way Did He Go?* by Ronald Searle. Copyright © 1956, 1957, 1958, 1959, 1960, 1961 by Ronald Searle.)

Learning

reinforcement. The schedule is usually described as a ratio between the number of nonreinforced responses and the number of reinforced responses. Thus, if reinforcement occurs after every fifth response, the schedule is described as a 5:1 fixed-ratio schedule. You may recognize that the fixed-ratio schedule is employed in industry when workers are paid on a piecework basis.

The response rate under a fixed-ratio schedule is generally steady and quite high. Pigeons have been trained on a fixed-ratio schedule in which the total number of reinforcements received is barely enough to keep them alive. It has been shown that the higher the ratio, the higher the response rate. Migrant workers are frequently paid on a piecework basis (fixed-ratio schedule). Each time they harvest a fixed amount of produce, they receive monetary reinforcement. The total pay is generally barely sufficient to maintain life. Thus, most migrant workers must work at a consistently high pace in order just to survive.

4. Variable-ratio (VR). In the variable-ratio schedule, as in the fixed-ratio schedule, reinforcement is delivered after a specific number of responses. However, in the variable-ratio schedule, the number of responses required before receiving reinforcement varies. For example, reinforcement may occur after seven responses, then after twenty responses, then after two responses, and so on. We can specify this schedule in terms of the average ratio of nonreinforced to reinforced responses.

Variable-ratio schedules characteristically produce an extremely high and steady rate of responding. Moreover, responses acquired under variable-ratio schedules are extremely resistant to extinction. If you think, for a moment, about the characteristics of variable-ratio schedules, the reason should become clear—the organism never "knows" but that its very next response could be the one that is reinforced.

Gambling is reinforced on a variable-ratio schedule. Inveterate gamblers continue to respond (place bets) at a very high rate, always hoping to make a killing or hit the jackpot on the very next bet. Figure 3.22 shows a man operating the "one-armed" bandit. The payoff on slot machines is on a variable-ratio schedule.

Operant Conditioning and Negative Reinforcement

Up to this point, we have been discussing positive reinforcement. We defined positive reinforcement as any event that strengthens the response that precedes it by virtue of its presentation. There are also *negative* reinforcers. Negative reinforcement is defined as any event that strengthens the preceding response by its *removal* or *termination*. For example, when a child touches a hot stove, he immediately withdraws his hand. The withdrawal of the hand terminates the pain, and the termination of the pain reinforces his withdrawal response.

Fig. 3.23
Rat working to escape shock.

Negative reinforcement may achieve very much the same results as positive reinforcement. An organism can learn to press a bar to terminate a shock as well as to receive food. We refer to situations involving the use of negative reinforcement of operant behavior as *aversive conditioning.* Aversive conditioning experiments are generally set up in one of two ways: one involves the *escape* from an aversive stimulus; the other, the *avoidance* of an aversive stimulus.

Escape Conditioning

In escape conditioning, the organism cannot avoid the aversive stimulus. It can escape only after the aversive stimulus has been presented. For example, suppose that we place a rat in a Skinner box which has been set up to deliver shocks. The animal cannot avoid the shocks, but can turn them off by pressing a bar. The animal soon acquires the bar-pressing response that terminates the aversive stimulus. Figure 3.23 shows a rat working to escape shock.

Avoidance Conditioning

Avoidance conditioning is similar in many ways to escape conditioning. In avoidance conditioning, some signal (for example, a tone) precedes the onset of the aversive stimulus. The animal can avoid the aversive stimulus by making the appropriate response when the signal comes on. If it responds to the signal quickly enough, it avoids the aversive stimulus.

Let's return to the bar-pressing example. In this situation, the animal learns to press the bar as soon as the warning signal sounds. If it does not respond quickly enough, it receives a shock that can be terminated only by pressing the bar. Ordinarily, escape conditioning (pressing the bar to terminate the shocks) must precede avoidance learning (pressing the bar when the warning signal sounds).

Many human situations involve escape and avoidance learning. Let's return briefly to the example of a child touching a hot stove. It should be clear that the child will eventually learn to avoid the hot stove. His "warning signal" will be the sight of the hot stove. We learn to avoid many dangerous situations in this

Learning

way—a particular object acts as a warning signal by reminding us of past experience.

Let's suppose that, after a long hard day, you finally get the opportunity to relax over a home-cooked meal. You are extremely hungry and the bowl of soup placed before you looks and smells particularly inviting. Without hesitation, you dig right in. To your dismay, the soup is extremely hot and scalds your tongue. You hurl forth a few profane expletives, bang your spoon against the table, and push back your chair. None of these reactions does anything to lessen the pain. You realize that *escape* or "getting away" *after* the pain has begun is not really good enough. It would have been better to *avoid* the pain entirely. You must learn what behavior is adaptive here, that is, what behavior will lead to avoiding the pain. As you sit glowering over the soup, you notice a small cloud of water vapor emanating from the bowl. If you are an intelligent person, you will learn that the water vapor is a "warning signal," telling you that the soup is too hot to eat. Hopefully, you will learn to avoid future pain by responding to this signal.

Punishment

Perhaps no question arouses more emotional reactions and less illuminating discussion than the debate over the use of punishment, especially on children. Advocates of punishment vehemently proclaim, "Spare the rod and spoil the child." Their opponents reply, with equal conviction, that punishment is a throwback to the primitive stages in our development as a species, that it is as outmoded as the dodo bird, and that it leaves in its wake psychological wounds that never completely heal. The truth probably lies somewhere between these two extremes. We say "probably," because the issue is extremely complex and is currently the subject of intensive investigation. Our tentative conclusions must be tempered by the recognition that we do not yet have all the answers, and probably will not have them for many years.

Before we discuss some of the things we *do* know about punishment, we must establish a working definition. We shall define punishment operationally as an aversive stimulus applied to an operant response. Punishment may be physical, like a shock to a rat's feet, or a rap on a child's bottom. In some organisms, punishment can often be verbal ("bad dog," "naughty boy").

When we speak of punishment in animal studies, we usually mean physical punishment which inflicts pain. For obvious ethical reasons, laboratory studies involving punishment in humans rarely employ physical punishment. If physical punishment is used, it is restricted to mild levels, where the threat of punishment is often "worse than its bite."

Let's now look at some of the things we know about the effects of punishment upon behavior. Its most general effect is to suppress the response that preceded it. However, timing is critical. Punishment must immediately precede or follow the response in order to achieve maximum suppression (Parke, 1969). The greater the severity of the punishment, the greater is the suppression effect (Reynolds, 1968). Human studies typically use noise as an aversive stimulus and have revealed that punishment is effective even after a few seconds delay, provided it is sufficiently strong. Weaker aversive stimuli must be applied immediately to be effective.

Delay of punishment may explain some of the difficulties in housebreaking a dog. Punishment is often delayed because the owners are not around when the prohibited act occurs. The owners may punish the dog when they get home, but this may be several hours too late. Because punishment suppresses the response immediately preceding it, the dog may learn, instead, to suppress tail-wagging and other greeting responses.

With human children, punishment seems most appropriate when used to suppress potentially harmful behavior. For example, if a child has a tendency to dart into the street without looking at the traffic, punishment will temporarily inhibit that response and, hopefully, alert him to the street's dangers. Punishment is most effective when it is used to suppress an undesirable response, and at the same time increase the likelihood that desired behavior will occur and be positively reinforced. Thus, when the street-darting behavior has been suppressed, the parents should take the opportunity to positively reinforce their child for avoiding the street altogether.

Furthermore, research with children suggests that punishment is more likely to be effective when it is administered by a warm and accepting person rather than by a cold and hostile person

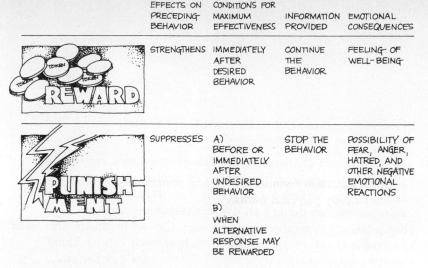

	EFFECTS ON PRECEDING BEHAVIOR	CONDITIONS FOR MAXIMUM EFFECTIVENESS	INFORMATION PROVIDED	EMOTIONAL CONSEQUENCES
REWARD	STRENGTHENS	IMMEDIATELY AFTER DESIRED BEHAVIOR	CONTINUE THE BEHAVIOR	FEELING OF WELL-BEING
PUNISHMENT	SUPPRESSES	A) BEFORE OR IMMEDIATELY AFTER UNDESIRED BEHAVIOR B) WHEN ALTERNATIVE RESPONSE MAY BE REWARDED	STOP THE BEHAVIOR	POSSIBILITY OF FEAR, ANGER, HATRED, AND OTHER NEGATIVE EMOTIONAL REACTIONS

Table 3.1
Summary of differences between reward and punishment and their effects on human behavior.

(Sears et al., 1957; Parke and Walters, 1967). Nevertheless, the administration of punishment is a very tricky affair. Punishment, particularly when it is severe and frequent, may lead to many undesirable emotions, including fear, anxiety, anger, and hatred. Children who are often punished by a parent, either physically or verbally, may come to fear and hate that parent. As a result, the parent's ability to guide the child's behavior, either through punishment or through positive reinforcement, may be forever undermined by the child's attitude toward him or her.

Moreover, strong punishment may induce so much anxiety that an individual will not be able to cope with everyday life situations. In one study, six- and seven-year-old children were required to learn a stimulus discrimination under low-intensity or high-intensity punishment (a loud noise). They had to avoid selecting stimuli similar to those associated with punishment. The task was readily mastered by children under low-intensity punishment, but the children experienced much greater difficulty when the punishment was "severe." The investigators hypothesized that the high-intensity punishment may have produced anxiety levels that were too high to permit adaptive learning to occur (Aronfreed and Leff, 1963).

The continued use of punishment in an environment from which escape is impossible (for example, in class with a teacher who scolds incessantly) may also cause the child to withdraw psychologically from the situation (for example, to daydream) and to become passive (Seligman et al., 1969). It is quite possible many children are school "drop-outs" long before they physically leave the school.

Table 3.1 summarizes some of the different ways in which rewards and punishments affect human behavior.

Operant Conditioning and Positive Reinforcement

Practical Implications of Operant Conditioning

In the previous chapter, we saw how biofeedback can apparently allow individuals to achieve a certain degree of control over so-called involuntary functions. In this chapter, we have seen that an organism can modify an operant response (such as bar-pressing) to receive reinforcement. Can an organism also learn to modify involuntary functions, such as heart rate or blood pressure, to obtain reinforcement?

In a series of ingenious studies, Neil Miller and his associates have demonstrated quite conclusively that operant control over autonomic responses is indeed possible (Miller, 1969). Using a variety of organisms and several different types of reinforcers, these investigators have shown that organisms can learn to control an astonishingly wide assortment of autonomic responses —increasing or decreasing salivary secretion, producing changes in heart rate or blood pressure, modifying intestinal contractions, and even changing the rate at which their kidneys form urine—all to obtain a reward (Miller, 1969).

The practical implications of these studies are enormous. It is quite possible that many psychosomatic disorders (physical symptoms resulting from psychological causes) have inadvertently been shaped in real-life situations through operant conditioning. For example, suppose that a businessman is particularly harassed by a series of economic setbacks. The resulting tension produces a number of physiological symptoms, among them irregular heart rhythm and increased blood pressure. If his business associates become solicitous about his health, they may voluntarily relieve him of some of the upsetting burdens and may even encourage him to take it easy for a while. However, this very release from harassment may serve to reinforce the man's tendency to respond with these kinds of bodily symptoms any time he is faced with upsetting circumstances.

If it is true that psychosomatic symptoms may be learned through operant conditioning, it is also possible that operant techniques may be employed to relieve these symptoms. Much research is now being conducted along these lines. Figure 3.24 illustrates one of the operant techniques employed to train patients to control abnormal heart rhythms.

One of the most intriguing concepts to come out of contemporary learning research is that the same principles of

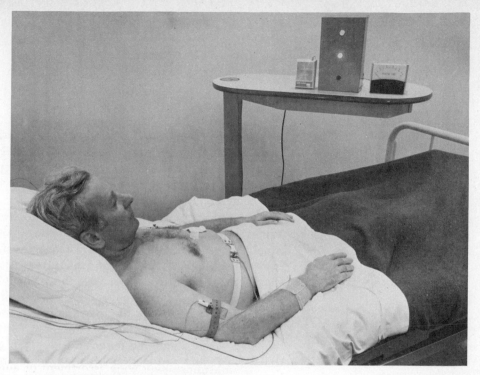

Fig. 3.24
A technician in the Laboratory of
Behavioral Sciences, Gerontology
Research Center, Baltimore,
Maryland, demonstrates a
technique used in attempts to
teach patients to control
abnormal heart rhythms. A
"traffic sign" with red, yellow,
and green lights shows the
subject how he is doing. An
intercom, to the left of the
"traffic sign," enables him to
communicate with the doctor. A
meter, to the right, shows him
what percentage of time he is
accomplishing his task. (NIH
Gerontology Photo.)

learning that guide the acquisition of adaptive behavior apply
equally well to the acquisition of maladaptive behavior. Any
behavior, whether adaptive or otherwise, that leads to
reinforcement is likely to be learned in a given situation. Some
students learn to study in order to reduce the anxiety associated
with an upcoming test, while other students learn to avoid this
anxiety by engaging in activities (like going to the movies), that
take their minds off the impending examination. Both of these
different forms of behavior, intended to alleviate anxiety, are
learned. The students who study, however, have learned adaptive
behavior that is likely to culminate in passing the course, while
students who go to the movies to take their minds off the
upcoming test, are engaging in maladaptive behavior that, if
practiced chronically, will increase the probability that they will
not pass the course.

Many new treatment procedures have been developed
recently to modify maladaptive behavior by the judicious
application of learning principles. We have previously referred to
these techniques as behavior modification. Consider the following
case involving a compulsive gambler.

A 37-year-old married man, the father of two, had frequently
recurring episodes, lasting several months at a time, during which
his entire life became dominated by compulsive betting on race
horses. Each morning he would open the newspaper to the racing
page, and engage in a series of time-consuming and ritualized
activities leading to the placing of his bets. During these episodes,

*Practical
Implications of
Operant
Conditioning*

he completely neglected his family and his marital obligations. His sexual activities declined to zero. He was referred to a behavior therapist after his wife, deeply concerned over steadily mounting debts, complained that she could no longer keep house and home together.

The treatment of this man consisted of the random administration of unpleasant electrical shocks during his ritualized, daily betting activities. There were nine treatment days over a two-week period, during which he received almost 700 shocks. By the fourth day, he reported that he had to force himself to open the daily papers. By the end of the treatment, he had lost all desire to buy the morning paper and to follow the races. Follow-up observations extending more than a year after treatment, have shown no renewed interest in gambling. Indeed, the man's family and marital situation, including his sexual behavior, underwent dramatic improvement during this period (Goorney, 1968).

Learning Through Imitation

We noted previously that punishment may have undesirable side effects. One effect that we did not mention is the possibility that the person who administers physical punishment may serve as an aggressive model for the child. Bandura noted this condition:

> When a parent punishes his child physically for having aggressed toward peers, for example, the intended outcome of this training is that the child should refrain from hitting others. The child, however, is also learning from parental demonstration how to aggress physically. And the imitative learning may provide the direction for the child's behavior when he is similarly frustrated in subsequent social interactions.
>
> (Bandura, 1967)

The role of imitation in aggressive behavior is discussed more fully in Chapter 12.

Much of human behavior is probably learned through imitation. When a child learns to speak, he observes and imitates both the facial expressions and vocal sounds produced by his parents. Subsequently, he learns to ride a bicycle, drive a car, read a novel, throw a baseball, and smoke a cigarette largely through observing others and imitating their actions. The expression "like father, like son" implies that children may *behave* like their parents as well as look like them.

Summary

1. Learning is defined as a relatively permanent change in behavior, resulting from experience or practice.

2. In the most basic form of learning, classical conditioning, a neutral stimulus is paired with another stimulus (unconditioned stimulus, UCS) which naturally gives rise to a given response (unconditioned response, UCR). The neutral stimulus acquires the capacity to elicit this response. The previously neutral stimulus is now called the conditioned stimulus (CS) and the response is called the conditioned response (CR).

3. When the CS is presented alone on a number of successive trials (extinction trials), the strength of the CR gradually decreases.

4. If an organism that has undergone experimental extinction is brought back into the experimental setting at a later time, the presentation of the CS alone may lead to the occurrence of the CR. This is called spontaneous recovery.

5. When a response to a given stimulus has been learned, the organism tends to make that response to similar stimuli as well; this is called stimulus generalization. Generally, the greater the similarity of the other stimuli to the original CS, the greater is the tendency for the CR to occur.

6. Learning to make distinctions among similar stimuli is called discrimination learning. In discrimination learning, the UCS is associated with the positive stimulus and not with the negative stimulus.

7. In higher-order conditioning, the CS is paired with a neutral stimulus, so that the neutral stimulus gradually acquires the capacity to elicit the CR. However, the ability to achieve higher-order conditioning is limited by the fact that the CS used in place of the UCS undergoes experimental extinction if it is not occasionally paired with the UCS.

8. The principles of classical conditioning have many practical implications. Unreasonable and irrational fears are often conditioned, and, through generalization and higher-order conditioning, spread to a wide variety of different stimuli.

9. In operant conditioning, the organism typically operates upon its environment to bring about a reinforcement. Reinforcement is most effective when it immediately follows the response to be learned.

10. The principle of immediacy of reinforcement has many practical applications in everyday life as well as in educational settings. Teaching machines, programmed learning, and computer-assisted instruction are some of the educational applications of the principle of immediate reinforcement.

11. Many responses initially have a low probability of occurring. However, by reinforcing successive approximations to the desired behavior, the final response can be "shaped." Moreover, a whole series of responses may be shaped individually and then chained together to form a complex sequence of responses.

12. Extinction, spontaneous recovery, and generalization occur in operant conditioning just as in classical conditioning.

13. To establish a discrimination in operant conditioning, we reinforce the response when it occurs in the presence of the positive stimulus and do not reinforce the behavior in the presence of the negative stimulus.

14. Food and water are primary reinforcers, since their reinforcement value depends little, if at all, on previous learning. However, any event regularly associated with a primary reinforcer comes to acquire reinforcing properties (it becomes a secondary reinforcer).

15. Some forms of behavior modification rely heavily on the use of tokens as secondary reinforcers.

16. When reinforcement is applied to a given behavior only a proportion of the times that it occurs, the behavior becomes more resistant to experimental extinction. Four different schedules of reinforcement have been studied: fixed-interval, variable-interval, fixed-ratio, and variable-ratio.

17. Punishment is operationally defined as an aversive stimulus applied to an operant response. The most general effect of punishment is to suppress the response that preceded it. Timing of punishment is critical: it must immediately precede or follow the response to achieve maximum suppression.

18. One of the most intriguing concepts to come out of contemporary learning research is that the same principles of learning that guide the acquisition of adaptive behavior also apply to the acquisition of maladaptive responses. Any behavior, adaptive or not, is likely to be learned if it is reinforced.

Terms to Remember

Acquisition   The period during which the organism learns the association between the conditioned stimulus (CS) and conditioned response (CR).

Aversive Conditioning   A form of operant conditioning which involves the use of negative reinforcement.

Avoidance Conditioning   A form of aversive conditioning in which the organism can avoid an aversive stimulus by making the appropriate response to a warning signal.

Classical Conditioning   A type of learning in which a previously neutral stimulus, through repeated pairings with an unconditioned stimulus, acquires the capacity to evoke the response originally made to the unconditioned stimulus.

Conditioned Response (CR)   The learned response to a conditioned stimulus.

Conditioned Stimulus (CS)   A stimulus which, through repeated pairings with an unconditioned stimulus (UCS), acquires the capacity to evoke a response it did not originally evoke.

Continuous Reinforcement   Reinforcement of a response every time it occurs.

Discrimination   Learning to respond differentially to similar stimuli.

Escape Conditioning   A form of aversive conditioning in which the organism can terminate an aversive stimulus by making the appropriate response.

Experimental Neurosis   Disturbed behavior in animals that results when they are required to make extremely difficult discriminations.

Extinction   The reduction in response that occurs (a) in classical conditioning when the conditioned stimulus (CS) is presented *without* the unconditioned stimulus (UCS); (b) in operant conditioning when the conditioned response (CR) is no longer followed by reinforcement.

Fixed-Interval Schedule (FI)   A schedule for reinforcing operant behavior in which reinforcement is administered after a fixed period of time.

Fixed-Ratio Schedule (FR)   A schedule for reinforcing operant behavior in which reinforcement is administered after the organism emits a fixed number of responses.

Higher-Order Conditioning   Conditioning of a response to a stimulus by pairing the neutral stimulus with another stimulus which was previously conditioned to elicit the response.

Instinctive Behavior   Unlearned complex patterns of responses characteristic of all members of a given species.

Learning   A relatively permanent change in behavior, resulting from experience or practice.

Negative Reinforcement   Any event that strengthens the response that precedes it by virtue of its removal or termination.

Operant Conditioning   A type of learning in which the response is instrumental in obtaining positive reinforcement or in escaping (or avoiding) negative reinforcement.

Partial Reinforcement   Reinforcement of a response only a proportion of the times that it occurs.

Positive Reinforcement   An event that strengthens the response that precedes it by virtue of its *presentation.*

Primary Reinforcement   Any event that has reinforcing properties which depend little, if at all, on previous learning.

Punishment   An aversive stimulus applied to an operant response.

Reinforcement   An event that strengthens the response that precedes or produces it.

Terms to Remember

Schedule of Reinforcement An established plan for allotting reinforcements under partial reinforcement.

Secondary Reinforcement Any event that acquires reinforcing properties through association with a primary reinforcement.

Shaping Modifying behavior by reinforcing only those responses that successively approximate the final desired behavior.

Spontaneous Recovery The recurrence of the previously extinguished conditioned response following a rest period.

Stimulus Generalization Once an organism has learned to associate a given behavior with a specific stimulus, it tends to show this behavior toward similar stimuli.

Superstitious Behavior Behavior learned simply by virtue of the fact that it happened to be followed by reinforcement, even though this behavior was not instrumental in obtaining the reinforcement.

Unconditioned Response (UCR) A response that occurs to an unconditioned stimulus automatically without requiring any learning.

Unconditioned Stimulus (UCS) A stimulus that naturally and automatically elicits an unconditioned response.

Variable-Interval Schedule (VI) A schedule for reinforcing operant behavior in which reinforcement is administered after a variable interval of time.

Variable-Ratio Schedule (VR) A schedule for reinforcing operant behavior in which the number of responses required for each reinforcement varies.

Recommended Readings

Ferster, C. B., and Skinner, B. F., *Schedules of Reinforcement,* New York: Appleton-Century-Crofts, 1957.

The first complete survey of types of schedules of reinforcement.

Geis, G. L., Stebbins, W. C., and Lundin, R. W., *The Study of Behavior: Reflex and Operant Conditioning,* Volume 1, Parts 1 and 2, New York: Appleton-Century-Crofts, 1961.

A programmed text which provides a thorough review of the principles of classical and operant conditioning.

Hilgard, E. R., and Bower, G. H., *Theories of Learning* (3rd ed.), New York: Appleton-Century-Crofts, 1966.

Thorough discussion of current theories and developments in the field of learning.

Kimble, G. A. (Ed.), *Foundations of Conditioning and Learning,* New York: Appleton-Century-Crofts, 1967.

Comprehensive treatment of the field of learning.

Reese, E. P., *Experiments in Operant Behavior,* New York: Appleton-Century-Crofts, 1964.

The basic principles of operant behavior are taught through experiments the reader performs.

Reynolds, G., *A Primer of Operant Conditioning,* Glenview, Illinois: Scott, Foresman and Co., 1968.

An excellent summary of the basic principles and terms used in operant conditioning.

Schoenfield, W. N., *The Theory of Reinforcement Schedules,* New York: Appleton-Century-Crofts, 1970.

Nine articles that approach behavior theory and schedules from a theoretical point of view.

Skinner, B. F., *Walden Two,* New York: Macmillan, 1948.

A novel whose characters live in a community where life is guided entirely by the principles of operant conditioning.

Smith, W. I., and Moore, J. W., *Conditioning and Instrumental Learning,* New York: McGraw-Hill Book Co., 1966.

A programmed text that serves as a review for many of the topics discussed in this chapter.

PSYCHOLOGY ISSUES

This is the first of four special *Issues* sections. Each *Issue* consists of passages from three articles or books. Most were written by psychologists.

The *Issues* do not try to illustrate every aspect of the psychological literature, but to show some of the many different interests psychologists have. They show psychologists using their expertise to solve real-life problems, responding to the ethical issues raised by their research findings, taking sides in psychological controversies, and using their special and diverse perspectives to illuminate some of the more fascinating social issues of today.

A.
Behavior Therapy

Behavior therapy (or modification) is a psychotherapy based on the techniques of learning theory. It differs from the depth therapies (psychoanalysis, for example) by assuming that emotional problems result from learned maladaptive behavior, rather than a basic personality disorder. Behavior therapy therefore aims at changing behavior, not the basic personality. It substitutes effective responses for maladaptive ones by conditioning new responses to the stimuli that evoke the problem behavior.

The three articles in this *Issue* show behavior therapy being used to eliminate some fairly common problems: disobedience in children (first article); heavy smoking and insufficient studying (second article); claustrophobia and fear of flying (third article). Each article takes a different behavioral approach, but each approach is pragmatic and aimed only at changing the problem behavior.

Behavior therapy is only one of many therapeutic options available for treating emotional problems. Although its usefulness has been widely accepted, some experts still question its ability to achieve lasting results.

REWARDING VIRTUE

Franklin Nelson

By the time he was 9, Joey seemed unmanageable. He teased his younger sister unmercifully and bossed and hit the few friends that still played with him. At school, his restlessness kept him from learning and his misbehavior was upsetting.

At home, he and his mother fought endlessly. She nagged and criticized him, and he frustrated and humiliated her. Joey was somewhat better behaved when his father was at home, especially when he threatened and punished the boy. However, this punishment quieted Joey only temporarily.

When he was not fighting with others, Joey seemed insecure and miserable. He knew everyone disliked him, but he couldn't stop misbehaving.

Finally, Joey and his parents went to see a psychotherapist. The therapist did not spend a long time exploring Joey's history; nor did he probe for deep underlying problems.

Reprinted with permission from *Newsday*, Long Island, 1973.

Instead, he helped Joey's parents learn how to change Joey's behavior.

He told them that they had relied too much on punishment to change Joey, and that, in the long run, this was making his behavior worse rather than better. He suggested, therefore, that they spend more time encouraging good behavior and less time discouraging bad behavior.

A point system was set up under which Joey could earn daily rewards by being better behaved. This point system was not designed to spoil Joey, but rather to give him a positive motivation for specific improvements in behavior. Joey was still punished if he misbehaved, but now the punishment was consistent, but mild.

The point system helped Joey to feel that improving his behavior was for his own good, a feeling that he had rarely had in the past.

In a relatively short time, Joey's behavior changed and the extremes of misbehavior at home and at school disappeared.

In the past, Joey's parents had criticized him so much that he was motivated to disobey rather than to please them. While each punishment quieted Joey temporarily, in the long run it strengthened his feeling that he was under attack, and this increased his resolve to fight back rather than to improve. In changing his parents' emphasis from bad behavior to good behavior, the therapist had succeeded in breaking a vicious circle.

Few of us receive extended training in how to raise children. When we have problems with them, we rely on our own childhood experiences or ask one of the neighbors. Most of the time, that is enough; sometimes it is not.

Behavior modification, the type of therapy illustrated here, is designed to help parents learn how to teach their children better behavior. Stated simply, behavior modification therapy suggests that emotionally disturbed behavior is learned, and that it can be unlearned as more desirable behavior is taught in its place.

This may come as a surprise to many laymen, as well as to many professionals, who clearly see that normal behavior is shaped by its consequences but who have come to believe that emotionally disturbed behavior is also amenable to the influence of reward and punishment.

In contrast to other therapies, behavior modification is directly focused on changing the disturbed behavior. It rejects the idea that there are deep-rooted problems which must be resolved before the behavior can change. Thus, Joey's unmanageable behavior in no way reflected an underlying problem; it *was* the problem.

Behavior modification therapy also rejects the idea that Joey's behavior was motivated by some unconscious need or, for that matter, that the basic motivation was anything inside of Joey. Instead, it suggests that the motivation for Joey's misbehavior was the imbalance between the amounts of punishment and reward, an imbalance more likely to result in defiance than in good behavior.

Because of its direct focus on changing the disturbed behavior, behavior modification therapy is both faster and more effective than others. Why shouldn't it be? It deals with the real issues that govern behavior change—reward and punishment—and not with mythical ones like unconscious motivations.

Prior to a clear understanding of how to change undesirable behavior, such myths were a convenient explanation of therapeutic failure; now, however, they are an obstacle to therapeutic success. If there were such a thing as unconscious motivation, Joey's improvement would have been only temporary. It was not.

In further contrast to other therapies, behavior modification does not try to unearth the conditions that originally led to the undesirable behavior. Such conditions are in the past, and are, therefore, beyond change. Sometimes what started the behavior is still motivating it, sometimes not. No matter; it is the parent's present behavior which must be changed for the child to change.

Sometimes a parent has difficulty in changing. However, parents can also learn better behavior without any recourse to searching for unconscious motivations or underlying problems.

The difficulty in making a change should not be exaggerated; in fact, children and parents can change for the better easier than one thinks.

In addition to its success with unmanageable behavior, behavior modification therapy is applicable to a wide range of conditions—excessive fearfulness, dependency, withdrawal, etc. Because the therapy is brief, it is appropriate with minor behavior problems as well as with more severe ones. Depending on the severity of the difficulty, the length of treatment may be as short as six to eight sessions over the course of two to three months. An added virtue is that these programs are practical and down-to-earth and thus are appealing to those children and adults who generally do not think they would profit from going to a therapist.

Operant Conditioning and Self-Control of Smoking and Studying

Adam Miller and Michael Gimpl
Saint Cloud State College

A. INTRODUCTION

As early as 1953 Skinner suggested that there were circumstances when a therapist should use operant conditioning to develop self-control techniques in the client. Since then there have been some recent successful efforts to implement his suggestion. Ferster, Nurnberger, and Levitt (1962) presented detailed self-control techniques for regulating eating behavior, while Stuart (1967) went further and reported not only successful control of eating but also transfer to smoking and other behaviors. Mertens and Fuller (1964) applied self-control procedures to alcoholics and Ober (1967) successfully decreased smoking using operant self-control. In addition, in laboratory studies of self-control with children Bem (1967) demonstrated verbal self-control for a motor response and Miller and Clark (1970) developed effective verbal self-reinforcers for a visual discrimination problem. The evidence is consistent that self-control procedures can be effective.

The special value of self-control procedures is that once they have been learned they are avail-

Reprinted from *The Journal of Genetic Psychology,* **119** (1971), pp. 181–186, by permission of The Journal Press, Provincetown, Massachusetts. Copyright © 1971 by The Journal Press.

able to the individual for modifying many behaviors. In behavioristic terms, once a learning set for self-control has been established an individual may be his own therapist or counselor or teacher in the future.

Heavy smoking and a low level of studying are behaviors that should be responsive to self-control techniques. Further, they have characteristics in common with a wide range of normal, neurotic, and psychotic behaviors that have been responsive to therapeutic increase or decrease with the use of operant techniques. So if self-control procedures proved successful for smoking and studying, applications should be appropriate to other behaviors.

In the present study operant self-control techniques were used to reduce smoking and increase study time for college students.

B. METHOD

1. Subjects

Forty-three undergraduate students, male and female, were selected from approximately 100 volunteers. Twenty-three were selected because they reported that they had studied less than 10 hours a week for at least one academic quarter, and 20 were selected because they had smoked at least one pack of cigarettes a day for at least a year.

2. Procedure

For nonstudiers or smokers the program of treatment during the three weeks of the experiment was generally the same. During week I subjects recorded their behavior. In week II they instructed themselves to increase study (or decrease smoking). And for week III they received one of three treatments: recording, self-instruction, or reinforcement.

a. Week I. Subjects were given written instructions of procedures and forms for recording their behavior. The subject recorded his responses (number of minutes studied or cigarettes smoked) during each one-half hour waking period. He also indicated whether he was giving an immediate report of the preceding one-half hour or was recalling his earlier behavior. In addition, if someone was present when the recorded response occurred and was willing to corroborate its occurrence, then the observer's name and phone number were recorded so that the experimenter could phone and verify the accuracy of the record. During all three weeks the subjects turned in their record forms daily to one of the two experimenters. Subjects were not instructed either to change their behavior or to keep it constant during week I.

b. Week II. The second week subjects were given written instructions, record forms, and self-instruction forms. The record forms duplicated those for week I and contained one additional column labeled "instructions." The general instructions for recording behavior were as those in week I.

In addition to the procedures of week I the subject gave himself instructions three times a day to change his rate of response a specified amount. For each subject an average daily rate was computed for week I. This average was the basis for setting goals for changing the daily rate of his responses.

In the morning when he arose he read aloud five times his goal for the number of responses until noon. At noon he again recited aloud five times his goal until evening. And in the early evening he read aloud five times his goal for the balance of the day. On the record form when a subject read his instructions aloud he checked the "instruction" column for the appropriate time.

For smokers the subject's own average from week I was reduced by 10% and this figure was the goal for the first two days of week II. An additional 10% was the goal for days 3 and 4 of week II, and a third 10% was the goal for the balance of the week.

For nonstudiers a 30-minute daily increase was set as the goal for the first two days of week II, an additional 30 minutes for the second two

days, and 30 more minutes for the balance of week II.

c. Week III. For the third week the subjects were randomly assigned to three treatment groups of nonstudiers and three corresponding treatment groups of smokers. The Recording group returned to the procedures of week I and subjects only recorded their responses. The Self-instructions group continued the procedures of week II. An average figure for the response was based on week II and new goals were set following the procedure used for week II. For nonstudiers 30-minute increases were again used and for smokers 10% decreases were used.

For the Reinforcement group subjects were told that they could earn points toward their final grade in the General Psychology course in which they were registered. They continued the procedures of recording and giving self-instructions as for week II. New goals for responding were established as for the Self-instructions groups. But subjects could earn points in two ways. Each time a subject read aloud the instructions to change behavior, and had an observer verify it, he received one point. Also, if the number of his responses equalled the number in the instructions, and was verified, he earned one point. He could earn a total of six points a day, two for each of the three self-instruction periods.

d. Dependent Variables. The major response variables measured in this investigation were two: the actual number of cigarettes that subjects reported they smoked, and the number of minutes subjects reported they studied.

* * * * * * * * * * * * * * * * * * * *

D. DISCUSSION

Contrasts between the findings for nonstudiers and smokers were several. First, the frequency of studying increased significantly, while smoking decreased significantly. This difference in direction of change was as planned. Second, the number of self-instructions decreased for smokers and increased for nonstudiers for no clear reason. Third, nonstudiers were more conscientious than smokers in keeping actual records of their behavior. The difference was almost in a ratio of two to one.

An additional contrast was that for both behaviors the change across weeks was significant, but only for studying was there evidence of differential effects among treatments. There are numerous reasons why this difference might have occurred, including differences among subjects, in complexity and strength of the responses and in the direction of change in responses.

One conclusion that seems justified is that the procedure of giving self-instructions and recording responses can predictably either increase or decrease the rate of responding.

A comparison of the relative effectiveness of the treatment procedures used in this study and those used in other studies is difficult because the criteria for success here were for short term reduction in smoking or increase in study, while other studies have tackled the more difficult objective of long term changes in behavior and a zero rate of smoking. The effectiveness of the procedures described here for such goals remains to be determined.

As Keutzer et al. (1968) have pointed out, theoretical analysis of self-control procedures has been necessary, in part, in order to legitimatize the term for behaviorists. Positive results, such as those of this study, of Bem (1967), of Miller and Clark (1970), and of Stuart (1967) should encourage further use and investigation of self-control procedures.

E. SUMMARY

Three treatment conditions were compared for their effectiveness in reducing smoking rates and increasing study time for 43 volunteers. The treatments were as follows: recording responses, self-instructions, and reinforcement for conforming to self-instructions. All subjects recorded re-

sponses the first week for a baseline and gave self-instructions the second week for modifying their rate of responding. In the third week smokers were separated into three groups and nonstudiers were separated into comparable groups.

For smoking an analysis of variance yielded significant decreases in smoking rate across weeks, but no significant differences among treatment groups. For studying an analysis of variance yielded significant increase in studying across weeks and interaction effects of treatments over weeks. The reinforcement condition produced the greatest increase.

References

Bem, S. L. Verbal self-control: The establishment of effective self-instruction. *J. Exper. Psychol.,* 1967, **74,** 485–491.

Ferster, C. B., Nurnberger, J. I., and Levitt, E. B. The control of eating. J. Math., 1962, **1,** 87–109.

Keutzer, C. S., Lichtenstein, E., and Mees, H. L. Modification of smoking behavior. A review. *Psychol. Bull.,* 1968, **70,** 520–553.

Mertens, G. C., and Fuller, G. B. The Manual for the Alcoholic. Willmar, Minn., Willmar State Hospital, 1964.

Miller, A., and Clark, N. Self-reinforcement established for a discrimination task. *J. Genet. Psychol.,* 1970, **117,** 1–6.

Ober, D. C. The modification of smoking behavior. Unpublished Doctoral dissertation, University of Illinois, Urbana, 1967.

Skinner, B. F. Science and Human Behavior. New York: Macmillan, 1953.

Stuart, R. B. Behavioral control of overeating. *Behav. Res. & Ther.,* 1967, **5,** 359–365.

Oriental Defense Exercises as Reciprocal Inhibitors of Anxiety

LOUIS GERSHMAN
Villanova University

and

JAMES M. STEDMAN
University of Texas
Medical School at San Antonio

Summary—In a case of claustrophobia and in another with fears of flying, Japanese defense activities of the Karate type proved to be effective counter-conditioners of anxiety. They were used in the former case *in vivo* and in the latter case both in imagination and *in vivo* [in real life].

Research and clinical evidence over the past ten years have substantially corroborated Wolpe's principle of reciprocal inhibition (1958): "If a response which is inhibitory of anxiety can be made to occur in the presence of the anxiety-

Reprinted from *Journal of Behavior Therapy and Experimental Psychiatry*, **2** (1971), pp. 117–119, by permission of Pergamon Press. Copyright © 1971 by Pergamon Press.

evoking stimuli, it will weaken the bond between these stimuli and the anxiety." The most frequently used counter-conditioner in the treatment of phobias has been muscle relaxation. In general, because of the ease with which relaxation can be learned by the patient and controlled by the therapist, the clinician tends to look for other counter-conditioners in the desensitization of fears only when the patient is unable to relax effectively.

Other counter-conditioners include assertive responses, sexual responses, and motor responses (Wolpe, 1958), emotive imagery (Lazarus and Abramovitz, 1962) and induced anger (Goldstein, Serber, and Piaget, 1970). One activity will function more satisfactorily than another for a particular person

with a particular problem. And if a therapist identifies a counter-conditioner which is idiosyncratic to a patient, it is likely to have special therapeutic efficacy.

Two cases will be described in which self-defense activities, Kung Fu and Karate, respectively, were used to counter-condition anxiety. These are oriental methods of self-defense. Karate, a Japanese system of unarmed self-defense and countcrattack converts the hand, fist, elbow, or foot into a weapon aimed at an opponent's weak spots. As taught in this country, Kung Fu, of earlier Chinese origin, is similar to Karate, but is considered more of an art and requires much more training to attain proficiency. It seems likely that these exercises inhibit anxiety in much the same way as assertive behavior does, by evoking responses related to anger.

Case 1

Mr. P, 31, married, gave a history of anxiety involving elevators, enclosed places, trains, buses, and locked rooms. Over the past 5 years, secondary generalization of anxiety had occurred to the wearing of tight-fitting clothing, underwear, and his wedding ring. These maladaptive behaviors interfered with P's occupational adjustment and family life. In the course of history-taking, P indicated that he was a protégé of Kung Fu, liked to engage in this activity, and felt like a "man" when he did. A trial showed that P's anxiety level of 50–60 *suds* at the beginning of the session plummeted to zero after one minute of Kung Fu. As a result, we decided to attack Mr. P's fear of locked rooms, using Kung Fu as the competing response. Though our description of the *in vivo* procedures to be followed raised P's *suds* level to 80, he agreed to give them a try. We proposed to lock P in a room for progressively longer times, starting with 10 seconds, and having him engage immediately in Kung Fu exercises as soon as the door was closed. At 10 seconds all feelings of anxiety were eliminated during the first trial. At 20 seconds, the Kung Fu exercises reduced his anxiety level to zero in two trials. Subsequent strategy involved two dimensions: (1) increasing the time spent in the locked room and (2) reducing the time spent on Kung Fu exercises. For example, one step in the hierarchy required P to spend the first 30 seconds going through Kung Fu exercises, while spending the remaining 15 seconds without the benefit of these inhibiting responses. As the end of the hierarchy approached P was able to sit comfortably in the room reading a newspaper. If he felt the least twinge of anxiety he was to start "Kung-Fu-ing," and quickly dissipate it. Eventually, a 45-minute trial was followed by a 1-hour trial. P had no difficulty remaining relaxed during the latter trial.

Following the elimination of anxiety in the locked room, P was enthusiastic about trying the method in elevators. At the end of the second session in an elevator, he was able to go up and down at will.

Generalization of extinction was apparent when P reported that he could again don tight underwear, and was no longer disturbed at wearing his wedding ring.

At a 6-month follow-up the patient had maintained his recovery.

Case 2

Mr. R, 28, a wealthy divorced executive, started to take flying lessons when his former wife remarried and moved with their 3-year-old child to a city several hundreds of miles away. R found it inconvenient and frustrating to travel by train every few weeks to see his child for whom he felt a great deal of affection. However, the flying lessons brought on anxiety from two sources— (1) an instructor who criticized him sharply whenever he made a mistake, and (2) the speed, altitude, landing, and other physical aspects of flying. R's tenseness produced soreness in the muscles of his left hand, arms, shoulders, and face, which he began to feel even while driving to the airport. The tension increased in the course of a flying session and led to errors in judgment.

Two hierarchies were constructed: (1) instructor's mannerisms and critical remarks, and (2) flying the plane; and R was trained in relaxation.

Flying the Plane Hierarchy
(in *increasing* order of anxiety)

1. Takes off. Thinks that he eventually will have to land the plane.
2. Gains altitude.
3. Plane drifts slightly off course.
4. Recognizes that he must make a correction.
5. Reduces speed then accelerates.
6. Says to himself, "Christ, how high am I!"
7. Heads toward airport— hard to judge distance and height.
8. On last leg of trip, close to airport. Feels that he is losing altitude too fast.
9. Is approaching tree tops and a power line.
10. Adds power, but holds too long.
11. Passes over tree tops too low.
12. The ground looms up, gets closer.
13. Is coming down. Hard to tell how far from the ground he is.

14. Has to make the final decision about what movement to make with the stick.

Though desensitization using relaxation was effective enough with the former hierarchy, it became apparent that it was . working very slowly with the latter. A new counter-conditioner was therefore sought. Since R had trained in Karate several years previously and frequently practiced its routines to maintain himself in physical condition, it was decided to try Karate as an anxiety-inhibitor.

At each presentation of a hierarchy item R was required to engage in vigorous *in vivo* Karate exercises. In two sessions, anxiety to all items in the plane-flying hierarchy was reduced to zero on the *sud* scale (Wolpe, 1969, p. 116). R also practiced at home. At a third session the items of the hierarchy were presented once again, this time under relaxation. Scores on all items were zero.

Next, the exercises were used *in vivo*. R lived about 10 minutes away from the flying field. He was requested to practice Karate routines for a few minutes (until he reached a zero *sud* score) before getting into his car and leaving for the airport. When he reached the flying field, he was to go to the men's room and spend another few minutes on Karate exercises.

When R boarded the plane at his next flying lesson the highest *sud* score that he experienced was 20. Most of the time, the score ranged between 10–15. This level of anxiety was not high enough to interfere with his flying. In fact, he was not sure whether his feeling was anxiety or excitement. He made three excellent landings with the instructor in the plane. Two lessons later he was permitted to fly solo. Subsequently, he continued his Karate exercises at home and before entering the plane, developing a great deal of confidence in flying solo.

When interviewed 6 months later the patient stated that he was flying without anxiety.

References

Goldstein, A. J., Serber, M., and Piaget, G. (1970) Induced anger as a reciprocal inhibitor of fear, *J. Behav. Ther. & Exp. Psychiat.* **1**, 67–70.

Lazarus, A., and Abramovitz, A. (1962) The use of 'emotive imagery' in the treatment of children's phobias, *J. Ment. Sci.* **108**, 109–195.

Wolpe, J. (1958) *Psychotherapy by Reciprocal Inhibition*, Stanford University Press, Stanford.

4 REMEMBERING AND FORGETTING

What is memory?

Measures of retention
Recall — Recognition — Relearning

Factors affecting remembering

Theories of forgetting
Disuse theory — Trace transformation
Interference theory — Motivated forgetting

The three types of memory
Short-term memory — Long-term memory
Intermediate memory

Improving memory

Have you ever been introduced to a person at a party and found that you couldn't recall his or her name a short time later? You probably attributed this failure to poor memory. Perhaps you were right. On the other hand, you may never really have learned the name to begin with.

There is an old German proverb: "He lies like an eyewitness." Capable attorneys never accept an eyewitness report at face value. They know that the original observations may have been inadequate and that memory itself is subject to distortions. A striking proof of this was unwittingly provided by a group of scientists well trained in observation. During a professional meeting, two men rushed into the meeting room, shouting and scuffling. One of the men was dressed in a clown suit; the other was wearing white pants, a red tie, and a blue jacket.

This incident had been carefully planned in advance. The scientists were asked to write reports, allegedly as part of a police investigation. Of the 40 scientists reporting, 34 misstated some of the facts. The suit of the second man was variously described as brown, striped, coffee-colored, or red. Some scientists reported on the details of the second man's hat, although in fact he wore no hat (Whalen, 1949).

Is this a demonstration of faulty memory? Not necessarily. Any discussion of memory presupposes that some learning has taken place. It is only after we have learned something that we can legitimately begin raising questions about the storage and retrieval of learned materials. In the case of the 40 scientists, it is wrong to conclude that memory is at fault when, in fact, the failure was probably caused by the ineffectiveness of the original learning. If something is not learned well to begin with, there will obviously be difficulties in retrieval.

What Is Memory?

The definition of memory poses a problem. So far, we have been making references to memory as if it were an object. In everyday speech, we continually refer to memory in this way. We speak of a good memory, a poor memory, a better memory for faces than

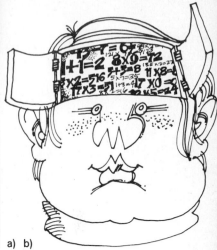

a) b)

c)

for names. We worry about failing memory and seek aids to improve it, as if it were a part of the body. Memory is not something that can be seen or felt. It is a construct; that is, it is inferred from certain behaviors of the individual. Consider the following examples: (1) You have read a novel and, at a later date, can write an essay on it. (2) You make some new acquaintances at a party, and when you see them again, you recognize their faces. (3) As a child you learned to play a musical instrument, and when you take it up again years later, you are surprised at how easily you relearn fingering exercises which caused so much consternation in childhood.

There are three main stages in each of these illustrations. The first stage involved some experience, or learning: reading a novel, meeting people, learning to play a musical instrument. The third stage (remembering stage) involved some activity or behavior that was clearly influenced by the first stage: writing the essay, recognizing the people, relearning the instrument. The middle or intervening stage involved retention of the prior experiences in such a way that they influenced later behavior. Behavior during this intervening time may not reflect the prior experiences at all. However, when you are able to write the essay, recognize the faces, and relearn the instrument, we may infer that you have somehow retained the prior, learned experiences. It is this retention stage that we refer to as memory. To the extent that you are unable to perform these activities, we infer that some forgetting has taken place.

Fig. 4.1
The three stages of memory: learning (a), retention (b), and remembering (c). (a, Anna Kaufman Moon—Stock, Boston. c, Daniel S. Brody—Stock, Boston.)

125

Since memory is unobservable, it must be inferred from the remembering stage. For this purpose, psychologists have devised different measuring techniques. As you will see, each of these ways of measuring retention may provide a somewhat different estimate of how much has been retained.

Measures of Retention

Recall

Recall is the method whereby the subject is required to reproduce what he has previously learned, entirely out of his unassisted memory. If we were to ask you to name all the presidents of the United States, recite the Pledge of Allegiance, or sing a popular song, we would be using the recall method for testing your retention. The most common type of recall test used in schools is the essay examination. If your instructor were to ask you on an exam to distinguish between classical and operant conditioning, he would be asking you to recall (without references or aids) previously learned material.

Recognition

Some of you may at one time or another have learned the names of the presidents of the United States. If you were to try to recall them now, you probably would not be able to remember all of them. You might then conclude that you had forgotten the names of some of the presidents. Box 4.1 contains a list of 60 names. If you check off those names which you recognize as presidents of the United States, you will probably find that your score on this test is considerably higher than it was when you tried to recall the names. This method of testing retention is known as recognition.

Our capacity to recognize previous events and experiences is often astounding. We meet thousands of people in a lifetime, read countless books, and learn hundreds of thousands of bits of factual information. Yet somehow we can sift the familiar from the unfamiliar. For example, you may not be able to recall the name of your third-grade teacher, but chances are you would

Harry S. Truman	Dwight D. Eisenhower	Abraham Lincoln	James A. Garfield
John N. Garner	Charles Fairbanks	Herbert E. Hoover	John C. Calhoun
Garret A. Hobart	James Madison	Alben W. Barkley	James Buchanan
Franklin Pierce	Chester A. Arthur	Leve P. Marton	Richard M. Johnson
John Adams	Thomas R. Marshall	Zachary Taylor	Franklin D. Roosevelt
Charles Dawes	George Washington	George M. Dallas	George Clinton
Calvin Coolidge	Charles Curtis	James Monroe	Andrew Jackson
Grover Cleveland	Aaron Burr	Rutherford B. Hayes	James K. Polk
Henry Wilson	John Quincy Adams	Lyndon B. Johnson	Thomas A. Hendricks
William Wheeler	Benjamin Harrison	Elbridge Gerry	William H. Taft
Ulysses S. Grant	Woodrow Wilson	Warren G. Harding	John Tyler
Thomas Jefferson	John F. Kennedy	Adlai E. Stevenson	Daniel D. Tompkins
Millard Fillmore	Martin Van Buren	William McKinley	John C. Breckenridge
Theodore Roosevelt	William H. Harrison	Andrew Johnson	Benjamin Franklin
William King	James Sherman	Henry A. Wallace	Richard Nixon

recognize it if you heard it. Similarly, how often have you seen a movie and been unable later to recall the title? Yet, if you were to see it listed, you would certainly recognize it.

Early experimental studies tended to support the view that recognition is easier than recall (Luh, 1922; Postman and Rau, 1957). However, this conclusion must be qualified somewhat in the light of later evidence. It has been found that the superiority of recognition over recall diminishes as the number of alternatives is increased (Davis et al., 1961). You may have noticed that a multiple-choice test with five or six alternatives for each question is usually more difficult than a similar test with fewer alternatives. The recognition task also becomes more difficult when the alternatives are quite similar to one another (Bahrick and Bahrick, 1964).

These experimental findings can be illustrated by an experience many of us have had. You may be able to recall, without difficulty, that a friend's phone number is 836-6720. But suppose someone asks you, "Is Beth's phone number 836-7620, 863-6720, or 836-6702?" At this point, you may just give up on trying to remember the right number, and look it up in the phone book.

Relearning

We have all had some experience in relearning material that we thought we had forgotten, and probably found that it was easier to learn the second time around. Relearning may detect evidence of retention, even though other methods suggest that nothing has

Box 4.1
Check off the names you recognize as presidents of the United States. Compare your score on this task with your recall score.

Measures of Retention

Fig. 4.2
Hermann Ebbinghaus. (National Library of Medicine, Bethesda, Maryland.)

been retained. For example, sometimes children born in one country immigrate to another, where a different language is spoken. Years later they may seem to have forgotten everything they knew about their native language and be unable to recall or even recognize words from it. But, if they attempt to relearn it, they are often surprised at how quickly it comes back to them.

Although relearning is the most sensitive method for testing retention, it is not frequently employed in any real-life situation because it is so difficult to use. The relearning method requires us to compare an original measure with a later measure of learning. In most practical situations we do not have the original measure of learning. For example, if you were to relearn the names of the presidents of the United States, you would probably require far less time than it took you originally. However, since there is no way of knowing how long it took you originally, it is impossible to make a comparison.

In a laboratory, where accurate measures of original learning are routinely obtained, the relearning method is often used to test retention. The relearning method was used by Hermann Ebbinghaus (1850–1909), a German psychologist who conducted the first systematic studies on remembering and forgetting.

Curve of Forgetting

Ebbinghaus was interested in studying the process of memorizing in its simplest and purest form. He recognized that the memorizing of prose, poetry, or other meaningful materials is influenced by past experiences, and by emotional and personality factors. Therefore, he designed learning materials that were essentially free of the influence of these factors. These materials consisted of three-letter combinations known as *nonsense syllables.* Each nonsense syllable was formed by putting a vowel between two consonants, like ZEB, NOV, KUL. Ebbinghaus constructed lists of these nonsense syllables and memorized them himself. He was careful to maintain the strictest possible experimental controls. He standardized the material to be memorized, and used exactly the same procedures throughout his investigations. He memorized each list, carefully recording how long it took him. Then he set his lists aside for a specified interval. At the end of that time, he relearned the same lists, again recording the amount of time required. The difference between the original learning time and the relearning time gave him a measure of retention.

Fig. 4.3
Ebbinghaus' curve of forgetting
Using himself as a subject, Ebbinghaus memorized lists
of nonsense syllables and then noted how long it took
him to relearn these lists. Notice that most of the
forgetting took place within one day and remained
relatively stable thereafter (Ebbinghaus, 1913).

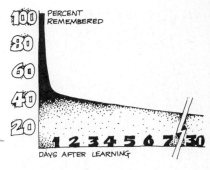

Figure 4.3 presents the results that Ebbinghaus obtained with
varying intervals of time between original learning and relearning.
Notice that most of his forgetting took place within the first few
hours; however, even after 30 days he retained some of his prior
learning. This curve is sometimes referred to as the typical curve
of forgetting, and much forgetting probably does follow this
course. For example, if someone were to ask you immediately
after class what a lecture was about, you would probably be able
to give a pretty complete summary. But one day later, you might
be hard-pressed to provide more than a scant outline of the
material covered. Of course, not all forgetting follows Ebbinghaus'
forgetting curve. We learn some things so well that we retain
them perfectly intact over long periods of time. Most military
verterans can repeat their serial number years after they have left
military service.

Factors Affecting Remembering

Have you ever walked out of an exam and said, "I couldn't
remember a thing. I must have forgotten everything I learned"? Is
this a valid conclusion? Not necessarily. As we mentioned earlier,
memory is unobservable and must be inferred from some measure
of performance (remembering stage). However, various
circumstances may influence performance during the remembering
stage. Since all we have to go by is performance during this stage,
it is not always possible to say exactly where the "breakdown"
occurred. For one thing, your original learning may have been
inadequate (learning stage), and you can only retain what you
have learned. What is learned poorly is likely to be poorly
retained. On the other hand, you may have learned well but
forgotten a great deal during the retention stage. In that case,
your conclusion would have been right. Finally, although you
may have learned and retained well, circumstances affecting you
during the remembering stage may have interfered with your
performance. It should be emphasized that remembering is made
up of activities which occur in the present and are influenced by
factors operating in both the present and the past. Among the
most important factors are those operating within the individual.

Individuals differ in many ways. We have different
personalities, physical appearance, intellectual abilities,

Factors Affecting
Remembering

motivations, and life experiences. Some of these factors affect the way we learn and our performances on tests of remembering. For example, highly intelligent individuals are usually superior learners. However, even individuals who have the same intelligence show broad differences in the degree to which they master and remember learning material. And, even if their mastery and retention are comparable, they may perform differently in a test situation

Let's look at two hypothetical cases. John is a bright student, confident of his own abilities and eager to perform well. He spends a great deal of time studying and preparing for upcoming exams. He enters the exam situation confident that he will do well and, generally, he does do well. Bob, an equally bright and motivated student, is assailed by self-doubts and is anxious about the possibility that he will do poorly. He may spend an equal amount of time sitting over his books, but the time may not be as productive because his anxiety interferes with his ability to concentrate. Even if he is able to overcome this handicap and studies diligently for the test, his anxiety may interfere with his performance in the test situation. He may find his "mind going blank," a common experience with highly anxious students.

You can probably think of other circumstances that may adversely affect performance in a test situation, such as fatigue, illness, or upsetting news. In the next chapter we examine procedures you can employ to optimize performance both during learning and in test situations.

Theories of Forgetting

You have probably all had the following exasperating experience: you spend a long time learning something, only to find that you have apparently forgotten most of it a short time later. Why does this happen? Does the mere passage of time make us forget, or are more active processes responsible? Is the extent of forgetting as great as it sometimes appears to be? Is forgetting selective? Are some things remembered better, and if so, why?

These are some of the challenging questions for which psychology has sought and is still seeking answers. This section is concerned with the various theories that have been proposed to explain why we forget. Keep the above questions in mind as you read.

Disuse Theory

The theory of disuse holds that learning produces a *memory trace* which automatically fades or decays with the passage of time. On the surface, this theory appears quite convincing. We have already observed that our retention of events is much better just after the event has occurred and seems to dissipate with the passage of time. In many ways the fading of the memory trace resembles the channels formed on sandy beaches after a rainstorm. With disuse, the memory trace tends to fade away, much as the channels on the beach disappear when water no longer runs through them.

Many of our everyday experiences seem to support the disuse theory. Students who have studied a course in school report later that, unless they have practiced some of the knowledge or skills they acquired in the course, they seem unable to remember any of the content. Similarly, medical doctors who specialize in a particular field frequently find it difficult to remember aspects of medical practice that fall outside their specialty. On the other hand, a person who is studying a course in which immediate applications are possible is likely to find that he retains much of what he learns.

As attractive or appealing as this theory seems, there is much evidence that forgetting involves far more complex processes than the mere fading of memory traces as a result of disuse. If all forgetting simply involved decay of memory traces, why are some things better remembered than others, even though the amount of practice is comparable? Why do we often fail to remember events exactly as they occurred? Obviously, disuse theory cannot explain questions like these. There must be more to forgetting than merely spontaneous decay of a memory trace.

Trace Transformation

Some theorists accept the notion of a memory trace, but suggest that there is a change in the pattern of the trace rather than a weakening of it. Such changes may account for many of the distortions in memory.

Theories of Forgetting

Original Story

The title of this story is "The War of the Ghosts." One night two young men from Egulac went down to the river to hunt seals, and while they were there it became foggy and calm. Then they heard war-cries, and they thought: "Maybe this is a war-party." They escaped to the shore, and hid behind a log. Now canoes came up, and they heard the noise of paddles, and saw one canoe coming up to them. There were five men in the canoe, and they said: "What do you think? We wish to take you along. We are going up the river to make war on the people." One of the young men said: "I have no arrows." "Arrows are in the canoe," they said. "I will not go along. I might be killed. My relatives do not know where I have gone. But you," he said, turning to the other, "may go with them." So one of the young men went, but the other returned home. And the warriors went on up the river to a town on the other side of Kalama. The people came down to the water, and they began to fight, and many were killed. But presently the young man heard one of the warriors say: "Quick, let us go home: that Indian has been hit." Now he thought: "Oh, they are ghosts." He did not feel sick, but they said he had been shot. So the canoes went back to Egulac, and the young man went ashore to his house, and made a fire. And he told everybody and said: "Behold I accompanied the ghosts, and we went to fight. Many of our fellows were killed, and many of those who attacked us were killed. They said I was hit, and I did not feel sick." He told it all, and then he became quiet. When the sun rose he fell down. Something black came out of his mouth. His face became contorted. The people jumped up and cried. He was dead.

One Subject's Version

The title of the story was "The War of the Ghosts." Two Indian warriors were in the vicinity of a stream or river or on the bank of the river and they overheard a war party in the vicinity. They were hiding in fear, not knowing whether it was friend or foe. When the canoe having the war party pulled up to the banks of the river or stream, the two warriors were asked to accompany the warriors in a canoe and they did not have the necessary weapons. One of the participants of the canoe said, "We have the arrows, the war weapons in the canoe." Only one of the two went because the other said that he did not want to go. The warrior that did go with the warriors to engage in battle found that there were people being killed all around him and he was feeling pretty good, not realizing that he had been hit. Coming back he related the story of the was that he engaged in to his townspeople. When he lay down, something came out of his mouth which was black, presumably black or dried blood, and he died.

Box 4.2
The authors read the original story to several different subjects and asked each subject to relate the story as accurately as possible. Note the difference between the original story and one subject's version of this story. (From F. C. Bartlett, *Remembering,* Cambridge University Press, publisher, 1954.)

Remembering and Forgetting

In many social situations, we tell about daily events in our lives—we recount news, gossip, and conversations we have had. We talk about books we have read and movies we have seen. How accurate are our reports? At the beginning of this chapter, we described an experiment in which scientists could not report accurately the details of an event they had witnessed. And, what is more to the point, the reports contained many distortions of remembered "facts."

These distortions in memory have been observed and studied by psychologists more than 40 years ago. Some psychologists have told or read stories to subjects and asked them to reproduce the stories as accurately as possible (see Box 4.2). Typically, these reproductions contained many distortions of the details presented in the original story (Bartlett, 1954). Supporters of the trace transformation theory say that these distortions result from transformations of memory traces that occur as time passes. Critics of both the disuse and the transformation theories point out that memory traces have not been demonstrated to exist. They also argue that both the fading and the distortions that occur in memory can be explained in terms of other processes.

Interference Theory

A more widely held theory maintains that it is not merely the passage of time that produces forgetting. This view holds that events intervening after the original learning may interfere with the retention of this learning. This interference, rather than time itself, is what causes forgetting.

A classic experiment demonstrated the effect of intervening activity on retention of previously learned material. Two undergraduates at Cornell University learned lists of nonsense syllables. Following the learning of each list, the subjects were tested to find out how much they recalled one, two, four, and eight hours later. Some of the lists were learned in the morning and some before going to sleep. Thus, the period intervening after learning involved either sleep or normal waking activity. Figure 4.4 shows that when the subjects were tested with sleep as their intervening activity, they retained more of what they had learned than when they spent their time in waking activities. If the mere passage of time were the only variable of importance, we would expect the two curves of retention to be the same. Since they were not the same, we conclude that the intervening activity is a determining factor in retention (Jenkins and Dallenbach, 1924).

Although these investigators established the importance of interference in forgetting, they were not able to specify which features of the intervening activities were responsible for the interference. Most subsequent studies have focused on determining the relationship between the type of intervening activity and the amount of forgetting.

Retroactive interference, often called *retroactive inhibition,* refers to the interfering effect of an intervening activity on retention of previous learning. If the intervening activity leads to improvement in retention, we refer to this effect as retroactive facilitation.

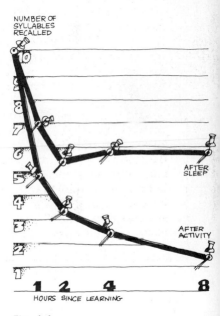

NUMBER OF SYLLABLES RECALLED

AFTER SLEEP

AFTER ACTIVITY

HOURS SINCE LEARNING

Fig. 4.4
This graph shows that more of the learned material was retained when sleep was the intervening activity (Jenkins and Dallenbach, 1924).

Theories of Forgetting

133

The typical experimental design for investigating retroactive interference and retroactive facilitation is as follows:

Experimental Group	Control Group
Learn task *A*	Learn task *A*
Learn task *B*	Perform unrelated activity
Test for retention of task *A*	Test for retention of task *A*

In a typical retroactive interference study, the two groups are compared with respect to their performance on the retention task. If the retention scores of the experimental group are lower than those of the control group, we may say that the difference is due to interference by the intervening activity. Various investigators have established the conditions under which this interference is greatest. Perhaps the best way to understand retroactive interference is to try the following experiment: For task *A*, require your subjects to learn to operate a combination lock. Then, have half of these subjects (experimental group) learn a different combination for a similar lock. Have the remaining subjects (control group) spend an equivalent amount of time resting. Test both groups for retention of task *A*. The experimental group should show retroactive interference.

This simple experiment demonstrates an important aspect of retroactive interference. When a subject is required to learn in sequence different responses to similar stimuli, learning of the second response interferes with retention of the original response. The greater the similarity of the stimuli, the greater the retroactive interference. It should be pointed out that the learning of the second task may also be similarly affected by the prior learning of task *A*. The interference of one task with the learning of a second, later task is called *proactive interference*.

Proactive and retroactive interference have considerable predictive value for many behaviors. For example, imagine the foyer of a large apartment house, with hundreds of mailboxes labeled with people's names. The mailman who makes the delivery every day has probably learned the location of everyone's name. Now, suppose someone switched all the names to different boxes. How do you think this switch will affect the mailman's learning the new order of names? It seems very likely that learning the new order will be confusing and difficult (proactive interference). If the names were then put back in their old places, we can safely predict that the mailman will experience much difficulty in remembering the original order (retroactive interference).

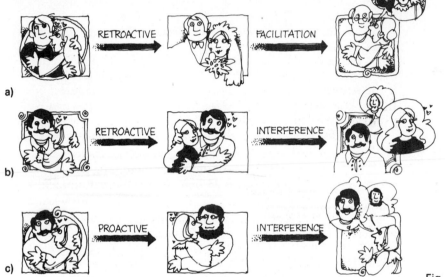

Fig. 4.5
a) Retroactive facilitation.
b) Retroactive interference.
c) Proactive interference.

We cannot dispute the fact that these interference effects occur. But whether or not the interference theory constitutes an adequate explanation for forgetting remains to be seen.

Motivated Forgetting

One theory that attempts to account for the selective nature of forgetting (that is, the fact that we forget certain things and remember others) maintains that we forget certain events or experiences because we are unconsciously motivated to do so. Supporters of this theory would say that a person forgets a dental appointment because he fears the pain. A person continues to

*Theories of
Forgetting*

135

Box 4.3
A case of psychological amnesia: disassociation of memory as the unconscious defensive response to intolerable emotional conflict. (No. 166 of 191 case illustrations in H. P. Laughlin, *The Neuroses*, Washington: Butterworths, 1967, pp. 779–780.)

1. *Parental approval vital*

Mr. G. R. was a 24-year-old college student. He was the only son of an extremely ambitious father who was a very successful engineer. His mother was perfectionistic, obsessional, and domineering. The young man was in his third year of university study, struggling to get through a pre-engineering course, in which he was not in the slightest bit interested. However, he felt he had to continue, largely as a result of irresistible parental pressure. He had already failed one year in this course.

His third year was further complicated by the fact that he had made a marriage which had been kept secret, in as far as his parents were concerned. He did not feel that he could possibly tell them of his marriage unless at the same time at least, he could also present them with a successful college record. This was impossible. The parental approval which had always been vital to him appeared forever lost!

2. *Precipitating event*

The marriage had involved emotional and time demands, which had still further interfered with his college performance. He had become extremely anxious about the probable results of examinations, which were due to begin in a few weeks' time. One Friday afternoon, after classes, he took part in a "bull session" in the college dormitory. This left him thoroughly convinced that he would not be able to pass his

gamble because he remembers the "hits" and forgets the many misses.

One of the key concepts of psychoanalytic theory is a form of motivated forgetting known as *repression* (ejection of anxiety-arousing material from consciousness). In Chapter 12 we discuss the concept of repression in greater detail. The most dramatic examples of repression are often found in cases of amnesia in which physical factors are not involved. Psychological factors must play a key role in these cases (see Box 4.3).

Although repression was first described in clinical settings, much recent research has been conducted in the laboratory, where the focus has been on repression as a form of motivated forgetting. Individuals tend to repress memories of events that are unpleasant in some way. Systematic laboratory studies of this phenomenon have shown that subjects tend to forget painful or unpleasant experiences more rapidly than those that are neutral or pleasant.

In one study, subjects were required to learn words as responses to various nonsense syllables. Each time the nonsense syllables were presented, the subjects were instructed to respond to each syllable with the appropriate word. Then electrodes were attached to their fingers so that a painful electric shock could be delivered. New words were flashed on the screen, some of them

*Remembering
and Forgetting*

examinations. This served as the precipitating event.

He started for home, but did not arrive there. Late that evening he was found wandering in the streets of a city some two hundred miles away from the site of his college.

3. Prompt identification and medical care

He was soon identified by papers in his wallet. There was also a picture of the few people who had been present at his wedding. One of these happened to be recognized by one of the local policemen. This friend had acted as best man at the wedding some six or seven months before. He was called to the police station to identify his friend. This he was quite promptly and positively able to

do, although at this time the patient had no conscious memory of ever having seen this man before.

The patient was admitted to the psychiatric service of a general hospital and treated psychotherapeutically. *Pentothal* interviews were accompanied by strong suggestions that he would gradually recover his memory. By the end of the week, things were pieced together and, with the exception of some of the events of the trip from college, the material was returned to consciousness.

4. Amnesia an extension of avoidance pattern of defense

Further psychiatric study over a period of time revealed that this man had always been disturbed by his parents'

attitudes. His established and usual method of handling these difficulties had been to attempt to ignore them. This was a pattern of avoidance. As he said, "I just pretend they're not there. In this way, I can deal with them. . . ."

His amnesic episode represented an episodic magnification and extension of this established pattern of defensive avoidance. Psychotherapy was able to resolve many of the problems. He accordingly was enabled to make marked improvement, with more realistic evaluation of his assets and future possibilities, and partly through some helpful modifications in certain of the parental attitudes.

accompanied by shock. Each new word was related in some way to a word on the original list. The subjects were then tested for retention of the original words. It was found that they remembered more of the original words that were related to "unshocked" words in the second list, than they did original words related to "shocked" words. Thus, the researchers concluded that the unpleasantness of shock led to the selective forgetting of words indirectly related to this unpleasant experience (Glucksberg and King, 1967).

Although motivated forgetting undoubtedly occurs, it probably accounts for only a small portion of all forgetting.

In this section we have discussed four different theories of forgetting. It is important to recognize that *each* theory may have a piece of the truth. We do not yet know enough to choose among these theories or to find the "true" theory.

The Three Types of Memory

Ask one of your friends to repeat a list of seven one-digit numbers which you recite to him at the rate of one per second. Your friend will probably be able to repeat the series without a mistake immediately after hearing them. After a delay of 20

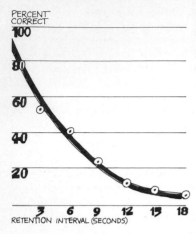

PERCENT CORRECT

RETENTION INTERVAL (SECONDS)

Fig. 4.6
Short-term memory

The experimenter spelled a three-unit nonsense syllable which the subject was asked to remember. To prevent rehearsal, the subject was required to count backwards by threes or fours from a three-digit number. The counting was paced by a metronome. At a given signal, the subject was asked to recall the three-unit nonsense syllable. As can be seen in this graph, forgetting was extremely rapid— falling to less than ten percent after an interval of only 18 seconds. The results obtained in this landmark study prompted much interest in short-term memory. (After Lloyd R. Peterson and Margaret J. Peterson, "Short-Term Retention of Individual Verbal Items," *Journal of Experimental Psychology,* **58,** 1959, pp. 193–198. Copyright © 1959 by the American Psychological Association. Used by permission.)

*Remembering
and Forgetting*

minutes ask him to repeat the numbers again. He will probably be unable to remember all the numbers in the original order. In other words, your friend's memory for these numbers was of short duration. But this same friend can probably recall the telephone numbers of several friends, the multiplication tables, and possibly even his social security number.

There appears to be more than one kind of memory. One is of extremely short duration and accounts for our ability to retain information long enough for immediate use, as in the case of the seven one-digit numbers. To take another example: when we look up a number in the phone book, we usually retain the number long enough to dial the party we wish to reach. However, if nobody answers or if the line is busy, we probably will have to look up the number again. This memory of short duration is known as short-term memory (STM).

Short-Term Memory (STM)

Most of the earlier studies of memory were concerned with assessing retention over relatively long periods of time—hours, days, and even months. A landmark study was conducted in 1959 (by Peterson and Peterson) that unleashed a flood of experimentation and speculation about forgetting that takes place within a matter of seconds (see Fig. 4.6). This study and subsequent studies have led many researchers to postulate a type of memory of extremely short duration called short-term memory (STM).

One of the outstanding characteristics of STM is its extremely limited capacity, in terms of the amount of information that can be temporarily stored at any given time. We use the term *memory span* to refer to the amount of information that an individual can absorb in STM and recall immediately. Most studies have found that the memory span is limited to between five and nine items. However, the memory span is influenced by factors such as the age, health, and intellectual level of the individual, as well as the type of material.

Short-term memory holds information just long enough so that it can be acted upon in some immediate way. When you call directory assistance and ask the operator for the number of a person living at a certain address, the operator has to retain the

a)

b)

information only briefly. By the time the next request comes in,
she has probably already forgotten the name and address you
gave her. This speed of forgetting in short-term memory is often
advantageous. A telephone operator would be utterly confused if
she retained all the names, addresses, and numbers she heard
during the course of a day.

The impact of most events on STM is like throwing a pebble
into a lake. It produces no more than a ripple, which fades away
and leaves no permanent record. Obviously, some information
that enters STM is not lost, but rather is permanently stored in
some way. The way in which information gets transferred from
STM to some permanent storage is not yet clearly understood.
However, there must be some interaction between STM and a

*The Three Types
of Memory*

139

more permanent type of memory—information must be filtered in such a way that the useful information is retained and the useless information is discarded. When you read this book, you do not remember every word. Somehow, you are able to select those words and thoughts that are important, compare them with what you have previously learned and retained, and transfer some of the new information into more permanent storage.

Long-Term Memory (LTM)

There are many memories which seem to be stored within the brain for long periods of time—a day, a year, or a lifetime. Our own names and addresses, the vocabulary and structure of the language we speak, and significant past events, all exemplify long-term memory (LTM).

There is a great deal of research going on to determine the underlying mechanisms for short- and long-term memory. Much of the research concerned with LTM has focused on a complex protein molecule called RNA (ribonucleic acid). RNA is a kind of chemical messenger for DNA (deoxyribonucleic acid). Presumably, RNA activates the DNA to produce specific proteins, and these proteins seem, in turn, to be the carriers of long-term memory.

Recent research suggests that anything leading to increased RNA production may improve memory, and that any inhibition of RNA production may interfere with memory. Much of the evidence comes from exciting and still controversial research on planaria (flatworms). When planaria are cut in half, each half regenerates into a new worm. If the planaria are conditioned to make a response, and then cut in two, each new worm retains what the original worm previously learned. However, when one half is treated with a substance that destroys RNA, the new worm which develops from that half shows no memory of the previously learned response (McConnell et al., 1959).

Whatever the underlying mechanisms for LTM ultimately prove to be, every moment of our waking lives testifies to the existence of this permanent repository of information. When we read, speak, or drive a car, we constantly draw upon this repository to guide our ongoing behavior.

If long-term memory is, in fact, a permanent storehouse of information and past experiences, then how can we explain such

Fig. 4.8
The orchestra conductor who uses no score and the men and women at their college reunion are calling upon long-term memory. (a, Philip John Bailey— Stock, Boston. b, Tim Carlson— Stock, Boston.)

things as a student's mind "going blank" during an examination for which he had studied quite diligently? Much of what we ascribe to forgetting may actually be a failure in retrieval (Shiffrin, 1970). *Retrieval* is the process whereby we somehow manage to sift through the complex filing system of LTM and find the specific information we need. You may recall the research discussed in Chapter 2 (Penfield, 1959) in which electrical stimulation of certain parts of the brain caused some patients to vividly recollect past experiences that they had apparently forgotten. Obviously the information was present in LTM, but apparently without the electrical stimulation it could not be retrieved.

Intermediate Memory

Studies of patients who have sustained head injuries have shown that these patients remember very few of the events that occurred just prior to their accident, whereas their retention of earlier events is relatively intact. For example, in a study of 1000 patients suffering head injuries, it was found that approximately 75 percent of these patients had forgotten events immediately preceding their accident, whereas only about 16 percent had forgotten earlier events (Halstead and Rucker, 1968).

Studies of this sort have led some psychologists to postulate a type of memory that comes between STM and LTM— intermediate memory (Halstead and Rucker, 1968). Presumably, during this intermediate phase memories become consolidated and become a part of LTM. Anything that interferes with this process, such as an injury to the brain, will prevent information from becoming part of LTM. In other words, events require an undisturbed period of time to be absorbed and integrated. The presumed functioning of intermediate memory may be compared to the action of plaster of paris after it has been poured into a mold. A period of time must pass before the plaster of paris hardens and can be said to be permanently fixed. If the hardening process is interrupted, for example, by overturning the mold, the plaster of paris never achieves the form destined for it by the mold.

A striking example of what happens when consolidation is prevented is the case of a man who had undergone brain surgery in an effort to alleviate severe, recurrent epileptic seizures. The surgery was performed on part of the limbic system. At the time of the operation, he was 27 years old. When he was examined two years later, he still gave his age as 27. The following observations were made by the psychologist who examined him:

> As far as we can tell this man has retained little if anything of events subsequent to his operation, although his IQ rating is actually slightly higher than before. Ten months before I examined him his family had moved from their old house to one a few blocks away on the same street. He still has not learned the new address, though remembering the old one perfectly, nor can he be trusted to find his way home alone. He does not know where objects constantly in use are kept; for example, his mother still has to tell him where to find the lawn-mower, even though he may have been using it only the day before. She also states that he will do the same jigsaw puzzle day after day without showing any practice effect and that he will read the same magazines over and over again without finding their contents familiar.

> (Milner, 1959, p. 49)

In this man's case, we see that both STM and pre-operation LTM remained intact. He was still able to perform tasks like mowing the lawn, that required him to draw on the long-term memory he already had. He could also remember the location of the mower long enough to find it, but could not remember it from day to day. After surgery, however, the consolidation of new information from STM to LTM was impossible.

Improving Memory

"How can I improve my memory?" This is a question asked by all kinds of people, from harassed students who would like to improve their grades, to ward politicians who want to remember the names and faces of their constituents. You can hardly pick up the daily paper in a large city without finding advertisements for courses in memory training.

On analysis, however, the question is vague. As we have seen, memory is extremely complex and any prescriptions for improving it must be equally complex. We have to ask specific questions: Who wants to remember what and when? Solutions will vary from one person to another, from one kind of material to another, and from one situation to another. For example, the way you study for an essay might be inappropriate in studying for a multiple-choice test. Essay exams stress the ability to recall and interrelate previously learned materials, while multiple-choice exams require the recognition of particular facts embedded among incorrect alternatives.

Clearly, there is no single, comprehensive answer to the question, "How can I improve my memory?" If you want to improve your memory, you must know what your objectives are, and the solution must be tailored to fit your problem. In our present state of knowledge, there is little that we can do to improve any of the three types of memory. Perhaps someday it will be possible to take a pill to improve memory. In the meantime, the best strategy is better management of the learning process. Techniques to improve the efficiency of learning and remembering are discussed in the next chapter.

Summary

1. People commonly ascribe their inability to remember past events, persons, places, and dates to faulty memory. In many cases, however, the original learning, rather than memory, is at fault. What is not well learned is unlikely to be retained well.

2. Memory is a construct inferred from certain behaviors of the individual. There are three stages involved in memory: learning, remembering, and retention. Memory, which refers to the retention stage, must be inferred from the remembering stage, during which the individual performs some activity or behavior that was influenced by the learning stage.

3. There are three commonly employed measures of retention: recall, recognition, and relearning.

4. Failure to perform well at the remembering stage may be due to poor original learning, inadequate retention, and/or circumstances occurring during the remembering stage that adversely affect performance.

5. Several theories have been formulated to account for forgetting: the disuse theory, the trace transformation theory, and the interference theory.

6. Retroactive interference occurs when an intervening activity interferes with the retention of prior learning.

7. Proactive interference occurs when the prior learning of a response to a given stimulus interferes with the acquisition of a new response to the same or similar stimuli.

8. Psychoanalytic theory postulates a form of motivated forgetting, called repression, in which people tend to repress memories of events that are unpleasant in some way.

9. Present evidence suggests that there are three types of memory: short-term memory (STM), long-term memory (LTM), and intermediate memory.

10. There is no single, comprehensive answer to the question, "How can I improve my memory?" More specific questions must be asked, like "Who wants to remember what and when?"

Remembering and Forgetting

Terms to Remember

DNA (Deoxyribonucleic Acid)   A complex protein molecule which is presumed to play an important role in the physiological basis of memory.

Disuse Theory of Forgetting   This theory holds that learning produces a memory trace which automatically fades or decays with the passage of time.

Interference Theory of Forgetting   This theory holds that events intervening after the original learning may interfere with the retention of this learning.

Intermediate Memory   A type of memory that comes between short-term and long-term memory. Presumably, during this phase memories are consolidated and become a part of long-term memory.

Long-Term Memory (LTM)   A type of memory of extremely long duration.

Memory   Retention of prior experiences in such a way that they influence later behavior.

Memory Span   The amount of information that an individual can absorb in short-term memory and recall immediately.

Memory Trace   A modification of nervous tissue presumed to underlie memory; a construct which is used to explain retention.

Motivated Forgetting   A theory which maintains that we forget certain events or experiences because we are unconsciously motivated to do so.

Nonsense Syllable   Three-letter combinations that do not make a word, for example, ZEB.

Proactive Interference   The interference of one task with the learning of a second.

Recall   A method of measuring retention whereby the individual must reproduce a previously learned response with a bare minimum of cues.

Recognition   A method of measuring retention whereby the individual must demonstrate that he can identify previously learned material.

Relearning   A method of measuring retention whereby the individual relearns material that has been partially or completely forgotten. The difference in the amount of practice required to achieve the original point of mastery provides a measure of the degree of retention.

Repression   Ejection of anxiety-arousing material from consciousness.

Retrieval   The process of sifting through material in long-term memory to find the specific information needed at a particular time.

Retroactive Facilitation   Improvement in retention caused by the nature of the activity intervening between learning and remembering.

Retroactive Interference (Retroactive Inhibition)   Loss in retention caused by the nature of the activity intervening between learning and remembering.

RNA (Ribonucleic Acid)   A complex protein molecule presumed to play an important role in the physiological basis of memory.

Short-Term Memory (STM)   A type of memory of extremely short duration.

Trace Transformation Theory of Forgetting   This theory explains distortions in memory in terms of changes in the pattern of the memory trace.

Recommended Readings

Adams, J. A., *Human Memory*, New York: McGraw-Hill Book Co., 1967.

Comprehensive study of the entire general field of memory research.

Ebbinghaus, H., *Memory: A Contribution to Experimental Psychology*, New York: Dover Publications, Inc., 1964.

A reprint of a classic in the field.

Gurowitz, E. M., *The Molecular Basis of Memory*, Englewood Cliffs, N.J.: Prentice-Hall, Inc., 1969.

A critical review of research on the chemical basis of memory.

Howe, M. J. A., *Introduction to Human Memory*, New York: Harper & Row Publishers, 1970.

A brief survey, in paperback, of much of the recent work in this field.

Kintsch, W., *Learning, Memory, and Conceptual Processes*, New York: John Wiley & Sons, Inc., 1970.

An overview of verbal learning which includes a modern treatment of recent work on memory.

Norman, D. A., *Memory and Attention: An Introduction to Human Information Processing*, New York: John Wiley & Sons, Inc., 1969.

A study of the way humans perceive, attend to, and remember events. Technical terms are explained as they are introduced.

5
MANAGEMENT OF LEARNING AND REMEMBERING

Factors within the individual

Characteristics of the task

Types of material — Meaningfulness
Amount of material

Method variables

Repetition — Knowledge of results — Recitation
Distribution of practice — Whole versus part
Logic versus rote — Overlearning

Learning methods

The S Q 3R Method — Programmed instruction

Transfer of training

Learning how to learn

Habit breaking

Incompatible-response method — Toleration method
Exhaustion method — Change-of-environment method

Suppose that your psychology professor has scheduled a midterm examination to take place in ten days. What would be the best strategy to pursue in preparing for this test? Should you wait until the last moment, and then study intensively for a ten-hour period just before the exam? Or would you be better off studying each day for an hour? Should you read through all the material several times, or would it be wiser to pause periodically and recite aloud what you have just read? Should you read through previous tests or the self-tests provided in your workbook? Or would it be better to actually take these tests, making sure to check your answers against the ones provided?

In all probability, students have sought the answers to questions such as these since the first examination appeared on the scene. In a broader sense, the issues implied in these questions underlie some of the fundamental factors associated with human learning and remembering. The previous two chapters dealt with some of the more general principles of learning and remembering. This chapter focuses on the practical management of these principles in order to achieve maximum benefits from our learning experiences.

When we discuss learning, it should be clear that we are not concerned with some abstract or esoteric subject. Learning is the survival instrument of the species; it is the survival instrument of the individual. Unlike organisms lower than man, which rely largely upon inherited bases for adaptation to the environment, we humans are capable of acquiring an almost unlimited range of responses to meet the exigencies of the environment. We are capable, through learning and cultural transmission of what we have learned, to reshape the environment to meet our needs. Clearly, the student who is able to take advantage of what we know about the learning process is more capable of surviving in the academic environment.

There are many factors that affect human learning. In addition to our practical interest in taking advantage of these factors for the everyday management of learning, as students of psychology we also have a broader interest in understanding the learning process. The factors which affect human learning can be put in three general groups: (1) those within the individual, (2) characteristics of the material, and (3) the methods used in learning.

Factors Within the Individual

Psychologists are forever seeking general principles that permit understanding, prediction, and control of behavior. However, when attempting to apply general principles, we must never lose sight of the fact that each individual is unique. The way in which each person responds to any given situation is influenced by many factors, both past and present. Since no two individuals have had identical sets of experiences, we should not be surprised when two individuals, confronted with the "same" situation, display enormously varied and diversified behaviors. For example, we have seen that any response followed by positive reinforcement tends to be repeated. In our culture, grades are commonly employed as reinforcers for study behavior. One student will work tirelessly to obtain a high grade in a course, completing every assignment, attending all classes, taking copious notes, and diligently preparing for all scheduled quizzes. Another student may "cut" many classes, rarely "crack" the textbook, and engage in minimal preparation for upcoming examinations. In short, he appears to be completely unmotivated by the incentive of a good grade. How do we explain the fact that one student behaves in accordance with the principles of reinforcement, whereas the other's behavior appears to contradict this principle?

Grades are a learned, or secondary, reinforcer. The use of grades as a positive reinforcer presupposes that, through prior experiences, grades have acquired reinforcement value. However, what is an effective reinforcer for one individual may not "work" for another. The student who will not exert any effort to obtain a good grade may, however, work for some other kind of reinforcement. He may demand something more tangible, such as a monetary reward for his efforts. Or he may be the kind of person for whom the learning experience itself is sufficiently rewarding to motivate him to diligent study. In each of these cases, reinforcement is effective, but the nature of the reinforcement depends upon the unique characteristics of the person. Clearly, for the proper management of the learning process, it is vital that we take into consideration individual differences such as these. Before we can successfully apply specific prescriptions for effective learning and remembering, we must first discover what makes an individual "tick"—why he is successful in certain types of learning situations and unsuccessful in others. For example, the same student who flinches at the thought of any course dealing with numerical concepts may be a "whiz" when it comes to calculating the batting average of his favorite ballplayer.

Although it is difficult to make general statements when you are dealing with individuals, there are certain personality factors that are known to affect the learning process adversely. Anxiety is one of the most common deterrents to efficient learning and subsequent performance on retention tests. However, anxiety is a double-edged sword—it can either facilitate or disrupt performance. For example, some people learn to reduce their anxiety about upcoming tests by organizing effective programs of study and preparation. For these people, anxiety serves to enhance performance. In other people, however, anxiety leads to diffuse, disorganized, and chaotic behavior. They find that they cannot study effectively under the constant tension of worry about how well they will perform on the test.

Many students experience overwhelming levels of anxiety when confronted with a test situation. Even when they have studied long and hard for an exam, their performance can be so eroded by anxiety that their grades do not reflect their actual level of learning. When this happens repeatedly, it becomes difficult to keep trying in the face of continued frustration. Indeed, each failure to perform well on a test provides additional fuel for their anxieties about tests. Just as success breeds success, so also does failure breed failure. Although this appears to be a hopeless situation, researchers working on this problem have developed promising techniques which have enabled many individuals to cope with test anxiety.

For many students, courses involving mathematics and numerical concepts evoke high levels of anxiety. One investigator selected those students who scored high on a "mathematics anxiety" questionnaire, and gave them a "treatment" consisting of a short-term course in which they learned to relax in the imagined presence of situations that aroused progressively greater degrees of anxiety (Suinn, 1971). For example, a tape recording described a situation that presumably elicited a relatively low level of anxiety ("consider two different summer job offers"). This was followed by a description of a neutral situation, one that should have aroused no anxiety. The students were then

Session No. 1

Scene 1

Now as you are relaxing like that I want you to picture a scene. I want you to picture a scene in which you have two different offers for summer jobs. One will pay you a pretty good salary, while the other one pays a lower salary but includes a room and board and travel expenses. Just picture yourself sitting down in a comfortable, relaxed manner. You are beginning to figure out which of the jobs is the most lucrative. As you work out the problem you remain relaxed and at ease. Just picture that scene.

Neutral Scene

Now let that scene go. Just let it dissolve away and picture another scene this time. Picture a peaceful scene. Just imagine that on a calm summer's day you lie on your back on a soft lawn and watch the clouds move slowly overhead. Just picture yourself on a lawn or meadow looking up at a blue sky and watching the clouds move slowly overhead. Notice especially the brilliant edges of the clouds as they slowly pass.

Relaxation

Now let that scene dissolve away. Just let it completely dissolve away and go back to relaxing. Just concentrate on letting your whole body relax more and more and deeper and deeper. Relax your forehead and your jaws. Relax your neck, shoulders, your chest and back, relax your stomach. Relax your hips and thighs, your knees, calves. Relax your ankles and feet. Relax your arms, your forearms. Relax your hands and fingers. Just let your whole body relax more and more. Get rid of any tension you might have in your body. Just let the relaxation take over.

Scene 1

Now once again as you are relaxing I want you to picture a scene in which you have two different offers for summer jobs and one of them will pay you a pretty high salary while the other one pays room and board, travel expenses, but a lower salary. Now just picture yourself sitting down in a comfortable, relaxed manner and beginning to figure out which of the jobs is the most lucrative and as you work on the problem you remain relaxed and at ease.

---

trained in relaxation techniques. The first scene was presented again, and the students were told to relax. This general sequence was repeated for scenes that became increasingly anxiety-producing. By the time the subjects arrived at the most anxiety-arousing scene ("imagine you are taking a final examination in mathematics"), they were expected to show considerable skill at relaxing in the presence of anxiety-producing stimuli.

The basic assumption underlying the use of "relaxation" techniques is that relaxation is incompatible with anxiety. If a person can learn to relax in anxiety-arousing situations, he can gain a measure of control over his anxiety. In doing so, he can reduce the debilitating effects of anxiety on learning and performance. The results of this study support both expectations. The subjects who received relaxation therapy obtained sharply reduced scores when retested on the "mathematics anxiety" questionnaire, and their performance on a test of mathematical ability improved markedly. Indeed, their performance on the mathematics test was superior to that of nonanxious control subjects. Box 5.1 presents some of the tape-recorded materials used in the first therapy session.

Box 5.1
Some of the tape-recorded materials used to train students with high mathematics anxiety (Suinn, 1971). See text for explanation.

Factors Within the Individual

It should be pointed out that this crippling anxiety may occur during the learning stage, the remembering stage, or both. When it occurs during the learning stage, anxiety may lead to behavior that is antagonistic to effective study. For example, the thought of studying for a test may be so anxiety-inducing that the person escapes the learning situation altogether—by daydreaming instead of studying, or by watching television or engaging in social activities with a group of friends. Naturally, if he does this, he will not perform well on an examination, because as we have already seen, what is not well learned is not well retained. In contrast, another student may study efficiently and learn well but be assailed by attacks of anxiety only during the remembering phase (the test itself). This is perhaps the most exasperating and discouraging circumstance, not only because it usually causes feelings of self-doubt and inadequacy, but also because the instructor may erroneously conclude that the student has failed to study and to learn the assigned materials.

Few would dispute the conclusion that anxiety is one of the most common and pervasive elements in the learning and remembering processes. However, many other variables operating within the individual also exert profound influence on learning and remembering. Motivation, prior experiences, and, of course, intellectual abilities are among the most important. An individual may have an enormous amount of talent, but if that talent is not directed along efficient and productive lines, it may go wasted. There are many procedures that can be used to achieve better management of both learning and remembering. We will discuss several of these in the remainder of this chapter. However, for any of these procedures to be effective, it must be implemented by the learner. The acquisition of improved learning techniques requires dedication and effort on the part of the learner, similar to the professional athlete's conscientious adherence to training rules in order to achieve and maintain his proficiency.

Characteristics of the Task

Over the course of a lifetime, we acquire an incredibly large and complex repertoire of learned behaviors. Rarely do we pause to reflect on the remarkable diversity of skills, knowledge, and accomplishments over which we have achieved mastery. Every moment of our waking lives provides mute testimony to the wide range of behaviors of which we are capable—reading the newspaper, buttoning our jackets, writing a letter, memorizing a part in a play, or calculating the correct change after making a purchase at the supermarket, to name but a few.

Learning tasks vary in many ways. They differ in terms of their complexity, the types of skills they require, their familiarity, and even in their degree of pleasantness. When a person is confronted with a learning situation, the characteristics of the task itself will certainly influence the strategy he uses in attempting to achieve mastery.

Types of Material

Most learning tasks can be broadly classified in terms of the extent to which they involve acquisition of motor responses or verbal behavior. Although it is often convenient to make this gross classification, we should bear in mind that all tasks do not fall neatly into one category or another. For example, when you are learning a complex motor skill, such as playing tennis, there are many verbal components (for example, reminding yourself how to grip your racket). Similarly, learning a verbal skill, such as reading, requires complex and integrated eye movements.

Learning motor skills

Learning to write, to drive a car, to hit a tennis ball, to eat with a knife and fork—these are all examples of the acquisition of motor skills. Proficiency in the performance of motor tasks is essential throughout our lifetime. There is no human activity that does not in some way involve motor activities. Even an infant starts out with a fairly sizable collection of gross motor movements— kicking, sucking, grasping, and so forth—which soon develop into intricate and precise skills that permit him to meet the demands of his environment. Creeping and crawling soon give way to walking, running, jumping, skipping, and climbing. By the time the child reaches school age, he has already acquired considerable proficiency in a number of skills such as drawing, coloring, finger painting, and cutting. He then learns reading and writing, the use of a knife and fork, and a vast array of other skills that will serve

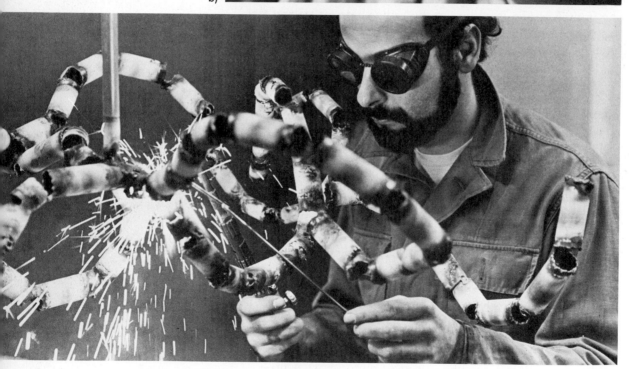

Fig. 5.1
The motor skills we learn early in life are constantly refined and applied to an increasingly varied array of activities as we grow up. (a, Stock, Boston. b, Patricia Hollander Gross—Stock, Boston.)

a)

b)

Management of Learning and Remembering

him throughout his life. The occupation he ultimately enters will require a wide variety of motor skills, whether it be fruit picking, secretarial work, or brain surgery.

Most motor skills seem to take on an independent existence of their own, occurring "automatically," without any conscious effort or thought. For example, think about writing. As a child, you had to concentrate on each step; you had to think about forming round o's, dotting your i's, and spelling out each word.

Fig. 5.2
The pursuit-rotor task

A disc of light moves about a flat surface at a speed and in a pattern preselected by the experimenter. The subject attempts to keep the tip of the stylus in contact with the lighted disc. (Courtesy of Research Media, Hicksville, New York.)

As an adult, writing is something you take pretty much for granted; you rarely stop to think about the way you hold your pen or how to form the letters. Motor skills typically progress from discrete, disconnected movements to the smoothly organized and integrated final skill.

Psychologists have studied the acquisition of a wide variety of motor skills such as typewriting, operating a telegraph, and playing a musical instrument. But since such real-life skills are extremely complex, investigators usually resort to such relatively simple skills as the pursuit-rotor task or the mirror-tracing task (see Figs. 5.2 and 5.3).

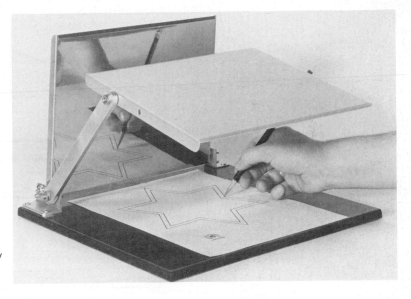

Fig. 5.3
Mirror-tracing task

The subject must trace between the lines of the star as quickly as he can. Since a shield blocks his view, he can see only the mirror image of the star. Thus, the star appears reversed to him. (Courtesy of Lafayette Instrument Company, Lafayette, Indiana.)

In the pursuit-rotor task, the subject is required to keep the tip of a stylus in contact with a moving disc of light. Two separate scores are kept: the amount of time on the target, and the number of hits, or times that contact is made. In the mirror-tracing task, the subject must trace a figure as quickly as possible. The task is difficult because the subject sees only the mirror image of his response; for example, when he moves his hand upward, he sees his hand move in the opposite direction.

*Characteristics
of the Task*

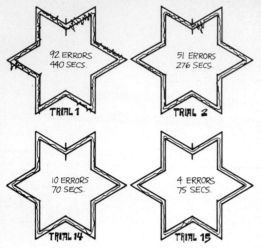

TRIAL NO. 1 AT THE BEGINNING S SMILED, THEN LAUGHED IN EMBARRASSMENT. "IT'S AWFUL! I CAN'T START TO GO IN THE RIGHT DIRECTION. NOW, IF I PUSH IT THAT WAY.... OH, I'M ONLY GOING BACK AND FORTH. HOW DO I EVER GO FORWARD?" THE HAND OF S, GRASPING THE PENCIL TIGHTLY, SHOOK AS IT BORE HEAVILY ON THE PAPER. LEANING OVER IN A HUNCHED, CRAMPED POSITION, S EXHIBITED MARKED ATTENTION. EXCLAMATIONS OF DISGUST WERE FREQUENT. HAVING GONE AROUND THE FIRST POINT, SHE REMARKED, "A LITTLE BETTER!" THERE WERE SIGHS AS SHE WENT ALONG THE SIDE OF THE SECOND POINT, MAKING MANY ERRORS. AFTER TRACING AROUND THE THIRD POINT, SHE SAID COMPLAININGLY, "OH-OH, STUCK AGAIN!" HER MOUTH WAS CLOSED TIGHTLY. JUST BEFORE THE FIFTH POINT SHE CROSSED THE LINE SEVERAL TIMES, EXCLAIMING, "OH, DEAR! I'M SLIPPING OUT AGAIN!" ACCORDING TO HER OWN INTROSPECTIVE REPORT SHE FELT "AWFULLY HOT." HER ATTENTION, SHE SAID, WAS NOT STEADY BECAUSE PART OF THE TIME SHE WAS TRYING TO THINK OUT THE PROCESS; THEN SHE DECIDED TO PAY ATTENTION. HER THOUGHTS ALSO DWELT ON THE INSTRUCTION TO KEEP BETWEEN THE LINES. SHE WAS CONSCIOUS OF THE FACT THAT SHE WAS MAKING MANY MISTAKES.

Fig. 5.4
Tracings of the star outline and comments made by one subject during the first trial in a mirror-tracing experiment. Note the increase in proficiency shown by the fourteenth and fifteenth trials. (From Ralph Garry and Howard L. Kingsley, *The Nature and Conditions of Learning*, 3rd edition. Copyright © 1970. Reprinted by permission of Prentice-Hall, Inc., Englewood Cliffs, New Jersey.)

ABCDEFGHIJKLMNOPQRSTUV

WAYS

Fig. 5.5
We gain increasing mastery of our verbal skills, just as we do of our motor skills.

ABCDEFGHIJKLMNOPQRSTUV

WAYS

The Head
Name Benjy Selling.
There are seven openings in your head your mouth is the top end of the food tube. The two openings of your nose lead to a tube that goes to your throat.

This nose tube joins your throat near the windpipe which goes to your lungs. Your two eyes and two ears connect to your Brain and the Brain is the most important organ in your head.

158

Fig. 5.6
A memory drum. The subject is required to learn material which is presented one frame at a time in the small opening. (Courtesy of Ralph Gerbrands Co., Arlington, Massachusetts.)

An interesting example of the behavior that generally accompanies the acquisition of a motor skill is presented in Fig. 5.4. A beginner characteristically makes a number of comments that seem to be irrelevant to the responses he is making. However, many of these comments appear to guide him as he increases his proficiency in the task. With continued practice, these comments tend to drop out as the subject concentrates more and more on the responses required for mastery of the task.

Much of what we have learned about the acquisition and retention of complex skills comes from studies involving relatively simple motor skills. The use of such devices as the pursuit-rotor and the mirror-tracing tasks has permitted investigation of the effects of different learning methods on the acquisition and retention of motor skills.

Verbal learning

One of the most significant aspects of human behavior is verbal learning. Most of our everyday learning involves the use of words, and formal education is almost exclusively verbal learning. For this reason, much psychological research is concerned with the study of verbal skills. Experiments in verbal learning generally take one of two forms: serial anticipation or paired-associate learning.

In *serial-anticipation learning*, the subject is required to memorize a list of nonsense syllables (words, digits, or symbols) in a fixed order. Usually the list to be learned is presented to the subject on a memory drum, a device which exposes one word at a time at a rate of speed predetermined by the experimenter. Figure 5.6 shows a subject using a memory drum.

Characteristics of the Task

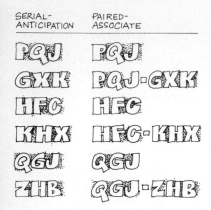

SERIAL-ANTICIPATION	PAIRED-ASSOCIATE
PQJ	PQJ
GXK	PQJ-GXK
HFC	HFC
KHX	HFC-KHX
QGJ	QGJ
ZHB	QGJ-ZHB

Fig. 5.7
Typical lists of nonsense syllables
used in serial-anticipation and
paired-associate learning.

The memory drum is also used in *paired-associate learning* to expose the stimulus materials. A word or syllable (the stimulus) is presented in one frame, and in the next frame the same stimulus is paired with another word or syllable (the response). The subject has to recite the response word whenever the appropriate stimulus is presented. Some typical lists of nonsense syllables used in serial-anticipation learning and paired-associate learning are given in Fig. 5.7. We have purposely used the same syllables in both lists to illustrate the differences between these two methods. In serial-anticipation learning the syllables always appear in the same order, while in paired-associate learning the order of the pairs varies from trial to trial.

Learning the alphabet and learning to count are examples of serial-anticipation learning. When you attempt to learn the vocabulary of a foreign language by associating the foreign words with English words, you are experiencing paired-associate learning. Paired-associate learning and the acquisition of a foreign language are in fact so closely related that students who excel in paired-associate learning in the laboratory generally excel in mastering a foreign language (Cooper, 1964).

One of the difficulties in studying verbal learning is that the subjects enter an experimental situation with differing degrees of experience and sophistication in the use of words. Not only that, but words have different meanings for different people, and particular words are more familiar to some people than to others. Thus, control of the experimental situation is extremely difficult. It is for this reason that most experiments on verbal learning use nonsense syllables. You might question the applicability of this research to real-life situations. However, bear in mind that virtually all of the language symbols that the young child encounters are, to him, nonsense materials. To the child learning to read, combinations of letters are as meaningful to him as nonsense syllables are to an adult. Only through long years of almost constant practice do the words appearing on a page of text become invested with the meaning they have for a literate adult. Moreover, many of the other tasks the child encounters in school are like nonsense materials, because they are unfamiliar and unlike any prior experiences he has had.

*Management
of Learning
and Remembering*

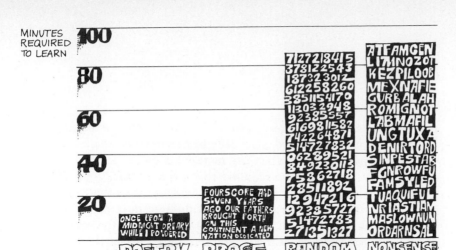

Fig. 5.8
Meaningful material (poetry and prose) requires less time to learn than nonsense materials (Lyon, 1914).

Meaningfulness

Take a look at this sentence: "Me anti meiha dmetan ot herm an." Clearly it is gibberish. Now put the book aside for a moment and try to repeat the sentence. You are probably experiencing some difficulty. Now do the same thing with the following sentence: "Meantime I had met another man." Surely you had no difficulty repeating this sentence. The difference between these two sentences illustrates one of the most important variables affecting verbal learning: meaningfulness. Material is meaningful because our previous experience with it forms associations in our minds. Clearly, the second sentence is more meaningful than the first. It consists of familiar words arranged according to the rules of grammar so as to produce a coherent thought. If you have not already noticed, the first sentence is composed of exactly the same letters as appear in the second sentence, arranged in precisely the same order, but grouped in such a way as to produce unfamiliar combinations.

The importance of meaningfulness in verbal learning was illustrated by an experiment in which subjects were required to memorize a list of 200 nonsense syllables, 200 numerals in random order, a 200-word prose passage, and 200 words of poetry. Figure 5.8 presents the results of this experiment. It is clear that much more time was needed to learn nonsense materials (random numerals and nonsense syllables) than to learn the meaningful materials. However, even nonsense syllables are not completely devoid of associations with meaningful words. Several experimenters (among them Glaze, 1928, and Archer, 1960) have devised lists of nonsense syllables that vary in the

Characteristics of the Task

161

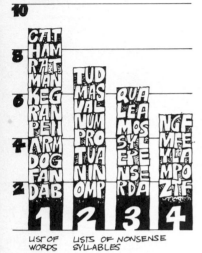

NUMBER OF
ITEMS
REMEMBERED

LIST OF WORDS · LISTS OF NONSENSE SYLLABLES

Fig. 5.9
Subjects learned one list of words and three lists of nonsense syllables. The nonsense syllables in List 2 had higher association values than those in Lists 3 and 4. List 4 contained nonsense syllables of lowest association value (McGeoch, 1930).

degree to which they suggest meaningful associations. A number of experimenters have used these lists to demonstrate that learning is more efficient when the material is more meaningful. In one study, subjects were required to learn four lists. One of the lists was composed of actual words, whereas the other three lists consisted of nonsense syllables that differed in terms of meaningfulness (McGeoch, 1930). Figure 5.9 presents the results of this experiment. It is clear that the more meaningful the material, the more effective the learning.

You can reproduce these same results by trying the informal experiment in Fig. 5.10 on some of your friends.

LIST 1	LIST 2	LIST 3
CAT	FAM	FHQ
FAN	CEN	KBP
KEG	LEM	MZJ
NOT	HAZ	BHJ
RUG	DOB	ZTF
TIP	PIL	LCF
DAB	BAL	QJH
SEX	MEX	HJG

Fig. 5.10
Study List 1 for 30 seconds. Write down, in order, all of the words you can remember. Repeat this procedure until you have learned all eight items on the list in the proper order. Record the number of trials needed to achieve mastery. Repeat this same procedure for Lists 2 and 3. Compare the number of trials required to learn each list. Note that List 1, since it is composed of actual words, is the most meaningful. List 3, which is composed of nonsense syllables of low association value, is the least meaningful.

Amount of Material

In memorizing a set of materials, it is obviously wise not to attempt more than you can accomplish efficiently. In the last

Management of Learning and Remembering

chapter, we said that there is a definite limit to the memory span of human subjects. The average memory span is seven or eight items for materials such as numbers or letters. To learn a list of ten letters or numbers requires about twice as much time as it takes to memorize seven or eight. Clearly, the amount of material to be learned is a significant factor in the efficiency of learning. The limitations on memory span are of particular importance because of the widespread use of numbers in everyday life—telephone numbers, social security numbers, student identification numbers. Since we learn a series of numbers more easily than a series of letters, it is perhaps fortunate that numbers are used for this purpose.

Method Variables

"There just aren't enough hours in the day" is a frequent lament of students trying to juggle busy schedules so as to accommodate study and social activities and still get a reasonable amount of sleep. For many years, researchers have worked on various aspects of this problem. Many volumes have been written suggesting various strategies that students might develop in order to use their time in the most efficient way possible. In the following sections, we discuss some of the methods of learning that have been explored both in the laboratory and in the classroom.

It has been suggested that we tend to overemphasize the role of the instructor in the learning process and minimize the role of the student. However,

> . . . it is the student, in the final analysis, who sets the standard of education. He sets this standard by his study behavior. Students are the most important instructors in the college. No matter how brilliant the lecturer or how good the facilities, most students would fail if they did not teach themselves by study outside the classroom. . . . That the student is seldom thought of as an instructor, in the truest sense of the word, is really the most startling indictment of our prevalent educational philosophy.
>
> (Fox, 1962)

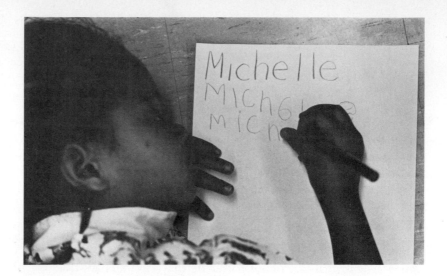

Repetition

Some things are recalled after only one hearing—a name, an address, a slogan. But these are exceptions. We usually have to read or hear unfamiliar or lengthy material several times before we master it.

Most people have a good memory for things that are associated with their own interests. For example, many of us can give a detailed account of a particularly pleasant vacation long after the events have faded into the distant past. One reason is that we are interested in this material, and so we keep it alive by talking and thinking about it. This repeated rehearsal is, in effect, additional practice, and where learning is concerned there is no substitute for practice. However, there are variables that tend to maximize the benefits of practice, as we shall see in the following sections.

Knowledge of Results

One of the most important variables that influence learning is feedback, or knowledge of results. When you are trying to learn something and someone tells you that you are on the right track, you feel encouraged to continue along the same lines. On the other hand, if someone says, "No, you are doing it wrong," he is telling you that you should pursue an alternative course. Without feedback, we can neither enjoy the pleasures of our accomplishments nor profit from our mistakes.

The role of feedback in a motor learning task was carefully demonstrated in an experiment by Thorndike (1932). Two groups

*Management
of Learning
and Remembering*

164

of blindfolded subjects were asked to draw a line equal in length to a four-inch piece of wood which they were free to touch and manipulate. They were required to draw 200 lines each day for a period of nine days. One group was given feedback for seven days, and then no feedback for two days. The other group received no feedback throughout the nine-day period. The performance of the group that received feedback improved daily, and was significantly superior overall. However, when feedback was withheld after the seventh day, performance deteriorated markedly. The group that received no feedback showed no improvement throughout the nine-day period.

Fig. 5.12
Feedback: how am I doing? (Patricia Hollander Gross—Stock, Boston.)

Studies on motor learning all indicate that knowledge of results leads to more efficient learning. However, the effects of immediate feedback or knowledge of results are not so clear in the case of verbal learning. Most studies indicate that performance is enhanced when knowledge of results is provided immediately; for example, one study demonstrated that students seem to profit more when classroom examinations are scored and returned immediately (Sarason and Sarason, 1957). On the other hand, another study suggested that older students may profit more when the return of the examinations is delayed for a day or longer (More, 1969). Apparently, older students are more likely to think about, review, and rehearse the materials that appeared on an examination when they are forced to wait for the results. Thus, when feedback is delayed on one examination, their better performance on a subsequent test may reflect the effects of this additional repetition.

Method Variables

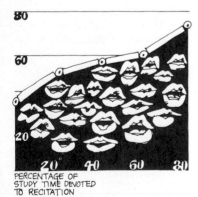

PERCENT
REMEMBERED
IMMEDIATELY
100

80

60

20

20   40   60   80

PERCENTAGE OF
STUDY TIME DEVOTED
TO RECITATION

Fig. 5.14
Recitation

Subjects spent varying portions
of study time in active recitation
of a list of 16 nonsense syllables.
Subjects who spent more time
in recitation showed better
immediate recall (Gates, 1917).

You may recall that we raised a question at the beginning of
this chapter concerning the efficiency of taking self-tests and
checking answers. The research on feedback, or knowledge of
results, is largely responsible for the popularity of workbooks
which include test items and answer keys. If you avail yourself of
this source of feedback information, you should note an
improvement in your performance. Furthermore, when you know
how you are doing, you are more likely to maintain an interest in
your work. In other words, knowledge of results enhances the
learning process through its effect on motivation.

Recitation

Have you ever had the frustrating experience of reading a page of
material and then discovering that you can recall none of its
contents? You reread the page several times and still nothing
"sticks." This experience seems to contradict the principle that
repetition enhances remembering. However, simple repetition is of
little value unless you are actively attending to what you are
doing. Too often you discover that your mind was drifting while
your eyes simply scanned the words on the page. One method of
dealing with this problem is to put the book aside from time to
time, and try to recite out loud what you have just read.

Figure 5.14 presents the results of a study in which the
subjects devoted varying percentages of study time to recitation.

The "zero group" devoted all of its time to reading, whereas the "80 percent group" devoted 80 percent of its study time to recitation and 20 percent to reading. It is clear that recitation led to marked improvements in learning. The groups that spent portions of their study time in recitation learned the material better than the group that spent none of its time in recitation (Gates, 1917).

A wide variety of other studies have shown that reading with recitation is superior to reading alone. Why? When you read something with the knowledge that you must soon recite what you have read, you are more likely to be motivated to remember and less likely to become inattentive. Moreover, recitation provides immediate knowledge of results, so that you can see how well you are doing and adjust and modify your responses accordingly. Finally, recitation provides active practice in recalling the material you wish ultimately to retain.

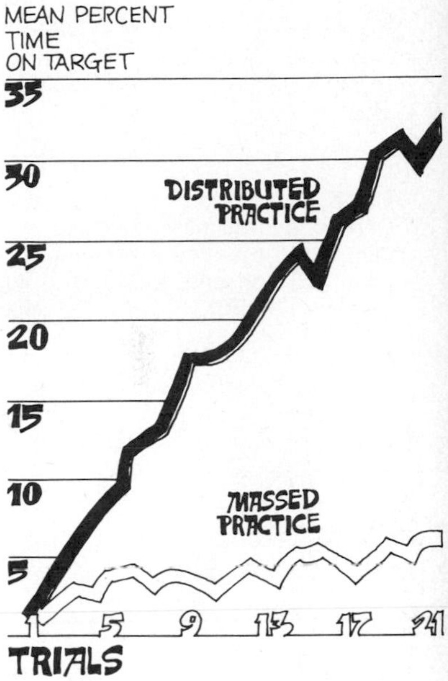

Distribution of Practice

Like medicine, practice can be administered in large doses at a single time or in small doses distributed over a period of time. When practice is *massed,* all of the learning is crowded into long, unbroken time intervals. When practice takes place in smaller doses with rest intervals intervening between practice sessions, it is referred to as *distributed* practice.

Figure 5.15 shows two learning curves for the pursuit-rotor task. One curve was obtained under conditions of massed practice (no rest period between trials), and the other curve under conditions of distributed practice (a 60-second rest period between trials). Clearly, distributed practice led to superior acquisition of this response.

Almost all motor tasks benefit from distribution of practice trials instead of massing of them. If you are learning to bowl, for example, it would be wiser to distribute your practice over five one-hour sessions than to concentrate it into a single five-hour session. In part, the inefficiency of massed practice stems from the accumulated effects of fatigue. You may have noticed what happens when you try to study for extended periods of time. You become tired, and so you do not function well.

Fig. 5.15
Massed versus distributed practice on a pursuit-rotor task

In massed practice, subjects received no rest between trials, while subjects in the distributed-practice condition received a 60-second rest between trials. Note the superiority of the group learning under conditions of distributed practice. (After L. E. Bourne and E. J. Archer, "Time Continuously on Target as a Function of Distribution of Practice," *Journal of Experimental Psychology,* **51,** 1956, pp. 25–33. Copyright © 1956 by the American Psychological Association. Used by permission.)

Method Variables

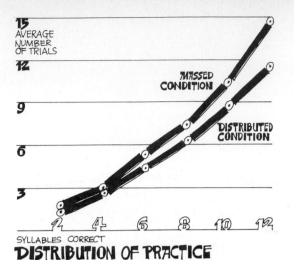

15 AVERAGE NUMBER OF TRIALS

12

MASSED CONDITION

9

DISTRIBUTED CONDITION

6

3

2   4   6   8   10   12

SYLLABLES CORRECT

DISTRIBUTION OF PRACTICE

Fig. 5.16
Comparison of massed versus distributed practice in learning a list of 12 nonsense syllables (Hovland, 1938).

The results on verbal learning tasks are not so clear-cut. Distribution of practice usually, but not always, leads to superior performance on verbal learning tasks.

Figure 5.16 presents the results of a study in which subjects were required to learn a list of 12 nonsense syllables. The subjects using *massed* practice were given a 6-second rest between trials. The subjects using *distributed* practice were given a 126-second rest between trials. The results show that the subjects who used distributed practice required fewer trials to learn the task (Hovland, 1938). Other research in this area, however, has not always produced such clear-cut differences between these two types of practice. Occasionally, distributed practice retards or has no effect on verbal learning (Underwood, 1961).

Many of you have probably developed the study strategy of cramming (massed practice) immediately before an examination. Just how effective is this method of study? Usually, cramming is not as effective as is study with some spacing between sessions. However, we cannot say exactly how the practice sessions should be distributed to achieve maximum learning efficiency, because too wide a range of factors is involved to permit formulation of any hard-and-fast rules. Nevertheless, the research does suggest certain strategies that will optimize the learning benefits to be derived from study. The student should budget his study time so that he is never faced with the necessity of massing his practice just prior to an examination. If the learning has been distributed over a period of time, the night before an examination can be advantageously spent in an intensive review. Distributed practice coupled with review is more efficient than distributed practice without review. In addition, either of these methods is superior to massed practice.

Whole versus Part

Suppose that you are expected to deliver a speech approximately 30 minutes long. You have decided to commit the entire speech to memory so that you will not need to refer to notes. What would be the best approach? Would it be better to try to learn the speech as a whole, or should you separate it into parts and learn one part at a time?

There is no simple answer to this question. The advantages and disadvantages of each method depend on several factors, including your motivation, the nature of the speech, and your previous experiences.

The principal disadvantage of learning something as a whole (the *whole-method*) is that it is frequently a long time before you have anything to show for your efforts. Suppose, for example, you decided to memorize the speech as a whole. Presumably, it would take you a considerable amount of time before you accomplished this feat. This long wait for reinforcement may discourage you. On the other hand, if you were to learn only a small part at a time (the *part-method*), you would have something to show for your efforts after only a few minutes' work. Thus, one of the advantages of learning one small part at a time is that we receive faster feedback on the progress of our performance. That is, we receive reinforcement when we have accomplished only a part of the task instead of having to wait until we have completed the entire task. Trying to learn the whole task at once is likely to be particularly frustrating to children and to adults who have had little experience in memorizing (Garry and Kingsley, 1970).

The part-method is superior when the task can be divided into distinctive units. For example, if you are learning tennis, you can practice your serve at one session and your forehand stroke at another practice session. The part-method is also superior when the amount of material to be learned is so great that any attempt to attack it as a whole exposes the learner to some of the disadvantages of massed practice.

The whole-method may be more advantageous when the material forms a relatively cohesive unit. With this type of material, the part-method has the disadvantage of requiring not only that we learn the parts themselves, but also that we learn to join them in sequence to form the whole.

Method Variables

Logic versus Rote

You have probably all taken courses that involved a great deal of rote memorization, for example, a foreign language, biology, or history. On the other hand, most of you have also taken other courses in which the primary emphasis was on understanding certain logical relationships, for example, philosophy, psychology, sociology, or English literature. You probably found that the courses involving rote memory were more difficult to master in the sense that they required more hours of study. The same finding has been demonstrated in the laboratory—that logically interrelated materials are more easily mastered than materials that must be learned by rote.

Try this simple experiment on several of your friends. Ask them to learn the following sequence of numbers: 581215519222629333. Suggest to half of your subjects that they group the numbers into sets of three and then memorize them (call this the "rote memorization condition"). Suggest to the other half that the numbers are arranged in a logical pattern; ask them to find the pattern and then memorize the numbers (call this the "logic condition"). Incidentally, in case you have not already discovered the pattern yourself, the series begins with the number 5 and continues by the alternate addition of 3 and 4 (5 + 3 + 4 + 3 + 4 + . . .). Record the time it takes for the subjects in each condition to learn the numbers. Three weeks later, ask each subject to recall these numbers for you. You will probably find that some of the subjects in the logic group are still able to recall the numbers, whereas none of the subjects in the rote memory group will be successful.

An actual experiment employing these same procedures found little difference in the learning of both groups. However, three weeks later, 23 percent of the subjects in the logic group recalled the numbers perfectly, whereas none of the subjects in the rote memory group were able to remember the numbers at all (Katona, 1940).

It should be clear that the educational process is concerned not only with the immediate learning situation, but also with long-term benefits. Although it may be possible to learn different facets of a subject equally well, long-term retention may differ markedly with the type of material. To investigate this question,

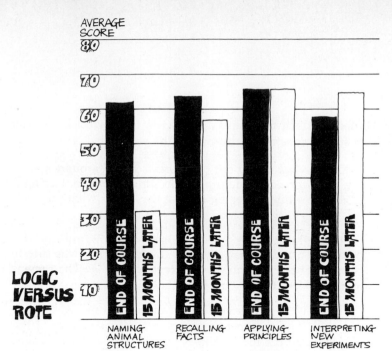

AVERAGE SCORE

LOGIC VERSUS ROTE

NAMING ANIMAL STRUCTURES | RECALLING FACTS | APPLYING PRINCIPLES | INTERPRETING NEW EXPERIMENTS

END OF COURSE — 15 MONTHS LATER

Fig. 5.17
Zoology students were tested at the end of a course and again 15 months later. The graph shows that they retained best the material that was logically interrelated (applying principles and interpreting new experiments). Rote materials were not retained as well (Tyler, 1933.)

one study used the content of a college zoology course. Students were tested on four different aspects of the course on a final examination and again 15 months later. The results of the study are shown in Fig. 5.17. It is clear that the students performed about equally well on all four facets of the final examination. However, there were marked differences in their retention scores obtained 15 months later. Material that was meaningfully related (applications of principles, interpretations of new experiments) was remembered best (Tyler, 1933).

Mnemonic devices

In view of the fact that some facets of many courses require rote memorization, are there any techniques that you can use to maximize your efficiency in retaining rote materials? There are, and they are known as mnemonic devices. One technique should be obvious: try to organize the material in some way that establishes meaningful relationships among otherwise unrelated materials.

A laboratory study has demonstrated that organizing rote materials in meaningful ways is an effective mnemonic device. Subjects were required to learn 12 lists of ten unrelated nouns. The control subjects were asked to learn the words in each list in their correct order; they were given no further instructions. The experimental subjects, on the other hand, were told to construct

Method
Variables

171

stories in which the nouns appeared in the correct order. Here are two stories constructed by two of the subjects:

> A *lumberjack dart*ed out of a forest, *skate*d around a *hedge* past a *colony* of *ducks.* He tripped on some *furniture,* tearing his *stocking* while hastening toward the *pillow* where his *mistress* lay.

> One night at *dinner* I had the *nerve* to bring my *teacher.* There had been a *flood* that day, and the rain *barrel* was sure to *rattle.* There was, however, a *vessel* in the *harbor* carrying the *artist* to my *castle.**

The results were dramatic, as can be seen in Fig. 5.18. Subjects in the experimental group recalled 94 percent of the words from all the lists, whereas the control subjects recalled only 14 percent (Bower and Clark, 1969).

You are probably familiar with a number of different mnemonic devices. For example, if you have studied music, you may have used "Every Good Boy Does Fine" to learn the names of the lines of the treble clef (E, G, B, D, and F), and you may have used the fact that the letters of the spaces form the word *face.* How many of you have heard, "On Old Olympus' Towering Top, A Finn And German Viewed Some Hops"? Students who have studied biology may recognize this as the mnemonic device used to remember the first letters of the twelve pairs of cranial nerves (olfactory, optic, and so on).

Mnemonic devices have been the subject of renewed interest in recent years. Formidable and rather formal procedures have been devised which permit individuals to retain a remarkable amount of information. Indeed, in one study, subjects were able to memorize lists of 700 paired words in an incredibly short period of time (Wallace et al., 1957).

Nightclub entertainers are frequently able to enthrall audiences with their uncanny feats of memory. A nightclub comedian may be able to rattle off one joke after another without seeming to pause for breath. Other so-called mental gymnasts can be shown hundreds of items by members of the audience and

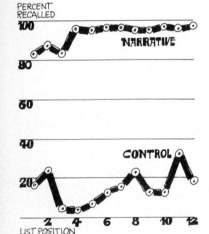

PERCENT RECALLED

NARRATIVE

CONTROL

LIST POSITION

Fig. 5.18
Meaningfulness and retention

Subjects who had constructed stories that incorporated the words to be remembered showed dramatically superior retention than the control group (Bower and Clark, 1969).

Management of Learning and Remembering

*From G. H. Bower and M. C. Clark, "Narrative Stories as Mediators for Serial Learning," *Psychonomic Science,* **14**: 4 (1969), pp. 181–182. Used by permission.

then repeat, from memory, all the items they have seen without error and in the order in which the items were presented. How are these incredible feats accomplished? Are such individuals blessed with supernatural powers of memory?

Recent research has revealed that various mnemonic systems are generally employed by these entertainers. Although the systems vary from one to another in details, they have several features in common. For example, many use visual imagery to aid recall. In one widely advocated mnemonic system, a set of peg-words is first associated with a set of numbers, as in the following jingle:

> one is a bun, two is a shoe, three is a tree, four is a door, five is a hive, six is sticks, seven is heaven, eight is a gate, nine is wine, ten is a hen . . .

Then the material to be recalled is associated with these peg-words through the use of bizarre imagery. For example, suppose you wanted to learn the following list of words, in order:

Fig. 5.19
How can bizarre images such as these aid in recall? See text for an explanation.

*Method
Variables*

pig, fly, run, dog, milk, doll, cup, cheese, chair, book. You might form the following bizarre associations to the peg-words: a pig sleeping in a bun, a fly wearing a shoe, a stocking with a run hanging on a tree, a dog opening the door, and so on (see Fig. 5.19). Presumably, once you have formed these associations, further learning is unnecessary, since the peg-words readily elicit the bizarre images, which, in turn, contain the critical response words.

Though we do not necessarily label them as such, we all use mnemonic devices to aid recall. These devices appear to be most successful when the associations stem from the individual's personal experiences (Paivio, 1969). Our memory banks differ, and what is meaningless to one individual may arouse a wealth of associations for another. The following verbatim account describes how one student used his own mnemonic device to aid recall:

> Sometimes you have to be inventive when you want to remember things. I remember once I tried so hard to learn the date 1874. It was the year the first ice cream soda was invented, and I wanted to remember it so I could impress my friends later. But somehow it kept slipping from me. I tried everything—I tried repeating it—I closed my eyes and I said it. Still, I couldn't seem to remember it a few minutes later when I tested myself. So finally I thought about the number 1874 and I saw it was 26 years before 1900. I don't know why that helped me, but later I had no trouble remembering it.

Although mnemonic devices may be useful for learning certain kinds of rote material, not all tasks lend themselves to their use. For example, there is probably no substitute for straight memorization when learning such things as the multiplication tables or the alphabet.

Overlearning

We have already said that what is learned poorly is likely to be poorly retained. Similarly, what is learned well is likely to be well retained. Are there any benefits to be derived from continued practice on material already well learned? Continued practice after mastery has been achieved is called overlearning. A classic study on overlearning showed that retention is indeed improved with a moderate amount of overlearning (Krueger, 1929).

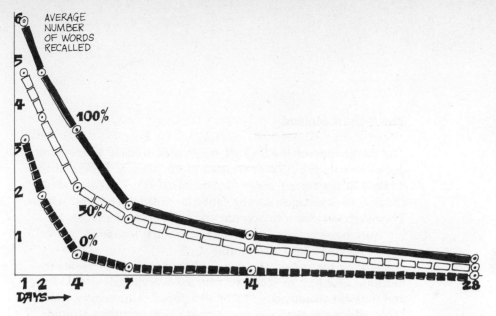

AVERAGE NUMBER OF WORDS RECALLED

100%

50%

0%

1 2 4 7 14 28

DAYS →

Three groups of subjects learned lists of single-syllable nouns. One group learned until they were able to repeat the lists perfectly. A second group continued to practice the lists for half again as many trials as was required for one perfect repetition (50 percent overlearning). The third group received 100 percent overlearning; that is, they continued to practice for an equal number of trials beyond that required for original mastery. The results of this study are summarized in Fig. 5.20.

You may note that overlearning did lead to superior retention. However, there is a point of diminishing returns; that is, the gain in retention achieved by 50 percent overlearning, as opposed to zero overlearning, was greater than the gain achieved by going from 50 percent overlearning to 100 percent. These results suggest that the student should not discontinue study at the moment he has barely mastered the material. Rather, he should continue his study for at least a short additional time. On the other hand, there is little to be gained by prolonging overlearning over a very long period of time.

Learning Methods

We have seen that efficiency of learning and remembering is influenced by a great many variables. As a result of the knowledge that has accumulated through the study of these variables, efforts have been made to devise comprehensive methods of study.

Fig. 5.20
Overlearning

After subjects had learned a list of words to the point that they were able to recite them without error, they were subdivided into three groups. One group received no additional practice (zero overlearning); another group practiced half again as long as it took for original learning (50 percent overlearning); and the third group practiced for as many trials as was required for original learning (100 percent overlearning). The effect of overlearning was to improve the retention of the learned materials; however, by the 28th day, retention was low for all groups. (Krueger, 1929).

Learning Methods

175

The S Q 3R Method

The designation of the S Q 3R method is in itself a mnemonic device to help the student remember the various aspects of the method in the correct order (Robinson, 1961). The method consists of five stages: survey, question, read, recite, and review. This method takes into account such important variables as motivation, repetition, knowledge of results, recitation, whole versus part, and logic versus rote.

During the *survey* phase, you should look over the main headings of a unit of study to gain an overview of the material and note the major points to be developed. This survey should take just long enough for you to see the main topics around which the material is organized. If there is a summary, it is worthwhile to read it, because it may also reveal something about the organization of the chapter.

Your actual work begins with the *question* stage. You should rephrase the first heading into the form of a question. For example, the first heading in this chapter is "Factors within the Individual." You should have asked yourself, "What are the factors within the individual that will influence the efficiency of learning and remembering?" By questioning yourself in this way, your curiosity will be aroused, you will be able to bring your own previous knowledge into the picture, and you will be more likely to recognize the important points.

Now *read* the material in that section with a view toward answering the question you previously raised. This stage should involve an active search for the answer rather than a passive plodding through the written material.

Once you have read the section, put the book aside and attempt to *recite* in your own words the main points of what you have just read. This recitation can be either oral or written. If you cannot do this, you should reread the section until you are successful at reciting the important ideas. However, you should aim at brevity; that is, do not try to memorize the entire section. The recitation phase is probably the most significant aspect of the S Q 3R method, since it is this behavior that is commonly required in class and on examinations.

After you have repeated this procedure for each headed section, you should *review* the entire lesson by looking over whatever notes you have taken. Reviewing serves as a check on memory and also pinpoints areas for further study.

Many students are probably aware of the fact that their study techniques are inefficient and could stand improvement. The S Q 3R method provides a technique which, if implemented conscientiously, will almost certainly improve your performance. It will, in effect, make you your own instructor. At first, this method may seem to take more time and effort than your previous method did. But remember that the S Q 3R method itself has to be learned, and this learning requires time and effort. With practice, you should be able to use the S Q 3R method as easily as any well-learned and thoroughly practiced skill.

Programmed Instruction

Think for a moment about the traditional tools of classroom instruction: the teacher and the textbook. To what extent is either of these geared to take advantage of what we know about learning? In the typical classroom situation, the student is generally a passive recipient of information rather than an active participant in the learning experience. The instructor has little or no control over factors that are vital for effective learning. He has no way of ensuring that the student is paying attention, nor can he provide reinforcements when the student has grasped a principle or concept. In general, the typical classroom situation provides little or no reinforcement that is contingent upon the student's responses. With the usual testing situation, reinforcement or feedback is so delayed that it probably has little or no effect on learning. Moreover, the instructor must pace his lecture for the "average" student, thereby boring the brighter student and leaving the slower one behind.

In recent years efforts have been made to overcome the difficulties inherent in the traditional classroom setting. One of the most important developments has been the emergence of programmed instruction, which systematically applies the principles of operant conditioning to the learning situation (see Fig. 5.21).

Several key features characterize programmed instruction. The information is presented in finely graded series of *small steps.* At each step, the student is required to provide answers to specific questions. Thus, he is actively involved in the learning situation.

Learning Methods

177

1	Learning should be fun.
	However, in the early stages of learning a subject, students often make many errors.
	Most people (do/do not) like to make errors.

do not	

2	When a student makes many errors in learning, he often decides that he does not like the subject.
	He would be more correct to decide that he does not like to make _____.

errors	

3	For a long time, educators, psychologists, and people in general thought it was impossible to
	learn without making a large number of <u>errors</u>.
	In fact, they even had a name for this kind of learning. They called it "trial-and-_____" learning.

error	

4	Recent developments in the psychology of learning have cast serious doubts as to the necessity of
	"trial-and-error" learning. If the learning material is carefully prepared, or PROGRAMED, in
	a special way, the student can master the subject while making very few errors. The material you
	are reading right now has been prepared, or _____ in this special way.

programed	

5	The basic idea of programed learning is that the most efficient, pleasant, and permanent
	learning takes place when the student proceeds through a course by a large number of small,
	easy-to-take steps.
	If each step the student takes is small, he (is/is not) likely to make errors.

is not	

Fig. 5.21
Programmed learning

Work through this program yourself. As you actively participate in the learning experience, note that the program proceeds by finely graded steps. Note also that the material has been prepared in such a way that you will rarely make an error. Moreover, since the correct answer is available, you are provided with immediate knowledge of results. (Reproduced by permission of Teaching Machines, Incorporated—A Division of Grolier Incorporated.)

6	A <u>program</u>, then, is made up of a large number of small, easy-to-take steps.
	A student can proceed from knowing very little about a subject to mastery of the subject by going through a _____.
	If the program is carefully prepared, he should make (many/few) errors along the way.

program   few

7	Programed learning has many features which are different from conventional methods of learning.
	You have already learned one of these principles.
	This principle is that a student learns best if he proceeds by small _____.

steps

8	The features of programed learning are applications of <u>learning principles</u> discovered in psychological laboratories.
	You have learned the first of these principles.
	You can guess that we call it the Principle of Small _____.

Steps

9	The principles on which programed learning are based were discovered in (psychological/astrological) laboratories.
	The first of these principles is the Principle of Small Steps.

psychological

10	The first principle of programed learning is
	<u>The Principle of</u> _____ _____.

Small Steps

	What is the first Principle of Programed Learning?
	_____ _____ ____ _____ _____

This *active participation* capitalizes on the advantages of recitation as opposed to passive reading. Moreover, the correct answer appears immediately after each step. Thus, the student receives *immediate feedback* on his answer, and this enables him to discover and correct any mistake he has made. Each step of the program is constructed in such a way that the learner will probably obtain a correct answer. Consequently, he is rewarded each step along the way. Presumably, this constant reinforcement makes learning a positive and pleasant experience.

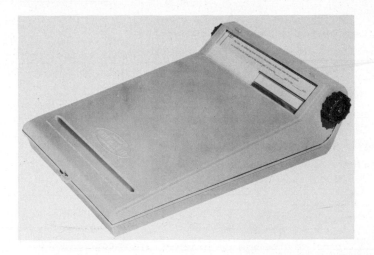

Figure 5.21 reproduces part of a learning program designed to teach the elements of programmed learning. In a program of this sort, each student proceeds through every step of the sequence without deviation. A program constructed in this way is called a linear program. In contrast, programs that allow students who make errors to branch to additional and more detailed material are called branching programs. Branching programs take into account wide differences in rates of learning by permitting each student to proceed at his own pace. Thus, students who make few errors are permitted to go directly through a learning sequence, while students who are having difficulty can get the more detailed explanations and steps they need.

Programmed instruction may take a number of different forms. It can be put into book form (as programmed texts) and

into teaching machines (Fig. 5.22). It can also be put into a computer; in that case it is called computer-assisted instruction (Fig. 5.23).

Fig. 5.23
Computerized instruction in the laboratory of Dr. William Uttal at the University of Michigan.

Transfer of Training

In the broadest sense, we might say that the whole purpose of education, formal or otherwise, is to impart knowledge and skills that the individual may apply (transfer) from one situation to another. When we teach a child to avoid a hot stove, we expect that he will transfer his learned avoidance behavior to other, similar situations. Similarly, when a person learns to add numbers, we expect that he will transfer this knowledge to courses that require the manipulation of numerical values (algebra or physics, for example) and to real-life situations (changing money in a foreign country, or doubling a recipe, for example).

This transfer of training is the very basis for our capacity to benefit from our past experiences. It is probably fundamental to our ability to recognize familiar faces, places, and things, to develop abstract concepts, and to utilize past experiences to build up a storehouse of learned behaviors that can be applied to many different situations.

Transfer of Training

181

SPANISH	ENGLISH
POPA	STERN
INTIMAMENTE	NEARLY
SUSPENSO	FAILURE
FRUTO	PROFIT
OCUPADO	OCCUPIED
DOBLE	DOUBLE
EDICIÓN	EDITION
INSTANTE	INSTANT

Fig. 5.25
Transfer of training in language
Try to guess the English meanings of the Spanish words while covering the right-hand column. After you check your answers, note that the first four cases involve negative transfer, and the last four positive transfer.

Fig. 5.24
Positive transfer
Even if the numerical designations on the face of this watch are unfamiliar to you, you probably have no difficulty telling the time. (Courtesy of Customtime Corp., Philadelphia, Pennsylvania.)

Management of Learning and Remembering

There are two different types of transfer. If a prior experience facilitates learning in a new situation, we say that *positive transfer* has occurred. However, prior experience does not always lead to facilitation of new learning. When prior learning interferes with learning in a new situation, we say that *negative transfer* has occurred.

Positive transfer is illustrated by the ease with which a person can learn to drive a particular car with an automatic transmission and transfer this learning to an almost unlimited variety of other cars with automatic transmissions. Similarly, if you learned to tell time on one kind of watch, you can easily tell time on other watches in spite of differences in size, shape, and the numerical designations on the face of the watch (see Fig. 5.24). It should be clear that a key factor in positive transfer is the similarity of stimuli in different situations. When the stimulus situations are similar and the same behaviors are required, as in reading the dials of two different watches, positive transfer usually occurs. This is precisely what is expected on the basis of stimulus generalization.

Negative transfer will typically result when individuals are required to learn new responses to stimuli to which other responses have previously been learned. The negative transfer will be maximal when the new responses are incompatible with the previously learned responses. If you have learned to drive a car with an automatic transmission, and have then been placed in the driver's seat of a car containing a standard transmission, you will appreciate the problem of negative transfer, for in all probability you will grind the gears and make the owner of the car wilt with apprehension.

Figure 5.25 provides an example of both positive and negative transfer in translating words from Spanish into English.

Learning How to Learn

It is a common observation that students who take many standardized psychological and educational tests show progressive improvement as they take test after test. They are obviously learning how to take these tests; that is, they are learning how to deal with the types of problems presented. Instead of learning specific responses (answers) to specific stimuli (test questions), they are learning general ways of thinking about and approaching the types of problems that come up in test situations. Or to put it another way, they are *learning how to learn*—they are developing certain strategies that can be transferred from one situation to another.

The classic experiments demonstrating learning how to learn have been performed on monkeys. The typical experiment

Fig. 5.26
The monkey is required to learn which of two stimuli is correct, that is, which one has a raisin hidden beneath it. The stimuli were varied from task to task. The problem always required learning which stimulus concealed the raisin. (Courtesy of Dr. Harry F. Harlow, University of Wisconsin Primate Laboratory.)

*Learning
How to Learn*

Fig. 5.27

This graph shows the performance of monkeys on a series of discrimination tasks. The animals perform at a chance level on the first trial, and show improvement on each successive trial. However, the rate of improvement increases markedly as the animals are given more and more problems. The monkeys are clearly *learning how to learn.* (Courtesy of Dr. Harry F. Harlow, University of Wisconsin Primate Laboratory.)

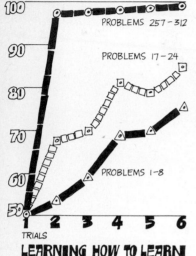

PERCENT
CORRECT
RESPONSES

PROBLEMS 257-312

PROBLEMS 17-24

PROBLEMS 1-8

TRIALS

LEARNING HOW TO LEARN

involved a discrimination task in which a monkey was required to choose between two different stimuli (Fig. 5.26). The monkey was shown two objects, such as a cube and a cup. A raisin was hidden under one of the objects. The monkey had to learn to select the object with the raisin under it, even when the object was moved in a systematic way from trial to trial. Initially, the monkey required a number of trials to master this task. Once it was mastered, two different objects were introduced, a funnel and a cylinder. Again a raisin was hidden under one of the objects, and the position of that object was systematically varied. The monkey required fewer trials to learn the solution to this second task. The same procedures were repeated for each subsequent task, each time using different stimulus objects. Eventually the monkey was able to select the correct object after only a single trial. If its first choice was correct, it would repeat its choice in the second trial. If its first choice was wrong, it would select the other stimulus object on the second trial (Harlow, 1949).

In this experiment the monkey formed a *learning set;* that is, it developed a general approach to the solution of similar problems. Figure 5.27 shows the progressive improvement in performance as more and more tasks were mastered. Learning sets have been demonstrated in a wide variety of higher organisms, including cats, rats, and humans.

Habit Breaking

So far, we have concentrated on the retention of learned behavior, primarily with a view toward improving learning and remembering. We have examined some of the factors that tend to strengthen the learned responses or habits we have acquired. However, there are numerous instances in which we have learned some undesirable response or habit and wish to weaken it. For example, how many of you have tried to kick the nicotine habit? How many of you have fears that you find intolerable? Many techniques for habit breaking have been employed, with varying degrees of success. In a sense, we have already discussed the weakening of learned responses, or habits, in our discussion of experimental extinction (Chapter 3). We saw that withholding

Management of Learning and Remembering

reinforcement following a learned operant response led to extinction of that response. Most methods of habit breaking rely upon extinction to some extent.

Incompatible-Response Method

One of the most effective techniques for habit breaking is called the incompatible-response method, and involves the extinction of an undesirable response and the acquisition of a new response in its place. The new response is incompatible with the original, undesirable response; that is, the two responses cannot occur simultaneously. In effect, we are substituting the new response for the old one.

A classic experiment, involving a three-year-old boy's fear of rabbits, made use of the incompatible-response method. The experimenter gave the boy some candy and showed him a caged rabbit at the same time, in the hope that his pleasurable responses to the candy would be incompatible with, and therefore cancel, his fear of the rabbit. There is, of course, some risk in using this technique. Since the two responses cannot occur simultaneously, the child may have learned negative responses to the candy instead of positive responses to the rabbit. It is important that the desired reaction be more intense than the one we wish to eliminate. In this experiment, the rabbit was kept caged in order to minimize the intensity of the fear reaction. Thus, the experimenter successfully substituted the desirable responses originally made to the candy for the undesirable fear of the rabbit (Jones, 1924).

Toleration Method

There are two different strategies for extinguishing an undesirable response. We have already seen that the incompatible-response method requires that the desired reaction be more intense than the one we wish to eliminate. Another technique, the toleration method, is to introduce very gradually the stimulus that elicits the undesired response. By the time it is presented at full strength, the undesired response has been extinguished or greatly reduced in intensity.

*Habit
Breaking*

The toleration method has been particularly successful in eliminating undesirable emotional responses such as fear. Suppose you have a younger sister who is afraid of the dark. How could you eliminate this fear response? You might install a dimmer switch in her bedroom. In the beginning, you might leave the light sufficiently bright so that her fear responses are minimal, and then gradually reduce the intensity of the light over a period of time, making sure that her fear responses remain minimal. Finally, it should be possible to turn the light off altogether. The effectiveness of this technique might be improved by combining it with the incompatible-response method. You could put some favorite toy, such as a teddy bear, into bed with her each night. Her favorable responses to the teddy bear might gradually come to replace her fear of the dark.

You may recognize that a combination of the toleration and incompatible-response methods was used in the study aimed at alleviating mathematics anxiety. Students learned to relax when confronted with situations that had previously aroused anxiety. After they learned to relax in low-anxiety situations, they were gradually brought up to the situation that elicited maximum anxiety (Suinn, 1971).

Exhaustion Method

A second technique for extinguishing the undesired response, the exhaustion method, requires the individual to make the undesired response in the presence of the stimuli that normally evoke it, so often that the response is eventually extinguished. The exhaustion method is sometimes called the sink-or-swim method, since the stimuli that elicit the undesired response are introduced and maintained at full strength. Thus, the exhaustion method involves a single, continuous attempt to extinguish a response, and is either a resounding success or an outright failure.

The exhaustion method is typically used to break horses. The rider tries to stay on the horse's back until the horse stops bucking. In other words, the bucking is exhausted. At that point, other responses replace the original one.

An interesting clinical case illustrates the successful application of the exhaustion method in a mental hospital. A woman patient would beg, borrow, or steal towels from all conceivable sources. The staff attempted various techniques to break this disruptive habit, including punishment and coercion. None of these methods worked. Finally, they decided to try the exhaustion method. No attempt was made to interfere with the woman's undesirable habit, and towels were made available almost everywhere she turned. She eventually accumulated so many towels in her room that there was barely any space to move around. After a few experiences of this sort, the undesired response was exhausted and did not occur again (Ayllon, 1963).

Change-of-Environment Method

In certain situations it is possible to isolate the individual from the stimuli that evoke the undesirable behavior. In the absence of cues that normally elicit the behavior, the individual will not make the undesired response. This technique is known as the change-of-environment method. In most situations, however, it is not possible to achieve the degree of isolation necessary to make this method permanently effective. For instance, you can put alcoholics in an environment where liquor is unavailable for a period of time. During that time they obviously won't drink. However, when they return to their old environment, all of the stimuli that elicit their drinking behavior will still be present, and they will probably return to their former habit almost immediately. The change-of-environment method is generally unsuccessful because no desirable behaviors are substituted for the undesirable one.

Summary

1. Learning is the survival instrument of the human species. Some of the factors that affect human learning include (a) factors within the individual, (b) characteristics of the materials to be learned, and (3) the methods of learning.

2. Personality factors, such as anxiety, may affect the efficiency of learning and subsequent performance on retention tests.

3. Proficiency in motor tasks is essential throughout a person's lifetime. Characteristically, the acquisition of motor skills is accompanied by vocalizations that appear to guide the learner as he increases his proficiency in the task.

4. Much research on the acquisition of verbal behavior involves serial-anticipation or paired-associate learning. It has been found that learning and retention are better, the more meaningful the material is that must be learned. In addition, limitations in the memory span limit the amount of material that can be assimilated during any given time interval.

5. Several of the method variables that affect both the learning and retention of materials are (a) repetition, (b) knowledge of results or feedback, (c) active recitation, (d) distribution of practice, (e) whether the material is learned as a whole or piecemeal, (f) whether the learning materials are logically interrelated or involve rote learning, and (g) overlearning.

6. The S Q 3R method is a widely advocated way to achieve mastery and long-term retention benefits from the study of textbook materials. The method involves five stages: survey, question, read, recite, and review.

7. Programmed instruction presents information in finely graded small steps, involves active participation, and provides immediate feedback about the adequacy of answers. Both linear and branching forms of programmed instruction have been employed.

8. In the broadest sense, the purpose of education is to impart knowledge and skills that the individual can apply or transfer from one situation to another. Prior experience may either facilitate or interfere with learning in a new situation. Facilitation is referred to as positive transfer, and interference as negative transfer.

9. There are numerous occasions when we have learned and retained habits which we want to break. Four general methods for habit breaking have been described: the incompatible-response method, the toleration method, the exhaustion method, and the change-of-environment method.

Terms to Remember

Change-of-Environment Method   A method of habit breaking in which the individual is removed from all cues that normally elicit the undesired behavior.

Distributed Practice   Learning material with rest intervals intervening between practice sessions (contrast with *massed practice*).

Exhaustion Method   A method of habit breaking in which the individual makes the undesired response in the presence of the stimuli that normally evoke it so often that the response is eventually extinguished.

Incompatible-Response Method   A method of habit breaking which involves the extinction of an undesirable response and the acquisition of a new response which is incompatible with the original undesired response.

Learning How to Learn   Developing certain strategies that can be transferred from one situation to comparable situations.

Learning Set   A general approach to the solution of similar problems.

Massed Practice   Learning material by crowding practice into long, unbroken time intervals (contrast with *distributed practice*).

Memory Drum   Apparatus, used in verbal learning experiments, which exposes one word or syllable at a time at a predetermined speed.

Mnemonic Devices   Techniques for organizing material to be learned, to maximize efficiency in remembering.

Motor Skill Learning   Learning which involves primarily the use of muscles.

Negative Transfer   The interference of prior experience in an earlier situation with learning in a new situation.

Overlearning　Continued practice after mastery has been achieved.

Paired-Associate Learning　A type of learning in which items (words, syllables) are learned in pairs. The subject must respond with the appropriate word or syllable when presented with the associated stimulus.

Part-Method　Method of learning in which the individual separates the material to be learned into parts, and learns one part at a time (contrast with *whole-method*).

Positive Transfer　The facilitation of learning in a new situation by prior experience in another situation.

Programmed Instruction　A method of instruction which systematically applies the principles of operant conditioning to the learning situation.

Pursuit-Rotor　Apparatus used in motor-skill learning experiments, in which the subject must keep the tip of a stylus in contact with a moving disc of light.

Recitation　In learning, actively repeating (or reciting) material one is trying to recall (as opposed to passive reading).

Rote Learning　Verbatim learning which does not require a logical understanding of the material to be learned.

Serial-Anticipation Learning　A type of learning in which the subject is required to memorize a list of words or syllables in a fixed order.

S Q 3R Method　A method of studying which involves five stages: survey, question, read, recite, review.

Teaching Machine　A device for presenting programmed instruction.

Toleration Method　A method of habit breaking in which the stimulus eliciting the undesired response is introduced gradually.

Whole-Method　Method of learning in which the individual learns the material as a whole unit (contrast with *part-method*).

Recommended Readings

DeCecco, J. P., *The Psychology of Learning and Instruction,* Englewood Cliffs, N.J.: Prentice-Hall, Inc., 1968.

A textbook in educational psychology designed for teachers in training.

Garry, R., and Kingsley, H.L., *The Nature and Conditions of Learning* (3rd ed.), Englewood Cliffs, N.J.: Prentice-Hall, Inc., 1970.

Presents a broad range of experimental and empirical information about learning. Relates learning variables to instruction.

Hicks, B. L., and Hunka, S. M., *The Teacher and the Computer,* Philadelphia: W. B. Saunders Co., 1972.

Text on computer-assisted instruction.

Holland, J. G., and Skinner, B. F., *The Analysis of Behavior: A Program for Self-Instruction,* New York: McGraw-Hill Book Co., 1961.

A good model of a program for self-instruction, covering such topics as classical and operant conditioning and schedules of reinforcement.

Mann, R. D., et al, *The College Classroom: Conflict, Change and Learning,* New York: John Wiley & Sons, Inc., 1970.

Discusses interpersonal dynamics which affect learning in the classroom. Emphasis is on the emotional part of what happens in the classroom.

Skinner, B. F., *The Technology of Teaching,* New York: Appleton-Century-Crofts, 1968.

Contains papers dealing with the history of programmed instruction and modern technology of education.

Voeks, V., *On Becoming an Educated Person* (3rd ed.), Philadelphia: W. B. Saunders Co., 1970.

Contains many useful suggestions on how to study effectively. Includes material on teaching machines and programmed learning.

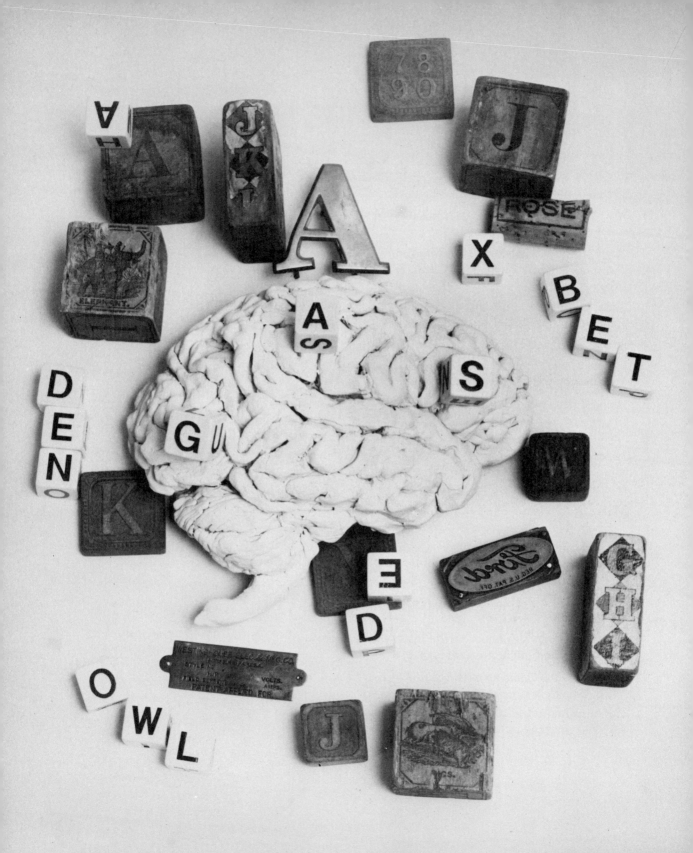

6 LANGUAGE AND THE THOUGHT PROCESSES

Language and thinking are perhaps the most significant of all human activities. They account for our ability to conceptualize the world around us, communicate with one another, and solve the problems of our everyday existence. In general, the various events involved in thinking, reasoning, and problem solving are referred to as *cognitive processes*.

Language

We humans like to think of ourselves as the superior animals living on earth. We readily point to our many accomplishments—our tremendously complex technology, our great and varied architectural and engineering feats, and our artistic and literary achievements. Yet perhaps our greatest accomplishment is our development of language. How is this unique? Unlike communication among lower organisms, human language involves the learning and use of an incredibly large and varied array of abstract symbols. A *symbol* is anything that stands for something else.

Words are among the most commonly employed symbols, and can be used to represent various aspects of experience. For example, the English word *chair* stands for an object, usually with four legs and a back, specially designed for us to sit on, one at a time. We cannot sit on the word *chair,* but we can use the word to represent the object we sit on. We call the physical chair the referent for the word *chair.* Effective communication among individuals is based upon some general acceptance of the meanings of words and symbols. Difficulties in communication often arise because people attach different meanings to the same words, gestures, and other symbols of their language.

Some words have such clearly defined referents that they evoke relatively similar images and associations in different people. Thus, when someone uses the word *chair* in conversation, there is unlikely to be any misunderstanding as to the referent—the referent is an object that you can point to. However, many words cannot be defined merely by pointing to an object, but rather must be defined through the use of other words. *Freedom, democracy,* and *radical* are words for which there are no commonly agreed-upon referents. When we use the word *freedom,* can we be

"THERE GO THE MOST INTELLIGENT OF ALL ANIMALS!"

Fig. 6.1
(Copyright © 1966, by Helen Thurber. From *Thurber & Company,* published by Harper & Row. Originally printed in *The New Yorker.)*

sure that we are evoking the same chain of associations in all our listeners? One person's idea of freedom may be someone else's idea of prison, as in the following example:

> The parents of a 17-year-old girl require that she be home by 10 P.M. on weekdays and no later than one A.M. on the weekends. The parents feel that the girl is given a great deal of freedom, and support their view by pointing to some of her friends who are not permitted out on weekdays and must observe earlier curfews on weekends. "You have more freedom than we had at your age," is their clinching argument. The girl, for her part, is able to identify friends whose parents invoke no restrictions whatsoever. She concludes, "I am kept a prisoner in my own home."

The problem of meaning in language is further complicated by the fact that language is organic—that is, it is constantly growing and changing. Many people today believe that the expression, "the exception proves the rule," means that a rule is confirmed when an exception is found. This logical absurdity stems from the fact that the word *prove* originally meant "put to a test." Thus, the original meaning of the above expression was "the exception tests the rule," and if we were inventing the expression today, we would have worded it, "the exception

Language

disproves the rule." The word *awful* provides another example. Two hundred years ago, a dramatist would have been ecstatic if a critic said his play was "awful." Today the same review might well plunge a playwright into a deep depression. The word "awful" previously meant "inspiring great awe," but today the same word evokes a disagreeable and unpleasant association.

If people who speak the same language have problems communicating, imagine the difficulty that arises when two people try to communicate in two different languages. This problem is compounded by the fact that many words cannot be translated directly from one language to another. For example, Eskimos have a variety of words to describe different types of snow. Some of these words have no counterparts in the English language (Brown and Lennenberg, 1954). Similarly, the Arabic language contains about 50 different words to describe what in English we would call simply a "pregnant camel" (Thomas, 1937).

Language is more than a means of communication. Rarely do we pause to reflect on the pervasive and dominant role it plays in our everyday lives, but it is involved in virtually all of our ongoing daily activities. When we think and reason, we manipulate the symbols of language. We use language to organize our daily lives. We wake up in the morning at 7:30 in order to make a 9:00 class. Language provides the symbols both for representing time and for ordering events in time. If we drive, we encounter hundreds of traffic signs directing us to turn left, merge right, or stop. Buying gas requires language, and so does listening to the radio, reading the paper, talking to yourself, and, of course, reading this book.

Moreover, it has been suggested that memory may be coded in the brain in terms of language symbols (Schachtel, 1959). We experience something, formulate and review the experience in language terms, and store the memory of that experience in language symbols. Our commonly observed inability to remember childhood events may be explained by the absence in childhood of the verbal symbols necessary to code and store these experiences.

Language can be the source of both pleasure and pain. A compliment can make your day, but a cutting remark can utterly destroy you. In the past, bearers of bad tidings were sometimes executed as soon as they had delivered their message. On the other hand, we enjoy a well-told story, and react with pleasure to words of affection and tenderness.

Until recently, some aspects of language study were thought to be outside the province of psychology. The study of the structure of language, for example, was formerly relegated to linguistic specialists. However, psychologists now recognize that all aspects of language constitute behavior. Therefore, a new field *psycholinguistics,* has emerged. Psycholinguistics studies language acquisition and use, and the formal structure of language.

Development of Language

From the moment we are born, we are literally immersed in a sea of language. When a newborn child arrives home from the hospital, he may be innundated by a wave of chatter from well-wishing friends and relatives. Conversations go on all around him. Strange faces hover over him making unintelligible sounds. He may hear a radio or television in the background while his brothers and sisters play beside him. For his part, he is capable of only a limited range of vocalizations—crying, gurgling and coughing. Even these early vocal productions contain many of the basic elements of speech. Indeed, during the first few months of life, the child produces all the basic speech sounds of which the human organism is capable (Osgood, 1953). Moreover, these same speech sounds are found in children of all geographical regions and cultures. It is somewhat sobering to realize that the young infant produces without effort or contemplation such exotic sounds as the German gutterals ("ch") and the French "u"— sounds that cause so much frustration in college students learning these languages for the first time.

Many of these vocalizations rapidly drop out of the child's repertory of vocal responses as his parents reinforce sounds characteristic of their native language (as in "ma-ma" and "da-da") and provide models of speech sounds for the child to imitate. Thus, a child born into an English-speaking home will soon stop making the German gutteral sounds, because these sounds are not heard in daily conversation and their production is not reinforced.

Between the ages of about three weeks and five months, even crying sounds will undergo subtle but significant modifications,

Language

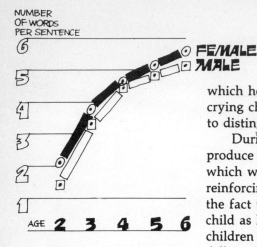

NUMBER OF WORDS PER SENTENCE

FEMALE
MALE

AGE 2 3 4 5 6

Fig. 6.2
Early language development. As the graph shows, girls tend to be ahead of boys in their acquisition of language skills.

which herald the beginnings of communication. At this age, crying changes in duration and pitch, and the parents soon learn to distinguish a discomfort cry from a pain or anger cry.

During the latter half of his first year, the child begins to produce enormously varied, continuous, and patterned sounds which we refer to as "babbling." These sounds are apparently reinforcing to the child, and this may account, at least in part, for the fact that babbling tends to dominate the vocalizations of the child as he approaches one year of age. It is interesting that children who are born deaf utter strange sounds that are quite different from the babbling of children with normal hearing.

At the age of about one year, the first sounds that can be identified as true speech appear. The child speaks his first recognizable words and attaches these symbols to the appropriate referents, although with a high degree of generalization to similar objects. Thus, a child may respond appropriately with the word "da-da" when he sees his father, but may embarrass his mother by saying "da-da" to many different men.

Thereafter, the child's acquisition of speech grows by leaps and bounds—from about 3 words at one year of age, to 50 by the age of two, and 1000 words by his third year (Lennenberg, 1969). By the time he reaches college age, he may have more than 180,000 words at his command, or 200,000 if he is highly literate (Miller, 1951).

During the early childhood years, in particular, there is a curious and educationally important discrepancy in the rate at which boys and girls acquire language skills. On the average, girls are more advanced than boys at each age level throughout the preschool and early school years (see Fig. 6.2). Failure to take these differences into account, at home and in the classroom, may partly explain why speech disorders are far more common among men than among women. For example, it has been estimated that about four times more men than women stutter. Persistent stuttering (as opposed to the normal hesitations that accompany the acquisition of speech) occurs before the age of six in about 90 percent of all cases (Goldenson, 1970).

The acquisition of speech is but one aspect of the mastery of language skills. Speech requires an orchestration of many complex motor and associative skills. Speaking and writing are called the *expressive* functions of language, because they are the means by which we communicate meanings to other people. This ability to use language in a coherent way should not be confused with the ability to understand language (the *receptive* function). The infant demonstrates an enormous capacity to respond to human speech long before he is able to reproduce it. Before the age of about one month, the infant does not distinguish between speech and other sounds occurring in his environment. At about the age of one month, he begins to smile and respond vocally to the sound of the human voice (Nakazima, 1966). He even develops some rather complex expectations; for example, he "expects" to hear a person's voice come from the spot where that person is standing. When an experimental setting is arranged so that the mother's voice does not appear to come from her face, the infant may become agitated and may even burst into tears (Aronson and Rosenbloom, 1971).

By the age of three months, the child begins to distinguish among the various qualities of human vocalization: an angry tone will evoke withdrawal responses, whereas a friendly tone will elicit cooing and smiling (Wolff, 1963). By eight months, some infants have developed firm ideas of the way their mother should sound, and show signs of distress when these expectations are violated. If a stranger's voice appears to be coming from his mother, the infant reacts differently than if his mother appears to be talking with her own voice (Cohen, 1973). By ten months of age, the child will obey such simple commands as "no" or "bring me the doll," especially when the commands are paired with gestures.

Throughout a person's life, his receptive vocabulary remains far greater than his expressive vocabulary. The receptive function of language can be likened to recognition in memory, and the expressive function can be likened to recall. Just as we are generally more proficient at recognizing prior experiences than at recalling them, we are likewise more proficient at understanding language than at reproducing it. If you have studied a foreign language, you may have observed that you understand far more of the language than you are able to actively use. You may be at a loss to conjure up the Spanish word for table, but if you hear the words *mesa* and *pesa* spoken, you may well recognize that *mesa* is the correct one. Similarly, a young child may have difficulty pronouncing certain words, but may be perfectly able to recognize the correct pronunciation. One mother told the following story about her 18-month-old daughter:

> Patty called her bottle "wa-wa." One day when her aunt was playing with her, Patty asked for her "wa-wa." Her aunt picked the bottle up and handed it to Patty saying, "Here's your wa-wa." Patty became very upset, stomping her feet and throwing the bottle on the floor. I'm not sure why, but Patty seems to resent adults speaking "baby-talk" to her.

Language in Chimpanzees

Communication systems are not uniquely human. They have been observed in a wide variety of different species, from insects through the primates. In lower organisms, the communication patterns appear to be established by hereditary factors and are highly resistant to modification. In humans, however, learning plays the dominant role. For many years, investigators have been intrigued by the notion that animals other than man can *learn* complex language systems.

Suppose you are asked to teach language to a chimpanzee. How would you go about doing this? The assignment is by no means easy. For years psychologists have tried to teach chimpanzees to speak. Their early efforts met with extremely limited success.

In one study, a chimpanzee named Gua was raised with a human infant. By the time she was 16 months old, Gua had a receptive vocabulary of about 100 words, but she made no attempts at human speech (Kellogg and Kellogg, 1967). In another study, a chimpanzee was able to employ meaningfully six simple words. The experimenters spent many months of painstaking effort to accomplish this modest feat (Hayes, 1951). Their failure to achieve greater success came as something of a surprise, since many other behavioral measures suggest that chimpanzees are quite intelligent. Indeed, chimpanzees appear to have about the same mental capacity as a three-year-old child. Why, then, are they unable to match the language ability of three-year-olds?

Perhaps our approach is wrong. As humans, we tend to regard all our behavior as intelligent behavior. We look for similar behavior in animals as evidence of their intelligence. It is possible that other animals lack the neural and muscular equipment

BOY, HAVE I GOT THEM CONDITIONED. EVERY TIME I DO THIS, THEY COME OVER AND TICKLE ME.

Fig. 6.3

necessary to produce patterned speech as it occurs in humans. Whether or not the chimpanzee has the necessary neuromuscular structures to produce human speech is still open to question (Lieberman, 1968). However, studies of the chimpanzees have led investigators to conclude that "vocalization is highly resistant to modification in this otherwise highly educable species" (Gardner and Gardner, 1971). It is possible that efforts to teach language to chimpanzees have been unproductive because we have failed to select behaviors that are more amenable to modification by learning. Perhaps chimpanzees do have the capacity to learn language, but in another form.

Think for a moment. What do people do who are born deaf? How do they acquire the ability to communicate with the rest of us? Just because they cannot communicate through speech does not mean that they cannot carry on conversations, think, and do all the other things we associate with language. In fact, people born deaf can form concepts, construct sentences, reason, and communicate meaningfully with others through the use of sign language.

Is it possible that a lower animal could also learn to communicate through sign language? Researchers observed chimpanzees in their natural surroundings, and noted that they make extensive use of gestures. Even in captivity, chimpanzees spontaneously develop begging and other gestures. These observations led a husband and wife team to try to teach sign language to a young female chimpanzee named Washoe (Gardner and Gardner, 1971).

Washoe was trained in the sign language taught in the United States and Canada. Her training began when she was approximately one year old. She first learned the sign for "come, gimme," which involves pivoting the wrist or knuckles in a

Language

SIGN	USAGE	FORM PLACE WHERE SIGN IS MADE (P)	CONFIGURATION OF ACTIVE HAND (C)
1. COME GIMME	FOR A PERSON OR AN ANIMAL TO APPROACH, AND ALSO FOR OBJECTS OUT OF REACH. OFTEN COMBINED = COME TICKLE, GIMME SWEET	AT ARM'S LENGTH, IN FRONT OF BODY	FLAT HAND, PALM UP
6. TICKLE (TOUCH)	FOR TICKLING AND CHASING GAMES	BACK OF FLAT HAND, PALM DOWN	INDEX FINGER EXTENDED FROM COMPACT HAND
12. DRINK	USED FOR THE OBJECT AND THE ACTION, AS IN YOU DRINK, ME DRINK, AND SWEET DRINK, THE USUAL PHRASE FOR SODA POP. ALSO USED FOR CONTAINERS, SUCH AS CUPS AND BOTTLES.	LIPS	THUMB EXTENDED FROM COMPACT HAND
16. PLEASE	ASKING FOR OBJECTS AND ACTIVITIES. FREQUENTLY COMBINED: PLEASE OPEN, PLEASE FLOWER. ALSO, WHEN ORDERED TO ASK POLITELY	CHEST, NEAR SHOULDER	FLAT HAND, PALM TOWARD SIGNER
23. IN	FOR GOING INDOORS, AND FOR INDICATING LOCATIONS, AS FOR OBJECTS PLACED INSIDE CONTAINERS	PALM OF CURVED HAND, PALM TOWARD SIGNER	FLAT HAND, PALM TOWARD SIGNER
32. PANTS (TROUSERS)	FOR DIAPERS, RUBBER PANTS, AND TROUSERS	HIPS	FLAT HANDS, PALMS TOWARD SIGNER
40. LOOK	FOR THE ACT OF LOOKING AND PEEKING, AND FOR OPTICAL DEVICES SUCH AS GLASSES, BINOCULARS, AND MAGNIFYING LENSES	SIDE OF EYE	INDEX FINGER EXTENDED FROM COMPACT HAND
48. BIRD	FOR BIRDS AND FOR BIRD-CALLS	LIPS	THUMB AND INDEX FINGER TOUCH, POINTING TO SIGNER
59. DIRTY	FOR DEFECATING, VOIDING THE BLADDER, OR THEIR PRODUCTS, FOR THE TOILET, AND FOR ITEMS THAT ARE SOILED	UNDERSIDE OF CHIN (USUALLY ACCOMPANIED BY SOUND OF TEETH CLACKING TOGETHER)	SPREAD HAND, BACK OF WRIST, TOWARD P
71. BUG	FOR INSECTS AND SPIDERS	NOSE	THUMB EXTENDED FROM SPREAD HAND
84. YOURS	INDICATING HER COMPANION'S POSSESSIONS, WHEN ASKED WHOSE THAT?	ON A PERSON'S CHEST	FLAT HAND, BACK TOWARD SIGNER

Table 6.1
Some of the signs learned and used by Washoe during the first three years of training. The signs are numbered according to the order in which they were learned. (Courtesy of Drs. R. Allen Gardner and Beatrice T. Gardner.)

Language and the Thought Processes

beckoning motion. In her first three years of training, Washoe mastered 85 different signs. Figure 6.4 shows her making the sign for "drink." (See Table 6.1 for examples of some of the signs Washoe learned.) Washoe also learned to combine signs to form primitive sentences. For example, she learned that by combining "come, gimme" with the sign for "tickle," she could ask her trainers to tickle her. Since Washoe is still a youngster, she will undoubtedly continue to master signs for many more years. Only time will tell how far she will progress in the acquisition of sign language.

Washoe is not the only success story. The problem of language acquisition in lower animals continues to intrigue psychologists. As we said earlier, the chimpanzee is a fairly

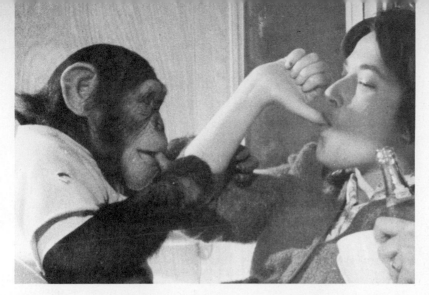

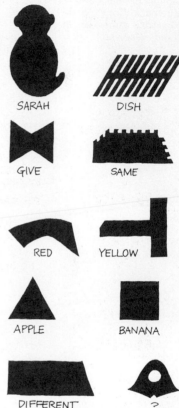

SARAH DISH

GIVE SAME

RED YELLOW

APPLE BANANA

DIFFERENT ?

intelligent animal. Like man, the chimpanzee is a visual animal.
We know that young children can be taught to recognize
symbols. You can ask a child, "Where is the spoon?" and the
child will point to a symbol that represents a spoon (such as a
picture in a book). Why can't we try the same sort of thing on a
chimpanzee?

In fact, efforts along these lines are now in progress. In one
study, a female chimpanzee, Sarah, began her language training
when she was about five years old. During the first five years of
training, she has acquired an expressive vocabulary of about 130
words. What is more, she can build sentences, follow written
commands, and ask and answer questions (Premack and Premack,
1972). How was this accomplished?

The first step was to teach Sarah a basic vocabulary. This was
done in the following manner. Plastic symbols were constructed
and mounted on bases. Each symbol represented a different word
or concept (see Fig. 6.5). Once she had learned the basic
vocabulary, the next step was to teach her concepts. Consider the
concept of redness, for example. We know that Sarah has
acquired the concept of redness, when she can apply the
appropriate symbol to all red objects, even though they differ
from each other in other ways. For example, Sarah knows to
apply the symbol for red when she sees an apple and a
persimmon at the same time. A *concept* is a representation of the
common attribute of objects which are different in other respects.

Is it possible to manipulate these concepts in such a way as
to construct the rudiments of communication? In other words, is
it possible to teach Sarah certain relational concepts? It is one
thing to teach her the concept "red," the concept "yellow," the
concept "apple," or the concept "banana." It is another thing to

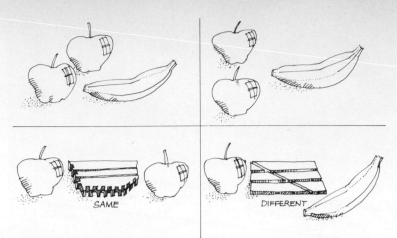

Fig. 6.6
Materials and procedures used to teach Sarah various relational concepts. (From "Teaching Language to an Ape," by Ann James Premack and David Premack. Copyright © 1972 by Scientific American, Inc. All rights reserved.)

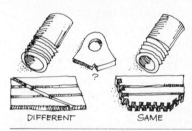
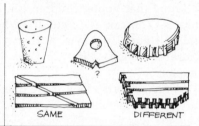

CONCEPTS "SAME" AND "DIFFERENT" WERE INTRODUCED INTO SARAH'S VOCABULARY BY TEACHING HER TO PAIR OBJECTS THAT WERE ALIKE (*TOP ILLUSTRATION*). THEN TWO IDENTICAL OBJECTS, FOR EXAMPLE APPLES, WERE PLACED BEFORE HER AND SHE WAS GIVEN PLASTIC WORD FOR "SAME" AND INDUCED TO PLACE WORD BETWEEN THE TWO OBJECTS. SHE WAS ALSO TAUGHT TO PLACE THE WORD FOR "DIFFERENT" BETWEEN UNLIKE OBJECTS.

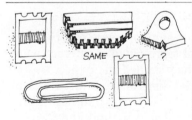
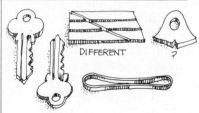

THE INTERROGATIVE WAS INTRODUCED WITH THE HELP OF THE CONCEPTS "SAME" AND "DIFFERENT." A PLASTIC PIECE THAT MEANT "QUESTION MARK" WAS PLACED BETWEEN TWO OBJECTS AND SARAH HAD TO REPLACE IT WITH EITHER THE WORD FOR "SAME" OR THE WORD FOR "DIFFERENT."

NEW VERSION OF THE INTERROGATIVE WAS TAUGHT BY ARRANGING AN OBJECT AND PLASTIC SYMBOLS TO FORM QUESTIONS: "WHAT IS [OBJECT A] THE SAME AS?" OR "WHAT IS [OBJECT A] DIFFERENT FROM?" SARAH HAD TO REPLACE QUESTION MARKER WITH THE APPROPRIATE OBJECT.

teach her concepts such as "The apple is on the banana," or "The apple is different from the banana." These two statements express the relationships "apple on" and "apple not equal to," a more sophisticated level of conceptualization than "redness."

In order to teach Sarah relational concepts, her trainer taught her symbols for these concepts (see Fig. 6.6). Sarah was so

Language and the Thought Processes

successful at learning these symbols that she even invented her own game, and taught it to her trainer. She began a sentence such as, "Banana is on . . .," and challenged the trainer to complete it. She arranged a number of possible choices (multiple-choice task), and accepted only one as the correct answer, for example, "Banana is on dish."

Theories of Language Development

Human language is a most extraordinary phenomenon. Despite wide differences among people all over the world, we all share one characteristic—we have developed ways of describing our environment and communicating with one another. So pervasive is the use of language by humans in all times and places that one might well dwell on the question of how language is acquired.

One popular view is that language is learned in much the same way as any other operant behavior (Skinner, 1957). We have already seen that any response that is followed by reinforcement tends to be repeated, or learned. When an infant makes a sound that is recognizable as a word or as an approximation of a word (for example, "da-da," for daddy, "ba," for ball), the parents usually show their approval, either verbally ("Good boy") or physically (hugs and kisses), and thus presumably reinforce this behavior. The infant is likely to repeat these sounds, as well as any others that are followed by reinforcement.

Several lines of evidence question the generality of the reinforcement theory of language development. One investigator made an extensive study of mother–child interaction during the child's first year of life and found, surprisingly, that mothers reinforce virtually *all* the vocalizations their children make, and not only those which approximate adult speech (Wahler, 1969).

Further criticism of the reinforcement theory comes from the observation that, as soon as we achieve some facility with language, we are able to produce an almost infinite variety of meaningful combinations of words that we may never have seen or heard before. Almost every sentence we speak or write is original and may be regarded as a creative act. If we learn language only by being reinforced for uttering specific words and word combinations, how can we account for the rich and varied

Language

sentence and paragraph structure of Bob Dylan, James Joyce, Winston Churchill, or even of our own personal letters?

Considerations of this sort have led some theorists to suggest alternative explanations for language development. One theorist believes that the human brain is highly specialized for language production. He suggests that the brain is prewired to make the various grammatical transformations that occur in any language (Chomsky, 1969). This would explain the remarkable capacity children have for generating grammatically correct sentences long before they have had any formal training in grammar.

Suppose you show a picture of a dog to a five-year-old girl and ask her to identify it. You then show her a picture of two dogs and ask her to complete the sentence, "There are two _____." The child will probably supply the correct plural form. You might wonder whether she knows the rules of plural formation, or whether she has simply memorized "One dog, two dogs." What if you showed her a completely unfamiliar form, and supplied a nonsense word for that form? If she supplies the correct plural form, her response could not possibly be due to prior memorization. Rather, she must have some knowledge of the rules of plural formation.

When preschoolers and first graders were presented with nonsense materials like those shown in Fig. 6.7, they were indeed able to apply the basic rules of grammar, even though they had received no formal instruction (Berko, 1958). For example, they were able to complete the following sentences:

This is a man who knows how to rick. He is ricking. He did the same thing yesterday. What did he do yesterday? Yesterday he _____.

This is a dog with quirks on him. He is all covered with quirks. What kind of a dog is he? He is a _____ dog.*

THIS IS A WUG.

NOW THERE IS ANOTHER ONE.
THERE ARE TWO OF THEM.
THERE ARE TWO _____.

Fig. 6.7
Preschoolers and first-graders were able to apply the basic rules of grammar to nonsense materials. (From Jean Berko, "The Child's Learning of English Morphology," *Word*, **14**, 1958, pp. 154–155. Reprinted by permission.)

Concept Formation

As we have seen, concept formation involves attaching a symbol to objects that share a common characteristic and ignoring their differences. Apples come in many sizes, shapes, and colors. In

*From Jean Berko, "The Child's Learning of English Morphology," *Word* **14** (1958), p. 150–177.

order to learn the concept "apple," you must be able to abstract some characteristic (or characteristics) that all apples have in common. This is not as easy as it might seem. True, "apple" is a concept. But an apple is also a fruit. What is the difference between the concept "apple" and the concept "fruit"? An apple can also be thought of as "food." Concepts have varying degrees of abstraction. Figure 6.8 presents two examples of different levels of abstraction.

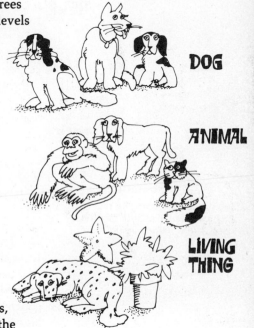

Fig. 6.8
Concepts vary in level of abstraction.

The first concepts we learn are relatively concrete. That is, they are at a low level of abstraction. For instance, we learn the concept "dog" before we learn the concept "animal," and certainly before we learn the concept "living thing." Numerical concepts are the most abstract, and have been demonstrated to be the most difficult to learn.

Concept learning has been studied extensively in the laboratory. Since all subjects come into the experimental situation with different language habits and different levels of literacy, the experimenter would have to control for these differences if he wanted to use an actual language in his experiment. A more effective way to investigate the acquisition of concepts is to invent a new language, and then study how concepts are acquired in this new language.

Before reading further, study the names given to each group of objects in Fig. 6.9. See if you can discover what the objects in each group have in common, that is, what the underlying concept

Concept
Formation

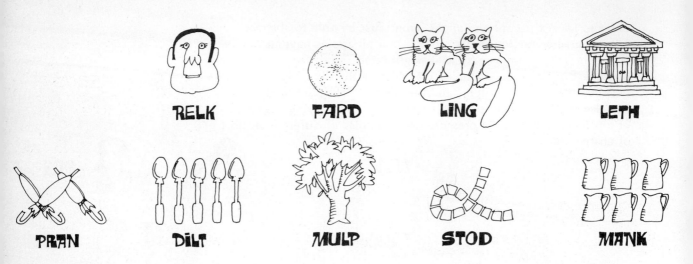

RELK   FARD   LING   LETH

PRAN   DILT   MULP   STOD   MANK

Fig. 6.9
See if you can learn the name of each concept. Test yourself by filling in the names in Fig. 6.10.

Language and the Thought Processes

is. If you have succeeded in learning these concepts, you should be able to attach the correct nonsense word to the appropriate concept in Fig. 6.10.

These same symbols were used in a study which investigated three different kinds of concepts: concrete objects, shapes, and numbers. This study found that subjects learned concepts (that is, learned to attach the proper symbols) in the following order: concrete objects, shapes, and finally numbers (Heidbreder, 1947). However, other investigators found that their subjects had a different experience. Apparently, individuals differ in the ease with which they form different types of concepts. Try testing a few of your friends on the concepts in Figs. 6.9 and 6.10, and see whether you observe individual differences.

How do we learn concepts? Reinforcement theorists believe that concepts are acquired through the processes of generalization and discrimination. When children learn to apply the label "dog" to the family pet, they tend to generalize this label to all animals they see, for example, to cats, cows, and horses. Parents usually reinforce their children for correctly calling a dog "dog," and correct them when they use the label inappropriately. Parents may even assist this discrimination by emphasizing a dog's distinctive characteristics (by saying, for example, "Dogs go 'bow-wow,' cats say 'meow' ").

Cultures do not all conceptualize in the same way our Western tradition does. In the European and English languages, which have common roots, a sentence consists of a subject and a verb. Therefore, our very language predisposes us to think in terms of things that *are* (nouns) and things that are *happening* (verbs). You may be surprised to learn that there are languages that do not make distinctions between nouns and verbs. The Hopi Indians, for example, classify things in terms of their duration. Short-lived events (such as lightning and ocean waves) are represented by something that is like our verbs; longer-lasting and more stable events (such as buildings and trees) are represented by something resembling our nouns.

A student of American Indian languages has hypothesized that the language of a particular culture reflects the experiences of the members of that culture, while the types of concepts a culture forms are, in turn, determined by that culture's language (Whorf, 1956). Thus, if a particular culture has no word for a particular concept, it will not be able to form that concept. Someone living in the South Sea islands, for example, would have no word for snow, and therefore would have no way to conceptualize snow. On the other hand, an Eskimo has seven totally different words to describe various kinds of snow. In the Hopi language, the same word is used to describe such different objects as flying insects,

Fig. 6.10
First study the names of the concepts shown in Fig. 6.9. See if you can identify the concepts by filling in the appropriate nonsense word.

Concept Formation

airplanes, and pilots (Whorf, 1947). In our own country, a study found that black children use relatively more words to describe skin color than do white children (Palmer and Masling, 1969).

Although the hypothesis that language determines concept categories may be interesting, it has not been confirmed experimentally. It is possible that cultures develop their concepts first, and then create a vocabulary to encompass these concepts. Moreover, the lack of a word to describe a concept does not necessarily mean that the concept does not exist. A child may call both an apple and a balloon a "ball," but he will not try to eat the balloon.

Some people say that there never was a generation gap before this generation. They say, "You never heard anyone talk about it before." Is this because there was no expression in the vocabulary for it, or because it *is* a relatively recent phenomenon?

The Thought Processes

What do the following behaviors have in common: daydreaming, solving a mathematical problem, reading today's psychology assignment, having a dream, having a nightmare?

All of these behaviors involved thinking—the internal manipulation of symbols that represent objects, people, places, events, or relationships. Thinking is unquestionably the most common type of behavior that humans engage in. There is hardly a moment in a person's life when thought processes are not going on. If you really want to see how pervasive these thought processes are, try to stop thinking for even a moment. There have probably been many times when you wished you could turn your thinking *off* and get a bit of respite. For example, when you have had a particularly stimulating evening, you may find that the recurrence of thoughts about the evening's events intrude upon your efforts to achieve sleep.

On the other hand, thinking is perhaps the most significant activity humans engage in. Thinking frees us from physical restraints, from the necessity of manipulating the physical events in our environment. To illustrate, suppose that you ask a friend how to get to his house. He tells you, "Go three blocks, make a left, proceed to the first stop sign, and make a right. My house is the third house from the corner on the left-hand side of the street." From just these simple directions you will be able to find his house. Imagine how complex our lives would be if we had to see or physically experience each step in the sequence before we could visit a place for the first time. All the great human accomplishments—architecture, mathematics, science, music, art, and literature—involve the manipulation of symbols. We do not have to physically manipulate two apples and three apples to arrive at the conclusion that there are five apples altogether. We can simply manipulate the symbols 2, 3, and 5. Through thinking and the manipulation of symbols involved in thinking, we are able to visit the ancient Greeks, solve contemporary problems, and anticipate events that have not yet occurred.

Kinds of Thinking

Although thinking is the most pervasive element in human behavior, it is one of the most difficult to study. By its very nature, it is not subject to direct observation. We must infer thinking from other behaviors. A further problem in the study of thinking is the necessity to distinguish among different kinds of thinking. Dreaming is certainly a different kind of behavior from purposeful and directed problem solving. For convenience, we shall distinguish between two broad classes of thought processes. One is autistic thinking, which is relatively uncontrolled and includes such activities as daydreaming and dreaming. The other is directed thinking, which is more controlled and purposeful and is typified by problem solving and creative thinking.

Autistic thinking

Autistic thinking is wishful, symbolic thinking, and is influenced by our needs, feelings, and wishes. Examples of autistic thinking include fantasy and dreams. Autistic thinking characteristically does not follow the laws of logic, and is engaged in primarily for self-gratification. It is effortless, spontaneous, and free from realistic and logical constraints.

We all engage in autistic thinking. It has recreational value, and frequently permits us to tolerate unpleasant circumstances and to achieve, in our imagination, goals which may be

The Thought Processes

impossible in real life. Autistic thinking can also play a vital role in planning for the future. The premedical student who imagines himself as a highly successful and respected doctor may find himself better motivated to overcome the many difficult obstacles that lie between him and this goal. Moreover, autistic thinking may play a significant part in many problem-solving situations, particularly when unusual or novel solutions are required. Many new ideas have come from dreams and freewheeling imagination. The following example was reported by a colleague:

> I had a dream one night in which numbers began to order themselves in columns and then began to subtract themselves from one another. When I awoke, I thought for a moment about what this dream meant. Suddenly I realized that the dream was revealing a new mathematical relationship. In the ensuing thirty minutes I wrote down these ideas as they came to me in fragmentary form from the dream. I prepared a paper which was subsequently published.

Extreme examples of autistic thinking sometimes occur under the influence of drugs, and take bizarre and distorted forms not unlike those found in extremely disturbed individuals. For example, two patients under the influence of drugs were asked to interpret the proverb, "a stitch in time saves nine." One

Fig. 6.11

Children often engage in autistic thinking. (Photo by Marcea Keegan—Photo Trends.)

responded, "If I would take one stitch ahead of time, I would know nine times better how to do another stitch." The other's interpretation was, "I could do something and it would help everyone else" (Rosen and Gregory, 1965).

Directed thinking

At the other extreme from autistic thinking is directed thinking—reasoning, problem solving, and creative thinking. Unlike autistic thinking, directed thinking requires considerable effort, is under the constraints of logic and reality, and is directed toward a specific goal or outcome.

Problem solving. We are often confronted by an obstacle which prevents us from reaching a goal. This confrontation stimulates many thought processes. When we concentrate our thoughts upon the anger or frustration caused by the situation, we accomplish little toward reaching the goal. However, when we direct our thinking toward overcoming the obstacle, we are engaging in problem-solving behavior.

Suppose, for example, that you want to go away for the weekend to visit an old friend, but you discover that the busline has cancelled its service to the town where your friend lives. You might swear at the reservations operator, or indulge in other

Fig. 6.12
Directed thinking can also have recreational value. (Harry Wilks—Stock, Boston.)

The Thought Processes

The problem is to hold both strings at the same time. You may use any of the objects shown on the table.

Two trains, 100 miles apart, are traveling toward one another. One is moving at 55 miles an hour, and the other at 45 miles an hour. A bird starts out at the front of one train and flies to the other. When it reaches the other train, the bird turns around and flies back to the first train. It continues to do this until the trains come together. Assume that the bird flies 60 miles an hour and loses no speed in turning. How far did the bird fly?

(Hint: How *long* did the bird fly?)

A DOCTOR AND HIS SON ARE INVOLVED IN AN AUTOMOBILE ACCIDENT. THE DOCTOR IS KILLED AND HIS SON IS BADLY INJURED. WHEN THE BOY IS BROUGHT INTO SURGERY, THE SURGEON EXCLAIMS, "I CAN'T OPERATE ON HIM, HE'S MY SON."

HOW IS THIS POSSIBLE?

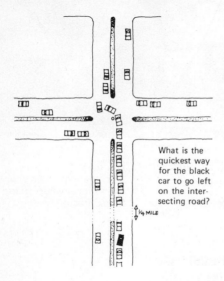

What is the quickest way for the black car to go left on the intersecting road?

¼ MILE

A LILY IS GROWING IN A POND. EACH DAY IT DOUBLES ITS SIZE. AFTER EXACTLY 30 DAYS, THE ENTIRE POND IS COVERED. HOW LONG WOULD IT TAKE 2 LILIES, DOUBLING THEIR SIZE EACH DAY, TO COVER THE ENTIRE POND?

BROTHERS AND SISTERS I HAVE NONE, BUT THIS MAN'S FATHER IS MY FATHER'S SON.

WHO AM I?

Connect the nine dots, drawing four straight lines, without lifting your pencil from the paper.

Fig. 6.13
Try to solve these problems before looking at the answers given in Fig. 6.14. (From *Personality and Psychotherapy*, by J. Dollard and N. E. Miller. Copyright © 1950 by McGraw-Hill Book Company. Used by permission of McGraw-Hill Book Company.)

Language and the Thought Processes

forms of nonproductive behavior, or you could try to find another way to get where you want to go. Looking for alternative solutions usually launches us into thought processes that can be described as problem-solving behavior.

How would you go about solving this problem? Once you know what your problem is, you will probably think of several different possible solutions. These possible solutions, or *hypotheses*, are an integral part of problem-solving behavior.

The first thing you might hypothesize is that someone else might be driving to the same town you want to go to. It is easy enough to test this hypothesis, providing you know of a bulletin board where you can post a notice. And, just in case this proves fruitless, you might formulate another hypothesis. Perhaps there is train or airplane service to that town, with special weekend or student discount rates. Problem solving characteristically involves the formulation and testing of several hypotheses. Either you find a hypothesis that proves to be correct, or you run out of hypotheses and fail to solve the problem. If you are able to verify one hypothesis, you may not be able to do anything about it. For example, suppose you find out that the only way to get to your friend's town is to take a flight that leaves Friday afternoon at the very time you have to be at an important meeting. Since you cannot miss the meeting, you might try to reschedule it, or decide to thumb your way to your friend Saturday morning.

Many different types of problems have been used to investigate problem-solving behavior. Several of these are shown in Fig. 6.13. See how many you can solve before turning to Fig. 6.14 for the answers.

Our ability to solve problems depends on a number of different factors. Past experience, motivations, emotions, flexibility may all affect our ability to attack and solve a particular problem. One of the most important determinants is *set*, or tendency to respond in a certain way.

In problem-solving situations, we tend to respond in ways that were successful in the past. We notice things that we expect to see or are accustomed to seeing. We tend to perceive things in such a way that our perceptions agree with our prior experience or expectations. In a sense the whole educational process may be described as an effort to provide appropriate learning sets for solving the various types of problems that one encounters in the various disciplines. For the most part, set is desirable, since it permits us to arrive at solutions to problems that we otherwise would not be able to solve. For example, in your math courses you learn multiplication, division, subtraction, and addition, and learning these operations will permit you to solve problems involving quantity in real life.

However, when a new type of solution is demanded, set may interfere with our ability to solve a problem (see Fig. 6.9b, f). Under these new circumstances, you might have to "break the set," or take a fresh approach to the problem. You might have to walk away from the problem and then come back and look at it from an entirely new viewpoint. Sometimes, the set is so difficult to break that the only way to solve the problem is to call in

The Thought Processes

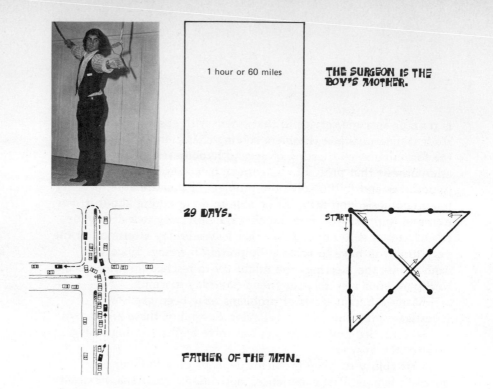

1 hour or 60 miles

THE SURGEON IS THE BOY'S MOTHER.

29 DAYS.

START

FATHER OF THE MAN.

Fig. 6.14
Solutions to problems presented in Fig. 6.13.

somebody who does not have the same set. That person can look at the problem in a new and different light, and perhaps, solve it. For example, earlier in this chapter, we described how difficult it was to teach language to chimpanzees. Success was achieved only when somebody "broke the set" of trying to teach human speech, and recognized that a different approach might be more profitable.

One of the classic studies involving the effects of set on problem-solving behavior is illustrated in Figs. 6.15 and 6.16 (Luchins, 1942). We suggest you try the following demonstration on two of your friends. Ask one of them to write out the solutions to the problems in Fig. 6.15. Each problem demands the same indirect solution ($B - A - 2C$). Then, ask this same friend, and the friend who has not done the problems in Fig. 6.15, to solve the problems in Fig. 6.16. Record the amount of time they each take. You will probably find that the second subject does the task faster than the first subject, who may be trying to apply the formula that solved the problems in Fig. 6.15. Note, particularly, the comparative performance of your friends on Problem 8. Although the indirect solution ($B - A - 2C$) works for the other problems in Fig. 6.16, Problem 8 can only be solved by a direct solution ($A - C$). Direct solutions will also work for the other problems. ($A - C$ for Problems 6, 8, and 10, and $A + C$ for Problems 7 and 9).

Language and the Thought Processes

216

Creativity. What does it mean when we say someone is creative? Most people associate creativity with originality. The ability to see things in a novel and inventive way is, indeed, one of the characteristics of the creative individual. However, originality by itself is not the only ingredient in creative processes. Simply because an idea is original or different, does not necessarily mean that it is productive or worthwhile. For example, a publisher may be the first to discover that he can dramatically reduce his production costs by publishing books with nothing but blank pages. However, this highly original idea would hardly qualify as a creative act. Creative acts are purposeful, directed toward novel solutions to problems, and are productive.

Fig. 6.15
The problem in this figure is to obtain the quantity shown in the last column when given empty jars (A, B, and C) as measures. After you have done this, try the problems in Fig. 6.16.

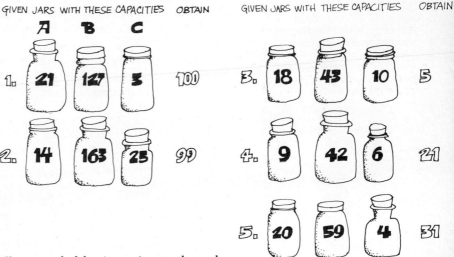

GIVEN JARS WITH THESE CAPACITIES · OBTAIN

	A	B	C	
1.	21	127	3	100
2.	14	163	25	99

GIVEN JARS WITH THESE CAPACITIES · OBTAIN

	A	B	C	
3.	18	43	10	5
4.	9	42	6	21
5.	20	59	4	31

Creative acts are generally preceded by intensive study and preparation. Contrary to popular belief, people do not show bursts of creativity in areas they know nothing about. Great mathematicians, artists, or composers must thoroughly understand the basic elements of their fields before they can produce works that we deem creative. On the other hand, creative works are not necessarily produced by the giants of science or art. At one time or another, we are all called upon to produce new and worthwhile creations that need not be earthshaking in their significance. Salesmen may come up with a new way to market a product; cab drivers may find a new shortcut to the airport; camp

The Thought Processes

counselors may make up thrilling new bedtime stories to tell the children in their charge; in fact, any one of us may see a new approach to some problem we face every day. As we pointed out earlier, virtually every sentence you speak or write can be viewed as a creative act.

In Chapter 11 we discuss the relationship between creativity and intelligence.

Imagery in Thinking

Most of the symbols we use in thinking involve language. We have already seen the significant role that language plays in cognitive behavior. However, not all symbols are verbal. Close your eyes for a moment and think about your psychology classroom. Do you have a visual image of it? Is the image faint or clear? If you say "clear," see if you can count the number of seats.

Individuals vary in the clarity of their visual imagery. Some people can reproduce images with such great detail that we say they have a "photographic memory," or eidetic imagery.

Fig. 6.16
Record the amount of time required to solve these problems for subjects who have first solved the problems in Fig. 6.15. Compare the time scores with those of subjects who have not worked on Fig. 6.15.

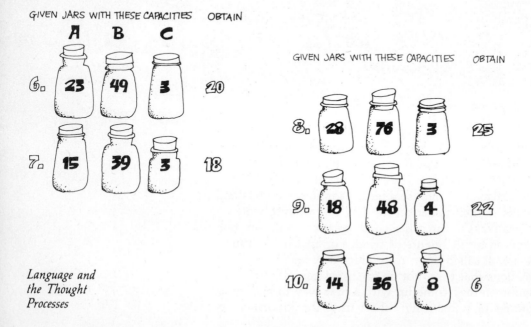

Language and the Thought Processes

A story that is frequently told in this connection involves a law student who was accused of cheating on a final examination. It seems that this student had reproduced, word for word, the details of a case cited in his textbook. The student claimed that he had studied this particular passage and was able to reproduce an exact image of it. In order to test his claim, he was given an unfamiliar passage to study for five minutes. He was then able to reproduce more than 400 words, including the details of punctuation, without a single error.

Fig. 6.17
Painting of a chicken dance, by Ernest Spybuck. (Photograph courtesy of Museum of the American Indian, Heye Foundation.)

Study the picture in Fig. 6.17 for 30 seconds. Now put the book down and try to answer the following questions. How many white circles are visible on the robe worn by the leftmost figure in the painting? What musical instrument is being played by the goup seated on the blanket? How many animals are in the picture? If you have answered these questions accurately, you may have eidetic imagery.

Do you wish you had eidetic imagery? Most people wish they did. But it really is not such an advantage. Children often have it, but adults rarely do. Few scientists and mathematicians possess eidetic imagery. The truth of the matter is that clear and persistent imagery tends to interfere with abstract thinking.

The Thought Processes

Summary

1. The events involved in thinking, reasoning, and problem solving are referred to as cognitive processes.

2. In many ways, man's greatest accomplishment is his development of language. Some words can be relatively easily defined by pointing to the object to which the word refers, the referent. Many words, however, must be defined through the use of other words.

3. Language is more than a means of communication; it is involved in virtually all of our ongoing daily activities. Moreover, it has been suggested that memory may be coded in the brain in terms of language symbols.

4. The newborn child is capable of producing only a limited range of vocalizations. However, his early vocal productions include many of the basic elements of speech, regardless of the geographical region and language culture into which he is born. Many of these vocalizations will drop from the child's repertory of vocal responses as his parents reinforce sounds characteristic of the culture, and provide speech sounds for the child to imitate.

5. During the latter half of his first year, the child begins to produce varied, continuous, and patterned sounds referred to as "babbling." At about the age of one year, the first sounds appear that are recognizable as true speech.

6. During the early childhood years, girls acquire language skills more rapidly than boys of comparable age.

7. The mastery of language involves the acquisition of both expressive function (the means by which we communicate meaning to others) and receptive function (the ability to understand language).

8. Communication systems are not uniquely human. In lower animals, communication patterns appear to be established by hereditary factors; in man, learning plays the dominant role.

9. The reinforcement theory, as exemplified by B. F. Skinner, holds that language is learned in much the same way as any other operant behavior: vocalizations that approximate human speech are rewarded so that a gradual shaping of vocalizations occur.

Language and the Thought Processes

10. Opposing the reinforcement position, Chomsky argues that the human brain is an organ that is highly specialized for the production of language. Chomsky suggests that it is prewired for making the grammatical transformations that occur in language.

11. Concept learning involves attaching a symbol to objects that share a common characteristic while ignoring the differences that exist. Concepts have varying degrees of abstraction.

12. Thinking involves the internal manipulation of symbols that represent objects, people, places, events, or relationships. Through thinking, we are freed of the necessity to manipulate physical events in our environment in order to determine the consequences of these manipulations.

13. Two broad classes of thinking can be distinguished: autistic thinking and directed thinking.

14. Most of the symbols we use in thinking involve language. However, not all symbols are verbal. Individuals vary in the clarity of their visual imagery. Some people can reproduce images with such detail that we say they have a "photographic memory," or eidetic imagery.

Terms to Remember

Autistic Thinking   Wishful, symbolic thinking which is influenced by the individual's needs, feelings, and wishes, as in daydreaming.

Cognitive Processes   The various events involved in thinking, reasoning, and problem solving.

Concept   An abstract idea or representation of the common attribute of objects which are otherwise different.

Concept Learning   Learning to attach a symbol to objects that share a common characteristic, while ignoring their differences.

Creative Thinking   Productive thinking which is directed toward novel solutions to problems.

Directed Thinking   Controlled, purposeful thinking which is directed toward a specific goal or outcome, as in problem solving.

Eidetic Imagery   Visual imagery that is so clear and detailed that the objects represented seem to be actually present; sometimes called photographic memory.

Expressive Function of Language   Communication of meanings to others, for example, by speech and writing.

Problem Solving   Behavior directed toward overcoming an obstacle or adjusting to a situation by using new ways of responding.

Psycholinguistics   The study of language acquisition and use, as well as the formal structure of language.

Receptive Function of Language   Understanding of language.

Set   A readiness to respond in a certain way because of prior experience or expectations.

Symbol   Anything that stands for something else.

Thinking   The internal manipulation of symbols.

Recommended Readings

Blumenthal, A. L., *Language and Psychology: Historical Aspects of Psycholinguistics,* New York: John Wiley & Sons, Inc., 1970.

Describes psycholinguistics research at the turn of the century, and shows how the development of contemporary psycholinguistics is related to the earlier tradition.

Bruner, J. S., and Oliver, R. R., *Studies in Cognitive Growth,* New York: John Wiley & Sons, Inc., 1966.

Describes cognitive growth in a number of different cultures.

Chomsky, N., *Language and Mind* (enl. ed.), New York: Harcourt Brace Jovanovich, Inc., 1972.

Discusses ways in which the study of language has evolved in the past, is developing today, and may be expected to develop in the future.

Hayes, J. P. (Ed.), *Cognition and the Development of Language,* New York: John Wiley & Sons, Inc., 1970.

Presents modern accounts, by leaders in the field, of research and theory on the development of language.

Neisser, U., *Cognitive Psychology,* New York: Appleton-Century-Crofts, 1967.

An extremely well-written review of the higher mental processes from a cognitive point of view.

Pollio, H., *The Psychology of Symbolic Activity,* Reading, Massachusetts: Addison-Wesley Publishing Co., 1974.

A book for the serious student interested in remembering and forgetting, concept formation, problem solving, language and language use, and the development of thinking.

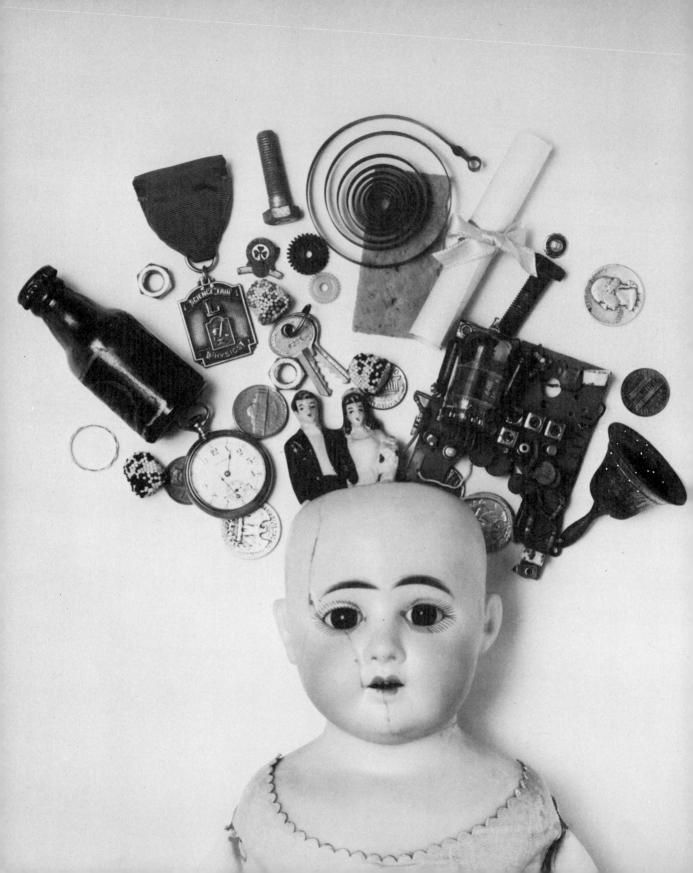

7
MOTIVATION

Measurement of motivational states

Biological drives

Hunger drive — Thirst drive
Sleep drive — Drive to avoid pain
Sex drive — Maternal drive

Stimulus needs

The need for stimulation
Contact comfort need

Learned motives

Fear and anxiety — Social motives

Motivation is unquestionably one of the most important variables affecting behavior. Indeed, most psychologists would agree that *all* behavior is motivated. This idea is so generally accepted that references to motivation occur frequently in everyday conversation. We constantly hear ourselves and others questioning the underlying causes of behavior: "Why does John drink so much?" "Why does Jane want to do such a thing?" "What are you trying to prove?"

Although the questions are easy to raise, the answers are not readily apparent. In trying to pinpoint the motives underlying any given behavior, we are often tempted to jump to conclusions. For example, we see someone go to a refrigerator, open it, and scan its contents. His behavior suggests that he is motivated by hunger. But when he produces a container of cold water and proceeds to pour himself a drink, we must revise our inference and conclude that his behavior was motivated by thirst.

To complicate matters, people whose behavior appears on the surface to be similar may, in fact, be prompted by a wide variety of motives. Some students study introductory psychology because they are curious about the subject, some are trying to solve their personal problems, and some are just fulfilling course requirements.

Since motives cannot be directly observed, we must infer their operation from behavior or from our knowledge of the circumstances accompanying that behavior. Motives have two distinct functions. They *energize,* or activate, behavior and they *direct* that behavior toward specific goals. As we become increasingly hungry, we become more active and also more likely to direct our activities toward goal objects that will satisfy this hunger—specifically, food.

The language for describing motivated behavior is still not settled. For our purposes, it is convenient to distinguish between two groups of motives: *biological drives,* in which there is clearly a physiological basis such as hunger and thirst; and *learned motives,* those which appear to be acquired from experience. Consider newborn children, whose physiological needs account for all of their behavior. They require food, sleep, and water; they must breath, excrete wastes, and avoid pain or discomfort. As children develop and begin to interact with their environment, learned motives play an increasingly important role in determining their behavior. They seek out playmates on their own, develop interests and skills, and strive for independence from their parents.

There is a third group of motivations, called *stimulus needs,* which function like biological drives but do not appear to have any underlying physiological basis. Nor do they appear to be learned. They are inferred from behavior which appears to be motivated by a need to be active and stimulated, and to explore and manipulate the environment.

We are often unaware of underlying motivations which operate in ourselves and others. The literature of psychoanalysis provides many examples of the unconscious motivation of behavior. A woman who takes care of her invalid father may be so protective that we are led to conclude that her behavior is motivated by love and concern for his health. Nevertheless, she may be bothered by a recurrent nightmare in which her father, or a person very much like her father, is repeatedly hurt or killed. Such evidence may lead us to suspect that she harbors considerable unconscious hostility toward her father. Clinicians commonly look for indirect indications of unconscious motivation, such as the content of dreams.

People often behave in ways which they themselves do not understand. The explanations they give may seem correct to them; however, a skilled observer may deduce other motives underlying their behavior. A student who claims that he does not study because grades are unimportant may, in fact, have unconscious anxiety about his ability. If he were to study and get a poor grade, he would be forced to face the issue of his own incompetence. We shall discuss unconscious motivation at greater length in Chapters 13 and 14.

Measurement of Motivational States

Since motives cannot be directly observed, they cannot be directly measured. However, techniques have been developed for measuring the strength of a motivational state. Four different measurement techniques are used.

1. General activity level

We have mentioned that one of the functions of motives is to energize behavior. Thus, we can expect that increased motivation will lead to increased restlessness or activity. Since it is usually not practical to observe and measure human activity level, many of the laboratory studies on motivation use lower animals in situations specially designed for measurement of activity level. One of the most commonly used devices is the activity wheel, which records running behavior (see Fig. 7.1). Various experiments have shown that the more highly motivated the animal—for example, the longer it is deprived of food—the more it will run. Of course, this observation holds true only within certain limits. If the deprivation is extended over too long a period of time, the animal's activity will diminish as a result of its weakened condition.

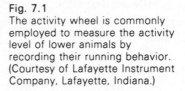

Fig. 7.1
The activity wheel is commonly employed to measure the activity level of lower animals by recording their running behavior. (Courtesy of Lafayette Instrument Company, Lafayette, Indiana.)

2. Performance rate

An inveterate gambler will spend hours carefully going over the daily racing form and making selections from it; a baseball enthusiast will spend every spare moment calculating batting averages and studying the latest statistics on individual players and favorite teams; a politician running for office will appear almost indefatigable as he shakes thousands of hands, kisses countless babies, and delivers speeches wherever there is an audience to listen. What do all these examples have in common? In each, an individual is responding at a high rate to satisfy a strong motivational state.

Once an organism has learned a response to satisfy a motive, its rate of responding can be used to measure the strength of that motivation. Rate-of-response measures are

Motivation

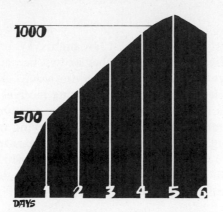

Fig. 7.2
Rate of responding as a measure of drive

A rat had been trained to press a bar to obtain food. When food was withheld, the rate of bar-pressing increased until the fifth day. After that, the weakening effects of starvation caused the response rate to decrease (Heron and Skinner, 1937).

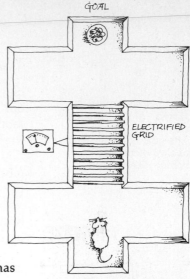

Fig. 7.3
The animal must cross an electrified grid in order to reach the goal. The number and intensity of shocks it will accept provide a measure of the strength of the animal's motivation.

commonly employed in the laboratory. For instance, a rat that has learned to press a bar to receive food will increase its rate of bar-pressing with increased hunger. Figure 7.2 summarizes the results of one study relating rate of responding to increased levels of hunger.

3. Overcoming an obstacle

You have probably observed that a highly motivated individual will sometimes endure a great deal of hardship in order to reach a desired goal. For example, an aspiring concert pianist will subject himself to long and arduous hours of practice in order to achieve his vocational goal. A person who hasn't had a bite to eat all day may be willing to drive miles late at night in a snowstorm to get a hamburger. High levels of motivation for a particular goal often enable people to overcome obstacles that stand between them and their goal.

In many laboratory studies, animals are confronted with obstacles that obstruct their goal-directed activities. The obstruction frequently consists of an electrified grid which they must cross to reach their goal (see Fig. 7.3). The stronger the motivation, the more pain the animals will accept to satisfy that motivation.

4. Selection among goals

In most real-life situations several motivations are operating at once, and behavior is generally determined by the strongest one. Suppose you are motivated to complete a term paper that is due in the morning. Suppose also that you missed your evening meal and are extremely hungry. To make matters worse, you have not

Measurement of Motivational States

Fig. 7.4
If a rat has learned to turn left
for food and right for water, and
is then deprived of food and
water, the goal object it selects
presumably indicates which
motivational state is stronger.

had much sleep the past few nights. Which motive will you act
on? Presumably, your behavior will be determined by whatever
motive is strongest. By observing your behavior, we can assess
the relative strength of competing motives.

In the laboratory situation, the relative strength of different
motives can be determined by observing which of several goals
the organism selects. A rat that has learned to turn left for food
and to turn right for water will make whichever response will
lead to satisfaction of the motive that is dominant at that
particular time (see Fig. 7.4).

T - MAZE

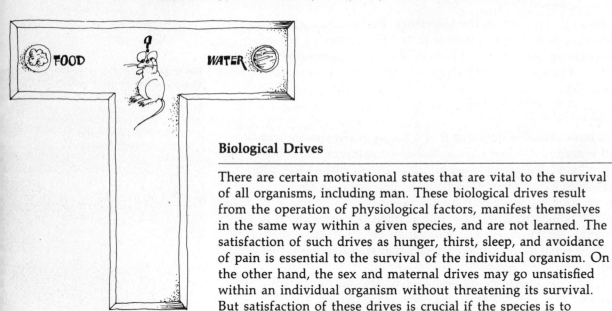

Biological Drives

There are certain motivational states that are vital to the survival
of all organisms, including man. These biological drives result
from the operation of physiological factors, manifest themselves
in the same way within a given species, and are not learned. The
satisfaction of such drives as hunger, thirst, sleep, and avoidance
of pain is essential to the survival of the individual organism. On
the other hand, the sex and maternal drives may go unsatisfied
within an individual organism without threatening its survival.
But satisfaction of these drives is crucial if the species is to
survive.

Hunger Drive

Suppose we notice that a little girl who has not eaten for a
relatively long while becomes increasingly restless and directs
more of her behavior toward finding food. She rummages through
the kitchen, hunting for the leftovers from last night's dinner.
After she eats, there is a decrease in both her restlessness and her
food-seeking behavior. Although we couldn't observe this child's
hunger drive directly, we could infer its presence. We observed

Motivation

230

the condition—the period of food deprivation—which led to the arousal of the drive. We also noted both the *activation* and the *directedness* of the ensuing behavior. Her behavior was directed toward a specific class of goal objects, that is, food. Finally, we observed her eating. This final response in the sequence of goal-directed behaviors, called the *consummatory response,* led to a decrease in the girl's drive level. We could infer the decreased level by observing the decrease in her restlessness and in her food-seeking behavior.

For a long time it was assumed that the hunger drive was aroused by local physiological causes such as stomach contractions (hunger pangs). But much recent evidence indicates that arousal can occur even when there are no stomach contractions.

It is now well established that the hypothalamus (see Chapter 2) is involved in the arousal of the hunger drive, as well as many other biological drives. There are several lines of evidence for this conclusion: (1) damage to various areas of the hypothalamus leads to changes in motivated behavior; (2) different areas in the hypothalamus are involved with different drives; and (3) excitatory and inhibitory centers that control motivation have been identified in the hypothalamus (that is, damage to a specific area of the hypothalamus can sometimes lead to activation of some kind of motivated behavior, and sometimes to cessation of that behavior).

In the case of hunger, two distinct centers have been identified in the hypothalamus. The *excitatory center* controls the onset of eating behavior. Electrical stimulation of this area causes a satiated rat to start eating; destruction of it causes a rat to stop eating entirely, and finally to die of starvation (Miller, 1958). The other area is called the *inhibitory center.* Electrical stimulation of this area causes a hungry rat to stop eating; destruction of it leads to a dramatic increase in eating behavior (Ehrlich, 1964). Figure 7.5 shows a photograph of a normal rat alongside a rat in which the inhibitory center of the hypothalamus was destroyed.

Both of these centers seem to be responsive to the physiological condition of the organism. When biochemical factors produce a state of imbalance in the blood (such as occurs during food deprivation), the excitatory center of the hypothalamus is activated. There is evidence that blood chemistry

Fig. 7.5
Destruction of the inhibitory center of the hypothalamus leads to excessive eating and subsequent obesity (Teitlebaum, 1964). (Courtesy of Dr. Philip Teitlebaum.)

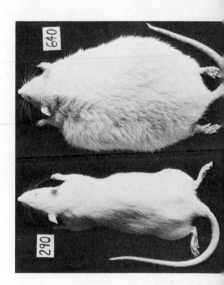

*Biological
Drives*

has an effect on hunger: if satiated animals receive blood transfusions from hungry animals, they show behavioral manifestations of hunger.

Knowing the role of blood chemistry and of the hypothalamus in activating eating behavior, we might be tempted to ask whether obese humans may overeat because of chemical imbalances in the blood or malfunctions of the hypothalamus. In a few instances, one or both of these factors may account for obesity. But present evidence indicates that obesity in most people is determined by a variety of learned, rather than physiological, factors. Obese people do overeat, but not in response to physiological stimuli.

A series of studies on obesity supports the view that obese people are more responsive to external than to physiological stimuli in regulating their food intake. If obese and normal people are given plain, dull, and uninteresting food, the normal people eat amounts appropriate to their physiological state, while obese people eat almost nothing. On the other hand, when their food is especially attractive, obese people eat huge amounts, regardless of their physiological state. Normal and underweight people eat amounts more nearly appropriate to their physiological states (Schachter, 1965).

One of the most potent environmental cues for eating behavior is time. During waking hours, there is usually a four- to six-hour interval between meals. In one study, subjects were deceived into believing that it was closer to mealtime than it actually was. Presumably, if obese individuals react more to external than to internal cues, they should eat more when they believe it is mealtime, even though they may not be physiologically "hungry" (Schachter and Gross, 1968).

The investigators manipulated two clocks, one running at twice normal speed, the other at half normal speed. Each subject arrived at 5:00 P.M. to participate in an experiment that supposedly concerned "the relationship of base levels of autonomic reactivity to personality factors." He was taken to a windowless room that contained only electronic equipment and a clock. Electrodes were attached to his wrists, his watch was removed ("so that it will not get gummed up with electrode jelly"), and the experimenter left the room for 30 minutes.

Two experimental conditions were employed. In one, the experimenter returned when the clock read 5:20. In the other condition, the experimenter returned when the clock read 6:05 (normal dinnertime for most of the subjects). The experimenter was carrying a box of crackers as he entered the room. He invited the subject to help himself after the electrodes were removed. Then he gave the subject a questionnaire to fill out and again left the room, leaving the subject alone with the box of crackers.

The experimenters predicted that obese subjects would eat more crackers when the clock read 6:05 than when it read 5:20, since their eating behavior is presumably triggered by external environmental cues. On the other hand, normal individuals should eat about the same amount regardless of what time they thought it was, since normal people presumably respond to internal physiological cues. The results are shown in Fig. 7.6. The obese subjects, as predicted, ate about twice as much when they thought it was 6:05. The normal subjects, on the other hand, ate less at 6:05. The experimenters attributed the unexpected behavior of the normal subjects to a desire not to spoil their dinner. Thus, it seems that obese individuals must eat when they think it is time to eat, whereas normal subjects are capable of exercising restraint. The results of this study indicate that, contrary to expectations, obese people are not the only ones whose eating behavior is influenced by external factors. Clearly, the normal individuals were also influenced by the external clock. In their case, however, the clock served as a cue to inhibit eating behavior.

Although hunger is a biological drive and therefore unlearned, its mode of satisfaction is influenced in humans by many learned factors. For example, there are striking differences in the kinds of food people choose when hungry. These choices are strongly affected by cultural factors. Moslems and orthodox Jews follow religious restrictions against eating pork or shellfish. Many, but not all, societies have a taboo against eating human flesh.

The hunger drive in humans is influenced by many other learned factors. We like to have our food prepared and served in a special way; we consider certain foods to be appropriate for breakfast but not for dinner; we enjoy eating in certain settings and with certain people, despite the fact that hunger drive can be satisfied in virtually any setting. Learned factors may become so dominant that an individual will prefer to starve rather than eat food that has become repulsive as a result of cultural learning.

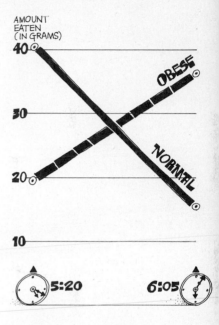

Fig. 7.6
Obesity and Eating

When obese subjects thought it was 6:05 P.M., they consumed twice as many crackers as when they thought it was 5:20 P.M. Normal subjects ate fewer crackers when they thought it was 6:05, presumably not to spoil their dinner. (Used by permission of Stanley Schachter.)

Biological Drives

Thirst Drive

Anyone who has been deprived of water for a long time will remember how intense thirst can become. Prolonged water deprivation leads to widespread physical manifestations such as nausea, impaired breathing, and dryness of the mouth, tongue, and throat.

Just as earlier theories about hunger stressed local factors such as stomach contractions, theories about thirst stressed local factors such as dryness of the throat. We now know that the hypothalamus is also involved in the activation of the thirst drive. When a salt solution is injected into the hypothalamus of satiated goats, they will drink water and even urine (Anderson and McCann, 1955). If distilled water is injected into the hypothalamus of water-deprived cats, they stop drinking, as if they were satiated (Miller, 1957).

In humans, thirst, like hunger, is influenced by a variety of learned social and cultural factors. Most Americans prefer to drink cold water even though the temperature of the water has nothing to do with its capacity to satisfy thirst. Moreover, water is by no means the only liquid used to quench thirst, and different societies vary in the liquids they choose for quenching thirst. Nor is drinking necessarily associated with arousal of the thirst drive—there are many occasions when drinking is part of a religious or social ritual.

Sleep Drive

From time to time various people have proposed that sleep is a form of behavior which, like an undesirable habit, can be broken. To prove their point, they have tried to remain awake for extremely long periods of time. All such efforts have been failures. As the period of sleep deprivation increased, the persons became increasingly irritable and reported sounds and sights that were not physically present. They had to be constantly stimulated and prodded in order to keep them awake. Eventually, all efforts to ward off sleep were to no avail and they fell into a deep and prolonged sleep (see Fig. 7.7).

The truth is that sleep is not a habit but a drive state, and shares many of the attributes of other biological drives, like thirst

and hunger. Satisfaction of the sleep drive is necessary for the survival of the organism. The longer an organism is deprived of sleep, the greater is the need for it. Deprivation leads to increased irritability. Once the sleep drive is satisfied, the organism will usually not go to sleep again until a certain amount of deprivation exists.

Fig. 7.7
(Stock, Boston.)

Certain brain centers are intimately involved in sleep and wakefulness. There are both excitatory and inhibitory centers in the hypothalamus. Destruction of the excitatory or wakefulness center leads to profound sleep, from which the organism can be aroused only by very strong stimulation. Destruction of the inhibitory, or sleep, center keeps the organism in a constant state of wakefulness. Further evidence that sleep involves brain centers has come from studies of Siamese twins who share a common blood supply but have separate brains. It has been observed that each twin has separate waking and sleeping cycles.

Most adults need from six to nine hours of sleep each night. The usual pattern is approximately 16 hours of wakefulness during the day and 8 hours of sleep at night. However, like other drives, sleep is subject to modification by learned factors. For example, people who work at night jobs are able to sleep during the day. People in occupations that require shifting back and forth between nighttime and daytime duty are able to do so without great difficulty, although they are often irritable just after each shift from night to day duty or vice versa. It is interesting that in northern Norway, where the sun shines day and night for weeks at a time in summer and does not appear at all during the

Biological Drives

winter, the population maintains the same pattern of sleep and wakefulness throughout the year.

Drive to Avoid Pain

The drive to avoid pain is one of the most compelling in all animals. Humans have developed highly sophisticated techniques to eliminate or reduce the intensity of pain and discomfort. Few of us are willing to sit in the dentist's chair without novocaine or some other pain-deadening aid. Indeed, anesthesiology has become a vital specialty in the practice of medicine. In addition, we are inundated with advertisements promising relief of headache, neuralgia, rheumatism, arthritis, and all kinds of bodily aches and pains.

What do you suppose it would be like to go through life without ever experiencing the throb of a toothache, a migraine headache, or a plain "bellyache"? We might be tempted to regard such a pain-free existence as a life of bliss. But in fact, studies of individuals born without the capacity to experience pain show that their lives are fraught with constant peril. Without pain, virtually all of the cues that we rely on as danger signals are absent. In rare cases, children are born without any sense of pain. If such a child were accidentally to touch a hot burner on an electric stove, he would not withdraw his hand from the burner immediately, as a normal child would. Instead of receiving a minor first-degree burn, this child could suffer extensive tissue damage from such an incident, perhaps ultimately resulting in serious infection or even the loss of his fingers. Many such children do not survive childhood because of their inability to recognize common danger signals arising from within, such as an inflamed appendix.

One 19-year old girl who was congenitally insensitive to pain was studied extensively by a group of physicians and psychologists. According to her parents, she had never experienced pain, despite numerous accidents resulting in burns, cuts, and fractures. Indeed, she had at one time fractured her ankle in an automobile accident and attended a dance immediately afterwards. She did not realize that anything was wrong until later, when she found that her swollen foot would not fit into her shoe (Cohen et al., 1955).

Other research has shown that individuals who survive childhood in spite of congenital insensitivity to pain avoid injuries by learning to recognize other cues (Sternbach, 1963).

Sex Drive

Unlike hunger and thirst, the satisfaction of the sex drive is not vital to the survival of the organism, but is of utmost importance to the survival of the species. Yet the sex drive does have certain characteristics in common with the other biological drives. When sexually aroused, the organism becomes more active and restless. It learns to make a variety of responses to gain access to a receptive partner. When sexual activity has been completed, the organism shows many of the usual characteristics of satiation. In lower animals, most of the behaviors associated with sex are unlearned and represent unconditioned responses to unconditioned stimuli. Sex hormones secreted by the testes in males and the ovaries in females appear to play a dominant role in the arousal of the sex drive. When the sex glands of lower animals are removed (castration in males, spaying in females) before the animals achieve sexual maturity (puberty), the sexual behavior characteristic of the mature animal never emerges. However, if removal takes place after sexual maturity, normal sexual behavior continues for a short period in most animals and then disappears. Normal sexual activity can be restored by injecting male sex hormones into a castrated male animal and female sex hormones into a spayed female animal. It is possible to reverse sexual roles by injecting female hormones into a male animal that was castrated before sexual maturity (Whalen and Edwards, 1966).

The effects of removing sex glands are much more variable in humans than in other animals. Castration before puberty sometimes prevents the development of the sexual behavior characteristic of the mature human male, and sometimes it does not. Castration after the attainment of sexual maturity may have varying effects on sexual behavior—it may decrease or remain the same in some individuals, or increase in others. In women, the effects of loss of hormonal functioning (as in menopause) or removal of ovaries (as in a hysterectomy) are equally variable. In some women sexual activity increases after menopause or

Biological Drives

237

Kathy is 9.
Her parents told her if she slept
with her hands under the covers
she wouldn't grow.

Kathy will grow up of course, but she'll have bad feelings about doing something that many people do. And her parents will have passed an old guilt on to a new generation.

But Kathy's parents can't take all the blame. When they were 9, they were probably told the same thing. And even though they know the folk tales about going blind and getting warts aren't true, they still believe it's bad for children to explore themselves.

The odd thing is they probably couldn't even give you a good reason. Like most parents, they probably don't know about the recent figures that show that almost all men and a majority of women have masturbated.

The truth is, even Kathy's parents didn't stop, though their parents told them to. They just felt more guilty about it. What they were doing was responding to the basic sexual desires which men and women have at all

stages of life. And because it is not always possible to fulfill these needs through sexual intercourse, there are many times in life when masturbation becomes the only alternative.

It may be too late now for Kathy's parents to change their feelings. But once they realize how universal this activity is, they can learn to stop passing on these unnecessary guilt feelings to their children. And let Kathy grow up a happy woman with a healthy attitude about her body.

This information is brought to you by the Community Sex Information & Education Service; a private non-profit organization dedicated to the prevention and solution of all sexual problems. Some of our other services include: telephone counseling, educational lectures and folders (including a pamphlet about masturbation) referrals for safe, legal abortions and arrangements for free VD and pregnancy tests. All of our services are free. And the person calling is *never* asked to give his or her name.

Sexual ignorance is not bliss

COMMUNITY SEX INFORMATION AND EDUCATION SERVICE INC.
For more information call your local chapter — (617) 232-2335

Fig. 7.8
(Prepared by
Sterling/Blumenthal, Inc.
Advertising.)

hysterectomy, possibly because they no longer fear becoming pregnant.

Learned factors play an important role in sexual satisfaction in humans. Indeed, cultural factors probably have more influence on the sex drive than on any other biological drive. In our society, no drive has been subject to more restrictions and prohibitions than sex, although considerably less so in recent years (see Fig. 7.8).

Attitudes toward sex vary enormously from culture to culture. For example, many cultures do not place the same prohibitions on premarital sexual intercourse as we find in the United States. One investigator studied 158 different societies and found that 70 percent do not place restrictions on premarital sexual relations (Ehrmann, 1961).

Interestingly, in societies were women are encouraged to participate actively in sex, they are frequently vigorous and aggressive sexual partners. But in societies that discourage active participation by the woman, women are often inhibited in their sexual behavior. In other words, societies that expect orgasms in

Motivation

women generally produce women who are capable of orgasms; but where orgasms in women are discouraged, women often seem to be incapable of orgasms (McCary, 1967).

Only in recent years have sexual taboos been sufficiently relaxed in this country to allow detailed investigations of sexual behavior. Before the pioneering efforts of Kinsey and his associates, investigations of sexual behavior were limited to the study of lower animals, to other cultures, or to abnormal sexual behavior reported in clinical settings. Based exclusively on interviews of thousands of American men and women, Kinsey's findings had a great impact on sexual attitudes and paved the way for later, more detailed studies of human sexual behavior.

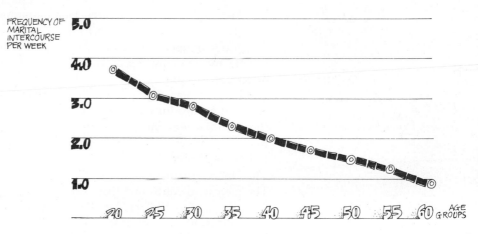

The results of Kinsey's studies dispelled many long-held notions about sexual practices in this country. For example, Kinsey reported that more than 90 percent of the men interviewed had masturbated by the age of 20, and approximately one out of three had achieved orgasm in a homosexual relationship. However, only 20 percent of the women reported that they had masturbated by the time they finished high school. Although some women reported that they had never experienced orgasm, many claimed to enjoy sexual activity. These studies indicated that the sex drives of men and women appear to reach their peaks at different ages. Men appear to be most active sexually by the age of 20 (see Fig. 7.9), while women reach their peak somewhere between the age of 25 and 30 (Kinsey et al., 1948, 1953).

Fig. 7.9
Decline of sexual activity in married men with increasing age. (Used by permission of the Institute for Sex Research, Inc., Indiana University.)

Biological Drives

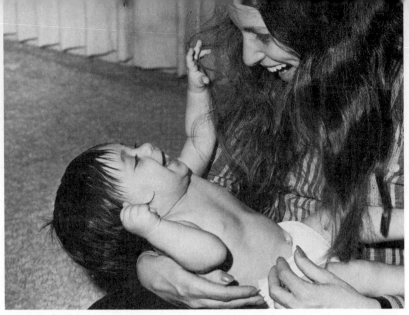

a)

Fig. 7.10
The behavior by which the
maternal drive is expressed in
women is perfected by
maturation and learning, and
may even be reversed by
unfortunate experiences so that
the mother rejects her infant.
The mother and child in (c) was
drawn by a young man in his
early twenties who was
undergoing a period of severe
mental disturbance. A
psychotherapist who knew him
has suggested that it represents
maternal rejection in the face of
the child's intense oral need. If
this interpretation is correct,
what do you think the artist felt
about the mothering he received
as an infant? (a, Liz Muller. b,
Anna Kaufman Moon—Stock,
Boston. c., from R. W. Pickford,
Studies in Psychiatric Art, 1965,
courtesy of Professor Pickford
and Charles C. Thomas,
Publisher, Springfield, Illinois.)

Although Kinsey's research was monumental for its time, it
was restricted to interview techniques, and suffered from the
difficulties inherent in this method, for example, bias in the
sample and inaccurate reporting. Recent studies, involving the
direct observation and recording of the sexual responses of
hundreds of men and women, have brought the study of human
sexual behavior into the laboratory. Among the many findings of
these studies was the observation that all the women involved in
the study achieved orgasm, and some achieved several orgasms in
a short period of time. In addition, these studies showed that
some men remain sexually active even at 70 or 80 years of age.
The men who continued their sexual activity into their later years
were those who had regular sexual experiences in their earlier
years (Masters and Johnson, 1966, 1970).

Maternal Drive

Research on the maternal drive has shown that it is one of the
most compelling motivations in lower species. It begins to
function soon after the female has conceived, and is manifested in
nest-building behavior.

When a mother rat is separated from her young by an
obstacle such as an electrified grid, she will tolerate very painful
shocks to reach her young. In fact, she will tolerate more shock to
satisfy the maternal drive than to satisfy either the hunger or the
thirst drive.

Motivation

240

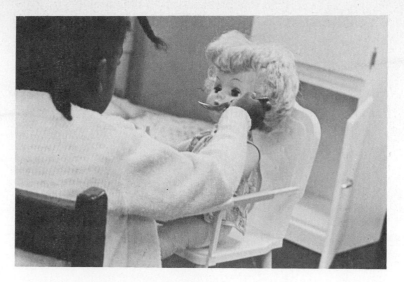

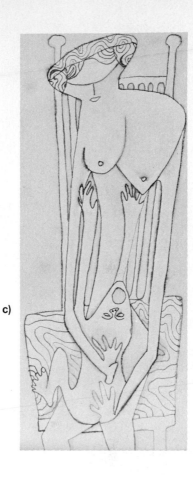

b)   c)

The behaviors associated with the maternal drive appear to be essentially unlearned in lower animals. But in humans, the maternal drive appears to be more the result of learning than of innate biological factors (see Fig. 7.10). Some human mothers turn their children over to other people to be taken care of; some even mistreat or abandon their young.

Stimulus Needs

If we limit our observations to lower animals, we note the extent to which basic biological drives dominate their behavior. They eat, breathe, drink, eliminate waste products, occasionally engage in sexual activities, and sleep. In contrast, humans spend far more of their time in activities that have no direct relation to biological drives. They appear to be motivated by a need to be active and stimulated, to explore and manipulate their environment, and to experience varied forms of stimulation. They do not receive stimulation passively but are constantly modifying their environment in order to produce new experiences. Evidence of stimulus needs can be seen in young children. When a child receives a new toy, he will examine it and manipulate it, try to make noises with it, and put it to all sorts of uses not intended by the manufacturer.

Stimulus needs are most obvious in humans, but they are also present in lower animals. In many ways they are like the biological drives, but apparently they do not satisfy physiological deprivations.

Stimulus Needs

Fig. 7.11
A subject in a sensory deprivation study is deprived of virtually all sensory stimuli while lying on his back in a soundproof chamber.

The Need for Stimulation

At any given moment the waking organism is bombarded by an indescribably large number of physical stimuli. Have you ever wondered what would happen if we were cut off from all or most of these stimuli? Imagine that you are in a bed in a soundproof room, wearing goggles that allow diffuse light to pass through but remove all patterned vision. In addition, you are wearing gloves that restrict your sense of touch. How long would you last in that situation? What effects would it have on your behavior? If you are like the many undergraduates who participated in studies of this sort, you would probably last only a few days, even if you were paid $20 a day. In addition, your ability to solve standard psychological problems would be impaired. Most strikingly, with increased exposure to this situation, you would undergo dramatic psychological changes. You might become irritable, begin to hallucinate, and experience other changes similar to those occurring in emotional disorders. Figure 7.11 illustrates one type of apparatus used in sensory deprivation studies.

Experimental findings from sensory deprivation studies strongly suggest that organized, meaningful sensory stimulation is necessary for normal brain functioning. Apparently the brain requires stimulation from the environment. If the environment fails to provide it, the brain will manufacture its own stimulation in the form of hallucinations and fantasies. The scientists who planned the Apollo missions were aware of this problem and made certain that the astronauts had adequate visual and auditory stimulation.

Not only do we require a certain amount of stimulation for normal functioning, but we actively seek out new forms of stimulation. The need for varied stimulation has been

Motivation

242

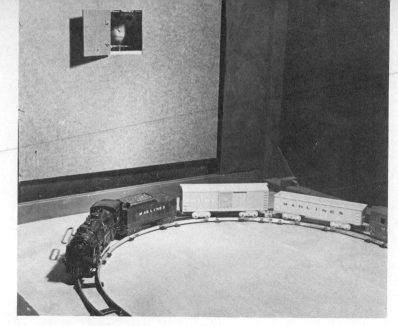

demonstrated with many different organisms, including man. Rats will spend a long time exploring a new environment. Birds may approach a strange object even though it is potentially threatening to their lives. Monkeys will learn to manipulate and open a latch when the reward is some form of visual stimulation (see Fig. 7.12). Human infants spend most of their waking hours exploring and manipulating their environment. They are drawn toward any object which is colorful, makes noise, or provides distinctive tactile experiences (see Fig. 7.13). Adults frequently take great pains to set up elaborate light shows and multi-channel stereo systems to provide themselves with new and varied stimulation.

Fig. 7.12
Monkeys will learn responses and continue to work for the reward of visual stimulation. Here we see a monkey who has learned to push open a window to see a toy train in operation. (Photo courtesy of Myron Davis.)

Fig. 7.13
An infant shows an almost insatiable curiosity. The five-month-old baby in this photograph will spend many hours playing with a toy for the sole purpose of visual, auditory, and tactual stimulation.

Stimulus Needs

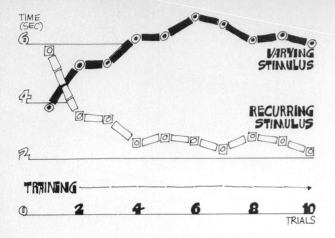

TIME (SEC)

VARYING STIMULUS

RECURRING STIMULUS

TRAINING

0   2   4   6   8   10

TRIALS

Fig. 7.14
Adult subjects spent more time looking at pictures that changed on every trial (varying stimulus), than at pictures that remained the same on each trial (recurring stimulus). (After D. E. Berlyne, "The Influence of Complexity and Novelty in Visual Figures on Orienting Responses," *Journal of Experimental Psychology*, **55**, 1958, pp. 289–296. Copyright © 1958 by the American Psychological Association. Used by permission.)

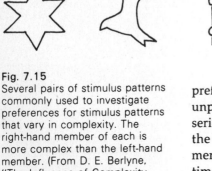

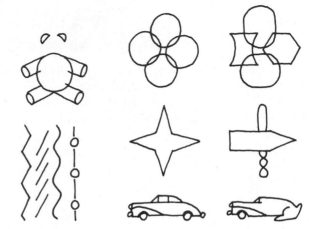

Fig. 7.15
Several pairs of stimulus patterns commonly used to investigate preferences for stimulus patterns that vary in complexity. The right-hand member of each is more complex than the left-hand member. (From D. E. Berlyne, "The Influence of Complexity and Novelty in Visual Figures on Orienting Responses," *Journal of Experimental Psychology*, **55**, 1958, pp. 289–296. Copyright © 1958 by the American Psychological Association. Reproduced by permission.)

Many studies have demonstrated that humans show a preference for patterns and experiences that are variable and unpredictable. In one study, human adults were asked to look at a series of pairs of animal pictures (see Fig. 7.14). One member of the pair of pictures was the same on every trial; the other member was changed from trial to trial. The subjects spent more time looking at the changing picture than at the recurring picture (Berlyne, 1958).

Another aspect of stimulus variability is the *complexity* of the stimulus patterns. Figure 7.15 shows several pairs of patterns in which the right-hand member is more complex than the left-hand member. Adults typically spend more time looking at the more complex of the two patterns.

The need for varied stimulation has obvious survival value for the organism. If an animal does not explore the world around it, how can it find the sources of food? How can it learn what areas are dangerous and must be avoided? At the human level, the need for varied stimulation leads to experiences that give

Motivation

Fig. 7.16
Contact comfort
Infant monkeys will spend more time clinging to a terrycloth "mother" than to a wire "mother," even when the wire "mother" provides food. (Courtesy of Dr. Harry F. Harlow, University of Wisconsin Primate Laboratory.)

people increased knowledge of the world around them. Some of our greatest accomplishments have grown out of our irrepressible need to learn what is beyond the here and now.

Contact Comfort Need

Until fairly recently, many psychologists believed that children come to love their mothers through a classical conditioning process. The mother, initially a neutral stimulus, acquires the capacity to elicit positive emotional responses in the infant as a result of her continuous association with positive reinforcements: she feeds the child when he is hungry, gives him water when he is thirsty, changes wet or soiled diapers, and provides comfort when the child is distressed.

Research on infant monkeys has suggested another possible explanation for the child's attachment to its mother. The investigators, noting that mothers provide a soft, warm surface when they hold or nurse the infant, hypothesized that this contact comfort may be the basis of the child's love for its mother. To test their hypothesis, they provided infant monkeys with various types of substitute "mothers." Some of these "mothers" provided a soft, warm surface, such as terrycloth; others were made of wire mesh or covered with sandpaper. Figure 7.16 shows a monkey with a wire and a terrycloth mother. Given a choice between a soft, comfortable terrycloth "mother" which supplied no food and a hard, uncomfortable wire "mother" which provided a continuous supply of warm milk, the monkeys showed a marked preference for the terrycloth "mother." It would therefore appear that the need for contact comfort was stronger

Stimulus Needs

Fig. 7.17
(Cary S. Wolinsky—Stock,
Boston.)

Fig. 7.18
(Dan O'Neill—Editorial
Photocolor Archives.)

than the hunger drive in determining the monkeys' attachment to a substitute mother (Harlow and Zimmerman, 1959; Harlow and Suomi, 1970).

These studies, if they are applicable at the human level, have important implications for child-rearing practices. Although experimental evidence on human infants is lacking, it appears that human infants also have a need for contact comfort. But most hospitals separate the mother from her child immediately after birth and keep the child in an aseptic nursery for several days. If there is, in fact, a comfort need that manifests itself at birth, the mother should be free to cuddle her child during the first days of life.

Learned Motives

There are many motivational states, particularly in humans, in which learned rather than biological factors appear to be the primary determinants. As we have seen, the satisfaction of basic biological drives dominates the experience of newborn children. As they develop and their basic physiological needs are routinely

Motivation

satisfied, learned motives assume a larger and more dominant role in their lives.

Why do some people strive so desperately for good grades, political office, or social approval? Why do some people stay "tied to their mother's apron strings" throughout their lifetimes? Why are some teachers so concerned about the outcome of student evaluations? These questions assume the existence of underlying notivational states. But, they obviously cannot be answered by reference to any of the biological drives or stimulus needs we have already discussed. For answers we must look to the motives that people learn in the course of their interaction with their environment.

Earlier, we discussed some of the measures used to infer the presence and intensity of motivations. When dealing with biological drives such as hunger and thirst, we can be fairly sure that our inferences are correct. Learned motives present more difficulties. There is little agreement on the definition of some of these motives. Even when psychologists can agree on how to define a specific learned motive, they do not always agree on how it should best be measured.

Fear and Anxiety

Learned fear is one of the most fundamental motives—most of us will do almost anything to avoid or escape from a fear-producing situation. Young children show fear to a very limited number of situations, such as sudden loss of support or sudden loud noises. As children grow older, they begin to fear many more and different kinds of things.

In one study, marked differences were found in the behavior of young children and college students at the sight of a snake. In 15 children, aged 14 to 27 months, only two showed distinct signs of fear. But of the 90 college students studied, two-thirds showed either distinct signs of fear or obvious dislike of the snake (Jones and Jones, 1928).

Several studies have demonstrated that fear can be attached to almost any situation or stimulus. A classic study using rats showed the mechanism by which fear may be acquired. The experimental apparatus was a box containing two compartments, one of them painted white. The rats learned to jump a barrier to

Learned Motives

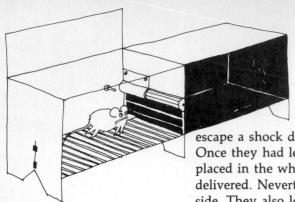

Fig. 7.19
After learning to jump to the black box to escape shock, the rat must learn to turn the wheel to escape from the white compartment. It learns wheel-turning even in the absence of shock. Presumably, learned fear has motivated the acquisition of this new response.

escape a shock delivered in the white compartment (see Fig. 7.19). Once they had learned the escape response the animals were placed in the white compartment again, but no shock was delivered. Nevertheless, they rapidly crossed over to the other side. They also learned a new response (turning a wheel) which permitted them to escape from the white compartment, even though no shock was delivered. Figure 7.20 shows that speed of wheel-turning increased with each successive placement in the white compartment. This result demonstrates that the animals had learned to fear the white compartment (Miller, 1948, p. 248).

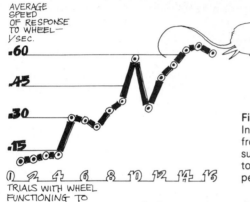

AVERAGE SPEED OF RESPONSE TO WHEEL— I/SEC.

.60
.45
.30
.15

① ② ④ ⑥ ⑧ ⑩ ⑫ ⑭ ⑯
TRIALS WITH WHEEL FUNCTIONING TO OPEN DOOR

Fig. 7.20
Initially, the rats learned to escape shock by running from the white compartment. With shock subsequently turned off, they learned to turn a wheel to escape from the white compartment. (Used by permission of Dr. Neal E. Miller.)

A distinction is often made between fear and anxiety. The word fear is usually applied to reactions to known stimuli, while anxiety is regarded as a fear reaction to unknown or unidentified stimuli, such as a premonition that something terrible is going to happen. We speak of *fear* of a dental drill, a surgeon's knife, or a rattlesnake. We say we are *anxious* about our future, the state of our health, or whether we will make a favorable impression in an interview. We will return to the topic of fear and anxiety in the next chapter.

Social Motives

As we have seen, learned motives result from the interaction of the individual with his environment. Man is preeminently a social being; that is, most of his behavior occurs in a social environment and is, of course, largely shaped by that environment, which includes other individuals, institutions, cultures, values,

Motivation

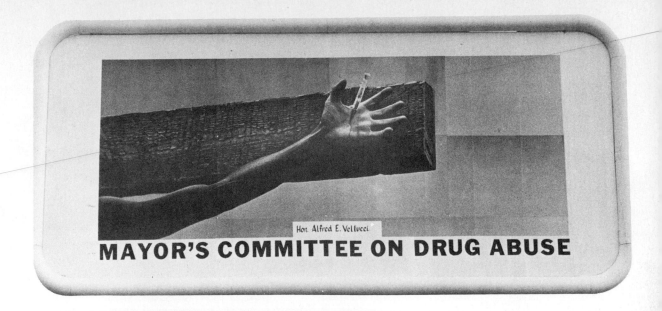

MAYOR'S COMMITTEE ON DRUG ABUSE

Hon. Alfred E. Vellucci

and ideals. Learned social motives are the result of the interaction of the individual with his social environment.

There have been many attempts to catalogue learned social motives. Some lists are extremely lengthy, and very few agree with one another in all particulars. We shall be discussing some of the more widely accepted of these motives.

Aggression

The question whether aggression is a learned motive or a biological drive is still subject to much debate. Although all of the facts are not in, much of the available evidence suggests that in our culture, aggression commonly results from the frustration of other motivations.

Aggression may be learned in much the same way as operant behavior. If children respond to a frustrating situation with aggressive behavior and are rewarded, they tend to repeat the aggressive behavior whenever they find themselves in that same situation. Imagine the following common occurrence: One child sees another with a toy that he wants. The other child refuses to give it up, so the first child hits him and grabs the toy. Later, in similar situations, the aggressive behavior will probably be repeated.

Many parents directly instruct their children to be aggressive, and reinforce instances of aggression by them. Indeed, many adults consider aggressiveness, particularly in males, to be desirable. In other cases, adults serve as models which children imitate. When a little boy points at a playmate and says "Bang,

Fig. 7.21
This poster gets its message across by exploiting our fear of pain and death. (Jeff Albertson—Stock, Boston.)

Learned Motives

249

a)

b)

c)

d)

Fig. 7.22
Models of aggressive behavior are not hard to find in our own society. (a, Marion Bernstein—Editorial Photocolor Archives. b, Arthur Sirdofsky—Editorial Photocolor Archives. c, Peter Menzel—Stock, Boston. d, Donald Wright Patterson, Jr.—Stock, Boston. e, R. P. Angier—Stock, Boston. f, Burk Uzzle—Magnum.)

Motivation

e)
f)

bang, you're dead," he is probably imitating his favorite television hero. Studies have shown that when children see aggressive behavior in others, they tend to act more aggressively themselves (Bandura and Walters, 1963).

It is interesting that aggression does not appear with equal intensity in all cultures. Indeed, members of some societies are remarkably free of aggressive behavior. Studies of primitive societies suggest that aggression is common when children are specifically trained in aggressive behavior. In one tribe in New Guinea, aggression is encouraged in boys from early infancy. The child cannot obtain nourishment from his mother without carrying on a continuous battle with her. Unless he grasps the nipple firmly and sucks vigorously, his mother will withdraw it and stop the feeding. In his frantic effort to get food, the child frequently chokes—an annoyance to both himself and his mother.

Learned Motives

Thus, the feeding situation itself is "characterized by anger and struggle rather than by affection and reassurance" (Mead, 1939). The people of another New Guinea tribe are extremely peaceful and do everything possible to discourage aggression. They regard all instances of aggressiveness as abnormal (Mead, 1939).

We will discuss aggressive behavior in more detail in Chapter 12.

Achievement motive

American society puts great emphasis on achievement. We are subjected to constant pressures to do well, to do better than the next person, to do our best—in business, in school, in athletics, even in play. This emphasis on doing well and achieving success characterizes the achievement motive.

Fig. 7.23
Look at this picture and write a five-minute story suggested by it. Tell what is happening, what led to the situation shown, what the man is thinking, and what will happen. You may get a rough idea of your own achievement motivation by comparing your story with those discussed in the text. (From "Business Drive and National Achievement," *Harvard Business Review*, July-August, 1962, pp. 99–112. Courtesy of Harvard Business Review and Dr. David C. McClelland.)

A method that is employed to measure the achievement motive involves a series of pictures. The subject is asked to make up a story about each picture as it is presented to him. The subject is instructed to tell what is happening in each picture, what led to the situation shown, what the characters are thinking, and what will happen. The pictures typically suggest situations such as work, study, father-son relationships, and daydreaming. The content of the subject's stories is then analyzed for evidence of the achievement motive.

One study investigated the achievement motive of business executives. Figure 7.23 shows one of the pictures used. Before reading further, follow the instructions given with this figure.

Now, here is a typical story written by a subject in this study.

The engineer is at work on Saturday when it is quiet and he has taken time to do a little daydreaming. He is the father of the two children in the picture—the husband of the woman shown. He has a happy home and is dreaming about some pleasant outing they have had. He is also looking forward to a repeat of the incident which is now giving him pleasure to think about. He plans on the following day, Sunday, to use the afternoon to take his family for a short trip.

(McClelland, 1962, p. 101)

None of the content of this story gives evidence of the achievement motive. The subject was completely concerned with the details of the family photograph and the relationships it suggests. He made no statement of goals or ways of achieving them.

Contrast the following story written by another subject:

The man is an engineer at a drafting board. The picture is of his family. He has a problem, and is concentrating on it. It is merely an everyday occurrence—a problem which requires thought. How can he get that bridge to take the stress of possible high winds? He wants to arrive at a good solution of the problem by himself. He will discuss the problem with a few other engineers and make a decision which will be a correct one—he has the earmarks of competence.

(McClelland, 1962, p. 101)

This subject only mentioned the family photograph in passing. He concentrated upon a specific problem and anticipated the formulation of a successful solution. According to this study, the second individual has a stronger achievement motive than the first (McClelland, 1962).

A variety of studies have investigated a number of variables in relation to the achievement motive. Among these variables are ethnic group, social class, and parental attitudes. In one study, a group of boys was divided into those scoring high and those scoring low in achievement motivation. Their mothers were asked, after the testing, to indicate which of 20 different behaviors exemplifying independence they expected their sons to achieve by the age of 10. Mothers who said that they expected their sons to be independent early in life tended to have sons with strong achievement motives (Winterbottom, 1953).

Learned Motives

Other studies have shown that other aspects of the family relationship influence the development of achievement motivation. For example, bright, high-achieving adolescents perceive their parents as less restrictive, more trusting, and more likely to encourage achievement, than do bright underachieving adolescents.

Most of the studies involving achievement have used males as subjects. Studies involving females have generally given inconsistent results. This fact may reflect cultural differences in expectations about men and about women. One of the goals of the women's liberation movement is to change current expectations about what women are capable of achieving. It will be interesting to see what experimental results are obtained in the future if social attitudes toward the roles and potential of women do undergo significant changes.

Dependency motive

In infancy, children are dependent upon others for satisfaction of all motivational states. The dependency motive is characterized by continued reliance on others for support and satisfaction. The extent to which children remain dependent on others as they grow older reflects parental attitudes and practices. Children whose parents encourage and reinforce independent action are likely to show relatively weak dependency motives. Children whose parents encourage them to depend on external rewards are likely to continue relying upon others for support, advice, and guidance. Thus, the dependency motive is learned through operant conditioning.

Approval motive

The approval motive is closely related to dependency. Individuals who have strong dependency motives often turn to others for approval of themselves or their actions. The desire for approval can become so strong that people will seek approval even though no other rewards are provided. Thus, the approval motive is characterized by a desire for those signs which indicate that others approve of us or our actions.

It is interesting that the signs which a particular person regards as indicating approval may be affected by his expectations in a given situation. A person who has often been praised expects praise. When he encounters silence instead, he behaves as if he has been criticized. On the other hand, if an individual has come to expect criticism or disapproval, he is likely to interpret silence as approval (Crandall et al., 1964).

Summary

1. Motivational states serve to energize or activate behavior, and to direct the behavior toward specific classes of goal objects.

2. Three broad classes of motivational states can be distinguished: biological drives, stimulus needs, and learned motives.

3. Since motives cannot be directly observed, they must be inferred from behavior and from the circumstances surrounding that behavior. Four measures are commonly used to determine the strength of motivation: (1) activity level, (2) performance rate, (3) overcoming an obstacle, and (4) selection among various goals.

4. Centers for the arousal of several biological drives (hunger, thirst, and sleep) are found in the hypothalamus.

5. The drive to avoid pain is one of the most compelling, in humans and lower animals alike. Rare cases in which children are born without the capacity to experience pain remind us of the importance of this drive for survival.

6. Unlike other biological drives, the sex and maternal drives do not have to be satisfied in order for the individual to survive.

7. There appear to be motivational states, operating most obviously at the human level, that require new and varied experiences for their satisfaction. We refer to these motivational states as stimulus needs.

8. Studies involving deprivation of sensory stimulation suggest that the brain requires organized and meaningful sensory stimulation for normal functioning. When such input is lacking, the brain will manufacture its own stimulation in the form of hallucinations, fantasies, and other internally produced forms of stimulation.

9. A stimulus need that has been shown to operate in the young of lower species, and probably in man, has been referred to as "contact comfort" need.

10. The satisfaction of basic biological drives dominates the lives of lower organisms and of human infants. However, with growth

and development, learned motives assume an increasingly important role in the life of the child.

11. Among the most important of learned drives are fear and anxiety. The word fear is commonly used to describe reactions to dangerous or aversive stimuli. Anxiety is regarded as a fear reaction to unknown or unidentified stimuli.

12. Social motives are acquired by the individual during the course of his interaction with his social environment.

13. The achievement motive, with its emphasis on doing well and achieving success, is particularly strong in American society.

14. The reliance upon others for support and satisfaction characterizes the dependency motive. The approval motive is closely linked to the dependency motive. Individuals with strong dependency motives commonly turn to others for approval.

Terms to Remember

Achievement Motive   The desire to do well and achieve success.

Aggression   Physical or verbal behavior intended to inflict harm or injury.

Anxiety   Fear reaction to unknown or unidentified stimuli; a premonition that something terrible will happen.

Approval Motive   The desire for those signs that indicate approval of the individual or of his behavior.

Biological Drive   A motive which stems from the physiological state of the organism, for example, hunger.

Consummatory Response   The final response in a sequence of goal-directed behavior.

Dependency Motive   The desire to rely on others for support and satisfaction.

Fear   Unpleasant emotional reaction to a known stimulus.

Hallucination   A sensory impression in the absence of an appropriate environmental stimulus.

Learned Motives   Motivational states in which learned, rather than biological, factors appear to be the primary determinant, for example, learned fear.

Motive   A condition which serves to energize and direct behavior toward specific classes of goal objects.

Sensory Deprivation   A condition in which the individual receives a minimum of sensory stimulation; this condition sometimes leads to hallucinations.

Social Motives   Learned motivational states which result from the interaction of the individual with his social environment, for example, aggression.

Stimulus Needs   A class of motivational states, involving a need for stimulation, for which no underlying physiological basis has been discovered.

Recommended Readings

Bolles, R. C., *Theory of Motivation,* New York: Harper & Row Publishers, 1967.
Views the concept of motivation both from a historical and from a contemporary perspective.

Brecher, R., and Brecher, E., *An Analysis of Human Sexual Response,* New York: American Library Association, 1966.
This highly readable paperback discusses some of the most significant research on sex.

Brown, J., *The Motivation of Behavior,* New York: McGraw-Hill Book Co., 1961.
Covers studies of primary and acquired sources of motivation in animals from both the behavioral and the physiological points of view.

McCay, J., *Human Sexuality,* Princeton, N.J.: Van Nostrand, 1967.
Discusses physiological and psychological aspects of sexual behavior.

McClelland, D. C., *The Achieving Society,* New York: The Free Press, 1967.

Motivation

Shows how the concept of achievement motivation can be applied to the study of economic development in a society.

Miller, N. E. (Ed.), *Neal E. Miller: Selected Papers,* Chicago: Aldine-Atherton, Inc., 1971.

Contains original papers by one of the leaders in the field of motivational research.

Murray, E. J., *Motivation and Emotion,* Englewood Cliffs, N.J.: Prentice-Hall, Inc., 1969.

Drawing material from a wide variety of sources, the author emphasizes the historical evolution of motivational concepts.

Murray, E. J., *Sleep, Dreams, and Arousal,* New York: Appleton-Century-Crofts, 1965.

A theoretical integration of the area of sleep, dreams, and arousal in terms of a postulated "motive to sleep."

Russel, W. A., *Milestones in Motivation,* New York: Appleton-Century-Crofts, 1970.

An orderly presentation of historical developments in motivation.

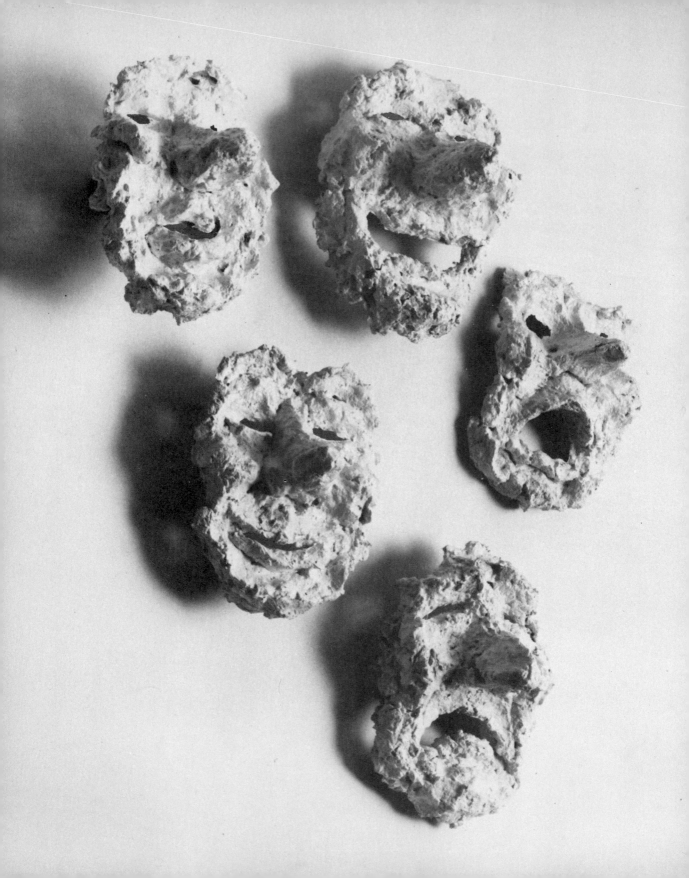

8
EMOTIONS

Try to imagine what life would be like if we had no emotions. We would be little more than drab, colorless machines, unable to experience the pride of achievement or the pangs of disappointment. We would derive no happiness from the companionship of others and would feel no grief at their loss. We would neither love nor hate. Nor would we be able to understand the joys and the sorrows of others. Indeed, we would not even envy those emotions we were denied.

What Are Emotions?

Every language is rich in the number and variety of terms used to describe states that we commonly think of as emotions. Most of us are quick to label various emotional states in ourselves and others. Yet it may surprise you to learn that psychologists have not yet reached a consensus on how to define and classify emotions, how to distinguish one from another, or how best to study them. While no definition of emotions is completely satisfactory, we may regard emotions as complex states involving cognitions, overt responses, internal changes, and motivational aspects. Let's look more closely at this description.

First, emotions involve cognitions. Two people confronted with the same situation may interpret it in different ways, and therefore respond with different emotions. In other words, our thoughts, beliefs, and prior experiences will color the way we view an event and, thus, profoundly influence our emotional reaction to that event. For example, someone who is concerned about the energy crisis may interpret the stack emissions of a power plant as an encouraging sign that their lights will stay on, while someone who is worried about the ravages of pollution may regard these same stack emissions with disgust.

Second, emotions involve overt responses. What are some of the overt responses that may accompany emotions? We have probably all seen a grief-stricken person cry, an angry person stomp his feet or kick a chair, and a happy person laugh. But does a person's behavior always reveal his underlying motivational state?

Let's imagine that, on your way into town on a bus late one afternoon, you catch a fleeting glance of a woman looking out of

Fig. 8.1
This group of police, deputies,
and student strikers was
photographed at Columbia
University in April, 1972. How
many different emotions would
you say are showing on those
faces you can see? (*Columbia
Spectator,* College News Photo
Alliance.)

a window. Even though you saw her for only a moment, you noticed that tears were streaming down her cheeks and her lips were turned down (Fig. 8.2). What emotion is the woman experiencing? Great sadness? Think for a moment. Don't some people cry when they receive very good news? Can you think of any other circumstances that might produce the tears and facial expression shown in Fig. 8.2? Turn the page for a full view of the woman (Fig. 8.3). Here we see that we would have misinterpreted her emotional state if we had relied solely upon the information provided by her facial expression.

We saw, in the last chapter, that it is not always possible to determine motives by observing behavior. Motives are always inferred; they are not directly observed. Similarly, we may not be correct if we assess people's emotional states purely by referring to their behavior. Many other factors must be taken into consideration. For example, we have been taught to conceal our emotions under certain circumstances—the phrase "Don't wear your heart on your sleeve" illustrates this.

Next, emotions involve internal, or physiological, changes. This is particularly true of intense emotional states. But are specific emotions associated with specific physiological states? Can fear and anger, for example, be differentiated on the basis of different types of bodily changes associated with each emotion? Later in this chapter we will look at these and other questions about the physiological bases of emotion.

Finally, emotions involve motivational changes. Most psychologists would agree that there is a close relationship between emotions and motivational states. Satisfaction or frustration of any motive may produce emotions. Pleasurable

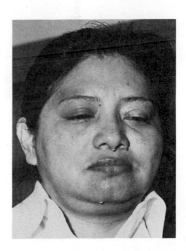

Fig. 8.2
What emotion is this woman experiencing? Turn to Fig. 8.3 for a clue. (Photo by Liz Muller.)

263

feelings generally accompany the satisfaction of motives—a good meal when we are hungry; a refreshing drink when thirsty; a good grade following intensive study; acceptance into a social group we have striven to get into. Even anticipation of satisfaction may be pleasurable. Observe the behavior of someone who has just been told to take the day off, or a child who has been promised a day at an amusement park.

Conversely, frustration of motivated behavior is commonly accompanied by negative feelings. For example, many of us know how depressing it is to have to lose weight or stop smoking. Sometimes, the mere anticipation of frustration can lead to fear or anxiety. For example, facing an impending examination when you don't think you are well prepared may produce feelings of anxiety.

The relation between emotions and motivation works both ways. Emotions themselves may provide the basis for motivated behavior. The desire to avoid an unpleasant emotion may also motivate an individual. For instance, a student who is not particularly concerned about an upcoming examination may be motivated to spend many hours preparing for it to avoid the unpleasant scene with his parents that occurs whenever he gets a B grade or lower.

On the other hand: Why do we go to the movies? What motivates us to attend a music festival? Why do we sometimes travel many hours to get to our favorite beach or ski slope? In these cases, our behavior may be motivated by a desire to experience pleasant emotions.

Emotions may also affect our motivation in situations that are unrelated to the emotion we are feeling. If you are sad or depressed, you may find no humor in the antics of your favorite comedian. On the other hand, if you have just received news that makes you excited and happy, you may approach an examination with uncharacteristic optimism.

Although we will be discussing the various emotional states separately, remember that many emotions may be operating simultaneously. For example, a person who is very angry may also be feeling despondent, anxious, or even elated. Indeed, it is not uncommon for emotional states to be in conflict with one another. The question of emotional and motivational conflict will be discussed in Chapter 12.

Fig. 8.3
Facial expressions alone may be a misleading clue to underlying emotions. (Photo by Liz Muller.)

Emotions

Physiological Bases of Emotion

Try the following test. Turn your television set to a movie or some drama so that you can see the picture but not hear the sound. How would you label the emotions that the actors are presenting? What cues are you using to make these judgments? How confident are you that you are correct? Now, turn on the sound and listen until you know what is going on. You may feel somewhat more confident in your assessments of their emotional states. But how do you know that your guesses are really accurate? Suppose you try this test again, with several friends present. If most of you agree, does this mean you have made a truly accurate judgment of the emotions the actors are portraying? In everyday situations, how do you know what any person, other than yourself, is really feeling? Since you cannot directly observe other peoples' feelings, it is obviously difficult to know whether you have made a correct judgment.

When we make judgments about another person's emotional state, we usually rely on outward signs of physiological activity: a tremor in the voice, a blush, trembling hands, sweating palms. Many studies have shown that varied physiological changes are associated with emotional states. Indeed, a number of different devices have been developed specifically to measure the physiological changes that accompany emotional responses. Some of the more common of these physiological changes involve pupil size, skin condition, heart rate, blood pressure, and respiration.

The Pupillometer

The pupils of our eyes have long been known as indicators of emotional arousal. Many magicians have an act which makes use of this response. A subject is asked to pick a card from a deck. After the card is returned to the deck, the subject is shown the cards one at a time. By carefully observing the subject's pupils to see which card produces increased pupil size, the magician is able to identify the correct card. If you try this trick on your friends, do not be discouraged if you don't meet with immediate success. Only a great deal of training will sensitize you to the extremely subtle changes in pupil size. In fact, a special device, called the pupillometer, was devised especially to measure changes in pupil size.

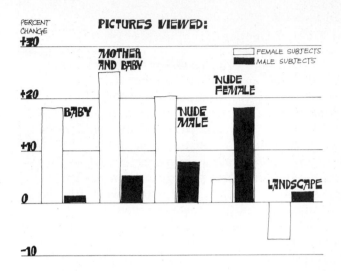

Fig. 8.4
Changes in pupil size as subjects viewed various pictures. (Used by permission of Dr. Eckhard H. Hess.)

The pupillometer was used in an interesting series of experiments to establish the effects of various types of stimulation on pupil size. In one study, male and female subjects were shown a series of pictures of a baby, a mother and child, a nude man, a nude woman, and a landscape. The results of this study are shown in Fig. 8.4. You will note that the pupil size of the female subjects increased markedly in response to the pictures of the baby, the mother and child, and the nude male; while the pupils of the male subjects showed their greatest increases to the picture of the female nude (Hess and Polt, 1960). Several studies have substantiated these findings. However, one study found that male homosexuals, as would be expected, showed a greater pupil response to pictures of their own sex (Hess et al., 1965).

Other studies have established that the pupil size increases with any kind of activating stimulation, not only visual. This suggests that the pupillometer might be useful in situations such as counseling, to detect stimuli that are interesting or significant to the client.

The Polygraph

Have you ever been caught in an extremely embarrassing situation? Recall, if you can, some of the physiological changes that occurred. Perhaps you could feel your face get warm and

Emotions

Fig. 8.5
Subject taking polygraph test
The capital letters on the polygraph charts represent the recordings of the following physiological phenomena: *A* is the tracing of the subject's muscular movements during the examination as picked up by the Reid Movement Chair; *B* and *C* are the tracings for the subject's respiration as recorded from two pneumographs placed over the subject's diaphragm and chest; *D* is the recording of the galvanic skin response (GSR) as picked up through two finger electrodes on the subject's left hand; *E* is the recording of the subject's relative blood pressure/pulse using a standard blood pressure cuff. (The instrument being used is the Reid Five Pen Polygraph manufactured by the Stoelting Company of Chicago. The photo portrays Reid examiners Frank S. Horvath as the examiner and Thomas B. Kelly as the subject.)

flushed, you might have noted a disruption of your normal breathing pattern, and a tendency to sweat. These changes involve the autonomic nervous system (Chapter 2), over which we normally exercise little or no control. The widespread involvement of the autonomic nervous system under conditions of strong emotional activation has led to the development of the polygraph.

The polygraph (Fig. 8.5), commonly known as the lie detector, measures galvanic skin response (GSR, a change in skin conduction that results from sweating), heart rate, blood pressure, and the rate of breathing. Contrary to popular belief, the polygraph is not used to detect lies, but to record emotional responses to selected stimuli. Most people will show changes in these four physiological measures when confronted with emotionally charged stimuli, such as the details of a crime they have committed. It is for this reason that law enforcement agencies rarely report details of a crime to the public. Thus, they are able to present these details (known only to the criminal), to the person taking the polygraph test, and observe any physiological changes that may occur. Presumably, only the guilty person will respond emotionally to these stimuli.

Because the records obtained from the polygraph are subject to misinterpretation and error, lie detection data are generally not admissible as evidence in court. An innocent person who happened to know the details of the crime might be found guilty by the lie detector. On the other hand, some people do not respond emotionally to the details of a crime they have committed; the lie detector test would find such a person innocent.

*Physiological
Bases of
Emotion*

Fig. 8.6
Fear has survival value to the extent that it prepares us physiologically for fight or flight. (Jack Prelutsky—Stock, Boston.)

Physiological Theories of Emotion

The strong emotions, such as anger and fear, have attracted the most interest. They are commonly regarded as undesirable because they tend to disrupt ongoing activity and are accompanied by negative feelings. But these same emotions may have survival value, when they activate adaptive behaviors in a time of emergency. For example, fear causes an increased flow of blood to the peripheral muscles, and this prepares the individual for either fight or flight. The commonsense view of the relation between these emotions and emergency reactions is based on the following sequence of events: a dangerous situation is perceived by the individual, fear is aroused, and the emergency response is activated. While this sequence does conform to many of our everyday experiences, there are notable exceptions, particularly in cases of extreme emergency.

Consider the following verbal report recounting a student's behavior in response to a sudden and threatening situation:

> When I was an undergraduate student, I lived off campus during my freshman year. I had to take a long walk to school each morning, and found that I could save time by cutting across a field and walking about 100 feet along a commuter

Emotions

268

railroad track. One morning I was completely lost in thought as I walked along the track, oblivious to the world about me and to where I was at the time. Suddenly the piercing shrill of a train whistle burst into my consciousness. Without thought or hesitation, I plunged headlong from the tracks and landed in a snow bank. The train missed me by inches. It's funny. At the time I jumped, I experienced no fear. The fear came moments later, as I lay in the snow bank and thought about my near miss.

If you think for a moment, many of you can probably tell of similar experiences, for example, avoiding an automobile accident by instantaneously applying the brakes, without thought or fear —only after the danger had passed did you experience the emotion of fear.

Acknowledging this common experience, one of the earliest physiological theories of emotion maintained that the perception of bodily changes is the critical factor underlying emotional states. This theory, called the *James–Lange theory*, proposed that environmental stimuli give rise to certain bodily changes by a reflex process. It is the subsequent perception of these bodily changes that results in the emotional experience. According to this theory, we see a bear in the woods, run away from it, and simultaneously undergo many physiological changes (increased heart rate, respiratory changes, muscular activities). It is the perception of these changes that leads us to identify our emotional state as fear. In the words of William James, "We feel sorry because we cry, angry because we strike, afraid because we tremble, and not that we cry, strike, or tremble because we are sorry, angry, or fearful, as the case may be" (James, 1890, p. 450).

Perhaps the greatest value of the James–Lange theory was that it unleashed a flood of experimentation concerned with autonomic changes associated with various emotional states. This theory would lead us to expect that each emotion should have a distinctive set of physiological changes associated with it. In other words, certain feelings in our body would be identified as fear, certain others as anger, and still others as love.

How do you know what you yourself are feeling? You should be able to identify your own emotions, since you can feel bodily changes in yourself. But do you always know what you are feeling?

Physiological Theories of Emotion

Suppose that your heart is pounding, the palms of your hands are wet and sticky, and your stomach is all churned up. Would you say with certainty that you feel excitement? Fear? Anger? Love?

Numerous attempts have been made to distinguish among the various emotions on the basis of distinctive physiological responses. These studies have met with limited success. In general, stimuli that produce strong emotions will lead to a general stirred-up state in the organism. To date, it has not been possible to assign unique physiological changes to specific emotions. There is one notable exception, however, involving the bodily changes associated with fear and anger.

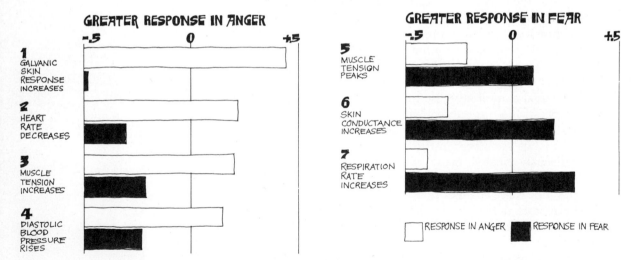

Fig. 8.7
Seven of the physiological measures that distinguish anger from fear. The graph shows changes from normal (zero). (After Albert F. Ax, "The Physiological Differentiation Between Fear and Anger in Humans," *Psychosomatic Medicine*, **15**, 1953, pp. 433–442, published by the American Psychosomatic Society. Used by permission of the author and publisher.)

In a classic study, subjects were made angry or fearful by a clever manipulation of the experimental setting. Various devices were attached to the subjects to permit the recording of 14 different physiological measures. The technicians were instructed to act in an abusive fashion in the anger-producing condition, and in a clumsy fashion in the fear-inducing condition. Altogether, seven different physiological measures clearly differentiated anger from fear (Ax, 1953). The results of this study are summarized in Fig. 8.7.

The physiological changes associated with anger are known to be produced by noradrenaline, a hormone secreted by the adrenal glands. However, fear is accompanied by the secretion of the hormone adrenaline. It is interesting that predators (such as lions) are characterized by high secretions of noradrenaline, and animals which rely on running away (fear) for survival have large quantities of adrenaline in their systems (Funkenstein, 1955).

In another study, hockey players were given urine analyses both before and immediately after a game. The players who participated actively in the game showed a sixfold increase in noradrenaline levels, while those players who were benched because of injury, and thus may have feared for their future with the team, showed increased quantities of adrenaline in their urine (Elmadjian, 1959).

The James–Lange theory focused on the autonomic changes that take place under strong emotions and on our perception of these changes. Crucial to this theory is the view that autonomic changes are communicated to the central nervous system, and that the central nervous system interprets these changes as specific emotions. One of the severest critics of this theory, W. B. Cannon, severed the connections between the autonomic and the central nervous system in dogs and found that the dogs continued to manifest emotional behavior (Cannon, 1929). Moreover, Cannon argued that the same autonomic changes occur in non-emotional states as occur in certain emotional states.

Based on the results of his own research, Cannon proposed an alternative physiological theory of emotions, the Cannon–Bard theory. This theory maintains that the physiological state and the emotional experience are triggered simultaneously by the hypothalamus. According to this theory, when it receives emotion-arousing stimulation, the hypothalamus activates the autonomic nervous system to produce a state of physiological arousal and, at the same time, sends impulses to the cortical structures so that the individual can interpret the emotional state. The Cannon–Bard theory says nothing about feedback from the physiological changes, which is the crucial element in the James–Lange theory.

The Cannon–Bard theory is supported by the observation that as long as the hypothalamus is intact, lower animals display certain emotions and corresponding physiological changes which disappear after the hypothalamus has been surgically removed (Cannon, 1929).

Cognitive Theory of Emotion

Cognitive Theory of Emotion

Let's go back to the emotional state we described earlier: pounding heart, perspiring palms, "butterflies" in the stomach. What label would you apply to the emotion? You might say; "How can I answer without knowing what has happened?" What if your dog had run out into the street and barely missed getting hit by a car? What if it was election night and the candidate you had actively campaigned for was running neck and neck with the most undesirable of the opposition candidates? What if you had just taken an "upper"? All of these situations lead to arousal states that are physiologically similar. Clearly , if you know only the physiological symptoms, you will have a hard time labeling the specific emotion. It seems obvious that, to identify an emotion we are experiencing, we must know the context as well as the state of physiological arousal. In most life experiences these two factors are intimately related. Consider the first situation we described. You would probably label the emotional experience aroused by your dog's near miss as fear. You might describe your election-night feelings as anxiety. How would you label the bodily sensations produced by the drug? Are the physiological symptoms alone sufficient to induce an emotion, as the James–Lange theory would predict? There is much evidence to indicate they would not.

In one study, more than 200 subjects were injected with adrenaline. Although the subjects all experienced similar physiological effects, they reported a wide variety of emotional experiences. Many of them described their feelings in an "as if" fashion. They made statements like, "I feel as if I were afraid," or "I feel as if I were awaiting a great happiness."

The few subjects who reported genuine emotional experiences had been provided with a context prior to the injection. For example, the experimenter spoke to the subjects about the subjects' sick children or dead parents. These topics produced little or no reaction before the injection. However, when these same topics were presented again after the injection, the subjects reported genuine emotional experiences (Marañon, 1924).

Presumably, the subjects in the study just described knew that they were being injected with a drug and were probably aware of some of the effects. This awareness might even explain why the majority of them experienced no emotion at all; they had a perfectly acceptable explanation—the drug—for their bodily feelings.

Suppose we could produce the same physical symptoms without the subjects knowing about the drug. They would experience face flushing, accelerated breathing, palpitations of the heart, and a slight tremor, but they would have no plausible explanation as to why they felt these things. How would they label their feelings? Would they describe them as pleasant or unpleasant?

In one study, an experimental situation was arranged so that the subjects experienced a state of physiological arousal for which some had an adequate explanation, while others did not. In addition, the subjects were exposed to two very different situations: one designed to induce a state of euphoria, the other to induce a state of anger. The investigators hypothesized that, in the absence of an adequate explanation for their physiological state, the subjects would label their feelings in terms of their immediate situation.

All the subjects were told that the study involved the effects of a vitamin supplement ("Suproxin") on vision. In fact, they were given an injection of adrenaline. After the subjects had agreed to the injection, one group was told to expect side effects, which the investigators described in the following way: "Your hand will start to shake, your heart will start to pound, and your face may get warm and flushed" (informed group). The other group was told that the injection was harmless and that there would be no side effects (uninformed group). Thus, the subjects all experienced similar physiological changes, but some were given adequate explanations for the changes, and some were not.

After the injection, the experimenters put a stooge, whom they identified as another subject, into a room with a real subject. The stooge had been instructed to create a situation designed to make the subject feel either euphoric or angry.

In the "euphoria" condition, the stooge behaved in a wild and strange manner. He crumpled paper, and played basketball using a wastepaper basket as his target. He made paper airplanes and threw them around the room. He picked up a hula hoop and twirled it around on his arm. In the "anger" condition, the stooge behaved differently. He acted annoyed and insulting toward the

Cognitive Theory of Emotion

subject. He expressed irritation with the situation and acted in a hostile fashion.

The experimenters observed the subjects' behavior in each of these conditions. In addition, the subjects filled out a questionnaire about their mood or emotional state.

In general, the subjects who had no reasonable explanation for their state of physiological arousal (the *uninformed* group) acted wild and happy when they were with the "euphoric" stooge, and hostile and aggressive when they were with the "angry" stooge. In addition, the subjects in the "euphoric" condition described themselves as feeling happy and good, whereas the subjects in the "angry" condition reported feeling irritated and angry. The subjects in the *informed* group, on the other hand, were far less influenced by the situation.

Thus, it seems that, given no explanation for a state of physiological arousal, we will interpret our emotional state according to what is happening around us (Schachter and Singer, 1962). Since all subjects experienced the same physiological symptoms under adrenaline, the James–Lange theory would have predicted that all subjects should experience the same emotional state. Clearly, these results contradict this theory.

Marijuana is a drug which produces altered physiological states. When a person smokes a "joint," how will he label his feelings? Will he say he is "high," or will he say he doesn't feel well? On the basis of the adrenaline studies, we might expect that the situation in which he finds himself will be the chief determinant of his emotional state.

One study found that subjects have to learn to label their physiological feelings as being "high":

> . . . being high consists of two elements; the presence of symptoms caused by marihuana use and the recognition of these symptoms and their connection by the user with his use of the drug. It is not enough, that is, that the effects be present; they alone do not automatically provide the experience of being high. The user must be able to point them out to himself and consciously connect them with his having smoked marihuana before he can have this experience. Otherwise, regardless of the actual effects produced, he considers that the drug has had no effect on him.
>
> (Becker, 1953, pp. 237–238)

Developmental and Learned Aspects of Emotions

Suppose that you volunteered to babysit for new neighbors while they moved into their house. You are left alone with their three-month-old infant while the parents set their house in order. You pick him up and suddenly he starts to cry. How would you interpret his crying behavior? Is he unhappy because you are holding him? Is he afraid because you are a stranger? Is he angry because his parents left him?

We would probably all agree that the baby is exhibiting some form of emotional behavior. On the other hand, it is very unlikely that the infant is actually experiencing as specific an emotion as unhappiness, or fear, or anger. Observations of many infants have indicated that their emotional behavior does not include any specific emotions like grief, disgust, love, hate, or jealousy. When these emotions are "seen" in an infant, it is adults who are labeling them in terms of their own experiences.

In fact, the emotional behavior of newborn babies is vague and undifferentiated. A wet diaper, a sudden loud noise, hunger and gas pains will produce a state which can be described as generalized excitement. This state can be differentiated from *quiescence,* during which the baby is calm and placid. The excitement stage is accompanied by physiological changes such as increased heart rate and alteration in breathing patterns. As the baby grows, differentiated emotional states begin gradually to develop. The earliest identifiable emotional responses are distress reactions to unpleasant stimuli and, a little later, delight responses to feeding, fondling, and other displays of affection. After three months, there is a rapid differentiation of responses associated with such states as anger, disgust, fear, and elation. Figure 8.8 shows the development of the various emotional states during the first two years of a child's life.

Although different situations will produce different responses, we have to learn how to label these responses as specific emotional states. For example, eight-month-old children may laugh and babble effusively at the sight of a new toy, and frown or even cry at the sight of a stranger. Even if they could verbalize at this age, it is unlikely that they would label their emotional states the same way we adults do. In fact, when preschool children first learn labels, they are expressed in terms of the

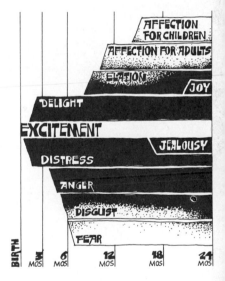

Fig. 8.8
Development of various emotions during the first two years of life. (Adapted from Bridges, 1932.)

*Developmental and
Learned Aspects
of Emotions*

Fig. 8.9
Do you see this behavior very
often? Probably not, if you live in
the United States. (Anna
Kaufman Moon—Stock, Boston.)

external situation. Thus, they will say, "I'm happy because we're going on a picnic," or "I'm mad because it's raining." Later, when they are about seven or eight years old, they begin to interpret their feelings in terms of emotional labels. Now they will say, "I feel happy," or "I feel angry." The emphasis has shifted away from the external situation to internal states or feelings, called affects.

Children learn not only how to label feelings associated with emotions, but also what emotions are appropriate in a given situation. For example, we don't learn how to cry, but we do learn when and where crying is appropriate. In our culture, boys learn that crying is seldom appropriate, whereas girls learn their crying is acceptable in any number of situations!

For those who doubt the crucial role of learning in emotion, you need go no further than to glimpse at the expression of emotion in cultures other than ours. Andaman Islanders and the Maori of New Zealand shed copious tears when greeting friends after a long absence, and when peace is established between warring tribes. It is reported that Japanese commonly smile after being scolded by a superior, or upon learning of the death of a favorite son. Earlier in this century, Chinese girls were provided with a book, *Required Studies for Women*, in which they received such admonitions as, "Do not let your teeth be seen when you

Fig. 8.10
Clues such as facial expression
help us interpret a person's
emotional state because we
learn how to express our
emotions by seeing how the
people around us do it.
(Copyright © 1972 by Children's
Television Workshop.)

smile," or, "If your father or mother is sick, do not be far from his or her bed. Do not even take off your girdle. Taste all the medicine yourself. Pray your god for his or her health. If anything unfortunate happens, cry bitterly" (Klineberg, 1938).

Appraisal of Emotion in Others

To a large extent, we learn the behaviors appropriate for expressing specific emotions. For example, we learn that a smile or a laugh signifies happiness; and a frown or a grimace, displeasure. Actors capitalize on these learned forms of emotional expression by using gestures, facial expressions, and voice inflections to communicate specific emotional states. However, as we saw earlier, judging people's emotional state from their behavior may lead to false conclusions. A wide variety of different situations may elicit the same behavior, and the same situation may give rise to many different behaviors. To complicate matters even further, the same emotional state may arise from a variety of different situations and lead to a variety of different behaviors. Let's look at a few examples.

On any Sunday afternoon in autumn and early winter, millions of American men sit glued to the "tube," watching football games. When a touchdown is scored by one of the teams,

*Developmental and
Learned Aspects
of Emotions*

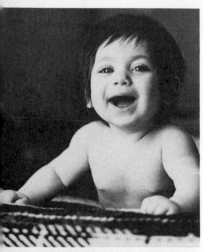

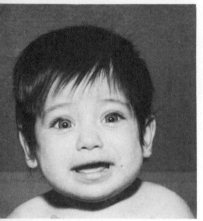

Fig. 8.11
The facial expressions of this
four-month-old infant clearly
reveal the pleasant (a)–unpleasant
(b) dimension of emotions. (a, Liz
Muller.)

many viewers will go into ecstasy, while others respond to the same event with anger or depression. The football "widows," on the other hand, may respond with supreme indifference, or even annoyance. Thus, the same situation gives rise to many different emotional states. Furthermore, even where a number of individuals share the same emotional state, their behaviors may be quite different. For example, some of those angered by the touchdown will sulk, while others will swear at the referee, the players, or anyone who happens to be in the room.

Many studies have demonstrated how hard it is to judge the nature of the underlying emotional state by observing behavior. In one study, medical students were asked to judge the emotions of children who had been exposed to various emotion-producing stimuli (for example, a sudden loss of support). When they were unable to see the stimulus situations that provoked the emotional behavior, the medical students were unable to agree on the children's emotion. Only when they were able to see the stimulus situation could they agree (Sherman and Sherman, 1929). It has been shown that we have the same trouble judging the emotions of adults (Coleman, 1949).

Although most studies have shown that we do not make very accurate judgments about the specific emotions of others, merely by observing their facial expressions, facial expression can provide valuable clues. For example, some emotions are usually regarded as unpleasant (for example, fear, grief) and others as pleasant (for example, love, joy). Look at the faces in Fig. 8.11. Clearly, the face on the left is expressing an unpleasant emotion, whereas we would certainly judge the face on the right to be expressing a pleasant emotion.

On the basis of a series of studies, it has been found that facial expressions can be classified according to three dimensions: pleasantness–unpleasantness; rejection–attention; and intensity (Schlosberg, 1952, 1954). Figure 8.12 shows some of the pictures used to rate facial expressions according to these three dimensions.

Emotions and Health

One of the most impressive characteristics of humans is our adaptability, our ability to get used to an almost endless variety

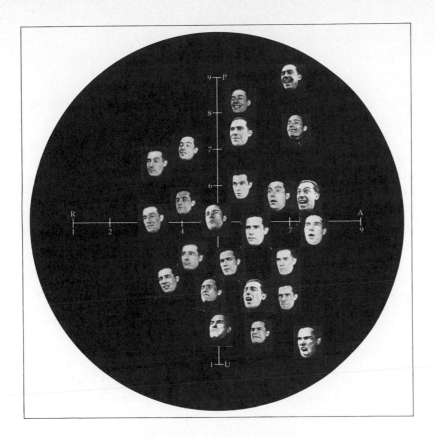

Fig. 8.12
Throughout a lifetime and, indeed, during the course of a single day, an individual may run through the entire gamut of emotions. Every interaction that an individual has with his environment is accompanied by some emotion. These emotions may range in intensity from such strong and dramatic states as love, rage, grief, and ecstasy to such relatively mild states as boredom, affection, and annoyance. Moreover, some emotions are generally regarded as unpleasant (for example, fear) and others as pleasant (for example, love). Finally, emotions may involve turning away from the stimulus (*rejection*, as in disgust), or turning attention toward the stimulus (*attention*, as in fear or surprise). The figure shows photographs of facial expressions as they were classified by subjects according to the pleasantness–unpleasantness (P–U) and rejection–attention (R–A) dimensions (Schlosberg, 1952).

of different circumstances. We have managed to survive under conditions of semistarvation, dire poverty, daily bombings, and the incredible brutality sometimes inflicted on us by others. We have learned to cope with virtually all climate conditions, from the tropical rain forests of South America, to the barren wastelands of the Sahara, to the numbing cold of the Arctic and Antarctic. We are able to adapt to a world that is forever changing, and throwing surprises at us almost daily. At times, however, our exposure to the continual kaleidoscope of changing circumstances has exacted a heavy toll.

General Adaptation Syndrome

What happens when someone is subjected to chronic and prolonged stress? One investigator has theorized that the prolonged stress resulting from emotional pressures, fatigue, or physical suffering produces a three-stage physiological reaction in the body: the alarm stage, the resistance stage, and the exhaustion

*Emotions
and Health*

stage. These three stages have been called the general adaptation syndrome (Selye, 1956).

1. Alarm stage. Our first reaction to stress involves such normal bodily defenses as increased secretions from the adrenal and pituitary glands, and widespread circulatory and digestive changes. These changes are adaptive in that they permit us to cope with stressful circumstances.

2. Resistance stage. If the stress continues, we appear to develop a resistance to the conditions that led to the initial alarm reaction, and many of the symptoms that occurred during the first stage disappear. We are, in fact, paying dearly for this seeming resistance. Continued high levels of secretion from the pituitary and adrenal glands are necessary to maintain this appearance of well-being.

3. Exhaustion stage. If exposure to stress persists, we pass the point of no return. The pituitary and adrenal glands are strained beyond their limits and can no longer maintain their secretions at this increased rate. We may even die from prolonged stress.

Psychosomatic Disorders

Intense emotions mobilize virtually all the body's systems: the circulatory system (heart, skin, and blood vessels), the endocrine glands (pituitary, adrenals, gonads), the respiratory system (mouth, nasal passages, and lungs), the digestive system (stomach, intestines), and the central nervous system. Figure 8.13 illustrates these diffuse reactions. As you might expect, anything that disturbs our emotional life will have widespread effects on our physical well-being. This is particularly true when emotional responses become classically conditioned to environmental stimuli (Chapter 3). For example, children who are severely punished for not eating will learn to react with fear to the feeding situation. Fear typically leads to inhibition of the entire digestive system. Thus, learned fear will interfere with normal digestive processes, and may have profound and long-term effects on the organs involved in digestion. Similar parallels may be drawn between emotional conditioning and other bodily systems.

In the not too distant past, the practice of medicine was thought to be concerned primarily with diagnosing and treating the physical symptoms of disease. In contrast, mental and emotional disorders were thought to be the exclusive province of clinical psychologists and psychiatrists. We now recognize that the human organism must be viewed as a totality in which physical and emotional factors constantly interact. Every so-called physical disorder may have a strong emotional component. Thus, people seem less resistant to the common cold when they are under stress or are suffering unusual emotional duress. Moreover, many doctors have observed that their patients' emotional health significantly affects their ability to recover from a physical illness.

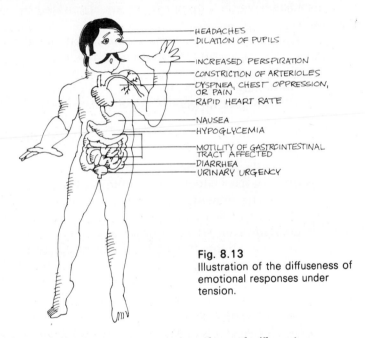

Fig. 8.13
Illustration of the diffuseness of emotional responses under tension.

For example, there have been many reports of people "hanging on" long after a serious physical disorder should have terminated their lives. On the other hand, some people with relatively minor disorders have succumbed as if welcoming death. As one leading investigator of the relationship between emotional and physical factors has observed, it is often "more important to know what kind of patient has the disease than what kind of disease the patient has" (Dunbar, 1943, p. 23). Clearly, then, the doctor of today must treat more than merely the physical aspects of

Emotions and Health

disease. Emotional factors should receive at least equal consideration.

Not only are emotional factors involved in many, if not all, physical illnesses, but there are certain disorders in which emotions appear to play the key role. Such conditions are commonly referred to as psychosomatic disorders. There is considerable evidence that a wide range of organic disorders (such as ulcers, heart disease, and asthma) have strong emotional components. Indeed, specialists in psychosomatic disorders conservatively estimate that 50 percent or more of many physical disorders have their origins in, or are aggravated by, emotional factors.

Psychosomatic symptoms appear to flare up and subside in relation to the amount of emotional stress the individual is experiencing at any given time. For example, a harassed housewife may develop severe and debilitating headaches when her husband goes to work in the morning, leaving her to take care of the children.

One of the questions that has puzzled investigators in this area is why some people develop ulcers, others headaches, and still others develop difficulties with other organ systems. Some investigators have suggested that the predisposition to certain psychosomatic ailments may be genetically determined. Such disorders as stomach ulcers and asthma have been found to run in families. However, we learn many of our emotional responses by imitating our parents and by being reinforced by them for this imitation. Thus, we cannot rule out the possibility that learned factors are involved.

Other investigators have speculated that, in a given individual, certain organ systems are more vulnerable to psychosomatic attack than others. For example, people who have a history of severe respiratory ailments are more likely to develop asthma than, say, a stomach ulcer. One study of 1200 asthmatic patients reported that 98 percent of asthmatic attacks were preceded by some respiratory infection (Bulatov, 1963).

Whatever the predisposing factors in psychosomatic illness may be, it is clear that learning plays a key role in the course and development of these disorders. We have already seen (Chapters 2 and 3) that responses of the autonomic nervous system are subject to voluntary control and can be conditioned. If autonomic responses are indeed influenced by circumstances in the environment, it is possible that the specific bodily reactions in psychosomatic disorders are learned in much the same way as any other behavior pattern. For example, one investigator was able to elicit respiratory patterns that resembled asthmatic breathing by reinforcing certain kinds of breathing (Turnbull, 1962).

It has been suggested that psychosomatic disorders may result from the accidental pairing of physiological responses and reinforcement (Lang, 1970). Here is an example:

> . . . a child may get little or no attention from crying, but the gasping or wheezing reactions that often follow crying spells may obtain immediate attention and concern for him. If this pattern is repeated, the infant might learn an asthmalike response as a means of obtaining parental attention and alleviating distress. In addition, an asthmatic reaction—as a means of reducing anxiety—might generalize to other types of stressful situations. By virtue of its anxiety-reducing quality, it would continually be reinforced, and hence tend to persist. Even when more adaptive ways of coping with anxiety were later acquired, the individual might still resort to asthmatic attacks under severe stress.*

Although it may be tempting to conclude that a given case of, say, asthma or ulcers, is psychosomatic, a note of caution is in order. These same conditions can result from physical causes in which emotions play only a minor role. Emotional stress has been implicated in a wide variety of physical ailments ranging from skin disorders, backaches, headaches, and asthma to hiccoughs, ulcers, and disturbances in menstruation. Let's look at three disorders—asthma, ulcers, and hypertension—in which emotional factors appear to be of paramount importance.

Asthma

Asthma attacks are characterised by breathing difficulties— wheezing, accumulation of mucus in the lungs, and irregular contractions of the bronchial tubes. Although an attack is frequently precipitated by inhaling such irritants as pollen and dust, emotional factors are believed to play a role in at least 75 percent of all cases. A person who is allergic to cat hair may, for

---

*From *Abnormal Psychology and Modern Life* by James C. Coleman, p. 510. Copyright © 1972 by Scott, Foresman and Company. Reprinted by permission of the publisher.

example, have an attack if they see even a porcelain figurine of a cat. Presumably as a result of prior conditioning, this person responds emotionally to cats and generalizes this response to similar stimuli.

It has also been demonstrated that suggestion and expectation play a role in precipitating asthma attacks. In one study, 40 patients suffering from respiratory disorders inhaled the mist of a salt solution which they were told contained dust or pollen. Of these patients, 19 developed typical asthmatic symptoms. What is more, the 12 patients showing the most severe attacks were "treated" with exactly the same mist that had induced the attack —they were told this time that the mist contained an asthma remedy. Their symptoms disappeared (McFadden et al., 1969).

The following account illustrates the role of expectancy in triggering an asthma attack:

> After moving into a new housing development, a group of men sought to "break the ice" by having weekly poker sessions in their homes. When it was my turn to host the group, I placed my dog in the basement so that he wouldn't interfere with the poker session with his continual begging for food. The cardplaying session went well until about midnight when the dog started to bark at the sound of a disturbance outside. One of the players, Charlie F., called out in distress, "You have a dog? I'm allergic to dogs." Within five minutes he had a full-blown asthmatic attack, with characteristic wheezing and difficulty in breathing. Clearly, his reaction was not brought about by the presence of dog hairs in his environment (they had been present throughout the preceding three and one-half hours) but to the sudden awareness that a dog was in the house. Presumably this knowledge triggered an emotional response which led directly to the asthmatic attack.

Ulcers

Many people have, at times, experienced acute stomach distress after a particularly bitter family quarrel, worry over finances, or a disappointing love affair. At these times, particularly when anxiety, hostility, and resentment are involved, the stomach becomes churned up. In some people, when these stresses are chronic, the lining of the stomach becomes engorged with blood, excessive acid-containing gastric juices are secreted, the stomach

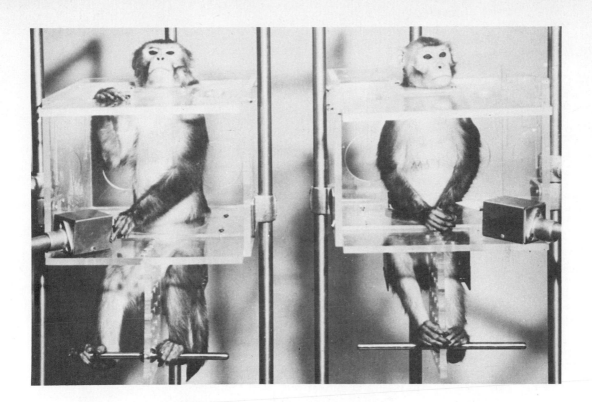

muscles contract, and small lesions are formed. The gastric juices enter these lesions and begin digesting the stomach or intestinal wall itself. These wounds are known as ulcers. Although similar conditions can result from physical causes such as faulty diet or disease, it is generally acknowledged that most ulcers are produced by internal emotional warfare.

A particularly dramatic observation of these physiological reactions to stress was provided by a patient who, because of an accident, could not take food through his mouth. It was necessary to expose the interior of his stomach, thereby making it possible to directly observe his stomach function. During the course of various interviews, it was noted that the patient became anxious, hostile, or resentful. At these times, there was a marked increase in acid secretions and stomach bleeding. It is interesting that when he was afraid, his stomach produced the opposite physiological reactions; that is, it calmed down (Wolf and Wolff, 1947).

Stress has been shown to produce ulcers in many laboratory animals. Figure 8.14 illustrates an experiment in which monkeys who were required to make "executive" decisions developed ulcers.

Fig. 8.14
The "executive monkey," on the left, was responsible for pressing a lever that prevented electric shocks from being delivered to both animals. The control animal, on the right, had no part in the decision-making. The executive monkey developed ulcers, while the control monkey did not (Brady, 1958). (Courtesy of Dr. Joseph V. Brady.)

Emotions
and Health

Hypertension

Under normal, relaxed conditions, our heartbeat is regular and our blood is distributed evenly throughout our entire body. Under conditions of stress, however, the familiar emergency reaction is observed: our blood is diverted from the organs of digestion to the muscles involved in fight or flight, and there is a sharp increase in blood pressure. We have already seen that this reaction is adaptive, since it enhances our ability to deal with the emergency. In most people, the body returns to its normal state after the crisis has passed. In some people, however, the blood pressure remains abnormally high during periods of calm as well as periods of stress. The condition of chronically elevated blood pressure is known as hypertension.

In only a minority of the cases is the cause of hypertension known and ascribable to physical causes. In the majority of the cases, the cause is unknown; however, emotional stresses appear to play a dominant role.

The following case illustrates hypertensive reactions in a young man:

Mark _____, a senior in law school, evidenced episodes of extreme hypertension whenever he was subjected to stress. He became aware of these episodes when he failed to pass his physical examination for induction into the Armed Forces because of exceptionally high blood pressure. In a later check at a medical clinic, under nonstressful conditions, his blood pressure was normal; however, under simulated stress conditions, his blood pressure showed extreme elevation; and this happened again when he returned for another physical examination at the induction center. Although most people show alterations in blood pressure under stress, Mark seemed to show unusual reactivity to a wide range of stressful conditions.*

*From *Abnormal Psychology and Modern Life* by James C. Coleman, p. 503. Copyright © 1972 by Scott, Foresman and Company. Reprinted by permission of the publisher.

Summary

1. Emotions may be regarded as complex states involving cognitions, overt responses, internal changes, and motivational aspects. Our thoughts, beliefs, and prior experiences profoundly influence our emotional reactions to events.

2. Many and varied physiological changes are associated with the various emotional states. These changes include skin conductance, heart rate, blood pressure, breathing rate, and pupil dilation.

3. There are two prominent theories of emotion. (a) The James–Lange theory relates emotion to the perception of bodily states that were activated by environmental stimuli by a reflex process. (b) The Cannon–Bard theory of emotions maintains that both the physiological state and the emotional experience are triggered simultaneously by the actions of the hypothalamus.

4. The emotions of the newborn child appear to represent an undifferentiated state of generalized excitement. The earliest identifiable responses involve distress reactions to unpleasant stimuli and, shortly after, delight responses to feeding, fondling, and other displays of affection. Beyond three months, there is a rapid differentiation of responses associated with anger, disgust, fear, and elation.

5. It is frequently difficult to judge the nature of the underlying emotional states in others by observing their behavior. In labeling the emotions of others, it appears that knowledge of the stimulus situation is the most important factor determining our judgment.

6. When an individual is subjected to chronic and prolonged stress, a three-stage physiological reaction (the general adaptation syndrome) occurs. This reaction includes an alarm stage, a resistance stage, and an exhaustion stage.

7. There are many physical disorders (psychosomatic illnesses) in which emotions appear to play a key role. Psychosomatic symptoms appear to flare up and subside in relation to the amount of emotional stress that the individual is experiencing at any given time.

Summary

Terms to Remember

Adrenaline　A hormone secreted by the adrenal glands which produces the physiological changes associated with fear.

Cannon–Bard Theory　The theory that both the physiological state and the emotional experience are triggered simultaneously by the actions of the hypothalamus.

Cognitive Theory of Emotion　The theory that the emotional experience is identified in terms of the situational context as well as the state of physiological arousal.

Emotion　A complex state involving cognitions, overt responses, internal changes, and motivational aspects.

General Adaptation Syndrome　A three-stage physiological reaction to prolonged stress, consisting of an alarm stage, a resistance stage, and an exhaustion stage.

James–Lange Theory　The theory that an emotional experience results from perception of bodily changes.

Noradrenaline　A hormone secreted by the adrenal glands which produces the physiological changes associated with anger.

Polygraph　Apparatus for recording several physiological measures simultaneously, such as galvanic skin response, heart rate, blood pressure, and rate of breathing. Commonly known as the lie detector.

Psychosomatic Disorders　Physical disorders such as ulcers, asthma, and hypertension, which have their origins in, or are aggravated by, emotional factors.

Pupillometer　A device used to measure changes in pupil size.

Recommended Readings

Darwin, C., *The Expression of the Emotions in Man and Animals*, Chicago: University of Chicago Press, 1965.

Reprint of Darwin's classic with an introduction by Konrad Lorenz, recipient of a Nobel prize in 1973.

Gray, J., *The Psychology of Fear and Stress,* New York: McGraw-Hill Book Co., 1971.

A short paperback which deals with the biological basis of emotional behavior.

Jacobson, E., *Biology of Emotions,* Springfield, Illinois: Charles C. Thomas Publisher, 1967.

An experimental approach to emotion, focusing on the biological aspects.

Levitt, E. E., *The Psychology of Anxiety,* New York: The Bobbs-Merrill Co., Inc., 1967.

A brief but comprehensive discussion of anxiety, based upon empirical findings.

Mandler, G., "Emotion," In Brown, R., et al (Eds.), *New Directions in Psychology,* New York: Holt, Rinehart and Winston, Inc., 1962, pp. 267–343.

Contains a thorough review of knowledge and research in the field of emotion.

Schachter, S., *Emotion, Obesity, and Crime,* New York: Academic Press, Inc., 1971.

A highly readable account of the author's research in these areas, as well as his reasons for supporting the cognitive theory of emotion.

PSYCHOLOGY ISSUES

B.
Ethical Implications
of Psychological Knowledge

The first article in this *Issue* — "Bay State In-mates Fear Brain Surgery, Chemical Mind-Control" — has been reprinted from a newspaper because it shows how much attention certain uses of psychological knowledge are attracting. Psychosurgery has a much longer history than you may realize. It dates back at least to ancient Greece and Rome, where physicians opened their patients' skulls to let out the vapors and humors thought to cause insanity.

In recent times psychosurgery has been used to treat certain mental disorders in institu-tionalized patients and prisoners, although it may be a less common practice than some people allege. The medical use of mind-altering drugs is a widely accepted fact of life.

Our proficiency with behavior control techniques — including surgical, chemical, and electrical procedures — is constantly improving. It is obvious that the very existence of techniques such as these can be considered a potential threat to personal freedom. The fact that many behav-ior control techniques are already in use suggests that the need to discuss the ethical implications of psychological knowledge has become urgent.

In fact, these implications are being dis-cussed, as the second and third articles in this *Issue* show.

Dr. José Delgado is an M.D. who is working on ESB, or behavior control by electrical stimu-lation of the brain (see Chapter 2, pp. 60 - 61). In an excerpt from his book *Physical Control of the Mind: Toward a Psychocivilized Society* (second article) he suggests some of the social and personal benefits we may derive from the techniques he is developing. At the same time, he urges extreme caution and moral integrity in their application.

Dr. Willard Gaylin is a psychiatrist and president of the Institute of Society, Ethics and the Life Sciences. The Institute, whose members come from many different disciplines, was formed for the purpose of serious and disci-plined study of the ethical issues being raised by developments in the life sciences. In an excerpt from an interview (third article), Dr. Gaylin raises some thought-provoking questions that demonstrate just how complex the ethical ques-tions are, and how important it is that they be carefully and intelligently considered from every angle.

Bay State Inmates Fear Brain Surgery, Chemical Mind–Control

By Jean Dietz
Globe Staff

Prison and mental hospital inmates in Massachusetts live in fear of psychosurgery and chemical means of controlling their minds.

Some Department of Mental Health and Correction officials dismiss their fears as groundless and evidence of "paranoia," while others display genuine concern about national reports of medical "tampering" with prisoners' behavior.

"There may have been abuses in the private sector, but not in public institutions. The fear stems from the popularity of such films as "A Clockwork Orange" and plays like "One Flew Over the Cuckoo's Nest," said a psychiatrist, who asked that his name not be used.

Despite such denials, a 27-year-old prisoner at Walpole, who has had two experi-

From the *Boston Globe*, Monday, May 28, 1973, p. 55. Reprinted by permission.

ences at Bridgewater State Hospital for the Criminally Insane, says his treatment increased his anxiety.

"I live in fear of becoming a vegetable, if I have to go back there. I have a terror of lobotomy (the removal of a part of the brain). If you refused medication, which is part of their behavior modification plan, they will get five or ten huskies on you and the doctor will shoot you up with drugs," he said in an interview early this month.

Although admitting he was not forced to take any drugs, he said: "This is because I'm smarter than the average dude out there. The average dude at Bridgewater is a zombie. His IQ is very low. There must be about 165 men at the Treatment Center for Sexually Dangerous Persons because they are now sending them out there straight from the courts."

During a month's stay at the Treatment Center where he underwent evaluation, the inmate said he met a "violent epileptic who said they kept

offering him tests at the Massachusetts General Hospital (MGH). He says they shot a tube up his head to see if there is any damage to it. They told him that electric brain surgery is a quick way to get out the door."

Absolutely no electricity is involved in the treatment of any patient at Bridgewater, except for routine electroencephalography (EEG), according to Dr. A. Louis McGarry, director of the Division of Legal Medicine in the Department of Mental Health.

"The only wires attached to anybody at the Treatment Center would be wires attached to the surface of the skull for standard EEG's," said McGarry.

"This is a routine test, done in every hospital. It does not involve cutting into the skin or bone or brain," he explained. "It is done to pick up abnormal brain waves, usually for the purpose of picking up epilepsy in one of its many forms."

There have been inmates who had neurological workups and examinations at the MGH on the regular neurological service where brain tumors, epilepsy or other brain damage are suspected, McGarry added. . . .

Although doctors at both MGH and Boston City Hospital state that no psychosurgery (surgery on the intact brain to produce psychological changes) has been performed on prison inmates at either institution, the issue is being seriously considered today.

In California, the prison system denied all plans to operate on "difficult" prisoners until letters were uncovered detailing "extensive plans" for a psychosurgical program in cooperation with the University Hospitals of California in San Francisco, Dr. Peter Breggin said here last week in an interview.

Breggin, who directs a project to examine psychiatric technology based at the Washington School of Psychiatry, says three prisoners were operated on in California in 1968 to "cure" them of allegedly violent tendencies.

"A lawyer interested in our work tracked one of these men down in Montana recently," Breggin said. "He is still in prison, but the report said that he had deteriorated intellectually and emotionally since the surgery."

Breggin said that attorneys for civil rights groups were also successful in stop-ping a behavior modification project at a prison in Vacaville, Calif., that came "right out of 'A Clockwork Orange.' "

"These were inmates of a maximum protection diagnostic unit who were given treatment with Anectine, a muscle-paralyzing drug related to curare," Breggin said.

Anectine paralyzes all voluntary muscles for about 60 seconds and makes it impossible for an individual to use his lungs. While the prisoner feels like "he is dying," Breggin said, he is told that the next time he feels an impulse to smash or attack, he will remember the sensation.

A court decision is now pending in Detroit in the case of a former prison inmate who was offered a choice of psychosurgery or hormonal castration by a chemical combination not approved for use in the United States by doctors at the Lafayette Clinic of Wayne State University. . . .

Both Dr. Vernon Mark of Boston City Hospital, and Dr. Thomas Ballantine of Massachusetts General Hospital, the two neurosurgeons most often attacked by Breggin as he speaks around the country, both state they have never operated on a prison inmate.

"I am not operating on anyone in the correctional system or in any prison," Dr. Mark said this week. "I consider Bridgewater State Hospital a prison."

"I don't think prison inmates should be subject to this type of surgery. I don't think a prisoner has the ability to give informed consent. The issue is more complex in mental hospitals," Dr. Mark stated.

"At Boston City Hospital a consumer advocacy committee has recently been added to review every case that has any possibility of coming to surgery in connection with treatment of seizures expressed in violence and rage," the neurosurgeon said further.

Ethical Considerations: Electrical Manipulation of the Psyche

By José M. R. Delgado, M. D.

When medical indications are clear and the standard therapeutic procedures have failed, most patients and doctors are willing to test a new method, provided that the possibility of success outweighs the risk of worsening the situation. The crucial decision to start applying a new therapeutic method to human patients requires a combination of intelligent evaluation of data, knowledge of comparative neurophysiology, foresight, moral integrity, and courage. Excessive aggressiveness in a doctor may cause irreparable damage, but too much caution may deprive patients of needed help. The surgical procedure of lobotomy was perhaps applied to many mental patients too quickly, before its dangers and limitations were understood; but pallidectomy and thalamotomy in the treatment of Parkinson's disease encountered formidable initial opposition before attaining their present recognition and respected status.

From *Physical Control of the Mind: Toward a Psychocivilized Society*, by José M. R. Delgado, pp. 216–218, Vol. 41 of World Perspectives Series, planned and edited by Ruth Nanda Anshen. Copyright © 1969 by José M. R. Delgado. Reprinted by permission of Harper and Row, Publishers, Inc.

While pharmacological and surgical treatment of sufferers of mental illness is accepted as proper, people with other behavioral deviations pose a different type of ethical problem. They may be potentially dangerous to themselves and to society when their mental functions are maintained within normal limits and only one aspect of their personal conduct is socially unacceptable. The rights of an individual to obtain appropriate treatment must be weighed with a professional evaluation of his behavioral problems—and their possible neurological basis—which necessitates a value judgment of the person's behavior in comparison with accepted norms. One example will illustrate these considerations.

In the early 1950s, a patient in a state mental hospital approached Dr. Hannibal Hamlin and me requesting help. She was an attractive 24-year-old woman of average intelligence and education who had a long record of arrests for disorderly conduct. She had been repeatedly involved in bar brawls in which she incited men to fight over her and had spent most of the preceding few years either in jail or in mental institutions. The patient expressed a strong desire as well as an inability to alter her conduct, and because psychiatric treatment had failed, she and her mother urgently requested that some kind of brain surgery be performed in order to control her disreputable, impulsive behavior. They asked specifically that electrodes be implanted to orient possible electrocoagulation of a limited cerebral area; and if that wasn't possible, they wanted lobotomy.

Medical knowledge and experience at that time could not ascertain whether ESB or the application of cerebral lesions could help to solve this patient's problem, and surgical intervention was therefore rejected. When this decision was explained, both the patient and her mother reacted with similar anxious comments, asking, "What is the future? Only jail or the hospital? Is there no hope?" This case revealed the limitations of therapy and the dilemma of possible behavioral control. Supposing that long-term stimulation of a determined brain structure could influence the tendencies of a patient to drink, flirt, and induce fights; would it be ethical to change her personal characteristics? People *are* changing their character by self-medication through hallucinogenic drugs, but do they have the right to demand that doctors administer treatment that will radically alter their behavior? What are the limits of individual rights and doctors' obligations?

As science seems to be approaching the possibility of controlling many aspects of behavior electronically and chemically, these questions must be answered. If, as in the case of this patient, the deviation of behavior conflicts with society so seriously as to deprive her of her personal freedom, medical intervention could be justified. The case of habitual criminal conduct is another example of this type of problem. Therapeutic decisions related to psychic manipulation require moral integrity and ethical education. Scientific training concentrates mainly in natural sciences and often neglects the study and assimilation of ethical codes, considering them beyond the realm of science. Perhaps it is often forgotten that the investigator needs a set of convictions and principles, not only to administrate grant money, to give proper credit to the work of others, and to be civilized with his colleagues, but especially to direct his life and his research, and to foresee the implications of his own discoveries.

The Real and Urgent Problems of Science and Ethics

Decisions in the biological sciences raise a rash of ethical questions. Will they be answered before we plunge into a brave new world of unprecedented control over life itself?

Gaylin: Before the Institute even began, Dan Callahan [who conceived the idea of the Institute and is its director] devoted two years to an extensive study of the abortion issue.

I was concerned with the enormous power of the psychiatrist and the coercive concept of normalcy. You see, medicine is entitled to certain forms of coercion. We can, for medical purposes, isolate people, immunize people, fluoridate the water. So, there's a tradition of coercion in medicine.

But coercion isn't even necessary. If your minister challenges some cherished piece of behavior, you're just as likely to change your religion as your behavior. But if a doctor says, "This is healthy," that has the imprimatur of the life-and-death giver, and you are likely to do what he orders without feeling coerced.

A portion of an interview by Ira Mothner, with psychiatrist Willard Gaylin. Reprinted by permission from *Intellectual Digest*, September 1973, pp. 67–68. Copyright © 1973 by Communications Research Machines, Inc.

That's what we do when we begin to define things as normal. If we say it is normal for children to see their parents nude, we extensively influence child-rearing habits. Since everybody wants to be a normal mother or father, something that was formerly forbidden is now healthy, permissible and normal.

What is normal? It's easy to defend ten fingers or a blood pressure of a fixed amount as normal, but what about attention span in the classroom? What's normal there? Is a child's attention span short because he's in a lousy classroom? Is it because of cultural differences, or is it because he is a hyperkinetic child, which implies that he's *sick* and entitles you to dole out the amphetamines?

. . . .

Q: As you say, there probably aren't any new ethical questions, but what about the new forms in which they're appearing?

Gaylin: The futuristic questions come up most poignantly in behavior control and genetic engineering. Obviously, you will always get a picture in the paper if you have an electrode planted in a man's brain. But the major problems, I suspect, will be in the utilization of psychological knowledge, the manipulation of men through various educational institutions.

Psychosurgery always attracts attention, even though, I believe, it's a less important problem. The very nature of surgery limits it as a procedure, and there is a natural revulsion—sometimes illogical—against having someone poke around in your brain. It's interesting to speculate about what precisely is the difference between the implantation of an idea early in life, as Dr. Skinner wants to do, and the implantation of an electrode. Which is truly the reversible or irreversible procedure? Which one most challenges the individual's autonomy?

Most people don't object when pacemakers are put in the heart to control the heartbeat. But if the same kind of device were placed in the brain to control behavior, they would.

Q: What if we could create a social pacemaker?

Gaylin: We have them. Dr. José Delgado has them. You put them in animals.

Q: And will they abort antisocial behavior?

Gaylin: Aggressive behavior. Dr. Delgado can stop a bull in its tracks by pressing a little button. He's done it. He puts an electrode in the brain. In addition, they are now designing a system that will feed miniaturized computers attached to the repressor. So, when the impulse starts, it will automatically trigger a repressive mechanism. It will inhibit the behavior and insure domestic tranquillity on the spot.

This raises certain problems that become particularly urgent when you must make a distinction between modifying behavior that only influences the individual and behavior that influences society. We get less exercised about the idea of using psychosurgery and electrodes to relieve internal agony than about using them to alter aggressive behavior. Then, we are not sure if we are slipping over from a concern for the individual's pain and anguish to a form of social control. Let me emphasize that I'm not opposed to social control. But if we do make a decision to sacrifice certain personal autonomies, certain private rights, for the public interest and good, it should be so labeled.

Most of us are frightened by this capacity to control behavior mechanically. But it will always be proposed as an alternative to lifetime incarceration for incurable conditions. We know that whatever is designed for these conditions—which are not common enough to be worth the money for the technology—will inevitably develop a momentum of its own and *will* be used more and more and more.

We can put the argument the other way. You want to do away with prisons, but you're worried that someone on probation will abscond. Why not implant a monitor deep within his body, so that you know he is still in Queens, where he belongs, still working on the job? And if he goes off somewhere, you've got him monitored by a central computer.

These are very frightening concepts, and I'm not sure they should be. People say, "My God, you're treating a human being as though he's a machine or a thing." But what are we doing when we lock him up in a cage for 15 or 20 years? I think you can neither take a hysterical, antitechnology approach, nor can you any longer take a gung-ho position—after the atom bomb and ecology disasters—and trust technology to solve all our problems.

9
SENSATION AND PERCEPTION

How many senses are there? Was your answer five? If it was, you are in good company from a historical point of view. Traditionally, we speak of seeing, hearing, smelling, tasting, and touching. However, as we shall see, there are many additional senses.

Try this exercise: Close your eyes and lift your left arm. Where is it? Did you say it is in the air? How do you know? Are you feeling it? Tasting it? Touching it? Since you are obviously not using any of the traditional five senses, some other sense must be operating, the so-called "muscle sense." We rely constantly on the muscle sense to tell us where the various parts of our body are, and we usually take it for granted. Only when we are deprived of this sense do we realize its crucial role in our ongoing behavior. For example, in the advanced stages of syphilis, the organism responsible for syphilis attacks many parts of the central nervous system. Occasionally, it destroys the nervous tissues in the spinal column that carry sensations from the leg muscles to the brain. When this happens, the patient loses the muscle sense in his legs, so that he literally does not know where his legs are. When he walks, he must continuously watch his legs in order to ascertain their position. If he is distracted for a moment from this surveillance, he may fall flat on his face.

What about the detection of warmth and cold? Sense of balance? Pain? It is almost impossible to get a consensus about the number of senses we have. Surely, there are more than a dozen. It is helpful to distinguish two broad classes of sensory receptors: _exteroceptors_, which provide information about the external world (for example, the receptors involved in seeing, hearing, smelling, tasting, and touching), and _interoceptors_, which monitor and provide information about internal states of the organism (for example, the receptors involved in the muscle sense, pain, and balance). The ongoing behavior of the individual requires the coordination and orchestration of the continuous flow of information arising from both the external environment and the internal environment.

Even looking at the so-called five external senses, we find that many of these can be broken down into separate senses. For example, in vision, we can speak of a black-white sense and a color sense. Even the color sense can be broken down into several separate senses.

Sensation
and Perception

It is beyond the scope of this book to discuss the various senses in great detail. We shall look at vision and hearing, because they are our most important senses. But first, let's examine the ways in which we measure sensitivity to environmental stimulation.

Measuring Sensation

Do you think you could see a candle 30 miles away on a clear, dark night? If it were very quiet, could you hear a watch ticking at a distance of 20 feet? If a bee's wing were to fall on your cheek from a distance of 0.4 inches, would you feel it? If a drop of perfume were diffused into a three-room apartment, do you think you could smell it? Or could you taste one teaspoon of sugar dissolved in two gallons of water?

For most people, the answers to these questions are "yes." In fact, these situations describe the minimum amount of stimulation that can be detected by the various senses. In other words, only stimulation at or above these levels is likely to be detected. The minimum amount of stimulation that can be detected by a given sense is known as the *absolute threshold* for that sense.

Even this so-called absolute threshold is not truly absolute. It varies from individual to individual and within the same individual at different times, depending on such factors as momentary changes in the receptors and the conditions under which they function. For example, after exposure to a continuous loud noise, it is difficult to detect a sound which would be readily heard after the ears have rested. The skin senses also show variations from time to time. Their sensitivity depends, in part, on the state of the surface blood vessels and on prior stimulation. After exposure to cold air, we are more sensitive to warmth, and vice versa. Certain illnesses or injuries can have devastating effects on our sensitivity to stimulation. The rubbing of clothing can be agonizing when we have a sunburn, and changes in humidity may be torture to a person suffering from arthritis.

Another aspect of the measurement problem involves the minimum increase or decrease of stimulation necessary to detect a *change* in stimulation. For example, imagine that you are in a room illuminated only by a 10-watt bulb. If a second 10-watt

Measuring Sensation

bulb were turned on, you would surely notice the increase in illumination. Suppose, however, that you were in a room illuminated only by a 100-watt bulb. If a 10-watt bulb were turned on, do you think you would notice any difference in illumination in this situation? Probably not. The change in stimulation necessary to detect a difference is known as the *difference threshold*. When the initial stimulation is low, less change in stimulation is required for a person to detect a difference. If you have a three-way lamp, observe how much more noticeable the change from 50 to 100 watts is than the change from 100 to 150 watts.

It is interesting that continued exposure to a given level of stimulation will, with most sense modalities, lead to an inability to detect that stimulation. This is known as *sensory adaptation*. If you enter a room where incense is burning, you will notice it immediately. After a short period of time, however, you will no longer smell it. When you first get dressed in the morning, you feel the clothes on your body. But after a while, you are completely unaware of the clothing, even though it is still stimulating your sensory receptors.

The traditional approach to sensation assumes that sensory receptors are normally in a resting state and are activated only when stimulated. In actuality, they are not sitting idly by; they are constantly sending impulses. In fact, what we are responding to when we become aware of a sensation is a *change* in stimulation. Adaptation occurs when there are no further changes in stimulation. You feel as if you were not being stimulated. For example, the clothes you wear provide constant stimulation, but not changing stimulation. That is why you no longer notice them after a while. We have all experienced the kind of adaptation that prompts us to say, "Come on in, the water isn't cold, once you get used to it."

Vision

You have probably heard someone compare an eye to a camera. The eye has a lens to focus an image, a diaphragm to regulate the amount of light entering (the iris), and a photosensitive surface (the retina) which acts much like the film in a camera (Fig. 9.1).

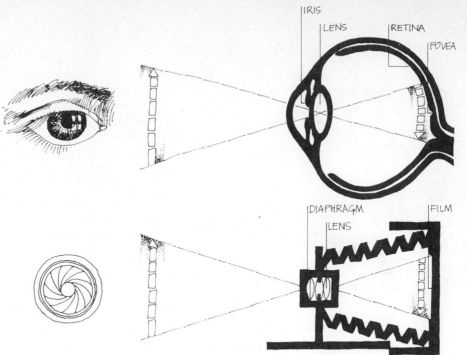

Fig. 9.1
The eye is similar to a camera

Both have a lens for focusing an image, a diaphragm (iris) for regulating the amount of light, and a photosensitive surface (film, retina) for receiving the image. Unlike the camera, the image in the retina activates electrical impulses which are relayed to the brain. In a sense, the brain "sees" the image, while in the camera the film "sees" the image. Moreover, the eye produces a clear image even when the individual is in motion. The camera must be held steady.

It is actually possible to take pictures with the living eye. This has been demonstrated in studies using a rabbit (Kühne, 1878) and a frog (Garten, 1908) (see Fig. 9.2).

Color Vision

Let's carry the analogy between the eye and the camera one step further. Just as we have to use one kind of film for color pictures and another kind for black-and-white, so the retina has different receptors, *rods* and *cones*, for black-and-white and for color vision.

The rods are extremely sensitive to light. Normal daylight bleaches out the photochemical substance associated with the rods, so that they can function only during periods of low illumination. No color is experienced with rod vision. You have probably noticed, when walking on a moonlit night, that you see

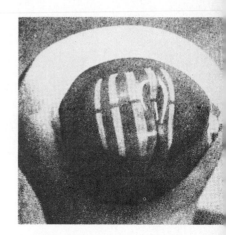

Fig. 9.2
In a replication of the original experiment, a frog was paralyzed and then put in a box for one half-hour and made to look at a pattern of bright stripes crossed at the center by a narrow bar. The retina was then removed and spread upon the knobby end of a white porcelain rod. (Courtesy of Dr. George Wald, Harvard University.)

RECEPTORS	SENSITIVITY	FUNCTION	LOCATION	ACUITY
RODS	HIGHLY SENSITIVE TO LIGHT (FUNCTION UNDER LOW ILLUMINATION)	MEDIATE BLACK-WHITE VISION	FOUND IN PERIPHERY OF RETINA	POOR
CONES	RELATIVELY INSENSITIVE TO LIGHT (FUNCTION UNDER HIGH ILLUMINATION)	MEDIATE COLOR VISION	FOUND PRIMARILY IN FOVEA (CENTRAL REGION OF THE RETINA)	GOOD

Table 9.1
The rods and cones compared

the world in different shades of gray. The cones, on the other hand, mediate color vision. They are far less sensitive to light than the rods, and they function under conditions of brighter illumination.

Have you ever been driving on a dark night, when an approaching car suddenly flashed its high beams in your eyes? The bright light bleaches the photochemical substance associated with the rods, and temporarily incapacitates them. When the car passes, there is not enough illumination for the cones to function, and you are momentarily blinded. Many serious accidents have occurred during this brief period of blindness.

While the rods are more sensitive to light, the nature of their connections with the central nervous system makes them less capable of making fine visual discriminations. In contrast to the rods, each cone is directly connected with the central nervous system, thereby permitting greater visual acuity. It is for this reason that day vision is far more acute than is night vision. Furthermore, the cones are more prolific in the central region of the retina (the fovea), while the rods are found in peripheral regions of the retina. Consequently, during daylight, our sharpest vision is located in the fovea, while in low illumination, such as in night vision, our sharpest vision is in more peripheral regions of the retina.

The next time there is a clear night, try making the following observation. Pick out a star which is just barely visible. Fix it in the center of your vision. It will probably disappear from view. Move your eye slightly to bring the image into a peripheral region. The star will come back into view. Table 9.1 summarizes some of the differences between the rods and cones.

Light, the physical stimulus for vision, consists of electromagnetic waves of extremely short wavelength. Color plate I (see endpapers) shows the entire electromagnetic spectrum, and the small region to which the human eye is attuned. As you can see, the visible spectrum consists of a very narrow range of wavelengths, from approximately 400 millimicrons to 700 millimicrons (a millimicron, mμ, is a thousandth of a millionth of a meter in length).

The portions of the electromagnetic spectrum which we respond to as light vary in three important ways: the specific wavelength, the intensity of the light at that wavelength, and the purity or homogeneity of the light (that is, the proportion of it that is of one particular wavelength). Three psychological experiences are related to these three physical dimensions: *hue* (what we refer to as color—red, green, orange, and so forth); *brightness* (how dark or light the color is); and *saturation* (how rich the color is). Generally speaking, a specific wavelength is seen as a specific hue or color. As you can see from color plate I, a wavelength of 400 mμ is seen as violet, 700 mμ as red. The perceived brightness of any particular hue is proportional to the amount of physical energy or radiation at that wavelength. A small amount of energy will make the color appear dark, whereas a large amount of energy will make it appear bright. If the incoming light contains only a specific wavelength or a very narrow band of wavelengths (say, between 395 and 405 mμ), the hue (violet, in this case) will appear rich or saturated. It will appear less saturated when the incoming light contains a wider spread of different wavelengths (say, from 380 to 420 mμ).

Red and green are probably the two most important colors in our everyday lives. They are conventionally used as signals, red signifying "stop" or "danger," and green meaning "go." Yet these colors are probably the poorest choices we could have made. Why do you think this is so?

First, rods and cones are not equally sensitive to all points on the visible spectrum. With equally intense lights of different wavelengths, some lights will appear quite bright and others will be barely visible. Figure 9.3 shows the relative brightness of equally intense lights of different wavelengths under cone vision. As you can see, our sensitivity to red is exceptionally poor. Red light must be very intense for us to see it. Red light is also less

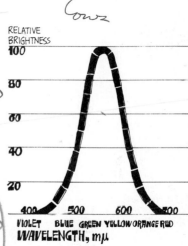

RELATIVE BRIGHTNESS

VIOLET BLUE GREEN YELLOW ORANGE RED
WAVELENGTH, mμ

Fig. 9.3
The cones are not equally sensitive to all wavelengths. The graph shows the relative brightness of equally intense wavelengths under cone or daylight vision.

Vision

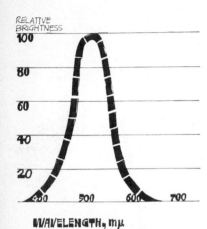

RELATIVE BRIGHTNESS

WAVELENGTH, mμ

Fig. 9.4
The rods are not equally sensitive to all wavelengths. The graph shows the relative brightness of equally intense wavelengths under rod or night vision.

Sensation and Perception

penetrating than is light of other wavelengths. The next time you drive your car in fog, notice how much sooner you can see a green traffic signal than a red one. Many multicar accidents that occur under foggy conditions may be caused by the drivers' failure to see the red brake lights of the cars in front of them in time to stop.

Figure 9.4 shows the relative brightness of equally intense lights of different wavelengths for rod vision. Again, we see that wavelengths in the red region are not very intense. The next time you watch color television, try tuning out the color. You will notice that the red objects appear dark gray or black. Since rod vision operates under conditions of low illumination, red objects will be difficult to see under these conditions, because they will appear dark gray or black. A night hunter who wears a red jacket invites disaster.

We do not see all colors equally well in peripheral vision. Color plate II shows the color sensitivity of the various areas of the eye. Note that red and green do not extend as far into the periphery as do yellow and blue. Thus, if you are driving down a street that has a red or green traffic signal on the side of the road, you might not even see it.

You can set up a very simple demonstration to illustrate the relationship of peripheral vision to color. Find some bright blue, green, yellow, and red pencils or pens. Sit in a well-lit room and fix your eyes on some point on the wall. Cover your left eye. Have a friend bring one of the pencils slowly around from behind your right ear toward the front of your face. As soon as you can tell what color the pencil is, say "Stop." Compare the stop points for each color. You should find that you see blue first, then yellow, and finally green and red.

A final argument against the use of red and green in warning systems involves color blindness. Color plate III is a reproduction of a color blindness test. Complete color blindness is very rare, but red–green color blindness is not uncommon (approximately eight percent of the male population and less than one percent of the female population has red–green color blindness). People with red–green color blindness can see yellow and blue as well as people with normal vision. Recognizing this fact, some states have designed green traffic lights with a bluish cast and red lights with a yellowish cast.

Hearing

The organs of hearing are as remarkable as the organs of seeing. Just as the eyes translate portions of the electromagnetic spectrum into visible light, so the ears transform vibrations of air molecules into the experience of sound. These air molecules are set in motion by the vibrations of physical objects. Under ideal conditions, our ears can hear vibrations from 20 cycles to 20 thousand cycles per second. We can respond to an enormous range of sound intensities; the most intense sound we can hear is approximately 5 million times greater than the softest sound we can hear.

Vibrating bodies may be described in terms of three physical dimensions: frequency, intensity, and complexity. When you press a piano key, the wire that is struck will vibrate at a given frequency. This frequency is usually described as the number of vibrations, or cycles, per second. If you now strike the same key with greater force, the same frequency will result, but the vibrations will be greater in amplitude (that is, intensity). Few objects vibrate at a single frequency alone. A piano string which vibrates at, say, 400 cycles per second also vibrates, with decreasing intensities, at 800, 1200, 1600, and other multiples of 400. This attribute of vibrating bodies is known as complexity.

Each of these physical dimensions has a psychological counterpart. Frequency is perceived as pitch, intensity as loudness, and complexity as timbre. The greater the frequency, the higher the pitch; the more intense the vibrations, the greater the loudness; and the more complex the sound, the richer the tonal quality (timbre). It is primarily timbre that gives each musical instrument its distinctive auditory qualities, and permits us to distinguish among the thousands of voices we hear in a lifetime.

The ear has three subdivisions: the outer ear, the middle ear, and the inner ear. The outer ear of modern man is the vestigial remains of an organ that once helped to collect sounds and direct them into the auditory canal. It is of little use now except as adornment, since we move our heads, rather than our outer ears, to bring sounds into focus. At the end of the auditory canal is a thin membrane, the eardrum, which is set into vibration by incoming sounds. The vibration of the eardrum activates three bones in the middle ear, which transform the air vibrations

Hearing

299

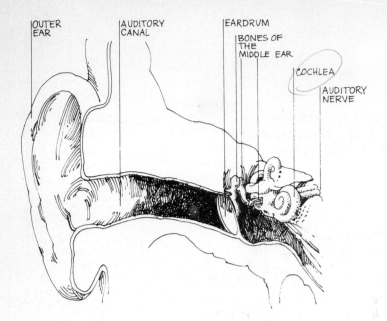

OUTER
EAR

AUDITORY
CANAL

EARDRUM

BONES OF
THE
MIDDLE EAR

COCHLEA

AUDITORY
NERVE

Fig. 9.5
Diagram of the ear.

into mechanical vibrations. The middle ear is separated from the inner ear by another thin membrane, the oval window, which carries the mechanical vibrations into a snail-like structure called the cochlea.

The cochlea is filled with a fluid which is set into motion by the mechanical vibrations of the bones in the middle ear. The movements of this fluid stimulate thousands of tiny hairlike structures, each of which is tuned to a different frequency, like the strings on a guitar. They, in turn, generate electrical impulses which are carried to the brain (see Fig. 9.5).

From this brief description, you can see that the ear is a marvel of engineering. Incoming air vibrations are first transformed into other air vibrations by the eardrum, then into mechanical vibrations in the middle ear, into vibrations of a fluid in the inner ear, and finally into the electrical impulses that go to the brain.

Now, when there is so much concern for the quality of our environment, a note of alarm has been sounded by scientists who fear that noise pollution may endanger our sensitive hearing mechanisms. We know that frequent exposure to intense noise can cause permanent and irreversible damage to our hearing organs. Mechanics working on jet engines have suffered impaired hearing, as have taxi drivers (in their left ears, which pick up the traffic noises). It is feared that men and women who spend a lot of time in discotheques and at rock concerts may, by the time they are 25, have their hearing capabilities reduced to the level of

*Sensation
and Perception*

our senior citizens. It is ironic that, in their search for louder and more exotic sounds, many people may be diminishing their capacity to achieve the very auditory experiences they most value.

What is Perception?

As we sit here writing material for this book, a five-month-old baby girl, Laurie Beth, sits on her mother's lap. Laurie Beth is selectively reaching for objects in her visual field. She grabs at hair, eyeglasses, wristwatches, and the arms of the chairs around her. A few months ago, she lay rather passively and responded at random to the stimuli around her. Now she actively responds to and interacts with her environment. A few months ago, her sensations were probably completely meaningless to her. The faces she saw were unrecognizable, and the objects were just there—they had no meaning. Now, these objects have obviously acquired some meaning for her. They are no longer an unrelated flow of sensory experiences, but a structured series of events that can be manipulated and drawn toward the mouth. She reaches out to touch things, and seems to respond to textural differences. The feel of a soft teddy bear seems to delight her. She directs her attention to each of us as we speak. Laurie Beth is rapidly changing from a sensory to a perceptual animal. She is learning to organize and interpret her sensory world. We call this activity perception.

The rest of this chapter will explore various aspects of the attention and perception processes.

Attention

Put your book down for a moment, and pay attention to whatever other stimuli you notice in your immediate vicinity. Do you hear a dog barking far away, the radio or television in another room, a clock ticking, cars in the street? While you were reading, you were somehow screening these stimuli out. How is this accomplished?

How many different things can you notice at one time? Some people report that they study best in the midst of a constant hubbub of chattering people and blaring music. This would seem to contradict the usual notion that absolute quiet is essential for reading or studying. Libraries, for example, are known for their rules prohibiting any kind of noise. Recent evidence appears to dispute this time-honored practice. One library, located in an urban community, allowed people to talk and played rock music. Many more people began using the library, and they spent more time there reading. Apparently, silence can be distracting to those accustomed to noise, as noise is to those accustomed to silence.

In fact, we can attend to only one thing at a time. When one sensory channel is activated, others appear to be gated out. Most of us have had the experience of driving with our car radio tuned to the news. Then, we approach a busy intersection where we have to pay attention to the traffic. A few minutes later, we realize that we missed several news items.

In one study, investigators recorded the electrical activity in the auditory system of cats (see Fig. 9.6). They sounded a click at regular intervals. When the cat was relaxed, the recording showed activity in the auditory system. However, when a mouse in a jar was placed before the cat, the auditory activity diminished markedly. In other words, the click was gated out when the visual channel was activated. When the mouse was removed, the recordings again showed activity in the auditory system (Hernandez-Peon et al., 1956).

What are the factors that cause us to pay attention to some stimuli in our environment, and to ignore others? Do motivational factors influence this selection? Emotional factors? Previous experience and knowledge? What about the characteristics of the stimuli, that is, intensity, contrast, and movement? These questions are enormously important to teachers, traffic engineers, politicians, publishers, salesmen, and advertising executives, to name but a few.

Characteristics of the stimulus

Modern automobiles are equipped with a red warning light to signal a loss of oil pressure. A warning signal alerts the driver to a dangerous condition. Therefore, the signal must be designed to fill this need, that is, to attract attention. How might you improve the design of this warning signal?

Suppose that you have to give a speech. What might you do to attract and maintain the attention of your audience?

Sensation and Perception

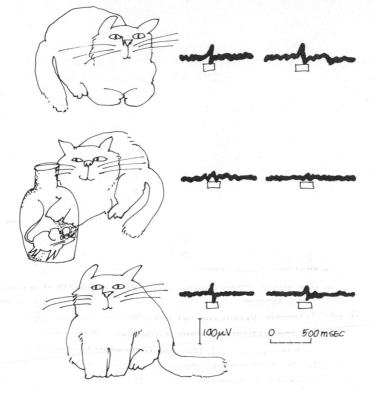

Fig. 9.6
"Gating out" in attention

Note the electrical activity of the auditory cortex when the cat is attending to a periodic clicking sound (top). The small open rectangles correspond to the duration of the click. When the cat directs its attention to the mouse, the auditory stimulus is "gated out." Note the reduced electrical activity as shown in the middle drawing. Finally, when the mouse is removed, the cat again responds to the clicking sounds (bottom). After R. Hernandez-Peon et al., "Modification of Electric Activity in Cochlear Nucleas During Attention in Unanesthesized Cats," *Science*, **123**, 1956, pp. 331–332.)

Imagine that you are commissioned by a firm to design a billboard to advertise one of their products. How might you design this billboard so as to attract attention to it?

Let's look at some of the stimulus characteristics that influence attention.

1. Intensity. The more intense the stimulus, the more likely it is to attract attention. The next time you are in a crowd of people, see how your eye automatically picks out people wearing bright colors. Or, when you walk into a restaurant, see how your attention is immediately directed to the strong odors coming from the kitchen. The intense siren of a police car, fire engine, or other emergency vehicle is designed to attract immediate attention.

2. Contrast. Stimuli that are distinctly different from their background usually attract our attention. Figure 9.7 illustrates how small type on a large and otherwise blank page attracts your attention. The principle of contrast is widely employed in advertising and in the marketing and packaging of products.

What is Perception?

DID THIS ATTRACT YOUR ATTENTION?

Fig. 9.8
Advertisers make good use of
the principle of contrast.
a) The neon sign lights up an
otherwise darkened sky.
b) The bank gets your attention
by using very large black letters
against a white and almost blank
background.
c) In a sea of words and
rectangular-shaped signs the
single letter outlined in a
diamond is the first thing you
notice.
(a, Philip Bailey—Stock, Boston.
b, Frank Siteman—Stock, Boston.
c, Patricia Hollander Gross—
Stock, Boston.)

a)
b)

c)

Figure 9.8 provides several examples of the use of contrast to
attract attention.

3. Movement. One of the best ways to illustrate the role of
movement in catching people's attention is to observe an infant's
reaction to stationary and moving stimuli. An object which may
be completely ignored while stationary is sure to command the

*What is
Perception?*

Fig. 9.9
When the rattle is held stationary over the infant's
head, she pays no attention to it (a). When the rattle
is moved, the infant's attention is drawn to it (b).
(Photos by Liz Muller.)

a)

b)

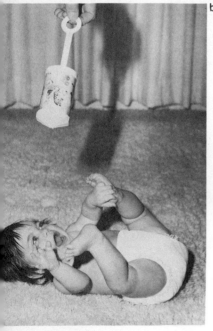

infant's attention as soon as it begins to move (see Fig. 9.9). Investigators have recently learned that some receptors in the retina are responsive only to moving stimuli. These receptors are active only when an image moves across the visual field. You may have noticed that more and more billboards use moving stimuli, or the illusion of movement.

Characteristics of the individual

One of the authors recently visited Disneyland with his family. If you had heard members of the family discuss their experiences afterward, you might have thought each had gone to a different place. The sixteen-year-old girl talked about the teenagers she had seen, and described certain details of dress and appearance she had particularly noticed. The seven-year-old boy found the amusement park full of exciting, and sometimes frightening, animals and prehistoric monsters; he barely noticed the teenage visitors. The five-year-old girl liked the cartoon characters who talked to all the children and posed with them for pictures. The mother noticed the various family groups who were also visiting (how many children? what ages?). Finally, the father paid considerable attention to the prices.

How would you explain the fact that each of these individuals attended to different aspects of the same situation? One possible explanation lies in each individual's motivations. Motivations tend to direct our attention. A hungry person is likely to notice food and related stimuli, such as appetizing odors or advertisements for food. A person walking on a dark, lonely road at night is likely to be alert to any sounds or movements. The same stimuli would not even be noticed during the day.

Advertising agencies are well aware of the effects of motivation on attention. Most agencies have detailed lists of human motivations. In preparing an advertising message, these agencies seek to identify the relevant motivations in the target audience, and to imply in some way that this product will satisfy these motives. Pick up any two magazines geared specifically for two different audiences, and compare the advertisements in terms of the elements used to attract the readers' attention. Figure 9.10 shows some sample advertisements placed in magazines geared for different audiences.

a) b)　　　　　　　　　　c) d)

The emotional state of an individual may determine which aspects of the environment he will attend to. A person who has just received extremely good news may, in his euphoric state, fail to notice signs of depression or unhappiness in others. Likewise, a person in a depressed emotional state may selectively attend to stimuli and events that reinforce his depression.

Previous learning and experience are other factors that affect what is selected for attention. Here is an exercise to try on your friends. Show one friend the two silhouettes in Fig. 9.11. Cover the vase at the bottom. Then ask him what he sees in Fig. 9.12. Show another friend the vase in Fig. 9.11 (covering the faces). Ask him what he sees in Fig. 9.12. In both cases you will have established a *set,* or expectancy, which should influence what the subject notices in Fig. 9.12.

Fig. 9.10
One of these advertisements appeared in *Esquire* magazine, one in *Ms.,* one in the *Wall Street Journal,* and one in *Let's LIVE.* See if you can guess which advertisement appeared in which magazine. Answers are on page 308. (a and d, courtesy of Houbigant Inc. b, courtesy of Life Laboratories Inc. c, courtesy of Fabergé Inc.)

What is Perception?

Fig. 9.11
Show one friend the top picture, and another friend the bottom picture. Then ask them both what they see in Fig. 9.12. (Photo by Jeff Albertson—Stock, Boston.)

Answer key to Fig. 9.10

a) *Wall Street Journal*
b) *Let's LIVE*
c) *Esquire*   d) *Ms.*

Fig. 9.12
This is called an ambiguous figure, since it is possible to see it either as two faces or as a vase.

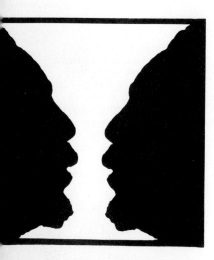

You may have observed that people in various occupational groups tend to notice aspects of their environment which are related to their occupations. For example, dentists tend to look at people's teeth; a man who sells cutlery will probably notice the knives and forks at a table setting; and a tailor is likely to notice the cut of a person's clothes.

Perceptual Organization

Before reading any further, look at Fig. 9.13. What do you see? At first you will probably see a meaningless series of blotches. Look again, and those meaningless blotches will take on the form of a tiger. You will see the tiger's head looking at you on the left side of the figure. Now that you see the tiger, you will no longer

see meaningless blotches. In fact, it may now be difficult to look at the figure and see it as meaningless. Such organization of our perceptual world is characteristic of our everyday perceptions. We do not see unstructured lines and shadows. We see structured forms—people, animals, objects.

The process of organizing experiences into meaningful and structured perceptions began when we were infants. Now that we are adults, we tend to take the organized world for granted. Rarely do we question the principles underlying this organization. Yet there are principles by which we organize or group physical dimensions into coherent units. These principles were most thoroughly investigated and elaborated by the Gestalt psychologists. This group maintained that we see things as unified *wholes* rather than as simply the sum of separate parts. The word *Gestalt,* in German, means "something complete, a whole, a total configuration." Thus, according to the Gestalt theorists, we see the lines below not as six separate and disconnected lines, but rather as three pairs of parallel lines.

|| || ||

The Gestalt psychologists have contributed much to our understanding of perceptual phenomena. Let's examine some of the ways in which we organize aspects of our visual world into meaningful, coherent perceptual wholes.

Fig. 9.13
Look at the figure on the left from all angles. What do you see? See text for an explanation. See page 310 for a discussion of the figure on the right.

What is Perception?

**Fig. 9.14
Camouflage**

The figure on the right contains the one on the left. However, the figure on the right is such a tightly organized whole that it **is** difficult to isolate parts.

Fig. 9.15

Can you see the name JASSENOFF in this photograph of a rug? The total pattern is so dominant that we fail to see that it contains the name. If you cannot find the name, rotate your book clockwise 90° and cover the bottom half of the photograph. The total pattern is the name and its mirror image. (Courtesy of Mike Lupo and Linda Moody; photo by Liz Muller.)

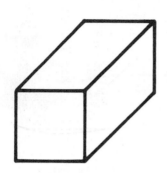

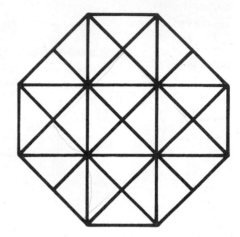

Figure and ground

One way we organize our perceptual experiences is to see objects against a background. When there are marked color or brightness differences, we tend to see a patterned figure on a ground. Look at the design to the right of the tiger in Fig. 9.13. You probably see a series of black figures against a white background. Continue to look at this design, but reverse the figure and ground. In other words, treat the black as the background and the white as the figure. You should now see the word *Tiger.*

In ordinary experience, figure–ground relationships are perfectly clear. We see objects and persons against a background. We almost never have trouble distinguishing figure from ground. A person, a table, a picture on the wall, and a mountain against the sky are all seen as coherent, organized wholes against a neutral, shapeless background. Indeed, as soon as you have seen the tiger in Fig. 9.13, you perceive it as a figure against a shapeless background.

Camouflage techniques rely heavily upon breaking up these figure–ground relationships. They purposely make it difficult to distinguish figure from ground. The figure is deliberately lost in the background, as you can see in Figs. 9.14 and 9.15.

Several patterns have unstable figure–ground relationships. For an example, refer back to Fig. 9.12. Sometimes you will see

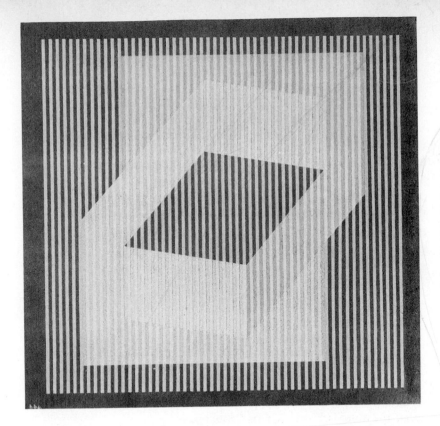

Fig. 9.16
Reversible figure–ground
Focus on the top edge of the central rectangle, and then on the bottom edge. What seems to happen to the three-dimensional relationships of the various planes as you do this? If you continue to look at this figure, the planes will keep shifting back and forth. (*Neither-Nor,* painting by Hannes Beckmann; courtesy of the Museum of Fine Arts, Boston.)

faces against a white background, sometimes a vase against a dark background. Note that it is impossible to see both simultaneously. Another example of a reversible figure–ground relationship can be seen in Fig. 9.16.

Proximity and similarity
We tend to see stimuli that are close together as a pattern, or an organized whole. Figure 9.17 illustrates the effect of proximity on perception.

Fig. 9.17
Proximity
a) When all of the elements are equally spaced, the entire figure looks like a checkerboard.
b and c) However, when the same elements are arranged so that some of them are placed closer to one another, our perception changes. Note that (c) forms a reversible figure–ground relationship. You can see four groups of dots against a white background, or you can see a white cross against a background of dots.

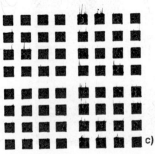

a)   b)   c)

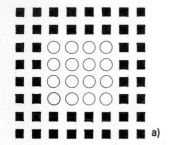 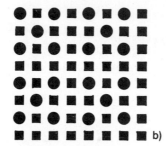 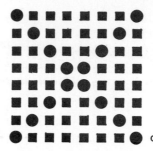

Fig. 9.18
Similarity

Note how the similar stimuli tend to form subgroups. We perceive different patterns because similar elements go together.

Objects that are similar tend to form subgroups. Figure 9.18 shows how our perception of the checkerboard changes as we vary the shape of some of its "squares."

Continuity

We tend to see elements as grouped together if they appear to be a continuation of a pattern. Figure 9.19 shows an example in which there appear to be two continuous patterns.

Fig. 9.19
Continuity

a) We see the curved line as one unit and the straight lines as another because of the principle of continuity.
b) Now we see what the figures look like if we do not put them together.

Sensation and Perception

Closure

No matter what we are looking at, there is always a gap in our visual field. This gap occurs at the point where the optic nerve enters the foveal region of the retina and is called the *blind spot*. We close this gap so successfully that we need a special demonstration to prove its existence. Figure 9.20 allows you to find the blind spot in your own visual field.

Fig. 9.20
The blind spot

Close your left eye and fixate the circle with your right eye. Hold your book about 12 to 14 inches from your eye and move it back and forth very slowly until you find your blind spot. To find the blind spot in your left eye, close your right eye and fixate the cross with your left eye.

We tend to perceive broken lines as continuous, and incomplete figures as complete and closed. Figure 9.21 illustrates this principle of closure.

The Constancies

Stop

Look at Fig. 9.22. Do you realize that when you see a person lying down, this is the image produced on your retina? Somehow, when you look at that person in real life, you do not see extremely huge feet and a distorted body. The camera records the image as it actually is. The perceiving individual makes

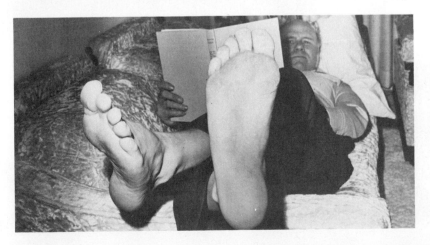

Fig. 9.21
Closure

Look at the lines in the left figure. You will probably see them as three groups of lines plus a single line to the left. This is due to proximity. Now look at the right figure, in which short horizontal lines have been added. Because of the principle of closure, you should now see three rectangles. The solitary line has moved to the right.

Fig. 9.22
Perceptual constancy

This is no trick of photography. The camera records what it sees. The image made by the feet is much larger than the image made by the head because the feet are closer to the camera. If we were viewing this same scene in real life, we would correct for these discrepancies and the man would not look distorted. (Photo by Liz Muller.)

What is
Perception?

313

adjustments in his interpretation of the image he receives so that his perceptions are consonant with his prior experience and knowledge.

In spite of incredibly wide variations in the conditions under which we view objects in our environment—we see them from many different angles, at varying distances, in different contexts, and under virtually limitless conditions of illumination—we tend to see these objects as relatively stable and unchanging. This is known as perceptual constancy. The various constancies discussed below are all based on prior learning.

Shape constancy

Take a few moments to look at various objects in the room about you. The door—do you see it as rectangular regardless of the angle you view it from? What about the paintings on the wall? The window? Hold a dinner plate in front of you, tilting it in various directions. Does it always look round in spite of the various positions in which you hold it (see Fig. 9.23)? The fact that we usually perceive objects that are familiar to us as retaining their shape in spite of widely contrasting visual images is known as shape constancy.

Fig. 9.23
Shape constancy

Because we have learned that dinner plates are circular, we see them that way despite wide variations in the viewing angles. The camera records the plates as we really see them. However, in actual situations, we interpret these retinal images so that they conform to our expectations of the world. (Photos by Liz Muller.)

314

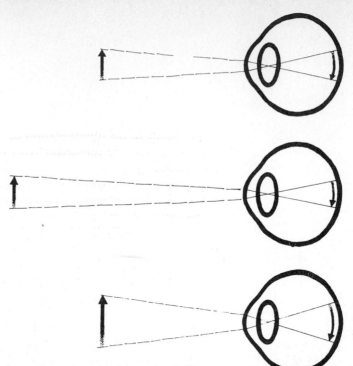

Fig. 9.24
Size of retinal image

The closer the object is to the eye, the larger its image in the retina. Identical objects viewed at various distances will produce retinal images of different sizes. Two objects, differing in size and held at the same distance, will produce retinal images of different sizes.

Size constancy

Imagine that you are out at night and you are looking at a full moon. You hold a circular object at arm's length so as to cover the moon. What size of object do you think would be just large enough to cover the image of the moon? A cantaloupe? A tennis ball? A nickel? A pea?

The truth is that an object the size of a pea, when held at arm's length, is sufficient to cover the image of the moon. Yet you perceive a small pea and a large moon (even though you do not perceive the moon as large as it really is). How is it possible for an object the size of a pea, held at a distance of only several feet, to completely blot out the moon? The answer is found in the fact that objects produce smaller retinal images, the farther they are from the perceiver (see Fig. 9.24).

You can demonstrate this fact with more familiar objects. Take a small circular ashtray and hold it in front of one of your eyes so that it blots out a large painting on the wall. Nevertheless, you do not perceive both objects as equal in size; you still see the ashtray as small and the painting as large. You have just demonstrated size constancy.

Brightness constancy

Imagine the following exercise: In a darkened room, put a piece of coal in a box, and shine a very bright light on the coal. Then, replace the coal with a piece of white paper, and shine a very dim

What is Perception?

light on the white paper. Will the coal look white because it has had a greater amount of light projected on it? Will the white paper look dark because it has had very little light projected on it? The answer to both of these questions is "no." The coal will look black even though a bright light is shining on it. The white paper will look white even though it is under very dim illumination. This exercise demonstrates the principle of brightness constancy.

We perceive brightness in terms of the proportion of the total light that is reflected. The coal in a bright light reflects only a small portion of the total light falling upon it. In contrast, the white paper reflects a high proportion of the total light shining on it. In general, bright objects reflect more light than dark objects. Thus, we tend to see bright objects as bright regardless of the conditions of illumination.

Distance and Depth Perception

Think for a moment of the many judgments you are constantly forced to make as you move through this three-dimensional world. For example, when you drive a car, you are continually called upon to estimate the distance of vehicles in front of you. You must be able to judge how soon to step on the brakes as you approach a stoplight. A slight error in judgment could be fatal. Every sport requires extremely fine judgments of depth and distance. It is amazing that we so rarely misjudge distance and depth. In large part, our success may be attributed to the fact that we have so many different cues for making these judgments.

What would happen if you were deprived of the vision of one eye? Could you still judge distance and depth? The answer is "yes," but not as well as with two eyes. We can obtain many cues to distance with a single eye (these are called monocular cues). However, there are other cues to distance which require the functioning of both eyes simultaneously (binocular cues). Let's look at the binocular cues that help us perceive distance in a three-dimensional world.

Binocular cues

Try this simple exercise. Close your right eye. Holding a pencil in front of you, line it up with a corner of the room, or any vertical

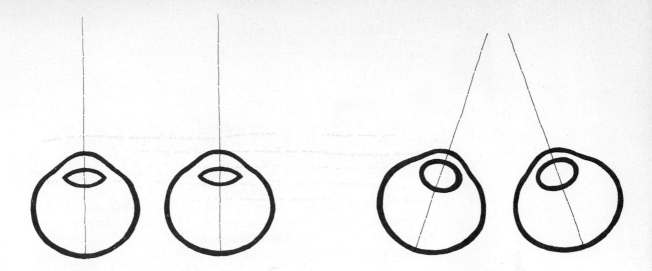

edge. Now, close your left eye and then your right eye, opening your left eye as you close your right eye. Alternate in this way between your left and right eyes. The pencil will seem to move with the opening and closing of each eye. Open both eyes simultaneously and focus on the corner of the room. You will see two pencils in your line of vision. Now, focus on the pencil with both eyes and you will see two corners in the background. This simple exercise demonstrates that the two eyes are getting slightly different images, because they are separated. They are actually seeing slightly different views of any object that they focus on. This slight discrepancy between the images reaching each eye is called *retinal disparity*. It is retinal disparity that gives the world its three-dimensional appearance. Retinal disparity is unquestionably the most important binocular cue to depth.

When you look at objects that are close to you, your eyes tend to turn toward each other (or converge) in order to focus. If an object is very close, you feel (and look) cross-eyed and you may notice muscular strain. As you look at objects that are farther and farther away, your eyes look in a more parallel direction to each other. We presume that the stimuli arising from the activation of the muscles that govern *convergence* also provide internal cues to depth and distance perception. Convergence typically works in concert with a particular monocular cue, as follows. When the eye focuses on a distant object, the lens flattens out. When it focuses on near objects, the lens bulges. We presume that the bulging and flattening of the lens provides an internal cue which informs us of the relative distance of objects. This phenomenon is known as *accommodation*. Figure 9.25 shows the eyes viewing near and far objects.

Fig. 9.25
Accommodation and convergence

Note that, for distant viewing, the lens is flattened (accommodation) and the eyes are on a parallel plane. For near objects, the lens bulges and the eyes turn toward each other (convergence).

What is Perception?

317

Fig. 9.26
This demonstrates the importance of binocular cues in depth perception. See text for an explanation. (Photos by Liz Muller.)

a)

b)

Both of the binocular cues, retinal disparity and convergence, function effectively over only relatively short distances. Convergence, for example, is useful for judging distance and depth over a distance of only a few feet. Even retinal disparity is limited to relatively short distances. There is a far greater disparity between the images your eyes receive when you are 5 feet from an object than when you are 50 or 100 feet away from the same object. Thus, even though we use both eyes, we make many judgments of distance and depth on the basis of monocular cues.

Monocular cues

Close your left eye. Spread your arms out to either side of you so they are parallel to the floor (see Fig. 9.26a). Now, quickly swing your arms around to the front, and see if you can make the index fingers of both hands touch (see Fig. 9.26b). Do this several times and note your accuracy. Now repeat this procedure with both eyes open. You will probably find that you have no difficulty bringing your index fingers together. This simple procedure demonstrates the importance of binocular cues in depth perception. Nevertheless, even without three-dimensional cues, our accuracy in judging depth remains relatively good. This is so because there are many cues provided by the environment. We learn to use these cues to judge distance and depth. Let's look at some of the more important ones.

1. Linear perspective. Parallel lines appear to converge in the distance; you probably noticed this as a child, when you were riding in a car along a straight road or looking down a stretch of railroad track. In general, objects that are nearer the point of convergence appear to be farther away (see Fig. 9.27a on page 320).

2. Texture. Closely related to linear perspective is the textural gradient of objects extending vertically in the visual field. When you look across a long, flat field, for example, nearby objects appear large and, therefore, coarser in texture. As the surface recedes, objects appear progressively smaller and finer in texture (see Fig. 9.27b).

3. Atmospheric conditions. One of the most common cues to distance is the relative clarity of objects that appear in our field of vision. Distant objects seem to be less clear because of atmospheric conditions. The difference in clarity is particularly noticeable in our smog-laden cities, where even relatively close objects are obscured by atmospheric haze (see Fig. 9.27c).

4. *Light and shadow.* When you look at Fig. 9.27d, you clearly see a crater. Turn the book upside down, and the crater suddenly becomes a mound. The reason is that we are accustomed to seeing light coming from above. When light falls upon a crater, the shadows are typically formed on one side of the crater and the bottom part has a relatively greater amount of illumination. The interplay of light and shadow causes us to interpret what we see as a depression. However, when we turn it upside down, we continue to perceive the light as coming from above. We now interpret the picture as a mound, because the distribution of light and shadows is the same as occurs when we look at a mountain or a mound in daylight. This perception is instantaneous and does not involve any thought; it is based upon our previous experiences with light and shadow.

5. *Interposition.* Close one eye, and place both hands in front of you in your line of sight so that the right hand partially obscures the left hand. It is easy to judge that the right hand is closer to your eyes than the left. Interposition occurs when one object partially obscures another in our field of vision (see Fig. 9.27e).

6. *Relative size.* We have already seen that the farther an object is from the viewer, the smaller the retinal image will be. If two familiar objects are approximately the same size, but one produces a smaller retinal image, we judge the object with the smaller retinal image to be farther away. Figure 9.27f provides an example of relative size as a cue to distance. As you can see in the left-hand photo, the two persons are roughly the same size. In the right-hand photo, you would judge the woman to be farther away because she appears smaller.

Note that, especially for unfamiliar objects, relative size is an ambiguous cue to distance. When one object appears larger than another, there are two possible explanations: either the one object is, in fact, larger, or the other object is farther away (see Fig. 9.28 on page 321).

7. *Motion parallax.* Distant objects moving at a given speed seem to be moving more slowly than closer objects that are moving at the same speed. A plane very high in the sky seems to be moving very slowly; when it is closer to the ground, it seems to be moving rapidly. In fact, the opposite is probably true—planes

a)

b)

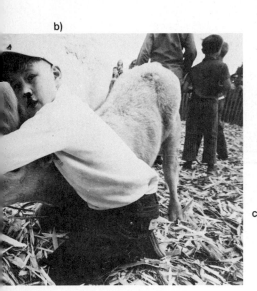

c)

Sensation
and Perception

Fig. 9.27
Various monocular cues for judging distance and depth. See text, pages
318–319, for an explanation. (a and b, copyright by Mark Silber, 1972. c (top),
Stephen J. Potter—Stock, Boston. c (bottom), Daniel S. Brody—Stock, Boston.
d, K. C. DenDooven. e, Liz Muller. f, Bruce Anderson.)

d) e)

f)

IS THE FIGURE ON
THE RIGHT SMALLER
THAN THE ONE ON
THE LEFT OR IS IT
FURTHER AWAY?

NOTE THAT WHEN ADDITIONAL
CLUES ARE PROVIDED
THE AMBIGUITY IS REMOVED.

Fig. 9.28
Relative size can be an
ambiguous cue to distance.

usually fly at higher speeds when they are at high altitudes.
Conversely, if you are in a plane at an extremely high altitude,
the plane does not seem to be moving very rapidly because the
ground does not appear to be moving rapidly in the opposite
direction. Indeed, the ground may appear to be moving slowly in
the same direction you are moving. When the plane comes in for
a landing, it is actually going at a slower speed. However, it
seems to be going extremely quickly because the objects in your
field of vision are going by so quickly in the opposite direction.

Illusions

So far, we have been discussing many of the factors that allow us
to make fairly accurate judgments of the world around us.
However, sometimes these judgments become distorted and
inaccurately reflect what is going on in the external world. When
this happens, we say that we are having an illusion. There are
many different types of illusions, and they involve most of the
sense modalities. The best known and most thoroughly
investigated are illusions of motion and the optical illusions.

Illusions of Motion

Have you ever thought of movies as illusions? When you watch a
movie, you are really looking at a series of still pictures projected
at high speed, so that they blend to produce the appearance of
continuous motion.

You can produce a similar illusion of motion by arranging a
series of lights in a pattern and turning them on in rapid
succession. The lights appear to move through the pattern in a
continuous sequence. This illusion of motion is referred to as the
phi phenomenon. It is widely used in neon signs and billboards.

Another example of apparent motion can be demonstrated
very simply. Take a pinpoint source of light into a completely
dark room. You can use a flashlight and cover most of its
illuminating surface with dark tape, so that only a very small bit
of light is visible. Place the flashlight in a fixed position. Now
move to another part of the room and stare at the light. To most

people, the light will appear to move spontaneously, by itself. This effect is known as the *autokinetic effect* ("auto" means self, "kinetic" means moving).

Optical Illusions

Although optical illusions have fascinated man for ages, there are still very few adequate explanations of why they occur. Figure 9.29 presents several examples of optical illusions. See how accurately you can answer the questions.

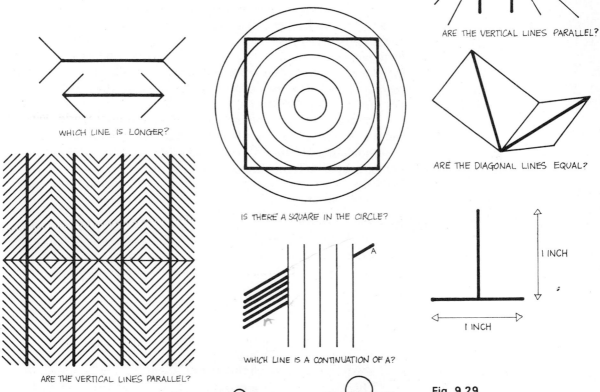

WHICH LINE IS LONGER?

IS THERE A SQUARE IN THE CIRCLE?

ARE THE VERTICAL LINES PARALLEL?

ARE THE VERTICAL LINES PARALLEL?

ARE THE DIAGONAL LINES EQUAL?

WHICH LINE IS A CONTINUATION OF A?

A

1 INCH

1 INCH

ARE THE INNER CIRCLES EQUAL IN SIZE?

Fig. 9.29
Selected optical illusions.

Factors Influencing Perception

We have discussed how prior experience, emotions, and motivations influence what we pay attention to in the world around us. The same variables also influence our perceptions of the world.

Even when people pay attention to the same stimuli, they do not always perceive them in the same way. As children, we probably all played the game of looking at cloud formations and telling what we saw. Some of us may have reported a huge monster preparing to devour a small animal, others a king sitting on a throne, and others a variety of plausible or preposterous perceptions. Again, we may ask: What are the factors that cause us to perceive stimuli and events in different ways? Why do some individuals perceive and report events in such bizarre and unusual ways that we call these people emotionally disturbed and hospitalize many of them?

The following excerpt from a conversation between a doctor and his patient in a mental hospital illustrates the extreme distortions in perception of time and space sometimes found among people suffering acute emotional disorders:

"How old are you?"

"Why, I am centuries old, sir."

"How long have you been here?"

"I have been now on this property on and off for a long time. I cannot say the exact time because we are absorbed by the air at night, and they bring back people. They kill up everything; they can make you lie; they can talk through your throat."

"Who is this?"

"Why, the air."

"What is the name of this place?"

"This place is called a star."

"Who is the doctor in charge of your ward?"

"A body just like yours, sir. They can make you black and white. I say good morning, but he just comes through here. At first it was a colony. They said it was heaven. These buildings were not solid at the time, and I am positive this is the same place. They have others just like it. People die, and all the microbes talk over there, and prestigitis you know is sending you from here to another world. . . . I was sent by the government to the United States to Washington to some star, and they had a pretty nice country there. Now you have a body like a young man who says he is of the prestigitis."

(White, 1932, p. 228)

You can probably tell of instances when your own mood, motivations, or expectations influenced the way you perceived a situation. You heard what you wanted or expected to hear, saw what you wanted or expected to see. One of the authors had the following experience as a graduate student:

The graduate school that I attended was located very near a ghetto area of the community. One of the undergraduate students had been stabbed in that area on the previous weekend. While I was returning home, just slightly after midnight, I was thinking about that stabbing. The area was very dark and foreboding. Suddenly, this figure came at me from out of the shadows with an object in his hand. I immediately perceived the object to be a knife and made some defensive movements. At this point, the perceived "would-be assailant" said, "Have a drink." The object in his hand was a bottle of whiskey.

Participants at athletic events are notorious for perceiving all decisions against their team as unjust and obvious errors. "The umpire is blind" is a common expression.

After the final football game of the season between Princeton and Dartmouth in 1951, many charges of foul play were leveled against both teams. The filmed replay of the game was shown to undergraduates from both schools. They were asked to record the number of infractions they detected on both sides. When Princeton students looked at the movie, they saw the Dartmouth team make more than twice as many infractions as their own team did. When the Dartmouth students looked at the movie, they saw both teams make about the same number of infractions; that is, they saw their own team make only half the number of infractions that the Princeton students saw them make. This, despite the fact that all students saw the same filmed replay of the game (Hastorf and Cantril, 1954).

Much additional research linking motivation and perception

Factors
Influencing
Perception

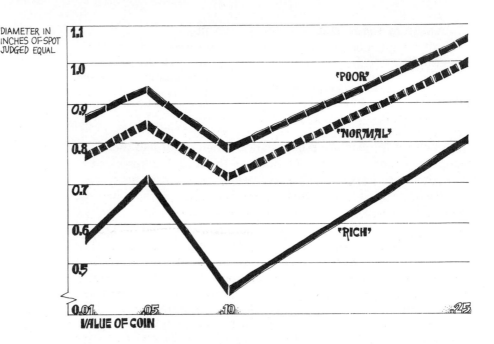

DIAMETER IN INCHES OF SPOT JUDGED EQUAL

1.1
1.0
0.9
0.8
0.7
0.6
0.5

'POOR'

'NORMAL'

'RICH'

0.01   .05   .10   .25

VALUE OF COIN

Fig. 9.30
Subjects were asked to judge the size of coins. This graph shows the results of their judgments in a normal state, and when they were hypnotized to believe they were "poor" or "rich." (After W. R. Ashley et al., "The Perceived Size of Coins in Normal and Hypnotically Induced Economic States," *American Journal of Psychology*, **64**, 1951, pp. 564–572. Used by permission of The University of Illinois Press.)

*Sensation
and Perception*

has been conducted in the laboratory. In one study, middle-class college students were individually hypnotized on two different occasions. Before they were hypnotized, they were asked to adjust the size of a light so that it would successively equal the size of a penny, a nickel, a dime, and a quarter. During the first session of hypnosis, the suggestion was planted that they had a prior history of poverty, with insufficient money to buy many of the necessities of life ("poor" condition). In the second session of hypnosis, the same students were told that they came from very wealthy families where there was never a financial problem, and never a shortage of either the necessities or the luxuries of life ("rich" condition). After each session of hypnosis, the subjects were again asked to adjust the size of the light to equal the sizes of various coins. In the "poor" condition, the subjects'
adjust the size of a light so that it would successively equal the larger than they did before hypnosis. In the "rich" condition, the subjects' adjustments suggested that they perceived the coins as considerably smaller than they had before hypnosis (Ashley et al., 1951). Figure 9.30 presents the results of this study.

Extrasensory Perception

Extrasensory perception, or ESP, is presumed to be a form of communication between individuals which does not rely on the use of any of the known senses. ESP includes (1) *mental telepathy*, in which an individual "reads" the mind of another person; (2) *clairvoyance*, the ability to perceive things that are not in sight or cannot be seen; and (3) *telekinesis*, the ability to influence future events.

ESP studies today are conducted with the same sorts of controls that are used in any other area of research in the behavioral sciences. In a typical experiment on mental telepathy, for example, a "sender" is given a thoroughly shuffled deck of specially prepared ESP cards. The standard deck of cards for these experiments consists of five sets of five cards. The five cards in each set contain the following figures, one on each card: a square, a circle, a triangle, a plus sign, and wavy lines. The "sender" concentrates on each card in turn, and tries to transmit his thoughts to a person seated either behind a screen or at some distance. On the basis of chance, we would expect the "receiver" to be correct, on the average, five times out of every run through the deck of 25 cards.

In some studies, individuals have achieved remarkable records of success. However, it is difficult to evaluate these findings, since the same individual may be successful at one time and unsuccessful at another. Earlier studies of ESP reported striking evidence in favor of its existence. But as more sophisticated experimental controls have been introduced in later studies, the evidence has been less impressive. Nevertheless, some psychologists have been impressed by both the experimental rigor and the number of studies showing positive results. One reviewer concluded that ESP should be accepted as proved unless we are willing to charge many universities and serious scientists with involvement in a "gigantic conspiracy" (Eysenck, 1964).

Nevertheless, psychologists have not generally accepted extrasensory perception as a proved phenomenon. This reluctance is due largely to the inability to imagine a satisfactory mechanism by which thought transference could occur. Some investigators have suggested that brain waves might be involved. However, the electrical power in brain waves is so minute, that it seems incredible that they could be transmitted over long distances and sorted out by another person's brain.

Unfortunately for serious-minded investigators, extrasensory perception is commonly associated with stage magicians, charlatans who claim mysterious "psychic" powers, and various mediums who claim to be able to communicate with the dead. Thus, when we think of ESP, we tend to think of the occult. As we know, it is difficult to break such a well-established "set." At present, it seems safe to say that most psychologists favor continued controlled studies of ESP, and have adopted a "wait and see" attitude.

Summary

1. There are many more senses than the traditional five: sight, touch, hearing, smell, and taste. Other senses include the muscle sense, pain, and sense of balance.

2. Two broad classes of sensory receptors may be distinguished: exteroceptors and interoceptors.

3. Measurement of the sensory capabilities of humans has established the degree of sensitivity of various sensory receptors to a broad range of physical energies. The minimum amount of stimulation that can be detected by a given sense is known as the absolute threshold for that sense.

4. The change of stimulation necessary for a person to detect a difference in stimulus intensity levels is known as the difference threshold. When the initial stimulation is low, less change in stimulation is required for a difference in stimulus intensity to be detected.

5. With most sense modalities, continued exposure to a given level of stimulation will lead to a reduced ability to detect that stimulation (sensory adaptation).

6. The eye is in many ways like a camera. The lens focuses the image, the iris regulates the amount of light entering the eye, and a photosensitive surface, the retina, acts much like the film in a camera.

7. Two broad classes of receptors are found in the retina: rods and cones.

8. The portions of the electromagnetic spectrum to which we respond as light vary in three ways: the specific wavelength, which determines the psychological dimension of hue; the intensity of the light at that wavelength, which determines brightness; and the purity of the light at that wavelength, which determines saturation.

9. Our ears transform the vibrations of air molecules into the experience of sound. The three physical characteristics of the vibrations are perceived as three corresponding aspects of sound: the frequency of the vibrations is experienced as pitch; intensity

(amplitude of the vibrations) as loudness; and complexity (the presence of other frequencies) as timbre.

10. The ear is composed of three parts: the outer ear, the middle ear, and the inner ear.

11. Perception is the organization and interpretation of sensory experience.

12. There is considerable evidence that we can pay attention to only one thing in our environment at a time. When one sensory channel is activated, it appears that others are gated out. What we pay attention to at any particular time is determined by the characteristics of the stimulus (intensity, contrast, movement) and the characteristics of the individual (prior experiences and motivation).

13. The principles of perceptual organization include figure and ground, proximity, similarity, continuity, and closure.

14. In spite of the incredible diversity of the conditions under which we view objects in our environment, we tend to see these objects as relatively stable and unchanging. The following visual constancies are based on prior experience: shape constancy, size constancy, and brightness constancy.

15. We are constantly forced to make judgments of distance and depth. Some of the cues for depth require only a single eye (monocular cues), and some require the simultaneous operation of both eyes (binocular cues).

16. At times our judgments become distorted and inaccurately reflect what is going on in the external world. We refer to such distortions as illusions.

17. Not all people perceive the same situation in the same way. Moods, motivations, expectancies, and prior experience influence the ways in which we perceive things and events.

18. Extrasensory perception is presumed to be a form of communication between individuals which does not rely on the known senses. Although much evidence appears to support the existence of ESP, most psychologists, in the absence of a

satisfactory mechanism by which to explain it, have taken a "wait and see" attitude, while encouraging continued controlled research.

Terms to Remember

Absolute Threshold   The minimum amount of stimulation that can be detected by a given sense.

Accommodation   A monocular cue to depth perception; the lens bulges for near objects and flattens out for far objects.

Autokinetic Effect   The apparent movement of a stationary pinpoint of light in a dark room.

Blind Spot   The point where the optic nerve enters the foveal region of the retina, creating a gap in the visual field.

Brightness   How dark or how light a color is; determined by the intensity of the light at that wavelength.

Brightness Constancy   The tendency to perceive objects in their correct brightness, regardless of the conditions of illumination.

Clairvoyance   A form of extrasensory perception; the ability to perceive things that are not in sight or cannot be seen.

Closure   In perception, the tendency to perceive broken lines as continuous, and incomplete figures as complete and closed.

Complexity   The presence of frequencies other than the fundamental frequency; the number and strength of these other frequencies determine the timbre of a sound.

Cones   One of the two types of receptors for vision located in the retina; the cones mediate color vision.

Continuity   In perception, we tend to see elements as grouped together if they appear to be a continuation of a pattern.

Convergence   A binocular cue to depth perception; in viewing a near object, the eyes tend to turn toward each other to focus.

Difference Threshold   The minimum increase or decrease of stimulation necessary for a person to detect a change in stimulation.

Exteroceptors   Sensory receptors which provide information about the external world (for example, the receptors involved in sight).

Extrasensory Perception (ESP)   A form of communication between individuals which does not rely on the use of any of the known senses.

Figure and Ground   In perception, the tendency to see things as objects against a background.

Fovea   The central region of the retina; contains only cones.

Frequency   The number of vibrations, or cycles, per second; determines the pitch we hear.

Gestalt Psychology   A school of psychology that stresses the view that we see things as unified wholes rather than as the sum of separate parts.

Hue   Scientific term for color; a specific wavelength is seen as a specific hue.

Illusion   A perception that is a distortion of an actual sensory experience.

interoceptors   Sensory receptors which provide information about internal states of the organism (for example, the receptors involved in the sense of pain).

Interposition   A monocular cue to distance perception; it occurs when one object partially obscures another in our field of vision.

Linear Perspective   Distance perception through the apparent convergence of parallel lines.

Loudness   The hearing sensation determined by the amplitude of the sound wave.

Mental Telepathy   A form of extrasensory perception in which one person "reads" the mind of another.

Motion Parallax A phenomenon whereby, when we move, near objects move across our visual field more rapidly than far objects.

Perception The organization and interpretation of sensory experiences.

Perpetual Constancy The tendency to see the world as relatively stable and unchanging, despite the wide variations in information received by the senses.

Phi Phenomenon Illusion of motion produced by a rapid succession of images that are really not moving, as in electric signs.

Pitch Highness or lowness of a sound; determined by the frequency of the sound wave.

Proximity In perception, the tendency to see things that are close together as a pattern or an organized whole.

Retina Photosensitive surface of the eye; it acts much like the film in a camera.

Retinal Disparity A binocular cue to depth perception; both eyes get slightly different images of an object because the eyes are separated from each other.

Rods One of the two types of receptors for vision located in the retina. No color is experienced with rod vision, only black, white, and gray.

Saturation The richness of a color; determined by the purity of the light at that wavelength.

Sensory Adaptation With most of our senses, continued exposure to a given level of stimulation will lead to an inability to detect that stimulation.

Set A readiness to perceive or respond in a certain way.

Shape Constancy The tendency to perceive objects that are familiar to us as retaining their shape, even though a variety of different visual images are received by the retina.

Similarity In perception, objects that are similar tend to form subgroups.

Terms to Remember

Size Constancy The tendency to perceive objects at their correct size, regardless of the size of the retinal image they produce at varying distances.

Telekinesis A form of extrasensory perception; the ability to influence future events.

Timbre The richness of a sound; determined by the complexity of the sound.

Recommended Readings

Bartley, S. H., *Principles of Perception* (2nd ed.), New York: Harper & Row Publishers, 1969.
A comprehensive treatment of human perception.

Forgus, R., *Perception: The Basic Process in Cognitive Development,* New York: McGraw-Hill Book Co., 1966.
Stresses the relationships between perception, learning, concept formation, and thinking.

Gibson, E. J., *Principles of Perceptual Learning and Development,* New York: Appleton-Century-Crofts, 1969.
Surveys theories of perceptual learning as well as the development of perception in the child.

Gibson, J. J., *The Senses Considered as Perceptual Systems,* Boston: Houghton Mifflin Co., 1966.
Departing from the traditional theories of perception, the author suggests that perception be separated from the sensory processes.

Gregory, R. L., *Eye and Brain,* New York: McGraw-Hill Book Co., 1966.
Relatively nontechnical account of how we see the world. Brings together experimental findings of psychology and physiology.

Gregory, R. L., *The Intelligent Eye,* New York: McGraw-Hill Book Co., 1970.
A fascinating analysis of the effects of learning on visual perception.

Mostofsky, D. I., *Attention: Contemporary Theory and Analysis,* New York: Appleton-Century-Crofts, 1970.

An original collection of papers representing the thinking currently associated with attention research throughout the world.

Stevens, S. S., and Warshofsky, F., *Sound and Hearing,* New York: Time–Life Books, 1965.

Highly readable account of hearing in humans and animals. Contains many illustrations.

Zubek, J. P., *Sensory Deprivation: Fifteen Years of Research,* New York: Appleton-Century-Crofts, 1969.

An edited volume containing a series of review articles covering the extensive research that has been carried out from 1954–1969 on the effects of a severe restriction of sensory stimulation on human functions.

10 CHILD DEVELOPMENT

The birth of the baby

The nature—nurture controversy
Principles of heredity — Maturation
Influencing development

The developing child

Prenatal influences — The neonate
The first two years
The preschool and middle years

The Birth of the Baby

Each of us begins life as a single cell. This cell, the product of fertilization of an ovum (egg) by a sperm, contains all the genetic information that will direct the growth of the organism throughout its life. About one day after fertilization, this cell divides into two living cells. Each of these cells, in turn, contains the same genetic information found in the original cell, the fertilized egg. The process of division continues, and by about two weeks a hollow ball has been formed. This ball contains three separate layers of cells, each of which will play a different role in the developing organism. The outer layer will develop into the skin, the nervous system, and the sense organs. Bones, muscles, and blood will develop from the middle layer. The inner layer will become the organs that comprise the digestive system.

Between the second and eighth weeks (the *embryo* stage), the baby's anatomy begins to take shape. By the end of the embryonic period, the developing organism, though only slightly more than an inch long, already contains such basic anatomical structures as limbs and distinguishable facial features.

From about the end of the second month until birth, the baby-to-be is referred to as the *fetus*. All the structures that will be required to sustain life as an independent organism are differentiated during this period. By about the fifth month, the heartbeat can be heard and the mother becomes aware of the spontaneous movements of the fetus. All the body systems are capable of functioning by the 28th week, and if an infant should happen to be born at this point, it might survive if intensive medical care is provided. Figure 10.1 illustrates some of the landmarks in the prenatal development of the human organism.

The Nature–Nurture Controversy

"The child is father of the man." This statement implies that much of what we become as adults is determined by what we were as children. What is the child?

In part, the child is a product of his heredity. Some qualities are irrevocably settled before birth. We cannot do anything about the child's sex, the tint of his skin, the shape and color of his eyes, or his tendency to be tall or short. These qualities are

Fig. 10.1
Stages in prenatal development

a) Living two-cell stage of human ovum 30 hours after fertilization. b) A living 3½-day-old human morula. c) Living human embryo at 4½ weeks. d) Living human embryo at 14 weeks. e) The birth of the baby. (a, b, c, and d, courtesy of Dr. Landrum B. Shettles. e, Wayne Miller—Magnum.)

a) b) c)

d) e)

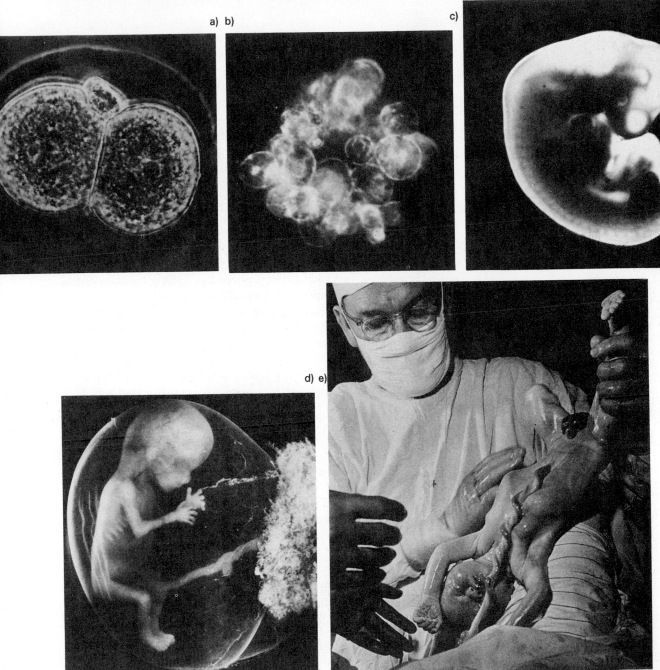

determined by chance. Each child is a mixture not only of his immediate parents but of his parents' parents and all generations that went before. Each baby is unique in his particular assortment of the hundreds of traits and tendencies that are transmitted through heredity. Each baby is different from babies in other families, and is also different from his own brothers and sisters.

The child is also a product of his environment. From the moment of conception, the fertilized egg is thrust into the unique uterine environment of the mother. Irregularities in this environment may have profound effects on the developing embryo. Later we shall look at some of the prenatal influences on the developing organism. Once the child is born, there are innumerable environmental forces operating upon him. Just as each child has his own unique heredity, so also is he exposed to a unique constellation of environmental factors.

Throughout recorded history, there has been a controversy over which is more important, heredity or environment. This is the issue of nature versus nurture. We now recognize that it is the interplay between hereditary and environmental influences that determines a person's mental and physical characteristics, and his emotional, social, and personality development. The hereditary scheme does not unfold in the absence of an environment. In turn, every environment operates upon an organism that has a genetic history.

Principles of Heredity

The original fertilized cell contains complex chemical substances known as *chromosomes,* on which are located the determiners of heredity called *genes.* There are 46 chromosomes in each cell of the human body (except the germ cells, which will be discussed below). Twenty-three of these chromosomes were obtained from each parent.

In the female, one of these 23 pairs of chromosomes consists of two X chromosomes. The cells of the male contain 22 pairs, plus an X and a Y chromosome. The X and Y chromosomes determine sex.

The body cells of a mature adult produce germ cells: the ovum in the female and the sperm in the male. Each germ cell contains half the usual complement of chromosomes. All female ova contain one X chromosome. Approximately half the sperm cells produced contain an X chromosome, and the other half contain a Y chromosome. Upon ejaculation of semen into the vagina of a woman who has ovulated (that is, whose uterus contains an unfertilized ovum), approximately two hundred million sperm cells begin a race to fertilize the egg. If a sperm containing an X chromosome wins the race, the fertilized egg will have two X chromosomes and the egg will develop into a female. If fertilized by a sperm carrying a Y chromosome, the fertilized egg will have the XY combination and the egg will develop into a male. Figure 10.2 shows how the X and Y chromosomes determine sex.

Fig. 10.2
Sex determination

Each egg produced by the female contains an X chromosome. Half of the male sperm cells contain an X chromosome, the other half a Y chromosome. The sex of the offspring is determined by the father.

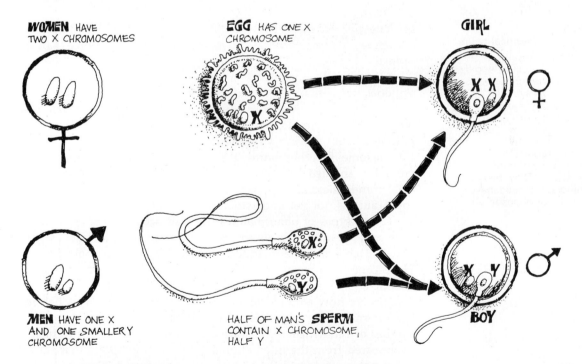

WOMEN HAVE TWO X CHROMOSOMES

EGG HAS ONE X CHROMOSOME

GIRL

MEN HAVE ONE X AND ONE SMALLER Y CHROMOSOME

HALF OF MAN'S SPERM CONTAIN X CHROMOSOME, HALF Y

BOY

We have said that each individual has a unique genetic makeup. There is, however, an exception. Identical twins develop from a single fertilized ovum. Thus, they each receive the same set of chromosomes and are exactly alike in their heredity. Fraternal twins, on the other hand, develop from two

The Birth of the Baby

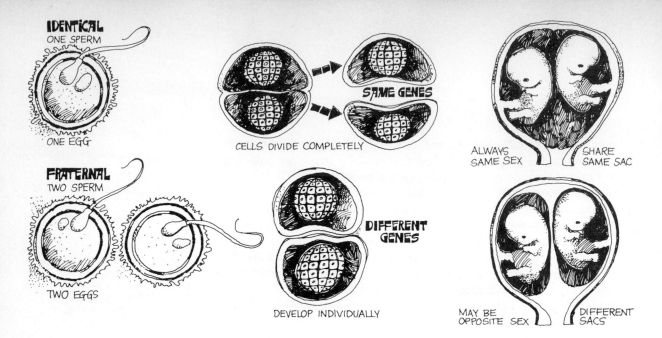

IDENTICAL
ONE SPERM

ONE EGG

CELLS DIVIDE COMPLETELY

SAME GENES

ALWAYS SAME SEX

SHARE SAME SAC

FRATERNAL
TWO SPERM

TWO EGGS

DEVELOP INDIVIDUALLY

DIFFERENT GENES

MAY BE OPPOSITE SEX

DIFFERENT SACS

Fig. 10.3
Fraternal and identical twins

Identical twins result from the fertilization of a single egg by one sperm. During the course of subsequent division, the cells divide completely and two separate organisms are formed. They share the same genetic makeup and are, of course, the same sex. Fraternal twins result from the fertilization of two eggs by two sperm. They, therefore, have different genetic makeup and may be of opposite sex.

Child Development

separate ova fertilized by two different sperm (see Fig. 10.3). Therefore, fraternal twins are no more alike in their heredity than are ordinary siblings.

Occasionally, for reasons not clearly understood, the fertilized egg does not contain the usual complement of chromosomes. In many cases, this will lead to some abnormalities in the developing organism. For example, in one form of feeblemindedness, known as mongolism or Down's syndrome, there is one extra chromosome. In other words, the child has 47 chromosomes instead of the usual 46. Why this extra chromosome leads to feeblemindedness and characteristic variations in physical appearance is not yet understood.

Other types of abnormalities can also occur. Some of these have made headlines in recent years. Occasionally, a female will have a Y chromosome in addition to the pair of X chromosomes. The recent controversy over the sex of females in international athletic competition resulted from this phenomenon. All female athletes are now required to submit to a series of sex tests before any international competition. Perhaps as a result of this, a number of renowned women athletes from Soviet countries have disappeared from the international scene. One suspects that they might not have passed the physical examination, for one reason or other. However, the most fascinating and controversial case involves the great Polish athlete Ewa Klobkowska, who passed the physical examination but was later disqualified when the study of her chromosomes revealed the presence of a Y chromosome. Is "she" female or male?

The body cells of some males (about one in a thousand) contain one X and two Y chromosomes. Because of the extra "male" chromosome, such men have been referred to as "supermales." Some investigators believe that the extra Y chromosome predisposes these men to extreme aggressiveness. Some have suggested, in fact, that individuals with the XYY combination are inclined to become criminals (Telfer et al., 1967). This matter is still under intensive investigation, and no definitive conclusions can be drawn at this time. However, it should be noted that many criminals do not have the XYY combination, and that many individuals with this combination do not become criminals.

Maturation

Have you ever observed the parental delight when baby takes his first step? The parents proudly proclaim that he has learned to walk. But has he, in fact, *learned* to walk? Or is his first step merely the culmination of months of muscular growth and neural development? These questions are not as easy to answer as they might seem. Behavioral changes may result from learning or from physiological changes that occur in the normal course of development (maturation). It is often difficult to distinguish changes that occur as a result of learning from those that are due strictly to maturation of the organism. Both kinds of change show increasing approximation to adult behavior over time.

The concept of maturation is of limited use in understanding the diversity of human behavior. Maturation sets the stage on which certain behaviors occur, but the full development of these behaviors is heavily dependent on learning. We do not acquire such skills as ice skating, bicycle riding, or dancing solely through maturation. Nor do we acquire our language skills simply through maturation.

The child must mature before he can engage in the many activities that are characteristic of the human species. At birth, his legs are not sufficiently developed to support the weight of his body. His brain, though it possesses the full complement of neurons, is still largely an undeveloped organ. The physical changes necessary for the development of language have not yet occurred. A host of interrelated physical developments must occur

The Birth of the Baby

before the child can walk, talk, think, and reason. Once the physical changes necessary for the exercise of a given function have taken place, the child is "ready" to benefit from practice.

Maturational readiness refers to the time interval during which the organism first becomes physically capable of acquiring a particular function or skill. The term implies that practice prior to this period will be largely wasted. This is an area of considerable interest to educators. Is there, in fact, an optimal time to begin teaching such things as reading and arithmetic? The answer to this question is both "yes" and "no." Many poor educational practices have stemmed from the view that there is "a magic age" at which all children are "ready" to speak, learn to read, and manipulate numerical concepts. The practice of placing children in grades according to chronological age is a reflection of this point of view. We now recognize that the "magic age" will vary from child to child, and from skill to skill within the same child. The inflexible use of time-bound sequences of educational experiences has probably hampered the development of many children (see Fig. 10.4). Much of the thrust of education today is in the direction of permitting children to learn at a pace that is consistent with their own maturational development.

Fig. 10.4
Individual differences in readiness

Fifth graders were tested in their reading and language skills and given a score that reflected the grade equivalent at which they were performing. As the graph shows, only about 20 percent of the fifth graders tested performed at a fifth grade level. Most performed above or below. (After *How Children Learn* by A. A. Frandsen. Copyright © 1957 by McGraw-Hill Book Company. Used by permission of McGraw-Hill Book Company.)

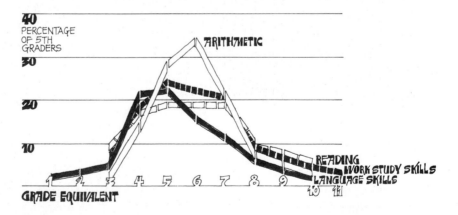

Critical periods

Some exciting findings in both animal and human studies have suggested that the time of maturational readiness is a critical period, in the sense that deprivation of particular experiences

Child Development

during this period may lead to permanent impairment.
Let's look at a few examples.

It has been observed that, shortly after hatching, a duckling or gosling will follow its mother around. This observation is not particularly dramatic. What makes it interesting is the fact that newly hatched ducklings and goslings will follow almost *any* moving object and become attached to it (see Fig. 10.5). This phenomenon is known as *imprinting*.

Studies on imprinting have revealed that there is a critical period of time in which imprinting can occur. For the mallard duckling, this period is between 13 and 16 hours. After the age of

Fig. 10.5
Konrad Lorenz (1903–) coined the term imprinting and demonstrated that imprinting will happen only during a critical period in the animal's early life. Here Lorenz plays foster Mother Goose to some imprinted goslings. (Photo by Thomas McAvoy, *Life.*)

The Birth of the Baby

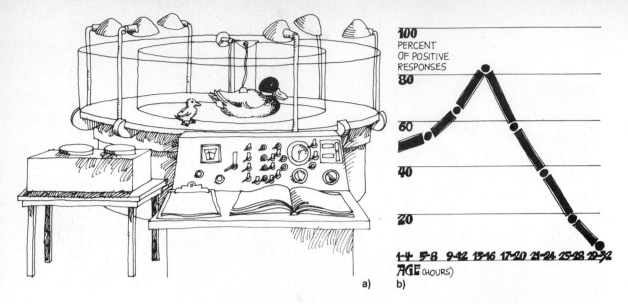

100
PERCENT
OF POSITIVE
RESPONSES
80

60

40

20

1-4 5-8 9-12 13-16 17-20 21-24 25-28 29-32
AGE (HOURS)

a)   b)

*Child
Development*

16 hours, the likelihood that imprinting will occur declines
rapidly in this species. Figure 10.6 shows the apparatus employed in
an imprinting study and the relationship between imprintability
and age (Hess, 1958).

Under natural conditions, the imprinting response has clear
adaptive value for the newly hatched gosling or duckling. The
mother provides protection for the young and will lead the young
to sources of food.

In natural settings, higher animals also form strong
attachments to their mothers. As with ducklings and goslings,
these attachments have obvious adaptive value, since the infant
cannot survive unless it is fed and cared for. These attachments
may persist for years.

In laboratory settings it is possible to systematically deprive
monkeys of contact with their mothers or other members of their
species. Recall our discussion of the experiments on contact
comfort need (Chapter 7), in which monkeys were "raised" by
surrogate cloth or wire "mothers." The initial studies seemed to
suggest that the cloth "mothers" were adequate substitutes for
the real mother. Infants showed the same sorts of affectional
responses toward the terrycloth "mothers" as control animals did
toward real mothers. For example, when novel fear-producing
stimuli were presented, these monkeys ran to their terrycloth
"mothers." They clung to them for a few minutes and then went
out to investigate the fear-producing stimulus (see Fig. 10.7). It
was only when these mother-deprived monkeys achieved
adulthood that it became apparent that something was wrong. For
example, when 18 female monkeys were released on an island

a) b)

c) d)

along with sexually experienced males, most of them resisted any attempt on the part of the males to engage in heterosexual activity. Indeed, after many months on the island, only four of these monkeys were successfully impregnated (Harlow, 1965). Clearly, the deprivation of contact with a real mother during the first few months of life led to a serious impairment in their ability to adjust to a normal adult heterosexual role. Furthermore, when the mother-deprived monkey gave birth to her own infant, she withdrew into a corner, completely ignoring the infant. She

Fig. 10.7
Attachment behavior in an infant monkey

When a frightening toy was introduced, the infant monkey ran promptly to its terrycloth "mother" and clung to it. After clinging for a few minutes, the monkey turned to investigate the strange object. (Courtesy of Dr. Harry F. Harlow, University of Wisconsin Primate Laboratory.)

Fig. 10.8
The effects of maternal deprivation

The mother monkey was separated at birth from her own mother and not given any opportunity to observe and interact with members of her own species. When she herself became a mother, she repulsed all efforts by her infant to establish physical contact. Here we see the mother resisting contact by forcing the infant's face into the wire mesh floor. (Courtesy of Dr. Harry F. Harlow, University of Wisconsin Primate Laboratory.)

Child Development

repeatedly rejected efforts on the part of the new infant to achieve contact with her. Figure 10.8 shows a mother pushing her infant's face into the wire floor.

In another study, infant monkeys were systematically deprived of social contacts for varying periods of time (3, 6, and 12 months). This deprivation was either *partial* (they could see and hear other monkeys, but were allowed no physical contact) or *total* (they could see no animal of any kind). Long-term studies of monkeys released after three months of total deprivation revealed that the monkeys made a complete social recovery and showed normal learning and sexual adjustment. However, monkeys either partially or totally deprived of social contact for six months showed an impairment in their ability to interact socially with other monkeys. These social inadequacies persisted for many years. Twelve months of total deprivation produces catastrophic results—these monkeys were not able to interact with other monkeys at all (Harlow and Harlow, 1966).

These studies show the extreme importance of social contacts during the formative months of life in primates. For obvious reasons, the effects of prolonged social deprivation in human infants cannot be systematically investigated in an experimental setting. However, a number of investigators have reported observations of children raised in a cold, mechanical manner and deprived of warmth, attention, and personal care. The effects are especially dramatic in institutional settings, where children frequently receive, at best, custodial care.

In one study, comparisons were made between babies raised in foundling homes and those raised in a nursery. The two settings varied in several different ways. One factor that clearly distinguished them was the degree of stimulation the children received. The children in the foundling home were deprived of toys or any other form of visual stimulation. Moreover, they were cared for by a staff of nurses, who provided only for their basic physiological needs and did not handle, fondle, or play with the children. In the nursery, on the other hand, the children received abundant stimulation. They had toys to play with, and they could see the children in neighboring cribs. They were visited regularly by their mothers or other caretakers, who lavished much warmth and attention on them. The differences between these two groups were most dramatic. The children in the nursery walked early, frequently scrambling over the bars of cribs to play on the floor. They appeared to show normal language and social development, and the curiosity characteristic of children of their age. In the foundling home, many of the children did not survive the first two years of life. Of those who did survive, many showed signs of deep depression, gazing indifferently as they lay in their cribs. By the age of two, only two of 26 children were able to walk or speak (Spitz, 1945).

A more recent study compared children from comparable backgrounds raised in two different types of institutions in Iran. The following is a description of the child-care practices in Institution A:

> On the average there were eight children per attendant . . . The attendants have no special training for their work and are poorly paid. The emphasis on the part of the supervisors seems to be on neatness in the appearance of the rooms, with little attention to behavioral development. In his crib the child is not propped up, and is given no toys. . . . Except when being bathed, the younger children spend practically their entire time in their cribs.
>
> (Dennis, 1960)

The Birth of the Baby

Contrast the above with the care provided in Institution B:

> The number of children per attendant is 3–4. Children are held in arms while being fed, are regularly placed prone during part of the time they are in their cribs, are propped up in a sitting position in their cribs at times, and are placed in play pens on the floor daily when above four months of age. Numerous toys are provided. Attendants are coached in methods of childcare, and supervisors emphasize behavioral development as well as nutrition and health.
>
> (Dennis, 1960)

Dramatic differences were observed in the motor behavior of children raised in these two institutional settings. By the age of two, only 42 percent of the children raised in Institution A were able to sit alone, whereas 90 percent of those raised in Institution B were able to do so. Only 8 percent of the children in Institution A could walk by the age of three. By contrast, 94 percent in Institution B could do so (Dennis, 1960).

The results of these studies are consistent both with observations from animal laboratories and with anecdotal reports about children raised in disturbed family settings. Largely as a result of these observations, many hospitals have instituted programs in which nurses who care for children are asked to handle and fondle them, and give them the personal care that was previously denied children in these settings. Even institutions that are seriously understaffed have invited women in the community to visit for a few hours daily to "play mother" to the infants. The decline in infant mortality over the last few decades can probably, in part, be attributed to these new practices.

Children raised in impoverished households often experience deprivation of stimulation not unlike that found in institutional settings that provide only custodial care. In many cases, there is only one parent (usually the mother), who is forced to find employment to maintain her entire family. In order to support her family, which may consist of several children, she has to leave them for long periods of time without adequate care or stimulation.

What happens to a child who has been deprived of intellectual, social, and positive emotional experiences during the critical years? The concept of critical periods stresses the importance of timing of stimulation, social and otherwise, in the sequence of development. The issue is crucial to programs based on the premise that individuals will "catch up," even though they have been deprived during their critical periods. Probably the best known of these programs is Project Headstart. Recognizing that children from impoverished homes were inadequately prepared to benefit from the educational system, Project Headstart has tried to provide these children with compensatory education. The children, age four and older, are given an opportunity to experience various forms of intellectual and social stimulation. The hope has been that this intensive preschool educational setting will counteract the deficiencies of earlier years. The rather limited success of Project Headstart has led to attempts to influence the development of deprived children even before the age of four.

Influencing Development

During the 1960's, mainly because of research showing the importance of early affectional ties for later social development, many parents and researchers concentrated on the emotional and social development of the child. Very few investigators were concerned with the child's intellectual development. We have now come to realize that a warm, accepting environment may not be enough to stimulate intellectual development.

Researchers concerned with intellectual development have been intrigued with the question: Is there a period of time, analogous to the "critical period" for social-emotional development, that is critical for intellectual development?

Some of the most exciting research on early intellectual development has come out of the laboratories of Harvard University. Observing that, by the sixth year of life, children seemed already to be clearly differentiated with respect to their ability to cope with intellectual tasks, the researchers set out to investigate at what age this differentiation takes place. Their research has led to a surprising conclusion—between the ages of 10 and 18 months (White, 1972).

The investigators assumed at first that the key periods of intellectual development probably came somewhere after the age of three. So they began their study with a group of youngsters

The Birth of the Baby

three to six years of age. They divided the children into two groups: those rated as outstanding in their ability to cope with problems in and out of the classroom (A group), and those who were unable to cope (C group). The investigators were able to identify a cluster of 17 specific intellectual and social abilities common to members of the A group. The C-group children did not show this same clustering. In the course of this study, the researchers were led to an inescapable conclusion:

> The youngest members of their A group, who were barely 3 years old, had exactly the same cluster of abilities as the 6 year old A's. They also seemed well ahead of the 6 year old C's in both social and intellectual skills. In other words, the researchers had come too late: whatever produced the differences between the two groups has occurred well before the age of 3.
>
> (Pines, 1971, p. 163)

When the mothers of these children were studied, it was found that the mothers of A-group children frequently provided an enriched intellectual environment for their children—toys to play with, and freedom to roam and explore. When the child ran into an obstacle, the A-group mother would speak to the child, stimulate his curiosity, and provide him with new ideas. The C-group mothers, on the other hand, placed many restrictions on their child's curiosity and opportunity to explore. The results seemed to indicate that these restrictions were severe enough to retard the intellectual development of these C-group children by the time they were a year and a half old. However, the destiny of the child is not rigidly set by the age of a year and a half. Given an altered environment, the child can change. Presumably, if the child remains in the same environment and the mother does not change, the child will continue along the same lines of development. Follow-up studies have shown that where no environmental changes were made, the A-group children remained outstanding and the C-group children continued to display social and intellectual inadequacies.

Intervention programs are based on the rationale that positive changes can be produced by altering the child's environment at a sufficiently early age. The environment provided by the mother in the United States is not always optimal. Indeed, people who live in relatively comfortable middle-class communities are not always aware of the devastating experiences to which young children living in impoverished areas are exposed.

One research team (Lally, 1971) has reported a number of situations judged to be typical of low-income families in the United States. The following is an anecdotal report of conditions in one impoverished household, as described by a nonprofessional member of the research team:

> . . . she [the mother] keeps the place a mess. It's just like a pig-pen there. She started working at a bar after the baby was born. This is a rough bar. She worked until 1:00 A.M. She worked there for awhile, but I don't know if she was fired or quit, but she is not working there any more. Her place is a mess. I went there on Monday morning and there were beer cans, and papers were all over the floor. Chi [the baby] was soaking wet and yelling; Rho [the mother] was in bed, and she said she was sick. I told her if she would get up and clean up a little bit and give the baby her food, she might feel a little better. This mother is on Welfare. When we first started working with her, she was having problems with Welfare because they cut off her money because she was living with the children's father, and he was supposed to leave money downtown for the children, and they cut her check. After he left, they reinstated her money, and she is getting more money now
>
> (Lally, 1971, p. 5)

Most investigators assume that children raised in environments of this sort will inevitably suffer profound and demoralizing behavioral deficits. Efforts are under way to counteract the effects of such deprivation and despair. Programs to provide supplementary outside intervention have been initiated in many major cities (Lally, 1971; Parmelee, 1973; Schaefer and Aronson, 1970) (see Fig. 10.9).

Since the mother is the most important feature in the infant's environment, intervention programs usually try to enlist the mother's participation in the program. The hope is that the mother will transfer what she learns in the intervention program to the care of her children at home. One of the most significant effects of intervention has been increased social interaction between the mother and her child.

We now recognize that both the mother and the community play a vital role in the development of the child. Approaches to

The Birth of the Baby

353

a) b)

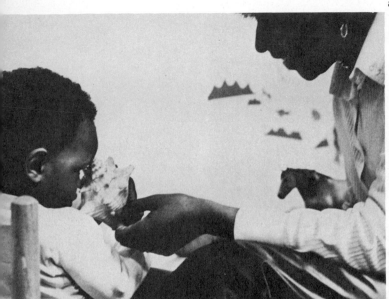 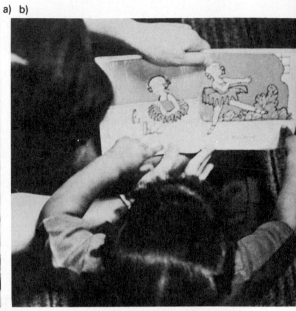

c) d)

e) f)

g)

Fig. 10.9
Intervention

Typical activities at Syracuse University's Children's Center program.

a) An activity in the sensory experience area of the toddler program. The child is feeling and listening to a seashell.

b) An activity on a rug in the sensory experience room, which contains reading and listening materials and comfortable places for story time. The child is starting to point to the ballerina's "foot" at the adult storyteller's request.

c) Lunch room activity. Toddlers eat meals family-style at a table with teacher. They choose from a wide variety of offerings and have learned to eat and enjoy a great many different kinds of foods.

d) The adult has partially hidden a colorful plastic doughnut under a printed cloth screen. Although the 8½-month-old cannot yet locate the doughnut when it is completely hidden, he is clearly reaching for the partially hidden toy.

e) This is the testing room. The infant is trying to solve a problem involving spatial concepts. How does one get a long linked chain into a rather narrow plastic jar? Bunching is too sophisticated a solution for this baby, but he has figured out how to 'feed' links of chain into the jar.

f) The same infant, working with a long link chain, has now victoriously found a new bunch-and-drip-into-jar technique for dealing with the problem.

g) An activity in the small-muscle area. The teacher is helping a couple of completely absorbed toddlers to fit puzzle pieces together. (Courtesy of Dr. J. Ronald Lally; photos by Roger Gregoire, Boston.)

355

the care and handling of children with behavioral and intellectual problems have changed dramatically. We used to isolate these children from their home and community environments by placing them in specialized institutions. Now, many of the large institutions are being closed and replaced by smaller facilities located within the communities where they are needed. Members of these communities are becoming actively engaged in the operation of these centers. Professionals, paid staff, and volunteers from the community are currently being trained to work with these children. The parents in the community are being encouraged to participate actively in the programs.

The Developing Child

When the child emerges from the warm, moist, somewhat crowded but usually uncomplicated uterine environment provided by the mother, he is held upside down and slapped rather unceremoniously on his backside. A thin, reedy cry is his first response to this indignity, and heralds, by the breathing necessary to activate the cry, his readiness to begin lifelong interaction with the world about him. At first, the child is little more than a bundle of highly organized protoplasm, capable of limited reflexive responses to the environment, and of carrying out basic biological functions. As a member of the human species, he is more a promise than a reality.

It is hard to believe how rapidly the baby changes (see Fig. 10.10). At first, the child is merely a passive recipient of sensory stimulation, reacting primarily to internal stimuli such as hunger and gas pains. Almost before the parents are aware of it, this helpless infant has become a veritable "monkey," climbing into every corner, helping himself to his favorite foods. In the beginning, he stares vacantly at the stimuli that pass across his field of vision. Before the end of his first year, his perceptual and motor coordination has advanced to the point where he can spot his favorite toy halfway across the room and quickly crawl or run over to get it. Even the sounds he makes have shown dramatic changes. Before, all he was capable of was a stream of unintelligible sounds primarily related to crying. Now he can produce coherent repeated patterns such as "da-da" and "ma-ma."

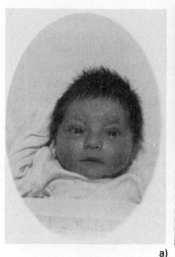

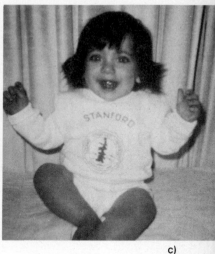

a)   b)   c)

Although all babies show the same general sequence of development, none of the achievements are rigidly fixed by the calendar. Parents who have several children will tell you that no two of them developed in exactly the same way. Yet all were healthy and intelligent. In later sections of this chapter we will refer to ages at which certain behaviors typically appear. These ages should be regarded as crude guides, since wide differences in development are normal and expected. Parents who are unaware of this wide variability will frequently make comparisons of their own children with those of a neighbor, sometimes with delight and sometimes with dismay. Neither of these reactions is necessarily appropriate. These reactions typically stem from the notion that a "normal" child will sit up, walk, and talk at specific ages. In fact, there is no clearly definable, "normal" child. Only when a particular development is extremely delayed is there cause for concern.

In the following sections we will look at some of the major landmarks in the development of the child, beginning with prenatal influences. For convenience, we have divided our discussion of child development after birth into the following stages:

1. The neonate, from birth through the first few weeks of life.

2. The first two years of life (excluding the neonate period).

3. Preschool and middle years, from two to twelve years of age.

Fig. 10.10
An infant's behavior and physical appearance undergo profound changes in short periods of time: (a) 2 days old, (b) 5 months old, (c) 8 months old. (c, Liz Muller.)

The Developing Child

Prenatal Influences

It was once believed that if the expectant mother exposed herself to certain types of situations, she could greatly influence what that child would subsequently become. Many expectant mothers became devotees of art museums, opera, and musical concerts in the expectation that these cultural activities would cause their children to appreciate the "finer things in life." When this view was repudiated, the pendulum swung in the other direction. For a while, researchers ignored the possibility of any form of prenatal influence. In short, it became a neglected area of research. However, as we indicated earlier, the child has an environment from the moment of conception. We now know that alterations in this environment can profoundly affect the developing organism. Some of the following factors may be related to later problems at birth and in infancy: the age of the mother, whether or not she has taken drugs or contracted an illness during pregnancy, her smoking and nutritional habits, and the number of previous pregnancies (see references in Parmelee and Haber, 1973). For example, when the mother contracts rubella (German measles) in the first few months of pregnancy, there is a high risk that her child will be born with a deficit such as deafness.

The developing baby-to-be is completely dependent on the mother for all its nutritional needs. Hence, it is reasonable to assume that serious deficiencies in the mother's diet will adversely affect the physical well-being of the baby. It used to be thought that the unborn baby had first claim on the nutritional resources of the mother, and that any inadequacies in her diet would be inflicted on the mother rather than on the developing child. It now appears that the opposite is true. The mother's body takes care of itself first, and then attends to the needs of the organism growing within her. Recent research has indicated that malnutrition, particularly during the fetal period, leads to an irreversible loss of brain cells in the unborn child (see Dayton, 1969, for example). Thus malnutrition in the pregnant mother may lead to permanent impairment of her offspring.

The most vulnerable children are those born into impoverished economic circumstances. Protein, so crucial to the development of the unborn child, is typically in short supply because of the prohibitive cost of high-protein foods such as

Fig. 10.11
Rooting behavior
When neonates are touched on the cheek, they turn their
head in the direction of the stimulation and try to suck the
stimulating finger. (From H. Prechtl and D. Beintema, "The
Neurological Examination of the Fullterm Newborn Infant,"
Little Clubs Clinics in Developmental Medicine, No. 12,
1964. Distributed by Heinemanns and Lippincotts.)

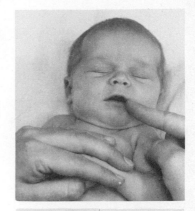

meats. Thus, many children of poverty start life with two strikes
against them. The incidence of malnutrition throughout the world
is alarming. If babies born to malnourished mothers do indeed
suffer permanent losses of brain tissue, then obviously society
must find a way to reduce malnutrition on a worldwide scale. It is
reassuring that many researchers are initiating intervention
procedures during the prenatal period and placing much emphasis
on nutrition (see Lally, 1971).

The Neonate

The newborn baby is an incompetent organism, utterly dependent
on adult intervention to terminate the nurturance previously
received through the umbilical cord and to initiate the first
breaths that signal his life as an independent individual. Within a
matter of hours, the infant is already a changed person. At this
early age, some infants appear to be capable of turning toward a
source of sound (Turkewitz et al., 1966). Before the age of two
days, most infants can follow a moving object with their eyes,
though not all the time. If an expanding shadow is cast on the
screen in such a way as to create the impression of imminent
collision (the "looming effect"), a neonate as young as two weeks
will react with alarm (Ball and Tronick, 1971). On the other hand,
if the shadow does not appear to be on a collision course, the
baby will follow the progress of the shadow with no apparent
emotion. Thus, it appears that the young neonate is not so
passive and unresponsive a creature as we used to think.

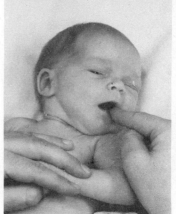

The neonate is also equipped with a number of adaptive
responses. The sucking response occurs at birth or shortly after,
and permits the infant to obtain nourishment, for the first time,
through his digestive system. When hungry, he engages in a
complex series of responses known as *rooting behavior:* he explores
his mother's body with his mouth, turns in the direction of any
tactual stimulation on the side of his face, and firmly grasps any
object on which he can obtain a hand hold (see Fig. 10.11). After
analyzing film records of this kind of behavior, one investigator
concluded that communication between mother and neonate may
be initiated by this rooting response: "The newborn has the
capacity to respond to the stimulation of its mother with activity
which orients the baby to its mother, stimulates her, and gives

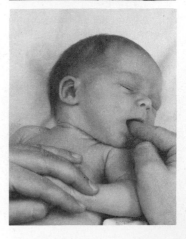

her information about the infant's 'capacities' " (Blauvelt, 1962).

The neonate's early days are spent mostly in sleep, which averages about 17 hours a day during the first three days (Parmelee et al., 1961). Two different types of sleep have been distinguished: regular sleep, with slow, even breathing and few body movements; and irregular sleep, with uneven breathing, frequent movements of the body, facial grimaces, and rapid eye movements (REM). REM sleep is more common during the neonatal period than at any later stage of life (Roffwarg et al., 1966). It thus appears that the mechanism for dreaming is present right from the very beginning.

Although neonates have many developmental characteristics in common, we should never lose sight of the fact that each baby is a unique human being. Babies come in a large assortment of colors, sizes, shapes, and weights. They also show many different behavioral characteristics. One baby may be placid and easygoing, sleeping through many different kinds of noise and commotion. Another baby may be sensitive to even slight changes, may cry frequently, and wake at the slightest noise. Some babies are difficult to hold; they wriggle and squirm and arch their bodies like a springboard. Others seem to love being held and hugged, perfectly content to cuddle up and even fall asleep in their mother's arms.

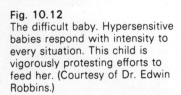
Fig. 10.12
The difficult baby. Hypersensitive babies respond with intensity to every situation. This child is vigorously protesting efforts to feed her. (Courtesy of Dr. Edwin Robbins.)

It has been estimated that about one in every ten children is hypersensitive. These children howl throughout the night, scream when they are washed, spit out their food, and reject efforts to hug and comfort them (see Fig. 10.12). Many of them grow up to be "problem" children. It is tempting to conclude that the violent

Child Development

displays of temperament during the first few days of life are more or less fixed characteristics of these infants—they become problems later on because they are problems to begin with. Such an interpretation is not necessarily valid. It is altogether too easy to forget that the difficult child may continue to be difficult *because of* the reactions he produces in his parents. A child who screams at all hours of the day and night is difficult to love. Parents may become outwardly hostile to the child, punishing him severely, or may retreat into apathy and indifference. Either alternative spells trouble for the growing child.

Several projects are under way in various sections of the country to identify the "difficult" infant and intervene early in his life. Such programs usually attempt to free the parents of their guilt-feelings about having a difficult child and to instruct them in ways to minimize frictions. Here is an example of a difficult child who, by his eighth week, had already made a shambles of his household:

> Here's a boy we've followed since 1956. We'll call him Bob. Bob was very difficult. When he was eight weeks old, he would not sleep more than half an hour at a time. He would wake up and shriek and scream for long periods.

> His mother could not stand the screaming for long. She would give in, give him a bottle. He would take it. Afterwards he would vomit. She really struggled to keep some kind of feeding schedule, but she just couldn't take the screaming. And she was distressed because he seldom smiled.

> Both parents feared he might be abnormal. We were able to reassure them. The physical and neurological exams showed that he was normal—simply very difficult.

> We advised them to handle Bob very gently and smoothly when he had to be fed and changed. This would help minimize his intense reactions. And to leave him alone the rest of the time. This was hard for them. But we told the mother that she just could not continue the pattern she was establishing. In just two weeks—of course, that's a long time in a baby's short life—she told us that Bob had become much easier to handle. And he had started to smile more often, which delighted her.*

---

*An interview reported by B. W. Wyden in "The Difficult Baby is Born That Way," *New York Times Magazine*, March 21, 1971.

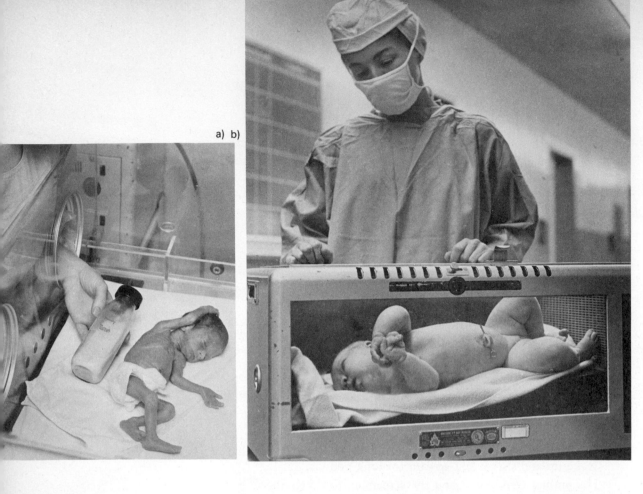

a) b)

Fig. 10.13
The premature baby. Note how small and thin the premature baby is compared to a full-term baby. (a, Photo Trends. b, Bob Mulligan—Photo Trends.)

Prematurity

Some children (approximately seven percent) arrive on the scene considerably before their expected date of birth. These premature infants are usually smaller, more fragile, and less developed physiologically than full-term babies (see Fig. 10.13). They generally require constant care and supervision, remaining in the hospital for several weeks or even months until they can be safely cared for at home. This enforced separation may impose many hardships on the parents, and may affect their attitudes toward the new baby. We have just seen how the attitude of the mother plays a significant role in the subsequent development of "difficult" children. Premature infants pose special problems of their own. It takes a while for them to catch up with full-term babies. A baby born two months early, for example, will, at four months, probably be about the same size and doing the same things as a full-term infant of two months. The following case history illustrates the reactions of a mother to her premature baby.

*Child
Development*

A 2 pound 3 ounce boy was born after a 7 month normal gestation. The cause of premature labor was unknown. He was discharged after 3 months in the hospital weighing 5 pounds 15 ounces. During these 3 months in which his mother had no contact with him except through the doctor's reports, her impression was that he was so fragile he might die at any moment. This notion was realistic in that, initially, she had been told repeatedly that his chances of survival were very slim. She wanted him to live, but hardly dared hope that he would. When she took him home, her fears concerning his survival were unchanged. She was also inclined to regard him as more rightfully belonging to the nurses and doctors at the hospital than to her. She kept herself detached from the baby and only gradually, as she realized he was going to survive, was she willing to become emotionally involved with him. She then went to the other extreme of fostering such excessive dependence that he developed a persistent fearfulness of separation from her.

(Parmelee and Liverman, 1968, p. 312)

The isolation imposed upon the premature baby may create difficulties for the baby as well as for the parents. In his sterile incubator existence, he tends to receive a minimal amount of visual, auditory, and social stimulation. It has been found that the unfavorable consequences of isolation may be counteracted by providing human stimulation, such as rocking and talking to the child (Siqueland, 1970).

No one really knows what causes prematurity. However, the incidence of prematurity seems to be highest among the lowest socio-economic classes (Parmelee and Haber, 1973). Thus, the problems of prematurity are often compounded by the generally unfavorable conditions that exist in these households—overcrowding, poor nutrition, and inadequate health care.

The First Two Years

The first two years of life are probably the most exciting to observe, since this is a time of rapid growth and development. Hardly a day passes that a perceptive mother fails to notice some physical or behavioral change in her baby. With astonishing rapidity, this helpless and largely passive creature becomes a

The Developing Child

bouncing, bubbling person, actively exploring and probing the world about him with an indomitable spirit and insatiable curiosity.

Motor development

Among the most prominent changes during the first two years are those in motor behavior, as the infant progresses from a horizontal to a vertical organism.

Early in the first year, many babies can raise their heads and elevate their chests using their arms as support. They can maintain a sitting position if sufficient support is provided. As the child progresses into the middle months of his first year, he becomes more competent in handling his body (see Fig. 10.14). He turns over, sits up, and develops considerable skill in manipulating and handling objects (see Fig. 10.15).

By the time he reaches his first birthday, he can usually walk with help, and pull himself into an upright position. Figure 10.16 shows the sequence of motor development which culminates in walking. The ages indicated reflect the norms for each particular motor skill. However, as we pointed out earlier, babies develop at different rates. One baby might begin walking as early as 10

Fig. 10.14
A six-month-old discovering her own body. (Photo by Liz Muller.)

Child Development

months, while another is just able to stand alone at 15 months. A trained observer can usually determine whether a slow rate of development is indicative of true retardation.

Once the infant has mastered the elements of walking, he spends much of his time scurrying from place to place. He falls, stumbles, and trips a great deal, but rarely injures himself seriously, because he remains loose and relaxed.

All the motor developments that take place during the first two years of life enlarge the horizons of the child. He interacts more and more with his environment as he gains greater freedom of movement.

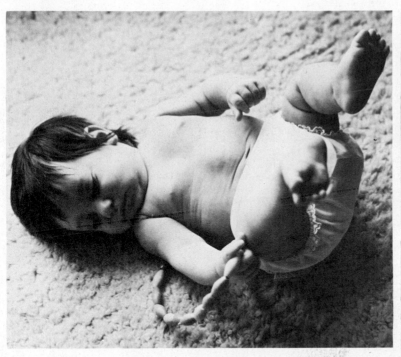
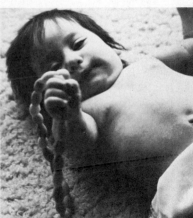
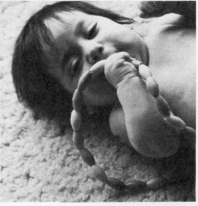

Fig. 10.15
Even as infants develop in other areas, they continue to explore their environment through their mouths. (Photos by Liz Muller.)

2 months (head up 45 degrees)

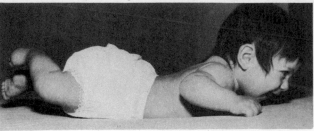

3 months
(chest up, arm support)

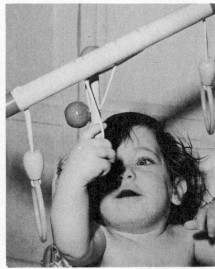

4 months
(sit with support)

5 months
(sit on lap, grasp object)

6 months
(sit on high chair, grasp dangling object)

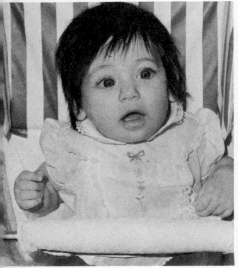

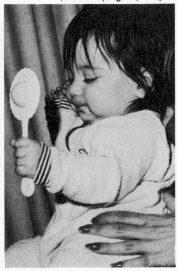

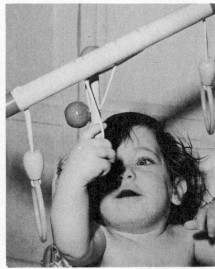

7 months
(sit without support)

8 months
(stand with help)

9 months
(stand holding furniture)

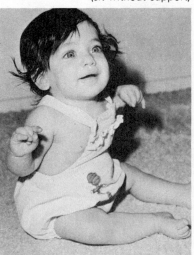

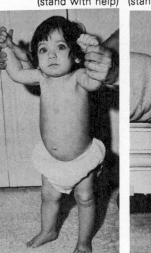

Child
Development

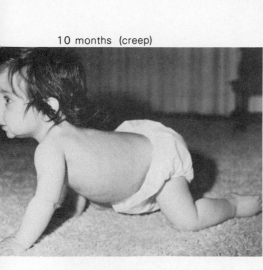

10 months (creep)

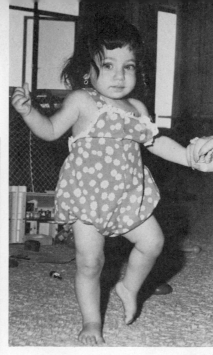

11 months
(walk when led)

12 months
(pull to stand by furniture)

13 months
(stand alone)

14 months
(walk alone)

Fig. 10.16
Sequence of posture and locomotion in infants

The ages shown are only meant to approximate the time at which these behaviors are observed in most infants in the United States. There is a wide range of individual differences. (Based on Shirley, 1933, and Frankenburg and Dodds, 1967; all photos except "2 months" and "3 months" by Liz Muller.)

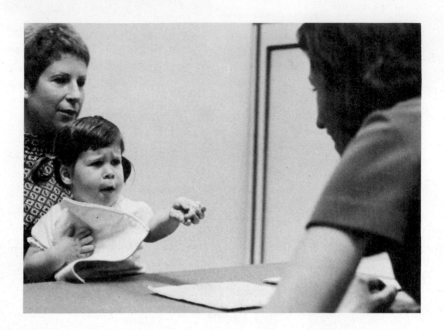

Fig. 10.17
Object permanence

This child is demonstrating her ability to find an object completely hidden under a cloth pad. (Courtesy of Arthur H. Parmelee, M.D., Director, Infant Studies Project, University of California, Los Angeles. This project is supported by UPHS contract No. 1-HD-3-2776 NICHD, "Diagnostic and Intervention Studies of High Risk Infants," and in part by grant HD-04612 NICHD, Mental Retardation Research Center, UCLA.)

*Child
Development*

Cognitive development

One of the most influential investigators of the cognitive development of children is the Swiss psychologist Jean Piaget. Piaget refers to the first two years of life as the *sensory-motor period* (Piaget, 1952). He describes a sequence of stages through which he believes all children progress. Much of the data which form the basis for Piaget's theories were obtained by observing his own three children as they developed. He combined naturalistic observation with the experimental method. Let's look at a typical example of his method.

If a child is shown an object, he may reach for it. But can the child conceive of the existence of that object when it is hidden from view? To answer this question, Piaget hid the object by throwing a piece of cloth over it to see whether the child attempted to retrieve the object from under the cloth (see Fig. 10.17). If the child did not retrieve the hidden object, Piaget assumed the child had not yet acquired a concept of permanence —the object ceased to exist once it was out of sight. Piaget found that most children developed the concept of object permanence at about the age of eight months.

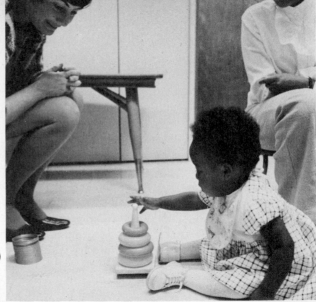

a) b)

c) d)

Fig. 10.18
Testing cognitive development

The infant in (a) is being tested on a sensory-motor scale. She must pull the pad with the toy on it. In (b), the youngster is learning spatial relationships by stacking rings on a cone. Photo (c) is another example of learning spatial relationships—this time by seeing how small objects fit in larger containers. In (d), if the child selects the correct picture, the bunny lights up. This is one of the methods used to test language. (Courtesy of Arthur H. Parmelee, M.D. See Fig. 10.17 for full credit.)

Once the child has developed the concept of object permanence, the parents may have to devise new ways of keeping forbidden objects from him. One mother reports:

Before, when I didn't want Danny to play with something, I simply hid it under a blanket or a newspaper. As soon as it was out of sight, Danny seemed to forget about it. I can't do that anymore. Now when I hide something, he either finds it or gets real upset.

According to Piaget, the child proceeds in an orderly sequence of predetermined stages from a reliance on reflexes to the development of symbolic thought. Children differ from one another in the rate, but not in the sequence of progress. In the beginning, the infant's interaction with his environment consists of little beyond the reflexes provided at birth. By the end of his first year, he develops a "theory" about his environment. For example, he will search for a missing or lost object. By the time the child reaches the final stage in the sensory-motor period, he is able to make symbolic representations of problems, and to invent solutions. The following is an example of sensory-motor invention that Piaget observed in one of his children:

> Jacqueline, at 1 year, 8 months, arrives at a closed door—with a blade of grass in each hand. She stretches out her right hand toward the knob but sees that she cannot turn it without letting go of the grass. She puts the grass on the floor, opens the door, picks up the grass again and enters. But when she wants to leave the room things become complicated. She puts the grass on the floor and grasps the doorknob. But then she perceives that in pulling the door toward her she will simultaneously chase away the grass which she placed between the door and the threshold. She therefore picks it up in order to put it outside the door's zone of movement.
>
> (Piaget, 1952, p. 339)

Piaget's theory has formed the basis for much of the testing and assessment of children's cognitive development (see Fig. 10.18 on page 369). ↳ figure changes out

Social development

One of the most delightful things to observe during this period is the infant's changing responsiveness to social stimulation. By the age of two months, the infant may bestow upon his parents his first smile in response to seeing or hearing them ("social smile"). The infant may have smiled at an earlier age, but it was more in response to internal stimuli (for example, the "gas smile"). Although the social smile has been reported as early as two weeks (Emde and Harmon, 1972), it is usually not until about the age of two months that it can be consistently elicited.

By the age of three months, many infants show a "wariness" to strangers which indicates a dawning awareness of the difference between the familiar and the foreign (Bronson, 1971). Nevertheless, most children do not clearly distinguish the mother from other familiar adults until sometime after the sixth month.

Child
Development

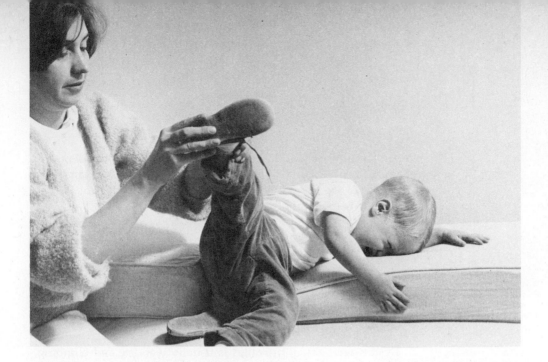

Fig. 10.19
Negativism is a not uncommon
sign of a child's growing
independence about two years
of age. (Lew Merrim—
Monkmeyer.)

Brief separation from the mother before six months of age produces no greater emotional response than separation from any other adult (Schaffer and Emerson, 1964). Somewhere around the sixth month, many infants display a marked fear of strangers (stranger anxiety). Whenever an unfamiliar person appears, the infant cries or screams and clutches at his parent. This reaction is often disconcerting to the well-meaning grandmother who comes from out-of-town for her long-anticipated visit with her grandchild. The intensity of stranger anxiety is markedly diminished if the infant has known many adults from an early age, as in the kibbutzim of Israel (Spiro, 1958).

The most dramatic changes that occur during these first two years are signaled by the child's first step and his first word. Most children speak their first real word by about the age of one year. Their ability to understand words and simple sentences expands at an incredible rate. With the advent of walking, the child now more actively explores his environment without adult assistance. He particularly enjoys playing a game in which an adult pretends to be ferociously pursuing him. At the same time that he is testing his autonomy by striking out to explore a new swing in the park, he demonstrates his dependence by rushing back and begging his mother to "Come, swing."

Perhaps the most frustrating sign of the child's growing independence is the *negativism* so frequently observed toward the end of the second year. At times, he will fight off all attempts to dress him (Fig. 10.19), refuse to obey commands, and throw

The Developing Child

temper tantrums when frustrated. Parents who accept this behavior as natural and do not attempt to fight it (for example, by spanking) are usually rewarded by a steady decline in negativistic behavior as the child grows older.

The Preschool and Middle Years

The years from two to twelve are usually subdivided into many different periods to reflect the many significant events in development that occur during this time. The years from two to five are called the preschool years, and the years from six to twelve are known as middle childhood.

By the age of two, the child is usually walking and climbing. He can scribble and open a box. During the next couple of years, we see many refinements in his skills. His walking becomes smoother and more stable. Much to the delight (and sometimes dismay) of his mother, he can help dry dishes. By the age of five, he can probably dress and bathe himself. Within the following year he may be able to print the entire alphabet and copy words. By the time he is eight or nine, he will most likely be writing script instead of printing, and may even start to develop his own style. We see the beginnings of adult reasoning in the ten- and eleven-year-old. At this age, the child stands on the threshold of adolescence.

Cognitive development

One of Piaget's most important contributions has been to explode the myth that children think the same way adults do, only not quite as well. Attempts of adults to produce educational materials for children sometimes go awry as a result of this misconception. They fail to recognize the nature of the thinking process that goes on in younger children. According to Piaget, children's thinking may follow completely different premises from those of adult thinking.

Children frequently bombard their parents with questions: Why? How? When? Parents assume that their children are asking for logical explanations when, in fact, they are unable to understand adult logic. If a child asks, "Why is it raining?" he may not be asking for a scientific explanation of precipitation. The following story was heard by the authors.

Child Development

A mother who had attended adult education classes on sex education for children was well prepared to answer any questions on sex posed by her three-year-old son. One day he asked: "Mommy, where do I come from?" The mother immediately went into a long, detailed explanation of the process of insemination, gestation, and birth. At the end of this discourse, the little boy scratched his head and said: "That's funny. Jimmy says he comes from Chicago."

According to Piaget, the child must undergo a sequence of developmental changes in his cognition before he can integrate complex concepts into a consistent logical framework. Suppose you pour the same amount of water into two identical glasses. By the age of four, the child can recognize that the two quantities are the same. Now, suppose you pour the water from one of the glasses into a tall, thin glass. Even though the young child sees you do this, he will report that the taller glass contains more water. Evidently he judges "more" in terms of height rather than quantity. It is only after the age of six or seven that most children will recognize that the quantities remain the same despite the difference in the height of the water.

Between the ages of seven and twelve, the child shows an ability to deal with logical relationships, but only if they are stated in concrete terms. For example, a child at this age would have little difficulty describing how a cat and a mouse are alike. For instance, he can report that they are both animals. But the abstract meaning of proverbs will frequently be beyond him. For example, if you ask him what the proverb "A rolling stone gathers no moss" means, he might merely rephrase the proverb in concrete terms, showing no grasp of its broader implications.

Piaget's work has stimulated extensive research throughout the world. However, Piaget is not without his critics. Many American psychologists object to the notion of an invariant sequence of developmental stages. They feel that Piaget's position tends to stress present genetic patterns while underplaying the role of environmental factors. The criticisms of Piaget, however, are directed to his theory rather than to his findings.

Language and social development

Shortly after the second year, there occurs what can only be regarded as a "language explosion" in the young child. In one study, a two-year-old child could speak 14 two-word sentences (such as "see doggie"), and six months later he was forming 2500 such combinations (Braine, 1963). This burgeoning language development opens a whole new world to him. He can convey his thoughts and feelings to others, interpret and make sense of his experiences, play word games, and invent fantasies.

Play activities undergo similar expansions. Whereas the young infant plays either by himself or with adults, beyond the age of two the child begins to play in the company of other children, playing side by side with a minimum of interaction. After the age of three, he begins to engage more in cooperative play, in which interaction is a vital element (see Fig. 10.20). A favorite form of play at this time is dressing up and acting like adults (see Fig. 10.21).

Fig. 10.20
Preschool children engage in cooperative play. (Photo by John R. Hamilton III.)

Fig. 10.21
A favorite form of play during preschool years involves doing what mommy and daddy do. (C. Wolinsky—Stock, Boston.)

During the preschool years, the child acquires a rich and
varied vocabulary, which he practices with none of the adult's
concern for social amenities. In short, he says everything that
comes to his mind:

> My four-year-old daughter was riding in the car with a
> college coed. She looked long and searchingly at the coed,
> and finally burst forth with an observation she had carefully
> formulated, "Marcia, you're ugly." "Yes, I know," Marcia
> replied with consummate patience and an acute awareness of
> her physical limitations. "God made me that way." The child
> replied with the candor only found in the preschool years,
> "God must have hated you." Needless to say, her parents
> squirmed uncomfortably throughout this exchange.

As children enter the school years, they begin to lose the
open and forthright innocence of their earlier days. They start to
practice guile and deception, forming small "in-groups" that revel
in the sharing of secrets (see Fig. 10.22).

Although the child's language abilities have increased
remarkably by the time he enters school, he often uses words
without any comprehension of their real meaning or implications.
The following story is an amusing illustration of a child's use of
words which, because of her limited experience, are meaningless
to her:

> A mother whose children had grown up returned after a lapse
> of several years to teaching first grade. During her first week
> she tried to stimulate rapport and conversation by asking the
> children to tell the group something interesting that had
> happened at home. "Interesting," to the children, apparently
> meant "unusual." They vied with each other in reports of
> how mother fell off the stepladder, the dog got run over in
> the drive, and father cut himself with the power saw and had

*The Developing
Child*

Fig. 10.23
During the middle years of childhood, same-sex play activities and peer-group formations are common. (a, Patricia Hollander Gross—Stock, Boston. b, Marion Bernstein—Editorial Photocolor Archives.)

Child Development

to have stitches. Discouraged by these accounts of carnage on the home front, the teacher changed the conversational topic for the second week. "Today," she said, "I'd like you to tell me a happy thought." There was a long silence. Then a little girl stood up; "I think I'm pregnant," she said. As this remark held no possibilities for conversation expansion, the teacher let it pass with a quiet "Thank you." It stayed in her mind, though, and that night she called the little girl's mother, who greeted her account with a gale of laughter. At breakfast that morning as she was shaking the Crispies into the children's bowls, she had said to her husband, "I think I'm pregnant." "That's a happy thought," he muttered.

(Landreth, 1967, pp. 202–203)

During these early school years, peer groups begin to assume greater importance to children than adults do. Many children form closely knit groups or "gangs" that, in many cases, establish elaborate and often secret rules and codes of conduct. The six-year-old is still somewhat of a baby and is not likely to be a full-fledged member of the "gang." He is still likely to cry easily and be regarded as a "tattle-tale." But by the time he is nine years old or so, he has become an integral member. These gangs are usually grouped by sex, and members of the opposite sex are frequently regarded with disdain or indifference (see Fig. 10.23).

Physically, girls change much more rapidly than boys during this period. Today, both boys and girls achieve sexual maturity earlier than they used to, probably because of better dietary and health practices (see Fig. 10.24). Many eleven- and twelve-year-old girls have already reached puberty, and often find that boys of the same age are too young for them.

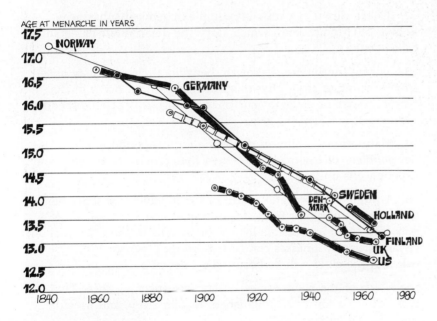

AGE AT MENARCHE IN YEARS

Fig. 10.24
Age of menarche (first menstrual period) in the U.S. and seven countries of western Europe has declined greatly from what it was 120 years ago. For example, in the mid-1840's an average Norwegian girl began menstruating at 17; today she is just over 13. The downward trend appears to be leveling off in some countries. The trend is probably chiefly due to advances in nutrition over the past century. (After "Growing Up," by J. M. Tanner. Copyright © 1973 by Scientific American, Inc. All rights reserved.)

The Developing Child

Summary

1. Each of us begins life as a single cell, a fertilized egg, which contains all the genetic information that will direct the growth of the organism throughout its life. The organism is a product of the interplay of both heredity and environment, with environmental influences beginning at the moment of conception.

2. The fertilized egg contains complex chemical substances known as chromosomes, which carry the determiners of heredity called genes.

3. During the course of growth, behavioral changes may arise from learning or from physiological changes that occur in the normal course of development (maturation). It is often difficult to distinguish between the two.

4. Maturational readiness denotes a critical period in the development of the organism, when the capacity to benefit from experience is optimal.

5. A number of prenatal conditions may adversely affect the developing embryo or fetus: for example, faulty maternal diet may lead to an irreversible loss of brain cells in the unborn child; certain drugs or illnesses contracted during pregnancy increase the risk that the child will be born with a deficit such as deafness.

6. Much of the neonate's early days are spent in sleep. Two types of sleep can be distinguished: regular sleep, and irregular sleep during which rapid eye movements are observed.

7. About one in every ten children is hypersensitive. Projects aimed at identifying such children and intervening early in their development give promise of minimizing the inevitable frictions caused by "difficult" children.

8. The first two years of life, called the sensory-motor period by Piaget, are a period of astonishingly rapid physical, motor, cognitive, and social development.

9. The ages between two and five are generally referred to as the preschool years; between six and twelve, as middle childhood.

10. A myth exploded by Piaget is that the thought processes of children are the same as those of adults. According to Piaget, the

Child
Development

child must undergo a sequence of developmental changes in his cognitions before he can integrate complex concepts into a consistently logical framework.

Terms to Remember

Chromosomes　Complex chemical substances within the cell nucleus which carry the determiners of heredity called genes.

Critical Period　The time period during which the capacity to benefit from experiences is optimal.

Embryo　The developing organism from about the second to the eighth week after conception.

Fetus　The developing organism from about the end of the second month after conception until birth.

Genes　Determiners of heredity located on the chromosomes.

Heredity　Whatever is passed on from parents to offspring through the genes (physical characteristics, personality, and so on).

Imprinting　A learning process that occurs with extreme rapidity during a critical period in the organism's life, for example, when a young duckling learns to follow its mother or any moving object.

Maturation　Biological changes that occur in the normal course of development after birth.

Maturational Readiness　The time interval during which the organism is first physically capable of acquiring a particular function or skill.

Middle Childhood　The years from age six to age twelve.

Mongolism or Down's Syndrome　A form of mental retardation associated with the presence of one extra chromosome (47 instead of the usual 46).

Negativism　Contrary behavior frequently observed in the child toward the end of the second year.

Neonate   The child from birth through the first few weeks of life.

Prenatal   The period of life before birth.

Preschool   The period from age two to age five.

Puberty   The time when children achieve sexual maturity; the onset of adolescence.

Rooting Behavior   A complex series of reflex responses occurring in the neonate; he explores his mother's body with his mouth, and turns in the direction of tactual stimulation occurring on the side of his face.

Sensory-Motor Period   The term used by Piaget to refer to cognitive development during the first two years of life.

Stranger Anxiety   A fear of unfamiliar or strange faces that develops in the infant somewhere around the sixth month after birth.

Recommended Readings

Bettelheim, B., *The Children of the Dream,* New York: The Macmillan Co., 1969.

The author describes child rearing on a kibbutz and how it differs from our system.

Elkind, D., *A Sympathetic Understanding of the Child: Six to Sixteen,* Boston: Allyn & Bacon, Inc., 1971.

A brief and informal discussion of some of the major aspects of child and adolescent development. Children are viewed in the context of the social relationships in which they live and learn.

Erikson, E. H., *Childhood and Society,* New York: W. W. Norton and Co., Inc., 1963.

A detailed statement of Erikson's theory of child development.

Kagen, J., *Understanding Children: Behavior, Motives, and Thought,* New York: Harcourt Brace Jovanovich, Inc., 1971.

Presents current psychological knowledge and ideas about children.

Lavatelli, C. S., and Stendler, F. (Eds.), *Readings in Child Behavior and Development* (3rd ed.), New York: Harcourt Brace Jovanovich, Inc., 1972.

A collection of theoretical statements and articles that reflect significant research and development in the field.

Lefrancois, G. R., *Of Children,* Belmont, California: Wadsworth Publishing Co., 1973.

A delightful, highly readable text on child development.

Mussen, P. H. (Ed.), *Carmichael's Manual of Child Psychology* (3rd ed.), 2 vols., New York: John Wiley & Sons, Inc., 1970.

Discusses the latest research findings on the biological basis of development, infancy and early experience, cognitive development, and child psychopathology.

Piaget, J., and Inhelder, B., *The Psychology of the Child,* New York: Basic Books, Inc., Publishers, 1969.

A concise summary of Piaget's theory of child development.

Stone, L. J., and Church, J., *Childhood and Adolescence* (3rd ed.), New York: Random House, Inc., 1973.

Comprehensive textbook on developmental psychology.

11
INTELLIGENCE

What is intelligence?

Measuring intelligence

Stanford–Binet test of intelligence
The Wechsler tests — Group tests
Requirements of a test

The value of intelligence testing

The tyranny of intelligence testing

The constancy of IQ
Intelligence: nature or nurture?

Extremes in intelligence

The mentally retarded
The mentally gifted

Creativity and intelligence

Aptitude and special tests

What Is Intelligence?

You have probably used the word "intelligent" many times in your life. What precisely do you mean when you say that someone is intelligent, or not so intelligent? Do you think your friends would agree with your concept of intelligence? Ask some of your friends, "What do you mean by intelligence?" You may be surprised at the number of different answers you get. Even psychologists have had a difficult time agreeing on a definition of intelligence. Some psychologists stress the ability of the individual to adapt to new situations and to profit from previous experiences. Others regard intelligence as a cluster of various types of abilities, such as reasoning, memory, verbal fluency, and competence with numerical concepts. Still other psychologists view intelligence as scholastic aptitude, the ability to do well in school.

The lack of universal agreement on a scientifically precise definition of intelligence often obscures a fairly basic agreement regarding the nature of the concept. For example, who would doubt that the individual described below showed a high level of intelligence?

> At the age of three, John Stuart Mill had learned the entire Greek alphabet and was able to translate long lists of Greek words into their English equivalents. By the age of twelve, he had mastered many of the Greek classics in their original form including the various philosophical treatises of Plato and the scientific writings of Aristotle. Before he was fifteen, he had studied chemistry, botany, mathematics, Latin and French. As an adult he wrote many scholarly books encompassing such diverse fields as history, law, and logic.

Similarly, most of us would agree that the person described below is *not* intelligent:

> At the age of three, William R. had not yet spoken his first word. By the age of fifteen, he was capable of communicating only simple thoughts and ideas. Moreover, he had difficulty comprehending reading materials beyond the second grade level. As an adult, he could obtain employment only in situations in which considerable supervision was required.

Note that in neither of these cases was intelligence directly observed. Like so many other phenomena we study in psychology, intelligence is a construct which we infer from behavior. Often these inferences are based on informal observations of the behavior of others. We listen to a person speak and, for reasons that are often difficult to pin down, we conclude that he is bright, average, or dull. A person who does well in school or in business is commonly judged intelligent. Another who experiences difficulties in school or who fails to climb the ladder to success in business is considered less intelligent. However, such informal judgments are usually based on only limited observations of behavior, under widely varying conditions, and do not permit precise comparisons of different individuals at different ages.

In effect, the psychologist formalizes many of the behavioral criteria by which we judge intelligence and provides an objective basis for comparing individuals. The various tests of intelligence represent the culmination of many years of effort along these lines. Although, as we shall see, these efforts have not been an unqualified success, tests of intelligence have had a major impact on education, counseling, and related fields.

Many psychologists define intelligence as what intelligence tests measure. Although this operational definition may appear circular, it does take into account all the factors that were investigated in the course of constructing the intelligence tests, and this is a fairly broad range of factors. Let's look at the way in which intelligence is measured.

Measuring Intelligence

Stanford–Binet Test of Intelligence

Around the turn of the century, the Paris schools faced a severe problem of overcrowding. Moreover, French educators had long been aware that many children did not seem to benefit from traditional educational experiences. These children swelled classroom enrollment and interfered with the progress of the other children. It had been assumed that these children were simply perverse, and that the only way to deal with them was to inflict punishment and humiliation. But these methods had not solved the problem. Continued failure of punitive methods prompted many educators to take a different view. Perhaps some children were not capable of benefitting from traditional education. If these children could be identified, they could be placed in special educational settings. A French psychologist, Alfred Binet, devised a test to identify such children. The test met with immediate success and was the precursor of many subsequent measures that have come to be known as intelligence or IQ tests.

In devising his original scales of intelligence, Binet started with the assumption that, on the average, the older children were, the better they would perform on his test. Moreover, a set of norms could be established defining average performance for each age group. Binet established his norms by grouping together items that a majority of children at a given age could pass. Thus, if a four-year-old could pass all the items at the six-year level, his mental age was six. Since his mental age exceeded his chronological age, he would be considered bright. On the other hand, if a child with a chronological age of six could pass all the items at the four-year level but none beyond, he had a mental age of four and would be considered dull.

Fig. 11.1
Alfred Binet. (National Library of Medicine, Bethesda, Maryland.)

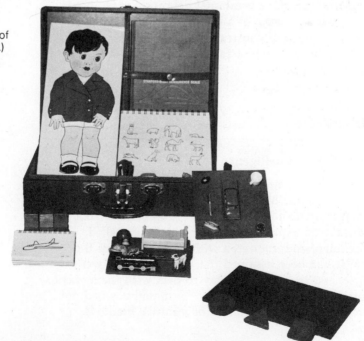

Fig. 11.2
Materials used in the Stanford–Binet test of intelligence.

The original Binet scale has undergone many revisions since it was introduced in 1905. The most famous revisions were accomplished at Stanford University, and the scales resulting from these revisions are known as the Stanford–Binet intelligence scales. Figure 11.2 shows some of the Stanford–Binet materials. Each child is tested individually, and there are a number of items at each age level. The child receives credit for each item he is able to answer correctly. The examiner continues to administer the test at progressively higher age levels until the child misses all the items at a particular age level. Box 11.1 shows some of the items from several different age levels.

Age Level	
Three-year	Copy a circle
Four-year	Why do we have houses?
Five-year	Copy a square
Six-year	What is the difference between a bird and a dog?
Seven-year	In what way are wood and coal alike?
Eight-year	What should you do if you found on the streets of a city a three-year-old baby that was lost from its parents?
Nine-year	What is foolish about: "Bill Jones' feet are so big that he has to pull his trousers on over his head."
Ten-year	What is grief?
Eleven-year	In what way are a knife-blade, penny, and a piece of wire alike?

Box 11.1
Sample items at various age levels from the Stanford–Binet Intelligence Scale, 1960 revision. (Reproduced by permission of the publisher, Houghton Mifflin Company.)

The concept of intelligence quotient (IQ) was introduced in one of the Stanford–Binet revisions. IQ reflects the relationship between chronological age (CA) and mental age (MA). By applying a single formula, it is possible to obtain a score that allows comparison of intellectual functioning among children of the same as well as different ages. Let's calculate the IQ's of the four-year-old with a mental age of six, and of the six-year-old

Measuring Intelligence

387

with a mental age of four. The IQ's are obtained from the following formula:

$$IQ = \frac{MA}{CA} \times 100.$$

Thus, the IQ of the four-year-old is

$$IQ = \frac{6}{4} \times 100 = 150$$

and the IQ of the six-year-old is

$$IQ = \frac{4}{6} \times 100 = 67.$$

When MA = CA, IQ = 100, which is the average IQ for the population. Figure 11.3 shows the distribution of IQ's on the 1937 Stanford–Binet revision.

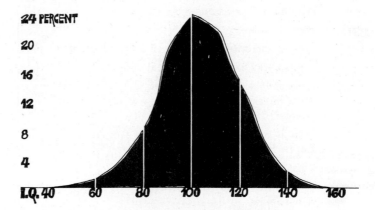

Not all intelligence quotients are defined in the same way. For adults and late adolescents, the concept of mental age is no longer appropriate. Some psychologists believe that mental growth, like physical growth, does not continue throughout life. Sometime during the adolescent years, the individual stops growing, both physically and mentally. Other psychologists argue that mental growth continues well beyond adolescence, and that what appears to be stabilization is artificial and merely reflects inadequacies in test construction. Whatever the case may be, there is relatively little growth in mental age beyond the

Intelligence

388

adolescent period as measured by intelligence tests. Consequently, there are several tests with a "derived" IQ score. The performance of individuals of the same age is compared, and certain statistical manipulations are performed so that the average score is 100. Thus, individuals who score on a par with their age level will obtain an IQ score of 100. An individual who performs considerably better than his age peers will have an IQ considerably above 100.

Although the Stanford–Binet remains one of the most widely used and respected instruments for measuring intelligence, it has several limitations. First, it is highly verbal in nature and tends to discriminate against those who have difficulties with the English language. In addition, it is of questionable value when employed with adolescents and adults. Moreover, since it yields only one overall index of intellectual performance, there is no way to assess the specific strengths and weaknesses of the person tested.

The Wechsler Tests

As we have pointed out, the Stanford–Binet intelligence test tends to discriminate against individuals who have limited use of the English language. The following case illustrates the difficulty of assessing the intelligence of a person who has a pronounced language handicap:

> Martha P., a friendly, highly motivated, and cooperative girl of twelve, had emigrated from Russia at the age of nine. Only Russian was spoken in her home. On the Stanford–Binet test, she received an IQ score of 96, well within the normal range. Nevertheless the test administrator received the distinct impression that her performance did not truly reflect her intellectual ability. A subsequent detailed analysis of the test results suggested that her language handicap may have impaired her performance. A few examples shed light upon the extent of this handicap. In the vocabulary, she made only four correct responses. Approximately one-half of those children with a chronological age of eight years get at least eight vocabulary words correct. Thus Martha, who was nearly twelve years of age, apparently had an English vocabulary of less than eight years. The types of errors Martha made are also quite revealing. For tap she replied "spinning thing" (obviously

Table 11.1
Comparison of some of the
characteristics of the
Stanford–Binet and Wechsler
tests.

Box 11.2
Verbal and performance subtests
of the WAIS with simulated
sample items. (Courtesy of The
Psychological Corporation.)

STANFORD-BINET	WECHSLER TESTS
INDIVIDUALLY ADMINISTERED, HIGHLY VERBAL	INDIVIDUALLY ADMINISTERED, BOTH PERFORMANCE AND VERBAL MEASURES
PRIMARILY FOR CHILDREN	SCALES FOR BOTH CHILDREN (WISC) AND ADULTS (WAIS)
YIELDS ONE OVERALL SCORE	YIELD VERBAL AND PERFORMANCE I.Q.'s PLUS PROFILES IN VARIOUS CATEGORIES
BASED ON "MENTAL AGE" CONCEPT	"DERIVED" I.Q.

Verbal Subtests

Sample Items*

Information

How many wings does a bird have?
Who wrote "Paradise Lost"?

General Comprehension

What is the advantage of keeping money in a bank?
Why is copper often used in electrical wires?

Arithmetic

Three men divided eighteen golf balls equally among themselves. How many golf balls did each man receive?
If two apples cost 15¢, what will be the cost of a dozen apples?

Similarities

In what way are a lion and a tiger alike?
In what way are an hour and a week alike?

Vocabulary

This test consists simply of asking, "what is a _____?" or "what does _____ mean?" The words cover a wider range of difficulty or familiarity.

Performance Subtests

Description of Item

Picture Arrangement

Arrange a series of cartoon panels to make a meaningful story.

Picture Completion

What is missing from these pictures?

Block Assembly

Copy a design with blocks.

Object Assembly

Put together a jigsaw puzzle.

Digit Symbol

1	2	3	4
X	III	I	0

Fill in the symbols:

3	4	1	3	4	2	1	2

*Examples given are similar to those used on WAIS Test.

thinking of top), in spite of the fact that she had the printed word in front of her. Similarly, for muzzle she replied "mixed up," obviously thinking of muddle. Based upon many examples of this sort, it was concluded that Martha's intelligence was probably much higher than the test score indicated.

Wechsler tests were developed to deal with difficulties of this sort. Although the original test was designed to assess adult intelligence, later versions also included a separate test for children. Like the Stanford–Binet, these tests are individually administered. The Wechsler tests still in use include the Wechsler Adult Intelligence Scale (WAIS) and the Wechsler Intelligence Scale for Children (WISC). The outstanding difference between the Wechsler tests and the Stanford–Binet is probably the addition of items not dependent on verbal ability (performance items). In fact, the WAIS and WISC are constructed to yield separate verbal IQ and performance IQ measures, as well as an overall IQ score. The IQ scores are derived measures, computed from tables. They do not represent a relationship between mental and chronological age. Table 11.1 summarizes characteristics of the Stanford–Binet and the Wechsler scales.

The WAIS and WISC contain very similar subtests. However, the WISC is designed for children aged five to fifteen, and the WAIS is used for people above the age of sixteen. Box 11.2 shows the various subtests of the WAIS and a sampling or description of items from each subtest.

Group Tests

Many of you probably remember taking a group test of intelligence sometime during your school career. You may have experienced many of the frustrations that are characteristic of any group testing situation. Perhaps you were not feeling well that day, or perhaps you did not understand some of the instructions. When large groups take a test, it is usually difficult for the individual to get any kind of attention or help. The examiner usually finds it impossible to deal with individual problems that may arise during the test. This is not to say that group tests have no value, but rather to caution you against putting too much weight on any one individual's performance on a group test.

Measuring
Intelligence

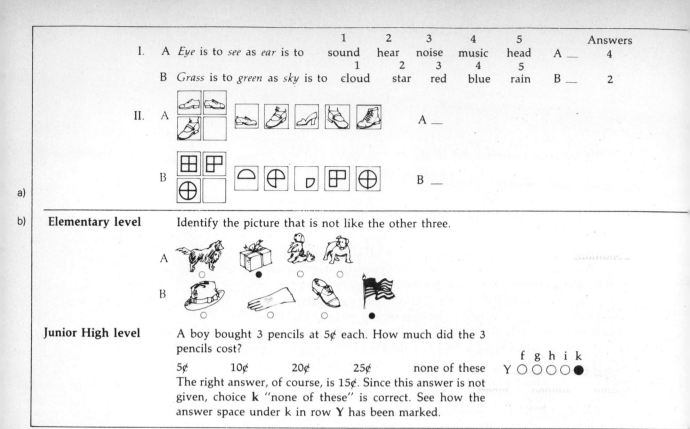

			1	2	3	4	5		Answers
I.	A	*Eye* is to *see* as *ear* is to	sound	hear	noise	music	head	A __	4
	B	*Grass* is to *green* as *sky* is to	cloud	star	red	blue	rain	B __	2

a)

II. A
    A __

B
    B __

b)

Elementary level

Identify the picture that is not like the other three.

A

B

Junior High level

A boy bought 3 pencils at 5¢ each. How much did the 3 pencils cost?

5¢   10¢   20¢   25¢   none of these

f g h i k
Y ○ ○ ○ ○ ●

The right answer, of course, is 15¢. Since this answer is not given, choice **k** "none of these" is correct. See how the answer space under k in row **Y** has been marked.

The following story, though not necessarily typical of the problems that may arise when a single group test is used to assess an individual's level of intelligence, may serve as an example of the type of thing that can happen when individual identity is lost:

Donald J. was a student in the eighth grade in a large metropolitan school system. At a given time and date, all children throughout the system were administered a group test of intelligence. Just prior to the test, Donald was summoned to the principal's office to discuss his eligibility to receive honors at a forthcoming graduation exercise. When he returned to the classroom, the testing had already been in progress for a period of time. The teacher handed him a copy of the test and told him to complete it before the time limit had expired. Since Donald had not received instructions on the taking of the tests, he doodled on the answer sheet instead of filling in the various alternatives. When he arrived at high school the following year, he was surprised to learn that his request for a precollege curriculum had been disapproved. Instead, he was assigned to a class of children who were experiencing all manner of mental and emotional difficulties. He remained in this special educational setting, in

Intelligence

Do the following sample problems:

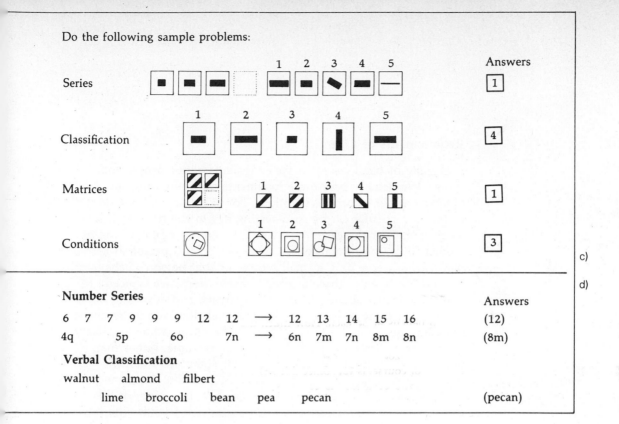

Series

Classification

Matrices

Conditions

Answers

1

4

1

3

c)

d)

Number Series

| 6 | 7 | 7 | 9 | 9 | 9 | 12 | 12 | → | 12 | 13 | 14 | 15 | 16 |

Answers (12)

| 4q | | 5p | | 6o | | 7n | → | 6n | 7m | 7n | 8m | 8n |

(8m)

Verbal Classification

walnut   almond   filbert

lime   broccoli   bean   pea   pecan

(pecan)

which more emphasis was placed upon the students' deportment than upon their scholastic growth.

Two years later, the city again required all of its students to take a group intelligence test. A few weeks later, Donald was again summoned into the principal's office. After checking his signature against the one appearing on the test form, the high school officials acknowledged that a serious error had been made. His test scores of two years ago had suggested that Donald was severely retarded; his most recent score placed his performance beyond that of most college graduates. When the circumstances of the first test were revealed by Donald, he was immediately placed in a precollege high school program. Subsequently, he graduated with distinction from college and is generally acknowledged as successful in his chosen profession.

Group intelligence tests are valuable primarily in large screening programs, where it is not possible to administer an individual test to each person. These tests are often used for selection purposes, such as in a military setting to identify individuals best suited for training in various specialties. Box 11.3 presents examples of items from several of the more widely used group intelligence tests.

Box 11.3
Sample items from some widely used group intelligence tests.
a) Kuhlmann–Finch junior high school test items. (Courtesy of Dr. Frank H. Finch and Dr. Frederick Kuhlmann, and the publisher, American Guidance Service.)
b) Otis–Lennon Mental Ability Test items for elementary school and junior high school. (From Otis–Lennon Mental Ability Test, copyright © 1967 by Harcourt Brace Jovanovich, Inc. Reproduced by special permission of the publisher.)
c) IPAT Culture Fair Intelligence Test items. (Copyright © 1957 by the Institute for Personality and Ability Testing, Champaign, Illinois. Reproduced by permission.)
d) Lorge–Thorndike Intelligence Test items. (Reproduced by permission of the publisher, Houghton Mifflin Company.)

Requirements of a Test

Every day of our lives we make judgments about people and things. We usually base these judgments on limited information obtained under informal conditions. For example, we may decide to buy a particular car by road-testing it. On the basis of this small sample of the car's "behavior," we are, in effect, trying to predict future performance. Or, when we meet a person at a party, we observe only a small sample of that person's behavior. Yet, on the basis of these informal observations, we typically make judgments about personality, interests, and even intellect. We rely on these observations, despite their limitations, because it is usually not practical to carry out all the observations necessary to provide a firm basis for judgment. For example, rather than take a course with a particular instructor completely "on the blind," most students try to get some information about the instructor and the course in order to predict their own, or the instructor's, future performance. They may ask friends who have had this particular instructor; they may note his grade distrubutions at the end of the previous semester; or they may even sit in on one of his classes.

We are all aware of the pitfalls of these informal types of observation. Yet the more formal testing procedures used in psychology and education are much like these informal methods. They also rely on limited samples of behavior in an attempt to predict future performance. However, formal testing is expected to meet several specific requirements.

Objectivity

A good test must be objective. This means that the scoring of the test should be free of the influence of subjective and personal factors. When different people score the same test, they should come up with the same test score for each individual.

Reliability

Suppose that you rely on your alarm clock to wake you at seven o'clock every morning to get to class on time. If your alarm clock is working properly (and you hear it), it will ring at seven o'clock and wake you up. But what if it is defective? Perhaps sometimes it runs slow. Even though you set it for seven o'clock, it actually rings at eight. At other times, it runs fast and you find yourself getting up at the crack of dawn.

A good test, like a good alarm clock, must be reliable; that is, it must yield consistent results. We can determine the reliability of a test in several different ways. We can compare the performance of the same individual on two different occasions, using the same or alternate forms of the test. We can compare his performance on two halves of the same test by comparing his performance on all the odd-numbered items with his performance on all the even-numbered items. If the test is reliable, the scores compared in these ways should be nearly identical.

Validity

A test is said to be valid if it measures what it purports to measure. This definition implies that, for an intelligence test to be valid, it must actually measure intelligence. However, as we have already pointed out, intelligence is not directly observed but must be inferred from behavior. Consequently, there is no direct method to demonstrate that an intelligence test is *really* measuring intelligence. The best we can do is determine that an intelligence test is measuring some aspect of *behavior* that we generally acknowledge as "intelligent" behavior. For example, an underlying assumption of most early intelligence tests was that intelligence is involved in the ability to do schoolwork. Indeed, many tests of intelligence were validated by showing that IQ scores predicted scholastic achievement. With these considerations in mind, we might say that a test is valid if it predicts performance in a criterion situation.

We will distinguish between two types of validity, both of which relate test performance to some criterion measure. To clarify the distinction, let's look at a hypothetical example. Let's imagine that we have developed a physiological measure which we believe will permit an extremely rapid assessment of intelligence. How might we go about determining the validity of this claim?

Predictive validity. It is generally accepted that scholastic performance reflects, in large part, the operation of intelligence. If our physiological measure permitted us to predict the future scholastic performance of subjects, we would have reason to accept the measure as a valid indicator of intelligence.

*Measuring
Intelligence*

a)
b)

Fig. 11.4
Do you think the girl in (a) had the same set of childhood experiences as the two little girls in (b) are having? If not, how do you think this might affect her ability to perform on an IQ test? What if most of the IQ tests she takes are standardized on populations whose experiences *are* similar to the two little girls'? (a, Norman Hurst—Stock, Boston. b, Harrison—Photo Trends.)

Intelligence

Concurrent validity. Suppose we selected three groups of individuals who we could agree represented three different levels of intellectual functioning. One group, for example, might consist of college professors; another, of high school graduates; and a third, of high school dropouts. If the physiological measure is a valid instrument for assessing intelligence, we would expect the professors to obtain the highest scores on this measure, and the high school dropouts the lowest. This method is called concurrent validity because it compares the scores on the new measure with an already existing criterion of intellectual performance (the number of years of education successfully completed).

In order to be valid, a test instrument must be reliable. For instance, suppose that a high score on an intelligence test leads to the prediction of superior school performance, and a low score to the prediction of poor school performance. If the test was not reliable, then the same individual might score high on one day and low on the next. How could we make valid predictions about his school performance? On the other hand, a test can be perfectly reliable, but have no validity at all. For example, the length of a person's big toe can be reliably measured, but it is unlikely to provide a valid basis for predicting school performance.

Standardization

A score by itself is meaningless. It takes on meaning only when it can be compared to some known standard. Most tests are standardized. They are administered to some large and representative group of people selected at random, and tested under comparable conditions. The resulting scores are subjected to acceptable statistical procedures, and norms, or standards, are devised. Any individual's score can be compared to these norms. The method of selecting individuals to make up the standardization group is extremely important in any application of these norms to specific individuals. Most tests of intelligence in the United States have been standardized on a white, English-speaking, urban school population, and thus their norms are of questionable value for interpreting the scores of individuals outside this group. We shall have more to say about this problem in later sections of this chapter.

The Value of Intelligence Testing

Intelligence test results have been used extensively in the field of education. This is reasonable, because the validity of intelligence tests is frequently established on the basis of performance in a formal educational setting. It was recognized early that IQ test scores provide a generally valid basis for ascertaining the individual's *present* level of intellectual functioning. This is particularly true of IQ tests administered individually.

Resourceful teachers have recognized the value of providing graded educational experiences for children at different levels of intellectual functioning. It is useful to know that a particular child is unusually bright, so that he can be stimulated with new and exciting materials at the level he is capable of handling. Otherwise, he may retreat into boredom and view school as a dull, unexciting sequence of tedious exercises. He may start using his intellect to invent ways of avoiding school or, if this fails, he may end up disrupting class routines. On the other hand, if more is demanded of a child than he is capable of delivering, he may come to fear school and he, too, may become a disruptive influence in the classroom.

The various group intelligence tests have been used extensively in the field of education. As we pointed out earlier, the use of group tests for individual diagnostic purposes is questionable. However, these tests have often been used to screen large numbers of individuals in order to identify those with possible intellectual problems. Those individuals so identified can then be referred for individual testing.

Both the military and private industry have long recognized the value of group intelligence tests for personnel screening. Some of the earliest success in this area was achieved by the military, starting as early as World War I. In World War II, the Army General Classification Test (AGCT) was employed as one of the bases for selecting candidates for Officer Training School. Considerable success was achieved, as you can see in Fig. 11.5. You may recall that one way of determining the validity of a test is to see how well it predicts success and failure. The AGCT was particularly good in this respect. A greater percentage of those who scored high on the AGCT were successful in receiving their commissions than those who scored low.

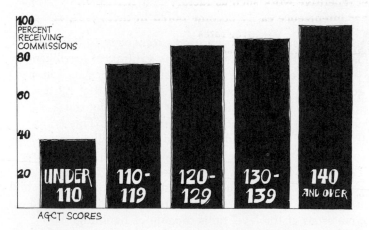

Fig. 11.5
The relationship between the Army General Classification Test (AGCT) and success in officer candidate school during World War II. Note that the higher the score on the AGCT, the greater the percentage of men who were successful in receiving their commission (Boring, 1945).

Today, many corporations administer group intelligence tests as a standard aspect of personnel selection and classification. These tests are part of a battery of psychological tests. The aim is not necessarily to select the most intelligent person, but rather to provide a match between level of intellectual functioning and the requirements of the job. A person may be overqualified, that is,

Intelligence

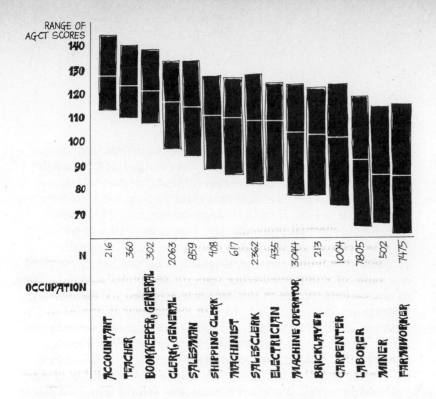

RANGE OF
AGCT SCORES

| N | 216 | 360 | 302 | 2063 | 859 | 408 | 617 | 2562 | 435 | 3044 | 213 | 1004 | 7805 | 502 | 7475 |

OCCUPATION: ACCOUNTANT, TEACHER, BOOKKEEPER, GENERAL, CLERK, GENERAL, SALESMAN, SHIPPING CLERK, MACHINIST, SALESCLERK, ELECTRICIAN, MACHINE OPERATOR, BRICKLAYER, CARPENTER, LABORER, MINER, FARMWORKER

Fig. 11.6
IQ and occupation

The range of AGCT test scores for several occupational groups. Each bar shows the range of scores for the middle 80 percent —the lowest and highest 10 percent are not shown. The horizontal white lines show the middle scores for each occupational group. Half score above and half score below this point. (After *Differential Psychology* by A. Anastasi. Copyright © 1958 by The Macmillan Company. Used by permission of Macmillan Publishing Co., Inc.)

too intelligent to find the job challenging and stimulating. Many studies have found that people of lower intelligence adapt best to routine, repetitive work such as factory and clerical work. Persons of higher intelligence easily become bored in these jobs, and have higher absentee and turnover rates.

Figure 11.6 shows the distribution of IQ's for various occupations. It is interesting that, although the average IQ of farm workers and miners is considerably lower than that of accountants and teachers, there is some overlapping. In other words, some farm workers score higher than some accountants. It appears that a certain minimum intellectual ability is necessary for entering a given occupational field. The fact that some individuals score much higher than the majority of others in the same field suggests that factors other than intelligence operate in job selection.

The Tyranny of Intelligence Testing

In the preceding section, we were careful to emphasize the fact that IQ scores are useful insofar as they provide insight into an individual's present level of intellectual functioning. The IQ score is not some magical number that stays with a person through a lifetime, fixed and immutable. Failure to recognize this fact has

The Tyranny of Intelligence Testing

led to much misunderstanding and many injustices. Individuals are often pigeonholed early in life—"borderline" IQ, "normal," "potential genius"—and it is often difficult for them to escape. A teacher sees a recent measure of a child's IQ on the transcript and notes that it is low. He adjusts his expectations of the child's academic performance accordingly. This is as it should be. However, the teacher should not label the child marginally educable for all time. Indeed, if he is a good teacher, he recognizes that the score is only an *estimate* (and therefore subject to error) of the student's *present* level of intellectual functioning. Throughout the school year, he will continually revise his estimate of the child's level of functioning in accordance with careful observations of his classroom progress. Once a teacher says, "His IQ is too low; I can teach him little," he is abdicating the responsibility of his profession, and is making the child the unknowing victim of a misunderstanding. An IQ score, we repeat, is not a magical number which, like a person's given name, will remain with him for life.

Students and parents have similar difficulties. One reason for the reluctance of a psychologist or guidance counselor to reveal an IQ score is the awareness that the score will often be misinterpreted and occasionally misused. One of the authors recalls the proud proclamation of an undergraduate acquaintance, an attractive girl of 18: "My IQ is 135; I don't have to study." Her statement was prophetic rather than diagnostic. She received a letter from the dean, at the end of her freshman year, encouraging her to seek matriculation elsewhere.

There are other characteristics of intelligence tests that limit the generality of their applications. As we pointed out earlier, most IQ tests used in the United States are highly verbal in nature, and they are typically standardized on English-speaking populations. Moreover, they are constructed by middle-class professionals and reflect middle-class values and morality. There is consequently a built-in bias favoring white, English-speaking, middle-class children. We shall return to this problem later in the chapter.

The Constancy of IQ

Earlier we defined reliability in terms of the consistency with which an instrument yields measurements or scores. The fact that

IQ tests are reliable (that is, yield similar scores for the same individual on two different occasions) has led many people to proclaim that the IQ is constant. If an individual obtains a score of 105 at age four, it is assumed that he will obtain a score of 105 at age twenty, plus or minus a few points due to error in the test. Such an assumption confuses short-term repeatability of measures with long-term predictability. Let's look at an analogy.

If you measure the weight of a two-year-old child on two successive days, you will receive consistent measures—that is, the test is reliable. What is more, the measures will validly reveal differences between several two-year-old children who differ in weight. How successful do you think you would be in predicting their adult weights? Similarly, how accurate do you think you would be in predicting the adult IQ of a child of two? The truth is that neither measure would accurately predict an adult value from a childhood measure. Just as the rate of change in physical growth fluctuates considerably before adult weight is reached, so also does IQ. One way to establish this fact is to measure changes in IQ of a group of individuals who achieved identical scores at an earlier age (see Fig. 11.7). It is readily apparent that gross errors in judgment would occur if we assumed that IQ remains

Fig. 11.7
Constancy of IQ

Four children with identical IQ scores at age 7 were retested annually over a period of ten years. Note the fluctuation in IQ for each child and the widespread differences that ultimately emerged. (Adapted from *Educational Psychology in the Classroom* by H. C. Lindgren. Copyright © 1956 by John Wiley & Sons, Inc.)

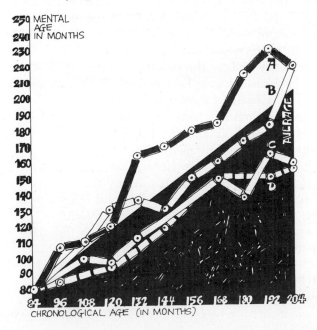

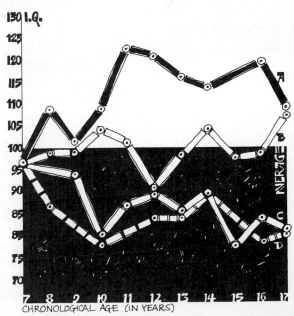

401

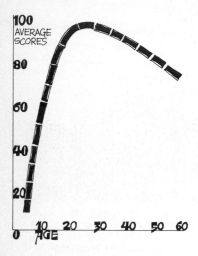

Fig. 11.8
Age and IQ

The scores shown in this figure represent the average score obtained by individuals at various ages. Note the declining scores obtained beyond the age of about thirty. (Adapted from *The Measurement and Appraisal of Adult Intelligence* by David Wechsler. Copyright © 1958 by The Williams & Wilkins Co., Baltimore.)

Intelligence

constant throughout life.

Proponents of the position that IQ is constant point to the fact that the IQ score predicts adult intelligence with greater accuracy, the closer the child is to adulthood. This finding is not surprising; but it does not lend weight to the assumption that IQ is constant. Whatever the forces are that determine the ultimate level of adult intelligence, these forces have been at work longer in the older child. If intelligence is negatively affected by an intellectually unchallenging environment, the cumulative effects will be greater in a ten-year-old child than in, say, a five-year-old. His score at age ten will, therefore, more closely approach his adult score.

The tyranny of IQ testing arises whenever a test result blinds us to the plasticity of the human organism. When we plan the lifelong course of a child's education on the basis of an early assessment of his intelligence, we may be doing him a grave injustice. If the IQ score reveals that the child has "low normal" intelligence, the parents, the teacher, and the child himself may conclude that there is not much of a future for this child in the intellectual sphere. The child may receive few inducements to intellectual growth, and considerable encouragement to make do with his limited abilities. In many cases, his later lack of accomplishment is simply a self-fulfilling prophecy.

To observe that the IQ measures of many individuals fluctuate over time is not to deny the fact that some individuals show fairly stable performance over long periods of time. What factors cause some individuals to show quite dramatic changes with age, while others remain relatively constant? Later in this chapter, we discuss changes in intellectual functioning that occur as a result of changes in the environment.

Certain changes in intellectual functioning are clearly related to the maturing and aging of the individual. Many studies have shown that intellectual abilities increase steadily and reach a peak somewhere between the ages of twenty and thirty (Wechsler, 1958). After the age of thirty, there is a gradual decline through old age. This is particularly true for performance items in which speed is crucial. However, the rate of this decline varies from individual to individual. Figure 11.8 shows the average scores on the WAIS obtained by individuals at different ages.

Fig. 11.9
Sir Francis Galton. (National
Library of Medicine, Bethesda,
Maryland.)

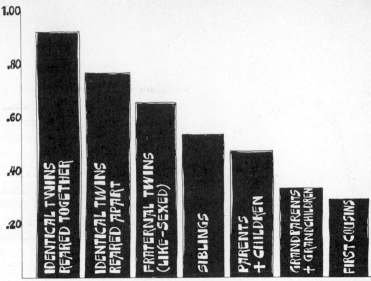

IDENTICAL TWINS REARED TOGETHER
IDENTICAL TWINS REARED APART
FRATERNAL TWINS (LIKE-SEXED)
SIBLINGS
PARENTS + CHILDREN
GRANDPARENTS + GRANDCHILDREN
FIRST COUSINS

Intelligence: Nature or Nurture?

Closely related to the view that IQ is constant is the position that
intelligence is genetically determined. The reasoning goes
something like this: "If IQ is determined at the moment of
conception, it must, like eyes, hair, and skin color, remain
constant throughout the individual's life." Fluctuations in IQ
similar to those reported in Fig. 11.5 must represent testing errors
—aberrations due to the conditions of testing, the state of health
of the person tested, and momentary factors such as mood,
anxiety, and motivation.

   More than a hundred years ago, Francis Galton, a pioneer in
the study of individual differences, made some observations that
became the focus of the nature–nurture controversy. He found
that men of accomplishment had many more distinguished
relatives than did an equal number of "average" people. He
concluded that this phenomenon was due to heredity, that
intelligence "runs in the family." Later studies have uncovered
similar evidence. If intelligence is genetically determined, then
individuals who are close relatives should show greater
similarities in their intelligence than individuals who are distantly
related or unrelated. Identical twins should show the greatest
similarity.

   In fact, many studies have reported the relationship between
degree of family relatedness and similarity of IQ test scores.
Figure 11.10 shows that there is a greater degree of similarity in
the IQ's of people who are closely related (siblings, parents and

Fig. 11.10
IQ and family relatedness

This figure shows an increasing
similarity of IQ scores with
increasing degrees of genetic
relatedness. The degree of
relationship is expressed in terms
of a statistical measure, the
correlation coefficient. The
higher the coefficient, the
greater the similarity in IQ's.
Thus, identical twins (reared
together) show the greatest
similarity in their IQ scores, and
first cousins show the least.
Unrelated individuals would
show a zero correlation (Burt,
1958; McNemar, 1942;
Newman et al., 1937).

*The Tyranny
of Intelligence
Testing*

403

children) than of those who are more distantly related (for example, first cousins). Note that the greatest degree of similarity is found in the IQ's of identical twins.

Some of the evidence used to support the position that intelligence is genetically determined can also be used to support the opposing position, if considered from a slightly different point of view. Look again at Fig. 11.10. Note that the IQ's of identical twins raised together are more alike than the IQ's of identical twins raised separately. If IQ's were determined strictly by genetic factors, then the IQ's of identical twins should be the same, no matter where and how they were raised. Similarly, fraternal twins are no more alike genetically than are any other siblings. Therefore, their IQ's should show the same degree of similarity as those of ordinary siblings. The fact that the relationship is higher for fraternal twins may be due to greater similarities in environment among fraternal twins than among siblings of different ages.

Additional support for the role of environmental factors comes from studies which show that city children score higher on IQ tests than do children from rural areas. There are many factors that might explain this difference. Some psychologists have argued that many intelligence tests contain items that are more familiar to a city child than to a child brought up on a farm. However, there is evidence to suggest that the difference in IQ's may be due to the fact that city schools were generally superior to rural schools at the time these studies were conducted. In one study, Southern-born black children who moved to Philadelphia showed significant gains in IQ test scores, whereas the mean IQ's of children born and raised in Philadelphia remained about the same (Lee, 1951).

It is clear that environmental factors do indeed play a crucial role in the intellectual development of a child. The most striking evidence comes from studies in which dramatic changes in IQ have occurred as a result of changes in environment. One investigator extensively studied 25 orphanage children. The IQ's of these children were ascertained early in life. Thirteen of these children were later moved from the orphanage to a state institution for retarded children. The IQ's of the children transferred to the state institution generally showed dramatic increases (see Fig. 11.11). In one case, the increase was 58 points (Skeels, 1966).

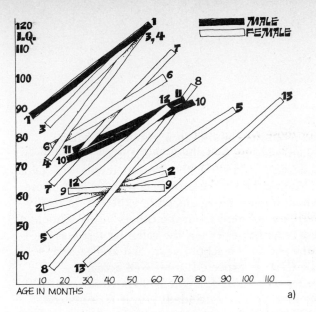

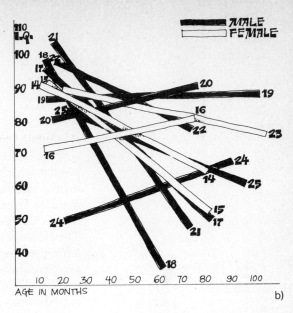

a)

b)

It may seem strange to regard a change from an orphanage to an institution for retarded children as a favorable change of environment. The fact is that the change was a very substantial improvement in the environment of these children. The children in the orphanage were given little more than custodial care, whereas those in the state institution received individual care from the nurses and even from the older retarded inmates. Although all 25 of these children were originally considered unfit for adoption, 11 of those transferred were eventually adopted, while none of those remaining in the orphanage were ever adopted. Moreover, all 13 of the transferred children grew up to lead normal adult lives. Only four of the orphanage children could be described as leading somewhat normal adult lives; only one managed to complete high school and obtain skilled employment.

What about the home environment? Bright parents tend to have bright children; and dull parents, dull children. Twenty-point differences in IQ have been found between children of professional parents and those of unskilled laborers (McNemar, 1942). This evidence has been regarded as support for the role of heredity. However, these data can be viewed in another way. Brighter parents are more likely to provide stimulating intellectual environments for their children and to stress the acquisition of those abilities that IQ tests measure. For example, children of professional parents are likely to be exposed to a rich and varied verbal environment.

The school situation is another aspect of a child's intellectual environment. One provocative study focused on the effects of teacher expectations on IQ scores. A group test of intelligence

Fig. 11.11
IQ and environment

a) Most of the children who went from an orphanage to a state school (poorer to better environment) showed dramatic increases in their IQ test scores. b) The majority of children remaining in the orphanage showed decreases in their IQ test scores. (From Vandenberg, 1968; based on data from Skeels, 1966.)

The Tyranny of Intelligence Testing

was administered to all the children in a public elementary school. The teachers were led to believe that the test could predict which children would show the greatest intellectual gains during the year. The teachers were provided with a list of those children from whom the greatest gains were expected. In reality, these children were no different from the others in the school. The findings were remarkable. When the same IQ test was administered at the end of the school year, first and second graders whom the teachers expected to do well actually performed far better than those for whom there were no such expectations. The investigator concluded: ". . . if teachers can, then probably healers, parents, spouses, and other ordinary people also can affect the behavior of those with whom they interact by virtue of their expectations of what that behavior will be" (Rosenthal, 1966, p. 412).

Children from impoverished backgrounds usually do poorly on intelligence tests. It used to be thought that children from these backgrounds were lazy or stupid. This view was consistent with the notion of racial and ethnic differences in intelligence that are determined by genetic factors. The idea that certain racial and ethnic groups inherit lower intelligence gets apparent support from the fact that, for the most part, these groups do differ in terms of achievement. They generally do not perform very well in school, and they rarely achieve positions of prominence in our society. Can these differences be attributed to genetic factors? If these children had equal opportunities to acquire the skills, experiences, and concepts measured in intelligence tests, we might be justified in concluding that racial and ethnic differences are indeed genetic in origin. However, as long as the majority of blacks, Puerto Ricans, Mexican-Americans, and Indians grow up in environments lacking these opportunities, we cannot attribute IQ differences to heredity. The poor performance of these groups may be, in part, a self-fulfilling prophecy—their parents, teachers, and the community in general expect them to do poorly, and so they fulfil these expectations.

There is another bias that bears repeating. Intelligence tests are, for the most part, made up by middle-class people using middle-class language experiences and concepts. In other words, IQ tests have a built-in bias that discriminates against children from different subcultures. For example, black children raised in

1. A "Gas Head" is a person who has a: (a) fast moving car; (b) stable of "lace"; (c) "process"; (d) habit of stealing cars; (e) long jail record for arson.

2. If you throw the dice and "7" is showing on the top, what is facing down? (a) seven; (b) "snake eyes"; (c) "boxcars"; (d) "little Joes"; (e) eleven.

3. Cheap chitlings (not the kind you purchase at a frozen food counter) will taste rubbery unless they are cooked long enough. How soon can you quit cooking them to eat and enjoy them? (a) 15 minutes; (b) 2 hours; (c) 24 hours; (d) 1 week (on a low flame); (e) 1 hour.

4. "Bird" or "Yardbird" was the "jacket" that jazz lovers from coast to coast hung on: (a) Lester Young; (b) Peggy Lee; (c) Benny Goodman; (d) Charlie Parker; (e) "Birdman of Alcatraz."

5. Hattie Mae Johnson is on the County. She has four children and her husband is now in jail for non-support, as he was unemployed and was not able to give her any money. Her welfare check is now $286.00 per month. Last night she went out with the highest player in town. If she got pregnant, then nine months from now how much more will her welfare check be? (a) $80.00; (b) $2.00; (c) $35.00; (d) $150.00; (e) $100.00.

6. A "handkerchief head" is: (a) a cool cat; (b) a porter; (c) an Uncle Tom; (d) a hoddi; (e) a preacher.

7. "Money don't get everything it's true_____." (a) but I don't have none and I'm so blue; (b) but what it don't get I can't use; (c) so make do with what you've got; (d) but I don't know that and neither do you.

8. Which word is out of place here? (a) splib; (b) Blood; (c) grey; (d) Spook; (e) Black.

9. How much does a short dog cost? (a) $0.15; (b) $2.00; (c) $0.35; (d) $0.05; (e) $0.86 plus tax.

10. Many people say that "Juneteenth" (June 10) should be made a legal holiday because this was the day when: (a) the slaves were freed in the USA; (b) the slaves were freed in Texas; (c) the slaves were freed in Jamaica; (d) the slaves were freed in California; (e) Martin Luther King was born; (f) Booker T. Washington died.

Answers: 1(c), 2(a), 3(b), 4(d), 5(a), 6(c), 7(b), 8(c), 9(a), 10(b).

Box 11.4
The "chitling" test. (From Lewis R. Aiken, Jr., *Psychological and Educational Testing.* Copyright © 1971 by Allyn and Bacon, Inc. Used by permission.)

the ghetto acquire concepts and language that are not tested in traditional IQ tests. A black sociologist, Adrian Dove, devised his own IQ test (the "Chitling Test") in a half-serious attempt to show that "we're just not talking the same language." Box 11.4 presents 10 items from this test. See how well you can do.

Extremes in Intelligence

Extremes in Intelligence

When you look at the distribution of IQ scores for a large number of randomly selected people, you usually find a wide range of values. There is a pattern to this distribution. Most people score around the middle of the distribution, and relatively few at the extremes. You can see this pattern in Table 11.2, which presents the distribution of IQ scores on the WAIS, with the descriptive terms applied to the various categories. On the basis of this table, in the population of the United States there should be about 4½ million people who can be classified as very superior and an equal number who can be classified as mentally retarded.

Table 11.2
Distribution of adult IQ scores on the Wechsler Adult Intelligence Scale. (From *The Measurement and Appraisal of Adult Intelligence* by David Wechsler. Copyright © 1958 by The Williams & Wilkins Co., Baltimore.)

I.Q.	VERBAL DESCRIPTION	% OF ADULTS
BELOW 70	MENTALLY RETARDED	2.2
70-79	BORDERLINE	6.7
80-89	DULL NORMAL	16.1
90-109	AVERAGE	50.0
110-119	BRIGHT NORMAL	16.1
120-129	SUPERIOR	6.7
ABOVE 130	VERY SUPERIOR	2.2

The Mentally Retarded

Although it is generally accepted that people with IQ's below 70 are mentally retarded, there are wide differences in the degree of retardation. Box 11.5 describes the characteristics of people with various degrees of retardation at different ages.

Take a few moments to contrast the characteristics of people in the "mildly retarded" group with those in the "profoundly

Intelligence

Degree of Mental Retardation	Preschool Age 0–5 Maturation and Development	School Age 6–20 Training and Education	Adult 21 and over Social and Vocational Adequacy
Profound (I.Q. below 20)	Gross retardation; minimal capacity for functioning in sensori-motor areas; needs nursing care.	Some motor development present; may respond to minimal or limited training in self-help.	Some motor and speech development; may achieve very limited self-care; needs nursing care.
Severe (20–35)	Poor motor development; speech is minimal; generally unable to profit from training in self-help; little or no communication skills.	Can talk or learn to communicate; can be trained in elemental health habits; profits from systematic habit training.	May contribute partially to self-maintenance under complete supervision; can develop self-protection skills to a minimal useful level in controlled environment.
Moderate (36–52)	Can talk or learn to communicate; poor social awareness; fair motor development; profits from training in self-help; can be managed with moderate supervision.	Can profit from training in social and occupational skills; unlikely to progress beyond second grade level in academic subjects; may learn to travel alone in familiar places.	May achieve self-maintenance in unskilled or semi-skilled work under sheltered conditions; needs supervision and guidance when under mild social or economic stress.
Mild (53–69)	Can develop social and communication skills; minimal retardation in sensori-motor areas; often not distinguished from normal until later age.	Can learn academic skills up to approximately sixth grade level by late teens. Can be guided toward social conformity.	Can usually achieve social and vocational skills adequate to minimum self-support but may need guidance and assistance when under unusual social or economic stress.

retarded" category. Most mildly retarded people are capable of taking care of themselves and even performing some kind of gainful employment. However, people who are profoundly retarded are almost certain to spend their lives under close supervision and custodial care. The fact that mild retardation does not necessarily incapacitate an individual in all areas is strikingly illustrated in the case of a teenage boy with an IQ of about 55 who is a noted concert organist. Although he has some difficulty in performing such everyday activities as dressing and buttoning his clothes, he was achieved proficiency on seven different musical instruments. He has memorized over a thousand different songs, and composed about 40 of his own.

Box 11.5
Developmental characteristics of the mentally retarded. (Reprinted by permission of The President's Committee on Mental Retardation, Washington, D.C.)

Extremes in Intelligence

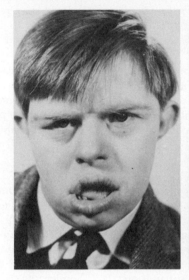

Fig. 11.13
Mongolism has genetic origins. (Reproduced by permission from R. F. Tredgold and K. Soddy, *Tredgold's Mental Retardation*, 11th edition (1970), published by Bailliere, Tindall & Cassell Ltd. and published in the U.S.A. by the Williams & Wilkins Company, Baltimore.)

Fig. 11.12
Cretinism can have prenatal origins. (Illustration from a mid-nineteenth century book on cretinism; National Library of Medicine, Bethesda, Maryland.)

Intelligence

What causes mental retardation? Before we try to answer this question, we must first point out that mental retardation is not a single disorder. Rather, it is a symptom of a large number of different conditions that affect the functioning of the individual. Thus, there are many causes of mental retardation, and most of them are still poorly understood. There are factors operating before birth that may lead to deficient intellectual functioning; these include infections contracted by the mother during pregnancy, or drugs and other toxic agents taken by the mother while carrying the child. Some forms of retardation, such as mongolism, are caused by genetic factors (see Fig. 11.13). Brain injuries during birth are responsible for a small percentage of cases. Finally, there are factors operating after birth that may lead to retardation. Certain infectious diseases, accidents resulting in brain damage, or diets deficient in substances vital for normal

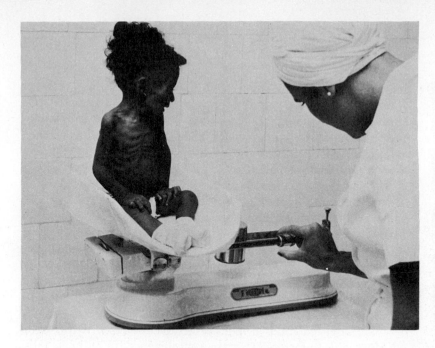

Fig. 11.14
Mental retardation can result
from a protein-deficient diet. This
one-year-old child who weighs
only nine pounds is suffering the
consequences of such a diet.
(Jean Speiser, UNICEF.)

development may cause retardation (see Fig. 11.14). Sometimes, the symptoms of mental retardation are observed in children raised under adverse environmental conditions.

The Mentally Gifted

The most comprehensive and long-term studies of the intellectually gifted were conducted under the general supervision of Lewis M. Terman. Approximately 1500 children with IQ's of 140 or higher were selected in 1921, and have been studied up to the present. The purpose of the study was to identify the characteristics of the mentally gifted and to follow their progress to see how they developed as adults. This study contradicted many popular misconceptions about the mentally gifted. You have probably heard people talk about "the thin line between genius and insanity." Many people stereotype the very bright as skinny, bespectacled bookworms. Terman's studies revealed that these mentally gifted children were better than average in emotional stability, physical health, and height and weight. Moreover, their academic and occupational accomplishments have become legendary. Approximately 90 percent of them attended

*Extremes in
Intelligence*

Fig. 11.15
Women have the same IQ distribution as men. Why do
you think fewer of them ever become distinguished
scientists, artists, politicians, or industrialists? (Reg. Innell
—Photo Trends.)

college. Although they were, on the average, about two years
younger than their classmates, they won three times as many
honors. When studied 25 years later, 150 out of 700 were judged
"very successful" by criteria such as holding responsible
managerial positions, or being listed in *Who's Who* or *American
Men of Science* (Terman, 1925; Terman and Oden, 1947, 1959).

It is evident that the mentally gifted make important
contributions to our society. Yet, if you were to look at the
names of people of accomplishment in the sciences, literature,
politics, and industry, you would find very few women's names
among them. Since the distribution of IQ's among women closely
parallels that of men, there are just as many mentally gifted
women as men. Therefore, on the basis of numbers alone, we
would expect better representation of women on the lists of
distinguished people.

Not all gifted children live up to their promise. At this point,
we must look to factors other than intelligence for an explanation.
It is not uncommon for a very bright girl to quit school to take
care of her home and family (see Fig. 11.15). Many would-be
career women "drop out" rather than fight the battle for equal
recognition in fields dominated by men. It is indeed sad that
society loses almost 50 percent of its potential pool of intellectual
and creative talents.

Creativity and Intelligence

As we have seen, IQ tests can identify people who are highly
intelligent. Yet many of these people are not characterized by an
ability to come up with new and creative ideas. Think for a
moment. Do you know people you would call "creative"? Why
would you call them creative? What characteristics or abilities do
they have? Now think of the people you consider "intelligent."
Are they creative? The distinction between creativity and
intelligence is an intriguing question.

A noted investigator of creativity distinguishes two classes of
thinking, convergent and divergent. *Convergent thinking* involves
the ability to arrive at a conclusion "in accordance with truth and
fact." *Divergent thinking* has more to do with the ability to see

Intelligence

new and unusual relationships that are nevertheless appropriate to the problem situation (Guilford, 1967). Many people view the creative person as characterized by divergent thinking. A test that is often employed to evaluate creativity involves unusual uses for common objects (Guilford, 1954). For example, what are the various uses of a shoe? A convergent thinker is likely to answer by citing the conventional use of a shoe—to protect your feet when you are walking. A divergent thinker may come up with such uses as a hammer, a bed for a doll, a drinking vessel, an ashtray, or a surface to draw on.

Researchers in the area of creative thinking believe that the conventional IQ test and formal education stress convergent rather than divergent thinking (Wallach, 1970). Since convergent and divergent thinking represent different and quite unrelated abilities, it may be argued that individuals with creative talents go unrecognized and largely ignored in our society (see Pankove and Kogan, 1968; Wallach and Wing, 1969). Indeed, an individual with too many new and unusual ideas may be regarded, in many settings (including the classroom), as a nuisance.

Many tests have been devised to measure creativity. Figures 11.16 and 11.17 show the different types of responses made by creative individuals and by randomly selected subjects on two tests of creativity.

Fig. 11.16
Welsh Figure Preference Test

Subjects are asked to state a preference for a series of drawings. Randomly chosen individuals tended to prefer the figures shown on the left, whereas creative individuals preferred the figures on the right. (Reproduced by special permission from the Welsh Figure Preference Test by George S. Welsh, Ph.D. Copyright 1949, published by Consulting Psychologists Press, Inc.)

Fig. 11.17
Drawing-completion test

Subjects were asked to elaborate on the set of line drawings shown at the far left. Randomly chosen individuals produced sets of drawings like the one shown second from the left. The two right sets of drawings were produced by creative individuals (Barron, 1958).

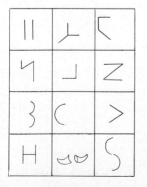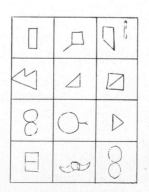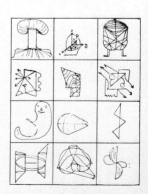

Aptitude and Special Tests

"What do you want to be when you grow up," a doting aunt asks her little nieces and nephews. "A truck driver," "An architect," "A teacher," they reply with little deliberation, and whirl off to engage in the thousand-and-one activities that capture the attention of early school-age children. The same question, with variations, will be repeated on countless occasions throughout their childhood by mother, father, teachers, clergymen, relatives, and friends. With each passing year, the question will take on added significance. Before too long, the little nieces and nephews have reached the age of serious decision making. And this very decision may be the most important one they will ever have to make. It they successfully appraise their own skills and motivations and the employment opportunities in whatever line of work they choose, they will receive deep satisfaction from the activities that will occupy approximately one-third of their adult waking hours. On the other hand, failure to obtain a happy match between their abilities and their interests may lead to a lifetime of dissatisfaction, disappointment, and frustration. What is more, chronic dissatisfaction with their work will contaminate every aspect of their lives, social and personal as well as occupational.

Psychologists have labored for many years to devise tests that can help people make career decisions. Many people have no need of these tests, since they can arrive independently at a choice that is consonant with their own abilities and interests. Other people are confused about their own motivations and are unable to identify areas of strength that relate to job opportunities. Some of these people seek the advice of professional counselors who, through the skillful use of tests and interviews, may be able to help identify sources of strength and weakness relative to various vocational goals.

The two broad classes of tests commonly used by vocational counselors involve the assessment of aptitudes and of interests.

Aptitude tests attempt to measure the individual's capacity to become proficient in a given activity or occupational field. You are probably already familiar with the Scholastic Aptitude Test (SAT), which predicts students' aptitude for college-level study. When used for occupational counseling, the objective of aptitude tests is to identify and isolate those skills and abilities required

Numerical Ability

Select the correct answer.

Add	13	A	14
	12	B	25
		C	16
		D	59
		E	None of these

Subtract	30	A	15
	20	B	26
		C	16
		D	8
		E	None of these

a)   b)

c)

Space Relations

Which one of the four figures can be made by folding the pattern shown?

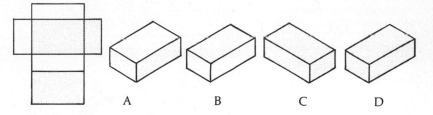

A   B   C   D

Answer: D

Fig. 11.18
Aptitude tests

a) One part of a widely used test of manual dexterity. The subject is required to insert a bolt in each hole and place a rivet over the bolt.

b and c) Sample items from a test of vocational aptitude that measures eight different ability areas. The sample items have been taken from two of the areas. (Reproduced by permission. Copyright © 1947, 1961, 1962 by The Psychological Corporation, New York, N.Y. All rights reserved.)

by various occupations. Presumably, people whose performance on those tests show them to possess the abilities demanded by a particular line of work are more likely to succeed in that line of work than people who do not show these abilities. Unfortunately, however, aptitude tests have not enjoyed the success in predicting occupational outcomes that intelligence tests have had in predicting scholastic performance. Figure 11.18 presents samples from two of the more widely used aptitude tests.

It is almost a truism that aptitude alone will not guarantee success and satisfaction in a given occupation. Certainly

Aptitude and Special Tests

Box 11.6
Two sample items from the Kuder Preference Record. The subject must choose from among three alternatives the one he likes best and the one he likes least. (From *Kuder Preference Record,* Form Bl, copyright 1948 by G. Frederic Kuder. Reprinted by permission of the publisher, Science Research Associates, Inc.)

Fig. 11.19
Kuder Preference Profile
The Kuder Preference Profile shown was obtained from a college student named Mary. "... The high Mechanical, Computational, and Clerical scores suggest a liking for routine, uncreative activities. When questioned about office work, Mary enthusiastically described her previous summer's work as a file clerk; her duties apparently consisted solely of alphabetizing folders, yet she had just loved it. Moreover, she had done well in secretarial training courses. Evidently both ability and interest fell in an area she had not considered a vocational goal." (Diagram "Kuder Profile of Mary Thomas" from *Essentials of Psychological Testing,* 3rd edition, by Lee J. Cronbach, Harper & Row, 1970. Based on *Kuder Preference Record,* Vocational Form C, copyright 1950 by G. Frederic Kuder. Used by permission of the publisher, Science Research Associates, Inc.)

Intelligence

motivations and interests are also of great importance. Many tests are designed to assess interest patterns as they relate to occupational fields. One of the most widely used of these is the Kuder Preference Record. Box 11.6 presents some sample items from this test. Figure 11.19 presents a sample profile from the Kuder Preference Record obtained by a single subject.

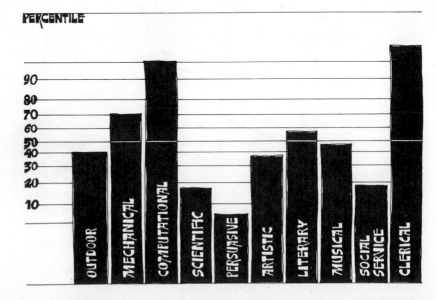

Summary

1. Intelligence is not directly observed, but must be inferred from aspects of the behavior of people. The psychologist formalizes many of the behavioral criteria by which we judge intelligence and provides an objective basis for comparisons among individuals.

2. The most famous and widely used revision of the original Binet scale, the Stanford–Binet intelligence scales, introduced the concept of IQ. The Stanford–Binet test is individually administered, is highly verbal in nature, and yields a single overall index of intellectual performance.

3. The Wechsler tests are also individually administered, but provide two separate estimates of intelligence (verbal and performance) as well as an overall IQ. However, these IQ scores are derived measures, computed from tables.

4. Group tests of intelligence may best be used in large screening programs, where it is not possible to administer an individual test to each person. Because of the limitations of such tests, their usefulness for individual diagnostic purposes is minimal.

5. The formal tests used in the fields of psychology and education attempt to obtain samples of aspects of an individual's behavior from which predictions of future behavior may be made. A good test must be (1) objective, (2) reliable, (3) valid, and (4) standardized.

6. IQ tests have been used advantageously in educational, military, and industrial settings. In industry, the intelligence test is frequently used as part of a battery of tests in an effort to find a match between individual interests and capabilities and the requirements of the job.

7. The fact that IQ scores are reliable has led many people to proclaim that the IQ is constant. Such a view confuses short-term repeatability of measures with long-term predictability, and ignores the plasticity of the human organism.

8. Closely related to the view that IQ is constant is the position that intelligence is genetically determined. The question of the

heritability of intelligence is complicated by the fact that most IQ tests are standardized on middle-class populations, and use middle-class language and concepts.

9. At both extremes of the distribution of IQ scores is a small proportion of individuals whose intellectual functioning is either so impaired that they can be considered retarded, or so advanced that they can be regarded as intellectually gifted.

10. Long-term studies of the intellectually gifted have dispelled many popular notions concerning their physical health and emotional stability: mentally gifted children are, as adults, better than average in emotional stability, physical health, and height and weight.

11. Distributions of IQ scores of men and women are closely parallel. The fact that so few women in our society have risen to positions of prominence in the sciences, literature, politics, and industry suggests the operation of cultural factors.

12. Studies of creativity suggest the possibility of two broad classes of thinking: convergent thinking, presumably tested in IQ scales; and divergent thinking, which involves the ability to see new and unusual relationships that are appropriate to a problem situation.

13. Psychologists have devised several tests to help people who are assailed by doubts concerning career or vocational objectives. Some of these tests attempt to measure the individual's capacity to achieve proficiency in a given activity or occupational field (aptitude tests). However, since aptitude alone will not guarantee success and satisfaction in a given occupation, other tests have been devised to assess interest patterns as they are related to occupational fields.

Terms to Remember

Aptitude Tests Instruments designed to measure an individual's capacity to achieve proficiency in a given activity or occupational field.

Convergent Thinking   Thinking that involves the ability to arrive at a conclusion "in accordance with truth and fact."

Derived IQ Score   The average score on an intelligence test for a given age group is set equal to 100; individuals who score on a par with their age level will obtain an IQ score of 100.

Divergent Thinking   Thinking that involves seeing new and unusual relationships that are appropriate to a problem situation.

Intelligence   The ability to adapt to new situations and to profit from previous experiences when confronted with new situations or problems; some people define intelligence as what intelligence tests measure.

Intelligent Quotient (IQ)   The individual's mental age divided by his chronological age and multiplied by 100: $IQ = (MA/CA) \times 100$.

Mental Age (MA)   The individual's score on an intelligence test based on a norm; an MA of 7 means that the individual has performed as well as the average seven-year-old.

Mental Retardation   Below-normal intelligence; generally, an IQ of 70 or less.

Mongolism   Mental retardation associated with genetic factors and manifested in certain physical characteristics as well as deficient intelligence.

Objectivity   In a test, the degree to which scoring is free of the influence of subjective and personal factors.

Reliability   The degree to which a test yields consistent results each time it is taken.

Standardization   The process by which norms, or standards, are obtained for comparing individual scores; a test is administered under comparable conditions to some large and representative group.

Validity   The extent to which a test predicts performance in a criterion situation.

Recommended Readings

Recommended Readings

Ahmann, J. S., and Glock, M. D., *Evaluating Pupil Growth: Principles of Tests and Measurements* (4th ed.), Boston: Allyn & Bacon, Inc., 1971.

Comprehensive discussion of the problems and techniques of evaluation.

Aiken, L. R., *Psychological and Educational Testing,* Boston: Allyn & Bacon, Inc., 1971.

Comprehensive textbook on the background and methodology of testing and contemporary issues and developments.

Blatt, B., *Exodus from Pandemonium: Human Abuse and a Reformation of Public Policy,* Boston: Allyn & Bacon, Inc., 1970.

Cites evidence of common, systematic, and shocking abuses perpetrated today in institutions for the mentally retarded.

Clarizio, H. F., Craig, R. C., and Mehrens, W. A., *Contemporary Issues in Educational Testing* (3rd ed.), New York: Harper & Row, Publishers, 1970.

Part IV deals with controversial issues in testing.

Cronbach, L. J., *Essentials of Psychological Testing* (3rd ed.), New York: Harper & Row, Publishers, 1970.

This comprehensive text provides a thorough review of psychological testing procedures and techniques.

DuBois, P. H., *A History of Psychological Testing,* Boston: Allyn & Bacon, Inc., 1970.

Comprehensive treatment of the history of testing.

Hutt, M. L., and Gribby, R. G., *The Mentally Retarded Child: Development, Education and Treatment* (2nd ed.), Boston: Allyn & Bacon, Inc., 1965.

A thorough treatment of mental retardation in children.

Robinson, H. B., and Robinson, N. M., *The Mentally Retarded Child,* New York: McGraw-Hill Book Co., 1965.

Discusses the origin, diagnosis, treatment, and everyday problems of mental retardation.

Thompson, T., and Grabowski, J., *Behavior Modification of the Mentally Retarded,* New York: Oxford University Press, Inc., 1972.

Discusses the application of operant conditioning techniques to the education of the mentally retarded.

PSYCHOLOGY ISSUES

C.
The Nature/Nurture Controversy

The nature/nurture controversy is one of the oldest and most hotly debated issues in psychology. It started in 1869 when Sir Francis Galton applied Charles Darwin's evolutionary theories to human intelligence. Galton (who also happened to be Darwin's cousin) observed that intellectual ability varied widely and, furthermore, that certain kinds of excellence seemed to run in families.

The articles in this *Issue* provide a sampling from the many writings on both sides of the controversy. The first two articles are excerpts from classic books in psychology: Henry H. Goddard's *Kallikak Family: A Study in the Heredity of Feeble-Mindedness* (1914) and John B. Watson's *Behaviorism* (1924). They are excellent examples of the kind of single-minded logic that has tended to characterize the controversy. The third article was published in 1969 and shows that the subject is far from closed, even now.

Goddard traced two family lines descended from a common ancestor ("Martin Kallikak") through six generations. One line resulted from Martin's marriage to a "respectable girl of good family" and consistently produced "good representative citizenship" — "doctors, lawyers, judges, educators, traders, landholders. . ." The other line resulted from Martin's affair with a feebleminded tavern girl and produced quite the opposite type of humanity — prostitutes, alcoholics, criminals, and feebleminded individuals. Goddard's data, like Galton's before him, was genealogical. He completely ignored the environmental differences that existed between the two branches of descendants.

Watson, on the other hand, was a behaviorist and completely rejected the notion of inherited mental traits; he believed that intelligence and all other tendencies and talents are shaped by environmental influences. Watson did admit that inherited physical structure may limit the ability to shape behavior, but his basic thesis was that "our hereditary structure lies ready to be shaped in a thousand different ways — the same structure — depending on the way in which the child is brought up."

The third article in this feature is a short section from an article that brought the nature/nurture controversy into the public arena by causing a storm of critical protest when it was published in late 1969. Arthur Jensen's article — "How Much Can We Boost IQ and Scholastic Achievement?" — claimed, among other things, that genetic factors contribute about 80 percent to IQ while all other factors together contribute only 20 percent. Jensen's findings are still the subject of heated debate which has exploded outward from the academic community.

THE KALLIKAK FAMILY

BY HENRY H. GODDARD

The foregoing charts and text tell a story as instructive as it is amazing. We have here a family of good English blood of the middle class, settling upon the original land purchased from the proprietors of the state in Colonial times, and throughout four generations maintaining a reputation for honor and respectability of which they are justly proud. Then a scion of this family, in an unguarded moment, steps aside from the paths of recti-

From Henry H. Goddard, *The Kallikak Family: A Study in the Heredity of Feeble-Mindedness*, New York: The Macmillan Company, 1914.

tude and with the help of a feeble-minded girl, starts a line of mental defectives that is truly appalling. After this mistake, he returns to the traditions of his family, marries a woman of his own quality, and through her carries on a line of respectability equal to that of his ancestors.

We thus have two series from two different mothers but the same father. These extend for six generations. Both lines live out their lives in practically the same region and in the same environment, except in so far as they themselves, because of their different characters, changed that environment. Indeed, so close are

they that in one case, a defective man on the bad side of the family was found in the employ of a family on the normal side and, although they are of the same name, neither suspects any relationship.

We thus have a natural experiment of remarkable value to the sociologist and the student of heredity. That we are dealing with a problem of true heredity, no one can doubt, for, although of the descendants of Martin Kallikak Jr. many married into feeble-minded families and thus brought in more bad blood, yet Martin Jr. himself married a normal woman, thus demonstrating that the defect is transmitted through the father, at least in this generation. Moreover, the Kallikak family traits appear continually even down to the present generation, and there are many qualities that are alike in both the good and the bad families, thus showing the strength and persistence of the ancestral stock.

The reader will recall the famous story of the Jukes family published by Richard L. Dugdale in 1877, a startling array of criminals, paupers, and diseased persons, more or less related to each other and extending over seven generations.

Dr. Winship has undertaken to compare this family with the descendants of Jonathan Edwards, and from this comparison to draw certain conclusions. It is a striking comparison, but unfortunately not as conclusive as we need in these days. The two families were utterly independent, of different ancestral stock, reared in different communities, even in different States, and under utterly different environment.

The one, starting from a strong, religious, and highly educated ancestor, has maintained those traits and traditions down to the present day and with remarkable results; the other, starting without any of these advantages, and under an entirely different environment, has resulted in the opposite kind of descendants.

It is not possible to convince the euthenist (who holds that environment is the sole factor) that, had the children of Jonathan Edwards and the children of "Old Max" changed places, the results would not have been such as to show that it was a question of environment and not of heredity. And he cites to us the fact that many children of highly developed parents degenerate and become paupers and criminals, while on the other hand, some children born of lowly and even criminal parents take the opposite course and become respectable and useful citizens.

In as far as the children of "Old Max" were of normal mentality, it is not possible to say what might not have become of them, had they had good training and environment.

Fortunately for the cause of science, the Kallikak family, in the persons of Martin Kallikak Jr. and his descendants, are not open to this argument. They were feeble-minded, and no amount of education or good environment can change a feeble-minded individual into a normal one, any more than it can change a red-haired stock into a black-haired stock. The striking fact of the enormous proportion of feeble-minded individuals in the descendants of Martin Kallikak Jr. and the total absence of such in the descendants of his half brothers and sisters is conclusive on this point. Clearly it was not environment that has made that good family. They made their environment; and their own good blood, with the good blood in the families into which they married, told.

So far as the Jukes family is concerned, there is nothing that proves the hereditary character of any of the crime, pauperism, or prostitution that was found. The most that one can say is that if such a family is allowed to go on and develop in its own way unmolested, it is pretty certain not to improve, but rather to propagate its own kind and fill the world with degenerates of one form or another.

Are "Mental" Traits Inherited?

By John B. Watson

Our hereditary structure lies ready to be shaped in a thousand different ways — the same structure — depending on the way in which the child is brought up. To convince oneself, measure the right arm of the blacksmith, look at the pictures of strong men in our terrible magazines devoted to physical culture. Or turn to the poor bent back of the ancient bookkeeper. These people are structurally shaped (within limits) by the kinds of lives they lead.

But every one admits this about bone and tendons and muscles — "now how about mental traits? Does the behaviorist mean to say that great talent is not inherited? That criminal tendencies are not inherited? Surely we can prove that these things can be inherited." This was the older idea, the idea which grew up before we knew as much about what early shaping throughout infant life will do as we now know. The question is often put in specific form: "Look at the musicians who are sons of musicians; look at Wesley Smith, the son of the great economist, John Smith — surely a chip off the old block if ever there was one." The behaviorist recognizes no such things as mental traits, dispositions or tendencies. Hence, for him, there is no use in raising the question of the inheritance of talent in its old form.

Wesley Smith was thrown into an environment early in life that fairly reeked with economic, political and social questions. His attachment for his father was strong. The path he took was a very natural one. He went into that life for the same reason that your son becomes a lawyer, a doctor, or a politician. If the father is a shoemaker, a saloonkeeper, or a street cleaner — or is engaged in any other socially unrecognized occupation, the son does not follow so easily in the father's footsteps, but that is another story. Why did Wesley Smith succeed in reaching eminence when so many sons who had famous fathers failed to attain equal eminence? Was it because this particular son inherited his father's talent? There may be a thousand reasons, not one of which lends any color to the view that Wesley Smith inherited the "talent" of his father. Suppose John Smith had had three sons who by hypothesis all had bodies so made up anatomically and physiologically that each could put on the same organization (habits) as the other two.[1] Suppose further that all three began to work upon economics at the age of six years. One was beloved by his father. He followed in his father's footsteps and due to his father's tutorship this son overtook and finally surpassed his father. Two years after the birth of Wesley, the second son was born; but the father was taken up with the elder son. The second son was beloved by the mother who now got less and less of her husband's time, so she devoted her time to the second son. The second son could not follow so closely in the footsteps of his father; he was influenced naturally by what his mother was doing. He early gave up his economic studies, entered society and ultimately became a "lounge lizard." The third son, born two years later, was unwanted. The father was taken up with the eldest son, the mother with the second son. The third son was also put to work upon economics, but receiving little parental care, he drifted daily towards the servants' quarters. An unscrupulous maid had taught him to masturbate at three. At twelve the chauffeur made a homosexual of him. Later falling in with neighborhood thieves he became a pickpocket, then a stool-pigeon and finally a drug fiend. He died of paresis in an insane asylum. There was nothing wrong with the heredity of any one of these sons. All by hypothesis had equal chances at birth. All could have been the fathers of fine, healthy sons if their respective

wives had been of good stock (except possibly the third son *after* he contracted syphilis).

Objectors will probably say that the behaviorist is flying in the face of the known facts of eugenics and experimental evolution — that the geneticists have proven that many of the behavior characteristics of the parents are handed down to the offspring — they will cite mathematical ability, musical ability, and many, many other types. Our reply is that the geneticists are working under the banner of the old "faculty" psychology. One need not give very much weight to any of their present conclusions. We no longer believe in faculties nor in any stereotyped patterns of behavior which go under the names of "talent" and inherited "capacities."

DIFFERENCES IN STRUCTURE AND DIFFERENCES IN EARLY TRAINING WILL ACCOUNT FOR ALL DIFFERENCES IN LATER BEHAVIOR

Grant variations in structure at birth and rapid habit formation from birth, and you have a basis for explaining many of the so-called facts of inheritance of "mental" characteristics. . . . Let us take up these two points:

1. Human Beings Differ in the Way They Are Put Together

2. Differences in Early Training Make Man Still More Different

How will these two points explain the so-called facts of inheritance of talent or mental characteristics? Let us take a hypothetical case. Here are two boys, one aged 7, the other 6. The father is a pianist of great talent, the mother an artist working in oil, a portrait painter of note. The father has strong large hands but with long, flexible fingers (it is a myth that all artists have long, tapering, finely formed fingers). The older son has the same type of hand. The father loves

---

[1] And by this statement we do not mean that their genetic constitution is identical.

his first born, the mother the younger. Then the process of "creating them in his own image" begins. The world is brought up on the basis largely of shaping the young you are attached to as you yourself have been shaped. In this case the older becomes a wonderful pianist, the younger an indifferent artist. So much for different training or different slanting in youth. But what about different structure? Please note this. The younger son, under ordinary conditions, could not have been trained into a pianist. His fingers were not long enough and the muscular arrangement of the hand was not flexible enough. But even here we should be cautious — the piano is a standard instrument — a certain finger span and a certain hand, wrist and finger strength are needed. But suppose the father had been fond of the younger child and said, "I want him to be a pianist and I am going to try an experiment — his fingers are short — he'll never have a flexible hand, so I'll build him a piano. I'll make the keys narrow so that even with his short fingers his span will be sufficient, and I'll make a different leverage for the keys so that no particular strength or even flexibility will be needed." Who knows — the younger son under these conditions might have become the world's greatest pianist.

Such factors, especially those on the training side, have been wholly neglected in the study of inheritance. We have not the facts to build up statistics on the inheritance of special types of behavior, and until the facts have been brought out by the study of the human young, all data on the evolution of different forms of human behavior and eugenics must be accepted with the greatest possible caution.

Our conclusion, then, is that we have no real evidence of the inheritance of traits. I would feel perfectly confident in the ultimately favorable outcome of careful upbringing of a *healthy, well-formed baby* born of a long line of crooks, murderers and thieves, and prostitutes. Who has any evidence to the contrary? Many, many thousands of children yearly, born from moral households

and steadfast parents become wayward, steal, become prostitutes, through one mishap or another of nurture. Many more thousands of sons and daughters of the wicked grow up to be wicked because they couldn't grow up any other way in such surroundings. But let one adopted child who has a bad ancestry go wrong and it is used as incontestable evidence for the inheritance of moral turpitude and criminal tendencies. As a matter of fact, there has not been a double handful of cases in the whole of our civilization of which records have been carefully enough kept for us to draw any such conclusions — mental testers, Lombroso, and all other students of criminality to the contrary notwithstanding. As a matter of fact adopted children are never brought up as one's own. One cannot use statistics gained from observations in charitable institutions and orphan asylums. All one needs to do to discount such statistics is to go there and work for a while, and I say this without trying to belittle the work of such organizations.

I should like to go one step further now and say, "Give me a dozen healthy infants, well-formed, and my own specified world to bring them up in and I'll guarantee to take any one at random and train him to become any type of specialist I might select — doctor, lawyer, artist, merchant-chief and, yes, even beggar-man and thief, regardless of his talents, penchants, tendencies, abilities, vocations, and race of his ancestors." I am going beyond my facts and I admit it, but so have the advocates of the contrary and they have been doing it for many thousands of years. Please note that when this experiment is made I am to be allowed to specify the way the children are to be brought up and the type of world they have to live in.

The Inheritance of Intelligence

By Arthur R. Jensen

"In the actual race of life, which is not to get ahead, but to get ahead of somebody, the chief determining factor is heredity." So said Edward L. Thorndike in 1905. Since then, the preponderance of evidence has proved him right, certainly as concerns those aspects of life in which intelligence plays an important part.

But one would get a quite different impression from reading most of the recent popular textbooks of psychology and education. Genetic factors in individual differences have usually been belittled, obscured, or denigrated, probably for reasons of interest mainly on historical, political, and idealogical grounds which we need not go into here. Some of the following quota-

From Arthur R. Jensen, "How Much Can We Boost IQ and Scholastic Achievement?" *Harvard Educational Review*, Vol. 39, No. 1, Winter 1969.

tions, each from different widely used texts in our field, give some indication of the basis for my complaint. "We can attribute no particular portion of intelligence to heredity and no particular portion to the environment." "The relative influence of heredity and environment upon intelligence has been the topic of considerable investigations over the last half century. Actually the problem is incapable of solution since studies do not touch upon the problem of heredity and environment but simply upon the susceptibility of the content of a particular test to environmental influences." "Among people considered normal, the range of genetic variations is not very great." "Although at the present time practically all responsible workers in the field recognize that conclusive proof of the heritability of mental ability (where no organic or metabolic pathology

is involved) is still lacking, the assumption that subnormality has a genetic basis continues to crop up in scientific studies." "There is no evidence that nature is more important than nurture. These two forces always operate together to determine the course of intellectual development." The import of such statements apparently filters up to high levels of policy-making, for we find a Commissioner of the U.S. Office of Education stating in a published speech that children " . . . all have similar potential at birth. The differences occur shortly thereafter." These quotations typify much of the current attitude toward heredity and environment that has prevailed in education in recent years. The belief in the almost infinite plasticity of intellect, the ostrich-like denial of biological factors in individual differences, and the slighting of the role of genetics in the study of intelligence can only hinder investigation and understanding of the conditions, processes, and limits through which the social environment influences human behavior.

But fortunately we are beginning to see some definite signs that this mistreatment of the genetic basis of intelligence by social scientists may be on the wane, and that a biosocial view of intellectual development more in accord with the evidence is gaining greater recognition. As Yale psychologist Edward Zigler (1968) has so well stated:

Not only do I insist that we take the biological integrity of the organism seriously, but it is also my considered opinion that our nation has more to fear from unbridled environmentalists than they do from those who point to such integrity as one factor in the determination of development. It is the environmentalists who have been writing review after review in which genetics are ignored and the concept of capacity is treated as a dirty word. It is the environmentalists who have placed on the defensive any thinker who, perhaps impressed by the revolution in biological thought stemming from discoveries involving

RNA-DNA phenomena, has had the temerity to suggest that certain behaviors may be in part the product of read-out mechanisms residing within the programmed organism. It is the unbridled environmentalist who emphasizes the plasticity of the intellect, that tells us one can change both the general rate of development and the configuration of intellectual processes which can be referred to as the intellect, if we could only subject human beings to the proper technologies. In the educational realm, this has spelled itself out in the use of panaceas, gadgets, and gimmicks of the most questionable sort. It is the environmentalist who suggests to parents how easy it is to raise the child's IQ and who has prematurely led many to believe that the retarded could be made normal, and the normal made geniuses. It is the environmentalist who has argued for pressure-cooker schools, at what psychological cost, we do not yet know.

Most geneticists and students of human evolution have fully recognized the role of culture in shaping "human nature," but also they do not

minimize the biological basis of diversity in human behavioral characteristics. Geneticist Theodosius Dobzhansky (1968) has expressed this viewpoint in the broadest terms: "The trend of cultural evolution has been not toward making everybody have identical occupations but toward a more and more differentiated occupational structure. What would be the most adaptive response to this trend? Certainly nothing that would encourage genetic uniformity. . . . To argue that only environmental circumstances and training determine a person's behavior makes a travesty of democratic notions of individual choice, responsibility, and freedom."

12
FRUSTRATION AND CONFLICT

Frustration

Motivational conflict

Approach–approach conflict
Avoidance–avoidance conflict
Approach–avoidance conflict
Multiple approach–avoidance conflict

Cumulative effects of frustration

Reactions to frustration

Aggression — Defense mechanisms

Frustration

How often do you experience frustration? You may be surprised to learn that you are frustrated more often than you realize. What *is* frustration? We may define frustration as a blocking or thwarting of goal-directed activities. Thus, anything that prevents you from reaching some goal is a frustrating circumstance. Did an alarm clock wake you this morning? Did you want to continue sleeping? If so, then the alarm blocked this desire, and you experienced frustration. Did you drive your car to school? Did you get stuck in a traffic jam? If you did, you again experienced frustration. Right now you are reading this textbook. Is there something else you would rather be doing? If you think carefully about your activities during any ordinary day, you will probably discover that you are frustrated a good part of the time.

How do you feel when you are frustrated? Most people think of frustration as an unpleasant emotional state. In this book, we define frustration in terms of the precipitating circumstances rather than in terms of the consequences, although we will be looking at some of these consequences later.

There are many circumstances that block us from reaching a particular goal. For example, you may want to remain in college next year, but you must take a year's leave of absence so that you can work to earn your expenses. Or suppose your two favorite rock groups finally came to town, but their concerts are both scheduled for the same night. Or perhaps your parents object to the length of your hair or your style of dress and threaten to withdraw financial support unless you make certain changes. These are all examples of frustration arising from environmental circumstances.

Not all frustrations arise from external barriers. Sometimes, limitations *within* an individual prevent him from reaching a desired goal. For example, an outstanding college basketball star may be rejected by the professionals because he is not tall enough. Or a young woman who is overweight spots an outfit that she really likes but finds that she cannot fit into it. Frustrations resulting from personal limitations often involve aspirations to goals that are beyond a person's capabilities.

The frustrations that are the most serious and difficult to resolve are those arising from a source other than external or

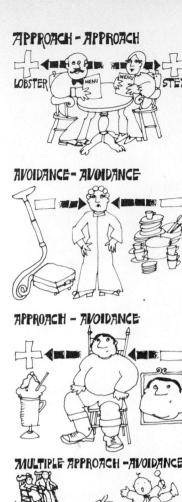

personal barriers. Conflicting attitudes or motives may prevent us from reaching a desired goal. This third condition is often called motivational conflict.

Motivational Conflict

Many different motivations operate concurrently. At any given moment, you may be hungry, tired, need to go to the bathroom, want to call a friend, and need to study for an examination. Some of these motivations are incompatible with each other. For example, the need to study is incompatible with your desire to sleep. It is easy to think of examples of motivational conflict. An avowed critic of automobile-induced air pollution finds it necessary to drive to work or school. A young woman's desire to go to nursing school conflicts with her desire to have a baby. A ten-year-old boy wants to go to summer camp, but doesn't want to leave his best friend behind. Some of these conflicts are relatively easy to resolve. Others cause prolonged and profound anxiety and confusion.

Motivational conflicts are subjective in nature and need not reflect the realities of the external situation. A teenage girl may be apprehensive about joining a particular social group. Although she is strongly drawn to this group because she has many interests in common with its members, she may be plagued with self-doubts about her own ability to fit in. A friend with a more objective view of the situation may find her behavior incomprehensible. The reassurance of this friend—"Don't be silly, everybody will love you"—may fall on deaf ears. Whatever the external reality may be, the girl is experiencing what is, to her, a genuine conflict.

Figure 12.1 shows the four basic types of conflict situations: approach–approach, avoidance–avoidance, approach–avoidance, and multiple approach–avoidance (Lewin, 1935; Miller, 1944).

Approach–Approach Conflict

We often find ourselves simultaneously motivated to approach two desirable but mutually exclusive goals. Because both of the goals are desirable, we refer to this type of situation as an approach–approach conflict. Suppose you press the "down"

Fig. 12.1
Schematic representation of four types of conflict situations.

Motivational Conflict

425

button for an elevator and two elevators arrive at the same time, both going down. Or you must decide which of two appetizing desserts to have after dinner. Or you are faced with a choice between two interesting television shows.

Once you choose between the two goals, you have resolved the conflict. The initial choice is determined by the relative strengths of the two approach tendencies. If one goal is decidedly more attractive, the decision is made rather easily. For example, if an applicant has been accepted by two equally desirable graduate schools, and one school offers him a fellowship and free tuition while the other does not, the applicant will have little difficulty deciding between the two schools.

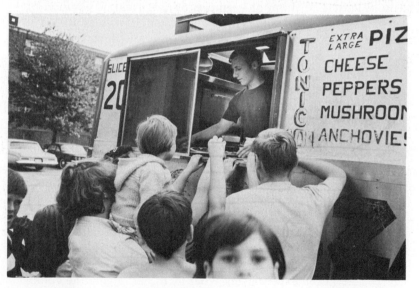

In general, approach–approach conflicts are relatively easy to resolve. A slight hesitation may accompany decision making in this type of conflict, but it is usually shortlived.

Avoidance–Avoidance Conflict

Sometimes we are faced with a choice between two undesirable goal objects—"caught between the devil and the deep blue sea." What we really want to do is avoid both goal objects by escaping the situation altogether. However, the circumstances may be such

Frustration and Conflict

426

that we are forced to choose one of the unpleasant alternatives. For example, a child may be forced by his father to choose between spinach and lima beans, both of which he dislikes. A senior in college must take a specific course for graduation, but learns that the only two instructors who teach it are disliked by everyone who has taken the course. Or, an individual with a throbbing toothache must bear the pain or submit to the dentist's drill.

Avoidance–avoidance conflicts generally result in much indecision and hesitation. If the conflict is intense, the individual may try to escape, if this is possible. For instance, the college senior may contemplate dropping out of school or he may petition for waiver of the course requirement. The young child faced with two extremely unpleasant alternatives may decide to run away from home, if only for an hour or two.

Approach–Avoidance Conflict

In the above examples of conflict, we discussed the goals as if they produced *either* an approach *or* an avoidance tendency. In fact, most goals have both positive and negative aspects. Ice cream is delicious, but loaded with calories. Smoking may be pleasurable, but carries a potential health hazard (Fig. 12.4). You may love your parents, but find them a nuisance at times. A teenager may want to listen to his parents, but fears censure from

Fig. 12.4
Approach–avoidance conflict: enjoying your bad habit. (Mark L. Rosenberg—Stock, Boston.)

Motivational Conflict

his peer group. When we have both positive and negative feelings about a goal object, we refer to these feelings as _ambivalent_.

Approach–avoidance conflicts usually involve much vacillation and indecision. A person who decides to give up smoking may find himself picking up and putting down a cigarette every few minutes. A student who feels inadequately prepared for an examination will be ambivalent about attending class that day. He may get into his car and drive directly to school. However, by the time he has parked his car, he may start to have second thoughts about going to class. The closer he gets to the classroom, the more real the danger appears to be and the more hesitant he may become in his approach.

This kind of vacillation and indecision is found in animals as well as in humans. In one experiment, rats were trained to run down an alley to obtain food. This training established the approach tendency. The rats were then given an electric shock while eating. The shock produced an avoidance tendency. As a result of this training, the rats experienced an approach–avoidance conflict about the food. Now, when the rats were placed at the starting point, they started out in the direction of the food, but stopped before they reached it. By manipulating the drive strengths associated with the food or shock (that is, by making the rat more hungry or making the shock more intense), the experimenter could control where the rat stopped. (Miller, 1959).

Anything that affects the motivational strengths associated with the approach or avoidance tendencies will affect the behavior toward or away from the goal object. For instance, suppose our hesitant student, described in the example above, hears rumors that the upcoming examination is unusually easy. If he believes these rumors, his motivation to approach is likely to increase.

In talking about approach–avoidance conflicts, it is helpful to introduce the concept of gradients of approach and avoidance. A _gradient_ is a change in the strength of the response tendency with decreasing distance from the goal object. What do we mean by distance from a goal object? Distance can be physical, psychological, or temporal. A lion which is three feet away behind bars is physically close but psychologically far away. We have all experienced the effects of temporal distance on approach–avoidance conflicts—at 8:55 A.M., a 9:00 A.M. examination is a lot closer than it was the previous evening.

Frustration
and Conflict

Fig. 12.5
The harness device used to measure strength of pull exerted by the rat. (Courtesy of Dr. Neal E. Miller.)

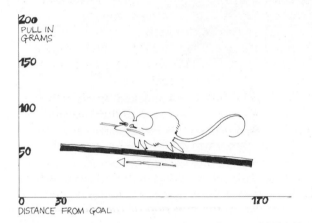

Fig. 12.6
Approach gradient.

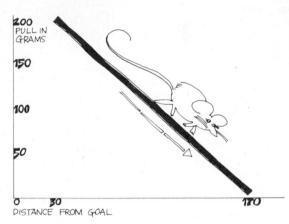

Fig. 12.7
Avoidance gradient.

An ingenious method for determining approach and avoidance gradients was devised by Brown (1948). Rats were placed in a harness device which permitted the experimenter to measure the amount of pull exerted by the animal (see Fig. 12.5). In one situation, rats were trained to run down an alley to obtain food. When they were restrained at various points along the way, the amount of pull provided a measure of the strength of the approach tendency at each point. The rats pulled harder on the harness, the closer they were to the goal. Figure 12.6 shows the approach gradient as a function of distance from the goal.

In order to obtain a measure of the avoidance gradient, rats were given an electric shock when they reached the end of the runway. The amount of pull on the harness away from the end of the runway was recorded at various distances along the runway. Figure 12.7 shows the avoidance gradient as a function of distance from the negative goal. Note that the avoidance gradient is much steeper than the approach gradient.

Motivational Conflict

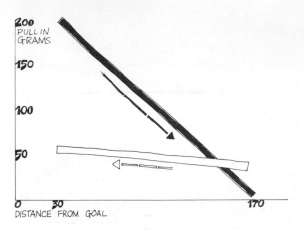

What happens if a rat is both fed and shocked at the same location? The rat will experience both approach and avoidance tendencies toward that location; that is, both the approach and the avoidance gradients will be set up at once. Figure 12.8 shows what happens when the two gradients are superimposed on one another. At some point (approximately 100–150 centimeters from the goal), the gradients cross and the strength of the tendency to approach is the same as the strength of the tendency to avoid. At this point, the organism will show vacillation and hesitation. If it moves toward the goal, the avoidance tendency will become greater and it is likely to turn away from the goal. On the other hand, if it moves too far from the goal, the approach tendency will become stronger and the animal will turn back toward the goal.

By this time you may have begun to suspect that approach–avoidance conflicts are much more difficult to resolve than the other types of conflict discussed above. Unlike the other types of conflict, it is virtually impossible to leave the scene of an approach–avoidance conflict. The individual cannot get far enough away because of the approach tendency; he cannot reach the goal because of the avoidance tendency. Presumably, the closer he gets to the goal, the more anxiety he experiences. At the same time, the closer he gets to the goal, the more he wishes to reach it.

Approach–avoidance conflicts often form the basis of enduring emotional problems that may last throughout life. For instance, a man may have strong homosexual desires. At the same time, he may react with guilt or shame or revulsion to the possibility of a homosexual relationship. If sexually approached by another man, he may experience tremendous anxiety and a strong desire both to approach and to avoid a homosexual encounter.

How are approach–avoidance conflicts resolved? Think about the last time you had conflict about attending a particular examination. You either went or you did not; therefore, you somehow resolved the conflict. A general strategy for resolving approach–avoidance conflicts is to do something which results in a change in the relative strengths of the two opposing tendencies. Let us suppose that you decided to go to that examination. You may have remembered that the exam covered old material and you would probably do well. Thus, the strength of the tendency to avoid was decreased. Or, you may recall that this instructor never gives make-ups, thus increasing your approach tendency. Suppose, on the other hand, you had decided to avoid the examination. You may have resolved this conflict in favor of avoiding by raising the avoidance gradient (realizing how unprepared you were) or by lowering the approach gradient (the instructor gives make-up exams and they are reputed to be easier than the original). Figure 12.9 illustrates the various ways in which an approach–avoidance conflict is resolved.

Fig. 12.9
Resolution of an approach–avoidance conflict.

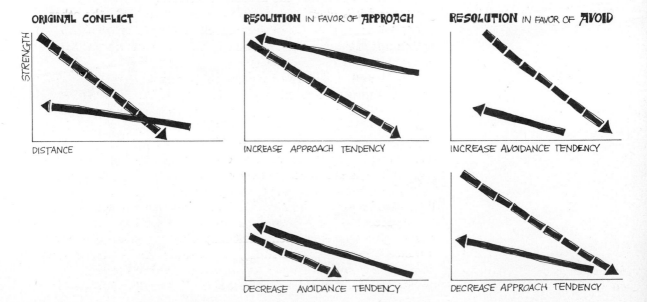

ORIGINAL CONFLICT

STRENGTH

DISTANCE

RESOLUTION IN FAVOR OF APPROACH

INCREASE APPROACH TENDENCY

DECREASE AVOIDANCE TENDENCY

RESOLUTION IN FAVOR OF AVOID

INCREASE AVOIDANCE TENDENCY

DECREASE APPROACH TENDENCY

431

Fig. 12.10
Multiple approach–avoidance conflict: you have to
make a difficult decision that has many personal,
social, and moral implications. (Daniel S. Brody—
Stock, Boston.)

Multiple Approach–Avoidance Conflicts

In most real-life situations, any particular goal may have both
positive and negative aspects. Think for a moment about some of
your own goals and desires in life, and you will find that they are
fraught with negative components. When you are studying for a
particular career, there are many things you must do that are
distasteful. There are long hours of arduous study, many dull
lectures to be attended, and many courses that you would prefer
not taking. Even a situation which appears to be highly positive
may have some negative aspects. We previously discussed
approach–approach conflicts as if each goal had only positive
elements. In reality, there are usually some negative aspects to
almost all goals in life. For example, those two delicious desserts
that you must choose between are both very fattening; or both of
those "down" elevators that arrive at the same time have been
known to get stuck between floors.

To complicate matters further, a host of motives operate
simultaneously within the individual. Each of these motives
demands its own goal. The goals may have both negative and
positive elements and may be incompatible with each other (see
Fig. 12.11).

Fig. 12.11
Conflicts in the life of the poor
harassed and bedeviled human
being.

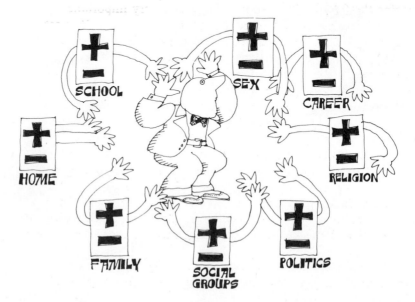

*Frustration
and Conflict*

An excellent example of a multiple approach–avoidance conflict that confronts many of today's youth appeared in an article in *Life* magazine:

> Once last summer Richie had arrived at Jones Beach with a group of "heads." A hundred yards away were two couples who were "straights." Richie waved at the couples, then started walking toward them. But midway he stopped. He glanced back at his "head" friends, then looked forward toward the others. Finally he sat down on a dune mid-distance between them, not able to commit to either side.
>
> (*Life*, May 5, 1972)

On the surface, this may appear to be an approach–approach conflict. But the fact that Richie had such great difficulty in resolving this conflict suggests that there were avoidance elements associated with each goal. In fact, Richie may not have been completely comfortable with either the "straights" or the "heads."

Cumulative Effects of Frustration

Imagine the following situation: You have a very important examination scheduled for nine o'clock in the morning. You set the alarm for 7:30, which leaves you enough time to dress and review your notes before taking the 15 minute drive to school. Unfortunately, the alarm does not go off and you do not wake up until 8:30. You dash madly around the house trying to get ready to leave. The clothes you wanted to wear are not back from the cleaners, your roommate is in the middle of a shower, and you can't find the keys to your car. At 8:55 A.M. you finally get yourself together and dash outside, to find that it is raining, and you have trouble starting the car. You run into traffic and get stopped by a policeman for going through a red light. At school you cannot find a place to park—except for spaces reserved for faculty. Finally you get there, only to find a note posted which indicates that the room has been changed to one on the other side of the campus.

We have defined frustration as a blocking or thwarting of goal-directed activity. The above situation describes a series of frustrating circumstances. Obviously, the final frustration—the changing of the examination site—would not have produced so intense a reaction, had it not been preceded by a series of other frustrations. It may have been, in effect, the last straw.

Frustration produces effects in the organism that have motivational characteristics similar to those of the aversive drive states. Thus, we would expect behavior to be energized under frustrating circumstances. In experimental studies, when we increase the amount of current with which we shock the animals, we increase the animals' pain drive. Similarly, when frustrating events accumulate, the frustration effect increases with each additional event.

Reactions to Frustration

Obviously, individuals differ widely in the variety and intensity of their reactions to frustration. Some people can tolerate enormous amounts of frustration without any disruptive effects on their ongoing behavior. For others, a minor perturbation becomes "the straw that breaks the camel's back." The amount of frustration that an individual is able to cope with is referred to as his *frustration tolerance*.

It is not fully understood why some people seem to have high tolerance to frustration, and are able to function with remarkable aplomb under circumstances that would drive others to the psychotherapeutic couch. Nor is it clear why other people have such short fuses that they appear to fall apart at the slightest hint of frustration or stress. Although there have been suggestions that genetic factors may be involved, it appears more likely that frustration tolerance involves learning, perhaps starting in infancy. There are as many differences among people in their levels of frustration tolerance as in the kinds of reactions frustration produces. You have probably observed the different reactions frustration produces in others and in yourself.

How would you have reacted to the situation described in the preceding section? Would you have thrown the alarm clock across the room? Would you have screamed at your roommate? Would you have had a temper tantrum when you found the note posted? Or would you simply have shrugged in resignation and decided to

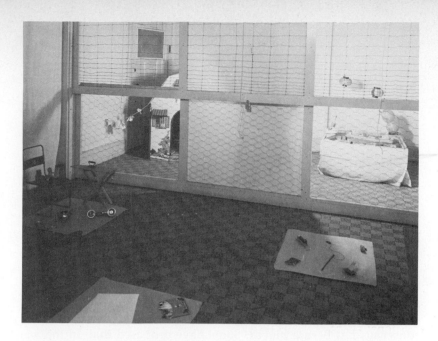

Fig. 12.12
Frustration situation

The screen separated the children from the more attractive toys and thus presented a frustrating barrier. (Photo courtesy of the University of Iowa Photographic Service and the Institute of Child Behavior and Development.)

forget the examination? At what point would you have blown your cool? Ask your friends how they would have reacted. You will probably find many different reactions to the situation.

The different types of reactions produced by a frustrating situation were investigated in an experiment involving nursery school and kindergarten children. In one part of the experiment, the children were individually placed in a room filled with broken or incomplete toys. For example, there was an ironing board with no iron, a chair without a table, various water toys but no water, papers but no crayons. The children were permitted to view a set of complete and more attractive toys in another part of the room. They were separated from these toys by a wire screen (see Fig. 12.12). Presumably, this situation was frustrating, because the children could see the goal (better toys) but were blocked from reaching it. Many of the reactions observed are fairly typical reactions to frustration. In the words of the experimenters:

> There is a decrease in the happiness of the mood in the frustrating situation; happy emotional expressions decrease in frequency and unhappy expressions increase. In frustration there is an increase in motor restlessness and hypertension as revealed by loud singing and talking, restless actions, stuttering, and thumb sucking. There is an increase in aggressiveness in frustration; hitting, kicking, breaking, and destroying all increase in frequency.
>
> (Barker et al., 1943, p. 456)

Since aggression is so common a reaction to frustration, let's look at aggression in more detail.

Reactions to Frustration

Aggression

The problem of man's cruelty and aggression toward man is most persistent and puzzling. Pick up a copy of today's newspaper. Note the number of articles in which some act of aggression or violence is reported. Many people have expressed great concern over the rash of violence in the United States and throughout the world—bombings, riots in the cities and colleges, muggings and murders in the streets, war. Yet history is filled with stories of man's violence and aggressiveness toward his fellow man, ever since "Cain rose up against his brother Abel and killed him."

Many theories have attempted to explain aggression, but no consensus has been achieved. Some have proposed that, in the course of evolution, aggressiveness was necessary for the survival of some species, including man. Since the fittest species (the most aggressive) survived and reproduced, the most successful and populous species would tend to be the most aggressive. Such theories imply that aggressiveness is an inborn trait that had survival value before the development of civilized societies. Furthermore, according to these theories, aggression is outdated in contemporary society and must be inhibited.

Other theorists argue that aggression is learned. They maintain that some societies teach their children to be aggressive by reinforcing aggressive acts and providing hostile models for the child to imitate. In our society, movies and television abound with acts of violence during children's viewing hours (see box).

Although theorists disagree about the basic causes of aggression, most acknowledge a close link between frustration and aggression. Frustration leads to aggressive tendencies, which may or may not be manifested in aggressive behavior. Conversely, aggressive behavior is frequently, but not always, preceded by frustrating circumstances (Miller, 1941).

Learning aggressive behavior

The specific forms of aggressive behavior, like all learned responses, are acquired through shaping, reinforcement, and imitation. Children who observe aggressive behavior in their parents often imitate the aggression displayed by their adult models. To what extent do models influence the acquisition of aggressive behavior in children?

Frustration and Conflict

436

An interesting experiment was designed to answer this question. Nursery school children were individually placed in a room with an adult model. Each child played with a toy on one side of the room while the adult played with toys on another. In the "aggressive model" condition, the adult picked up a Bozo clown, hit it, punched it, hammered it, and shouted such expressions as "Sock him" and "Pow." In the control condition, the adult played quietly with tinker toys. After this session, all of the children were moved to another room and were frustrated by having some toys taken away. Only the children exposed to the aggressive model responded with aggression in this second situation (Bandura et al., 1961).

In a later experiment, it was found that children imitated the aggressive behavior of adult models even when they were presented on film rather than in real life (Bandura et al., 1963). Moreover, the behaviors of the children were very similar to those of the adult models (see Fig. 12.13).

A major controversy concerns the extent to which seeing violence on television and in the movies leads to imitations of this violence in real life. A series of studies suggested that

Fig. 12.13
Imitating aggressive behavior
Nursery school children viewed a film in which an adult was seen throwing, hitting with a hammer, and kicking a "Bozo clown." Afterwards the children were observed displaying the same forms of aggressive behavior. (Photo courtesy of Dr. Albert Bandura.)

*Reactions
to Frustration*

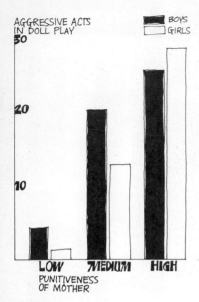

AGGRESSIVE ACTS
IN DOLL PLAY

BOYS
GIRLS

30

20

10

LOW   MEDIUM   HIGH
PUNITIVENESS
OF MOTHER

Fig. 12.14
Punishment and aggression

The greater the punitiveness of
the mother, the more aggressive
behavior is displayed by the
children in doll play. (Adapted
from "Some Childrearing
Antecedents of Aggression and
Dependency in Young Children,"
by R. R. Sears, J. W. M. Whiting,
V. Nowlis, and P. S. Sears,
Genetic Psychology Monographs,
47, 1953, pp. 135–234.
Reproduced by permission of
The Journal Press.)

*Frustration
and Conflict*

viewing violence may increase the likelihood that the viewer will
himself become aggressive if he is frustrated, and if he feels that
the violence he viewed was justified (Berkowitz, 1968).

Punishing aggressive behavior

What happens when you punish aggressive behavior? Punishment
of aggression seems to lead to more aggression. Figure 12.14
shows that the more punishment the mother inflicts, the more
aggressiveness is shown by her child in doll play (Sears et al.,
1953). In addition, a study of highly aggressive adolescent boys
revealed that their fathers were extremely punitive at home. The
boys were typically "well-behaved" at home, but were highly
aggressive at school (Bandura and Walters, 1959).

It appears that punishment of aggressive behavior leads to
inhibition of that behavior in the presence of the punishing agent,
but to an increase in aggressive behavior when that agent is
absent. Evidently, the child learns to discriminate between the
occasions when aggressiveness is punished and those when there
will probably be no punishment.

Expression of aggression

Aggressive behavior can take many forms. It may be physical,
such as hitting, kicking, shooting, or stabbing. Or it can take the
form of a verbal attack—screaming, name-calling, or a
vituperative outburst of four-letter invectives. The following
excerpt from Dick Gregory's account of his experience in trying
to integrate a school in Greenwood, Mississippi, illustrates both
physical and verbal forms of aggression:

> The next thing you know, you're knocked down in the gutter
> with that cracker's foot on your chest and a double-barrelled
> shotgun on your throat. And he's saying "move, nigger, and
> I'll blow your brains out." . . .

> (*Newsday,* March 9, 1968)

When aggression follows frustration, the aggressive impulse is
usually first directed against the source of frustration. Thus, in
the previously described experiment in which children's access to
toys was blocked, the children's first acts of aggression were
directed against the wire screen which stood in the path to their
goal. Many of you may recall having had a toy taken from you

by another child. Did you strike out at him in retaliation? Perhaps such encounters resulted in a barrage of name-calling as well.

Often, it is not possible or not safe to express aggression directly against the frustrating obstacle. The aggressive impulse may be inhibited because of a fear of possible punishment or harmful consequences. Thus, if a worker is frustrated by his supervisor, he may be tempted to strike out against the supervisor. However, he may inhibit this impulse because of the threat of retaliation. Instead, he may go home and start a family argument. We then say that he has displaced his aggression. When we displace aggression, we direct it toward a source other than the original cause of the frustration (see Fig. 12.15).

The following account provides an amusing illustration of displaced aggression by a four-year-old girl whose mother had punished her by shutting her in a clothes closet:

> After a rather long silence, the mother inquired from her side of the door, "What are you doing?" The child said, "I've spat on your hat, I've spat on your coat, I've spat on your shoes. Now I'm waiting for more spit."
>
> (Landreth, 1967, p. 327)

Fig. 12.15
Displaced aggression

Some observers have interpreted the urban riots of the late 1960's as an instance of displaced aggression. According to this theory, the rioters were striking out against the *symbols* of ghetto oppression. (Pictorial Parade, Editorial Photocolor Archives.)

Reactions to Frustration

Sometimes we displace aggression because we cannot identify the original source of frustration. We may feel angry but have no target against which to direct this anger. Bureaucratic organizations frequently heap frustrations upon individuals. However, anyone trying to deal with such an organization usually does not know whom to blame, because the locus of decision making is frequently unspecified. Has this ever happened to you? You register for your courses for the following semester. The registration card comes back and you see that some of the courses you had planned to take are either not assigned or else scheduled at the wrong time. You then have to stand in a long line at the registrar's office in order to reschedule your program. When you ask how this mistake was made, everyone just shrugs his shoulders.

A common form of displaced aggression is scapegoating. A *scapegoat* is an innocent victim who becomes the target of displaced aggression. The term comes from an ancient Hebraic ceremony described in the Old Testament:

> ... and Aaron shall lay both his hands upon the head of the live goat, and confess over him all the iniquities of the people of Israel, ... and send him away into the wilderness ... the goat shall bear all their iniquities upon him ...

> (Leviticus 16: 21–22)

Minority groups are often the victims of scapegoating. Well-known historical examples include the Christians of ancient Rome, the Jews of Nazi Germany, and the blacks in the United States, who, at one time, were lynched at an average rate of one every three days.

Releasing aggressive feelings

Numerous therapy procedures, in addition to the various encounter groups springing up across the country, are based on the assumption that it is undesirable to have pent-up aggressive feelings (see Fig. 12.16). These procedures and groups encourage the venting of hostile and aggressive impulses, in the belief that expressing hostility in verbal or symbolic form is a "safe" way of releasing aggressive tendencies and results in a lessening of these feelings.

Research on this point is far from conclusive. In one study, subjects who were given an opportunity to express their anger

Fig. 12.16
Some modern therapies encourage group members to express hostile and aggressive feelings. These therapies are based on the belief that this is a safe way to release aggressive tendencies. (Ian Berry—Magnum.)

against an antagonist ended up disliking the antagonist more, and were more physiologically aroused by his presence, than subjects who were not given the opportunity to vent their feelings (Kahn, 1966). In another study, children showed no reduction in their aggressive feelings even though they were allowed to express physical or verbal aggression against a child who had frustrated them (Mallick and McCandless, 1966). These studies are intriguing insofar as they run contrary to popular belief. Further research is needed before definitive statements can be made.

Defense Mechanisms

So far in this chapter, we have looked at the various sources of frustration and some of the resulting behavior. We have seen that some reactions to frustration might be considered constructive, others destructive, and still others may represent a compromise. Suppose your car does not start in the morning, preventing you from going to work or school. You might display one or more of several different behaviors. You might call for assistance, kick the car, take an alternative means of transportation, or withdraw from the situation entirely by going back to bed.

There are many frustrating situations in life for which there are no appropriate or constructive behaviors. This is particularly true in approach–avoidance conflicts. There are many such conflicts which, for reasons beyond our own control, we cannot satisfactorily resolve. Think for a moment about your own present life situation. Can you think of any conflicts that exist now and have persisted for a period of time? If you are a student now and are dependent on your parents for financial support, you might desire freedom from the various restrictions and controls that they still exercise over you. To repudiate your parents might result in a withdrawal of support. Many students do not resolve this conflict until they graduate from college and are able to become gainfully employed on their own. Lifelong ambivalence toward one's parents is not uncommon. To take another example, some form of sexual conflict may start in adolescence and persist throughout the lives of many individuals.

Conflicts like these give rise to prolonged and persistent anxiety. We have all developed techniques for dealing with such anxiety. These techniques do not really solve the problem, but they protect us against the excessive anxiety produced by the

Reactions
to Frustration

unresolved conflicts. The various anxiety-reducing techniques are generally referred to as defense mechanisms, and were first described in the writings of Sigmund Freud. They defend the individual against his own feelings of inadequacy, guilt, and unfavorable self-evaluations when he is faced with continuing conflict or frustration. Although there are individual differences, we all use defense mechanisms to some extent. We have probably all heard a failing student blame his poor performance on the instructor—"He doesn't know how to teach." And we have probably encountered an instructor who attributes the poor attendance in his class to the low level of student motivation. Both of these are examples of projection, which will be discussed below.

How do we decide whether the student's failure was due to poor instruction or whether he was using a defense mechanism to protect himself from an awareness of his own inadequacy? All defense mechanisms involve some degree of self-deception, and may be accompanied by some distortion of reality. To judge the student's behavior accurately, we would need to know something about his underlying motivations, and whether or not he was deceiving himself about the cause of his failure.

We can sometimes make inferences as to whether or not a person is using a defense mechanism by observing his behavior. If his reactions are inappropriate to the situation (for example, laughing at a failing grade), we can guess that he is probably protecting himself through the use of a defense mechanism.

Let's look at some of the most frequently used defense mechanisms. Although we will be looking at the "normal" uses of defense mechanisms here, we will later examine them as they appear in more exaggerated, or abnormal, ways (Chapter 14).

Repression

Some of us experience some feelings or impulses that are unacceptable to us and thus produce anxiety. For example, a man might find that he has developed strong sexual feelings toward another man, and consequently feel guilty and anxious. How might he overcome this feeling of anxiety? Psychologists have found that people can suppress the anxiety-producing thoughts by consciously trying to think of other things, or by engaging in activities that distract them from the anxiety-arousing impulses.

However, another process, called *repression*, operates automatically and involuntarily to cause an individual to "forget" undesirable impulses or feelings. Repression does not occur with all anxiety-producing material. It is difficult to specify all the conditions under which it occurs. However, several facts are clear: (1) the thought or impulse must have great significance to the individual; (2) it must be extremely anxiety-arousing, probably involving feelings of guilt; (3) repression leads to relief of the acute phase of anxiety.

Repression may be described as burying an impulse, or feeling, alive. We say "alive," because banishing objectionable thoughts or impulses from consciousness does not eliminate their dynamic force:

> They continue to lead a subterranean life beneath a conventional surface, yet they are liable to manifest their influence in traits of personality, in special interests, in some system of beliefs or code of values, or in more marked form as neurotic, psychosomatic, or psychotic symptoms.
>
> (Noyes and Kolb, 1963, pp. 41–42)

Moreover, the repressed impulses may express themselves in such disguised forms as dreams, fantasies, and slips of the tongue. Repressed impulses may also arouse vague feelings of discomfort or anxiety which, if they work their way toward consciousness, may become quite intense.

Under certain conditions, the repressed material can be brought into consciousness, where the associated anxiety can be dealt with and understood. Such techniques as hypnosis, sodium pentothal interviews, and, as we will see later (Chapter 14), various types of psychotherapy have been used for this purpose (see Fig. 12.17).

Fig. 12.17
Jean-Martin Charcot (1825–1893) used hypnotism to remove the symptoms of hysteria. One of his students, Sigmund Freud, later used hypnosis to bring repressed memories to the surface. (National Library of Medicine, Bethesda, Maryland.)

*Reactions
to Frustration*

The following case illustrates the extent to which repression may interfere with memories of unpleasant experiences, and may even affect ongoing behavior:

A young man who had recently become engaged was walking along the street with his fiancée. Another man greeted him and began to chat in a friendly fashion. The young man realized that he must know this apparent stranger, and that both courtesy and pride required that he introduce the visitor to his fiancée. The name of the other man, however, eluded him completely; indeed, he had not even a fleeting recognition of his identity. When in his confusion he attempted at least to present his fiancée, he found that he had also forgotten her name.

Only a brief behavior analysis was necessary to make this incident comprehensible as an example of normal generalized repression. The apparent stranger was in fact a former friend of the young man; but the friendship had eventually brought frustration and disappointment in a situation identical with the one described. Some years before, our subject had become engaged to another young woman, and in his pride and happiness he had at once sought out this friend and introduced the two. Unfortunately, the girl had become strongly attached to the friend and he to her; at length she broke her engagement and married the friend. The two men had not seen each other until this meeting, which repeated exactly the earlier frustrating situation. It is hardly surprising that the newly engaged man repressed all recognition of his former friend, all hints as to his identity, and even the name of the fiancée.

(Cameron and Magaret, 1951, pp. 367–368)

Denial

One of the simplest mechanisms of defense is denial, in which the individual "screens out" disagreeable events or materials by ignoring them. Denial is assumed to operate unconsciously by a protective mechanism of nonawareness; in this way it is different from a conscious effort to suppress or repudiate reality, for example, by lying. A person may refuse to discuss topics that make him anxious, look away from unpleasant sights, or faint at times of emotional crisis (see Fig. 12.18). By denying the reality, he protects himself from the associated anxiety. For example, a

Fig. 12.18
Denial is an unconscious defense against the anxiety an unpleasant or disturbing reality may cause us. (Norman Hurst—Stock, Boston.)

mother who refuses to admit to herself that her child is incurably handicapped may go from doctor to doctor looking for a different opinion. Or the relatives of a patient with a terminal illness may convince themselves that he is getting better.

The following case illustrates the mechanism of denial among the parents and sisters of a dangerous delinquent boy:

> A large physically mature boy of fourteen was brought to a juvenile court by police officers who reported that his theft of a bicycle was the latest in a long series of minor offenses. . . . His neighbors complained that he struck and injured other children, that he was noisy and disorderly in his general conduct, and that he seemed to be out of control of his family . . .
>
> It was impossible to obtain from the parents reliable evidence concerning the boy's early development. Consistently, in their reports, in their attitudes and in their general treatment of him, his parents and his sisters denied his retardation. . . . The parents explained that their son was "just playing" when in his vigorous activity he knocked the mother down, or nearly choked to death another child. . . . Over and over again the parents repeated their repudiation of their boy's diagnosis of retardation. His sister expressed the family attitude in her description of her brother. "He's so bright and so good—he is just like Jesus."
>
> (Cameron and Magaret, 1951, p. 169)

Reactions to Frustration

Reaction formation

An individual may protect himself from unacceptable motives or feelings by developing conscious attitudes and behaviors that stress *opposite* motivations. Thus, a mother who has strong, but unacceptable, underlying hostility toward an unwanted baby may become overprotective and smother the child in affection. People with intense unconscious sexual conflicts may protect themselves from feelings of guilt by devoting a large part of their lives to eradicating smut and pornography, and other forms of social "evils," real or imagined. One clue to whether their behavior represents reaction formation is the degree of exaggeration that it displays. The famous line from Shakespeare, "The lady doth protest too much, methinks," is a common way of acknowledging reaction formation.

Reaction formation may help a person adjust to his situation by preventing him from recognizing tendencies within himself that he regards as threatening or beneath his dignity. In extreme cases, however, it may lead to a rigidity of behavior and beliefs that seriously complicates his relationships with others. For example, the person who has devoted his life to eradicating pornography may inflict excessive punishment on his teenage son for reading books that are only slightly racy, and hardly pornographic.

Intellectualization

Sometimes a person defends himself against the anxiety produced with a conflict by avoiding or cutting off his emotional involvement. He deals with the situation strictly on an intellectual plane. A man who has been recently divorced may discuss the causes for the breakup in a completely unemotional, detached, and clinical fashion. If we were to take his behavior at face value, we might think that he had no emotional involvement whatsoever.

The process of intellectualization is illustrated in the following account by a London prostitute:

> The act of sex I could go through because I hardly seemed to be taking part in it. It was merely something happening to me, while my mind drifted inconsequentially away. Indeed, it was scarcely happening to me; it was happening to something

lying on a bed that had a vague connection with me, while I was calculating whether I could afford a new coat or impatiently counting sheep jumping over a gate.

(Cousins, 1938)

Rationalization

Rationalization is probably the most common defense mechanism. We often find plausible reasons for engaging in certain behaviors when we cannot face up to the real reasons. We fool ourselves into believing that our behavior is motivated by feelings and desires that are socially acceptable. For example, we persuade ourselves to watch a television program instead of doing some unpleasant work, on the grounds that we "need a little relaxation —all work and no play makes Jack a dull boy."

We also use rationalization to muffle the disappointment of blocked or frustrated aspirations and desires. If we have difficulty achieving a satisfactory academic record in school, we may excuse ourselves by saying that "grades are not important," "the educational hierarchy is a tool of modern, corrupt society," or "most classroom instruction is not relevant." A well-known example of this type of rationalization is Aesop's fable of the fox who couldn't reach the grapes and rationalized, "The grapes are probably sour anyway."

It is, of course, often difficult to determine the dividing line between rationalization and objective, dispassionate consideration of the facts. We may suspect rationalization if the person overreacts, that is, if he becomes upset when his motives are questioned and has difficulty recognizing contradictory evidence.

Projection

When we attribute our own unacceptable desires, impulses, traits, and thoughts to others, or even to inanimate objects, we are projecting. At one time or another, most of us have resorted to projection to protect us against an unfavorable self-evaluation. When we have prepared inadequately for an examination, we may attribute our poor performance to the lack of preparation of the instructor—"How can I learn anything? He's so disorganized, he never prepares his lectures." Conversely, a disorganized and poorly motivated instructor with many failing students may ascribe their failure to inadequate preparation and motivation on

Fig. 12.19
Projection

Both motorists backed out of
their driveways without looking
in their rear-view mirrors. Who is
to blame?

their part. A young woman who is in conflict about her feelings
for her boyfriend may decide to "cool it" because "he really
doesn't love me." Or a tennis player who carelessly splinters his
racket on the ground may defend himself by sheepishly saying,
"It was a lousy racquet." A person who holds hostile attitudes
toward a particular social group may attribute this hostility to
members of that group, accusing *them* of hating *him.*

There have been many laboratory studies on various aspects
of the projection mechanism. One well-known study
demonstrated projection among college students. Members of a
fraternity were asked to rate themselves and each other on four
undesirable traits—stinginess, obstinacy, disorderliness, and
bashfulness. Of the subjects who possessed one or more of these
traits, some displayed self-awareness, while others did not. Those
subjects who had the traits, but did not recognize them in
themselves, had a greater tendency to attribute these traits to
others than did subjects who either did not have the traits or
recognized them in themselves (Sears, 1936).

Projection often involves transferring blame to some object or
person other than oneself (see Fig. 12.19). In this way the person
evades responsibility for his own acts.

Regression

We have seen that, as infants, we are completely dependent and
relatively helpless organisms. As we progress from infancy
through childhood and into adulthood, we gradually cease
depending on others for gratification of our needs, and begin to

*Frustration
and Conflict*

function as independent individuals. With increased autonomy come the burdens of greater responsibility. This transition is not an easy one to make, and an adult often finds himself looking back wistfully on the carefree and protected days of childhood. When confronted with overwhelming stress, he may find refuge in behavior that brought satisfaction at an earlier age. For example, an adult who feels neglected and unappreciated may throw a temper tantrum that, in childhood, brought him parental attention. This kind of behavior is called regression. A child who experiences sudden separation from his parents may regress to such infantile behaviors as thumbsucking and bedwetting.

Compensation

Compensatory reactions are defenses against feelings of inferiority stemming from real or imagined deficiencies or weaknesses. For example, a person who sees himself as weak or frail may compensate by engaging wholeheartedly in activities in which physical prowess is not required, such as scholarly or artistic pursuits. In some instances of compensation, the person tries to achieve eminence in an activity in which his "deficiency" is most pronounced. The literature abounds with apparent examples of such compensation. For Franklin D. Roosevelt, polio apparently provided the impetus for outstanding achievements in politics. Moses, who was a stutterer, became a great leader. Glenn Cunningham became a great track star despite suffering extensive and severe burns on both of his legs when he was a child. Napoleon Bonaparte, who was extremely short in stature, strove to rise to the heights of military and political power.

Summary

1. Frustration, which is a blocking or thwarting of goal-directed activities, may occur as a result of environmental circumstances or limitations within the individual. The most serious and difficult-to-resolve frustrations arise from conflicting attitudes or motives (motivational conflicts).

2. Many different motivations operate concurrently, and at times they are incompatible with one another. Four basic types of conflict situations have been described: approach–approach conflict, avoidance–avoidance conflict, approach–avoidance conflict, and multiple approach–avoidance conflicts.

3. Individuals differ widely in the variety and intensity of their reactions to frustration. The amount of frustration with which an individual is able to cope is called his frustration tolerance.

4. One of the common reactions to frustration is aggression. Specific forms of aggressive behavior are learned. Children who observe aggressive behavior in their parents will often imitate the aggression displayed by the adult models. Moreover, when aggressive behavior is punished, there appears to be less aggressive behavior in the presence of the punishing agent but greater aggressiveness when that agent is absent.

5. Aggressive behavior may take many forms, physical and verbal, which may be directed toward the frustrating agent or displaced toward a source other than the original cause of frustration.

6. There are many conflict situations that persist over long periods of time—some for a lifetime. Many of these conflicts give rise to prolonged and persistent anxiety. The individual may adopt various defense mechanisms to protect himself against the excessive anxiety produced by unresolved conflicts. A few of the most common defense mechanisms are repression, denial, reaction formation, intellectualization, rationalization, projection, regression, and compensation.

Terms to Remember

Aggression   Physical or verbal behavior intended to inflict harm or injury.

Ambivalence   Mixed feelings (both positive and negative) toward a person or situation.

Approach–Approach Conflict   A conflict in which the individual is simultaneously motivated to approach two desirable but incompatible goals.

Approach–Avoidance Conflict   A conflict in which the individual is simultaneously motivated to both approach and avoid a goal object.

Approach Gradient   A change in the strength of the approach tendency with decreasing distance from the goal object.

Avoidance–Avoidance Conflict   A conflict in which the individual is simultaneously motivated to avoid two undesirable alternatives.

Avoidance Gradient   A change in the strength of the avoidance tendency with decreasing distance from the goal object.

Compensation   A defense mechanism in which the individual makes up for a real or imagined deficiency or weakness in one area by striving to excel in another.

Conflict   The simultaneous arousal of two or more incompatible motives or attitudes.

Defense Mechanisms   Behavior patterns aimed at reducing anxiety in the individual; presumed to be unconscious.

Denial   A defense mechanism in which the individual unconsciously denies the existence of events that have aroused his anxiety.

Displaced Aggression   Aggression directed toward a source other than the original cause of frustration.

Frustration   A blocking or thwarting of goal-directed activities.

Frustration Tolerance   The amount of frustration that an individual is able to cope with effectively.

Gradient   A gradual change in the strength of the response tendency, as shown by a rising or falling curve in a graph.

Intellectualization   A defense mechanism in which the individual defends himself against the anxiety produced by a conflict by cutting off his emotional involvement, and dealing with the conflict on a strictly intellectual level.

Multiple Approach–Avoidance Conflict   A conflict in which the individual is simultaneously motivated to both approach and avoid two or more goal objects.

Projection   A defense mechanism in which the individual attributes his own unacceptable desires, impulses, traits, and thoughts to others.

Rationalization   A defense mechanism in which the individual finds socially acceptable but false reasons for his behavior.

Reaction Formation   A defense mechanism in which the individual protects himself from unacceptable motives or feelings by repressing them, and assuming the opposite attitudes and behaviors.

Regression   A defense mechanism in which the individual reverts to an immature form of behavior that brought satisfaction at an earlier age.

Repression   A defense mechanism in which the individual unconsciously excludes unpleasant thoughts, feelings, and impulses from conscious awareness.

Scapegoat   An innocent victim who becomes the target of displaced aggression.

Suppression   Conscious inhibition of anxiety-producing thoughts, feelings, and impulses (contrast with repression, which is unconscious).

Recommended Readings

Arkoff, A., *Adjustment and Mental Health,* New York: McGraw-Hill Book Co., 1968.

Frustration and Conflict

Contains concise discussions of frustration, conflict, defense, and anxiety.

Freud, A., *The Ego and Mechanisms of Defense,* New York: International Universities Press, 1946.

A detailed and interesting account of defense mechanisms by Sigmund Freud's daughter.

Johnson, R. N., *Aggression: In Man and Animals,* Philadelphia: W. B. Saunders Co., 1972.

Comprehensive treatment of all aspects of aggressive behavior in humans and animals.

13
PERSONALITY

*Factors affecting personality
development*

Theories of personality

*Type theories — Trait theories
Psychoanalytic theories
Social learning theories*

Assessment of personality

*Interviews — Rating scales
Personality inventories
Projective techniques*

Fig. 13.1
All these people are listening to the same speaker, but do you think they are all reacting the same way? Why not? (Jeff Albertson—Stock, Boston.)

Personality

In popular usage, the word personality most often occurs in evaluative statements, such as "He has a good personality," "She has a bad personality," or "He has no personality at all." When psychologists study personality, their purpose is not to make value judgments, but to try to describe those persistent and enduring *behavior patterns* of an individual that tend to be expressed in a wide variety of life situations.

Each person's personality is unique; no two individuals will always behave in precisely the same way even under the same conditions. We all eat, drink, sleep, engage in recreational activities, read, and have conversations with our friends. What differentiates us and provides the basis for personality study is the *way* in which we engage in these various activities. We each have different food preferences and eating habits; different things "turn us on"; we converse in different ways and on different topics.

In spite of these differences, our behavior is highly predictable. Moreover, much of our behavior is based on the assumption that people about us will behave in expected ways. For example, when we drive an automobile, we are constantly making assumptions about the behavior of other drivers, for example, that they will drive on the right side of the road, and that they will stop for traffic signals. Our survival in spite of the fact that there are thousands of unique personalities behind the wheels of the other cars attests to the predictability of behavior. Indeed, it is when individuals behave in unexpected ways that headlines are made.

So far, we have seen that although personality is unique, certain consistent patterns of behavior are shared by many individuals. There is also consistency within each individual. Just as we expect most people to behave in certain ways, we expect individuals to behave in ways that are consistent with our past observations of them. Think about some person you know extremely well. You can probably predict how he or she would behave in a wide variety of situations.

Factors Affecting Personality Development

Why is it that two children born to the same parents and brought up in similar environments may differ widely in their personality characteristics? One may be affable, easygoing, and relaxed, while the other is a "completely obnoxious brat." At birth, differences already exist among children. Some cry quite frequently and are very active; others are more placid. Babies eat and sleep according to different schedules. These variations produce different reactions among adults. A child who is responsive to parental affection will certainly elicit different responses than an infant who squirms and refuses to be held. These inborn tendencies and initial contacts form the basis for the development of those enduring behavior patterns we refer to as personality.

As much as two siblings may differ from one another, they share many more personality characteristics than do any other two individuals raised in two different cultures. To understand this, we must recognize that different cultures have different values. The various members of each culture—parents, relatives, neighbors, peers—selectively reinforce and shape different behaviors. Children learn to do what is expected of them, and different cultures expect different things. There are even differences among subgroups in the same culture. For example, in the United States, middle-class parents tend to value and reinforce self-direction and independence in their children.

Factors Affecting Personality Development

457

Working-class parents, however, appear to be more concerned that their children learn to conform to the expectations of others, particularly those in authority (Kohn, 1963).

During the first few years of a child's life, most of his experiences are provided directly by the parents, particularly the mother. Parents are the primary agents for transmitting their culture. They interpret their culture's values in their own way, according to their understanding of these values. There are wide differences in people's understanding of cultural values, and corresponding to these differences are wide variations in child-rearing practices. This is one reason why there is such diversity in the personality development of children, even in the same culture. For example, some parents feel that punishment makes children "good," and therefore inflict a great deal of punishment. Other parents, trying to achieve the same goal ("good" children), use positive reinforcement instead of punishment. Children raised under these different circumstances will inevitably develop different personality characteristics.

As children grow older, their social contacts broaden dramatically to include teachers, neighbors, storekeepers, and members of their peer group. When they learn to read, they become exposed to a wide variety of different values and ideas, some of which may profoundly influence their thinking and behavior.

Critical and largely unpredictable events—such as the death of a parent, an accident resulting in a permanent physical disability, or moving to another state or country—may also have an enormous impact on personality development. The following account by the mother of a teenage girl is not at all unusual:

> Karen's changed. I just don't understand it. Ever since we moved out here to _____ somehow—I think—it has something to do with the friends she has here. They have such different ideas about everything—sex, drugs, you name it. They don't have any respect for their parents. Karen didn't used to be like that when we lived in _____

Theories of Personality

There is no universally accepted theory of personality. In some cases, the lack of agreement is due to the fact that the goals of the theorists are different. Some theorists are interested in developing an overall basis for *describing* personality. Others seek to understand *how personality develops*. Even among theorists seeking explanations for personality development, there are differences in the extent to which they emphasize biological as opposed to social and cultural factors.

Let's look first at those theories that emphasize the description of personality.

Fig. 13.2
A Medieval "type" theory of personality held that each individual was composed of four humors, with one humor dominating the other three. This dominant humor determined the person's physical and emotional character, or temperament. The four humors were (a) melancholic (sad), (b) sanguine (cheerful), (c) choleric (angry), and (d) phlegmatic (impassive). (National Library of Medicine, Bethesda, Maryland.)

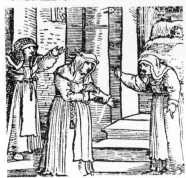

a)

b) c)

d)

Type Theories

It is not uncommon to hear someone described as "the artistic type," "the scholarly type," "the bossy type," "the independent type," or "the nervous type." The idea of classifying people into specific types dates far back into history (see Fig. 13.2). Type theorists search for primary characteristics that can be used to describe the whole personality. Either a person fits into a specific category or he does not. For example, Carl Jung postulated that individuals are either extroverts or introverts. Extroverts like to be with other people, are outgoing, and are likely to choose occupations in which there is much contact with other people, such as selling or social work. Introverts, on the other hand, prefer to be alone and are likely to choose work that allows them to avoid people (Jung, 1923).

It is not unlikely that among your acquaintances, there are some who are definitely extroverts and some whom you would call introverts. In other words, the observable behavior of some of your friends conforms most of the time to our conception of the

Theories of Personality

459

A test of introversion–extroversion was administered to a
group of clinically normal adults. Most of the scores fall in
the middle range—which is neither introversion nor
extroversion. Very few cases fall at the two extremes
(Newmann and Yacorzynski, 1942).

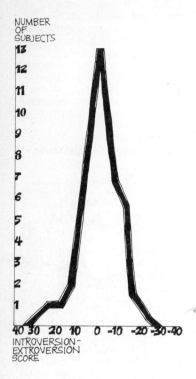

NUMBER
OF
SUBJECTS

13
12
11
10
9
8
7
6
5
4
3
2
1

40 30 20 10 0 -10 -20 -30 -40
INTROVERSION–
EXTROVERSION
SCORE

extroverted personality type, while other friends' behavior fits the
introverted personality type. However, you will probably find
that most of your friends cannot be labeled in this way. Most
people do not neatly fit into either of these categories (see Fig.
13.3). Under one set of circumstances they may display those
behaviors we label as extroversion, while under different
conditions they show behaviors we identify as introversion. For
example, a college professor may be a quiet, contemplative, and
introspective person in a seminar, and a wild cut-up at a cocktail
party.

Because of the limitations of type theories, many
psychologists feel that classifying personalities into *any* system of
single-dimension categories is an inadequate way of describing
personality. They feel that personality can be adequately
described only by using a large number of dimensions.

Trait Theories

Suppose you wanted to introduce someone to a friend and were
asked, "What's his personality like?" Generally, when we think
of a person, we think of a combination of things that make up
his personality. So you might say, "He is very outgoing, a little
selfish, and not too dependable."

Can you think of more words that could be used to describe
traits of individuals? The English language has about 40,000
words that can be used to describe behavioral differences or traits
(Norman, 1967). With this seemingly endless list available, how
does one decide how many traits are necessary and sufficient to
describe personality and predict behavior? R. B. Cattell, a leading
proponent of trait theory, felt that some traits are more "basic"
than others (Cattell, 1946). The problem was to decide which
ones. Through the use of sophisticated statistical techniques,
Cattell came up with a series of personality variables that can be
used to describe a number of basic personality dimensions. Many
of these variables may be expressed as opposites—honest versus
dishonest, sociable versus shy, conceited versus modest. However,
these opposites are to be regarded as the extreme points on a
continuum, with individuals falling between the two extremes.

By measuring these traits, using a number of different test
instruments, we can construct a profile for an individual or for a

Personality

group sharing some common characteristic. This profile presumably represents the extent to which the individual or the group in question displays the various traits that make up personality. Figure 13.4 is a sample group profile. We will be discussing some of the instruments used in personality assessment later in this chapter.

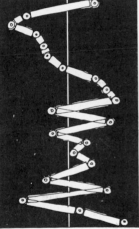

TRAIT DESCRIPTION
FOR SCORES ON LEFT
SIDE OF GRID

CENTILE RANK
0% 10 20 30 40 50% 60 70 80 90 100%

TRAIT DESCRIPTION
FOR SCORES ON RIGHT
SIDE OF GRID

RESERVED, CRITICAL — OUTGOING, WARMHEARTED
LESS INTELLIGENT — MORE INTELLIGENT
EMOTIONALLY LESS STABLE — EMOTIONALLY STABLE
SUBMISSIVE, ACCOMMODATING — AGGRESSIVE, ASSERTIVE
SERIOUS, QUIET — HAPPY-GO-LUCKY, ENTHUSIASTIC
LESS RIGID, CASUAL — STAID, PERSEVERING
TIMID, SHY — VENTURESOME, UNINHIBITED
TOUGH-MINDED, REALISTIC — SENSITIVE
TRUSTING, ADAPTABLE — SUSPICIOUS
PRACTICAL, CAREFUL — IMAGINATIVE, IMPRACTICAL
UNSOPHISTICATED, NAÏVE — SHREWD, SOPHISTICATED
CONFIDENT, SERENE — APPREHENSIVE, WORRYING
CONSERVATIVE, TRADITIONAL — EXPERIMENTING, ANALYTICAL
GROUP ADHERENT — SELF-SUFFICIENT
FOLLOWS OWN URGES — CONTROLLED
RELAXED — HIGH TENSION LEVEL

INTROVERSION — EXTROVERSION
LOW ANXIETY — HIGH ANXIETY
RESPONSIVE EMOTIONALITY — TOUGH POISE
SUBDUED GROUP ADHERENCE — INDEPENDENCE
LOW NEUROTICISM — HIGH NEUROTICISM

Fig. 13.4
Sample personality profile of a group

A personality test was administered to a group of 937 male drug addicts while they were in prison. The profile shown in the figure presents the average position of the group on each of these scales. Note, for example, that the addicts tended to be outgoing, emotionally unstable, impractical, and apprehensive. Profiles may also be constructed for individuals. (16 Personality Factor Questionnaire. Copyright 1949–1967 by the Institute for Personality and Ability Testing, Champaign, Illinois. Reproduced by permission.)

Many psychologists are not satisfied with the trait approach to personality theory. They argue that merely assigning traits to an individual does not express the full complexity of the personality as it manifests itself in ever-changing life situations. For example, we may describe a person as honest, loyal, and fair-minded. But is he always honest? Under what circumstances might he be dishonest? Is an individual who scores high on aggressiveness always aggressive? Or does the expression of this tendency depend on the situation? For example, a professional football player may be as ferocious as a lion on the field, but gentle as a lamb in his home.

Another objection to trait theories of personality is that they ignore the question of how personality is formed. Assigning the label "aggressive," even if it is accurate, gives no insight into how the person may have developed this trait.

Theories of Personality

461

Psychoanalytic Theories

Psychoanalysis is more than a theory of personality. It is also concerned, as we will see in the next chapter, with the diagnosis and treatment of psychopathology. However, in this section, we will concentrate on those aspects of the theory that are concerned with the development of personality. Since Sigmund Freud is the founder of psychoanalytic theory and the most widely known of the psychoanalytic theorists, let's look first at some of the concepts he proposed.

Basic Freudian concepts

Freud believed that personality is divided into three parts: the id, the ego, and the superego. The *id* consists of the primitive and instinctual drives of the individual. The id operates on the *pleasure principle;* that is, it is concerned only with the immediate satisfaction of basic biological drives. The individual is unaware of the operation of the id. A very young infant is under the complete control of the id, seeking only to satisfy his basic needs —"he wants what he wants when he wants it." As he gets older, the ego develops. The *ego* functions on the *reality principle;* the ego permits the individual to postpone the gratification of basic drives until the "proper" time. A person who is hungry is functioning on the level of the id if he demands food immediately. If he is able to wait some time before eating, his ego is in control. The id and the ego are in constant conflict, since the ego must control the impulsive, and sometimes unrealistic, demands of the id. The *superego* develops still later in the life of the individual. As the child begins to perceive the values and beliefs of the significant people around him, he incorporates these values into his own personality. This process is referred to as *identification.* The superego is analogous to what most people call the conscience.

According to Freud, these three parts of the personality are delicately balanced in the normal individual. Dominance by either the id or the superego could lead to serious personality problems. Thus, a person with a weak superego may not successfully inhibit his id impulses, and may thereby bring himself into conflict with society. If the superego is too strong, the person achieves gratification of his instinctual urges only at the cost of tension, anxiety, and guilt.

This three-part structure is only a part of the Freudian conception of personality. Freud also considered personality development. As the individual matures, he goes through a number of stages, each of which is important to the development of his personality.

Before discussing these stages, it is important to understand Freud's conception of sexuality. Sexuality is the cornerstone of Freud's theory and has generated much controversy largely because his use of the concept has been misunderstood. According to Freud, the pleasurable feeling that the individual gets from stimulation of the sensitive areas of the body is basically sexual. Freud called the various sensitive areas of the body *erogenous zones.* As the individual matures and passes through the various stages of development, the focus of pleasure shifts from one part of the body to another. The principal erogenous zones, in the order of their developmental importance, are the mouth, the anus, and the genitals.

Oral stage. The infant's principal source of sexual or erotic pleasure during the first year of life is the mouth. In this first stage of personality development, the oral stage, pleasure is derived from sucking and biting. If the infant's experiences during this stage have been particularly satisfying, such oral activities as eating, kissing, and talking will continue in a normal way into adulthood. But if the infant has experienced frustration during the oral stage, it is possible that his later personality will reflect this in behaviors such as overeating and greediness.

Anal stage. During the anal stage, which occurs between the ages of one and three, the infant derives pleasure from both elimination and retention of feces. If he is highly frustrated during the course of toilet training, he may become obstinate and excessively frugal as an adult.

Phallic stage. Somewhere around the fourth year of life, the focus of erotic pleasure shifts to the genital zone. During this so-called phallic stage, the child derives pleasure through manipulations in the genital zone (masturbation). A critical event, which must be resolved at this time if the child is to advance to more mature psychosexual stages, is the Oedipus complex in boys and the Electra complex in girls.

The boy unconsciously develops strong sexual feelings toward his mother. These feelings are threatening to him because they

a) b)

a)

c)

b) c)

Fig. 13.5
During the latency stage girls do "girl things." (a, Bruce Anspach—Editorial Photocolor Archives Newsphoto. b, Anna Kaufman Moon—Stock, Boston. c, Dan O'Neill—Editorial Photocolor Archives.)

Fig. 13.6
While girls are doing "girl things," boys are doing "boy things." (a, Bob Van Lindt—Editorial Photocolor Archives. b, Photo Trends. c, Frank Siteman—Stock, Boston.)

place him in direct conflict with his father; this conflict is known as the *Oedipus complex.* The boy fears that his father will retaliate by castrating him. Thus, *castration anxiety* develops, perhaps because the boy has observed that females lack a penis. To protect himself against this anxiety, he represses his incestuous urges and identifies with his father.

The situation is somewhat different with girls. The girl blames her mother for her lack of a penis, a condition known as *penis envy.* She shifts her attachment to her father and sees her mother as a direct rival. This is known as the *Electra complex.* Freud believed that girls never completely lose their attachment to their fathers. He regarded this attachment as normal, and felt that it would later form the basis for heterosexual relations with a husband. The girl resolves the Electra complex by identifying with her mother and by seeking a substitute father image, a boyfriend.

Latency stage. Presumably by about the age of six, the normal child has successfully repressed the Oedipus or Electra complex. Sexual urges become dormant for the next few years. Reaction formation is a common defense mechanism at this stage and may be inferred from the almost universal plaint of boys at this age, "I hate girls." During this period, children practice many of the behaviors associated with their emerging sex roles. Girls do "girl things" and boys do "boy things."

Genital stage. With the advent of puberty, the beginning of adolescence, the focus of erotic pleasure returns to the genital zone. The individual who has successfully passed through all the preceding stages is well prepared for assuming the normal adult heterosexual role.

Evaluation of Freudian theory

There is little question that Freud's theorizing had a major impact on the study of personality. The broad range of concepts which he developed has stimulated much research aimed at testing his ideas.

Many aspects of his theory are still widely accepted. Few psychologists question the importance of early childhood experiences in the development of personality, and few doubt that Freud made major contributions to the study of personality.

Theories of Personality

Freud was responsible for emphasizing the role of unconscious factors, motivational conflict, and defense mechanisms in behavior.

However, much of Freud's work has been the subject of severe criticism. Freud based virtually all of his formulations upon his observations of emotionally disturbed patients who were undergoing psychoanalytic therapy. Moreover, the setting was Vienna of the late 1890's and the early 1900's, a setting with many of the same special characteristics that we associate with Victorian England. Questions have been raised concerning the validity of generalizing observations from this setting to today's population. In addition, many people question the applicability of Freud's findings to other cultures at other times. Indeed, much anthropological evidence has cast doubt on the generality of his conclusions.

Many critics also object to the emphasis Freud placed on sexuality and on biological instincts. These critics think that he tended to gloss over the role of social and cultural factors in the development of personality.

Finally, many of Freud's statements do not readily lend themselves to scientific verification. For example, how would you scientifically determine that a person is assailed by feelings of guilt related to his Oedipal strivings, and that these feelings are the underlying determinants of his behavior?

Departures from Freud

It is interesting that some of Freud's severest critics were originally his own disciples. These theorists used Freud's findings as a point of departure, but they departed so far from Freud that they developed their own theoretical schools.

Two of Freud's contemporaries, Carl Jung and Alfred Adler, proposed ideas which shifted the focus of the theory away from sexuality. One of Jung's key concepts was that of the *collective unconscious.* Jung believed that, in the course of evolution, certain shared experiences, predispositions, and symbols became part of man's genetic makeup. For example, one might cite the universality of certain dreams (such as dreams of falling) as evidence of Jung's collective unconscious. To Adler, the key conflict in an individual's personality involved feelings of inferiority and superiority. Adler is responsible for the popular terms "inferiority complex" and "superiority complex."

Other theorists, such as Karen Horney, Erich Fromm, and Erik Erikson, attempted to redress what they felt was an overemphasis on biological determinants in Freud's theory. Instead, they focused on the role of social and cultural factors in the development of personality.

Karen Horney (1885–1952) objected to Freud's relegating social and cultural factors to a minor role in the development of personality. She pointed out that many stresses arise from inconsistencies within the individual's own society (for example, we subscribe to the commandment "Thou shalt not kill," yet we send people to war).

Erich Fromm (1900—) maintains that through increased automation and depersonalization, society has deprived individuals of satisfying personal and social relationships with each other. He feels we must find new meanings in life and productive ways of satisfying personal and social motives.

Erik Erikson (1902—) sees the individual and society not as two separate interacting entities, but rather as a totality that cannot be separated artificially.

Social Learning Theories

While the various psychoanalytic theorists derive their data from observations of patients in clinical practice, other theorists approach the study of personality from an experimental point of view. Learning theorists start out with the basic assumption that personality is learned and, therefore, the principles of learning are applicable (see Chapter 3). There have been many different groups of social learning theories. In this section, we will look at two of the most prominent.

Dollard and Miller

Dollard and Miller point out that there are four basic elements in the learning process: drive, cue, response, and reward. When a drive is active in the presence of various environmental stimuli (cues), responses that serve to reduce or satisfy that drive are acquired. This drive reduction is rewarding. For example, a hungry (drive) rat in a Skinner box (cues) will learn to press a bar (response) to obtain food which satisfies its hunger drive (reward) (Dollard and Miller, 1950).

At this point, you might be thinking, "This is all very interesting, but how does one develop a theory of personality based on hungry rats learning bar-pressing responses?" Dollard and Miller attempted to apply the principles of learning derived from laboratory experiments to psychoanalytic phenomena. Let's look at some of the similarities in basic concepts between Freud's theory and learning theory. First, both stress the importance of drive as an energizer of behavior. Second, both theories postulate that drive or tension reduction is rewarding; that is, the organism will act in ways that lead to tension reduction. Third, both have developed elaborate theories of motivational conflict, and both are concerned with the ways in which motivational conflicts are resolved.

It might be instructive to look at a single phenomenon and compare the approach of the learning theorists to that of Freud. Earlier (Chapter 12) we discussed displaced aggression, which sometimes occurs under frustrating circumstances. Although the concept of displacement originated in psychoanalytic theory, it can readily be handled by learning theory. Let's look at an experiment in which displacement was demonstrated in human subjects.

A questionnaire that assessed attitudes toward certain minority groups was administered to a group of boys both before and after exposure to frustrating conditions. As a result of the frustration, the boys expressed a greater number of hostile attitudes toward the minority groups. A psychoanalyst might say that the boys were *displacing* their aggression from the source of the frustration (the experimenters) to the minority groups. Learning theorists, however, would say that the subjects were *generalizing* hostile feelings from the experimenters to the minority groups (Miller and Bugelski, 1948).

In effect, Dollard and Miller translated many psychoanalytic concepts into operationally defined terms that permit experimental testing.

Bandura and Walters

One of the criticisms of Dollard and Miller's work is that it relies heavily on animal research to develop a personality theory. Bandura and Walters felt that a comprehensive theory of personality can be developed *only* by studying humans, and that

interpersonal processes cannot be ignored in a theory of
personality. Since interaction among people is an essential
characteristic of human behavior, they used social settings to
study human behavior.

Bandura and Walters have focused on a kind of
learning-imitation which emphasizes the role of social factors. We
saw earlier (Chapter 12) that when children observed adults
displaying aggressive behavior, they imitated these aggressive
models. They imitated these behaviors even when the models
they observed were on film. Thus, Bandura and Walters suggest
that models are the primary source of learned behaviors (Bandura
et al., 1961, 1963).

Assessment of Personality

Suppose you are asked to write a description of your own
personality. How objective do you think you could be? We are
often not aware of many characteristics within ourselves. Our
defense mechanisms operate so well in achieving self-deception
we really cannot see ourselves as others see us (see Fig. 13.7). For
example, you might say that you are "firm," while others would
describe you as "stubborn."

Since we cannot be expected to give a fair and accurate
assessment of our own personalities, we must look elsewhere for
this assessment. But why is it desirable to assess personality in
the first place?

There are several reasons why psychologists strive to develop
better and better instruments for assessing personality. People are
frequently confused about their life goals and about their ability
to succeed in various activities. In order to help them make
decisions, tests are used in conjunction with vocational
counseling, as illustrated in the following case:

Frank P. went to the counselling center on campus because he
was confused about his life and vocational objectives and his
entire life appeared to be without focus. In his first two years
at college he had switched his major no fewer than four
times—from English literature, to mathematics, to chemistry,
to philosophy. Although his academic record was good, he
expressed great concern about his inability to find a major

469

that struck a deep responsive chord within him. The results of testing revealed him to have an extremely high IQ with varied interests, including mathematics, science, psychology, and writing. Personality inventories suggested that personal–social relations played a significant role in his motivational makeup. When all the facts were put together, it was recommended that he consider psychology as a major field.

He followed the recommendation and has since become a respected professional in the field.

Potential employers often use test instruments for determining a person's suitability for a job. Individuals with emotional problems may benefit from diagnoses and prognoses based on test results. Finally, psychological instruments are often useful in testing the assumptions and predictions arising from some theory of behavior.

The multitude of different techniques for assessing and describing personality attests to the widespread interest in this area. One approach that has fascinated people for ages has been to divine personality in relation to heavenly bodies. In a book on astrological signs (Goodman, 1968), the following descriptive terms are used to describe the Aquarian personality:

> The Aquarian is so much a dreamer that he lives on rainbows. But he is basically a realist. He is fascinated by politics, sports, children, horses, automobiles, elderly people, medical discoveries, authors, astronauts, alcoholics, pianos, pinwheels, prayers, and baseball.

> He loves the security of crowds but he has spells of gloominess when he wants to be left alone. He is fixated on friendship, but does not have many intimate friends. He can empathize with others but enjoys defying public opinion. He stings.

> Aquarians are so broad in outlook that they are rarely prejudiced, "unless there are severe planetary influences in the natal chart."

Criticisms of astrological personality descriptions are aimed primarily at their lack of validity and at the broadness of the descriptions, most of which could fit almost anybody. Can you think of somebody born under Aquarius—or any other sign, for that matter—who does *not* fit the description shown above, at least in part?

Psychologists have attempted to develop sophisticated techniques for the measurement and description of personality. As we saw in our discussion of intelligence tests (Chapter 11), a good test must have two characteristics. It must be reliable, that is, yield consistent results on repeated testing of the same individual. It must also be valid, that is, it must measure what it purports to measure. These same requirements hold for personality assessment.

Let's now look at some of the methods that have been developed to assess personality.

Interviews

When you applied to college, were you required to come in for an admissions interview? How often have you been interviewed in the course of seeking employment? Although the interview is not commonly regarded by nonpsychologists as a method of personality assessment, its purposes are usually diagnostic (does the person have the necessary characteristics?) and prognostic (how well will he do?). The interview procedure has much in common with the naturalistic procedures described in Chapter 1.

Interviews may be structured or unstructured. In the *unstructured* interview there is no set pattern of questions. The interviewer remains flexible and is free to explore tangents and probe more deeply whenever he feels such inquiry is warranted. In the *structured* interview, a standard set of questions is used. Although the structured interview does not provide as varied information as the unstructured does, it has the advantage of permitting more precise comparison of the responses given by different people.

In any interview situation, the outcome may be influenced by the characteristics of the interviewer. Even such subtle behaviors as nodding the head or mumbling "uh hum" may serve as cues to or reinforcers of the behavior of the interviewee.

Rating Scales

Look at Fig. 13.8. You will see a number of sample items as they might appear in different types of personality rating scales. Think of several people whom you know quite well. Referring to Fig. 13.8a, place a check mark at a point which you feel best describes

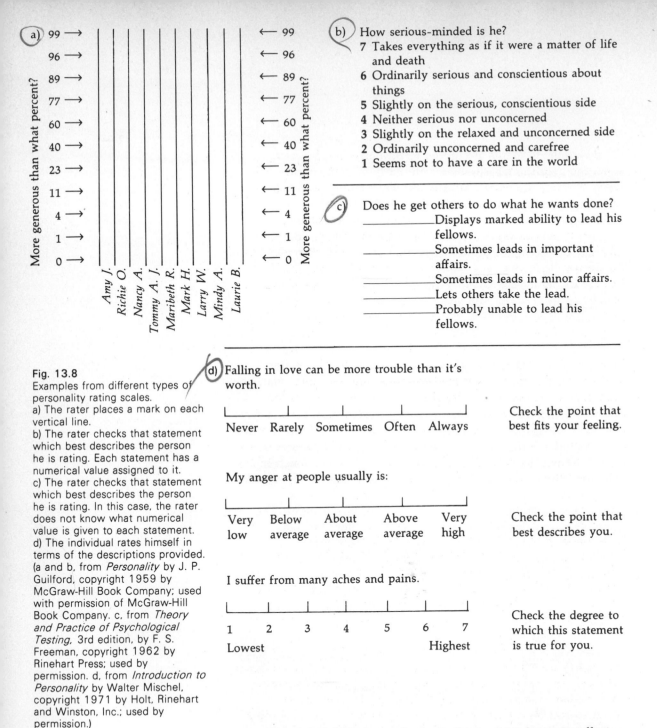

a) 99 →
96 →
89 →
77 →
60 →
40 →
23 →
11 →
4 →
1 →
0 →

More generous than what percent?

Amy J.
Richie O.
Nancy A.
Tommy A. J.
Maribeth R.
Mark H.
Larry W.
Mindy A.
Laurie B.

← 99
← 96
← 89
← 77
← 60
← 40
← 23
← 11
← 4
← 1
← 0

More generous than what percent?

b) How serious-minded is he?
7 Takes everything as if it were a matter of life and death
6 Ordinarily serious and conscientious about things
5 Slightly on the serious, conscientious side
4 Neither serious nor unconcerned
3 Slightly on the relaxed and unconcerned side
2 Ordinarily unconcerned and carefree
1 Seems not to have a care in the world

c) Does he get others to do what he wants done?
_____ Displays marked ability to lead his fellows.
_____ Sometimes leads in important affairs.
_____ Sometimes leads in minor affairs.
_____ Lets others take the lead.
_____ Probably unable to lead his fellows.

d) Falling in love can be more trouble than it's worth.

| | | | | |
Never Rarely Sometimes Often Always

Check the point that best fits your feeling.

My anger at people usually is:

| | | | | |
Very low   Below average   About average   Above average   Very high

Check the point that best describes you.

I suffer from many aches and pains.

| | | | | | |
1   2   3   4   5   6   7
Lowest   Highest

Check the degree to which this statement is true for you.

Fig. 13.8
Examples from different types of personality rating scales.
a) The rater places a mark on each vertical line.
b) The rater checks that statement which best describes the person he is rating. Each statement has a numerical value assigned to it.
c) The rater checks that statement which best describes the person he is rating. In this case, the rater does not know what numerical value is given to each statement.
d) The individual rates himself in terms of the descriptions provided. (a and b, from *Personality* by J. P. Guilford, copyright 1959 by McGraw-Hill Book Company; used with permission of McGraw-Hill Book Company. c, from *Theory and Practice of Psychological Testing*, 3rd edition, by F. S. Freeman, copyright 1962 by Rinehart Press; used by permission. d, from *Introduction to Personality* by Walter Mischel, copyright 1971 by Holt, Rinehart and Winston, Inc.; used by permission.)

each of these individuals on the trait shown. You have, in effect, made a judgment about a personality characteristic of each of these people. If you were to complete the entire scale, you could then construct a profile of your judgments along a number of different personality dimensions.

The item shown in Fig. 13.8a illustrates one type of rating scale, the graphic rating scale. There are a number of different types of rating scales in common use. Figure 13.8b and c presents sample items from two other kinds of scales.

Rating scales are useful only when the person making the judgments is well acquainted with the person he is rating. Incidentally, rating scales can be self-administered, in which case the person is making judgments about himself, as in Fig. 13.8c. Besides assuming familiarity with the person being rated, rating scales require that the judgments be objective. A frequent problem with rating scales involves the *halo effect,* in which the judgment of each trait is influenced by the rater's overall impression of the individual. Thus, if the rater likes the person, he might rate him high on all traits. Conversely, if the rater dislikes the person, he may tend to judge him low on all traits. Students in colleges and universities all over the country are currently rating the effectiveness of their instructors. If an instructor makes an extremely favorable impression because of one characteristic (for example, because he is a high grader or has a good sense of humor), he may receive high overall ratings. This is an example of the halo effect.

Personality Inventories

Personality inventories differ from other types of tests (intelligence, aptitude, and achievement tests) in that there are no "right" or "wrong" answers. An individual is expected to answer a series of questions about himself. Like the other types of tests, personality inventories are scored objectively and permit comparison of an individual's standing on a given characteristic with that of some standardization group.

The most serious problem encountered in the construction of personality inventories arises from the fact that individuals, either purposely or inadvertently, may not provide truthful answers. One method that has been used to identify individuals who are not answering truthfully is to insert key items which may reveal inconsistencies in the individual's pattern of responses. For example, if someone answered all of the following items "False," we might well suspect his honesty on the rest of the inventory: "I sometimes feel angry"; "sometimes my friends disappoint me"; "I never have thoughts which I am ashamed to share with others."

Assessment of Personality

A personality inventory may be designed to measure a single trait or dimension of personality. In this case, the total score provides a quantitative measure of where the individual stands on that characteristic. Other inventories measure several aspects of personality simultaneously.

There are two ways of standardizing a personality inventory. One is to standardize it on the basis of a group of subjects displaying the characteristic measured by the test. For example, a measure for homosexuality could be standardized on a group of homosexuals; an individual's score would then be compared to this reference group. Another way to standardize a personality inventory is to use a reference group that is "normal" with regard to the particular characteristic being measured. We would then be interested in the individual's deviation from the norm. Such deviations may permit us to identify personality problems.

There are literally thousands of personality inventories in use today. One of the most widely employed is the Minnesota Multiphasic Personality Inventory (MMPI). On this instrument, the individual is required to respond to 550 statements as "True," "False," or "Cannot Say." The following are sample items from this inventory: "It does not bother me particularly to see animals suffer"; "People often disappoint me"; "My sleep is fitful and disturbed"; "At times I feel like smashing things."*

The MMPI is an example of a test that was developed on the basis of groups of patients with known personality disorders. Scoring of the test yields a profile of scores. The responses of the individual taking the test are then compared with the profiles of various clinical groups.

We indicated above that individuals may distort their responses to items on personality inventories. Many people tend to answer items so as to present a socially acceptable picture of themselves. The level of "social desirability" of an item is a constant source of difficulty for the test constructor. One method of overcoming this difficulty is to force the subjects to choose between two items that are judged to be equal in either social desirability or social undesirability. The Edwards Personal

---

*Reproduced by permission. Copyright 1943, renewed 1970, by the University of Minnesota. Published by the Psychological Corporation, New York. All rights reserved.

Preference Schedule exemplifies this approach to personality test construction. Based on the assumption that the motivational dispositions of individuals reveal important dimensions of personality, the test attempts to measure 15 basic needs of the subject.

Projective Techniques

Another problem with personality inventories is that their purposes are generally transparent. Consequently, as we have seen, the individual may distort his answers to present a favorable picture of himself. He may do this consciously, but unconscious forces may also be at work. We have already discussed mechanisms as a way of protecting ourselves from anxiety. Being asked to admit to unfavorable personality characteristics may give rise to anxiety and bring defensive reactions into play. Projective techniques are an attempt to overcome this difficulty.

A further criticism of personality inventories is that they present a picture of personality that is limited by the structure of the test and of the items. Projective methods are frequently referred to as "unstructured" tests, since the individual is free to respond in an unlimited variety of ways to the test materials. The materials themselves are frequently ambiguous in form; that is, they do not have any obvious meaning.

Unknowingly, you have probably been using projective techniques throughout your life. Have you ever looked at cloud formations or abstract art and tried to state what they looked like to you? You may have noted that the wide variety of different answers given in these situations seem to reveal more about the beholder than about what is beheld. Projective methods provide a more systematic way of presenting ambiguous types of stimuli. To the trained and experienced observer, the responses to a standardized set of ambiguous stimuli may reveal important aspects of personality.

Rorschach test. Have you ever splattered ink on a piece of paper and then folded the paper over the blot? You may have obtained something similar to Fig. 13.9. What do you see in the blot? Do you see any human figures? Do they appear to be stationary, or

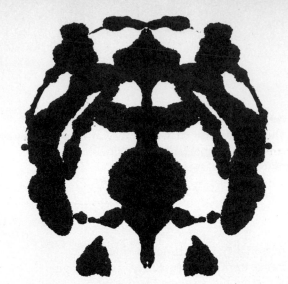

Fig. 13.9
An ink blot similar to those used in the Rorschach test.

are they doing something? Does what you see involve the entire blot or just a portion of it?

Presumably, the responses you are making are revealing certain aspects of your personality. In fact, one of the most widely used projective personality tests, the Rorschach test, employs a series of ten ink blots similar to the one shown in Fig. 13.9. The subject is asked to describe what he sees in the blot, or what it looks like.

The responses are scored in a number of different ways. Look again at the questions above. They reflect several of the elements of the response which are analyzed. For example, did you see any human figures? Animals? Landscape? Such responses would reflect what is referred to as content, which is one of the scoring categories. Other categories include the popularity of the response, and whether the response involves the whole blot or only a part of it.

Intensive training is required before an individual is qualified to administer, score, and interpret Rorschach responses. Although some standardized scoring methods are available, the experience of the examiner plays a significant role in the interpretation of the responses.

Thematic Apperception test (TAT). The TAT is a more structured projective technique than the Rorschach. It consists of 20 cards, 19 of which show actual scenes taken from photographs or paintings, and one of which is blank.

The subject is shown a card and asked to make up a story about it. He is told to describe what is going on, and what the

Personality

476

character or characters are doing, thinking, and feeling. He is asked what preceded the events shown and what will be the outcome. In the case of the blank card, he is asked to imagine a picture and make up a story.

The following story was related by a married male adult in response to a TAT card showing a group of casually dressed men lying close to one another in a field:

(Pause) I don't get much from this. If it were in the service, why it's a possibility that they might be just relaxing from the fatigue. (Pause) This gives me the impression that it's just four lazy men. (Pause) It's hard for me to imagine anything out of this primarily because I don't care for (Pause) the relatively—relative closeness there—ah—of how they're lying (Pause) one so close to another with apparently more ground to spread out in. Ah—ah—I don't know why one should—should rest on another. (Pause) It looks like it might be a hobo jungle. (Pause) As far as I'm concerned, it—it's repulsive to me.

Q: Why?

Well, ah I—ah I just—ah—something like that doesn't—ah (Pause) I get nothing from it. I—I—I can't—I see no reason for men to be bunched up sleeping together like that unless they were cold. Apparently they're not. (Pause) They're not dressed for cold weather. (Pause) They're—there's one lying on one man—no on this—well—all three of them, all three of the fellows are resting on another man, apparently in one form or another, they're touching him. (Pause) It's hard for me to get anything out of the picture. I don't know what would bring it about (Pause; sigh) unless it were—unless it was a hobo jungle. I've never been in one, all I've seen is an ex—is pictures similar to this one.

(Rosen and Gregory, 1965, pp. 181–182)

The examiner evaluates the content and formal characteristics of the stories and attempts to discover something about the person's motives and conflicts. As can be seen in this example, the cards can sometimes elicit thoughts and images that are disturbing to the subject, and may reveal unconscious underlying conflicts.

The TAT has also proved useful in research designed to measure the achievement motive (see Chapter 7).

Assessment of Personality

a)

b)

I like
Most people
My greatest worry
Men
Women
My father
This test

c) Supply the missing captions.

d) Which two faces do you like best? Which two do you like least?

Fig. 13.10
Examples of different types of projective techniques used in the study of personality.
a) The subject is provided with a number of cardboard figures and asked to create a dramatic scene in front of several different backgrounds.
b) The subject has to complete each sentence.
c) The subject has to supply the missing captions.
d) The subject is asked to choose the two faces he likes best and the two he likes least.
(a, photo courtesy of The Psychological Corporation. b, from *Personality* by J. P. Guilford, copyright 1959 by McGraw-Hill Book Company; used with permission. c, reproduced by permission from the Rosenzweig P-F Study, copyright 1948. d, after a test devised by L. Szondi, copyright 1959 by the J. B. Lippincott Company.)

Other projective techniques. There are a number of other projective techniques in common use. Figure 13.10 presents examples from some of the more widely used of these methods.

The projective tests are not usually used in isolation. Various test procedures are combined so that the examiner's evaluation is based on a broad sampling of behaviors in different types of situations.

Summary

1. Personality consists of those persistent and enduring behavior patterns of an individual that tend to be expressed in a wide variety of life situations.

2. Even at birth, differences in crying and activity level are discernible, and these variations produce different reactions among adults. These inborn tendencies and initial contacts form the basis for the development of those enduring behavior patterns referred to as personality.

3. Individuals coming from different cultural settings may manifest widely varying personality characteristics, because the members of each culture selectively shape and reinforce different behaviors.

4. During the first few years of a child's life, the parents act as the primary agents for transmitting their culture. As the child grows older, his social contacts broaden dramatically.

5. Type theories of personality search for primary characteristics that can be used to describe the whole personality (for example, extroversion versus introversion).

6. Trait theories attempt to overcome the limitations in type theories by describing personality in terms of a large number of dimensions.

7. One of the most influential theories of personality, psychoanalytic theory, was initially developed by Sigmund Freud. Personality is divided into three parts: the id, the ego, and the superego. The developing individual passes through several stages, during which the focus of pleasure shifts from the mouth to the anus and then to the genitals.

8. While the various psychoanalytic theories derive their data from observations of patients in clinical practice, learning theorists start out with the basic assumption that personality is learned, and therefore the principles of learning are applicable.

9. A number of instruments have been designed to assess various aspects of personality. The results of testing are used for vocational counseling, determining a person's suitability for a

position, assisting in the diagnosis and prognosis of emotional problems, and testing the assumptions and predictions arising from some theory of behavior.

10. Some of the methods that have been developed to assess personality include interviews, rating scales, personality inventories, and projective techniques, such as the Rorschach test and the Thematic Apperception Test.

Terms to Remember

Anal Stage   In psychoanalytic theory, the stage of psychosexual development during which the infant derives pleasure from both elimination and retention of feces.

Castration Anxiety   A boy's fear that his father will castrate him in retaliation for his Oedipal feelings.

Collective Unconscious   In Jung's theory, a portion of the unconscious containing certain shared experiences, predispositions, and symbols which are inherited and found in all members of a given race or species.

Ego   In psychoanalytic theory, the aspect of the personality that regulates and controls the impulsive expressions of the id and deals with the demands of reality.

Electra Complex   Unconscious sexual feelings of a girl for her father.

Extroversion   The tendency to be outgoing and to engage in occupations or activities in which there is much contact with people (contrast with introversion).

Genital Stage   In psychoanalytic theory, the stage of psychosexual development in which the focus of erotic pleasure returns to the genital zone and the individual achieves mature heterosexual relations.

Halo Effect   The tendency, when making judgments about a particular trait, to be influenced by your overall impression of the individual you are rating.

Id In psychoanalytic theory, the primitive and instinctual drives of the individual. The id is concerned only with the immediate satisfaction of basic biological drives.

Identification The process of incorporating into one's own personality the values and beliefs of another person, usually a parent.

Introversion The tendency to be inward, to prefer being alone, and to engage in activities in which there is little contact with people (contrast with extroversion).

Inventory A series of objective questions designed to measure a single trait or several aspects of personality simultaneously.

Latency Stage In psychoanalytic theory, the stage of psychosexual development in which sexual urgings become dormant.

Oedipus Complex Unconscious sexual feelings of a boy for his mother.

Oral Stage In psychoanalytic theory, the first stage of psychosexual development, during which the mouth is the principal source of sexual or erotic pleasure.

Personality Those persistent and enduring behavior patterns of an individual that tend to be expressed in a wide variety of life situations.

Phallic Stage In psychoanalytic theory, the stage of psychosexual development in which the focus of erotic pleasure is the genital zone.

Pleasure Principle The tendency to seek immediate satisfaction of basic urges.

Projective Techniques Methods of assessing personality in which the individual is confronted with ambiguous materials and asked to interpret them.

Psychoanalysis A school of psychology, founded by Sigmund Freud, which emphasizes the unconscious determinants of behavior; a theory of personality and the diagnosis and treatment of psychopathology.

Terms to Remember

Rating Scale   A device for making judgments about oneself or others on certain defined traits.

Reality Principle   The principle of adapting the demands of the id to the realities of the environment.

Rorschach Test   A projective test of personality consisting of a series of ink blots.

Superego   In psychoanalytic theory, internal controls and standards derived from early influences; corresponds to the "conscience."

Thematic Apperception Test (TAT)   A projective test of personality in which the subject makes up stories for a set of pictures.

Trait   A characteristic used to describe a basic personality dimension.

Type Theories   Theories of personality that attempt to classify people into specific types, using primary characteristics to describe the whole personality.

Recommended Readings

Blum, G. S., *Psychoanalytic Theories of Personality,* New York: McGraw-Hill Book Co., 1953.

Integrated treatment of various psychoanalytic theories of personality.

Hall, C. S., and Lindzey, G., *Theories of Personality* (2nd ed.), New York: John Wiley & Sons, Inc., 1970.

Comprehensive review of the approaches of the leading personality theorists.

Pervin, L. A., *Personality: Theory, Assessment, and Research,* New York: John Wiley & Sons, Inc., 1970.

Uses the actual case of a normal college student to illustrate the different theoretical approaches and the relationships among theory, assessment, and the individual.

Wiggins, J. S., et al., *The Psychology of Personality,* Reading, Massachusetts: Addison-Wesley Publishing Co., 1971.

Comprehensive and well-written textbook that promotes the thesis that personality is best considered from many, often conflicting, points of view.

Zubin, J., Eron, L. D., and Schumer, F., *An Experimental Approach to Projective Techniques,* New York: John Wiley & Sons, Inc., 1965.

Thorough treatment of the various projective techniques.

14
ABNORMAL BEHAVIOR AND PSYCHOTHERAPY

Fig. 14.1
Not until the end of the nineteenth century was insanity considered a medical problem. Philippe Pinel was the first to effectively promote the view that insane persons were not incurable "wild beasts" who were insensible to pain, but victims of specific organic disorders. He advocated their liberation from the filthy asylums in which they were treated like prisoners. In 1798 he unshackled his patients at two of Paris' insane asylums. Once insanity was properly viewed as a medical problem and asylums were transformed into hospitals, the great strides of nineteenth-century psychiatry became possible. (a, "Madness" from Charles Bell, *Essays on the Anatomy of Expression,* London, 1806. b, Pinel striking off the chains of the insane at Salpêtrière; engraving, 1876. c, interior of the Eastern Hospital for the Insane, Konkakee, Illinois, 1895. Photos from the National Library of Medicine, Bethesda, Maryland.)

What Is Abnormal?

There are many different ways of defining "abnormal." Unfortunately, these definitions are often at variance with one another. For example, legal definitions are frequently in conflict with definitions arising from the fields of psychology and psychiatry. In some states, for instance, an individual is considered mentally ill only if he is unaware of the consequences of his actions. Thus, a person who plants a bomb "to gain revenge against all of the people who are out to get me" might be ruled legally sane if he knew that detonation of the bomb might kill people. Psychologists, however, might judge the same individual "insane" because of the severe distortions in his perceptions of the motives of others.

The word abnormal means "away from the normal"; thus, the question, "What is abnormal?" implies that there is a clearly defined "normal" and that departures from this constitute the abnormal. In many fields of human endeavor, it is not difficult to define what is normal. For example, in the field of medicine, scientists and doctors have a reasonably good idea of the structure and functions of the various parts of the body. The line between normal and pathological functioning is usually fairly clear. When it comes to psychological functioning, however, we have no established model of normality against which to judge abnormality. This is not meant to imply that no definitions of

Attitudes Toward Self	Emphasizing self-acceptance, adequate self-identity, realistic appraisal of one's assets and liabilities.
Perception of Reality	A realistic view of oneself and the surrounding world of people and things.
Integration	Unity of personality, freedom from disabling inner conflicts, good stress tolerance.
Competencies	Development of essential physical, intellectual, emotional, and social competencies for coping with life's problems.
Autonomy	Adequate self-reliance, responsibility, and self-direction—together with sufficient independence of social influences.
Growth, Self-Actualization	Emphasizing trends toward increasing maturity, development of potentialities, and self-fulfillment as a person.
Interpersonal Relations	Capacity for forming and maintaining intimate interpersonal relations.
Goal Attainment	Does not strive to achieve perfection but sets goals which are realistic and within the individual's capabilities.

Box 14.1
Characteristics of the "normal" individual. (From *Abnormal Psychology and Modern Life* by James C. Coleman. Copyright © 1972 by Scott, Foresman and Company. Reprinted by permission of the publisher.)

"normal" have been attempted. Box 14.1 presents some of the characteristics that are thought to describe healthy mental functioning. Note that we have not portrayed the normal individual as always happy, contented, and free from conflicts. On the contrary,

> ... he may often fall short of his ideals; and because of ignorance, the limitations under which an individual lives in a complex world, or the strength of immediate pressures, he may sometimes behave in ways that prove to be shortsighted or self-defeating. Consequently, he knows something of the experience of guilt at times, and because he tried to be fully aware of the risks he takes he can hardly be entirely free from fear and worry.
>
> (Shoben, 1957, p. 189)

What is Abnormal?

What are some of the different ways of defining the abnormal? One approach would be to define the normal as behavior that is approved and accepted within a given culture. Thus, those behaviors that fail to comply with cultural values or standards would be called abnormal. This cultural definition of abnormality implies that no behavior is abnormal so long as it is accepted by society. Thus, its advocates would argue that there is no such thing as a "sick society":

> A critical example is whether an obedient Nazi concentration-camp commander would be considered normal or abnormal. To the extent that he was responding accurately and successfully to his environment and not breaking its rules, much less coming to the professional attention of psychiatrists, he would not be labeled abnormal. Repulsive as his behavior is to mid-twentieth-century Americans, such repulsion is based on a particular set of values. Although such a person may be made liable for his acts—as Nazi war criminals were—the concept of abnormality as a special entity does not seem necessary or justified. If it is, the problem arises as to who selects the values, and this, in turn, implies that one group may select values that are applied to others. This situation of one group's values being dominant over others is the fascistic background from which the Nazi camp commander sprang.
>
> (Ullmann and Krasner, 1969, p. 15)

The cultural definition of abnormality has some serious shortcomings. Its critics argue that "it rests on the questionable assumption that socially accepted behavior is never pathological, and it implies that normality is nothing more than conformity" (Coleman, 1972, p. 15).

Another way to define the abnormal is in terms of the significance of an individual's behavior. If his behavior interferes with his ability to achieve goals or to resolve motivational conflicts, we may regard him as maladjusted. If a young woman is highly motivated to achieve a satisfying heterosexual relationship but constantly engages in self-defeating behavior (picking arguments, overeating, avoiding social occasions), we may say she is maladjusted and, in a sense, abnormal.

Critics of the adjustment point of view argue that some behaviors may be well adapted to achieving goals, but the goals themselves may reflect abnormality. Hitler was eminently successful in achieving many of his goals, but one would be hard-pressed to regard him as "normal."

A third basis for a definition is the one used by many professionals in the mental health field. They classify certain types of behaviors as abnormal, for example, those indicating disordered thought processes or loss of contact with reality, or irrational emotional outbursts. A person who manifests some or many of these behaviors is deemed abnormal.

In actual practice, the diagnosis of abnormality involves some combination of all these definitions. Suppose you are told about some woman who fired all her servants because "their personalities clashed with the wallpaper." Would you say she is abnormal? The reason for the dismissal is certainly not consistent with cultural values. It is maladjustive if her goal is to maintain an orderly household. Finally, her behavior betrays bizarre thought processes. (How would you go about ascertaining that personalities clash with wallpaper?)

From this brief sample of the woman's behavior, then, we have come to question her normality. Of course, we would not attempt a definitive diagnosis on the basis of such little evidence. Diagnostic judgments are made on the basis of observations of behavior in a variety of settings—therapeutic interviews, personality test results, reports of friends or relatives, to name a few.

The above example was taken from a case history of a woman patient suffering from a severe form of emotional disturbance. A more extended excerpt appears below. As you read the case history, try to relate her various behaviors to the three ways of defining abnormal behavior discussed above. While reading this, and other illustrative cases appearing throughout this chapter, it may be profitable to bear in mind such questions as: How did her behavior affect her own life? How did her behavior affect the lives of her family, her friends, and her employees?

Maya M. was a recent patient of a private mental hospital. She comes from a wealthy family and has enjoyed the best of privileges in life. She went to an exclusive private girls school and majored in fine arts in an Eastern college. She married an industrial executive and continued to live a successful life, throwing large gala gatherings attended by governors, senators, corporation presidents, diplomats. She gave birth to a son and was quite unhappy at having to take time away from her social life. Within a year of his birth, Maya developed a deep depression. She was despondent about the oncoming birthday party and felt she could not do him justice. Her depths of despair seemed real enough but quite inappropriate to the topic of her concern. She began to berate herself for having her child born before she could properly prepare the program for his first birthday party. She seemed to recover from her depression before long but retained some bizarre behavior. She fired all her servants on the basis that their personalities clashed with her wallpaper. She had a bedroom window torn out and replaced with a window that was triangular shaped because the three points imparted a feeling of "godliness" to her. She began writing notes to herself and having them translated into Chinese since this helped to unify the East and the West in the Universe. Her notes were often incomprehensible and irrational. Many phrases were sound associations, for example, "Clang, chang, brang, bang, ultramang." She became very literal in her interpretation of instructions. For example, her French recipe called to her to "prepare the lamb"; she did exactly this by talking soothingly to the lamb chop, describing her intentions so that it would know what to expect and be properly "prepared." She was hospitalized by her husband. Subsequently she plunged into another highly agitated fit of despair.

Following six months of treatment she was released from the hospital. Her social activities have been sharply curtailed, but she has been permitted and encouraged to be with her husband and her son. She says herself that it is the first time she has really felt part of the family.

(Suinn, 1970, p. 406)

A Note of Caution

In the case history presented above, we see instances of bizarre and outlandish behavior. Before proceeding further, it is important to point out that abnormal behavior is not always bizarre. Unfortunately, the public's acquaintance with most abnormal behavior comes from the mass media (newspapers, television, and movies), in which only the extreme forms of emotionally disturbed behavior are usually depicted. We read about and see rapists, mass murderers, or child abusers. Such accounts tend to portray mental patients as dangerous "raving maniacs" whose behavior patterns are so totally different from the "normal" that they appear to be almost a species unto themselves.

As a matter of fact, the behavior of most emotionally disturbed persons, whether institutionalized or not, is often not distinguishable from the "normal." There is no sharp dividing line where "normal" ends and "abnormal" begins. Some individuals are in an almost constant state of turmoil, unable to cope with the everyday requirements of living. All of us are, at one time or another, beset with worry, guilt, or self-doubts. Mostly, it is a question of degree. The magnitude of the problems as the individual sees them, and the success he has coping with them, may vary by minute degrees from "normal" to "abnormal." In this normal–abnormal continuum, even the same person may shift his position at different periods of his life and under special circumstances. An otherwise well-adjusted individual may, at times, be so overwhelmed by life's problems that his ability to make effective adjustments may be impaired. Conversely, changes in one's life situation for the better (a job promotion, an improved marital relationship, or an easing of financial burdens) may result in better adjustment.

A final note of caution: As you read this chapter, you may find that you "recognize" many of the symptoms of disturbed behavior in yourself or others. This is not uncommon. Just as many medical students are likely to perceive symptoms of physical illness in themselves as they read about various disorders, so also are students of psychology prone to imagine themselves victims of psychological disorders. If you have such thoughts as you read, you should not take them too seriously. It is only through increased knowledge and awareness of the factors underlying emotional disorders that we can gain those special insights that permit us to adjust more effectively to our life situation.

In the remainder of this chapter, we will discuss some of the broad classes of emotional disorders and several of the therapeutic techniques that have been developed to alleviate them.

The Neuroses

A college student appeared at the counseling center with a complaint that he was deathly afraid of examinations. Although he prepared himself well for tests, the mere mention of an exam would arouse fear in him. He had thus far achieved a fair but not outstanding grade point average. He had previously been involved in a confrontation with an instructor whom he accused of having administered an unfair test in that there was not enough time to answer all the questions. It soon became evident that such antagonistic behavior was a displacement of his frustration with himself. He soon realized that the time limit had not been long enough because he had wasted most of his time in attempting to control his anxieties. He had already skipped two other examinations by remaining in bed petrified with his fears of failure.

(Suinn, 1970, p. 242)

The above excerpt from a case history illustrates many of the characteristics of neurotic behavior. The neurotic individual is almost constantly unhappy, feels threatened and anxious in situations that most people would not consider dangerous, and avoids threatening situations instead of coping with them. He tends to cling rigidly to behavior patterns that are maladaptive because they provide an immediate, though temporary, relief from anxiety. However, these behaviors do not solve the real problem. For example, the student in the above illustration on two occasions managed to avoid the acute anxiety associated with examinations by staying in bed, but he was still plagued with his fear when later examinations came up.

What does neurotic behavior accomplish? In the short run, the person "solves" his problem by some kind of avoidance. In the long run, he persists in self-defeating behaviors. He typically reacts to a threatening situation by calling into play one or more of the defense mechanisms (see Chapter 12), usually in an exaggerated fashion. Neurotic behavior is a prime example of allowing the tail (defense mechanisms) to wag the dog (the person's life).

Neurotic individuals usually do not require hospitalization and are not likely to be dangerous to themselves or others. In the

Box 14.2
Dimensions of anxiety. (From *Abnormal Psychology and Modern Life* by James C. Coleman. Copyright © 1972 by Scott, Foresman and Company. Reprinted by permission of the publisher.)

1. **Realistic or Pathological.** Anxiety is considered realistic when it is appropriate in degree to the objective threat; it is considered pathological when it is out of proportion to the actual threat.

2. **Specific or General.** Anxiety may be elicited by certain specific situations which the individual perceives as threatening; or it may be elicited by a view of the world as a generally dangerous and hostile place.

3. **Aware or Unaware.** The individual may be acutely aware of his anxiety, as in an anxiety attack; he may feel vaguely apprehensive and anxious; or his anxiety may be repressed and kept out of awareness.

4. **Acute or Chronic.** The individual may evidence sudden intense anxiety in the face of a threatening situation; or he may maintain a chronic, continuously high level of anxiety.

5. **Positive or Negative.** At mild levels, anxiety may lead to increased effort and improved performance; at intermediate and higher levels, it may lead to the disorganization of behavior.

These dimensions of anxiety are not necessarily discrete, of course, but rather occur in varying combinations.

sections that follow, we will look at specific types of neurotic patterns. We will be giving examples of "textbook" cases throughout this chapter. We should point out, however, that patients generally display various combinations of symptoms. Rarely, in real life, is there a "pure" type.

Anxiety Reactions

We previously (Chapter 7) defined anxiety as a fear reaction to unknown or unidentified stimuli, a premonition that something bad will happen. Box 14.2 presents the dimensions of anxiety. A person suffering an *anxiety reaction* is usually in a constant state of anxiety and tension. Occasionally, he may have an "anxiety attack" in which he experiences intense and unbearable anxiety. These attacks are accompanied by widespread bodily symptoms, such as heart palpitations, profuse sweating, and breathing problems, as well as such psychological symptoms as inability to concentrate, difficulty in decision making, and a pervasive feeling of discouragement.

Anxiety is not in itself neurotic. Everyone experiences anxiety from time to time. However, the anxiety neurotic *constantly* feels threatened even though, to an outsider, there appears to be no real danger. For the individual suffering an anxiety reaction, the threat, although unidentifiable, is very real. The following case

The Neuroses

illustrates both the "free-floating" nature of anxiety reactions and the acute phases of an anxiety attack:

> The twenty-six-year-old wife of a successful lawyer came to a psychiatric clinic with the complaint that she had "the jitters." She said she felt that she was going to pieces. She had fears of being alone, of screaming, of running away, and of committing suicide. These fears were all intensified when she came near an open window. She suffered from constant headache, fatigue and nervousness, from episodes of abdominal cramps and diarrhea. Twice in the past year there had been "attacks," in which she had become dizzy and had broken out into a cold sweat. Her hands and feet became clammy, her heart pounded, her head seemed tight, she had a lump in her throat and could not get her breath.
>
> (Cameron and Magaret, 1951, p. 307)

In the anxiety reaction, anxiety is diffuse and without focus (free-floating). In the other neurotic reactions discussed below, anxiety is at least partially alleviated by the development of specific symptoms which protect the individual against underlying anxiety. Except for incomplete repression, the anxiety neurotic generally does not have these defenses.

Phobic Reactions

Phobias are unreasonable, intense, and persistent fears of situations or objects that do not constitute any real danger to the person. Because they tend to occur under fairly specific circumstances, a large number of phobias have been identified and named according to the situations in which they occur. A few well-known examples are claustrophobia (fear of closed places), acrophobia (fear of high places), and nyctophobia (fear of darkness or night).

Although the anxiety is elicited by a specific situation or class of objects, the individual is unaware of the reason for his fear. The situation that initially gave rise to the fear is repressed, usually because of guilt associated with it.

Some theorists believe that the phobic object is symbolic of some underlying conflict. These theorists might search for some underlying sexual conflict, for example, to explain a phobic fear of snakes.

Abnormal Behavior and Psychotherapy

494

Other theorists use learning-theory principles to explain phobias. They argue that fear was originally conditioned to the phobic object because of its direct or indirect association with a negative emotional state.

The following case illustrates the dynamics underlying a woman's fear of open spaces (agoraphobia):

Ellen R., a thirty-two-year-old woman, developed a severe case of agoraphobia in which she became terrified each time she attempted to leave her house. The phobia became so serious that she gave up her job, and remained home at all times. When she sought psychological help, it was found that when she was in her early teens she had been sexually promiscuous with several boys in the neighborhood. The patient changed her behavior when the family moved to another neighborhood, and she entered a new school. She experienced intense guilt feelings about her behavior, and she repressed all memories of it. The phobia which developed later in her life was based on the fear that she might lose control of herself, and be led into a life of prostitution. Without realizing what had happened, the patient had reactivated the entire episode some weeks earlier when she was going through some old papers and found a group photograph of herself at the time she had been promiscuous. The chain of unconscious associations triggered by the picture was responsible for the appearance of the agoraphobia at that particular time.

(Kisker, 1964, p. 255)

Phobic fears are most likely to develop when the person has strong guilt feelings which he has repressed. The phobic reaction can usually be prevented if the person is able to discuss his guilt feelings with a confidante before repression has set in. Later in this chapter, we will look at one method that has been successful in treating phobic reactions (desensitization therapy).

Obsessive–Compulsive Reactions

The biggest thing I've got is this obsession which spoils everything I do. If I had the courage I'd kill myself and get rid of the whole lot—it goes on and on, day after day. The obsession governs everything I do from the minute I open my eyes in the morning until I close them at night. It governs

The Neuroses

what I can touch, and what I can't touch, where I can walk, and where I can't walk. It governs whatever I do. I can touch the ground but I can't touch shoes, can't touch hems of coats, can't use the toilet without washing my hands and arms half a dozen times—and they must be washed right up the arms.

(Marks, 1965, p. 1)

This case illustrates the pattern of symptoms in an obsessive–compulsive reaction. An *obsession* is a recurring thought or impulse that persistently intrudes itself into the individual's consciousness. The *compulsive behavior* is a means of suppressing the anxiety associated with the unpleasant persistent and recurring thoughts or impulses.

All of us at varying times have had obsessive thoughts and engaged in compulsive behaviors. For example, after an important exam, have you found yourself plagued with thoughts such as, "What was the third question?—How did I answer it? Did I leave anything out?" Have you ever engaged in such compulsive behaviors as knocking on wood, doodling, or counting telephone poles as you ride along in a car? We seem to have no control over even these relatively minor obsessions and compulsions. We usually recognize them as being foolish and irrational at the time they occur. It is only when these obsessive–compulsive behaviors seriously interfere with our daily lives that we classify them as neurotic. The obsessive–compulsive neurotic may also recognize the irrationality of his behavior, but feels powerless to stop it. Moreover, he experiences great anxiety if his compulsive actions are thwarted.

Dissociative Reactions

No form of neurotic behavior has attracted such widespread attention as dissociative reactions. These involve some impairment of memory functions, usually as a defense to avoid or escape from an anxiety-arousing situation. Amnesia is a common example. The amnesia victim figuratively escapes a threatening situation by a partial or complete loss of memory of his personal identity. Sometimes the individual also literally escapes the situation by fleeing, at the same time forgetting his own identity and taking on a new identity.

Abnormal Behavior and Psychotherapy

A relatively rare form of dissociative reaction occurs when two or more independent and often opposite personalities exist within the same individual. *Dr. Jekyll and Mr. Hyde* (a story by Robert L. Stevenson) and the movie *The Three Faces of Eve* represent two examples of multiple personalities, the first drawn from literature, the second from an actual case history (Thigpen and Cleckley, 1954). The following excerpt illustrates how dramatic the separation of personality characteristics can be in this form of dissociative reaction:

A 28-year-old married woman was admitted to a hospital, depressed and retarded, after a suicidal attempt. Several days later she became angry and assaultive, claimed that it was her fault that she was depressed. She then stated that "Mary" was the depressed person; she was Cynthia. As Cynthia she reported frequently leaving home, picking up sailors and lesbians, and acting in a loose and lascivious manner. As Mary she acted as a dutiful, quiet, submissive housewife and mother, angry and depressed over her husband's poor relationship to her. Periodically she abruptly assumed the character of Cynthia and became loud, boisterous, and uninhibited. In the depressed state she accepted the dictates of her superego, repressed the rage toward her husband, and dutifully attempted to assume her responsibilities as a housewife, as Mary. When overwhelmed by rage, she expressed her rage through defiance and acted her aggressive and sexual urges as Cynthia. Only the latter dissociation recognized the former.

(Noyes and Kolb, 1963, p. 54)

Conversion Reactions

In conversion reactions (sometimes called hysteria), the individual suffers sensory or motor impairment (for example, blindness or paralysis) without any physical cause. As in all the neurotic reactions, these physical symptoms serve to defend the individual from anxiety.

One of the features of conversion reactions is that the person seems to be indifferent to his disability and tends to resist treatment. This has sometimes been called *la belle indifférence* ("beautiful indifference," or apathy). The symptoms are not faked; they are genuine. The following case shows both the defensive value of conversion reactions and the attitude of the patient toward his disability:

> The patient was a young college student involved in a minor traffic accident on his way home from classes. Although he was slightly bruised, medical examination showed no serious physical involvement and the patient was discharged from the hospital. He awakened the next morning with a numbness in his legs and found himself unable to move them. He was returned by ambulance to the hospital for extensive neurological and X-ray examinations with negative results.
>
> Throughout, the patient seemed bemused by the procedures, intrigued by the machinery, and taken by the nurses. The diagnosis: conversion reaction.
>
> This college student was interviewed by a psychologist and the following facts came to light. Just prior to the accident, he had another of many arguments with his family over his education. He preferred to seek employment in order to obtain an income. His parents, both from immigrant backgrounds, had forced him to continue his schooling in spite of constant bickering. He was on an allowance on the condition that he remain in school. Money had always been a problem since the patient tended to squander it on social activities, girl friends, and his motorbike. The patient admitted that he had not prepared himself for final examinations and was certain he would have failed them since he was incapable of successfully cramming. The draft had already taken some of his peers and he was positive that he would also be called once he lost his student deferment from the draft. The accident itself came as a surprise since he had always been reasonably cautious on his motorbike. Yet, he had driven in a carefree and even reckless fashion when the accident occurred. When he was first released from the hospital he felt "kinda lucky that I wasn't killed, but kinda sorry I wasn't scraped up more than I was." The impression was that a disabling injury would have been painful but useful.
>
> (Suinn, 1970, p. 238)

The Psychoses

As we have mentioned, the neurotic individual is rarely so disturbed as to require hospitalization. In contrast, people suffering from the most extreme forms of emotional disturbance—psychoses—must often be committed to institutions. Although the various psychotic conditions may differ in a number of ways, they have many characteristics in common. In general, the psychotic person shows a loss of contact with reality, disturbed thought processes, and personality disorganization, and is not able to function normally in society. See if you can identify these characteristics in the case of Leonard K.:

> Mr. Leonard K., age 55, was referred to the hospital by his family after an episode of reckless promises, extravagant claims, and grandiose commitments. He had usually been a calm and reserved person, but gradually began to show a change in personality. Once a fastidious dresser, he had suddenly surprised his wife by neglecting to shave, wearing suits that had been wrinkled because he slept in them, and refusing to wash. He became more and more expansive, talkative, and occasionally violent. By the time he was committed for treatment he believed himself to be a state senator, and spoke of his planned travels to "executive emperor" (words he had difficulty in communicating). He was known to stand wherever a crowd was willing to listen and loudly pronounce his views on war, religion, birth control, and nearly any topic that was suggested. His views were more on the order of "solutions" to world problems than opinions. His wife described him as having been an almost too mild person prior to the recent outbursts. His gradual loss of memory led him to confabulation (filling in memory gaps by creating events to relate). His shift to grandiosity was believed to be an attempt to compensate for his lowered self-confidence and esteem.
>
> (Suinn, 1970, p. 332)

Many theorists believe that the psychoses represent an exaggerated or more intense degree of neurotic reaction. They view psychoses as differing from neuroses only in the severity of the symptoms. Others argue that psychoses are distinct and fundamentally different forms of emotional disturbance.

There is similar disagreement concerning the underlying causes of psychoses. Everyone agrees that some forms of psychosis clearly stem from known physiological causes. However, there are many psychotic conditions for which no physiological factors can be specified; these are called *functional* psychoses. But, even in these psychoses, biological or genetic

The Psychoses

factors, or both, are thought to play an important role.

Some theorists maintain that there is no difference between psychoses in which there is a known organic cause and those for which no physical cause has been identified. They argue that subtle biological factors are at work in all psychoses—"No twisted thought without a twisted molecule."* Evidence for this position comes from studies in which samples of blood serum, urine, or spinal fluid taken from psychotics have had toxic effects upon lower organisms. Similar samples taken from nonpsychotic individuals have not produced these effects (Gamper and Krall, 1934; Heath, 1960). These theorists also point out that individuals have been known to display psychotic-like behavior while under the influence of certain drugs (for example, LSD); this behavior is sometimes referred to as a "bad trip." The fact that a chemical substance can induce such behavior suggests that chemical changes within the individual may be a key factor in all psychoses. Furthermore, certain drugs which are known to counteract the effects of LSD have been helpful in alleviating some psychotic symptoms.

Other theorists ascribe the functional psychoses to environmental factors. Some believe that early childhood experiences are crucial factors in the development of psychotic behavior. They point to case histories, like the following, to illustrate the role of early childhood experiences in the development of psychotic reactions:

As we began to learn about the family background, it became clear that the patient conducted his hospital life in the same autocratic, pompous, and captious manner in which the father had governed the parental household. [The father] was an ingenious and successful foreign-born manufacturer, but at home he ruled his roost like an Eastern potentate, a role for which he also claimed divine sanction and inspiration via a special mystical cult that he shared only with a very few special friends. The patient would permit only a chosen few of the staff into his sanctum, just as the father had secluded himself in his bedroom during most of the time that he spent

*Quoted from a speech by Ralph Gerard as reported in L. G. Abood, "A Chemical Approach to the Problem of Mental Disease," in D. D. Jackson, ed., *The Etiology of Schizophrenia*, New York: Basic Books, 1960.

at home, with only his wife and the children's governess permitted to enter and attend to his needs. [The father], successful inventor and merchant, would sit there in his underclothes reading religious books by the hour. The entire household participated in the religious rites, the mother sharing his beliefs completely and continuing to do so even after his death, which according to the cult meant continuing life in a different form; the widow did not dare to disavow his teachings, because she believed he would know of it.

More than imitation and caricaturization of the father's behavior was involved. Both the patient and his only sister were emotionally deprived children who were isolated from the parents and from the surrounding community because the family milieu was so aberrant.

(Fleck, 1960, pp. 337–338)

Some of the environmentalists feel that unusually stressful circumstances experienced at *any* age can precipitate a psychotic episode. The following case illustrates the effects of sudden catastrophic events on a 37-year-old woman:

An unmarried woman of 37 entered a psychiatric hospital in a state of extreme agitation, weeping, moaning and wringing her hands. From her cousins who accompanied her, it was learned that the close-knit rural family to which the patient belonged had been recently and abruptly dissolved. The patient's brother, to whom she was strongly attached, had been killed in an accident; and shortly afterward, the patient's aged father and her ailing mother died within a week's time.

(Cameron and Magaret, 1951, p. 257)

A number of studies have shown that not all people are equally susceptible to the effects of stressful circumstances. For example, when individuals are placed in an isolated room in which they are systematically deprived of sensory stimulation, some individuals begin to display characteristic psychotic-like behavior shortly after being isolated. Others are able to withstand the stress of sensory deprivation for much longer periods before they display any psychotic-like symptoms (Bexton et al., 1954). It would seem that everybody has a "breaking point" (see the discussion of the general adaptation syndrome in Chapter 8).

The Psychoses

Box 14.3
Comparison of neuroses and functional psychoses. (From
Abnormal Psychology and Modern Life by James C.
Coleman. Copyright © 1972 by Scott, Foresman and
Company. Reprinted by permission of the publisher.)

	Neuroses	Functional Psychoses
General Behavior	Maladaptive avoidance behavior, with mild impairment of personal and social functioning.	Severe personality decompensation; marked impairment of contact with reality; severe impairment of personal and social functioning.
Nature of Symptoms	Wide range of psychological and somatic symptoms, but no hallucinations or other extreme deviations in thought, affect, or action.	Wide range of symptoms, with extreme deviations in thought, affect, and action—for example, delusions, hallucinations, emotional blunting, bizarre behavior.
Orientation to the Environment	Slight, if any, impairment of orientation to environment with respect to time, place, and person.	Frequent loss of orientation to environment with respect to time, place, and person.
Insight (Self-Understanding)	Frequently, some understanding of own maladaptive behavior, but with a seeming inability to change it.	Markedly impaired understanding of current symptoms and behavior.
Physically Destructive Behavior	Behavior rarely dangerous or physically injurious to anyone.	In some cases behavior may be dangerous to self or others.
Etiology (Causes)	Emphasis on failure to acquire needed competencies, and/or on learned maladaptive behaviors.	Emphasis on maladaptive learning, decompensation under excessive stress, and possible biochemical irregularities.

Although it cannot be demonstrated yet, it is quite probable that the so-called functional psychoses represent the interplay of both environmental and organic factors. It is known, for example, that stress can produce profound biochemical changes in an individual. At the same time, as we have just seen, stress under some conditions can precipitate a psychotic episode.

No matter what the explanation for psychotic behavior, there is no question that the psychoses represent a very serious personal, social, emotional, and medical problem. Mental patients occupy more than half the hospital beds in this country.

*Abnormal Behavior
and Psychotherapy*

Psychoses can strike members of all ethnic and social groups at any age, often with no warning signs. They appear to occur more frequently among males, urban dwellers, and single or divorced people. Apparently, there is no relationship to intelligence (Goldenson, 1970). These statements are not meant to imply that such factors as sex and marital status *cause* psychotic breakdowns. On the contrary, it is quite possible that some people are not able to achieve successful marital relationships, for example, because of psychotic or prepsychotic conditions.

Box 14.3 shows some of the behavioral differences between neuroses and functional psychoses.

Let's now discuss some of the different types of psychotic reactions. In view of the long history of psychoses in the human species, it is somewhat surprising that we know so little about their causes. Even the classifications of psychotic behavior are confusing, inconsistent, and subject to much current dispute. Therefore, the way in which we classify psychotic disorders in this chapter is only one of many possible alternatives. Moreover, there is considerable overlapping of symptoms displayed by patients classified in the various categories of psychotic behavior. Just as each individual is unique, so also are the patterns of behavior displayed by each psychotic patient. We will look first at those disorders for which there is a known physical cause. Then we will examine psychotic reactions for which the causes are very much in doubt—manic–depressive reactions and schizophrenia.

Organic Psychoses

Look again at the case of Leonard K. presented on page 499. He was diagnosed as suffering from general paresis, a disease of the brain associated with the final stages of syphilitic infection. Early detection and treatment with drugs has greatly reduced the incidence of this psychotic condition.

Brain damage resulting in psychotic behavior may stem from a variety of causes, including diseases of the nervous system (such as syphillis), brain tumors, brain injuries, and overdoses of drugs or alcohol. One category of organic psychoses that many people are familiar with is associated with aging. Many older people are able to function quite well and show only a slight

The Psychoses

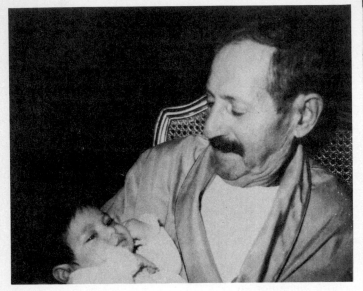

Fig. 14.2
Sam B. is an 85-year-old great-great-grandfather who remains
alert, vitally interested in and interesting to the world about him.

Fig. 14.3
Senility is an organic psychosis associated with
aging. (Copyright Mark Silber, 1972.)

decrease in mental ability (see Fig. 14.2). Others, however, suffer
a type of psychosis known as senility (see Fig. 14.3). Most senile
patients show a gradual deterioration of mental abilities. Some
become forgetful and confused; others hostile and irritable; a few
become suspicious of even their closest relatives. Perhaps the
most striking symptom involves impairment in memory functions.
The senile person often confuses present-day happenings with
past events. The following case illustrates such disturbances:

> During the past five years he had shown a progressive loss of
> interest in his surroundings and during the last year had
> become increasingly "childish." His wife and eldest son had
> brought him to the hospital because they felt they could no
> longer care for him in their home, particularly because of the
> grandchildren. They stated that he had become careless in his
> eating and other personal habits, was restless and prone to
> wandering about at night, and couldn't seem to remember
> anything that had happened during the day but was
> garrulous concerning events of his childhood and middle
> years.*

*From *Abnormal Psychology and Modern Life* by James C. Coleman, p. 550.
Copyright © 1972 by Scott, Foresman and Company. Reprinted by
permission of the publisher.

*Abnormal Behavior
and Psychotherapy*

Manic–Depressive Reactions

The primary characteristic of the manic–depressive reactions is extreme distortions of mood. The individual may show mood fluctuations from normal to either a manic phase or a depressive phase. The manic phase is characterized by high excitement, elation, and overactivity. The manic patient may run wildly about the room, singing, shouting, and gesturing dramatically. His conversation is often erratic, reflecting confused thoughts and ideas.

This excerpt from the case history of Madeline K. illustrates the manic phase:

> Her husband had returned home to find her twirling around the living room bizarrely draped in her wedding gown tied with a bathtowel and wearing a lampshade. She gaily greeted him, laughed with an ear-piercing shrillness, and invited him to stay for the exciting "coming-out" party she was giving. Strewn on the table were a thousand handwritten invitations signed with a flourish and addressed to such dignitaries as the President of the United States, the justices of the Supreme Court, the Emperor of Japan. She made incessant noises: singing her own ballads, shouting mottoes which she devised, reciting limericks, making rhyming sounds, and yelling obscenities. She had recorded her speech for presentation to the Library of Congress. The following is an excerpt:
>
> (Singing) By yon bonny briefs—my briefs are entirely outrageous but God take me you'd best like it—(in normal voice) the world is round the world is crown'd—illusions of Georgie, once a porgie—can't you see? —I am worth more than all the cherries in the universe—red is beautiful, red is ripe—bow ye before me and receive my blessing—thank God I'm not the devil—the freshest thing on this earth is a newborn clod—to work is to win—twin is as twin does—I sing a song of sexpot—hand me your head on a platter and I will forgive you all your sins—my plan will earn you a hundred-thousand-fold—mishmoshmoneymash—sliperydickerypop—dam it all full speed abreast—my head is gold, my hands are silver, my tail is platinum—Where am I? What time is it? Who goes there?—Gee but it's marvelous to be alive . . .
>
> (Suinn, 1970, p. 367)

The symptoms in the depressed phase are almost the complete opposite of those in the manic phase. Patients in the depressed phase show an extreme slowing down of mental and physical activity. They feel dejected, worthless, and guilty, and frequently attempt suicide. The following excerpt describes Madeline K.'s behavior in the depressed phase.

> An acquaintance had noticed her gradual refusal to leave her apartment and her apathetic attitude toward herself and the world around her. She looked immensely weary and had not slept soundly for days. She seemed mute, but would occasionally reply if a question were repeated long enough. Through careful probing it was found that she believed herself responsible for the "epidemics of the world" which she said was her punishment for her earlier sickness. She felt an urge to do penance for a lifetime of sin but could not remember the exact nature of her sin. For the past three weeks she had remained indoors pondering her own evil nature, and fearful of going out and possibly infecting others through the sheer enormity of her evilness. Life looked hopeless, she felt as though she was living in a shadow of despondency, despair enveloped her very existence. In the hospital she typically retired to a dark corner and would sit motionless for hours, heaving an occasional deep sigh. She seemed on the verge of weeping but her sorrow was never able to break loose. She was easily led by the nursing aides to different rooms, but once there she resumed her previous posture and ruminating.
>
> (Suinn, 1970, pp. 367–368)

Many patients do not display both the manic and depressive stages. Instead, they alternate between normal and one of the extremes.

Schizophrenic Reactions

Approximately 50 percent of all psychotic patients have been diagnosed as schizophrenic. What is schizophrenia? This is a highly controversial question. There is even considerable disagreement as to whether schizophrenia is a single mental disorder or, instead, many different disorders with similar symptoms. Although patients diagnosed as schizophrenic share certain symptoms, they also display some distinctively different behaviors. These differences constitute the most widely accepted basis for differentiating the types of schizophrenia. We shall look at four of these types: simple, hebephrenic, catatonic, and paranoid.

Simple schizophrenia is characterized by extreme apathy, withdrawal, and emotional dulling. Some cases of simple schizophrenia develop gradually over a period of many years, as the person increasingly withdraws into a simple and usually solitary way of life. This disorder often goes undetected because its onset is not sudden. The case of Kent illustrates many of these characteristics of simple schizophrenia:

> Kent had always seemed to his immediate family an unusually withdrawn person. In fact, he was laughingly dubbed "The Shy One" during childhood, a nickname which seemed so appropriate even later in life that it stuck. In elementary school he participated in few group sports or activities, preferring to be alone. While the other children enjoyed remaining at the school playground when classes were over, Kent left by himself and spent most of his hours in his room at home. In high school he was a model student in the sense that he never was a disciplinary problem, knew enough to get by, and was always polite. Few teachers felt that he was reachable, none noticed any topic about which he could become "fired-up." At the university he spent more of his time with the animals and in the fields than with his fellow students. He joined a fraternity but this seemed more for the convenience of the living arrangement. Parties generally found him a quiet observer although he occasionally allowed himself to be prompted into participating. He soon became the butt of many jokes because of his tendency to work in the yard while others were busy meeting and chatting with coeds. The joking barbs never seemed to penetrate his almost too even-tempered disposition. None of his friends ever felt they knew him in any real sense . . .
>
> (Suinn, 1970, p. 401)

The *hebephrenic schizophrenic* characteristically displays emotions that are inappropriate to the situation. His behavior is often silly and foolish; his conversation is rambling and incoherent and contains many neologisms (words he made up himself). He sometimes has scattered and disorganized *delusions* (false beliefs) and *hallucinations* (sensory experiences in the

The Psychoses

507

absence of appropriate sensory stimulation). Many of the features of hebephrenic schizophrenia are discernible in the following case:

> Edna K. was a 45-year-old wife of a laborer. Her illness had progressed rapidly and she was quite severely disturbed by the time of her admission to the hospital. It was impossible to obtain a meaningful description of her condition directly from her. The following is an excerpt from her intake interview:
>
> *Dr.* I am Dr. _____. I would like to know something more about you.
> *Pt.* You have a nasty mind. Lord!! Lord! Cat's in a cradle.
> *Dr.* Tell me, how do you feel?
> *Pt.* London's bell is a long, long dock. Hee! Hee! (Giggles uncontrollably.)
> *Dr.* Do you know where you are now?
> *Pt.* D___n! S___t on you all who rip into my internals! The grudgerometer will take care of you all! (Shouting) I am the Queen, see my magic, I shall turn you all into smidgelings forever!
> *Dr.* Your husband is concerned about you. Do you know his name?
> *Pt.* (Stands, walks to and faces the wall) Who am I, Who are we, Who are you, Who are they. (Turns) I . . . I . . . I . . . I!!! (Makes grotesque faces)
>
> Edna was placed in the women's ward where she proceeded to masturbate. She always sat in a chosen spot and in a chosen way, with her feet propped under her. Occasionally, she would scream or shout obscenities. At other times she giggled to herself. She was known to attack other patients. She began to complain that her uterus was attached to a "pipeline to the Kremlin" and that she was being "infernally invaded" by Communism.
>
> (Suinn, 1970, p. 402)

The identifying symptom of *catatonic schizophrenia* is extreme withdrawal into muteness and physical immobility. The catatonic frequently assumes and rigidly maintains a position for long periods of time. Sometimes, he exhibits "waxy flexibility," a state in which his body may be molded, like wax, into different positions. The following description of a catatonic patient illustrates these classic symptoms.

Abnormal Behavior and Psychotherapy

Manuel appeared to be physically healthy upon examination.
Yet he did not regain his awareness of his surroundings. He
remained motionless, speechless, and seemingly unconscious.
One evening an aide turned him on his side to straighten out
the sheet, was called away to tend another patient, and forgot
to return. Manuel was found the next morning, still on his
side, his arm tucked under his body, as he had been left the
night before. His arm was turning blue from lack of
circulation but he seemed to be experiencing no discomfort.
Further examination confirmed that he was in a state of waxy
flexibility.

(Suinn, 1970, p. 403)

Paranoid schizophrenia has received the greatest amount of
attention from the mass media and the general public. When a
severe psychotic condition is portrayed in a film, the symptoms
shown are usually those of paranoid schizophrenia. The primary
symptom is fragmented and illogical delusions. These are most
often delusions of persecution ("They are out to get me"), but
they are sometimes delusions of grandeur ("I am Napoleon," or "I
am God"). Paranoid schizophrenics are sometimes dangerous
because they may attempt to get revenge on those whom they
perceive as threatening. "Mad Bombers" are frequently paranoid
schizophrenics. Sirhan B. Sirhan, the convicted assassin of Senator
Robert F. Kennedy, was diagnosed as a paranoid schizophrenic.
Paranoid schizophrenics often have hallucinations in which they
claim to be receiving orders, usually from outer space, God, or
famous people in history. The following conversation illustrates
the illogical delusions of a paranoid schizophrenic:

Dr. What's your name?
Pt. Who are you?
Dr. I'm a doctor. Who are you?
Pt. I can't tell you who I am.
Dr. Why can't you tell me?
Pt. You wouldn't believe me.
Dr. What are you doing here?
Pt. Well, I've been sent here to thwart the Russians. I'm the
only one in the world who knows how to deal with
them. They got their spies all around here though to get
me, but I'm smarter than any of them.
Dr. What are you going to do to thwart the Russians?

The Psychoses

Pt. I'm organizing.

Dr. Whom are you going to organize?

Pt. Everybody. I'm the only man in the world who can do that, but they're trying to get me. But I'm going to use my atomic bomb media to blow them up.

Dr. You must be a terribly important person then.

Pt. Well, of course.

Dr. What do you call yourself?

Pt. You used to know me as Franklin D. Roosevelt.

Dr. Isn't he dead?

Pt. Sure he's dead, but I'm alive.

Dr. But you're Franklin D. Roosevelt?

Pt. His spirit. He, God, and I figured this out. And how I'm going to make a race of healthy people. My agents are lining them up. Say, who are you?

Dr. I'm a doctor here.

Pt. You don't look like a doctor. You look like a Russian to me.

Dr. How can you tell a Russian from one of your agents?

Pt. I read eyes. I get all my signs from eyes. I look into your eyes and get all my signs from them.

Dr. Do you sometimes hear voices telling you someone is a Russian?

Pt. No, I just look into eyes. I got a mirror here to look into my own eyes. I know everything that's going on. I can tell by the color, by the way it's shaped.

Dr. Did you have any trouble with people before you came here?

Pt. Well, only the Russians. They were trying to surround me in my neighborhood. One day they tried to drop a bomb on me from the fire escape.

Dr. How could you tell it was a bomb?

Pt. I just knew.*

Other Nonpsychotic Mental Disorders

In earlier sections of this chapter, we looked at neurotic disorders in which the control of anxiety plays a dominant role. We also

---

*From *Abnormal Psychology and Modern Life* by James C. Coleman, p. 276. Copyright © 1972 by Scott, Foresman and Company. Reprinted by permission of the publisher.

discussed the various psychotic states in which the individual displays severe distortions in his mental processes and his perceptions of place and time. In this section we will consider some disorders that commonly bring the individual into conflict with society. This category is a "mixed bag" which includes disturbances in personality as well as alcoholism, drug dependence, and compulsive gambling. We will restrict our discussion to the psychopathic personality and alcoholism.

The Psychopathic Personality

The psychopath (also called the antisocial personality) is something of an enigma. Unlike the neurotic, who is assailed by anxiety, the psychopath is characterized by the absence of both anxiety and the various defenses against it. He may engage in cheating, lying, or stealing with no associated feeling of guilt or remorse. Moreover, the psychopath rarely displays the bizarre and distorted perceptions of the psychotic. He may outwardly be an extremely charming person with an engaging personality who impresses people with his disarming frankness. He often knows how to say the right thing at the right time. But under this veneer of social desirability is a ruthless person who does not hesitate to take advantage of others in the pursuit of his goals. Since he is so often "successful" in his business, social, or sexual exploits, he sees little reason to change. He is, therefore, highly resistant to all forms of therapy. In extreme cases, the psychopath is capable of committing the most appalling crimes with no sense of guilt. Psychopaths constitute a high percentage of the delinquent and criminal population. Many embezzlers, confidence men, child molesters, and murderers are psychopathic.

The following letter was written by a young man in prison to a girl he had never met. In this letter we see the ease with which he lies about his present circumstances, ignores his future prospects, and expresses an affection that he could not actually have felt:

Dear June,

Of course you know my cousin, David! Well, I had a long talk with him about beautiful women. He said that you are the most beautiful thing on earth. The way he described you he made me think that I've known you all my life. You must

*Other
Nonpsychotic
Mental Disorders*

be a second Jean Harlow. I've dreamed about you, from the very first day he told me. I'd give a million dollars to have you in my arms. Sometimes I think I am in love with you although I've never seen you. Maybe someday I will see you. June, my darling, I love you. I love you with all my heart and soul. Please believe me?

June, my love, although I've never seen you I would like you to be my wife. I have lots of money and life would be a bowl of roses for you. I know that you will never regret it. Because I will make you the happiest woman on this earth . . .

I am six feet tall, weight is 190 lbs., light complexion, sharp and always in the chips, I can take you anywhere you desire. Money doesn't mean a thing to me. You can have anything your little soft, warm heart desires. I own a cafe on Seventh Avenue. Business is very successful. Money flows in like a bristling brook. I have an apartment and a . . . Chrysler convertible sedan, black with white-wall tires. Everything works by the push of a button. Life will be a luxurious one for you.

In the winter, I vacation in Miami, Florida. In the summer, I go to Canada. If I can have you as my companion and later, my sweetheart and finally my wife, we both could enjoy these luxuries together.   Love,

(signed) James
(Banay, 1943, p. 171)

Alcoholism

Alcohol abuse is one of the most serious problems of both physical and mental health in the United States. In 1970, there were nearly 100 traffic fatalities a day in which the consumption of alcohol was at least partly to blame. It is now estimated that excessive drinking is the third most common cause of death in the country, and the incidence of deaths due to alcohol appears to be rising (Coleman, 1972). Moreover, approximately nine million Americans find their life adjustments so severely impaired by the consumption of alcohol that they are labeled alcoholics. Excessive drinking touches about 36 million family members (wives, husbands, and children of alcoholics); this means that one out of every six people in this country is directly or indirectly involved in the problems of alcoholism (Chafetz, 1971).

1. Increased Consumption. One of the first signs that a drinker may be becoming an alcoholic is increased consumption of alcohol. This increase may seem gradual, but a marked change will take place from month to month. Often the individual will begin to worry about his drinking at this point.

2. Extreme Behavior. When the individual, under the influence of alcohol, commits various acts which leave him feeling guilty and embarrassed the next day, his alcoholic indulgence is getting out of hand.

3. "Pulling Blanks." When the individual cannot remember what happened during an alcoholic bout, his alcoholic indulgence is becoming excessive.

4. Morning Drinking. An important sign that a frequent drinker may be becoming an alcoholic appears when he begins to drink in the morning—either as a means of reducing a hangover or as a "bracer" to help him start the day.

A person who exhibits the preceding pattern of behavior is well on the road to becoming an alcoholic. The progression is likely to be facilitated if he receives environmental support for heavy or excessive drinking—for example, if his spouse provides such support, or if an occupational pattern or socio-cultural environment tolerates or even approves of the excessive use of alcohol.

Box 14.4
Early warning signs of approaching alcoholism. (From *Abnormal Psychology and Modern Life* by James C. Coleman. Copyright © 1972 by Scott, Foresman and Company. Reprinted by permission of the publisher.)

It is not always easy to distinguish between the so-called social drinker and the alcoholic. Both show impaired physical and mental functioning under the effects of alcohol. However, in the alcoholic, this impairment becomes chronic and seriously interferes with his work, his relationships with others, and his general ability to function. Box 14.4 presents some of the early warning signs of approaching alcoholism.

What are the effects of prolonged and excessive drinking? Alcohol acts as a depressant which inhibits the higher brain centers that usually exercise control over behavior. Thus, an intoxicated person is likely to act upon impulses that would normally be held in check. He may experience a sense of well-being, increased competence, and power (McClelland, 1971). The consumption of alcohol frequently brings with it a dramatic relief from tension and anxiety. In fact, one investigator has proposed that alcoholism represents a conditioned response to anxiety (Schaefer, 1971). The alcoholic pays a high price for this relief. In addition to widespread bodily damage (such as liver and heart complications), prolonged heavy drinking can lead to destruction of brain cells (Claeson and Carlsson, 1971) as well as impairments in judgment, sense of responsibility and intellectual functioning.

*Other
Nonpsychotic
Mental Disorders*

The following case history shows how alcohol can encompass and destroy all phases of a person's life and exemplifies the Japanese proverb, "First the man takes a drink, then the drink takes a drink, and then the drink takes the man":

R. P., a married man fifty years of age . . . had always been of unusual temperament, having a difficulty in mixing with other people, so that even his own relatives did not visit him. He was always restless, never being able to enjoy a holiday because he wanted to get back to work. He owned a wine and spirit business, and had at one time a dozen retail shops of his own. Five years before his admission into the hospital his disposition began to change. He commenced to grumble about everything at home, became irritable at trifles, swore volubly at his wife and children—a thing he had never done before. For some indefinite time he had been drinking secretly. Three years after this he fell into the hands of the police while drunk, and lost all of his licenses in consequence. His ordinary daily program at that time consisted in going out after breakfast, and returning drunk at midday, sleeping in the afternoon, going out again and returning drunk once more. He showed no care whatever for his family. His son, who was delicate, sometimes had to carry him home. While drunk he exposed himself to his family, including his daughter. During their convalescence from influenza he turned his children out of the house. He would send his wife on errands and refuse to readmit her till she had obtained what he happened to want—usually more alcohol. He took no interest in anything, neglected his business and threatened suicide but made no real attempt at it.

(Henderson et al., 1962)

Techniques of Therapy

It has been estimated that one person in ten will require some form of treatment for emotional problems at some time in his life. Many medical problems require fairly standard treatment, such as an antibiotic for a known bacterial infection. But the type of treatment given for emotional problems very often depends on the training, experience, and personality of the therapist, as well as on the problems the patient has. It has been said that there are as many different forms of therapy as there are therapists.

Abnormal Behavior and Psychotherapy

However, most therapists are usually identified with a specific school, or theoretical approach. They all share a common goal: to bring about changes in behavior. When psychological methods are used, we refer to the treatment as *psychotherapy.* When medical methods are used, the treatment is called *medical therapy.* Since all forms of therapy overlap to some extent, they should not be considered separate and discrete entities.

The objective of changing behavior is not unique to therapy. Salesmen, propagandists, advertisers, and teachers, to name a few, also have this objective. However, the therapy situation differs in the relationship between the parties involved. The patient is generally seeking help from the therapist, whom the patient perceives as having no motive other than a desire to help.

At one time or another, most of us have sought out a close friend, a relative, or a clergyman just to discuss personal problems. We may have been hoping to alleviate anxiety, fear, or guilt. These relationships might be described as informal psychotherapy. They are generally limited in duration, and usually occur in the context of a relationship other than psychotherapy. The "therapist" in these situations often has had no professional training in therapy, and he usually gives "off-the-cuff" advice.

When a person seeks professional help, the relationship between patient and therapist is usually restricted to the therapy situation. There are many different types of formal psychotherapy. They may differ in the methods employed, or in their assumptions about the underlying purpose of therapy. For example, some therapies focus on the overt symptoms, while others view these symptoms as manifestations of deep unresolved unconscious conflicts. The various therapies differ also in the extent to which the therapist controls the course of therapy. Some therapies emphasize helping the patient achieve "insight" into his problems. In others, the emphasis is on making the patient "happy" or able to function efficiently.

Psychotherapies

Although there are numerous kinds of psychotherapy, we will restrict our discussion to three of the most widely practiced forms: psychoanalysis, client-centered therapy, and behavior therapy.

Psychoanalysis

We have already mentioned that psychoanalysis is a theory of personality as well as a technique of psychotherapy. Let's briefly review some aspects of the theory in order to understand its application to the therapeutic situation (see also Chapter 13).

During the critical stages of psychosexual development, a person may experience conflicts that are not successfully resolved. The thoughts, feelings, and impulses associated with these conflicts lead to anxiety. The person must find ways of dealing with or fending off the pain associated with this anxiety. One of the most common ways of accomplishing this is to repress unacceptable urges. Although repression alleviates the acute phase of the anxiety, it does not eliminate anxiety, but rather "buries it alive." In addition, a person often develops neurotic symptoms as a way of dealing with his anxiety. Because the original source of the anxiety has been repressed, he is unaware of his underlying conflicts. The psychoanalyst tries to bring submerged (repressed) impulses and thoughts to the surface so that the individual can deal with them. Let's look at some of the techniques used in psychoanalysis.

In the classic psychoanalytic session, the patient, while sitting in a comfortable chair or lying on a couch, is required to *free associate,* that is, say anything that comes to mind. He is free to choose any topic, but must report all thoughts that go through his mind as well as any associated feelings. He is instructed not to try to construct a logical and coherent narrative, but simply to follow and report his thoughts as they occur spontaneously. The therapist usually sits behind the patient in order not to distract him.

Think about the state you are in when you are completely relaxed, perhaps just before falling asleep. Your mind is filled with a multitude of disconnected thoughts, feelings, and desires. Psychoanalysts believe that the thoughts occurring during such periods of relaxation provide a fairly direct route to the unconscious. Over a number of sessions of free association (usually over a relatively long period of time), the patient will presumably achieve insight into the conflicts that have been thrust into his unconscious.

As much as the patient may want to be helped, he constantly fights to protect himself from anxiety-arousing experiences. As "dangerous" thematic material begins to emerge during the course of free association, the patient may resist further encroachments into the unconscious. He may suddenly "clam up," talk excessively about an unrelated topic, or deny something he previously said. This *resistance* can also manifest itself in other ways. The patient may be late for his therapy appointment or forget it altogether. Or he may decide to discontinue therapy, as did the patient in the following example:

> A young man had achieved a reputation for brave and dashing military exploits. For this, and because he was handsome and well-to-do, he was a romantic figure. But his physical relations with his wife were a disappointment to both him and her, and he began psychoanalytic treatment for this and some other symptoms. The early weeks of his analysis brought a sincere contrasting of the world's impression of him with his own realization of weakness. This encouraging phase was succeeded by a period of slowed up production culminating in a dream. He was exploring a house which looked very good on the outside. But as he went further through the halls of this interesting and handsome building he came to a corner of one room where he stopped short, horrified. For on the floor in that corner lay something dreadful, disgusting, terrible—"too awful to look at. Perhaps it was a decaying dog—a cur—a beast—something of mine." He did not dare to look at it but turned and fled from the building.
>
> A few days later the patient wrote that he was feeling better and believed he would discontinue his analysis.
>
> (Menninger, 1958, pp. 101–102)

Although the controls over unconscious processes are lessened during a state of relaxation, psychoanalysts believe that these controls are minimized during sleep. Thus, unacceptable impulses that cannot find expression during waking hours may be expressed in dreams. Even in dreams, however, certain controls are still in effect. Consequently, some of the thematic material may take a disguised or symbolic form. We speak of the *manifest content* of a dream as the image and events that constitute the dream as it appears to the dreamer. The *latent content* is the actual meaning of the dream—the repressed motives seeking expression. The object of dream interpretation is to uncover the unconscious wishes and impulses by studying the symbols as they appear in the manifest content of the dream. The following excerpt is taken from the fortieth hour of psychoanalytic therapy of an unmarried 28-year-old man:

Cl. I had another of these dreams last night. I woke up in a sweat and was frightened almost to death.

Th. Tell me about it.

Cl. It's pretty much the same thing, I was driving a big truck along a dark country road at night. I saw a woman walking along it ahead of me, and I could have avoided her easily. But (great agitation) I didn't seem to want to! I just held the truck to the curve of the road on the right side, and I hit her! I hit her! and it was awful! I stopped and went around to her, and she was still alive but dying fast, and she was terribly battered!

Th. Tell me about the woman. Just say whatever comes to mind now. Think about the woman and just say whatever occurs to you.

Cl. Well, she was nobody I've ever known. She seemed small and sort of helpless. She was just walking along the road. It's not always the same woman in these dreams, but they're usually little old ladies like this one. She had dark hair and was terribly, terribly disfigured after the truck hit her. Mother's hair is almost snow white now, but this woman was dark. I've never known anybody like her. (pause)

Th. It seems important to you not to know who this woman was. Go on.

Cl. But I don't know who she was! She was just a little old woman on a dark country road. It was horrible! The accident messed her up so dreadfully! I felt nauseated and revolted by all the mess as well as by the horror of what I had done. But—and this is very strange—I didn't feel any real remorse in the dream, I don't think. I was terrified and sick at the sight but not really sorry. I think that's what wakes me up. I'm not really sorry.

Th. Almost as if you were glad to have got rid of this little old lady. Go on. Just say whatever comes to mind.

Cl. (after a long pause) I guess the horror of the sight is that she was so messy and bloody. Mother, the only older woman that I know really well, is always so neat and clean and well taken care of. This woman in the dream seemed, I don't know, evil somehow in spite of her being so helpless.

Th. Your mother is quite a burden on you at times, isn't she?

Cl. Why, no! How can you say that? She's a wonderful person, and I'm glad to do what I can for her. She means more to me than anybody else.

Th. These things are pretty painful to think about at times, but I'm pretty impressed by your knowing only your mother as a helpless little old lady and your dreaming so repeatedly about killing just such a person. And *you* are the one who dreams it!

(Shaffer and Shoben, 1956, pp. 516–517)

In the course of psychoanalysis, the patient usually forms a complex emotional relationship with the therapist. He tends to identify the analyst with some adult figure who played a significant role in his childhood. He unconsciously transfers to the therapist the emotions and feelings he had toward that person; this process is called *transference.* Without understanding the reason, the patient frequently alternates between attitudes of love and hate toward his therapist. Through the interpretation of this transference relationship, the patient is helped to gain insight into the source of earlier conflicts and emotions.

Traditional psychoanalysis is a long, time-consuming, and expensive process. The patient may undergo as many as five psychoanalytic sessions a week over a period of many years. Recently, some psychoanalysts have attempted to shorten the total time required.

Client-centered therapy

Psychoanalysis is historical in the sense that it probes into the past experiences of the patient. It goes deep into the unconscious in its search for root causes and conflicts. It relies to a considerable extent on interpretations made by the psychoanalyst, and tends to stress intellectual rather than emotional factors. In contrast, client-centered therapy is ahistorical in that it is concerned primarily with the current adjustment of the

Techniques of Therapy

519

individual. It does not search deeply for underlying causes, but relies heavily on the patient to direct his own course of therapy. The goal of client-centered therapy is the emotional, rather than intellectual, growth of the individual. The following excerpt is from the case history of an 18-year-old boy:

In his previous statements during the session, the client has said, "I don't want to be inferior in anything. . . ." "I try and cover the inferiority up as much as possible." The excerpt begins near the end of the interview.

Cl. Yes, but you can never destroy the things you're inferior in. They always remain where everybody can see 'em, right on the surface. No matter how well you can talk, no matter how well you can dance, no matter how good a time you are to the persons who are with you, you certainly can't wear a veil.

Th. M-hm. It's *looks* again, isn't it? . . .

Cl. Yeah. I wish I was like my brother. He's dark just as the rest of the family is. Me—I'm light—puny. He's heavier-built than I am, too. Guess I was just made up of odds and ends. I'm too darn light. I don't like my face. I don't like my eyebrows and my eyes. Bloodshot, little cow-eyes. I hate my pimple chin and I detest the way my face is lopsided. One side is so much different from the other. One side, the chin bones stick out further and the jaw bones are more pronounced. My mouth isn't right. Even when I smile, I don't smile the way other people do. I tried and I can't. When other people smile, their mouths go up—mine goes down. It's me; backward in everything. I'm clumsy as the devil.

Th. You feel sort of sorry for yourself, isn't that right?

Cl. Yes, self-pity, that's me. Sure I know I pity myself, but I got something to pity. If there were two of me I would punch myself right in the nose just for the fun of it.

Th. M-hm.

Cl. Sometimes I get so disgusted with myself!

Th. Sometimes you feel somewhat ashamed of yourself for pointing out all of those physical inadequacies, right?

Cl. Yes, I know I should forget them—yeah, forget them—I should think of something else. And that's—I hate myself because I'm not sure. That's just another thing I can hate myself for.

Th. You're sort of in a dilemma because you can't like yourself, and yet you dislike the fact that you don't like yourself.

Cl. M-hm. I know it isn't natural for a person not to like himself. In fact, most people are in love with themselves. They don't know quite so much of themselves. I've known people like that.

Th. M-hm.

Cl. But not me. (Pause). I don't see how anybody loves me, even Mom. Maybe it's just maternal love. They can't help it, poor things. (Pause.)

Th. You feel so worthless you wonder how anyone would think much of you.

Cl. Yeah. But I'm not gonna worry about it. I've just gotta make up for it, that's all. I've just gotta forget it. And try to compensate for it.

Th. M-hm. (Pause.)

Cl. I've always tried to compensate for it. Everything I did in high school was to compensate for it.

Th. M-hm. You've never had much reason to think that people really cared about you, is that right?

Cl. That's right. Oh, if you only knew how they—

Th. M-hm.

Cl. Everything anyone ever said or ever did they were just trying to get something out of me. Or else they were—

Th. It sort of made you feel inadequate not having the security of having people show that they cared a lot for you.

Cl. That's right.

Th. M-hm.

Cl. No one ever did . . .

(Snyder, 1947, pp. 82–85)

Just as Sigmund Freud is considered the father of psychoanalytic theory, Carl Rogers is regarded as the progenitor of client-centered therapy. Rogers and his followers present a basically optimistic approach to life. Since they do not regard the people who seek their help as "sick," they use the term client instead of patient. They believe that if people are not torn by conflicts, they will become productive and healthy human beings. Client-centered therapists provide a warm, friendly, and nonthreatening environment which allows the client to accept aspects of himself that he previously viewed negatively.

Rogers makes a key distinction between the *phenomenal self* (the way the individual views himself) and the *ideal self* (the way he would like to be). The way a person views himself may be at variance with the way he would like to be. The unhappy or maladjusted individual would probably show the greatest discrepancy between his phenomenal self and ideal self. The well-adjusted person might be expected to show less disparity.

A study was designed to test this important aspect of Rogers' theory. First, subjects were given a set of cards, each containing a sentence such as "I am a submissive person," "I am a hard worker," or "I really am disturbed." The subjects were asked to pick out the cards that best described them. Then they were asked to go through the same cards again, and choose those that described the kind of person they would like to be. Two groups of subjects were employed in this study. One, the experimental group, was comprised of individuals seeking treatment for emotional problems. The other group, the control group, was made up of people who were not looking for help. The subjects seeking therapy showed the least similarity between the way they described themselves (phenomenal self) and the way they would like to be (ideal self). The control subjects showed a high degree of similarity between phenomenal self and ideal self. After the experimental subjects received client-centered therapy, they showed a greater similarity between their phenomenal and ideal selves (Butler and Haigh, 1954).

Carl Rogers has recently stated that constructive personality change in the client depends on three fundamental attitudes of the therapist: (1) genuineness in the relationship, (2) acceptance of the client, and (3) an accurate understanding of the client's phenomenal world. These attitudes are more significant than the orientation, amount of training, and the techniques of the therapist (Rogers, 1969).

Behavior therapy

Behavior therapy is the application of the principles of conditioning (both classical and operant) to the modification of maladaptive behavior. The focus of behavior therapy is on the symptoms rather than the underlying causes. The adherents of this type of therapy regard neurosis in a strikingly different way than psychoanalysts do. Psychoanalysts regard neurosis as the result of complex unconscious conflicts. Behavior therapists ignore the unconscious, and regard neurosis as a collection of bad habits. Since all habits (good and bad) are learned, they can also be unlearned. Thus, behavior therapists view neurotic symptoms as "bad" or maladaptive habits that can be modified by using the principles of conditioning.

A variety of techniques are employed in behavior therapy, all of them based on the principles of conditioning discussed in Chapter 3. Let's look at several of these methods.

Extinction. Many undesirable habits are learned simply because positive reinforcement has unwittingly been associated with the occurrence of the response. For example, a parent may pay attention to a crying child only when the crying becomes extremely intense. Thus, the parent is inadvertently providing positive reinforcement for loud crying. Extinction therapy would consist of eliminating the positive reinforcement for the undesired behavior. Experimental extinction procedures have been used successfully, for example, to tame overly aggressive children (Hamblin et al., 1969), to reduce misbehavior in school (Madsen et al., 1968), and to decrease delusional behavior in a psychotic patient (Ayllon and Michael, 1959). The following case history illustrates the application of extinction procedures in a hospital setting:

> The patient had weighed over 250 pounds for many years. She ate the usual tray of food served to all patients, but, in addition, she stole food from the food counter and from other patients. Because the medical staff regarded her excessive weight as detrimental to her health, a special diet had been prescribed for her. However, the patient refused to diet and continued stealing food. In an effort to discourage the patient from stealing, the ward nurses had spent considerable time trying to persuade her to stop stealing food. As a last resort, the nurses would force her to return the stolen food.
>
> To determine the extent of food stealing, nurses were instructed to record all behavior associated with eating in the dining room. This record, taken for nearly a month, showed that the patient stole food during two thirds of all meals.

Procedure. The traditional methods previously used to stop the patient from stealing food were discontinued. No longer were persuasion, coaxing, or coercion used.

The patient was assigned to a table in the dining room, and no other patients were allowed to sit with her. Nurses removed the patient from the dining room when she approached a table other than her own, or when she picked up unauthorized food from the dining room counter. In effect, this procedure resulted in the patient missing a meal whenever she attempted to steal food.

(Ayllon, 1963)

As can be seen in Fig. 14.4, the withdrawal of food quickly eliminated the food-stealing response. In addition, the patient lost approximately 80 pounds over a 14-month period.

Fig. 14.4
Extinction in behavior therapy
An overweight patient in a mental hospital frequently stole food. When positive reinforcement (food) was withdrawn following each instance of stealing, the undesirable response (food stealing) was extinguished. Occasional instances of food stealing are shown by the white dashed arrows. No stealing occurred between the 18th and 41st weeks. (Additional information and related research can be found in _The Token Economy: A Motivational System for Therapy and Rehabilitation_ by T. Ayllon and N. H. Azrin, published by Appleton-Century-Crofts, 1968. Used by permission of Dr. T. Ayllon.)

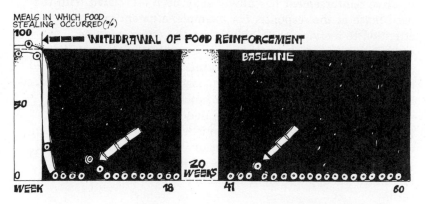

MEALS IN WHICH FOOD STEALING OCCURRED(%)

WITHDRAWAL OF FOOD REINFORCEMENT

BASELINE

20 WEEKS

WEEK   18   41   60

Abnormal Behavior and Psychotherapy

Desensitization. It is difficult to maintain two opposing emotional states at the same time. For example, can you be both anxious and relaxed? Desensitization procedures involve training the subject to relax in the presence of a situation that previously aroused anxiety or fear (see Chapter 5). These techniques have been particularly successful in the treatment of phobic fears.

For everyone there are certain things, situations, or events that arouse greater amounts of anxiety than other stimuli do. Each of us could probably construct a hierarchy in which we listed stimuli in order, from those that produce the least fear to those that produce the most. Desensitization therapy begins by teaching the patient to relax. When he has learned this behavior, the patient is told to imagine a situation which is low on his hierarchy (least fear-producing). If he continues to relax while imagining this situation, he is asked to imagine the next item on his hierarchy. As soon as a stimulus disturbs his state of relaxation, he is told to stop and concentrate on relaxing again. In this way, the patient is gradually led through a series of increasingly anxiety- or fear-arousing stimuli until he is able to tolerate the situation that is highest on his list.

You may recall the college student who was terrified of examinations (page 492). Desensitization therapy was started with this patient:

> He first made up a hierarchy of circumstances which he felt produced fear responses. He was then instructed in relaxation of muscle groups. The lowest item on his anxiety hierarchy list, being asked a question by his kid brother, was then presented while the patient was relaxing. When it was evident that this situation was well tolerated, the next item on the list was evoked, and so on. Within a month, the student reported being able to undertake examinations with only a modicum of tension. The patient returned, however, during final examinations with a recurrence of his paralyzing fear. Retraining continued with an emphasis on generalizing the relaxation responses to a wider variety of evaluational situations. Excellent progress has been noted and the student has recently been notified of his acceptability for graduate admissions.
>
> (Suinn, 1970, p. 242)

One of the most successful techniques in behavior therapy has combined desensitization with modeling. In modeling, the patient observes another individual (the model) go through a series of responses to situations increasingly high on the patient's anxiety hierarchy. A considerable amount of research has been conducted with subjects suffering from phobic fear of snakes. In one study, the subjects observed a model handle and play with a snake. Gradually, they were encouraged to participate in the handling of the snake (see Fig. 14.5). The combination of modeling and desensitization procedures resulted in a marked decrease in the subjects' fear of snakes (Bandura et al., 1969).

A criticism frequently leveled against desensitization, as well as other behavior therapy techniques, is that it treats the

Fig. 14.5
Treating a snake phobia
A combination of desensitization therapy and modeling was successfully used to treat snake phobia. The photographs show the models interacting with a live snake. Both live and film demonstrations were employed in the study (Bandura et al., 1969). (Courtesy of Dr. Albert Bandura.)

Abnormal Behavior and Psychotherapy

symptom without removing the underlying cause. The critics predict that the patient may give up one symptom and substitute another in its place. Joseph Wolpe, a leader in the application of desensitization therapy, has countered this criticism by pointing to date he has collected. He studied 249 cases of neuroses, including many phobias, that had been successfully treated by behavior therapy, and found that only four patients had acquired new symptoms (Wolpe, 1969).

Positive reinforcement. You may recall (Chapter 3) that pairing a positive reinforcer with a response that is to be learned is an extremely effective conditioning procedure. Contingent reinforcement (making a specific behavior a prerequisite for obtaining positive reinforcement) has been successfully employed in a variety of different settings. Mute psychotic children have acquired speech (Lovaas, 1968), and high school dropouts have learned academic skills (Clark et al., 1968) as the resent of the successful application of positive reinforcement techniques. The following case history illustrates the use of positive reinforcement in a hospital setting.

Shortly after the patient had been admitted to the hospital she wore an excessive amount of clothing which included several sweaters, shawls, dresses, undergarments and stockings. The clothing also included sheets and towels wrapped around her body, and a turban-like head-dress made up of several towels . . .

To determine the amount of clothing worn by the patient, she was weighed before each meal over a period of two weeks. By subtracting her actual body weight from that recorded when she was dressed, the weight of her clothing was obtained.

Procedure. The response required for reinforcement was stepping on a scale and meeting a predetermined weight. The requirement for reinforcement consisted of meeting a single weight (i.e., her body weight plus a specified number of pounds of clothing). Initially she was given an allowance of 23 pounds over her current body weight. This allowance represented a 2 pound reduction from her usual clothing weight. When the patient exceeded the weight requirement, the nurse stated in a matter-of-fact manner, "Sorry, you weigh too much, you'll have to weigh less." Failure to meet the required weight resulted in the patient missing the meal at which she was being weighed.

(Ayllon, 1963)

As can be seen in Fig. 14.6, the excessive dressing response was successfully eliminated.

One of the most rapidly growing practices in institutional settings involves a slight variation of positive reinforcement techniques. Patients are permitted to earn varying numbers of tokens (secondary reinforcers) for engaging in specific constructive behaviors. These tokens may then be exchanged for various luxuries or privileges. We have already seen the successful application of a *token economy* in a study described in Chapter 3. Although the use of token economies in therapy began only recently, the practice has spread rapidly to many different settings. Perhaps the most dramatic results have been obtained in mental hospitals. Patients who had previously shown little or no responsiveness to other people and things have become responsible, interested in their environment, and have been able to perform productive tasks within the hospital setting. A number

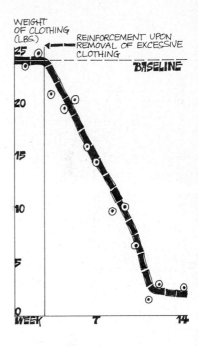

Fig. 14.6
Reinforcement in behavior therapy

A response, excessive dressing, is eliminated when food reinforcement is made dependent upon removal of superfluous clothing. Once the weight of the clothing worn by the patient drops to three pounds, it remains stable. (Additional information and related research can be found in *The Token Economy: A Motivational System for Therapy and Rehabilitation* by T. Ayllon and N. H. Azrin, published by Appleton-Century-Crofts, 1968. Used by permission of Dr. T. Ayllon.)

Techniques of Therapy

of patients who had been hospitalized for long periods of time and considered hopelessly psychotic have since been released from the hospital after living for a time in a token economy.

Aversive conditioning. Several years ago a young lady contracted a case of hiccoughs. Ordinarily, this would not be a cause of concern, since hiccoughs are rather common and generally harmless. In her case, however, the hiccoughs continued to plague her, and medical attention was sought. When she was unable to obtain relief through the use of various medical techniques, she was referred to traditional psychotherapists. The hiccoughs persisted to such an extent that she suffered a severe loss of weight and was unable to sleep. It was clear that unless a way was found to stop the hiccoughs, she could not long survive. In desperation, the family of this young lady went to a psychologist who was practicing behavior therapy, then a relatively new form of therapy. He attached electrodes to her body that delivered a painful, but not physically damaging, electric shock. He made the delivery of the shock contingent upon her hiccoughing; that is, whenever she hiccoughed, she would receive a painful electric shock (aversive conditioning). Within a short time, the hiccoughs disappeared. From the point of view of the behavior therapist, she was cured.

This case illustrates the successful application of aversive conditioning techniques. Aversive conditioning has also been used to cure a nine-month-old child of vomiting (Lang and Melamed, 1969), to eliminate stuttering (Goldiamond, 1965), and to treat bed-wetting (Wickes, 1958).

Aversive conditioning is often used in conjunction with positive reinforcement. The aversive stimulus is used to inhibit maladaptive behavior, and the positive reinforcement to strengthen constructive responses.

Group Therapies

So far, we have discussed therapeutic techniques involving the treatment of one patient at a time. A variety of different techniques have been developed for the simultaneous treatment of several people. These group therapies have emerged for a variety of reasons—economic necessity, shortage of trained therapists, and because some people seem to benefit from sharing and working out problems in a group situation. Many groups

Fig. 14.7
Sensitivity sessions allow
individuals to work their
problems out in a group
situation. (Dan O'Neill—Editorial
Photocolor Archives.)

simply represent an extension of traditional psychotherapeutic
techniques. For example, Rogerian and psychoanalytic therapists
handle groups as well as individuals. Other groups represent a
complete departure from these traditional techniques, to the
extent that some groups have leaders who are not professionally
trained, while others have no leader at all.

Probably the most popular form of group therapy today is
the *encounter group.* This kind of group usually consists of six to
twelve participants, and the members are encouraged to focus on
their feelings and express them openly and honestly (see Box
14.5).

Encounter groups have been springing up on college
campuses throughout the country. It is too early to ascertain how
successful the group experience has been in terms of long-term
favorable behavioral outcomes. An extremely comprehensive
study revealed some of the possible benefits, as well as the
potential dangers, of encounter groups. Of the 251 college
students participating in the study, 95 percent felt that the
encounter group experience should be included in the college
curriculum. Seventy-five percent of the students felt that the
experience had led to positive changes in themselves. On the
negative side, approximately 10 percent of those participating
appeared to be sufficiently adversely affected to warrant
subsequent psychotherapeutic treatment (Lieberman et al., 1971).

Somewhat similar to the encounter groups are *T-groups.* At
first, T-groups were used primarily in industrial and business

*Techniques
of Therapy*

529

Mary, who was 27, had recently separated from her 29-year-old husband, Bill. Since Mary had tried to be the perfect wife, it came as quite a shock to her when Bill, after one year of marriage, told her he was no longer in love with her. Feeling responsible for the difficulties in her marriage, and anxious about her ability to establish meaningful marital or other interpersonal relationships, Mary joined an encounter group which met one evening a week for 2½ hours. The group was cofacilitated by two nonprofessional leaders who were being trained by and working under the local Growth Center, the group's sponsor. The male facilitator was a 27-year-old high school teacher and the female facilitator was a 35-year-old housewife with three children. The group consisted of 4 male and 5 female participants ranging in age from 19 to 40.

At first during the meetings, Mary remained relatively quiet and listened politely as others spoke. She made only positive comments when she did speak—avoiding saying anything negative to anyone.

During the fourth meeting, one of the members—Sid, aged 38—confronted Mary about her uniform politeness and seeming superficiality, an exchange in which the facilitator also took part:

Sid: Mary, I would like to get to know you better, but your polite sweet manner puts me off. Frankly, your sweetness makes me a little angry with you.

Fcltr: In your anger, Sid, what do you need to say to Mary?

Sid: (in a loud and moderately angry voice) Damn it, Mary, come out from behind that phony sweet façade of yours! Stop putting me off!

Mary: (with a polite smile and pleasant tone) Gee, I'm sorry, I really don't want to put you off.

Fcltr: Mary, become aware of your smile and tone of voice.

Mary: (again smiling) I guess I was smiling (followed by a childish chuckle).

Sid: Mary, you're impossible! (said in a tone implying that he did not think Mary capable of being aware of her pattern of behavior).

Mary: (in a more somber tone) I really don't understand, Sid, why you are angry at me. I'm trying to . . . (long pause followed by an embarrassed look).

Fcltr: Would you be willing to look at Sid and express your embarrassment to him?

Mary: Yes (then looking at Sid). I stopped my sentence because I was going to say . . . "I'm trying to be polite so that you'll like me."

Sid: Mary, that's the trouble. I don't like your politeness—it seems phony to me.

Box 14.5
Encounter group therapy of a neurotic disorder. (From *Abnormal Psychology and Modern Life* by James C. Coleman. Copyright © 1972 by Scott, Foresman and Company. Reprinted by permission of the publisher.)

settings. They are sometimes called *sensitivity groups,* because their aim is to develop more sensitive feelings and attitudes toward one's fellow workers.

Medical Therapies

A number of techniques are used with emotionally disturbed individuals that do not involve direct behavioral manipulation. Instead, various kinds of medical treatment are used, either alone or in combination with certain psychotherapeutic techniques. It should be pointed out that these medical therapies can be administered only by medical doctors.

Electroshock therapy

In certain types of disorders, particularly those involving depressed states, the use of electroshock therapy has alleviated

Abnormal Behavior and Psychotherapy

I'd feel closer to you if I knew what you *really* were thinking and feeling.

Mary: You know it's true that I don't really feel all the nice things I say—but to imagine not being polite and sweet . . . just really scares me.

Fcltr: What is your fear?

Mary: I'm afraid nobody will like me.

Sid: I'm liking you right now.

Mary: You know when you said you like me, it made me feel anxious and confused. (She looks to facilitator.) I'm at a loss to figure out what's going on with me. Why do I feel confused?

Fcltr: Mary, right now the "why" of your confusion is secondary to the fact that you *are* feeling confused *right now.* Try to get the feel of your confusion. In other words, become aware of your sensations and let them emerge on their own.

Mary: (mildly distressed) I feel overcome by a growing sense of emptiness which I feel in my stomach.

Fcltr: Let your emptiness have its say. You're at the point at which you don't get support from others and you can't quite get it from yourself.

Mary: (mildly fearful) I feel awful. I feel like nothingness—I feel so empty.

Fcltr: (noting Mary's eyes becoming moist) What do your tears have to say to us, Mary?

Mary: (breaking into deep sobs) I feel unloved and unappreciated for what I am; I so much need everyone's approval. I really don't like myself. (Mary continues crying for several minutes, then adds as she looks down at the floor) Now I feel silly; everyone must think I'm a jerk!

Fcltr: Mary, you will get yourself into trouble by imagining what people are thinking. Right now, look at each person in the group and tell us what you see.

(As Mary looks around the group, she sees the members looking at her sympathetically; several have been moved to tears by her outpouring of feeling.)

Mary: (responding to the warmth and support she sees around her) I feel so happy, so free right now. I want to express my warm feelings to all of you. (She goes around the group making contact by touching, holding, or talking to each member.)

As the group sessions continued, Mary became able to drop her "polite good-girl" role, to begin to understand and trust herself, and to improve her competence and authenticity in relating to others.

the acute symptoms. Electrodes are attached to the patient's head and an electric current is applied briefly. The patient immediately goes into convulsions, and may remain unconscious for a time. Since the electric current travels more quickly than the nerve impulse, unconsciousness occurs before the patient can feel any pain. When the patient awakens, there is often at least a partial alleviation of the symptoms. Ordinarily, the patient shows short-term memory impairment. The treatment is usually repeated over a period of weeks or months. To date, we have no real understanding of why electroshock works—when it works. In recent years electroshock therapy has largely been supplanted by chemotherapy.

Chemotherapy

Chemotherapy is the use of various chemical substances (drugs) to treat disorders. Two main classes of chemotherapeutic agents are employed by psychiatrists: tranquilizers and psychic energizers.

Certain disorders are characterized by hyperactivity, extreme anxiety, and hostile and destructive behavior. Individuals suffering from these disorders are usually not amenable to normal psychotherapy because their behavior interferes with the conduct of the therapy session. Such people have often been helped by the administration of *tranquilizers.* A recent study compared two groups of schizophrenic patients: one group was given a combination of tranquilizers and psychotherapy, the other received only psychotherapy. The patients receiving psychotherapy alone showed no improvement in their condition, while the group receiving the combined treatment gave evidence of significant improvement (Grinspoon et al., 1968).

Tranquilizers are also commonly used by people suffering from far less serious disorders. Many businessmen, housewives, and students use them for relief of tensions and anxiety. Since they sometimes lead to undesired side effects such as dizziness, nausea, and low blood pressure, and many of them are potentially addictive, they should not be taken without medical advice.

Other drugs, known as *psychic energizers* or *antidepressants,* are used in the treatment of depressed, withdrawn, apathetic individuals. A review of studies employing a total of almost 6000 patients showed that four widely used antidepressants led to improvement in approximately 65 percent of the patients (Wechsler et al., 1965).

Summary

1. The word abnormal means, literally, "away from normal." Three different approaches to the definition of the abnormal are commonly used: the cultural definition, the adjustive significance of the behavior, and the classification of certain types of behavior as abnormal.

2. The normal–abnormal dimension is a continuum; there is no sharp dividing line between normal and abnormal. At times, an "abnormal" individual may behave quite normally; conversely, a "normal" person may, on occasion, engage in behavior that is considered abnormal.

3. The neurotic individual appears almost constantly unhappy, threatened, and anxious in situations that most people would not view as dangerous, and characteristically responds to threatening situations with avoidance instead of coping with them.

4. Several broad classes of neurotic reactions have been described: anxiety reaction, phobias, obsessive–compulsive reactions, dissociative reactions, and conversion reactions.

5. In psychotic reactions, the individual shows a loss of contact with reality, disturbed thought processes, and personality disorganization, and is unable to function normally in society.

6. Two broad classes of psychotic disturbances, for which no definite cause has been established, are the manic–depressive and the schizophrenic reactions.

7. Four basic types of schizophrenic reactions have been described: (1) simple schizophrenia, (2) the hebephrenic reaction, (3) catatonic schizophrenia, and (4) paranoid reactions.

8. In addition to the neuroses and psychotic states, there is a "mixed bag" of personality disorders which bring the individual into conflict with society. These include the psychopathic personality, alcoholism, drug dependency, and compulsive gambling.

9. It has been estimated that one person in ten will require some form of treatment for emotional problems at some time in his life. Psychological methods of treatment are called psychotherapy.

Medical methods of treatment are referred to as physiological therapy.

10. Three common forms of psychotherapy are psychoanalysis, client-centered therapy, and behavior therapy.

11. Therapeutic techniques have been developed for the simultaneous treatment of several people. Some groups represent an extension of traditional psychotherapeutic techniques, while others, such as encounter groups and sensitivity groups (T-groups), represent a departure from traditional methods.

12. Some emotionally disturbed individuals are treated with medical therapy, such as electroshock therapy or chemotherapy, used either alone or in combination with certain psychotherapeutic techniques.

Terms to Remember

Abnormal   (1) Those behaviors that fail to comply with cultural values or standards (cultural definition). (2) Behaviors that interfere with the individual's ability to achieve goals or to resolve motivational conflicts (adjustment definition). (3) Certain types of behaviors, for example, disordered thought processes.

Alcoholism   Physiological dependence on alcohol.

Anxiety   Fear reaction to unknown or unidentified stimuli, a premonition that something bad will happen.

Anxiety Reaction   A type of neurosis characterized by constant anxiety and tension.

Aversive Conditioning   A technique used in behavior therapy in which punishment or aversive stimulation is used to eliminate undesired behavior.

Behavior Therapy   A therapeutic technique based primarily on the application of the principles of conditioning to the modification of maladaptive behavior.

Catatonic Schizophrenia   A psychotic reaction characterized by extreme withdrawal into muteness and physical immobility.

Chemotherapy   A therapeutic technique involving the treatment of emotional disorders through the use of drugs.

Abnormal Behavior and Psychotherapy

534

Client-Centered Therapy   A nondirective type of psychotherapy concerned primarily with the current adjustment of the individual.

Compulsive Behavior   Impulse to perform some act repeatedly.

Contingent Reinforcement   A specific behavior is made a prerequisite to obtaining positive reinforcement.

Conversion Reaction   A type of neurosis characterized by sensory or motor impairment without any physical cause.

Delusion   A belief that is contrary to reality.

Desensitization   A therapeutic technique which involves training an individual to relax in the presence of a situation that previously aroused anxiety or fear. In desensitization therapy, the individual is gradually led through a series of increasingly anxiety- or fear-arousing stimuli until he is able to tolerate the situation that previously was the most anxiety-arousing for him.

Dissociative Reaction   A type of neurosis which involves some impairment of memory functions, usually as a defense to avoid or escape from an anxiety-arousing situation.

Dream Analysis   A psychoanalytic technique aimed at uncovering the unconscious wishes and impulses as they appear in the manifest content of the dream.

Electroshock Therapy   A type of medical therapy in which electricity is used to produce convulsions and unconsciousness.

Encounter Group   A small therapy group which focuses on expressing feelings openly and honestly.

Extinction Therapy   A technique of behavior therapy which consists of eliminating positive reinforcement for an undesired behavior.

Free-Floating Anxiety   Anxiety that is diffuse and without focus.

Free Association   A psychoanalytic technique for probing the unconscious; the individual reports his thoughts and feelings as they occur spontaneously.

Functional   Having no identifiable physiological basis.

Terms to Remember

Group Therapy   Psychotherapy in which two or more people are treated simultaneously.

Hallucination   A sensory experience in the absence of appropriate sensory stimulation.

Hebephrenic Schizophrenia   A psychotic reaction characterized by inappropriate emotional behavior, delusions, and hallucinations.

Ideal Self   In Rogerian theory, the way the individual would like to be.

Latent Content   In psychoanalytic theory, the actual meaning of a dream, the repressed motives that express themselves in the manifest content.

Manic–Depressive Reaction   A type of psychosis characterized by extreme distortions of mood.

Manifest Content   In psychoanalytic theory, the image and events that constitute the dream as it appears to the dreamer.

Medical Therapy   Treatment of emotional disturbance by medical methods.

Neurosis   Emotional disturbance characterized by maladaptive behavior aimed at avoiding anxiety.

Obsession   A recurring thought or impulse that persistently intrudes itself into the individual's consciousness.

Obsessive–Compulsive Reaction   A type of neurosis characterized by persistent and recurring thoughts or actions.

Organic Psychoses   Psychoses associated with known physiological causes.

Paranoid Schizophrenia   A psychotic reaction characterized by fragmented and illogical delusions.

Phenomenal Self   In Rogerian theory, the way the individual views himself.

Abnormal Behavior and Psychotherapy

Phobia   An unreasonable, intense, and persistent fear of situations or objects that do not constitute real dangers.

Phobic Reaction   A type of neurosis characterized by intense fear of a situation or object which the individual realizes constitutes no real danger to him.

Psychic Energizers (Antidepressants)   Drugs used to relieve depressed, withdrawn, apathetic individuals.

Psychoanalysis   A technique of psychotherapy in which the psychoanalyst endeavors to bring to the surface repressed impulses and thoughts so that the individual can deal with them.

Psychopathic Personality   A personality disorder characterized by the absence of both anxiety and the various defenses against it.

Psychosis   A severe form of emotional disturbance involving loss of contact with reality, disturbed thought processes, and personality disorganization. Psychotic individuals must usually be hospitalized.

Psychotherapy   Treatment of emotional disturbance by psychological methods.

Resistance   Tendency to resist or avoid treatment when anxiety-arousing material is being uncovered.

Schizophrenia   A type of psychosis characterized by personality disorganization, withdrawal from reality, disturbed thought processes, and emotional distortions.

Senility   A type of psychosis caused, in part, by brain changes due to aging.

Sensitivity Group (T-Group)   A type of small group which emphasizes the development of sensitive feelings and attitudes toward others.

Simple Schizophrenia   A psychotic reaction characterized by extreme apathy, withdrawal, and emotional dulling.

Token Economy   A reinforcement technique, sometimes used in hospitals, in which the individual is rewarded for socially accepted behavior with a token that can be exchanged for a desired object or activity.

Tranquilizer   A drug used to reduce anxiety and tension.

Terms to Remember

Transference   A process whereby an individual projects onto the therapist emotions and feelings he had toward another significant person.

Recommended Readings

Bergin, A. E., and Garfield, S. L. (Eds.), *Handbook of Psychotherapy and Behavior Change: An Empirical Analysis,* New York: John Wiley & Sons, Inc., 1970.

Applies general psychological principles to problems of adjustment and behavior modification, and emphasizes research findings as a frame of reference for evaluating psychotherapy.

Coleman, J., *Abnormal Psychology and Modern Life* (4th ed.), Glenview Illinois: Scott, Foresman and Co., 1972.

A thorough discussion of the causes, dynamics, and treatment of various types of emotional disorders.

Keen, E., *Three Faces of Being: Toward an Existential Clinical Psychology,* New York: Appleton-Century-Crofts, 1970.

Case studies are used to show the integration of humanistic concerns and therapeutic goals. Summarizes the relationship of existential psychology to natural science.

Millon, T. (Ed.), *Theories of Psychopathology,* Philadelphia: W. B. Saunders Co., 1967.

A paperback collection of readings dealing with the major theories of abnormal psychology and personality structure.

Neuringer, C., and Michael, J. L. (Eds.), *Behavior Modification in Clinical Psychology,* New York: Appleton-Century-Crofts, 1970.

A series of papers dealing with several areas of behavior modification techniques applied to various areas in clinical psychology.

Patterson, C., *Theories of Counseling and Psychotherapy,* New York: Harper & Row Publishers, 1966.

Describes various theoretical points of view and presents case histories.

Abnormal Behavior and Psychotherapy

Rogers, C., *Client-Centered Therapy,* Boston: Houghton Mifflin Co., 1951.

A well-written statement of the nondirective approach in psychotherapy by its founder.

Rosenthal, D., *Genetic Theory and Abnormal Behavior,* New York: McGraw-Hill Book Co., 1970.

Focuses on the contribution of heredity to various mental disorders.

Stone, A. A., and Stone, S. S. (Eds.), *The Abnormal Personality through Literature,* Englewood Cliffs, N.J.: Prentice-Hall, Inc., 1966.

Literary excerpts are used to illustrate behavior characteristics of various types of mental disorders.

Strupp, Hans H., *Psychotherapy and the Modification of Abnormal Behavior,* New York: McGraw-Hill Book Co., 1971.

Using a research-oriented approach, this paperback text describes the major theories of psychotherapy.

Ullman, L. P., and Krasner, L., *A Psychological Approach to Abnormal Behavior,* Englewood Cliffs, N.J.: Prentice-Hall, Inc., 1967.

A text which attempts to demonstrate that abnormal behavior is no different in its development and maintenance from other learned behaviors.

15
SOCIAL PSYCHOLOGY

The individual in society

Socialization — Culture and society — Role

Characteristics of crowds and groups

Group dynamics

Communication — Leadership — Group action

How groups influence behavior

Conformity — Obedience

Attitudes

The nature of attitudes — Development of attitudes
Cognitive dissonance
Prejudice — Changing attitudes

b)
Fig. 15.1
A young man before (a) and after (b) joining the "hippie" community.

Social Psychology

The Individual in Society

Do you think of yourself as a free and independent individual? Think for a moment about a typical day in your life. To what extent are you free of social pressures and restraints? Are the clothes you wear, the food you eat, your attitudes, your likes and dislikes, truly and completely under your personal control?

If you think carefully, you will probably conclude that everything you do is influenced by the values, attitudes, and pressures of others. The very language you speak and the symbols with which you think are products of the society you live in. From the moment you get up in the morning, every aspect of your daily life is governed by the rules, regulations, and controls imposed on you by your parents, your friends, your teachers, and perhaps even the policeman on the corner.

How about people who have left home and taken up residence in a so-called nonconformist community? Are they any less subject to group pressures? Figure 15.1 shows a young man before and after he became a "hippie." Do you think he is now free of social pressures?

It is clear that social forces exert a compelling and pervasive influence on all aspects of our lives, from the cradle to Medicare. These influences are the concern of social psychology. Social psychologists study the individual in society—the various social forces that interact to influence his behavior and thinking, and the ways in which the individual interacts with and modifies social groups to which he belongs.

Socialization

Man is preeminently a social animal. Each of us is, in fact, the product of a social act—sexual intercourse. From the moment of birth, we and those around us are totally and inescapably enmeshed in a web of complex social interactions. Even as infants, our presence has a profound influence on the lives of those around us; we, in turn, are completely dependent on others for nurturance, support, and instruction. As we grow, we learn the language of our parents, what behaviors are acceptable to those about us, how to express certain emotions and feelings, and how and when to conceal them. In short, we learn the socially

A movement which has had widespread appeal in recent years was advocated in a best-selling book, *Games People Play* (Berne, 1964). The movement is referred to as Transactional Analysis and involves the analysis of what people do and say to one another. In a recent book, *Born To Win* (James and Jongeward, 1971), the following analysis of cultural differences and changing cultural values appears:

"Cultural scripts are the accepted and expected dramatic patterns that occur within a society. They are determined by the spoken and unspoken assumptions believed by the majority of the people within that group. Like theatrical scripts, cultural scripts have themes, characters, expected roles, stage directions, costumes, settings, scenes, and final curtains. Cultural scripts reflect what is thought of as the 'national character.' The same drama may be repeated generation after generation.

"Script themes differ from one culture to another. The script can contain themes of suffering, persecution, and hardship (historically, the Jews); it can contain themes of building empires and making conquests (as the Romans once did). Throughout history some nations have acted from a 'top-dog' position of the conqueror; some from an 'underdog' position of the conquered. In early America, where people came to escape oppression, to exploit the situation, and to explore the unknown, a basic theme was 'struggling for survival.' In many cases this struggle was acted out by pioneering and settling. Some people managed both.

"Early pioneers were always on the move looking for new 'stages,' taking risks, and setting the scene for the settlers who followed. Even though some of the scenery, acts, characters, and actions changed, the basic theme often remained the same. Today this similar pioneering script is being acted out by the astronauts though with different costumes and settings. Coonskin caps have given way to complicated headgear, horses to space ships, grandma's Sunday pot roasts to food sucked from plastic bags.

"In contrast to always being on the move, as were the pioneers, the early American settlers' script was to dig in and put down roots. Settlers tilled the soil, built homes and towns, established businesses, worked hard to acquire material goods and to build the population. Their struggle was hard, and their lives short and precarious.

"Currently a large segment of American society—certainly not all of it—is no longer preoccupied with the struggle for individual survival. A modern-day settler has a life expectancy approaching eighty years. Rather than working independently, he is likely to be part of a large corporation or of a government structure. Rather than eking out a bare physical existence, he may find himself caught up in the pleasures and problems of affluence.

"As times change new script themes emerge: getting educated, making money, seeking pleasure, and searching for life's meaning. Today the American stage is overcrowded with people and goods, and the curtain rises on a new scene. When a large percentage of individuals take on themes that are different from the current premises of their culture, the dramatic style of the entire culture begins to change. Whereas some transitions are relatively painless, some are fraught with anguish and even bloodshed.

"Many modern youths, born into a different setting from that of their parents, are rejecting earlier script themes as having no value or relevance to *their* lives. Yet, many are again facing the 'struggling for survival' theme as it re-emerges in terms of the survival of the human race and the preservation of the natural environment."

accepted ways of behaving in our society, a process called *socialization.*

Culture and Society

Societies differ from one another in what their members consider to be socially accepted behavior. For example, do you consider it

Box 15.1
Transactional analysis. (From Muriel James and Dorothy Jongeward, *Born to Win: Transactional Analysis with Gestalt Experiments,* Addison-Wesley Publishing Company, Inc., 1971.)

a) b)

Fig. 15.2
The society to which we belong provides the models for our own behavior. Do you think it is a mere accident that the children in (a) are building a highrise clubhouse, or that the two men in (b) shake hands when they meet? (a, Harry Wilks—Stock, Boston. b, Anna Kaufman Moon —Stock, Boston.)

*Social
Psychology*

socially acceptable for a woman to run the household and be responsible for the economic activities of the family, while the man spends his time decorating himself, dancing, and gossiping with other men? If you were born and raised in the United States, you would probably question the appropriateness of this behavior. However, if you were a member of the Tchambuli tribe in New Guinea, you would find nothing extraordinary about it. Male children of the Tchambuli tribe are prepared for a life of dependence which, by Western standards, might be considered "feminine." The females are trained to be self-assertive and independent (Mead, 1939).

This example shows the effect of contrasting patterns of culture on human behavior. By culture, we mean the customs, traditions, beliefs, values, and attitudes that characterize a social group. Studies of various cultures have shown the extreme malleability of human behavior. Margaret Mead, one of the foremost authorities on cultural differences and their effects on human behavior, made the following observation:

The differences between individuals who are members of different cultures, like the differences between individuals within a culture, are almost entirely to be laid to differences in conditioning, especially during early childhood, and the

BERRY'S WORLD

"I'll tell you why I'm leaving you—because I've got a college education, and I can't develop my full potential doing housework!"

© 1972 by NEA, Inc.

Fig. 15.3
Socially acceptable behavior not only varies from culture to culture, but may also change over time within the same culture. The situation this cartoon is commenting on is only one example of the many standards of behavior that are undergoing change in our own society. (Reprinted by permission of Newspaper Enterprise Association.)

form of this conditioning is culturally determined. Standardized personality differences between the sexes are of this order, cultural creations to which each generation, male and female, is trained to conform. (Mead, 1939, p. 191)

The members of a given culture do not necessarily all behave and think in identical, prescribed ways. Nor do they all necessarily share common beliefs, values, and attitudes. Within any culture there may be various *subcultures;* these are segments of the larger culture which are characterized by their own customs, traditions, beliefs, values, and attitudes. For example, the rules governing eye contact vary according to one's subculture. Urban white Americans, for instance, avoid direct eye contact with a stranger once they are within recognition distance. On the other hand, many blacks look directly at one another, even if they are strangers. For some reason, it is much easier for people to accept differences in the way people of completely different cultures behave, than differences in the behavior of individuals belonging to subcultures of their own society. To black Americans, the eye behavior of whites gives the impression that they are being ignored, that they are not there. In fact, urban whites avoid eye contact with *anyone* with whom they are not familiar (Hall and Hall, 1971).

The Individual in Society

a) b)

c) d)

Fig. 15.4
Some American subcultures. (a
and b, Jeff Albertson—Stock,
Boston. c, Bruce Anspach—
Editorial Photocolor Archives
Newsphoto. d, Tim Carlson—
Stock, Boston.)

Individuals may be influenced simultaneously by several
different subcultures in the same society. They may live in a large
metropolitan urban area, or a small rural community. They may
be members of a particular ethnic group and observe a specific
religious faith. They may belong to an academic, business, or
hippie community. Their behaviors and life styles may reflect the
influence of these many subcultures.

Role

An individual occupies many different positions in the social structure. He may be a college student, a son, a part-time employee in the cafeteria, and an active member of a student protest group. Certain types of behaviors are considered appropriate to each of these positions. As a student, he is expected to attend classes, study, take examinations, and pass his courses. As a son, he is called upon to be respectful to his parents. As an employee, he is expected to be industrious and to submit to the authority of his employer. As a member of a protest group, he is expected to be an articulate spokesman against authority.

The patterns of behavior expected in given social positions are called roles. Roles may vary in permanence. After the student graduates, many of his roles as a member of the college community will terminate and he may assume new roles as husband, father, and businessman.

At any given time, the different roles a person plays may be in conflict with one another. For example, as a member of a protest group, he may be expected to speak out against the same professor to whom, as a student, he is expected to be attentive in class. Moreover, the patterns of behavior expected in a given position are not always clear-cut. The expectations depend on the social context. Whereas the parents may expect the son to be respectful and obedient, his peer group may call upon him to cut the ties of parental domination. Thus, he may be in conflict concerning his manner of dress, hair style, and whether or not to try certain drugs. Conflicting roles continue to plague us throughout our lives. H. G. Wells, when surveying the many expectations of him in the roles of famous author, husband, and father, was reported to have proclaimed in despair, "I am not a person; I am a mob."

Characteristics of Crowds and Groups

Situation 1

In a large metropolitan area, a number of people gathered at the base of a skyscraper and began looking up. They saw a man perched on a ledge, apparently preparing to jump. Before long, the numbers swelled, and someone shouted, "Jump!" In a moment, the one voice became many, each one yelling, "Jump! Jump! Jump!"

Situation 2

Many hours prior to an important sports event at the Melbourne Football Stadium, a number of people gathered to wait in line to buy tickets.

Situation 3

Several students enrolled in a seminar course are seated around a table discussing the assigned topic with their instructor.

In what way are all of the above situations similar, and how do they differ? All involve a collection of people gathered together for some specific purpose. However, here the similarity ends. Situation 1 is an example of a crowd. Situations 2 and 3 illustrate two kinds of groups which differ in terms of their degree of organization and the permanence of the association among their members. Let's look more closely at each of these situations so that we can better understand how they differ.

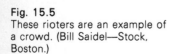

Fig. 15.5
These rioters are an example of a crowd. (Bill Saidel—Stock, Boston.)

Social Psychology

A *crowd* may be described as . . . a temporary group, focused on a common object of attention, in which mutual stimulation among members is a main basis of behavior. This mutual stimulation typically includes a *milling* of persons in close physical contact, *collective excitement* aroused by an unusual event, and the *social contagion* of mood and action from one member to another.

(Schellenberg, 1970, pp. 312–313)

Clearly, the first situation exemplifies a crowd; see Fig. 15.5 for another example of a crowd.

The most striking characteristic of crowds is that individual members may behave in ways that are inconsistent with their usual patterns of behavior. If one person were the sole witness to the scene described in Situation 1—the man perched on the ledge —it is highly unlikely that he would urge that man to jump. Many investigators of crowd behavior have suggested that an individual may act out of character in a crowd because he can express, with almost complete anonymity, certain underlying motives that do not usually receive social approval. Perhaps because of the lack of restraints, organization, and structure, crowd behavior is highly unpredictable. We will discuss the violent aspects of crowd behavior in Chapter 16.

In contrast to a crowd, a *group* has some degree of organization and there are rules governing the behavior of its members. Until recently, the scene described in Situation 2 would have been considered merely a collection of unrelated individuals, totally devoid of organization and structure. Recent studies, however, have demonstrated that people waiting in a line (queue) may constitute a group in the sense that there are regulations guiding their behavior while they are in the line (Mann, 1970).

Most of you have probably had the experience of waiting in line for a movie, at a supermarket, or to register for classes. Perhaps you have even had to wait for a long time to buy tickets for a particularly popular concert or game. Think for a moment about your behavior and that of others in the line. Were you aware of any implicit rules governing your position in the line? For example, was there any way to protect your position if you had to leave the line for a period of time? Were there any procedures to protect the line from infiltrators?

Characteristics of Crowds and Groups

Fig. 15.6
The spectators are an example of an informal
group. (Stephen J. Potter—Stock, Boston.)

Fig. 15.7
This class is an example of a formal group. (Charles M.
Hagen—Stock, Boston.)

Every year, football fans form 22 long, overnight queues to
purchase tickets for the Australian equivalent of the World Series.
A series of studies of the behavior of these groups has
demonstrated the capacity of such collections of people to evolve
a miniature social structure, complete with implicit rules and
regulations. For example, there is an informal understanding
about the minimum amount of time you must occupy a position
in order to establish your claim. Once your claim is established, if
you leave a possession to mark your place, you may not absent
yourself for more than two to three hours. Generally, physical
force is not used to eject an infiltrator: "The queue rarely acts
together to expel the violator; the onus for rejecting him falls
squarely on the shoulders of the person who 'let him in' " (Mann,
1970). Shortly before the ticket booth opens, there is a period of
maximum danger of infiltration. At this time, the line visibly
shrinks as people bunch together, making it more difficult to
break in. Figure 15.6 is another example of a group.

The seminar described in Situation 3 (see Fig. 15.7) is also a
group. However, that is a more formal and highly structured

situation in which the rules are more explicit and there is a clearly designated leader. A considerable amount of research has been conducted on these more formal types of groups. We will discuss some of the findings in the next section.

Group Dynamics

There are many different types of groups. Think for a moment about the number of different groups to which you belong. You are a member of a family group and a peer group, and you may belong to a fraternity or sorority, an athletic team, and a political club, as well as several classroom groups. As a member of these groups, you are simultaneously influenced by, and able to influence, others in these groups. Groups themselves can vary in a number of different ways—size, degree of structure and formality, the extent to which they exercise control over their members, the amount of participation expected, the degree of stability, and the extent to which they are organized into a hierarchical structure.

Group dynamics is the study of the ways in which groups develop and function, and of the factors affecting the interactions among members of a group and between different groups. As we will see, groups differ in their modes of communication, types of leadership, and bases for making decisions and taking action.

Communication

All groups have a definite communication structure which specifies who may interact with whom and on what occasions. Some groups, such as encounter groups and seminar groups, permit a free flow of communication among all members. Other groups place a restriction on the communication flow. For example, in a classroom lecture the flow of communication is primarily from one person (the instructor) to the rest of the group. In organizations in which there is a centralization of authority—the military, many large corporations, and various institutions—a hierarchical pattern prevails. In such situations, an individual is typically free to communicate only with people at his own level and those who are one level above or below him.

Group Dynamics

WHEEL

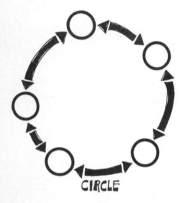

CIRCLE

Fig. 15.8
Communication patterns

Two patterns of communication involving small groups. In the "wheel" all communication is through a central figure. In the "circle" each group member may communicate only with two other members. These represent two different degrees of centralization in communication patterns that have been investigated in small group situations. The "wheel" represents maximum centralization.

Social
Psychology

Because of the complexity of many real-life group situations, most research has been conducted under controlled laboratory conditions, where the number of participants can be limited and the flow of communication can be precisely controlled. These laboratory situations are somewhat artificial, and do not necessarily permit generalization of the findings to larger real-world groups. Nevertheless, certain basic principles may be uncovered which can then be tested in group situations outside the laboratory.

Many different patterns of communication have been described. In one study, subjects were separated from one another by partitions, but they could send messages to other subjects through slots in the partitions. The experimenter could control the flow of communication by opening and closing these slots. Several communication patterns were used in studying the effect of interaction processes on the efficiency of five-member groups in arriving at solutions to relatively simple problems (see Fig. 15.8 for two of the patterns used). The most general finding was that the greater the centralization of structure, the more efficient was the problem-solving behavior of the group (Leavitt, 1951). One of the criticisms leveled against this study was that the problem task was extremely simple, consisting primarily of sorting and exchanging information.

A review of studies which varied the complexity of the problem-solving task suggests that centralized communication networks are more efficient for simple tasks. However, for complex tasks, decentralized communication patterns appear to be superior (Shaw, 1964). The reviewer concluded that

> . . . centralized networks are generally more efficient when the task requires merely the collection of information in one place. Decentralized networks are more efficient when the task requires, in addition to the information collection process, that further operations must be performed on the information before the task can be completed.
>
> (Shaw, 1964, p. 144)

Leadership

For years, people who have been interested in leadership have searched for certain qualities that characterize effective leaders.

This has led to the trait approach to leadership, which looks for certain general characteristics possessed by leaders but not by nonleaders. Most of the studies using this approach have failed to reveal any single important dimensions that consistently define effective leadership (Jenkins, 1947). This finding is not surprising when you consider the wide range of situations in which leaders emerge. Think of the many groups in which the leader is designated "president." Certainly, it is unlikely that the following presidents would possess a common pattern of personality traits— president of the United States, president of the PTA, president of a women's liberation movement, and president of a nudist colony. Obviously, an effective leader must possess those qualities that permit both the individual members and the group as a whole to achieve their goals. Although the requisite qualities will vary somewhat from group to group, not all individuals are equally likely to assume leadership positions, while some individuals may become leaders of several different groups.

Although no specific personality trait will guarantee leadership in all situations, the results of various studies suggest that the possession of certain characteristics will increase the likelihood that an individual will become either a leader or a follower. A review of studies concerned with the personality characteristics of leaders revealed that certain personality traits are more likely to be found among individuals in leadership positions. Compared to other members in their group, leaders tend to be more intelligent, dominant, better adjusted, and somewhat less conservative (Mann, 1959). It should be emphasized that an individual who is able to function as a leader in one group is not necessarily able to become a leader in other situations. However, a leader of one group is more likely to become the leader of another group if the groups' tasks are similar (Carter et al., 1950).

In many group situations, two different leadership functions emerge: a *task specialist* and a *social specialist* (Bales, 1958). The task specialist organizes and directs the group toward the achievement of its goals. He is not necessarily liked by the group members, but he performs a vital function by keeping the group "on the job." In performing this function, many tensions and morale problems may arise. It is the social specialist who, through joking, cajolery, and generally lifting the *esprit-de-corps,* maintains

Group Dynamics

harmony and dissipates tensions within the group. Occasionally, both of these functions are performed by a single individual. But more often they are allocated to different people.

Group Action

Productivity

The popular expression, "Two heads are better than one," implies that two or more individuals working together toward the solution of a problem will be more successful than if they worked individually. The culmination of this point of view is found in the technique of _brainstorming_, which was widely practiced a number of years ago. Brainstorming is a technique which emphasizes group participation to elicit ideas and solve problems. The assumption is that the interaction among the group members will stimulate each individual to heights of creativity to which he could not aspire alone.

One investigator concluded that "the average person can think up twice as many ideas when working with a group than when working alone" (Osborn, 1957). However, other studies using a diverse sampling of subjects have tended to refute this finding (Taylor et al., 1957; Dunnette et al., 1963). They report that individuals produce a greater number of ideas when working _alone._ These studies suggest "that a group tends to 'fall in a rut' and to pursue the same train of thought. The effect of this is to limit the diversity of approaches to a problem, thereby leading to the production of fewer different ideas" (Dunnette et al., 1963). Individuals working alone appear to have a particular advantage where sustained creative effort is required.

You should not conclude, at this point, that individual performance is superior to a group effort in all types of situations. Certain tasks require a diversity of approaches for their solution. For example, the design of a new piece of equipment for use in an airplane might best be achieved by a team possessing many different skills—electronic, mathematical, psychological, and aeronautical. When the talents of a variety of different people can be pooled to contribute to the solution of a problem, group performance is likely to be superior to the performance of an individual working alone. A good example, with which you may

... Mr. K. is a successful businessman who has participated in a number of civic activities of considerable value to the community. Mr. K. has been approached by the leaders of his political party as a possible congressional candidate in the next election. Mr. K's party is a minority party in the district, though the party has won occasional elections in the past. Mr. K. would like to hold political office, but to do so would involve a serious financial sacrifice, since the party has insufficient campaign funds. He would also have to endure the attacks of the political opponents in a hot campaign.

Imagine that you are advising Mr. K.

Listed below are several probabilities or odds of Mr. K's winning the election in his district. **Please check the lowest probability that you would consider to make it worthwhile for Mr. K. to run for political office.**

Box 15.2
Sample problem situation employed to investigate the "risky shift" phenomenon. The subject could decide to take no risk (Mr. K. should not run for office) or he could state a willingness to take a risk when the chances of success were 1, 3, 5, 7, or 9 chances in 10 that Mr. K. would win. The lower the odds accepted by the subject, the greater the risk he is willing to take. Each subject made twelve such decisions working alone both before and after group discussion. Decisions made after group discussion shifted toward greater riskiness (Stoner, 1961). (From "Risk and Conservatism in Group Decision-Making" by G. R. Madaras and D. J. Bem, *Journal of Experimental Social Psychology*, **4**, 1968, pp. 350–365. Used by permission of Academic Press, Inc.)

already have had some experience, is the solution of crossword puzzles. Here, the superiority of the group stems from the variety of different verbal responses that are available for the solution (Thorndike, 1938).

Decision making

In actual practice, most of the important decisions that are made in government, business, finance, and education are the products of group efforts. Since so many of the important decisions in life are in the hands of groups, we might ask, "What are the differences in the kinds of decisions groups will make as opposed to individuals working alone?" One difference that has been observed is that decisions made by group consensus tend to be more risky than decisions made by the group members as individuals (Kogan and Wallach, 1967). This rather startling finding contradicts the common belief that groups tend toward more conservative courses of action.

In the original study of what is called the *risky shift* phenomenon, subjects were required to choose between a risky, but desirable, alternative and a more certain, but less desirable, alternative. The problems ranged over a wide variety of topics involving possible loss of money, prestige, and life. Box 15.2 is an example. First, the subjects made their decisions while working alone. They were then placed in groups of six and required to arrive at a unanimous selection of a level of risk. Finally, each individual was again required to state his own risk preferences for each problem. A shift toward greater riskiness was found in both the group decisions and the subsequent individual decisions. This risky shift was not found in a control group that did not participate in the group discussions and decisions (Stoner, 1961). A number of subsequent studies have verified this phenomenon

Group Dynamics

with many different populations and a variety of different problems (Kogan and Wallach, 1967).

The explanation for the risky shift phenomenon is still not clear. A variety of explanations have been offered. Some investigators have suggested that it may be related to the fact that there is less personal responsibility when a decision is made by a group and, therefore, less danger of blame in the event that the group decision proves to have been a bad one. Others have proposed that our culture rewards an individual who appears to be somewhat more daring than his peers. In a group situation, an individual discovers the risk levels of the other members. He may find that his initial position was no more daring than that of his peers. Consequently, he adjusts his risk level upward in order to maintain his self-image as a daring individual.

Whatever the explanation, it is clear that the risky shift phenomenon may have extremely important implications in real-life situations. Governments are constantly making decisions in crisis situations where one of the risks may be war. Individuals who are unwilling to challenge authority on their own may do so as a member of a group. Even the irrational behavior sometimes found in crowds may involve the risky shift phenomenon.

How Groups Influence Behavior

We have seen that an individual's behavior may be different when he acts as part of a group than when he acts alone. Groups exert a continuing and pervasive influence on all aspects of a person's life: his beliefs, attitudes, likes and dislikes. Many investigators have demonstrated that a number of psychological processes are subject to group influences and pressures.

When a person adapts his behavior to be consistent with his perception of group values, we say he is *conforming*. When he yields to the pressures of those in authority, we say he is *obedient*. Both conformity and obedience have been the subject of extensive investigation.

Conformity

Look at the three lines in Fig. 15.9. Which line do you think matches the line in Fig. 15.10? You have undoubtedly selected line *b* as the appropriate match. Do you think there are any

Fig. 15.9
Which of these lines matches the one in Fig. 15.10?

Fig. 15.10
The test line.

*Social
Psychology*

Fig. 15.11
Conformity

When the subjects were not under pressure to conform, their judgments were virtually without error (solid line). When subjects made judgments in the face of group pressure, they made many errors (broken line). (After "Opinions and Social Pressure" by Solomon E. Asch. Copyright © 1955 by Scientific American, Inc. All rights reserved.)

conditions under which you could be convinced to select either line *a* or line *c?* Surprisingly, a series of investigations showed that, under certain experimental conditions, many individuals can be pressured into making an obviously incorrect judgment (Asch, 1951, 1955, 1956). Let's look at several of the experimental manipulations that have identified some of the factors involved in conformity behavior.

The basic experimental design involved groups consisting of several subjects who were required to match lines similar to those shown in Figs. 15.9 and 15.10. Only one of the subjects in each group was naive, that is, was not aware of the design of the experiment. Unknown to him, the others were confederates working for the experimenter. The confederates were instructed to agree on an incorrect judgment on 12 of the 18 trials and to exert pressure on the naive subject to accept this judgment. The results are summarized in Fig. 15.11. As you can see, the average number of correct estimates given by the naive subjects is lower on all trials in which the confederates "ganged up" on the naive subjects. When the naive subjects were not exposed to group pressures, their judgments were virtually perfect.

Not all subjects were equally influenced by group pressures. Some subjects maintained their independence and never yielded to group pressures, while others agreed with the incorrect judgments of the majority almost all the time. The naive subject in Fig. 15.12 was among the independent subjects. Note the obvious concern on his face as he leans forward to check his judgment.

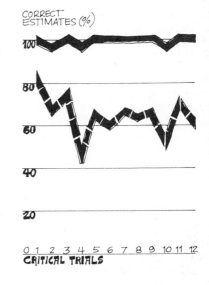

CORRECT ESTIMATES (%)

100

80

60

40

20

0 1 2 3 4 5 6 7 8 9 10 11 12
CRITICAL TRIALS

Fig. 15.12
All of the subjects except number 6 were confederates working for the experimenter. They were instructed to give the same wrong answers to several of the problems. (Photo courtesy of William Vandivert.)

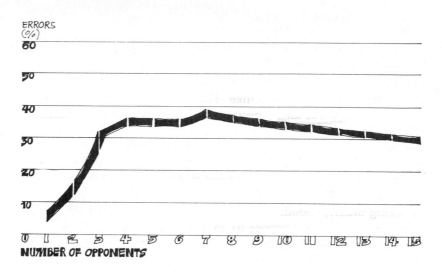

ERRORS (%)

NUMBER OF OPPONENTS

*Social
Psychology*

In a variation of the original experimental design, the number of individuals pitted against the naive subject was systematically varied (see Fig. 15.13). The effect of group pressures rose rapidly until, with three confederates opposing the judgment of the naive subject, his errors were approximately 32 percent. Increasing the number of confederates beyond three did not appear to make a substantial difference in the number of errors the naive subject made. Thus, the size of the opposition group appears to be important only up to a certain point.

In both of the above situations, the naive subject stood alone against a unanimous majority. What would happen if the unanimity were disturbed by introducing a second subject (either a confederate instructed always to give correct answers, or another naive subject)? The effect of this manipulation was striking. The support of only a single individual was enough to decrease the errors made by the naive subjects to about one-fourth of the errors made when they were pitted alone against the confederates. The errors remained relatively low even when the supporting partner left the room. However, when the partner "deserted" to the majority after the sixth trial, the error scores of the naive subjects showed an abrupt rise. Their frequency of errors increased to about the same level as in the original experimental session, in which the naive subject was opposed by the unanimous majority.

Experiments on conformity behavior go beyond the laboratory into real-life situations. In many business and industrial settings, workers often resist every effort by the management to introduce change. They frequently develop a set of _norms_—standards and expectations shared by a group—which call for the maintenance of the status quo. They express their resentment of change by various job actions: work slowdowns, sick days, sloppy and inefficient production. In a sense, the management is in the position of the minority subject in the conformity studies discussed above. How does it go about achieving orderly, nondisruptive, and acceptable change when the norms of the majority oppose it? In the conformity studies discussed so far, the object has been to learn the conditions which influence an individual to conform to group pressures. Other studies have been concerned with how group norms may themselves be modified in order to permit change.

In one study conducted in a pajama factory, the company wished to introduce several changes in production procedures. In order to determine the best method of overcoming worker resistance, an experiment was conducted. In the control group, the workers were merely informed that the changes were necessary to reduce costs and that a new piece-rate schedule was being introduced. In two of the experimental groups, which differed from each other in minor details, the workers and their leaders were actively involved in a discussion of the cost problem. They agreed that streamlining was possible, and even made constructive suggestions of their own. In the subsequent 32-day observation period, the production levels of the control subjects fell below previous levels and remained so throughout the experiment. All the experimental groups showed an initial drop, but this was followed by an abrupt rise to levels that remained higher than those prevailing before the change (Coch and French, 1948).

In an ongoing field study, investigators are attempting to induce passengers to form a line while awaiting bus services to Harvard Square in Cambridge, Massachusetts. Groups of varying numbers of confederates form a line at the bus stop and then note whether or not other people join the queue. So far, they have established that the size of the line is an important variable, with a 10-person queue reliably able to induce others to join (Mann, 1970).

Obedience

From time to time, people are horrified when they learn of heinous crimes committed in the name of obedience. In Nazi Germany, for instance, millions of Jews were mutilated, raped, and executed by soldiers following orders. More recently, we were shocked by the revelations of the massacre at My Lai in Vietnam by soldiers who protested that they were just obeying orders. Are these atrocities bizarre departures from the norm by abnormal individuals, or can any responsible and respected person be persuaded to inflict punishment upon another human being?

In a dramatic study of destructive obedience, the investigator attempted to learn the extent to which a subject can be induced to inflict pain on another subject in response to an authority figure (the experimenter). The study was conducted under the pretext that the experimenter was trying to determine the effect of punishment on learning. Each of the 40 subjects was told to test another subject (a confederate of the experimenter) on a learning task and to administer an increasing amount of punishment each time the "learner" made an error. Punishment was "administered" through a shock generator controlled by the subject. The intensity of the shock could be varied from slight (15 volts) through 30 different steps to severe shock (450 volts). Actually, the apparatus was not connected, but the "learner" was instructed to respond as if in pain. Whenever the subject hesitated to deliver punishment, he was prodded by the experimenter by such statements as "Please continue," or "You have no other choice, you *must* go on" (Milgram, 1963).

Suppose you were a subject in this experiment. At what point would you stop administering the shock? Keep in mind that you have nothing to lose by stopping—you will incur only the displeasure of the authority figure. You might be surprised to learn that, in the actual experiment, 65 percent of the subjects obeyed the commands of the experimenter fully, and "administered" the highest amount of shock possible (see Fig. 15.14). While doing this, however, many subjects reacted with acute discomfort and tension. The following observation was made of one of the subjects:

> I observed a mature and initially poised businessman enter the laboratory smiling and confident. Within 20 minutes he

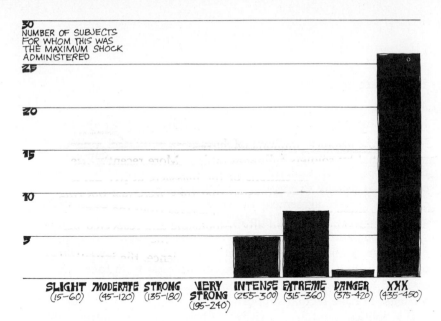

NUMBER OF SUBJECTS FOR WHOM THIS WAS THE MAXIMUM SHOCK ADMINISTERED

SLIGHT (15-60) MODERATE (45-120) STRONG (135-180) VERY STRONG (195-240) INTENSE (255-300) EXTREME (315-360) DANGER (375-420) XXX (435-450)

Fig. 15.14
Obedience

Subjects were told to administer increasing amounts of shock to a "learner." All 40 subjects administered shocks scaled "intense" or higher. Only 14 subjects broke off before the end (see text). (After "Behavioral Study of Obedience" by Stanley Milgram, *Journal of Abnormal and Social Psychology,* **67,** 1963, pp. 371–378. Copyright © 1963 by the American Psychological Association and used by permission.)

was reduced to a twitching, stuttering wreck, who was rapidly approaching a point of nervous collapse. He constantly pulled on his earlobe, and twisted his hands. At one point he pushed his fist into his forehead and muttered: "Oh God, let's stop." And yet he continued to respond to every word of the experimenter, and obeyed to the end.

(Milgram, 1963, p. 377)

It should be emphasized that the above experiment involved *destructive* obedience. Not all obedience is undesirable. Clearly, the harmonious working of any group or society requires that its members obey certain rules and laws, and conform to norms within acceptable ranges.

Attitudes

Attitudes are among the most important determinants of an individual's social behavior. They are acquired early in life during the course of socialization, and they continue to be modified throughout life. Attitudes largely determine our likes and dislikes, the stands we will take on various issues, and the way we react to the various situations that we encounter in life. The remainder of this chapter is devoted to the ways in which attitudes are acquired and modified.

Attitudes

The Nature of Attitudes

An attitude is a learned predisposition to respond in a specific way, negatively or positively, toward people, ideas, or situations. Attitudes typically involve an affective (or feeling) component, a cognitive (or thought) component, and a behavioral component. For example, when an individual endorses a candidate for political office, he is usually expressing positive feelings toward that candidate (affect), agreement with many of his ideas (cognition), and a decision to vote for him at election time (behavior).

Although attitudes are somewhat similar to opinions and beliefs, we can make some distinctions. A *belief* is the acceptance of a proposition as fact. Beliefs are not necessarily in favor of or opposed to something; they are simply statements which are assumed to have factual support. For example, you may believe that a political candidate is either a liberal or a conservative, and point to his voting record as evidence. This belief does not necessarily predispose you to feel or act in any specific manner for or against this candidate. However, if you hold certain attitudes toward liberalism or conservatism, then this belief may influence your feelings and actions toward this candidate.

Opinions express judgments and feelings for which the factual support is far weaker than for beliefs. Sometimes, we are so convinced that our opinions are correct that we hold them to be beliefs. Because opinions more frankly express the feelings of an individual than beliefs do, they are more likely to reveal attitudes.

We are not always aware of our own attitudes. We may have acquired many of them early in life under circumstances that we have since forgotten. We are more aware of our beliefs, since we are able to express them verbally. As a consequence, attitudes may conflict with beliefs. For example, a person may assert his belief that all individuals in our society, regardless of race or creed, should have equal rights to live in any neighborhood they choose. He may point to the Constitution and to Supreme Court rulings to support this belief. Yet he may find himself uncomfortably disturbed upon learning that a member of a group different from his own is planning to move into his neighborhood. This person's disturbed feelings are more indicative of his attitudes than his verbal statements are.

If it is difficult to determine our own attitudes, how do we ascertain the attitudes of others? What a person says may not always be consonant with what he does. Do we determine his attitudes from his verbal statements or from his actions? In one study, landlords, in response to telephone inquiries, all stated that they would rent apartments to black or interracial couples. Yet many of these same landlords would not even show the apartments to the couples when they appeared in person (McGrew, 1967).

"He said his first words today: 'Get out of Vietnam!' "

Fig. 15.15
Our first attitudes are formed in our home. (Drawing by Alan Dunn. Copyright © 1966 by The New Yorker Magazine, Inc.)

Development of Attitudes

The moment a child is born, he is thrust into a social setting in which he will be learning attitudes. At first he will learn them primarily from his parents, who will reward him for expressing certain attitudes and punish him for others. During the first few years, the parents provide virtually the only input the child has for the formation of attitudes (see Fig. 15.15). The child acts the way his parents do, and responds positively and negatively to the same things and situations. Indeed, when interview techniques are employed with children in order to determine their attitudes on various topics, they very often cite their parents as the reason for

Attitudes

behaving in a certain way. When children were asked about their selection of playmates, the following answers were typical:

> *First-grade girl.* "Mamma tells me not to play with black children. . . ."
>
> *Second-grade boy.* ". . . mother and daddy tell me . . . not to play with colored people or colored persons' things."
>
> *Fourth-grade boy.* "Mother and daddy tell me to play with white boys. . . ."

(Horowitz and Horowitz, 1938)

Many of these basic attitudes remain with the child throughout his life. A study of political and religious attitudes of high school seniors showed high degrees of agreement with parental affiliations (Jennings and Niemi, 1968).

As children grow older and move out into other social situations, there is a marked broadening of outside influences on the formation of attitudes. They learn the goals and the norms of their various peer groups, and adjust their own attitudes so as to be socially acceptable to these groups. During adolescence, this "moving out" is dramatic. Adolescents typically spend less time with their family than they did at earlier ages, more time with their peer groups. These years of adolescence have been referred to, by some psychologists, as a period of storm and stress. The emerging adult attempts, often unsuccessfully, to reconcile the many opposing social pressures and often contradictory attitudes that he encounters. What is often interpreted by parents as defiance of authority is merely compliance by the adolescent with the norms of his peer groups. Many of these changes are superficial, insofar as they do not represent deep-seated alterations of the basic elements of personality. They may involve new hair styles, different forms of facial adornment, and new styles of dress. Other changes may reflect changing life styles in the broader society, to which the older generations may be resistant. New patterns and norms governing sexual behavior exemplify this kind of change.

Some of the most striking changes in attitudes occur during the college years, when students are exposed to the many and varied attitudes and norms of the college community. Some of these new attitudes might diverge considerably from those the student held during high school. Many studies have demonstrated the impact of peer influence on the modification of attitudes during the college years. One study, conducted at a college noted for its "liberal" faculty, demonstrated that the attitudes held by students as freshmen showed a swing toward a more liberal viewpoint by the time they were seniors (Newcomb, 1943). Moreover, these more liberal attitudes tended to persist over a 20-year period (Newcomb, 1963).

Cognitive Dissonance

A person may sometimes behave in ways that are inconsistent with his existing attitudes, or he may hold contradictory attitudes. Such disparities take on many of the motivational characteristics that we discussed in relation to conflict behavior (Chapter 12). For example, some students are not able to modify their behavior and attitudes to conform to norms that are markedly different from their own. One of the colleges in this country has a reputation for encouraging students to adopt their own life styles, to be independent, to show resourcefulness and initiative. One student at this school withdrew after her first year, complaining that the pressure to conform to the norm of "being different" was too much for her! The case of this young lady shows the contradictory pressures that characterize many adolescent conflicts: the pressure to conform to previously acquired norms and attitudes conflicts with the pressure to adopt new life styles in conformity to peer group norms. She "resolved" her conflict by withdrawing from the situation.

Although people differ in the amount of inconsistency they can tolerate, a basic assumption of cognitive dissonance theory is that inconsistency is intolerable to an individual. According to this theory, when two or more cognitions (such as beliefs and opinions) are in disagreement (dissonant), a state of tension results. This inconsistency (dissonance) motivates the individual to adjust these cognitions so as to reduce the dissonance and thereby reduce the tension (Festinger, 1957). For example, suppose a person who enjoys smoking is confronted with evidence that smoking is harmful. He is faced with two dissonant cognitions: "I enjoy smoking" and "Smoking is harmful." The dissonance

Attitudes

(inconsistency between these two cognitions) results in a state of tension. How can he reduce the dissonance? He may reject or minimize the information ("most people who smoke don't get lung cancer"); he may rationalize that, by giving up smoking, he will gain weight and excess weight is also harmful to health; or he may give up smoking.

When there is dissonance between attitudes and behavior, the individual usually modifies his attitudes rather than his behavior. For example, when subjects were induced to lie to other subjects by telling them that an extremely tedious and boring task was, in fact, interesting, they subsequently rated the task as more interesting than did a control group of subjects who had not committed themselves to the lie (Festinger and Carlsmith, 1959). The experimental subjects reduced their cognitive dissonance by revising their attitude toward the task to fit their behavior.

If a person goes through a lot of trouble or pain to attain something, he tends to view it as more valuable or important than if he attained it through a minimum of effort. In one study, a group of female college students volunteered to participate in group discussions of sexual behavior. The subjects were randomly divided into three groups, which differed in the severity of initiation required for participation in the group discussion. In the group subjected to severe initiation, the girls were required to read aloud some embarrassing material to the experimenter. All the subjects then listened in on discussions that were designed to be extremely dull in order to maximize the dissonance of the subjects who had undergone severe initiation. The investigators found that subjects in the severe condition tended to have the most favorable attitudes toward the group's activities (Aronson and Mills, 1959).

A dramatic example of cognitive dissonance in a real-life situation was provided by the behavior of passengers who survived an air disaster. On October 13, 1972, a Uruguayan Air Force plane crashed into a remote and inaccessible peak in the Chilean Andes. Twenty-nine people died in the crash or shortly afterwards; sixteen survived 69 days of subzero temperatures and threatened starvation. The survivors later revealed that they had stayed alive by eating the flesh of the dead. With the strong prohibitions against cannibalism in Western civilization, how were they able to convince themselves that eating human flesh was appropriate under these circumstances? One young man compared the cannibalism to a heart transplant, pointing out that the heart of a dead person is used to keep another person alive. Others found support for their behavior in the tenets of their religious faith, pointing to the communion ceremony, in which the individual symbolically drinks the blood and eats the flesh of Christ.

Prejudice

Prejudice is defined as any kind of prejudgment, negative or positive. Social psychologists have generally been concerned with prejudice in the negative sense. Note that prejudice is an attitude (a predisposition to act), which may or may not be associated with behavior. The behavioral expression of prejudice is *discrimination.*

Ordinarily, prejudice and discrimination are maintained by perceiving the person or group against whom the prejudice is directed as different from one's own group. They may be seen as having different status, ideals, and values, and as behaving in different ways.

Prejudices, like other attitudes, are wholly learned. They may be acquired early in life through interactions with other individuals who communicate, directly or indirectly, negative feelings and attitudes toward certain individuals or groups. Many parents directly teach their children to hold unfavorable attitudes toward certain groups. However, there are also many indirect and subtle forces at work. A parent may communicate prejudices by a tone of voice or a gesture. Indeed, studies have found that many children express racial and religious prejudices at early ages (Radke et al., 1949; Ammons, 1950). These early attitudes are frequently superficial, and may only represent the child's parrotting of parental statements.

Prejudices are frequently supported by *stereotypes,* which are preconceived ideas about the attributes of people belonging to certain groups. For instance, in 1932 Princeton University students saw Germans as scientifically minded, industrious, and stolid; they saw Chinese as superstitious, sly, and conservative; and Turks as cruel, very religious, and treacherous (Katz and Braly, 1933). However, stereotypes change, as you can see in Box

Attitudes

Germans	Percent checking trait			Chinese	Percent checking trait		
Trait	1933	1951	1967	*Trait*	1933	1951	1967
Scientifically minded	78	62	47	Superstitious	34	18	8
Industrious	65	50	59	Sly	29	4	6
Stolid	44	10	9	Conservative	29	14	15
Intelligent	32	32	19	Tradition loving	26	26	32
Methodical	31	20	21	Loyal to family ties	22	35	50
Extremely nationalistic	24	50	43	Industrious	18	18	23
Progressive	16	3	13				

Turks	Percent checking trait		
Trait	1933	1951	1967
Cruel	47	12	9
Very religious	26	6	7
Treacherous	21	3	13
Sensual	20	4	9
Ignorant	15	7	13
Physically dirty	15	7	14

Box 15.3
Stereotypes change over time
(Katz and Braly, 1933; Gilbert,
1951; Karlins et al., 1969).

15.3, which compares the 1932 results with similar surveys conducted at Princeton in 1950 (Gilbert, 1951) and 1967 (Karlins et al., 1969). Some caution is necessary in interpreting these results. Although the stereotypes may indeed have changed, we must also keep in mind that the type of student attending Princeton in 1932 may have been very different from the types attending in 1950 and 1967.

Prejudice occurs in all walks of life, and its victims range from the aged, the mentally ill, homosexuals, women, and ex-convicts, to those who differ in religion and skin color. Many groups have been formed to combat the constant harassment and discrimination directed against their members. The Gay Liberation Front, the National Organization of Women, and a group called Insane Liberation are some of the more recent groups of this sort (see Fig. 15.16).

Of all forms of prejudice, the one that has received the most attention in this country has been racial prejudice. The following observation by a prominent black psychologist depicts the pervasive effects of racial prejudice on the developing attitudes of the children who are its victims:

Human beings who are forced to live under ghetto conditions and whose daily experience tells them that almost nowhere in society are they respected and granted the ordinary dignity and courtesy accorded to others will, as a matter of course, begin to doubt their own worth. Since every human being depends upon his cumulative experiences with others for clues as to how he should view and value himself, children

Social Psychology

who are consistently rejected understandably begin to question
and doubt whether they, their family, and their group really
deserve no more respect from the larger society than they receive.
These doubts become the seeds of a pernicious self- and
group-hatred and the Negro's complex, debilitating prejudice
against himself.

(Clark, 1965, pp. 63–64)

Fig. 15.16
Many of the groups that have
long been victims of prejudice
have begun to organize to
combat the discrimination
directed at their members.
(Owen Franken—Stock, Boston.)

Changing Attitudes

Although attitudes are relatively stable, they are not immutable—
they can and do change, as we have seen. We have already
discussed the three components of attitudes: affective, cognitive,
and behavioral. Attempts to change attitudes have generally
focused on changing one of these components. The assumption is
that changing one component will create pressures to change the
remaining components.

Many of the efforts by the United Nations and the mass
media to reduce racial prejudice and stereotypes have focused on
supplying information about the consequences of prejudice and
facts which show that minority group members have the same
basic motivations and needs as everyone else. These efforts are an
attempt to change the cognitive components. Advertising, too,
which in a sense is exclusively devoted to attitude change,
frequently attempts to produce favorable attitudes in the
consumer by presenting informational material (see Fig. 15.17).
The assumption behind this approach is that a favorable

Attitudes

The great new Sunbeam Shavemaster Shaver

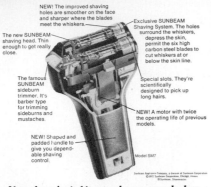

NEW! The improved shaving holes are smoother on the face and sharper where the blades meet the whiskers.

The new SUNBEAM shaving head. Thin enough to get really close.

The famous SUNBEAM sideburn trimmer. It's barber type for trimming sideburns and mustaches.

NEW! Shaped and padded handle to give you dependable shaving control.

Exclusive SUNBEAM Shaving System. The holes surround the whiskers, depress the skin, permit the six high carbon steel blades to cut whiskers at or below the skin line.

Special slots. They're scientifically designed to pick up long hairs.

NEW! A motor with twice the operating life of previous models.

Model SM7

If you haven't tried it yet, ask someone who has.

We did. We asked 104 previous electric shaver owners who now own the new Sunbeam Shavemaster Shaver.

We asked them to compare it to their previous shaver.*

Here are the percentages: 92% thought it was as close or closer; 93% thought it was as fast or faster; 94% thought it was as smooth or smoother; and 78% thought it was as easy or easier to handle. What's more, 91% said they would recommend it to a friend.

The improvements we made are working. This new Sunbeam Shavemaster Shaver deserves to be called great. Try it yourself and see if you don't agree.

*telephone survey: 69 previous Sunbeam owners, 35 previous competitive brand owners.

Sunbeam. Built with integrity, backed by service.

WHY SAFETY SELLS IN SWEDEN.

Of all motorized countries, Sweden has the best safety record.

Before a Swede can get a driver's license, he not only has to pass a complicated driving test, but also a comprehensive medical examination.

Cars are subject to spot inspections at any time. Cars found unsafe are taken off the road.

Swedish road signs go to extremes. A thorough system of descriptive signs stretches from the middle of big cities to the middle of nowhere. The sign in the picture, for example, warns that the road dead-ends at a ferry dock.

Obviously, Sweden are deeply committed to traffic safety. And they carry their commitment with them when they buy a car.

This is one of the reasons Volvo comes equipped with four-wheel power disc brakes.

Volvo is the only car in the world with a dual braking system that has three wheels on each circuit. If one circuit fails, you still have 80% of your braking power.

Volvo was the first mass-produced car to come equipped with three-point seat belts.

Volvo, you see, didn't get to be the largest selling car in Sweden by accident.

Volvo.

We build them the way we build them because we have to.

VOLVO

Travelers offers you the one thing you want most from an insurance company: insurance for less money.

Chances are you've been hearing a great deal these days about how great steel-belted radial-ply tires are.

(And the fact is, steel-belted radials are the most advanced type of tire you can buy. No matter what kind of car you drive.)

Well, here's something we at Uniroyal would like to tell you about our steel-belted radials:

World-wide, we've sold more steel-belted radials than any other American tire company.

You see, back in the fifties, we at Uniroyal made a judgement: the steel-belted radial would be the tire of the future. So we went to France, home of the steel-belted radial, to develop our own version of this remarkable tire. (No mean feat, since a radial tire, by nature of its construction, is extremely difficult to produce; and steel belts, by nature of the very material itself, are very difficult to work with.) By 1961, we had a steel-belted radial in production there. And we've had it in continuous production ever since.

Uniroyal is now making a steel-belted radial-ply tire, the Zeta 40M, here in America. And we feel the 10-year head-start we've had in Europe over every other American tire manufacturer, in perfecting what is a rather difficult tire to produce, has to give us—and, thereby, you—a distinct and obvious advantage.

Here's what you can expect from a Uniroyal steel-belted radial.

A radial tire has a definite edge in that the side walls of the tire flex a great deal more than those of a conventional bias-ply tire. This means that much more tread stays on the road at all times. And more rubber on the road means greater control and ease of handling on turns, more stability at high speeds, in passing and on wet surfaces, not to mention superior response in braking.

Clairoix, France—1961: Uniroyal tested its first steel-belted radial.

Another advantage of having more rubber remain on the road is that your tire will last a great deal longer. (It's not uncommon for a radial-ply tire to last well over 40,000 miles.) This longer wear may well serve to make up for the initially larger investment that steel-belted radials represent.

And finally, for our double steel belts. Their greater strength (steel belts, obviously, are much stronger than fabric or glass belts) offers you a tire with exceptional hazard protection, making it an extraordinarily safe tire.

(Incidentally, don't let anyone sell you just a radial tire or just a steel-belted tire. They're not the same as a steel-belted radial.)

With the Uniroyal Zeta 40M steel-belted radial-ply tire you get the performance of a radial plus the strength of steel belts. And it's made by a company that's had more experience in making this type of tire than any other American tire company.

Should your family be riding on anything less?

UNIROYAL

America's most experienced world-wide maker of steel-belted radials.

The cost of insurance, like the cost of practically everything else these days, seems to be going up and up and up with no end in sight.

Through our Office of Consumer Information, we've been hearing you out on this matter for a year now. We've been working on ways to do something about it for considerably longer. And we've come up with an idea that can actually lower the cost of our insurance as much as 20 per cent.

Basically, our idea is to sell insurance in a "wholesale" kind of way.

Working through companies or organizations, we can afford to charge less for individual auto insurance, home-owners, and what have you. Because when we sell to a lot of people at the same time and in the same place, the costs of selling and servicing are lower.

Not only that, our agents and brokers can write a simplified policy that's much easier to understand. And easier to pay for, because premiums can be automatically deducted from your paycheck.

We tried our idea at several large companies. It worked even better than we thought it would. And now we think it can save money for millions of other people, too.

If you're interested, if you'd like to know more, simply call The Travelers Office of Consumer Information and ask.

And if you have anything else on your mind, like whether "no-fault" auto insurance can really save you money or how health care can affect you or even some purely personal insurance problem, we'll do our best to help you there, too.

Call toll-free weekdays, from 9 to 5 Eastern Time
(800) 243-0191.

Call collect from Connecticut
277-6565.

Or you can write, if you prefer, to The Travelers Office of Consumer Information, One Tower Square, Hartford, Connecticut 06115.

Currently available in all but four states.

THE TRAVELERS

Fig. 15.17
Four advertisements that attempt to affect attitudes by appealing to the cognitive component.

attitude will result in the desired behavior (buying the product), and that changing the cognitive component will produce the favorable attitude.

Other efforts have attempted to change attitudes by modifying behavior. If a person can be induced to behave in a way that is incompatible with certain attitudes he holds, those attitudes may change so as to be consonant with the behavior. It has often been noted by debaters that, when forced to defend a position with which they initially disagree, they are often swayed in the direction of the contrary attitude. It is almost as if they "talk themselves into it." This aspect of attitude change has been studied in the laboratory. Students were given materials expressing attitudes that contradicted their own, and were asked to give an informal talk defending the positions expressed in these materials. On two out of three issues, their own attitudes showed considerable change in the direction of the message in the prepared materials. There was little change on the third issue. Control subjects, who merely listened to the talk, showed far less attitude change (Janis and King, 1954).

In another study, subjects in one group were provided with a script which they were to read to an audience. Subjects in a second group were given the same script, but were asked to improvise a talk based on it. In both groups, the subjects were defending positions at variance with their own attitudes. The subjects who improvised the talk showed greater change toward the position they were publicly advocating, than did subjects who merely read a prepared script (King and Janis, 1956).

In a study undertaken outside the laboratory, the attitudes of white housewives were ascertained before and after they moved into biracial housing projects, where circumstances forced them to adjust to the presence of blacks and to interact with them. In the fully integrated units, most of the attitudes changed in a favorable direction. In two units, however, there was considerable segregation, with black and white families living in separate buildings or separate parts of the project. White housewives living in these units showed little change one way or another (Deutsch and Collins, 1951).

It should not be assumed, however, that the answer to prejudice is simply to bring people holding prejudices into closer contact with members of the group against which the prejudice is directed. Much depends on the nature and quality of the contacts that subsequently develop.

As we have seen, some efforts at attitude change have focused on the cognitive component, and others on the behavioral aspect of attitudes. In most cases, the changes in affective states have been viewed as consequences (dependent measure) of altered behavioral or cognitive components. One investigator has concentrated his efforts on determining the extent to which the manipulation of affect, or feelings, will lead to cognitive changes. In one study, he administered a scale measuring the attitudes of the subjects on a number of issues: foreign aid, blacks moving into white neighborhoods, and so on. Then the subjects were hypnotized, and it was suggested to them that, upon awakening, they would feel differently about a particular issue. For example, one subject was told, "When you wake up, you will be very much in favor of Negroes moving into white neighborhoods. The mere idea of Negroes moving into white neighborhoods will give you a happy exhilarated feeling." The attitude scale was again administered a few days after the hypnotic session. It was found that the subjects changed their feelings in the direction suggested under hypnosis. Moreover, they now expressed changed cognitions which were in greater agreement with their changed feelings. For example, one subject who had favored foreign aid prior to hypnosis now argued that foreign aid would interfere with the development of self-reliance (Rosenberg, 1960).

Persuasive communication

Hardly a day passes when we are not literally assaulted by countless efforts to influence our attitudes in one way or another. Open a magazine or newspaper, or turn on the television set. All the commercials you see and hear are designed to produce favorable attitudes toward various products. A political campaign is an expensive and concerted effort to influence attitudes. All of these deliberate attempts to influence attitudes may be regarded as *propaganda.* Although the word propaganda has come to have a negative connotation, it should not be considered, in and of itself, either good or bad.

Propaganda has much in common with education, since both processes are designed to affect attitudes and behavior. However, they differ both in their objectives and in the types of appeals that they use. One goal of education is to impart information and knowledge (the cognitive component), whereas propaganda more frequently appeals to the emotions (affective component). Moreover, the objective of the propagandist is to persuade you to *his* way of thinking, whereas the educator attempts to bring your ideas in line with facts. This distinction is not always clear-cut, since propagandists frequently serve as educators insofar as they impart knowledge and information. Likewise, an educator may employ persuasive appeals to convince the student to adopt his point of view on a particular issue. Indeed, many educators may turn out to be more successful propagandists than those making their careers in the field of propaganda.

One factor that has frequently been investigated with respect to persuasive communication is the *source* of the communication. It has been found that the status and prestige of the individual advocating a position is often an important determinant of attitude change.

In one study, high school students were asked to rate the "fairness" of arguments attributed to three different sources. All subjects listened to the same speech, which advocated greater leniency in the treatment of juvenile delinquents. One group was told that the speaker was a judge in the juvenile courts (positive source); a second group was told that the speaker was drawn from the audience (neutral source); and a third group was also told that the speaker was drawn from the audience, but a preliminary interview revealed the speaker to have a previous criminal record (negative source). The investigators found that the presentation was rated "fair" about twice as often when it was delivered by the positive source than when it was presented by the negative source. Moreover, greater attitude changes were found in connection with the "judge's" speech (Hovland et al., 1953).

Another study confirmed the above results when the subjects were tested immediately, but revealed an interesting effect when they were retested weeks later. In this study, all subjects read the same communication. One group was given a high-credibility source for the communication; another group was given a low-credibility source, such as a Hollywood gossip columnist. When the subjects were tested immediately after reading the communication, the attitudes of the first group (given the high-credibility source) were found to have changed far more

Attitudes

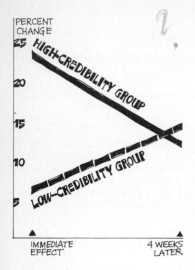

PERCENT
CHANGE

HIGH-CREDIBILITY GROUP

25

20

15

10

5

LOW-CREDIBILITY GROUP

IMMEDIATE
EFFECT

4 WEEKS
LATER

Fig. 15.18
The sleeper effect

When subjects are tested
immediately, a high-credibility
source produces greater attitude
change than a low-credibility
source. However, with the
passage of time, the amount of
change is about the same
regardless of the original source.
This is known as the "sleeper"
effect. (After "The Influence of
Source Credibility on
Communication Effectiveness"
by C. I. Hovland and W. Weiss,
Public Opinion Quarterly, **15**,
1951, pp. 635–650. Used by
permission.)

Social
Psychology

than the attitudes of the second group. When retested four weeks
later, however, the attitudes of both groups were found to have
changed about the same amount (see Fig. 15.18). It appears that
the subjects in the second group had forgotten the source but
remembered the content and were influenced by it. This change
over time is known as the *sleeper effect* (Hovland and Weiss, 1951).

The content of the message has also been shown to be a
factor in the effectiveness of a persuasive communication. One
question that has been explored is the efficacy of presenting both
sides of an issue, rather than only one side. It was found
(Hovland et al., 1949) that a one-sided argument is more effective
for reinforcing a person's original attitudes, but that presenting
both sides is more effective for changing a person's attitudes
(Hovland et al., 1949).

The content of a message may vary in a number of different
ways. You have probably all seen commercials on television
promoting the use of safety belts. Some of these commercials
show the consequences of failure to wear safety belts by
portraying broken bodies. Others give statistics concerning the
number of injuries and deaths attributed to the failure to wear
seat belts. Which of these two types of commercials do you think
is more successful? Research on the effect of fear-arousing
messages has led to conflicting results. For example, one study
demonstrated that fear-producing messages were more effective
than informational messages (Berkowitz and Cottingham, 1960).
Another study obtained the opposite result (Janis and Feshbach,
1953).

An attempt to reconcile these conflicting results proposes that
the degree of concern prior to hearing the message may affect the
outcome. If the audience is already very concerned and fearful
about an issue, a fear-arousing message may trigger defensive
reactions that will reduce anxiety, and thus cancel the
effectiveness of the message. For example, doctors report that
patients who fear they may be suffering a serious or incurable
illness often do not seek medical advice, because they are afraid
of a confirming diagnosis; while patients whose worst fears have
been confirmed by diagnosis seek other medical advice, in the
hope of receiving a more favorable report. On the other hand, the
fear-arousing message may be more successful in changing
attitudes when the audience is not already concerned about an
issue (McGuire, 1960).

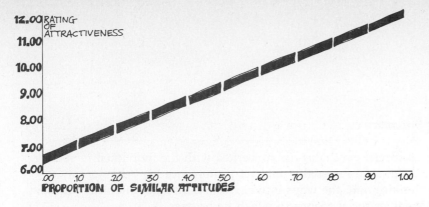

Fig. 15.19
Similarity of attitudes

When an individual perceives the attitudes of a stranger as highly similar to his own, he tends to rate the stranger as more attractive. (After "Attraction as a Linear Function of Proportion of Positive Reinforcements" by D. Byrne and D. Nelson, *Journal of Personality and Social Psychology,* **1,** 1965, pp. 659–663. Copyright © 1965 by the American Psychological Association and used by permission.)

Resistance to change

It may seem that attitudes are susceptible to so many influences that they should be in a constant state of flux. In fact, most attitudes are highly resistant to change. Remember that we have many mechanisms that defend us against the intrusion of unwanted ideas or attitudes. We may selectively attend only to those elements of a message with which we agree. Or we may distort our perception of a message in such a way as to make it conform to the attitudes we hold. The tendency to selectively perceive and distort may have a far-reaching impact on diplomatic relations. Suppose a representative from one nation believes that another nation is unfriendly, warlike, and hostile. When he meets with representatives of that nation, he may perceive any gesture, including genuine peaceful overtures, as threatening and as betraying some ulterior motive.

Charles Darwin, a great nineteenth-century biologist, always carried a pencil and pad with him in case he made observations that contradicted his theory of evolution. He recognized his tendency to selectively forget conflicting evidence.

We have seen that close contact with a group against which a person holds unfavorable attitudes may, under certain circumstances, alter these attitudes in a favorable direction. Many people make every effort to avoid this contact. Segregation, in part, represents just such an effort. Information that contradicts views that we hold also tends to produce tension. Thus, we usually avoid information and attitudes inconsistent with our own. A heavy smoker will probably avoid reading the latest scientific report linking smoking to lung cancer and heart disease. How often does a person committed to a particular political ideology attend lectures or read statements opposing his views?

Finally, contrary to the popular maxim that "opposites attract," people generally associate with others who hold and support similar views (see Fig. 15.19). One study demonstrated that we tend to be more attracted to people whom we perceive as having attitudes similar to our own (Byrne and Nelson, 1965).

Attitudes

Summary

1. Social psychology is concerned with the individual in society —the social forces that interact to influence his behavior and thinking, and the ways in which the individual interacts with and modifies social groups to which he belongs.

2. The socialization process involves learning socially accepted ways of behaving. Societies themselves differ from one another in what their members consider to be socially accepted behavior. Studies of various cultures have demonstrated the extreme malleability of human behavior.

3. As a social organism, each individual spends much of his time in the presence of other people. When in a crowd, the individual may behave in ways that are inconsistent with his usual patterns of behavior. In contrast to a crowd, a group has some degree of organization and there are rules governing the behavior of its members.

4. Groups differ in their modes of communication, types of leadership, and bases for making decisions and taking action.

5. An individual is said to be conforming when he adapts his behavior to be consistent with his perception of group values. When he yields to the pressures of those in authority, he is said to be obedient.

6. Attitudes, which are learned predispositions to respond in specific ways toward people, ideas, or situations, are important determinants of an individual's social behavior. Attitudes typically involve an affective, a cognitive, and a behavioral component.

7. During the early years of life, attitudes are primarily influenced by the child's parents. With increasing age and exposure to a wider variety of social situations, there is a broadening of outside influences on the formation of attitudes.

8. A basic assumption of the theory of cognitive dissonance is that inconsistency is intolerable to an individual. When two or more cognitions are dissonant, a state of tension results. The dissonance motivates the individual to adjust these cognitions so as to reduce the dissonance, and thereby reduce the tension.

9. Prejudice is defined as any kind of prejudgment, positive or negative.

10. Efforts to alter attitudes have often been directed toward one of the components of attitudes: cognitive, behavioral, and affective.

11. Many attitudes remain highly resistant to change. There are many mechanisms that defend the individual against the intrusion of unwanted ideas or attitudes. We may selectively attend only to those elements of a message with which we agree, or we may distort our perception of the message in such a way that it conforms to attitudes that we hold.

Terms to Remember

Attitude   A learned predisposition to respond in a specific way, negatively or positively, toward people, ideas, or situations. Attitudes typically involve an affective (or feeling) component, a cognitive (or thought) component, and a behavioral component.

Belief   Acceptance of a proposition as fact.

Brainstorming   A problem-solving technique which emphasizes group participation to elicit ideas.

Cognitive Dissonance   Lack of agreement between one's beliefs, feelings, or behavior resulting in a state of tension.

Conformity   The process of adapting one's behavior so as to be consistent with one's perception of group values.

Crowd   A temporary group, focused on a common object of attention, in which mutual stimulation among the members is an important basis of behavior.

Culture   The customs, traditions, beliefs, values, and attitudes that characterize a social group.

Discrimination   Behavioral expression of prejudice.

Group Dynamics   The ways in which groups develop and function, and the factors affecting the various interactions between and within groups.

Norms   Standards and expectations shared by a group.

Obedience   Yielding to the pressures of those in authority.

Opinion   A judgment or feeling for which the factual support is far weaker than for beliefs.

Prejudice   Any kind of prejudgment, negative or positive; an atttiude or opinion formed before examining all the facts.

Propaganda   Communication that deliberately attempts to influence attitudes.

Risky Shift   The tendency of people to be more willing to take risks when making group decisions than when making individual decisions.

Role   The pattern of behavior expected in a given social position.

Sleeper Effect   The phenomenon that communication ascribed to a low-credibility source initially has little effect on attitude change, but may have a greater effect once the source is forgotten.

Socialization   The process of learning the socially accepted ways of behaving in a particular society.

Social Psychology   The study of the individual in society—the various social forces that interact to influence his behavior and thinking, and the ways in which the individual interacts with and modifies social groups to which he belongs.

Social Specialist   A type of group leader who specializes in maintaining harmony and dissipating tensions within the group.

Stereotype   Preconceived idea about the attributes of people belonging to certain groups.

Subculture   A segment of a larger culture, charcterized by its own customs, traditions, beliefs, values, and attitudes.

Task Specialist   A type of group leader who specializes in organizing and directing the group toward the achievement of goals.

Recommended Readings

Bem, J. J., *Beliefs, Attitudes, and Human Affairs,* Belmont, California: Brooks/Cole Publishing Co., 1970.

An up-to-date attempt, in paperback, to explain how people form beliefs and attitudes and their effects on behavior.

Brown, R., *Social Psychology,* New York: The Free Press, 1965.

Chapter 11 contains a good discussion of attitude change.

Cartwright, D., and Zander, A., *Group Dynamics,* New York: Harper & Row, Publishers, 1968.

Collection of studies on the formation and functioning of small groups.

Evans, R. I., and Rozelle, R. M. (Eds.), *Social Psychology in Life,* Boston: Allyn & Bacon, Inc., 1970.

Contains research reports dealing with the involvement of social psychology in real life settings.

Freedman, J. L., Carlsmith, J. M., and Sears, D. O., *Social Psychology,* Englewood Cliffs, N.J.: Prentice-Hall, Inc., 1970.

Research-based text that includes discussions on group dynamics, attitude changes, and conformity.

Lindzey, G., and Aronson, E., *Handbook of Social Psychology,* 2nd ed., 5 Vols., Reading, Massachusetts: Addison-Wesley Publishing Co., 1968.

A reference work covering all the major areas of social psychology.

Mann, R. D., Gibbard, G. S., and Hartman, J. J., *Interpersonal Styles and Group Development: An Analysis of the Member–Leader Relationship,* New York: John Wiley & Sons, Inc., 1967.

Examines the changing relationship between members of groups and their formal leader.

Zimbardo, P. G., and Ebbesen, E. B., *Influencing Attitudes and Changing Behavior,* Reading, Massachusetts: Addison-Wesley Publishing Co., 1969.

An exciting treatment, in paperback, of the study of attitude change.

PSYCHOLOGY ISSUES

**D.
Psychologists and
Society**

In this fourth *Issues* section three psychologists extend their theories beyond the confines of the laboratory and into the broad problem areas of social change. The first and second articles—excerpts from Philip Zimbardo's "Pathology of Imprisonment" and a passage from B. F. Skinner's *Beyond Freedom and Dignity*—argue for fundamental changes in social institutions. The third article, a passage from Carl Rogers' "Interpersonal Relationships: USA 2000," tries to predict the direction certain social changes might take.

Philip Zimbardo is a social psychologist who designed and carried out an interesting experiment in role playing. He wanted to see what would happen to "mature, emotionally stable, normal, intelligent college students from middle-class homes" if they were suddenly transformed (through role playing) into prisoners or guards in a mock prison modeled after real life. The result was a strongly worded call for specific prison reform. Professor Zimbardo's editorial shows what kind of insight psychology can bring to specific social problems.

B. F. Skinner is a behaviorist whose interest in social change got its first major ex-

posure in his utopian novel *Walden II*. Skinner goes a good deal farther than Zimbardo. He advocates the development of a new technology based on the principles of behaviorism. This technology of behavior would redesign our social and physical environments so that they would shape only socially beneficial behaviors. Skinner believes that the principles of behaviorism, properly applied to solving the world's problems, could create a world without those problems.

Carl Rogers developed client-centered psychotherapy. This article describes what he thinks interpersonal relationships will be like in the year 2000. He is neither advocating nor designing change, he is trying to foresee it.

Pathology of Imprisonment

By Philip G. Zimbardo

In an attempt to understand just what it means psychologically to be a prisoner or a prison guard, Craig Haney, Curt Banks, Dave Jaffe and I created our own prison. We carefully screened over 70 volunteers who answered an ad in a Palo Alto city newspaper and ended up with about two dozen young men who were selected to be part of this study. They were mature, emotionally stable, normal, intelligent college students from middle-class homes throughout the United States and Canada. They appeared to represent the cream of the crop of this generation. None had any criminal record and all were relatively homogeneous on many dimensions initially.

Half were arbitrarily designated as prisoners by a flip of a coin, the others as guards. These were the roles they were to play in our simulated prison. . . .

At the end of only six days we had to close down our mock prison because what we saw was frightening. It was no longer apparent to most of the subjects (or to us) where reality ended and their roles began. The majority had indeed become prisoners or guards, no longer able to clearly differentiate between role playing and self. There were dramatic changes in virtually every aspect of their behavior, thinking and feeling. In less than a week the experience of imprisonment undid (temporarily) a lifetime of learning; human values were suspended, self-concepts were challenged and

From Philip G. Zimbardo, "Pathology of Imprisonment," *TransAction/Society*, 9 (6), 1972, pp. 4–8.

the ugliest, most base, pathological side of human nature surfaced. We were horrified because we saw some boys (guards) treat others as if they were despicable animals, taking pleasure in cruelty, while other boys (prisoners) became servile, dehumanized robots who thought only of escape, of their own individual survival and of their mounting hatred for the guards. . . .

The consultant for our prison, Carlo Prescott, an ex-convict with 16 years of imprisonment in California's jails, would get so depressed and furious each time he visited our prison, because of its psychological similarity to his experiences, that he would have to leave. A Catholic priest who was a former prison chaplain in Washington, D. C. talked to our prisoners after four days and said they were just like the other first-timers he had seen. . . .

Each of us carries around in our heads a favorable self-image in which we are essentially just, fair, humane and understanding. For example, we could not imagine inflicting pain on others without much provocation or hurting people who had done nothing to us, who in fact were even liked by us. However, there is a growing body of social psychological research which underscores the conclusion derived from this prison study. Many people, perhaps the majority, can be made to do almost anything when put into psychologically compelling situations — regardless of their morals, ethics, values, attitudes, beliefs or personal convictions. My colleague, Stanley Milgram, has shown that more than 60 percent of the population will deliver what they think is a series of painful electric shocks to another person even after the victim cries for mercy, begs them to stop and then apparently passes out. The subjects complained that they did not want to inflict more pain but blindly obeyed the command of the authority figure (the experimenter) who said that they must go on. . . .

With regard to prisons, we can state that the mere act of assigning labels to people and putting them into a situation where those labels acquire validity and meaning is sufficient to elicit pathological behavior. This pathology is not predictable from any available diagnostic indicators we have in the social sciences, and is extreme enough to modify in very significant ways fundamental attitudes and behavior. The prison situation, as presently arranged, is guaranteed to generate severe enough pathological reactions in both guards and prisoners as to debase their humanity, lower their feelings of self-worth and make it difficult for them to be part of a society outside of their prison. . . .

The riots in prison are coming from within — from within every man and woman who refuses to let the system turn them into an object, a number, a thing or a no-thing. It is not communist inspired, but inspired by the spirit of American freedom. No man wants to be enslaved. To be powerless, to be subject to the arbitrary exercise of power, to not be recognized as a human being is to be a slave.

To be a militant prisoner is to become aware that the physical jails are but more blatant extensions of the forms of social and psychological oppression experienced daily in the nation's ghettos. They are trying to awaken the conscience of the nation to the ways in which the American ideals are being perverted, apparently in the name of justice but actually under the banner of apathy, fear and hatred. If we do not listen to the pleas of the prisoners at Attica to be treated like human beings, then we have all become brutalized by our priorities for property rights over human rights. The consequence will not only be more prison riots but a loss of all those ideals on which this country was founded.

The public should be aware that they own the prisons and that their business is failing. The 70 percent recidivism rate and the escalation in severity of crimes committed by graduates of our prisons are evidence that current prisons fail to rehabilitate the inmates in any positive way. Rather, they are breeding grounds for hatred of the establishment, a hatred that makes every citizen a target of violent assault. Prisons are a bad investment for us taxpayers. Until now we have not cared, we have turned over to wardens and prison authorities the unpleasant job of keeping people who threaten us out of our sight. Now we are shocked to learn that their management practices have failed to improve the product and instead turn petty thieves into murderers. We must insist upon new management or improved operating procedures.

The cloak of secrecy should be removed from the prisons. Prisoners claim they are brutalized by the guards, guards say it is a lie. Where is the impartial test of the truth in such a situation? Prison officials have forgotten that they work for us, that they are only public servants whose salaries are paid by our taxes. They act as if it is their prison, like a child with a toy he won't share. Neither lawyers, judges, the legislature nor the public is allowed into prisons to ascertain the truth unless the visit is sanctioned by authorities and until all is prepared for their visit. I was shocked to learn that my request to join a congressional investigating committee's tour of San Quentin and Soledad was refused, as was that of the news media.

There should be an ombudsman in every prison, not under the pay or control of the prison authority, and responsible only to the courts, state legislature and the public. Such a person could report on violations of constitutional and human rights.

Guards must be given better training than they now receive for the difficult job society imposes upon them. To be a prison guard as now constituted is to be put in a situation of constant threat from within the prison, with no social recognition from the society at large. As was shown graphically at Attica, prison guards are also prisoners of the system who can be sacrificed to the demands of the public to be punitive and the needs of politicians to preserve an image. Social scientists and business administrators should be called upon to design and help carry out this training.

The relationship between the individual (who is sentenced by the courts to a prison term) and his community must be maintained. How can a prisoner return to a dynamically changing society that most of us cannot cope with after being out of it for a number of years? There should be more community involvement in these rehabilitation centers, more ties encouraged and promoted between the trainees and family and friends, more educational opportunities to prepare them for returning to their communities as more valuable members of it than they were before they left.

Finally, the main ingredient necessary to effect any change at all in prison reform, in the rehabilitation of a single prisoner or even in the optimal development of a child is caring. Reform must start with people — especially people with power — caring about the well-being of others. Underneath the toughest, society-hating convict, rebel or anarchist is a human being who wants his existence to be recognized by his fellows and who wants someone else to care about whether he lives or dies and to grieve if he lives imprisoned rather than lives free.

The Design of a Culture

By B. F. Skinner

A culture is very much like the experimental space used in the analysis of behavior. Both are sets of contingencies of reinforcement. A child is born into a culture as an organism is placed in an experimental space. Designing a culture is like designing an experiment; contingencies are arranged and effects noted. In an experiment we are interested in what happens, in designing a culture with whether it will work. This is the difference between science and technology.

A collection of cultural designs is to be found in the utopian literature. Writers have described their versions of the good life and suggested ways of achieving them. Plato, in *The Republic*, chose a political solution; Saint Augustine, in *The City of God*, a religious one. Thomas More and Francis Bacon, both lawyers, turned to law and order, and the Rousseauean utopists of the eight-

From B. F. Skinner, *Beyond Freedom and Dignity*, New York: Alfred A. Knopf, 1971.

eenth century, to a supposed natural goodness in man. The nineteenth century looked for economic solutions, and the twentieth century saw the rise of what may be called behavioral utopias in which a full range of social contingencies began to be discussed (often satirically).

Utopian writers have been at pains to simplify their assignment. A utopian community is usually composed of a relatively small number of people living together in one place and in stable contact with each other. They can practice an informal ethical control and minimize the role of organized agencies. They can learn from each other rather than from the specialists called teachers. They can be kept from behaving badly toward each other through censure rather than the specialized punishments of a legal system. They can produce and exchange goods without specifying values in terms of money. They can help those who have become ill, infirm, disturbed, or aged with a minimum of institutional care. Troublesome contacts with other cultures are avoided through geographical isolation (utopias tend to be located on islands or surrounded by high mountains), and the transition to a new culture is facilitated by some formalized break with the past, such as a ritual of rebirth

(utopias are often set in the distant future so that the necessary evolution of the culture seems plausible). A utopia is a total social environment, and all its parts work together. The home does not conflict with the school or the street, religion does not conflict with government, and so on.

Perhaps the most important feature of the utopian design, however, is that the survival of a community can be made important to its members. The small size, the isolation, the internal coherence — all these give a community an identity which makes its success or failure conspicuous. The fundamental question in all utopias is "Would it really work?" The literature is worth considering just because it emphasizes experimentation. A traditional culture has been examined and found wanting, and a new version has been set up to be tested and redesigned as circumstances dictate.

The simplification in utopian writing, which is nothing more than the simplification characteristic of science, is seldom feasible in the world at large, and there are many other reasons why it is difficult to put an explicit design into effect. A large fluid population cannot be brought under informal social or ethical control because social reinforcers like praise and blame are not exchangeable for the

personal reinforcers on which they are based. Why should anyone be affected by the praise or blame of someone he will never see again? Ethical control may survive in small groups, but the control of the population as a whole must be delegated to specialists — to police, priests, owners, teachers, therapists, and so on, with their specialized reinforcers and their codified contingencies. These are probably already in conflict with each other and will almost certainly be in conflict with any new set of contingencies. Where it is not too difficult to change informal instruction, for example, it is nearly impossible to change an educational establishment. It is fairly easy to change marriage, divorce, and child-bearing practices as the significance for the culture changes but nearly impossible to change the religious principles which dictate such practices. It is easy to change the extent to which various kinds of behavior are accepted as right but difficult to change the laws of a government. The reinforcing values of goods are more flexible than the values set by economic agencies. The word of authority is more unyielding than the facts of which it speaks.

It is not surprising that, so far as the real world is concerned, the word utopian means unworkable. History seems to offer support; various utopian designs have been proposed for nearly twenty-five hundred years, and most attempts to set them up have been ignominious failures. But historical evidence is always against the probability of anything new; that is what is meant by history. Scientific discoveries and inventions are improbable; that is what is meant by discovery and invention. And if planned economies, benevolent dictatorships, perfectionistic societies, and other utopian ventures have failed, we must remember that unplanned, undictated, and unperfected cultures have failed too. A failure is not always a mistake; it may simply be the best one can do under the circumstances. The real mistake is to stop trying. Perhaps we cannot now design a successful culture as a whole, but we can design better practices in a piecemeal fashion. The behavioral processes in the world at large are the same as those in a utopian community, and practices have the same effects for the same reasons.

The same advantages are also to be found in emphasizing contingencies of reinforcement in lieu of states of mind or feelings. It is no doubt a serious problem, for example, that students no longer re-

spond in traditional ways to educational environments; they drop out of school, possibly for long periods of time, they take only courses which they enjoy or which seem to have relevance to their problems, they destroy school property and attack teachers and officials. But we shall not solve this problem by "cultivating on the part of our public a respect it does not now have for scholarship as such and for the practicing scholar and teacher." (The cultivation of respect is a metaphor in the horticultural tradition.) What is wrong is the educational environment. We need to design contingencies under which students acquire behavior useful to them and their culture — contingencies that do not have troublesome by-products and that generate the behavior said to "show respect for learning." It is not difficult to see what is wrong in most educational environments, and much has already been done to design materials which make learning as easy as possible and to construct contingencies, in the classroom and elsewhere, which give students powerful reasons for getting an education.

A serious problem also arises when young people refuse to serve in the armed forces and desert or defect to other countries, but we shall

not make an appreciable change by "inspiring greater loyalty or patriotism." What must be changed are the contingencies which induce young people to behave in given ways toward their governments. Governmental sanctions remain almost entirely punitive, and the unfortunate by-products are sufficiently indicated by the extent of domestic disorder and international conflict. It is a serious problem that we remain almost continuously at war with other nations, but we shall not get far by attacking "the tensions which lead to war," or by appeasing warlike spirits, or by changing the minds of men (in which, UNESCO tells us, wars begin). What must be changed are the circumstances under which men and nations make war.

We may also be disturbed by the fact that many young people work as little as possible, or that workers are not very productive and often absent, or that products are often of poor quality, but we shall not get far by inspiring a "sense of craftsmanship or pride in one's work," or a "sense of the dignity of labor," or, where crafts and skills are a part of the caste mores, by changing "the deep emotional resistance of the caste superego," as one writer has put it. Something is wrong with the contingencies which induce men to work industriously and carefully. (Other kinds of economic contingencies are wrong too.)

Walter Lippmann has said that "the supreme question before mankind" is how men can save themselves from the catastrophe which threatens them, but to answer it we must do more than discover how men can "make themselves willing and able to save themselves." We must look to the contingencies that induce people to act to increase the chances that their cultures will survive. We have the physical, biological, and behavioral technologies needed "to save ourselves"; the problem is how to get people to use them. It may be that "utopia has only to be willed," but what does that mean? What are the principal specifications of a culture that will survive because it induces its members to work for its survival?

INTERPERSONAL RELATIONSHIPS: USA 2000

By Carl Rogers

What do the coming decades hold for us in the realm of intimacy between boy and girl, man and woman? Here, too, enormous forces are at

Reproduced by special permission from *The Journal of Applied Behavioral Science*, "Interpersonal Relationships: USA 2000," by Carl R. Rogers, pp. 265–280, 1968. Published by NTL Institute for Applied Behavioral Science.

work, and choices are being made which will not, I believe, be reversed by the year 2000.

In the first place the trend toward greater freedom in sexual relationships, in adolescents and adults, is likely to continue, whether this direction frightens us or not. Many elements have conspired together to bring about a change in such behavior, and the advent of "The Pill" is only one of these. It seems probable that sexual intimacy will be a part of "going steady" or of any continuing special interest in a member of the opposite sex. The attitude of prurience is fast dying out, and sexual activity is seen as a potentially joyful and enriching part of a relationship. The attitude of possessiveness — of owning another person — which historically has dominated sexual unions — is likely to be greatly diminished. It is certain that there will be enormous variations in the quality of these sexual relationships — from those where sex is a purely physical contact which has almost the same solitary quality as masturbation, to those in which the sexual aspect is an expression of an increasing sharing of feelings, of experiences, of each other.

By the year 2000 it will be quite feasible to insure that there will be no children in a union. By one of the several means currently under study, each individual will be assured of lasting infertility in early adolescence. It will take positive action, permissible only after a thoughtful decision, to reestablish fertility. This will reverse the present situation where only by positive action can one *prevent* conception. Also by that time computerized matching of prospective partners will be far more sophisticated than it is today and will be of great help to an individual in

finding a congenial companion of the opposite sex.

Some of the temporary unions thus formed may be legalized as a type of marriage — with no permanent commitment, with no children (by mutual agreement) and — if the union breaks up — no legal accusations, no necessity for showing legal cause, and no alimony.

It is becoming increasingly clear that a man-woman relationship will have *permanence* only to the degree to which it satisfies the emotional, psychological, intellectual, and physical needs of the partners. This means that the *permanent* marriage of the future will be even better than marriage in the present, because the ideals and goals for that marriage will be of a higher order. The partners will be demanding more of the relationship than they do today.

If a couple feel deeply committed to each other, and mutually wish to remain to-

gether to raise a family, then this will be a new and more binding type of marriage. Each will accept the obligations involved in having and raising children. There may be a mutual agreement as to whether or not the marriage includes sexual faithfulness to one's mate. Perhaps by the year 2000 we will have reached the point where through education and social pressure a couple will decide to have children only when they have shown evidence of a mature commitment to each other, of a sort which is likely to have permanence.[1]

What I am describing is a whole continuum of man-woman relationships, from the most casual dating and casual sex relationship, to a rich and fulfilling partnership in which communication is open and real, where each is concerned with promoting the personal growth of the partner, and where there is a long-range commitment to each other which will form a sound basis for having and rearing children in an environment of love. Some parts of this continuum will exist

---

[1] A proposal suggesting the licensing of births, and "substantial" payments to women who have no children during the normal reproductive period, ages 15–44, has been submitted to the Massachusetts Legislature. A sign of the times?

within a legal framework, some will not.

One may say, with a large measure of truth, that much of this continuum already exists. But an awareness of and an open acceptance of this continuum by society will change its whole quality.

Suppose it were openly accepted that some "marriages" are no more than ill-mated and transitory unions, and will be broken. If children are not permitted in such marriages, then one divorce in every two marriages (the current rate in California) is no longer seen as a tragedy. The dissolving of the union may be painful, but it is not a social catastrophe, and the experience may be a necessary step in the personal growth of the two individuals toward greater maturity.

16
CONTEMPORARY ISSUES

Drugs

Marijuana — LSD — Heroin

The stresses of contemporary life

Anonymity and bystander apathy — Violence

Women's liberation: the fight for equality

The energy crisis

In the past decade, many new terms have found their way into our vocabulary—hippie, pothead, skyjack, ripoff, uptight, hangup, bag, and generation gap, to name a few. It seems as if the age we live in is totally different from any other time in history. Is this really true? Perhaps the same psychological problems existed in past times, but have now simply found a more modern vocabulary. For example, more than 2000 years ago, the great philosopher Socrates was, in a sense, the victim of a "generation gap" when he was put to death, ostensibly for corrupting the youth and causing them to be disrespectful toward their elders. And there was a serious drug problem during much of the nineteenth century, when doctors routinely prescribed laudanum, a derivative of opium, as a pain reliever. Violence has been a part of man's history since time immemorial.

We seem to be plagued by the same problems that have harassed man throughout recorded history. What makes the problems we face today seem so unique to our times? For one thing, the *rate* at which change is taking place is greater than ever before. We hardly have time to adjust to one social crisis before a dozen others demand our attention. Second, population and the technology that supports it have expanded so abruptly that some of the issues we face are of an unprecedented scale and urgency— pollution, ecology, crowding in the cities, and shortages of vital energy and other natural resources.

Many of us find ourselves bewildered by this fast-moving and fast-growing world. Psychologists, as individuals, have been perplexed by the enormity of the issues that vie for their attention. They recognize that the behavioral scientist must play a key role in the attempt to understand the root causes of these problems, as well as their impact on the individual and on relations among individuals. One prominent psychologist has described some of the sources of dissatisfaction and unrest in today's complex technological world:

> As more and more people throughout the world become more and more enmeshed in a scientific age, its psychological consequences on their thought and behavior become increasingly complicated. The impact comes in a variety of ways: people begin to feel the potentialities for a more abundant life than modern technology can provide; they become aware of the inadequacies of many present political,

social, and religious institutions and practices; they discern the threat which existing power and status relationships may hold to their own development; they vaguely sense the inadequacy of many of the beliefs and codes accepted by their forefathers and perhaps by themselves at an earlier age.

The upshot is that more and more people are acquiring both a hope for a "better life" and a feeling of frustration and anxiety that they themselves may not experience the potentially better life they feel should be available to them. They search for new anchorages, for new guidelines, for plans of action which hold a promise of making some of their dreams come true, some of their aspirations become experientially real.

(Cantril, 1958, pp. vii–viii)

This chapter focuses on several of the major problems that we face today and that psychology can help us understand. With so many major issues competing for our attention, our choice of topics unquestionably reflects the authors' personal biases. Obviously, we could just as well have addressed ourselves to issues other than drugs, apathy and violence, Women's Liberation, and the energy crisis.

Drugs

Many people use the terms drug use and drug abuse interchangeably. These terms really have two different and distinct meanings. When a person drinks a cup of coffee, enjoys his favorite alcoholic drink, inhales the smoke from a cigarette or "joint," or swallows a tranquilizer, he is a drug *user*. The person who uses these or other drugs to such an extent that he is unable to function without them may be considered a drug *abuser*.

Few people would deny that drug abuse (including alcoholism —see Chapter 14) is one of the most serious problems we face today. Drug abuse itself is unquestionably a symptom of deeper psychological causes. Unfortunately, at the present state of our knowledge, we are better able to describe the effects of drugs on behavior than to specify the underlying causes of drug abuse.

Some drugs are particularly worrisome because their continued use leads to addiction. For example, a chronic heroin abuser finds that continued use leads to increased *tolerance:* his body not only can stand (tolerate) more of the drug, but actually requires greater and greater dosages to achieve the same effect. Before long, he develops a physiological dependence on the drug; this state of physiological dependence is called *addiction.* Should he try to "kick the habit," his body will react violently.

Addiction should be distinguished from *habituation,* which is psychological, rather than physiological, dependence. Withdrawal from habituation is more likely to be accompanied by emotional rather than physical distress. A person trying to give up cigarettes, for example, is often nervous, tense, and irritable; the physiological symptoms he may have are usually minor.

The chemical nature of a drug determines whether continued abuse will lead to addiction or habituation. Drugs such as heroin, morphine, codeine, and the barbiturates are addicting. Habituating drugs include marijuana, cocaine, and the amphetamines. Box 16.1 presents some facts about 14 of the more commonly used drugs.

Some people favor a relaxation of the laws governing the use and distribution of drugs. Others advocate the enactment and enforcement of stricter drug control laws. The proponents of both positions feel that there is adequate scientific justification for their point of view. Let's examine a few of the more widely used drugs and see what evidence there is about their short-term and long-term effects on behavior.

Marijuana

The chances are that either you or someone whom you know has tried marijuana at least once. Although estimates on its use vary, most experts agree that the use of marijuana has experienced a sharp rise in the past decade, especially among the teenage and college populations.

Marijuana was first made illegal in the United States in 1937. It is interesting that the law was passed by Congress more as a result of public clamor and unsupported charges appearing in the news media, than because of expert medical testimony. In fact, in committee hearings, one medical authority challenged the validity of most reports indicting marijuana as dangerous. He was severely chastised, browbeaten, and badgered by committee members for "trying to throw obstacles in the way of something that the Federal Government is trying to do" (Synder, 1970).

Marijuana is a mild hallucinogen—a mind-affecting drug—which is taken primarily for the psychological effects it produces. The effects vary according to the user's past experiences and present expectations, the strength and quantity of the drug used, and the circumstances under which it is used. The most commonly reported effects are distortion in time and space, intensification of sensory experiences, and dreamlike thought processes. There are occasional reports of panic reactions, particularly among young users. However, these reactions may reflect the personality characteristics of the individual more than the effects of the drug—some people experience panic in any new or changed circumstance. The physiological effects include increased heartbeat, increased thirst, and tingling of the scalp (Becker, 1963). As reported earlier (Chapter 8), in order to experience a psychological effect, the user must learn to label these physiological effects as a "high."

Marijuana users do not require increasingly large doses in order to experience a high. Marijuana is, therefore, habituating rather than addicting. The term pothead is sometimes erroneously applied to anyone who has used marijuana on more than one occasion. This use of the term is equivalent to calling anyone who occasionally takes a drink containing alcohol an alcoholic. The term pothead is best reserved for a person whose psychological dependence on marijuana is so great that its use has become a way of life.

Although the long-term effects of marijuana on behavior have not yet been determined, the short-term effects appear to be no greater than those associated with many commonly used drugs, such as alcohol, tranquilizers, and antihistamines. The judgment of individuals under the influence of marijuana seems to be somewhat impaired, even though they may have a subjective experience of improved awareness and judgment. There is also the possibility that, during a high, complex motor skills, such as those used in speech and driving, may suffer some impairment (Hollister, 1971; Clark and Nahashima, 1968).

The most commonly expressed fear concerning marijuana use is that it represents a first step toward the "hard" drugs, which

Box 16.1 ▶
Facts about drugs. (From *Resource Book for Drug Abuse Education,* developed as a part of the Drug Abuse Education Project of the American Association for Health, Physical Education, and Recreation and the National Science Teachers Association (NEA), 1969.)

Drugs

Name	Slang Name	Chemical or Trade Name	Source	Classification	Medical Use	How Taken
Heroin	H., Horse, Scat, Junk, Smack, Scag, Stuff	Diacetyl-morphine	Semi-synthetic (from morphine)	Narcotic	Pain relief	Injected or sniffed
Morphine	White stuff, M.	Morphine sulphate	Natural (from opium)	Narcotic	Pain relief	Swallowed or injected
Codeine	Schoolboy	Methylmorphine	Natural (from opium), semi-synthetic (from morphine)	Narcotic	Ease pain and coughing	Swallowed
Methadone	Dolly	Dolophine, Amidone	Synthetic	Narcotic	Pain relief	Swallowed or injected
Cocaine	Corrine, Gold dust, Coke, Bernice, Flake, Star dust, Snow	Methylester of benzoyleogonine	Natural (from coca, NOT cacao)	Stimulant, local anesthesia	Local anesthesia	Sniffed, injected, or swallowed
Marijuana	Pot, Grass, Tea, Hashish, Gage, Reefers	Cannabis sativa	Natural	Relaxant, euphoriant; in high doses, hallucinogen	None in U.S.	Smoked, swallowed, or sniffed
Barbiturates	Barbs, Blue devils, Candy, Yellow jackets, Phennies, Peanuts, Blue heavens	Phenobarbital, Nembutal, Seconal, Amytal	Synthetic	Sedative-hypnotic	Sedation, relief of high blood pressure, hyperthyroidism	Swallowed or injected
Amphetamines	Bennies, Dexies, Speed, Wake-ups, Lid poppers, Hearts, Pep pills	Benzedrine, Dexedrine, Desoxyn, Meth-amphetamine, Methadrine	Synthetic	Sympathomimetic	Relief of mild depression, control of appetite and narcolepsy	Swallowed or injected
LSD	Acid, Sugar, Big D, Cubes, Trips	D-lysergic Acid diethylamide	Semi-synthetic (from ergot alkaloids)	Hallucinogen	Experimental study of mental function, alcoholism	Swallowed
DMT	AMT, Businessman's high	Dimethyl-triptamine	Synthetic	Hallucinogen	None	Injected
Mescaline	Mesc.	3, 4, 5-tri-methoxyphen-ethylamine	Natural (from peyote)	Hallucinogen	None	Swallowed
Psilocybin		3(2-dimethyl-amino) ethylin-dol-4-oldihydro-gen phosphate	Natural (from psilocybe)	Hallucinogen	None	Swallowed
Alcohol	Booze, Juice, etc.	Ethanol, Ethyl alcohol	Natural (from grapes, grains, etc., via fermentation)	Sedative hypnotic	Solvent, antiseptic	Swallowed
Tobacco	Fag, Coffin nail, etc.	Nicotiana tabacum	Natural	Stimulant-sedative	Sedative, emetic (nicotine)	Smoked, sniffed, or chewed

Usual Dose	Duration of Effect	Effects Sought	Long-term Symptoms	Physical Dependence Potential	Mental Dependence Potential	Organic Damage Potential
Varies	4 hr	Eupnoria, prevent withdrawal discomfort	Addiction, constipation, loss of appetite	Yes	Yes	No*
15 milligrams	6 hr	Euphoria, prevent withdrawal discomfort	Addiction, constipation, loss of appetite	Yes	Yes	No*
30 milligrams	4 hr	Euphoria, prevent withdrawal discomfort	Addiction, constipation, loss of appetite	Yes	Yes	No
10 milligrams	4-6 hr	Prevent withdrawal discomfort	Addiction, constipation, loss of appetite	Yes	Yes	No
Varies	Varied, brief periods	Excitation, talkativeness	Depression, convulsions	No	Yes	Yes?
1-2 cigarettes	4 hr	Relaxation; increased euphoria, perceptions, sociability	Usually none	No	Yes?	No
50-100 milligrams	4 hr	Anxiety reduction, euphoria	Addiction with severe withdrawal symptoms, possible convulsions, toxic psychosis	Yes	Yes	Yes
2.5-5 milligrams	4 hr	Alertness, activeness	Loss of appetite, delusions, hallucinations, toxic psychosis	No?	Yes	Yes?
100–500 micrograms	10 hr	Insightful experiences, exhilaration, distortion of senses	May intensify existing psychosis, panic reactions	No	No?	No?
1-3 milligrams	Less than 1 hr	Insightful experiences, exhilaration, distortion of senses	?	No	No?	No?
350 micrograms	12 hr	Insightful experiences, exhilaration, distortion of senses	?	No	No?	No?
25 milligrams	6-8 hr	Insightful experiences, exhilaration, distortion of senses	?	No	No?	No?
Varies	1-4 hr	Sense alteration, anxiety reduction, sociability	Cirrhosis, toxic psychosis, neurologic damage, addiction	Yes	Yes	Yes
Varies	Varies	Calmness, sociability	Emphysema, lung cancer, mouth and throat cancer, cardiovascular damage, loss of appetite	Yes?	Yes	Yes

(Question marks indicate conflict of opinion. It should be noted that illicit drugs are frequently adulterated and thus pose unknown hazards to the user.)

*Persons who inject drugs under nonsterile conditions run a high risk of contracting hepatitis, abscesses, or circulatory disorders.

definitely do impair bodily and mental functions. Statements such as "Eighty percent of heroin and morphine addicts had previously used marijuana" raise the specter of millions of youths developing a craving for bigger and better highs as a direct result of their experiences with marijuana. This kind of "evidence" is quite misleading. Using this line of reasoning, we might establish an even greater indictment of milk, since 100 percent of all morphine and heroin addicts have "used" milk at one time or another. Such evidence simply fails to take into account the millions of people who use marijuana on occasion and have no interest in drugs which are clearly dangerous. To date, no direct causal link has been established between marijuana use and addiction to any of the hard drugs. However, it is possible that prolonged and continuous abuse of marijuana may pave the way to experimentation with other drugs. As one of the leading authorities on marijuana, William McGlothlin, has observed, "I'm fairly convinced that the *heavy* use of marijuana by an adolescent can contribute to poor judgment and magical thinking— particularly as regards the use of other drugs" (Gross, 1972). Moreover, since marijuana is often used in a group setting, an individual may succumb to group pressure and experiment with a drug that gives him a bigger high.

LSD

There are a number of hallucinogenic drugs in use today: LSD, psilocybin, mescaline, DMT, and STP. The most well known, frequently used, and thoroughly researched is LSD. LSD (lysergic acid diethylamide) is an extremely potent hallucinogenic drug. As little as four-millionths of an ounce produces marked behavioral changes. Or, stated another way, one ounce can provide more than a quarter of a million average doses. An average dose takes effect extremely rapidly, and the effects usually last from 8 to 12 hours. The use of LSD is accompanied by marked physical changes, including elevated blood pressure, temperature, and pulse rate.

The psychological effects of LSD are not always predictable. They seem to vary in the same person from time to time, and depend on such factors as the amount and purity of the drug taken, the circumstances under which it is used, and the personality characteristics of the individual. Experiences under LSD are sometimes referred to as "trips," which can be either good or bad, or both. The presence of a "guide" does not guarantee that the user will have a good trip.

Since LSD is chemically similar to substances occurring at the synapses, it may block or facilitate relaying of neural messages. This may account for *synesthesia,* the translation of one sensory experience into another—feeling an odor, seeing a sound, or hearing a light. It is not unusual for the user to experience marked changes in sensation and perception, including distorted perceptions of the self. For example, one person, while under LSD, reported, "I don't feel like I'm reacting to my own body now. I feel like I'm away from it . . . My feet feel like they're a million miles apart" (Pollard et al., 1965). Distorted perceptions of time are also common. Another individual "tripping" on LSD reported, ". . . I don't know what time it is. I can't even think what time it is . . . it feels like I've been here for weeks and days . . ." (Pollard et al., 1965).

Many experiments have been concerned with describing the psychological effects of LSD. The following excerpt is taken from the verbal report of a young man who took LSD as part of an experiment:

Everything's really going haywire now. At least it feels like it. Everything's just sort of spinning around. And settling down now. Nope, there it goes again. Feels like I'm in four places at once. Here comes the war again. I feel like I'm lying on two different planes or something. I'm scared. Awful scared. Awful tight. I want to relax and I can't. I don't feel like I can. Got that pain in my right arm again. Feel like I'm floating away, floating away. My legs are quivering. My teeth feel like they're moving. They aren't. They want to move. Feel like I'm cut in half. Like I'm being pushed down. Funny. Can't control that feeling. I'm tight but not tight, all at once. Just sort of sitting here in this room not doing much. I don't know. I don't like this . . . I feel like I want out. Feels, feel like I'm being pushed down, down, down, down. That's what it feels like. Like I'm being stood on. I want to lift up my right arm and I can't. Very uncomfortable.

(Pollard et al., 1965, p. 129)

Drugs

LSD produces marked variations in emotional states, ranging from inner contentment and oneness with the world to episodes of unmitigated terror. What is sometimes frightening to the user is that he may experience contrasting emotions at one and the same time. For example, he may simultaneously feel both euphoric and grief-stricken. These mood contrasts are somewhat similar to those found in manic–depressive psychosis (see Chapter 14). LSD may also produce other psychoticlike effects—hallucinations, occasional delusions, and feelings of depersonalization or loss of self-identity (Snyder and Lampanella, 1969). The most common comparison is between the schizophrenic reaction and the drug-induced psychoses. However, there are important symptom differences as can be seen in Box 16.2.

Why do people take LSD? The reasons are almost as varied as the types of effects produced. Some individuals say they take LSD because they are curious, because their friends encourage and sanction it, because they want to experience a high, or because they think they will achieve psychological, philosophical, and religious insights. Some individuals, aware of the heightened sensory and perceptual experiences it produces, believe that LSD will make them more creative. However, in this respect, LSD is a complete failure. Artists who have created works while under the influence of LSD have later repudiated the work (Gubar, 1969; McGlothlin and Arnold, 1971).

It is quite probable that many people are only dimly aware of the reasons they take LSD (or other drugs). The justifications cited above may merely be defenses against acknowledging such deeper underlying feelings as inadequacy or insecurity. Perhaps many LSD users are seeking instant gratification or simple solutions to complex problems and conflicts. Here again is an indication that drugs *are* problems, but are also symptomatic of more pervasive psychological processes (Horowitz, 1969).

How dangerous is LSD? One of the delusions occurring in many LSD trips is that the person thinks he has developed magical powers and is capable of flying through the air. You may remember reading about incidents in which a person, while on an LSD trip, jumped off a rooftop, with predictable consequences. The fact is that the perceptual distortions can be so overpowering that normal judgment is suspended and the individual may attempt almost any act, no matter how foolhardy or dangerous.

The similarities between the symptoms of schizophrenia and those produced by the psychotomimetic drugs (most commonly LSD-25, mescaline, and psilocybin) have led many investigators to speculate that their biochemical bases may be the same. But schizophrenia and drug-induced symptoms differ significantly, not only in many particular respects, but most importantly, in overall pattern.

	Schizophrenic Reactions	*Drug-Induced Psychoses*
Mood	Daydreaming and extreme withdrawal from personal contacts, ranging from sullen reluctance to talk to actual muteness.	Dreaming, introspective state, but preference for discussing visions and ruminations with someone.
Communication	Speech vague, ambiguous, difficult to follow; no concern about inability to communicate; past tense common.	Speech rambling or incoherent but usually related to reality; subjects try to communicate thoughts; present tense used.
Irrationality	Great preoccupation with bodily functions; illnesses attributed to unreasonable causes (the devil, "enemies").	Great interest in the vast array of new sensations being experienced; symptoms attributed to reasonable causes.
Hallucinations	Frequent, very "real" hallucinations, usually auditory and extremely threatening; attempts to rationalize them rejected.	Hallucinations predominantly visual; rare auditory hallucinations not so personal or threatening; subjects attempt to explain them rationally.
Delusions	Delusions common, usually of paranoid or grandiose pattern.	Delusions rare, occurence probably due to individual personality conflicts.
Mannerisms	Bizarre mannerisms, postures, and even waxy flexibility manifested by certain patients.	Strange and bizarre mannerisms rare.

Some people, when on a "bad trip" or "bummer," experience feelings of panic when overwhelmed by a flood of unprecedented thoughts, emotions, and perceptions. They are powerless to "turn off" the drug and, in their confused state, may think that they are losing their minds.

Box 16.2
Schizophrenia and drug-induced psychoses. (From *Abnormal Psychology and Modern Life* by James C. Coleman. Copyright © 1972 by Scott, Foresman and Company. Reprinted by permission of the publisher.)

Heroin

There can be no question about the dangers of heroin use. What may start out innocently enough as a desire to experience a new kind of high, may progress with extreme rapidity to an almost continuous type of nightmare existence. As one addict expressed it, "Heroin has all the advantages of death, without its permanence" (*Time,* 1970). Many addicts find permanence when they take an overdose.

The heroin user may begin by snorting or inhaling the drug, progress to "skin popping" (injecting it beneath the skin), and end up "mainlining" it (injecting it directly into his bloodstream; see Fig. 16.2). If a hypodermic syringe is not available, he may sever an artery and pour the heroin in with a spoon. Once a user is "hooked," his entire life becomes centered upon this white

Drugs

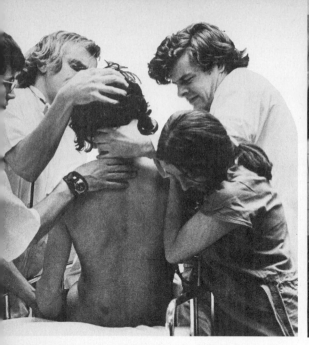

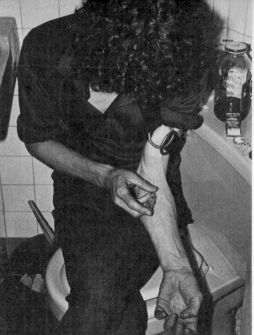

Fig. 16.1
Cases of drug overdose are more common in
hospital emergency rooms now than ever before.
(Cary S. Wolinsky—Stock, Boston.)

Fig. 16.2
Mainlining.
(Peter Menzel—Stock, Boston.)

powder. He will do *anything*—lie, steal, cheat, even kill—to get
that next fix. After a while, he does not even experience a high;
he simply needs the drug to avoid the terrors of withdrawal. The
habit demands more and more, and still more, of the drug. Before
long, it may cost him more than $100 a day, seven days a week—
about $40,000 a year! Even a highly paid corporation executive
would find it difficult to support such a habit. Usually, the only
way the addict can get that much money is through crime or
prostitution. Thus, crime associated with heroin addiction is not a
direct effect of the drug, but stems from the need to support the
habit. In fact, heroin is an extremely effective depressant, which
markedly reduces such motivational states as hunger and sex.

The victims of heroin addiction are legion—the addict
himself, his family, and those he has robbed or otherwise
brutalized in his quest for the "big H." In recent years another
innocent victim of heroin addiction has come to light, the
newborn infant of an addicted mother. Studies of infants born to
heroin-addicted mothers have found that more than two-thirds
start out life as addicts. Within 96 hours of birth, most will show
signs of withdrawal, including extreme irritability, tremors, and
vomiting. The incidence of withdrawal symptoms in the newborn

*Contemporary
Issues*

depends on how long the mother has been addicted, on the amount of heroin she has taken, and on how close to delivery she was when she took her last dose (Zelson et al., 1971).

The Stresses of Contemporary Life

We live an an age unlike any other. For the million or so years that man has been on this earth, there has generally been an abundant supply of natural resources, including land area for agriculture, energy resources for industrial development, and many of the other commodities necessary to feed, clothe, and shelter man. In this century, we have seen a culmination of events that may spell imminent disaster. The rate of population growth is so great that by the year 2020, it has been estimated, the earth's population will exceed 10 billion. The land and power resources to support a population of this size at more than a subsistence level are simply not available (Rocks and Runyon, 1972).

The stresses caused by this technological and population growth are already casting their shadows before them. The industrial revolution has brought about the virtual evacuation of rural areas and massive migration to the cities. Many new problems have appeared, and old ones have been exacerbated—overcrowding, pollution, drug addiction, crime, and violence.

Anonymity and Bystander Apathy

People in large urban areas frequently live a life of virtual anonymity. It is quite common for neighbors not to know one another. Social and familial ties tend to be looser than in small rural communities. People living in big cities often complain that they have become little more than computer code numbers. Most of the people the urban dweller meets during the course of his day are complete strangers. People ride side by side on crowded buses and subways and rarely exchange a word or greeting. It is easy to feel anonymous and without identity in situations like these.

One of the unfortunate consequences of big city anonymity is what has come to be known as bystander apathy. People have been known to ignore accidents, crimes, and even murders that occurred right under their noses. A number of years ago, a young lady was brutally killed during the early hours of the morning. Thirty-eight people viewed the assault from their apartment windows. Although the attack continued for more than half an hour, no one came to her rescue or even notified the police.

A number of incidents similar to this have been reported. In each case, there were large numbers of people who could have rendered assistance to the victim, and yet none did so. Such reports have led some people to conclude that the city dweller has become dehumanized and made callous by his environment. Obviously, some people do respond in emergencies. How, then, do we explain the behavior of those who do not?

A series of investigations has attempted to clarify some of the variables operating in bystander apathy. In one experiment, subjects (primarily female) were supposedly participating in a group discussion. Each subject was placed in a separate room containing a communication system. During the course of the discussion, one "subject" (a stooge) simulated a seizure. The following is a verbatim account:

> I er um I think I I need er if if could er er somebody er er er er er er er give me a little er give me a little help here because er I er I'm er er h-h-having a a a a real problem er right now and I er if somebody could help me out it would it would er er s-s-sure be sure be good . . . because er there er er a cause I er I uh I've got a a one of the er sei_____er er things coming on and and I could really er use some help so if somebody would er give me a little h-help uh er-er-er-er-er c-could somebody er er help er uh uh uh (choking sounds) . . . I'm gonna die er er I'm . . . gonna die er help er er seizure er (chokes, then quiet).
>
> (Latané and Darley, 1969, p. 261)

The communication system was set up in such a way that it was impossible for any subject to communicate with the others and to find out what, if anything, they were doing in this emergency. The experimenter recorded how soon the subject reported the emergency to him. The main independent variable in this experiment was the number of other people thought to be in the discussion group. Figure 16.3 shows that all the subjects who thought they were alone with the victim reported the emergency.

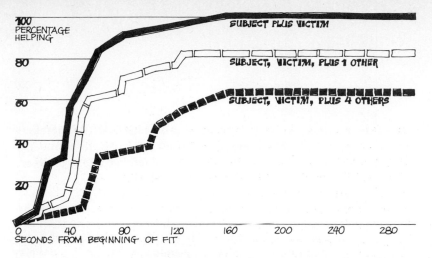

Fig. 16.3
Bystander apathy

The fewer the bystanders, the greater is the likelihood that assistance will be offered to a victim. Moreover, the speed of rendering assistance is faster. (After "Bystander Intervention in Emergencies: Diffusion of Responsibilities" by J. M. Darley and B. Latané, *Journal of Personality and Social Psychology*, **8,** 1968, pp. 377–383. Copyright © 1968 by the American Psychological Association and used by permission.)

When subjects thought that there were four others who could report the emergency, only 62 percent responded. Moreover, their responses were not as fast (Latané and Darley, 1969).

The investigators of bystander apathy have developed a two-factor explanation for their findings. (1) A bystander is affected by the reactions of the others who are present. If they do not appear to regard the situation as an emergency, he will perceive the situation as being less serious than if he were alone. (2) The greater the number of people present, the more diffuse will be the responsibility of any one individual alone.

The experimenters note that glib labels, which are often used by the mass media to explain bystander apathy, may be misleading. They suggest that "situational factors, specifically factors involving the immediate social environment, may be of greater importance in determining an individual's reaction to an emergency than such vague cultural or personality concepts as 'apathy' or 'alienation due to urbanization'." (Latané and Darley, 1969, p. 268).

Violence

At times, it seems as if man were born to violence. Wars, street riots, muggings, murder, and rape, all testify both to man's capacity for violence and his willingness to engage in it. Some behavioral scientists and social philosophers maintain that aggression and violence are basic, inherited components of man's makeup. They point to evolutionary history, and reason that man, a weak animal in comparison to the beasts of the jungle, could not have survived without his "killer instinct." Other scientists, looking at the same evidence, challenge the view that man's violent tendencies are inherited. They assert that violence results

The Stresses of Contemporary Life

from the failure of society to provide satisfaction for its members' needs. According to this view, dissatisfaction, frustration, and unhappiness, particularly as they occur in teeming cities, provide excellent breeding grounds for acts of violence:

> . . . a child of parents at the bottom of the socio-economic scale who comes into the world with the same basic intellect as a child of parents at the top is less likely, for lack of stimulation and opportunity, to develop it. Moreover, poverty often interferes with the development not only of intelligence but also of a healthy personality. There is evidence, too, of an association between poverty on the one hand and, on the other, ignorance and distrust of democratic ideals and institutions. Violence, too, breeds in an atmosphere of deprivation and despair.
>
> (National Institute of Mental Health, 1969, p. 2)

Still other scientists, disagreeing with the hereditary position, claim that violence is the consequence of cultural conditioning, and is transmitted from generation to generation in much the same way as social values, beliefs, and attitudes are transmitted. According to this view, the only way to end violence is to change the structure and the values of societies that encourage, countenance, and reinforce it.

Whatever the truth may be, aggression and violence are problems that have plagued man throughout recorded history. The majority of Americans expect that violence will continue to characterize human relationships. A recent survey revealed that 58 percent agree that "human nature being what it is, there must always be war and conflict" (Stark and McEvoy, 1970).

What is violence? According to the dictionary, violence is "characterized by extreme force; marked by abnormally sudden physical activity and intensity" (*Webster's Third New International Dictionary*). It is interesting that not all Americans agree on what kinds of acts exemplify violent and nonviolent behavior. Do the following behaviors constitute acts of violence—shooting of looters, beating of students, passive sit-ins, burning of draft cards? It may surprise you to learn that, in a recent survey (*Time*, 1971), 57 percent of the respondents regarded shooting of looters as nonviolent, while 58 percent considered draft-card burning as violent. Moreover, as many as one-third of the respondents

	PERSONS KILLED BY RIOTERS	PERSONS KILLED BY AUTHORITIES
FOOD RIOTS OF 1766	0	31
WILKITE RIOTS OF 1768	0	11
GORDON RIOTS OF 1780	0	310
LUDDITE RIOTS OF 1811–1813	1	30
"SWING" RIOTS OF 1830	0	9
DETROIT RIOT OF 1967	2 OR 3	28 OR MORE
ATTICA PRISON RIOT OF 1971	0	36

Table 16.1
Deaths in riots (Rude, 1964; "Kerner" Commission, 1968; *Life,* 1971).

viewed beating of students as nonviolent, while fully 22 percent regarded passive sit-ins as violent. Most of us would agree, however, that roiling, destructive crowds participating in urban riots are engaging in violent behavior.

Riots

Studies of urban riots that occurred in Detroit and Newark in the late 1960's have revealed some surprising facts about the characteristics of the people who participated in these riots. It was commonly supposed that the rioters were the uneducated, "hard-core" unemployed. Contrary to this supposition, the rioters were not the poorest, not the hard-core unemployed, and not the least educated. Rioters appeared to be most clearly differentiated from non-rioters by their sense of racial unity. The rioters were more likely to regard themselves as superior to whites, they preferred to be called "blacks" rather than "Negroes," and in general, they displayed strong feelings of racial pride (Caplan, 1968).

In eight major riots occurring in 1967, virtually all of the damage was confined to the ghetto areas. Paradoxically, the blacks appeared to be destroying "their own" property, burning their own neighborhoods and looting local stores. One explanation of this paradox proposed that the attacks were directed against the *symbols* of ghetto oppression (Delany, 1968).

Most of the crowd action in a riot is directed toward the destruction of property. Rarely do rioters direct their activities toward the destruction of human life (Rude, 1964). Yet many lives are lost in riots. Who kills whom in a riot? Analysis of many riots has revealed that most of the deaths are caused by the authorities rather than by the rioters themselves. In describing the New Orleans riot of 1870, General Sheridan said, "At least nine-tenths of the casualties were perpetrated by the police and citizens by stabbing and mashing in the heads of many who had already been wounded or killed by policemen. . . . It was not just a riot, but an absolute massacre by the police" (quoted in Delany, 1968). Table 16.1 shows that an overwhelmingly greater

*The Stresses of
Contemporary Life*

proportion of deaths was inflicted by persons in authority than by the rioters themselves.

Suicide

Suicide is an act of violence directed against oneself. In many instances of both attempted and successful suicide, it is clear that the individual did not really intend to die. For example, a person may take an overdose of pills and then call someone to inform him of this fact. In such cases, it may be that the suicidal attempt was a cry of despair and a desperate call for help. Although hard data on the number of suicides are difficult to obtain, since the cause of death is frequently listed as accidental, it is estimated that, in this country, more than 20,000 people take their own lives each year. Moreover, at least 200,000 people make some form of suicidal attempt (Goldenson, 1970).

Is there a difference between the person who "talks suicide" and the person who successfully completes a suicide? Two investigators distinguished among threatened, attempted, and completed suicide (Farberow and Shneidman, 1955). Extending these categories, another investigator has suggested that there is a *continuum of suicidal concern* which includes the "intellectualizers," the "threats," the "attempts," and the "completed suicides" (Braaten, 1963). The "intellectualizers" entertain occasional suicidal impulses and thoughts; the "threats" use more frequent and intensive suicidal language; the "attempts" actually carry out acts that could result in death; and the "completed suicides" culminate in the death of the individual. There are even differences among the completed suicides: there are those whose cries for help fall upon deaf ears; those who leave lengthy letters justifying their action; and those who decide to commit the act, find the means, and do so without communicating the reasons for their decision.

It is a common belief that, once a person attempts to commit suicide and fails, he has "acted out" his self-destructive impulses and is relatively secure from futher attempts. However, a recent survey conducted at a suicide prevention center revealed that 60 percent of the "completed suicides" had made a previous attempt on their own lives (Wold, 1970). On the other hand, some individuals make an unsuccessful attempt on their lives and, upon recovery, go on to lead normal and productive lives. Some psychologists and psychiatrists have suggested that the attempt at suicide may serve as a catharsis or an emotional outlet for these individuals.

It is interesting that in all countries more males commit suicide than females. In the United States, the ratio is approximately three to one. More "attempts" are made by females, but these are much less likely to be successful than attempts by males. The suicide rate increases with age, and it is higher for unmarried than for married people. Figure 16.4 shows that widowed and divorced men are in the highest risk category. Apparently marriage does not drive men to suicide, since, among **men, the suicide level** is lowest among married males.

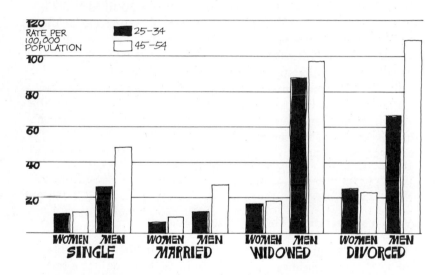

Fig. 16.4
Suicide and marital status (Vital Health Statistics, 1970).

In general, the suicide level among blacks is considerably lower than among whites: 3.9 versus 11.4 per 100,000 (Goldenson, 1970). However, a recent study presented evidence that there has been a sharp rise in suicide among urban blacks over the past fifteen years (Seiden, 1970).

Most suicides occur among people who are not suffering from severe emotional disorders at the time of the attempt. Only about one-third of all suicides are committed by individuals suffering acute emotional disorders, and most of these are severely depressed patients. Apparently, any sudden change in an individual's life situation, such as the loss of a loved one or the

The Stresses of Contemporary Life

breaking up of a marriage, may precipitate an attempt on one's own life.

Although suicide is the second most frequent cause of death among college students (Seiden, 1966), an exhaustive study of suicides in the Los Angeles area revealed that the rate is only about one-half as great as among non-college peers (Peck and Schrut, 1971).

A study of suicides over a ten-year period at the Berkeley campus of the University of California revealed a number of interesting findings. This study was unusual in that the non-suicide student population served as control subjects against which the suicidal students could be compared. Approximately 26 percent of the deaths occurred among students 30 to 34 years of age, although this age group constituted only six percent of the student body. About 34 percent of the suicides were among students referred for psychiatric treatment, although only ten percent of the entire student body had been seen at the mental health facilities on campus. The greatest number of suicides did not occur during the period prior to final examinations, when the anxieties and stresses are presumed to be greatest, but during the first six weeks of the semester (Seiden, 1966). This finding, however, is consonant with the view that a change in a person's life situation may precipitate a suicidal act.

Women's Liberation: The Fight for Equality

Many minority groups and subcultures within the nation—blacks, Puerto Ricans, Chicanos, American Indians, to name but a few— are fighting for equal rights and opportunities. All of these groups are referred to as minorities since each one constitutes only a small part of the entire population, and they have not been satisfactorily integrated into American society. We are now witnessing a fight for equality by a group which constitutes a majority, the women of America—they outnumber men by several million. This fight has been a long uphill battle.

In the last few years, women by the thousands have been joining the women's liberation movement. The core concern of the movement has been to open up to women the full range of options that have been available to men, and to give women the

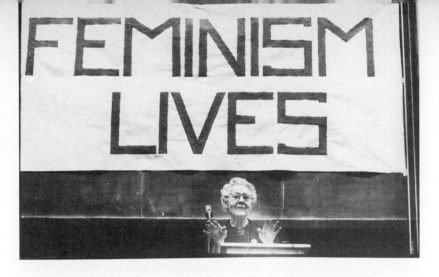

Fig. 16.5
(Ellis Herwig—Stock, Boston.)

opportunity to take a place in society that is consonant with their abilities. These women argue that the practice of assigning all women to the same role of full-time homemaker ignores the uniqueness of each woman.

One of the problems that women have had to overcome is the stereotype that they are inferior to men. This stereotype is held not only by "male chauvinist pigs"—women also tend to regard themselves as inferior to men. In one study, female college students were asked to rate a number of professional articles. Half of the women thought that the articles were written by women, and half thought that they were written by men. Identical articles received lower ratings when they were attributed to female authors (Goldberg, 1968). This stereotype of inferiority is deeply rooted in folklore, religious teachings, literature, and even in the mass media today. For example, the morning prayer of the Orthodox Jew reads, ". . . Blessed art Thou, oh Lord our God, King of the Universe, that I was not born a woman." Here is an excerpt from the New Testament: " For a man . . . is the image and glory of God: but the woman is the glory of man . . . Neither was the man created for the woman; but the woman for the man." And from the Koran, the sacred book of the Moslems: "Men are superior to women on account of the qualities in which God has given them preeminence."

Is it any wonder that women are regarded as inferior to men? What is the evidence to support this deeply embedded view? Compared to men, women have rarely achieved prominence in the sciences, arts, or politics. But does this prove that women are less capable in these areas? In the Soviet Union, one-third of the engineers and three-quarters of the physicians are women. Why do women make such a poor showing in these fields in the United States? Much research documents the fact that women are not inferior to men in intelligence. However, they are clearly

Women's Liberation: The Fight for Equality

differentiated in terms of early childhood experiences and the psychological impact these experiences have on adult role choices.

From the moment of birth, forces are set in motion which prepare the child for his later adult role. Long before boys start to look like boys and girls start to look like girls, certain types of behavior, attitudes, and aspirations are differentially reinforced. Boys are encouraged to be more aggressive and dominant. They are even given different types of toys—guns, erector sets, trains, and chemistry sets. Girls, on the other hand, are encouraged to be passive and submissive, and are given dolls to play with. During the school years, boys are expected to excel in mathematics and the sciences. Girls who develop similar aspirations are frequently discouraged by both adults and their peers. By the ninth grade, 25 percent of the boys, but only 3 percent of the girls, are considering careers in science or engineering (Bem and Daryl, 1970).

Arguments between adherents to and opponents of women's liberation have frequently created more heat than light. Nevertheless, it is clear that women are denied access to many types of opportunities that, if granted, would add substantially to the human resources of the nation. At a time when we need all the brain power we can get to help solve many of the social and technological problems that beset us today, we may be accused of squandering a vital resource that comprises slightly more than 50 percent of the nation's capacity.

The Energy Crisis

The human species has been on earth for two million years or so. Until the past few hundred years, our numbers have increased gradually and our demands on the earth's resources have been well within the earth's ability to supply. Within the past few centuries, however, this picture has altered remarkably. Our numbers have grown so sharply that, of all the people who have lived on earth since our species emerged from the primordial jungles, approximately one out of three is alive at this moment. Moreover, with the advent of the industrial revolution, we discovered that energy-powered machines can be made to do much of our work for us. In a mere flash of cosmic time came a steady parade of technological advances: the steam engine and the train; the internal combustion engine and the automobile; jet-powered aircraft and space vehicles venturing ever further into the unknown void. All of these devices have extended our capacity to do work. They have also put us in a new position of dependency in which muscle power has been superseded by energy drawn primarily from the fossil fuels.

Whereas primitive human beings had to rely exclusively upon their own muscle power and ingenuity to survive, the contemporary American has the energy equivalent of 100 around-the-clock slaves working on his behalf 365 days a year. Moreover, the per capita use of energy in the United States is approximately eight times the per capita energy consumption in the other nations on earth (Runyon and Rocks, 1973).

It is now clear that oil and natural gas, the energy sources upon which we have most depended, are in critically short supply (Rocks and Runyon, 1972). Moreover, there is little hope that the remaining supplies can be extracted at a sufficient rate to meet our exuberantly growing demands. Alternative energy modes, such as solar, nuclear, and geothermal power, should become feasible sometime during the coming century. It is clear, therefore, that the major theme of our times must become energy conservation: if there is little hope of finding more energy over the next few decades, we must learn to live with less now. The development of a strategy to conserve energy presents an awesome challenge to the behavioral sciences. Let's see what the field of psychology can contribute.

Changing Scripts

Borrowing some terms from transactional analysis, we might say that most of the young people of America are "scripted" in childhood to drive an automobile during their teenage years and to gain exclusive possession of a car by their early twenties. Most expect to drive a large, comfortable, energy-consuming automobile complete with air conditioning, power brakes, and power steering. Some, however, strive to own a small, "sexy" sports car, which is also profligate of energy. Businessmen are "scripted" to drive a "climate-conditioned" car to work, enter an air-conditioned office, and have at their disposal a host of

The Energy Crisis

energy-using devices (electric typewriters for their secretaries, intercommunication systems, computer facilities, and so on). Housewives expect to have a second car for shopping and transporting the children to and fro. In addition, we all desire the latest labor-saving devices in the home: dishwashers, automatic clothes washers and dryers, electric can openers, garbage compactors, electric toothbrushes.

Fig. 16.6
(Daniel S. Brody—Stock, Boston.)

The facts of the energy crisis make it clear that many of these scripts will have to be rewritten. One cause for optimism is the extreme flexibility of the human organism. Since habits and expectations are learned, they may be unlearned and new ones substituted in their place. However, as we have seen throughout this text, behavior modification can best be accomplished by providing incentives and rewards.

Energy Conservation: The Use of Incentives and Rewards

Survey data have already provided a great deal of information concerning areas of energy waste. In the automotive area alone, for example, we know that 82 percent of commuting workers use the automobile (U.S. Government, 1972). Moreover, 68 percent of these automobile commuters drive alone to work. When used in this way, the automobile represents an enormous waste of gasoline. Buses and commuter railroads are five to ten times more efficient in their use of energy to move people from place to place (Rice, 1972). However, if we could increase the passenger load per car, enormous energy and economic savings could be achieved.

From our knowledge of psychology, we may anticipate that voluntary programs are likely to be ineffective. Individuals are more likely to change deeply ingrained habits if incentives for change are provided. How can we provide such incentives? Three suggestions can readily be made:

1. Convert lanes in superhighways, throughways, and freeways for use only by mass transit (buses) and automobiles with near-capacity passenger loads. Presumably, the positive reinforcement of traveling relatively unimpeded to and from work and education will encourage more commuters to form car pools. The negative incentive of being stuck in endless traffic jams while others move freely in the segregated lane will cause others to imitate their peers. With fewer cars on the road there will be fewer traffic jams, less automotive pollution, and greater energy savings. The passengers in such cars will gain the additional satisfactions of saving money and being able to sleep or to read their newspaper on the way to work.

2. Reduce the tolls on roads, bridges, and tunnels for those cars with passenger loads beyond some minimum number. Here the financial incentive is obvious.

3. Provide easier access to parking areas and reduce the parking fees for automobiles with large passenger loads.

As we have seen throughout this text, it requires ingenuity, a willingness to break set patterns of thinking and doing, and attractive incentives in order to modify human behavior and bring about social changes. The energy crisis is an area that will require conservation of energy on a massive scale if we are to maintain personal, social, economic, and political viability. As a citizen and student of behavior, you will be called upon to participate in the solution to this and other challenging issues of our day. It is our sincere hope that this course has provided you with knowledge and insights that will make this participation more rewarding, both personally and socially.

The Energy Crisis

Summary

1. Perhaps the problems we face in contemporary civilization are made to appear unique because (a) the rate at which change is taking place is greater than ever before, and (b) population and supporting technology have burgeoned, bringing about crises in pollution, ecology, crowding in the cities, and availability of energy and other natural resources.

2. Drug abuse is a serious problem in itself, but is also symptomatic of deeper psychological issues.

3. Addiction should be distinguished from habituation. In habituation, there is psychological rather than physiological dependence.

4. Among the stresses attributed to the population explosion and crowding in urban areas are bystander apathy, violence, riots, and suicide.

5. One of the problems that women face in their fight for equality is that the stereotype of inferiority is deeply rooted in folklore, religious teachings, literature, and the mass media. Indeed, many women share these stereotypes. The view that women are intellectually inferior receives no support from psychological investigations.

6. The fact that man is threatened with the depletion of vital resources, including energy, poses challenging problems for the psychologist. The need to conserve energy will require the rewriting of many personal and cultural "scripts." The use of incentives and rewards will play a significant role in causing individuals to modify their behavior so as to reduce their dependence on energy-using devices.

Terms to Remember

Addiction   Physiological dependence on a drug.

Drug Abuser   A person who uses drugs to such an excess that he is unable to function without them.

Drug User   A person who uses drugs, but not to excess (contrast with *drug abuser).*

Habituation   Psychological dependence on a drug.

Mainlining   Injecting a drug directly into the bloodstream.

Synesthesia   The translation of one sensory experience into another, such as feeling an odor or seeing a sound.

Tolerance   The body's ability to withstand and require increased dosages of a drug.

Recommended Readings

James, M., and Jongeward, D., *Born to Win: Transactional Analysis with Gestalt Experiments,* Reading, Massachusetts: Addison-Wesley Publishing Co., 1971.

Primarily concerned with transactional analysis theory and its application to the daily life of the average person.

Latané, B., and Darley, J., *The Unresponsive Bystander—Why Doesn't He Help?,* New York: Appleton-Century-Crofts, 1970.

Studies the causes for intervention or its lack by witnesses of emergency situations.

Rice, Richard A., "System Energy and Future Transportation," *Technological Review,* 1972.

An article describing the energy efficiencies of various transportation modes.

Rocks, L., and Runyon, R. P., *The Energy Crisis,* New York: Crown, 1972.

Highly readable and convincing argument that the energy crisis is alarmingly real.

Rocks, L., and Runyon, R. P., "Energy and Foreign Policy: How Dependent Must We Be," proceedings of The Washington Journalism Center Conference on Energy and the Environment, October, 1973.

Runyon, R. P., and Rocks, L., "The Energy Crises: A Perspective," Address given before The Academy of Political Science, July 19, 1973. (*Proceedings* in press.)

A paper describing the reasons for the energy crisis, and anticipated economic, social, political, and personal effects of a prolonged energy shortage, as well as suggested remedial measures.

Snyder, S. H., *Uses of Marijuana,* New York: Oxford University Press, Inc., 1971.

Discusses patterns of marijuana use through the centuries, observed behavioral effects, known and expected dangers, and research.

REFERENCES

Abood, L. G., "A Chemical Approach to the Problem of Mental Disease," in Jackson, D. D. (ed.), *The Etiology of Schizophrenia,* New York: Basic Books, 1960.

Aiken, L. R., Jr., *Psychological and Educational Testing,* Boston: Allyn and Bacon, 1971.

Allen, K. E., and Harris, F. R., "Elimination of a Child's Excessive Scratching by Training the Mother in Reinforcement Procedures," *Behavior Research and Therapy,* **4** (1966), pp. 79–84.

Ammons, R. B., "Reactions in a Projective Doll-play Interview of White Males Two to Six Years of Age to Differences in Skin Color and Facial Features," *Journal of Genetic Psychology,* **76** (1950), pp. 323–341.

Anastasi, A., *Differential Psychology,* New York: The Macmillan Co., 1958.

Anderson, B., and McCann, S. M., *Acta Physiologica Scandinavia,* **33** (1955), pp. 333–346.

Archer, E. J., "A Re-evaluation of the Meaningfulness of All Possible CVC Trigrams,"

Psychological Monographs, **74** (1960).

Aronfreed, J., and Leff, R., "The Effects of Intensity of Punishment and Complexity of Discrimination upon the Learning of an Internalized Inhibition," Unpublished manuscript, University of Pennsylvania, 1963.

Aronson, E., and Mills, J., "The Effect of Severity of Initiation on Liking for a Group," *Journal of Abnormal and Social Psychology,* **59** (1959), pp. 177–181.

Aronson, E., and Rosenbloom, S., "Space Perception in Early Infancy: Perception within a Common Auditory-Visual Space," *Science,* **172** (1971), pp. 1161–1163.

Asch, S. E., "Effects of Group Pressure upon the Modification and Distortion of Judgment," in Guetzkow, M. H. (ed.), *Groups, Leadership, and Men,* Pittsburgh: Carnegie Press, 1951.

Asch, S. E., "Opinions and Social Pressure," *Scientific American,* **193** (1955), pp. 31–35.

Asch, S. E., "Studies of Independence and Conformity.

A Minority of One Against a Unanimous Majority," *Psychological Monographs,* **70,** 9 (1956).

Ashley, W. R., Harper, R. S., and Runyon, D. L., "The Perceived Size of Coins in Normal and Hypnotically Induced Economic States," *The American Journal of Psychology,* **64,** 4 (1951), pp. 564–572.

Ax, A., "The Physiological Differentiation Between Fear and Anger in Humans," *Psychosomatic Medicine,* **15** (1953), pp. 433–442.

Ayllon, T., "Intensive Treatment of Psychotic Behavior by Stimulus Satiation and Food Reinforcement," *Behavior Research and Therapy,* **1** (1963), pp. 53–61.

Ayllon, T., and Michael, J., "The Psychiatric Nurse as a Behavioral Engineer," *Journal of the Experimental Analysis of Behavior,* **2** (1959), pp. 323–334.

Bachrach, A. J., *Psychological Research* (2nd ed.), New York: Random House, 1965.

Bahrick, H. P., and Bahrick, Phyllis O., "A Re-examination of the Interrelations Among

Measures of Retention," *Quarterly Journal of Experimental Psychology,* **16** (1964), pp. 318–324.

Bales, R. F., "Task Roles and Social Roles in Problem-Solving Groups," in Maccoby, E., Newcomb, J. M., and Hartley, E. L. (eds.), *Readings in Social Psychology,* New York: Holt, Rinehart and Winston, 1958.

Ball, W., and Tronick, E., "Infant Responses to Impending Collision: Optical and Real," *Science,* **171** (1971), pp. 818–820.

Banay, R. S., "Immaturity and Crime," *The American Journal of Psychiatry,* **100** (1943), pp. 170–177.

Bandura, A., "The Role of Modeling Processes in Personality Development," in Hartup, W. W., and Smothergill, Nancy L. (eds.), *The Young Child,* Washington: National Association for the Education of Young Children, 1967, pp. 42–58.

Bandura, A., Blanchard, E. B., and Ritter, B., "Relative Efficacy of Desensitization and Modeling Approaches for Inducing Behavioral, Affective, and Attitudinal Changes," *Journal of Personality and Social Psychology,* **13** (1969), pp. 173–179.

Bandura, A., Ross, D., and Ross, S., "Transmission of Aggression Through Imitation of Aggressive Models," *Journal of Abnormal and Social Psychology,* **63** (1961), pp. 575–582.

Bandura, A., Ross, D., and Ross, S. A., "Imitation of Film-Mediated Aggressive Models," *Journal of Abnormal and Social Psychology,* **66** (1963), pp. 3–11.

Bandura, A., and Walters, R. H., *Adolescent Aggression,* New York: Ronald Press Co., 1959.

Bandura, A., and Walters, R. H., *Social Learning and Personality Development,* New York: Holt, Rinehart and Winston, 1963.

Bard, P., and Mountcastle, V. B., "Some Forebrain Mechanisms Involved in the Expression of Rage with Special Reference to Suppression of Angry Behavior," *Research Publications of the Association for Research on Nervous and Mental Diseases,* **27** (1947), pp. 362–404.

Barker, R. G., Dembo, T., and Lewin, K., "Frustration and Regression: an Experiment with Young Children," *University of Iowa Studies in Child Welfare,* **18,** 1 (1941), xv+314.

Barker, R. G., Dembo, T., and Lewin K., "An Experiment with Young Children," in Barker, R. G., Kounin, I. S., and Wright, H. F. (eds.), *Child Behavior and Development,* New York: McGraw-Hill, 1943, pp. 441–458.

Barron, F., "The Psychology of Imagination," *Scientific American,* **199,** 3 (1958), pp. 150–166.

Bartlett, F. C., *Remembering: A Study in Experimental and Social Psychology,* London: Cambridge University Press, 1954.

Becker, H. S., "Becoming a Marihuana User," *American Journal of Sociology,* **59** (1953), pp. 235–242.

Becker, H. S., *Outsiders: Studies in the Sociology of Deviance,* New York: The Free Press, 1963.

Bem, S. L., and Daryl, J., "We're All Nonconscious Sexists," *Psychology Today,* **4,** 6 (1970), pp. 22–26, 115–116.

Berko, Jean, "The Child's Learning of English Morphology," *Word,* **14** (1958), pp. 150–177.

Berkowitz, L., "Impulse, Aggression and the Gun," *Psychology Today,* **2,** 4 (1968), pp. 18–22.

Berkowitz, L., and Cottingham, D. R., "The Interest Value and Relevance of Fear Arousing Communications," *Journal of Abnormal and Social Psychology,* **60** (1960), pp. 37–43.

Berlyne, D. E., "The Influence of Complexity and Novelty in Visual Figures on Orienting Responses," *Journal of Experimental Psychology,* **55** (1958), pp. 289–296.

Berne, E., *Games People Play,* New York: Grove Press, 1964.

Bexton, W. H., Heron, W., and Scott, T. H., "Effects of Decreased Variation in the Sensory Environment," *Canadian Journal of Psychology,* **8** (1954), pp. 70–76.

Blauvelt, H. H., "Capacity of a Human Neonate Reflex to Signal Future Response by Present Action," *Child Development,* **33** (1962), pp. 21–28.

Boring, E. G., (ed.), *Psychology for the Armed Services,* Washington D.C.: Combat Forces Press, 1945.

Bourne, L. E., Jr., and Archer, E. J., "Time Continuously on Target as a Function of Distribution of Practice," *Journal of Experimental Psychology,* **51** (1956), pp. 25–33.

Bower, G. H., and Clark, M. C., "Narrative Stories as Mediators for Serial Learning," *Psychonomic Science,* **14** (1969), pp. 181–182.

Braaten, L. J., "Some Reflections on Suicidal Tendencies Among College Students," *Mental Hygiene,* **47** (1963), pp. 562–568.

Brady, J. V., "Ulcers in 'Executive' Monkeys," *Scientific American,* **199,** 4 (1958), pp. 95–100.

Braine, M. D. S., "The Ontogeny of English Phrase Structure: The First Phase," *Language,* **39** (1963), pp. 1–13.

Brenner, J. M., and Kleinman, R. A., "Learned Control of Decreases in Systolic Blood Pressure," *Nature,* **226,** 5250 (1970), pp. 1063–1064.

Bridges, K. M. B., "Emotional Development in Early Infancy," *Child Development,* **3** (1932), pp. 324–341.

Bronson, G., "Infants' Reactions to an Unfamiliar Person," Paper presented at meetings of the Society for Research in Child Development, 1971.

Broughton, W. J., "Sleep Disorders: Disorders of Arousal?" *Science,* **159** (1968), pp. 1070–1078.

Brown, J. S., "Gradients of Approach and Avoidance Responses and Their Relation to Motivation," *Journal of Comparative and Physiological Psychology,* **41** (1948), pp. 450–465.

Brown, R. W., and Lennenberg, E. H., "A Study in Language and Cognition," *Journal of Abnormal and Social Psychology,* **49** (1954), pp. 454–462.

Bulatov, P. K., "The Higher Nervous Activity in Persons Suffering from Bronchial Asthma," In *Problems of Interrelationship Between Psyche and Soma in Psychoneurology and General Medicine, Institute Bechtereva,* 1963, 317–328

(*International Journal of Psychiatry,* September, 1967, p. 245.)

Burt, C., "The Inheritance of Mental Ability," *American Psychologist,* **13** (1958), pp. 5–10.

Butler, J. M., and Haigh, G. V., "Changes in the Relation Between Self-Concepts and Ideal Concepts Consequent upon Client-Centered Counseling," in Roger, C. R., and Dymond, R. F., (eds.), *Psychotherapy and Personality Change,* Chicago: The University of Chicago Press, 1954.

Byrne, D., and Nelson, D., "Attraction as a Linear Function of Proportion of Positive Reinforcements," *Journal of Personality and Social Psychology,* **1,** 6 (1965), pp. 659–663.

Cameron, N., and Magaret, A., *Behavior Pathology,* Boston: Houghton Mifflin Co., 1951.

Cannon, W. B., *Bodily Changes in Pain, Hunger, Fear and Rage,* (2nd ed.), New York: Appleton-Century-Crofts, 1929.

Cantril, H., *The Politics of Despair,* New York: Basic Books, 1958.

Caplan, N. S., and Paige, J. M., "A Study of Ghetto Rioters," *Scientific American,* **219,** 2 (1968), pp. 15–21.

Carter, L. F., Haythorn, W., and Howell, M., "A Further Investigation of the Criteria of

Leadership," *Journal of Abnormal and Social Psychology,* **45** (1950), pp. 350–358.

Cates, J., "Psychology's Manpower: Report on the 1968 National Register of Scientific and Technical Personnel," *American Psychologist,* **25,** 3 (1970), pp. 254–263.

Cattell, R. B., *Description and Measurement of Personality,* Yonkers, N. Y.: World Book, 1946.

Chafetz, M. E., "A New Day of Hope for Alcoholics," *American Journal of Psychiatry,* **127,** 2 (1971), pp. 118–119.

Chomsky, N., "Language and the Mind," *Readings in Psychology Today,* Del Mar, Calif.: CRM Books, 1969.

Claeson, E., and Carlsson, C., "Swedish Scientist Links Alcohol to Brain Disorder," *Psychiatric News,* **6,** 4 (1971), p. 20.

Clark, K. B., *Dark Ghetto: Dilemmas of Social Power,* New York: Harper and Row, 1965.

Clark, L. D., and Nahashima, E. N., "Experimental Studies in Marihuana," *American Journal of Psychiatry,* **125** (1968), pp. 379–384.

Clark, M., Lachowitz, T., and Montrose, I. B., "A Pilot Basic Education Program for School Dropouts Incorporating a Token Reinforcement System,"

Behavior Research and Therapy, **6** (1968), pp. 183–188.

Coch, L., and French, J. R. P., Jr., "Overcoming Resistance to Change," *Human Relations,* **1** (1948), pp. 512–532.

Cohen, L. D., Kipnis, D., Kunkle, E. C., and Kubzansky, P. E., "Observations of a Person with Congenital Insensitivity to Pain," *Journal of Abnormal and Social Psychology,* **51** (1955), pp. 333–338.

Cohen, Saralee, "Infant Attentional Behavior to Face-Voice Incongruity," Unpublished Ph.D. dissertation, University of California at Los Angeles, 1973.

Coleman, J. C., *Abnormal Psychology and Modern Life,* Glenview, Ill.: Scott, Foresman and Co., 1972.

Coleman, J. C., "Facial Expression of Emotion," *Psychological Monographs,* **329,** 296 (1949).

Cooper, C. J., "Some Relationships Between Paired-Associate Learning and Foreign Language Aptitude," *Journal of Educational Psychology,* **55,** 3 (1964), pp. 132–138.

Corballis, M. C., and Beale, I. L., "On Telling Left from Right," *Scientific American,* **224,** 3 (1971), pp. 96–104.

Cousins, S. (pseud.), *To Beg I am Ashamed,* New York: Vanguard, 1938.

Cowles, J. T., "Food-Tokens as Incentives for Learning by Chimpanzees," *Comparative Psychology Monographs,* **14,** 71 (1937).

Crandall, V. C., Good S., and Crandall, V. J., "Reinforcement Effects of Adult Reactions and Nonreactions on Children's Achievement Expectations: a Replication Study," *Child Development,* **35** (1964), pp. 485–497.

Cronbach, L. J., *Essentials of Psychological Testing,* New York: Harper and Row, 1970.

Darley, J. M., and Latané, B., "Bystander Intervention in Emergencies: Diffusion of Responsibilities," *Journal of Personality and Social Psychology,* **8,** 4 (1968), pp. 377–383.

Davis, R., Sutherland, N. S., and Judd, B. R., "Information Content in Recognition and Recall," *Journal of Experimental Psychology,* **61** (1961), pp. 422–429.

Dayton, D. H., "Early Malnutrition and Human Development," *Children,* **16** (1969), pp. 210–217.

Delany, L. T., "The Other Bodies in the River," *Psychology Today,* **2,** 1 (1968), pp. 26–31, 59.

Delgado, J. M. R., "Cerebral Heterostimulation in a Monkey Colony," *Science,* **141** (1963), pp. 161–163.

Dement, W. C., "An Essay on Dreams: the Role of Physiology in Understanding Their Nature," in Barron, F. et al, *New Directions in Psychology,* Vol. II, New York: Holt, Rinehart and Winston, 1965.

Dement, W., and Kleitman, N., "The Relation of Eye Movements during Sleep to Dream Activity: an Objective Method for the Study of Dreaming," *Journal of Experimental Psychology,* **53** (1957), pp. 339–346.

Dennis, W., "Causes of Retardation Among Institutional Children: Iran," *Journal of Genetic Psychology,* **96** (1960), pp. 47–59.

Deutsch, M., and Collins, M. E., *Interracial Housing: A Psychological Evaluation of a Social Experiment,* Minneapolis, Minn.: University of Minnesota Press, 1951.

Diamond, E., "The Most Terrifying Psychic Experience Known to Man," *New York Times Magazine,* December 7, 1969, pp. 56–57.

Dollard, J., and Miller N. E., *Personality and Psychotherapy,* New York: McGraw-Hill Book Co., 1950.

"Drugs on Campus," Newsweek, January 25, 1971, p. 52.

Dunbar, F., *Psychosomatic Diagnosis,* New York: Harper and Row Publishers, 1943.

Dunnette, M. D., Campbell, J., and Jaastad, Kay, "The Effect of Group Participation on Brainstorming Effectiveness for Two Industrial Samples," *Journal of Applied Psychology,* **47** (1963), pp. 30–37.

Ebbinghaus, H., *Memory,* New York: Columbia University Teachers College, 1913. (Reprinted by Dover Publications, New York, 1964.)

Ehrlich, A., "Neural Control of Feeding Behavior," *Psychological Bulletin,* **61** (1964), pp. 100–110.

Ehrmann, W., "Premarital Sexual Intercourse," in Ellis, A., and Abarbanel, A. (eds.), *The Encyclopedia of Sexual Behavior,* Vol. II, New York: Hawthorn Books, 1961.

Elmadjian, F., "Excretion and Metabolism of Epinephrine," *Pharmacological Review,* **11** (1959), pp. 409–415.

Emde, R. N., and Harmon, R. J., "Endogenous and Exogenous Smiling Systems in Early Infancy," *Journal of the American Academy of Child Psychiatry,* **11** (1972), pp. 177–200.

Eysenck, H. J., *Sense and Nonsense in Psychology,* Baltimore: Penguin Books, 1964.

Farberow, N. L., and Shneidman, E. S., "A Study of Attempted, Threatened and Completed Suicide," *Journal of Abnormal and Social Psychology,* **50** (1955), p. 230.

Festinger, L., *A Theory of Cognitive Dissonance,* Stanford: Stanford University Press, 1957.

Festinger, L., and Carlsmith, J. M., "Cognitive Consequences of Forced Compliance," *Journal of Abnormal and Social Psychology,* **58** (1959), pp. 203–211.

Fleck, S., "Family Dynamics and Origin of Schizophrenia," *Psychosomatic Medicine,* **22** (1960), pp. 337–339.

Fox, L., "Effecting the Use of Efficient Study Habits," *Journal of Mathematics,* **1** (1962), pp. 75–86.

Frankenburg, W. K., and Dodds, J. B., "The Denver Developmental Screening Test," *The Journal of Pediatrics,* **71,** 2 (1967), pp. 181–191.

Freeman, F. S., *Theory and Practice of Psychological Testing,* New York: Holt, Rinehart and Winston, 1962.

French, J. D., "The Reticular Formation," *Scientific American,* **196,** 5 (1957), pp. 54–60.

Fromm, Erika, "Age Regression with Unexpected Appearance of a Repressed Childhood Language," *International Journal of Clinical and Experimental Hypnosis,* **18,** 2 (1970), pp. 79–88.

Funkenstein, D. H., "The Physiology of Fear and Anger," *Scientific American,* **192** (1955), pp. 74–80.

Gallup, G., "Generation Gap Shown in Sex View," *American Institute of Public Opinion,* 1970.

Gamper, E., and Krall, A., "Weitere Experimentell-Biologische Untersuchungen zum Schizophrenic Problem," *Zeitschrift für die gesamte Neurologie und Psychiatrie,* **150** (1934), pp. 252–271.

Gardner, Beatrice T., and Gardner, R. A., "Two-Way Communication with an Infant Chimpanzee," in Schrier, A. M., and Stollnitz, F. (eds.), *Behavior of Nonhuman Primates,* New York: Academic Press, 1971, pp. 117–184.

Garry, R., and Kingsley, H. L., *The Nature and Conditions of Learning* (3rd ed.), New Jersey: Prentice-Hall, Inc., 1970.

Garten, S., "Veränderungen der Netzhaut durch Licht," in *Graefe-Saemisch Handbuch der Augenheilkunde,* 2nd edition, 1908.

Gates, A. J., "Recitation as a Factor in Memorizing," *Archives of Psychology,* **6**, 40 (1917).

Gericke, O. L., "Practical Use of Operant Conditioning Procedures in a Mental Hospital," *Psychiatric Studies and Projects,* **3**, 5 (June, 1965), pp. 3–10.

Gesell, A., et al., *The First Five Years of Life,* New York: Harper Bros., 1940.

Gilbert, G. M., "Stereotype Assistance and Change Among College Students," *Journal of Abnormal and Social Psychology,* **46** (1951), pp. 245–254.

Glaze, J. A., "The Association Value of Nonsense Syllables," *Journal of Genetic Psychology,* **35**, 2 (1928), pp. 255–269.

Glucksberg, S., and King, L. J., "Motivated Forgetting Mediated by Implicit Verbal Chaining: a Laboratory Analogy of Repression," *Science,* **58** (1967), pp. 517–519.

Goldberg, P., "Are Women Prejudiced Against Women?" *Trans-Action,* **5** (1968), pp. 28–30.

Goldenson, R. M., *The Encyclopedia of Human Behavior: Psychology, Psychiatry, and Mental Health,* Vol. II, New York: Doubleday and Co. Inc., 1970.

Goldiamond, I., "Fluent and Nonfluent Speech (Stuttering). Analysis and Operant Techniques for Control," in Krasner, L., and Ullman, L. P. (eds.), *Research in Behavior Modification,* New York: Holt, Rinehart and Winston, 1965.

Goodman, L., *Sunsigns,* New York: Bantam Books, 1968.

Goorney, A. B., "Treatment of a Compulsive Horse Race Gambler by Aversion Therapy," *British Journal of Psychiatry,* **114** (1968), pp. 329–333.

Grinspoon, L., "Marihuana," *Scientific American,* **221**, 6 (1969), pp. 17–25.

Grinspoon, L., Ewalt, J. R., and Shader, R., "Psychotherapy and Pharmacotherapy in Chronic Schizophrenia," *American Journal of Psychiatry,* **124** (1968), pp. 67–74.

Gross, L., "A Parents' Primer on Pot," *West,* Los Angeles Times, May 7, 1972.

Gubar, G., "Drug Addiction: Myth and Misconceptions," *Pennsylvania Psychiatric Quarterly,* **8** (1969), pp. 24–32.

Guilford, J. P., "A Factor Analytic Study Across the Domains of Reasoning, Creativity, and Evaluation, I: Hypotheses and Description of Tests," *Reports from the Psychological Laboratory,* Los Angeles: University of Southern California, 1954.

Guilford, J. P., *Personality,* New York: McGraw-Hill Book Co., 1959.

Guilford, J. P., *The Nature of Human Intelligence,* New York: McGraw-Hill Book Co., 1967.

Haber, A., and Kalish, H. I., "Prediction of Discrimination from Generalization after Variations in Schedule of Reinforcement," *Science,* **142,** 3590 (1963), pp. 412–413.

Hall, E., and Hall, Mildred, "The Sounds of Silence," *Playboy,* June, 1971.

Halstead, W. C., and Rucker, W. B., "Memory: a Molecular Maze," *Psychology Today,* **2,** 1 (1968), pp. 38–41, 66–67.

Hamlin, R. L., Buckholdt, D., Bushell, D., Ellis, D., and Ferritor, D., "Changing the Game from 'Get the Teacher' to 'Learn,'" *Trans-Action,* **6** (1969), pp. 20–31.

Harlow, H. F., "The Formation of Learning Sets," *Psychological Review,* **56** (1949), pp. 51–65.

Harlow, H. F., "Love in Infant Monkeys," *Scientific American,* **200,** 6 (1959), pp. 68–74.

Harlow, H. F., "Sexual Behavior in the Rhesus Monkey," in Beach, F. (ed.), *Sex and Behavior,* New York: Wiley and Sons, Inc., 1965.

Harlow, H. F., and Harlow, M. K., " Learning to Love," *The American Scientist,* **54** (1966), pp. 244–272.

Harlow, H. F., and Suomi, S. J., "Nature of Love-Simplified," *American Psychologist,* **25** (1970), pp. 161–168.

Harlow, H. F., and Zimmerman, R. R., "Affectional Responses in the Infant Monkey," *Science,* **130** (1959), pp. 421–432.

Hastorf, A. H., and Cantril, H., "They Saw a Game: a Case Study," *Journal of Abnormal and Social Psychology,* **29** (1954), pp. 129–134.

Hayes, Catherine, *The Ape in Our House,* New York: Harper and Row Publishers, 1951.

Heath, R. G., "A Biochemical Hypothesis on the Etiology of Schizophrenia," in Jackson, D. D. (ed.), *The Etiology of Schizophrenia,* New York: Basic Books, 1960.

Heath, R., and Mickle, W., "Evaluation of Seven Years Experience with Depth Electrode Studies in Human Patients," in Ramey, E. R., and O'Doherty, D. (eds.), *Electrical Studies on the Unanesthetized Brain,* New York: Hoeber Medical Div., Harper and Row Publishers, 1960, pp. 214–247.

Heidbreder, E., "The Attainment of Concepts: I. Terminology and Methodology," *Journal of General Psychology,* **35** (1946), pp. 173–189.

Heidbreder, E., "The Attainment of Concepts: III. The Problem," *Journal of Psychology,* **24** (1947), pp. 93–138.

Henderson, D., Gillespie, R. D., and Batchelor, I. R. C., *Textbook of Psychiatry* (9th ed.), London: Oxford University Press, 1962.

Hernandez-Peon, R., Scherrer, H., and Jouvet, M., "Modification of Electric Activity in Cochlear Nucleus During 'Attention' in Unanesthetized Cats," *Science,* **123** (1956), pp. 331–332.

Heron, W. T., and Skinner, B. F., "Changes in Hunger During Starvation," *Psychological Record,* **1** (1937), pp. 51–60.

Hess, E. H., "Imprinting in Animals," *Scientific American,* **198,** 3 (1958), pp. 81–90.

Hess, E. H., and Polt, J. M., "Pupil Size as Related to Interest Value of Visual Stimuli," *Science,* **132** (1960), pp. 349–350.

Hess, E. H., Seltzer, A. L., and Shlien, J. M., "Pupil Response of Hetero- and Homosexual Males to Pictures of Men and Women: a Pilot Study," *Journal of Abnormal Psychology,* **70,** 3 (1965), pp. 165–168.

Hollister, L. E., "Marihuana in Man: Three Years Later," *Science,* **172** (1971), pp. 21–29.

Horowitz, E. L., and Horowitz, R. E., "Development of Social Attitudes in Children," *Sociometry,* **1** (1938), pp. 301–338.

Horowitz, M. J., "Flashbacks: Recurrent Intrusive Images after the Use of LSD," *American Journal of Psychiatry,* **126,** 4 (1969), pp. 147–151.

Hovland, C. I., "Experimental Studies in Rote-Learning Theory III. Distribution of Practice with Varying Speeds of Syllable Presentation," *Journal of Experimental Psychology,* **23** (1938), pp. 172–190.

Hovland, C. I., Janis, I., and Kelly, H., *Communication and Persuasion,* New Haven, Conn.: Yale University Press, 1953.

Hovland, C. I., Lumsdaine, A., and Sheffield, F., *Experiments on Mass Communication,* Princeton, N.J.: Princeton University Press, 1949.

Hovland, C. I., and Weiss, W., "The Influence of Source Credibility on Communication Effectiveness," *Public Opinion Quarterly,* **15** (1951), pp. 635–650.

James, M., and Jongeward, D., *Born to Win,* Reading, Mass.: Addison-Wesley Publishing Co., 1971.

James, W., *The Principles of Psychology* Vols. I and II, New York: Holt, 1890.

Janis, I. L., and Feshback, S., "Effects of Fear-Arousing Communications," *Journal of Abnormal and Social Psychology,* **48** (1953), pp. 78–92.

Janis, I. L., and King, B. T., "The Influence of Role Playing on Attitude Change," *Journal of Abnormal and Social Psychology,* **99** (1954), pp. 211–218.

Jenkins, J. G., and Dallenbach, K. M., "Oblivescence During Sleep and Waking," *American Journal of Psychology,* **35** (1924), pp. 605–612.

Jenkins, W. O., "A Review of Leadership Studies with Particular Reference to Military Problems," *Psychological Bulletin,* **44** (1947), pp. 54–79.

Jenkins, W. O., McFann, H., and Clayton, F. L., "A Methodological Study of Extinction Following Aperiodic and Continuous Reinforcement," *Journal of Comparative and Physiological Psychology,* **43** (1950), pp. 155–167.

Jennings, M. K., and Niemi, R. G., "The Transmission of Political Values from Parent to Child," *American Political Science Review,* **62** (1968), pp. 169–184.

Johnson, H. M., Swan, T. H., and Weigand, G. E., "In What Position do Healthy People Sleep?" *Journal of American Medical Association,* **94** (1930), pp. 2058–2068.

Jones, H. E., and Jones, M. C., "Fear," *Childhood Education,* **5,** 3 (1928), pp. 136–143.

Jones, M. C., "The Elimination of Children's Fear," *Journal of*

Experimental Psychology, **7** (1924), pp. 382–390.

Jouvet, M., "Recherches sur les Structures Nerveuses et les Mecanismes Responsables de Différentes Phases du Sommeil Physiologique," *Archives Italiennes de Biologie,* **100** (1962), pp. 125–206.

Jung, C. G., *Psychological Types,* New York: Harcourt Brace Jovanovich, 1923.

Kahn, M., "The Physiology of Catharsis," *Journal of Personality and Social Psychology,* **3** (1966), pp. 278–286.

Kamiya, J., "Operant Control of the EEG Alpha Rhythm and Some of its Reported Effects on Consciousness," in Tart, C. (ed.), *Altered States of Consciousness,* New York: Wiley and Sons, Inc., 1969.

Karlins, M., Coffman, T. L., and Walters, G., "On the Fading of Social Stereotypes: Studies in Three Generations of College Students," *Journal of Personality and Social Psychology,* **13** (1969), pp. 1–16.

Katona, G., *Organizing and Memorizing,* New York: Columbia University Press, 1940.

Katz, D., and Braly, K. W., "Racial Stereotypes of 100 College Students," *Journal of Abnormal and Social Psychology,* **28** (1933), pp. 280–290.

Kellogg, W. N., and Kellogg, L. A., *The Ape and the Child: A Study of Environmental Influence on Early Behavior,* New York: Hafner Publishing Co., 1967 (Originally published by McGraw-Hill Book Co., New York, 1933.)

"Kerner" Commission, *Report of the U.S. National Advisory Commission in Civil Disorders,* Washington, D.C.: U.S. Government Printing Office, 1968.

King, B. T., and Janis, I. L., "Comparison of the Effectiveness of Improvised Versus Nonimprovised Role-Playing in Producing Changes," *Human Relations,* **9** (1956), pp. 177–186.

Kinsey, A. C., Pomeroy, W. B., and Martin, C. E., *Sexual Behavior in the Human Male,* Philadelphia: W. B. Saunders Co., 1948.

Kinsey, A. C., Pomeroy, W. B., Martin, C. E., and Gebhard, P. H., *Sexual Behavior in the Human Female,* Philadelphia: W. B. Saunders Co., 1953.

Kisker, G. W., *The Disorganized Personality,* New York: McGraw-Hill Book Co., 1964.

Klineberg, O., "Emotional Expression in Chinese Literature," *Journal of Abnormal and Social Psychology,* **33** (1938), pp. 517–520.

Kogan, N., and Wallach, M. A., "Risk Taking as a Function of the Situation, the Person, and the Group," in Mandler, G., et al., *New Directions in Psychology,* Vol. 3, New York: Holt, Rinehart and Winston, 1967.

Kohn, M. L., "Social Class and Parent-Child Relationships: an Interpretation," *American Sociological Review,* **68** (1963), pp. 471–480.

Krueger, W. C. F., "The Effect of Overlearning on Retention," *Journal of Experimental Psychology,* **12** (1929), pp. 71–78.

Kuhne, W., 1878, cited in Wald, G., "The Eye and Camera," *Scientific American,* **183,** 2 (1950), pp. 32–41.

Lally, J. R., *Development of a Day Care Center for Young Children,* Syracuse University Children's Center Progress Report. February, 1971.

Landreth, C., *Early Childhood: Behavior and Learning,* New York: Alfred A. Knopf, 1967.

Lang, P., "Autonomic Control," *Psychology Today,* **4,** 5 (1970), pp. 37–41.

Lang, P. J., and Melamed, B. G., "Avoidance Conditioning Therapy of an Infant with Chronic Ruminative Vomiting," *Journal of Abnormal Psychology,* **74** (1969), pp. 1–8.

Latané, B., and Darley, J. M., "Bystander 'Apathy,'" *American Scientist,* **57** (1969), pp. 244–268.

Laughlin, H. P., *The Neuroses,* Washington: Butterworths, 1967.

Leavitt, H. J., "Some Effects of Certain Communication Patterns on Group Performance," *Journal of Abnormal and Social Psychology,* **46** (1951), pp. 38–50.

Lee, E. S., "Negro Intelligence and Selective Migration: A Philadelphia Test of the Klineberg Hypothesis," *American Sociological Review,* **16** (1951), pp. 227–233.

Lennenberg, E. H., "On Explaining Language," *Science,* **164,** 3880 (1969), pp. 635–643.

Lewin, K., *A Dynamic Theory of Personality,* New York: McGraw-Hill Book Co., 1935.

Lieberman, M. A., Yallum, I. D., and Miles, M. D., "The Group Experience Project: a Comparison of Ten Encounter Technologies," in Bank, L., Gottsegen, G. G. and Gottsegen, M. G., (eds.), *Encounter: Confrontations in Self and Interpersonal Awareness,* New York: Macmillan, Co., 1971.

Lieberman, P., "Primate Vocalizations and Human Linguistic Ability," *Journal of the Acoustical Society of America,* **44** (1968), pp. 1574–1584.

Lindgren, H. C., *Educational Psychology in the Classroom,* New York: John Wiley and Sons Inc., 1956.

Lovaas, O. I., "Some Studies on the Treatment of Childhood Schizophrenia," in Shuen, J. M. (ed.), *Research in Psychotherapy,* Washington, D.C.: American Psychological Association, 1968, pp. 103–129.

Luchins, A. S., "Mechanization in Problem Solving. The Effect of Einstelling," *Psychological Monographs,* **54,** 248 (1942).

Luh, C. W., "The Conditions of Retention," *Psychological Monographs,* **31,** 22 (1922).

Luria, A. R., "The Functional Organization of the Brain," *Scientific American,* **222,** 3 (1971), pp. 66–78.

Lyon, D. O., "The Relation of Length of Material to Time Taken for Learning and the Optimum Distribution of Time," *Journal of Educational Psychology,* **5** (1914), pp. 1–9, 85–91, 155–163.

Madaras, G. R., and Bem, D. J., "Risk and Conservatism in Group Decision-Making," *Journal of Experimental Social Psychology,* **4** (1968), pp. 350–365.

Madsen, C. H., Jr., Becker, W. C., Thomas, D. R., Koser, L., and Plager, E., "An Analysis of the Reinforcing Function of 'Sit Down' Commands," in Parker, R. K. (ed.), *Readings in Educational Psychology,* Boston: Allyn and Bacon, 1968.

Mallick, S. K., and McCandless, B. R., "A Study of Catharsis of Aggression," *Journal of Personality and Social Psychology,* **4** (1966), pp. 591–596.

Mann, L., "The Social Psychology of Waiting Lines," *American Scientist,* **58,** 4 (1970), pp. 390–398.

Mann, R. D., "A Review of the Relationship Between Personality and Performance in Small Groups," *Psychological Bulletin,* **56** (1959), pp. 241–270.

Marañon, G., "Contribution a l' Étude de l'Action Émotive de l'Adrénaline," *Revue Française d'Endocrinologie,* **2** (1924), pp. 301–325.

Marks, J. M., *Patterns in Meaning in Psychiatric Patients,* London: Oxford University Press, 1965.

Masserman, J. H., *Principles of Dynamic Psychiatry,* Philadelphia: W. B. Saunders Company, 1961.

Masters, W. H., and Johnson, V. E., *Human Sexual Response,* Boston: Little, Brown, 1966.

Masters, W. H., and Johnson, V. E., *Human Sexual Inadequacy,* Boston: Little, Brown, 1970.

McCarthy, D., "Language Development in Children," in Carmichael, L. (ed.), *Manual of Child Psychology* (2nd ed.), New York: Wiley and Sons, Inc., 1954, pp. 492–630.

McCary, J. L., *Human Sexuality,* Princeton, N.J.: Van Nostrand, 1967.

McClelland, D. C., "Business Drive and National Achievement," *Harvard Business Review,* July-August 1962, pp. 99–112.

McClelland, D. C., "The Power of Positive Drinking," *Psychology Today,* **4,** 8 (1971), pp. 40–41, 78–79.

McConnell, J. V., Jacobson, A. L., and Kimble, D. P., "The Effect of Regeneration upon Retention of a Conditioned Response in the Planarian," *Journal of Comparative and Physiological Psychology,* **52** (1959), pp. 1–5.

McFadden, E. R., Jr., Luparello, T., Lyons, H. A., and Bleeker, E., "The Mechanisms of Action of Suggestion in the Induction of Acute Asthma Attacks," *Psychosomatic Medicine,* **31,** 2 (1969), pp. 134–143.

McGeoch, J. A., "The Influence of Associative Value upon the Difficulty of Nonsense-Syllable Lists," *Journal of Genetic Psychology,* **37** (1930), pp. 421–426.

McGlothlin, W. H., and Arnold, D. O., "LSD Revisited: A Ten Year Follow-up of Medical LSD Use," *Archives of General Psychiatry,* **24** (1971), pp. 35–49.

McGrew, J., "How Open are Multiple Dwelling Units?"

Journal of Social Psychology, **72** (1967), pp. 233–236.

McGuire, W. J., "A Syllogistic Analysis of Cognitive Relationships," in Hovland, C. I., and Janis, I. L. (eds.), *Attitude Organization and Change,* New Haven: Yale University Press, 1960.

McNemar, Q., *The Revision of the Stanford-Binet Scale,* Boston: Houghton Mifflin, 1942.

Mead, M., "Sex and Temperament," in *From the South Seas,* New York: Morrow, 1939.

Mees, C. E. K., "Scientific Thought and Social Reconstruction," *Electrical Engineering,* **53** (1934), pp. 383–384.

Menninger, K., *Theory of Psychoanalytic Technique,* New York: Basic Books, 1958.

Milgram, S., "Behavioral Study of Obedience," *Journal of Abnormal and Social Psychology,* **67** (1963), pp. 371–378.

Miller, G. A., *Language and Communication,* New York: McGraw-Hill Book Co., 1951.

Miller, N. E., "The Frustration-Aggression Hypothesis," *Psychological Review,* **48** (1941), pp. 337–342.

Miller, N. E., "Experimental Studies of Conflict," in Hunt, J.McV. (ed.), *Personality and the Behavior Disorders,* Vol. I, New York: Ronald Press, 1944, pp. 431–465.

Miller, N. E., "Studies of Fear as an Acquirable Drive: 1. Fear as Motivation and Fear-Reduction as Reinforcement in the Learning of New Responses," *Journal of Experimental Psychology,* **38** (1948), pp. 89–101.

Miller, N. E., "Experiments on Motivation: Studies Combining Psychological, Physiological and Pharmacological Techniques," *Science,* **126** (1957), pp. 1271–1278.

Miller, N. E., "Central Stimulation and Other New Approaches to Motivation and Reward," *American Psychologist,* **13** (1958), pp. 100–108.

Miller, N. E., "Liberalization of Basic S-R Concepts: Extensions to Conflict Behavior, Motivation, and Social Learning," in Koch, S. (ed.), *Psychology: A Study of a Science,* Vol. II, New York: McGraw-Hill Book Co., 1959, pp. 196–292.

Miller, N. E., "Learning of Visceral and Glandular Responses," *Science,* **163** (1969), pp. 434–445.

Miller, N. E., and Bugelski, R., "Minor Studies in Aggression: II. The Influence of Frustrations Imposed by the In-Group on Attitudes Expressed Toward Out-Groups," *Journal of Psychology,* **25** (1948), pp. 437–442.

Milner, B., "The Memory Deficit in Bilateral Hippocampal Lesions," *Psychiatric Research Reports,* **11** (1959), pp. 43–52.

More, A. J., "Delay of Feedback and the Acquisition and Retention of Verbal Materials in the Classroom," *Journal of Educational Psychology,* **60** (1969), pp. 339–342.

Nakazima, S. A., "A Comparative Study of the Speech Developments of Japanese and American English in Childhood. II. The Acquisition of Speech," *Studia Phonologica,* **4** (1966), pp. 38–55.

National Institute of Mental Health, *The Mental Health of Urban America,* Washington D.C.: Public Health Service Publication No. 1906, 1969.

Newcomb, T. M., *Personality and Social Change,* New York: Dryden Press Inc., 1943.

Newcomb, T. M., "Persistence and Regression of Changed Attitudes: Long Range Studies," *Journal of Social Issues,* **19** (1963), pp. 3–14.

Newman, H. H., Freeman, F. N., and Holzinker, K. J., *Twins: a Study of Heredity and Environment,* Chicago: University of Chicago Press, 1937.

Neymann, C., and Yacorzynski, G., "Studies of Introversion-Extraversion and Conflict of Motives in Psychoses," *Journal of Genetic Psychology,* **27** (1942), pp. 241–255.

Norman, W. T., *2800 Personality Trait Descriptors: Normative Operating Characteristics for a University Population,* Ann Arbor: Department of Psychology, University of Michigan, April, 1967.

Noyes, A. P., and Kolb, L. C., *Modern Clinical Psychiatry,* Philadelphia: W. B. Saunders Co., 1963.

Olds, J., and Milner, P., "Positive Reinforcement Produced by Electrical Stimulation of Septal Area and Other Regions of Rat Brain," *Journal of Comparative and Physiological Psychology,* **47** (1954), pp. 419–427.

Osborn, A. F., *Applied Imagination* (Rev. ed.), New York: Scribner, 1957.

Osgood, C. E., *Method and Theory in Experimental Psychology,* New York: Oxford University Press, 1953.

Paivio, A., "Mental Imagery in Associative Learning and Memory," *Psychological Review,* **76** (1969), pp. 241–263.

Palmer, R. J., and Masling, J., "Vocabulary for Skin Color in Negro and White Children," *Developmental Psychology,* **1** (1969), pp. 396–401.

Pankove, E., and Kogan, N., "Creative Ability and Risk-Taking in Elementary School Children," *Journal of Personality,* **36** (1968), pp. 420–439.

Parke, R. D., "Effectiveness of Punishment as an Interaction of Intensity, Timing, Agent Nurturance and Cognitive Structuring," *Child Development,* **40,** 1 (1969), pp. 213–235.

Parke, R. D., and Walters, R. H., "Some Factors Determining the Efficacy of Punishment for Inducing Response Inhibition," *Monographs of the Society for Research in Child Development,* **32,** 109 (1967).

Parmelee, A. H., "Diagnostic and Intervention Studies of High-Risk Infants," Third Year Contract Proposal (NIH-NICHD 71-2447), March 1973.

Parmelee, A. H., and Haber, A., "Who is the Risk Infant?" *Clinical Obstetrics and Gynecology,* **16,** 1 (1973), pp. 376–387.

Parmelee, A. H., Jr., and Liverman, L., "Prematurity," in Green, M., and Haggerty, R. J. (eds.), *Ambulatory Pediatrics,* New York: W. B. Saunders Co., 1968, pp. 312–324.

Parmelee, A. H., Schultz, H. R., and Dislrow, M. A., "Sleep Patterns in the Newborn," *Journal of Pediatrics,* **58** (1961), pp. 241–250.

Pavlov, I. P., *Conditioned Reflexes,* New York: Oxford University Press, 1927.

Peck, M. L., and Schrut, A., "Suicidal Behavior Among College Students," *HSMHA Health Reports,* **86,** 2 (1971), pp. 149–156.

Penfield, W., *The Excitable Cortex in Conscious Man,* Springfield, Ill.: Charles C. Thomas, 1958.

Penfield, W., "The Interpretive Cortex," *Science,* **129** (1959), pp. 1719–1725.

Peterson, Ruth C., *Scale of Attitude Toward War,* Chicago: University of Chicago Press, 1931.

Peterson, L. R., and Peterson, Margaret T., "Short-Term Retention of Individual Verbal Items," *Journal of Experimental Psychology,* **58** (1959), pp. 193–198.

Piaget, J., *The Origins of Intelligence in Children,* New York: International Universities Press, Inc., 1952.

Pines, Maya, "A Child's Mind is Shaped before Age 2," *Life Magazine,* December 17, 1971, pp. 63, 67–68, 71, 90.

Pollard, J. C., Uhr. L., and Stern, Elizabeth, *Drugs and Phantasy,* Boston: Little, Brown and Co., 1965.

Postman, L., and Ra, Lucy, "Retention as a Function of the Method of Measurement," *University of California Publication in Psychology,* Berkeley, **8** (1957), pp. 217–270.

Prechtl, H., and Beintema, D., "The Neurological Examination of the Fullterm Newborn Infant," *Little Club Clinics in Developmental Medicine,* No. 12. London: Spastics Society Medical Information Unit and Wm. Heinemann Medical Books, Ltd., 1964.

Premack, A. J., and Premack, D., "Teaching Language to an Ape," *Scientific American,* **226** (1972), pp. 92–99.

Radke, M. J., Trager, H. G., and Davis, H., "Social Perceptions and Attitudes of Children," *Genetic Psychology Monographs,* **40** (1949), pp. 327–347.

"Redefining Violence," *Time,* June 14, 1971, p. 49.

Reid, J. E., and Inbau, F. E., *Truth and Deception,* Baltimore: The Williams and Wilkins Co., 1966.

Reynolds, G. S., *Primer of Operant Conditioning,* Glenview, Ill.: Scott, Foresman, and Co., 1968.

Rice, Richard A., "System Energy and Future Transportation," *Technological Review,* 1972.

Robinson, F. P., *Effective Study* (Rev. ed.), New York: Harper and Row Publishers, 1961.

Rocks, L., and Runyon, R. P., *The Energy Crisis,* New York: Crown Publishing Co., 1972.

Roffwarg, H. P., Muzio, J. N., and Dement, W. C., "Ontogenetic Development of the Human Sleep-Dream Cycle," *Science,* **152** (1966), pp. 604–619.

Rogers, C. R., "The Therapeutic Relationship: Recent Theory and Research," in Sarason, I. G. (ed.), *Contemporary Research in Personality,* Princeton, N.J.: Van Nostrand Inc., 1969.

Rorvik, D., "How to Relieve Headaches by Warming your Hands," *Journal,* June, 1972, pp. 82–83.

Rosen, E., and Gregory, I., *Abnormal Psychology,* Philadelphia: W. B. Saunders Co., 1965.

Rosenberg, M. S., "Cognitive Reorganization in Response to the Hypnotic Reversal of Affect," *Journal of Personality,* **28** (1960), pp. 39–63.

Rosenthal, R., *Experimenter Effects in Behavioral Research,* New York: Appleton-Century-Crofts, 1966.

Routtenberg, A., and Lindy, J., "Effects of the Availability of Rewarding Septal and Hypothalmic Stimulation on

Bar-Pressing for Food under Conditions of Deprivation," *Journal of Comparative and Physiological Psychology,* **60** (1965), pp. 158–161.

Rude, G., *The Crowd in History: A Study of Popular Disturbances in France and England, 1730–1848,* New York: Wiley and Sons, Inc., 1964.

Runyon, R. P., and Rocks, L., "The Energy Crisis: A Perspective," Address given before the Academy of Political Science, July 19, 1973. (*Proceedings* in press.)

Sarason, I. G., and Sarason, B., "Effects of Motivating Instructions and Reports of Failure on Verbal Learning," *American Journal of Psychology,* **70** (1957), pp. 92–96.

Schachtel, E. G., *Metamorphosis,* New York: Basic Books, 1959.

Schachter, S., "Obesity and Eating," *Science,* **150** (1965), pp. 971–979.

Schachter, S., and Gross, L., "Manipulated Time and Eating Behavior," *Journal of Personality and Social Psychology,* **10** (1968), pp. 98–106.

Schachter, S., and Singer, J. E., "Cognitive, Social and Physiological Determinants of Emotional State," *Psychological Review,* **69** (1962), pp. 379–399.

Schaefer, E. S., and Aaronson, M., "Infant Education Research

Project," Paper presented at the conference: Conceptualizations of Preschool Curricula, Center for Advanced Study in Education, the City University of New York, May, 1970.

Schaefer, H. H., "Accepted Theories Disproven," *Science News,* **99,** 11 (1971), p. 182.

Schaffer, H. R., and Emerson, P., "Patterns of Response to Physical Contact in Early Human Development," *Journal of Child Psychology and Psychiatry,* **5** (1965), pp. 1–13.

Schaller, G. B., *The Mountain Gorilla,* Chicago: University of Chicago Press, 1963.

Schellenberg, J. A., *An Introduction to Social Psychology,* New York: Random House, 1970.

Schlosberg, H., "The Description of Facial Expressions in Terms of Two Dimensions," *Journal of Experimental Psychology,* **44** (1952), pp. 229–237.

Schlosberg, H., "Three Dimensions of Emotion," *Psychological Review,* **61** (1954), pp. 81–88.

Sears, R. R., "Experimental Studies of Projection: I. Attribution of Traits," *Journal of Social Psychology,* **7** (1936), pp. 151–163.

Sears, R. R., Maccoby, Eleanor E., and Levin, H., *Patterns of Child Rearing,* Evanston, Ill.: Row, Peterson, 1957.

Sears, R. R., Whiting, J. W. M., Nowlis, V., and Sears, P. S., "Some Child Rearing Antecedents of Aggression and Dependency in Young Children," *Genetic Psychology Monographs,* **47** (1953), pp. 135–234.

Seiden, R. H., "Campus Tragedy: the Study of Student Suicide," *Journal of Abnormal Psychology,* **71** (1966), pp. 389–399.

Seiden, R. H., "We're Driving Young Blacks to Suicide," *Psychology Today,* **4** (1970), pp. 24–28.

Seligman, M. E. P., Maier, S. F., and Solomon, R. L., "Unpredictable and Uncontrollable Aversive Events," in Brush, F. R. (ed.), *Aversive Conditioning and Learning,* New York: Academic Press, 1969.

Shaffer, L. F., and Shoben, E. J., *The Psychology of Adjustment* (2nd ed.), Boston: Houghton Mifflin Co., 1956.

Shaw, M. E., "Communication Networks," in Berkowitz, L. (ed.), *Advances in Experimental Social Psychology,* New York: Academic Press, 1964, *I,* pp. 111–147.

Sherman, M. C., and Sherman, I. C., *The Process of Human Behavior,* New York: W. W. Norton, 1929.

Shiffrin, R. M., "Forgetting: Trace Erosion or Retrieval Failure?" *Science,* **168** (1970), pp. 1601–1603.

Shirley, M. M., *The First Two Years,* Institute of Child Welfare, Monograph No. 7, Minneapolis: University of Minnesota Press, 1933.

Shoben, E. J., Jr., "Toward a Concept of the Normal Personality," *American Psychologist,* **12** (1957), pp. 183–189.

Simon, C. W., and Emmons, W. H., "Responses to Material Presented During Various Levels of Sleep," *Journal of Experimental Psychology,* **51** (1956), pp. 89–97.

Siqueland, E. R., "Biological and Experimental Determinants of Exploration in Infancy," Paper presented at the First National Biological Conference, 1970.

Skeels, H. M., "Adult Status of Children with Contrasting Early Life Experiences: a Follow-Up Study," *Monographs of the Society for Research in Child Development,* **31,** 105 (1966), pp. 1–65.

Skinner, B. F., *Verbal Behavior,* New York: Appleton-Century-Crofts, 1957.

Smith, A., and Burklund, C. W., "Dominant Hemispherectomy: Preliminary Report on

Neuropsychological Sequelae," *Science,* **153,** 3741 (1966), pp. 1280–1282.

Snyder, S. H., "What we have Forgotten about Pot—a Pharmacologist's History," *New York Times Magazine,* December 13, 1970.

Snyder, S., and Lampanella, V., "Psychedelic Experiences in Hysterical Psychosis and Schizophrenia," *Communications in Behavioral Biology,* **3** (1969), pp. 85–91.

Snyder, W. U., *Casebook of Non-Directive Counseling,* Boston: Houghton Mifflin, 1947.

Sperry, R. W., "Hemisphere Deconnection and Unity in Conscious Awareness," *American Psychologist,* **23** (1968), pp. 723–733.

Spiro, M. E., *Children of the Kibbutz,* Cambridge: Harvard University Press, 1958.

Spitz, R. A., "Hospitalism: an Inquiry into the Genesis of Psychiatric Conditions in Early Childhood," *Psychoanalytic Study of the Child,* **1** (1945), pp. 53–74.

Stark, R., and McEvoy, J., III., "Middle-Class Violence," *Psychology Today,* **4,** 6 (1970), pp. 52–54, 110–112.

Sternbach, R., "Congenital Insensitivity to Pain," *Psychological Bulletin,* **60** (1963), pp. 252–264.

Stone, L. J., and Church, J., *Childhood and Adolescence* (3rd ed.), New York: Random House, 1973.

Stoner, J. A. F., "A Comparison of Individual and Group Decisions Involving Risk," Unpublished master's thesis, Massachusetts Institute of Technology, 1961.

Suinn, R. M., *Fundamentals of Behavior Pathology,* New York: Wiley and Sons, Inc., 1970.

Suinn, R. M., "The Application of Short-Term Video-Tape Therapy for the Treatment of Test Anxiety of College Students," Unpublished report, Colorado State University, 1971.

Supa, M., Cotzin, M., and Dallenbach, K. M., "Facial Vision: the Perception of Obstacles by the Blind," *American Journal of Psychology,* **57** (1944), pp. 133–183.

Szondi, L., Moser, U., and Webb, M. W., *The Szondi Test,* Philadelphia: J. B. Lippincott Co., 1959.

Taylor, D. W., Berry, P. C., and Block, C. H., "Does Group Participation When Using Brainstorming Facilitate or Inhibit Creative Thinking?" Technical Report No. 1, 1957. Yale University, Department of Psychology, Office of Naval Research.

Teitlebaum, P., "Appetite," *Proceedings of the American*

Philosophical Society, **108** (1964), pp. 464–472.

Telfer, M. A., Baker, D., Clarke, G. R., and Richardson, C. E., "Incidence of Gross Chromosomal Errors Among Tallcriminal American Males," *Science,* **159** (1967), pp. 1249–1250.

Terman, L. M. (ed.), *Genetic Studies of Genius,* Vol. I, Stanford, Calif.: Stanford University Press, 1925.

Terman, L. M., and Merril, M. A., *Stanford-Binet Intelligence Scale,* Boston: Houghton-Mifflin Co., 1960.

Terman, L. M., and Oden, M. H., *The Gifted Child Grows Up,* Stanford, Calif.: Stanford University Press, 1947.

Terman, L. M., and Oden, M. H., *Genetic Studies of Genius, Vol. V. The Gifted Child at Midlife,* Stanford, Calif.: Stanford University Press, 1959.

Thigpen, C., and Cleckley, H. M., "A Case of Multiple Personality," *Journal of Abnormal and Social Psychology,* **49** (1954), pp. 135–151.

Thomas, W. I., *Primitive Behavior: an Introduction to the Social Sciences,* New York: McGraw-Hill, 1937.

Thompson, T., "Richie," *Life,* May 5, 1972, pp. 58–72.

Thorndike, E. L., *The Fundamentals of Learning,* New

York: Teachers' College Press, 1932.

Thorndike, R. L., "The Effect of Discussion upon the Correctness of Group Decisions When the Factor of Majority Influence is Allowed For," *Journal of Social Psychology,* **9** (1938), pp. 343–362.

Turkewitz, G., Birch, H. G., Moreau, T., Levy, L., and Cornwell, A. C., "Effect of Intensity of Auditory Stimulation on Directional Eye Movements in the Human Neonate," *Animal Behavior,* **14** (1966), pp. 93–101.

Turnbull, J. W., "Asthma Conceived as a Learned Response," *Journal of Psychosomatic Research,* **6** (1962), pp. 59–70.

Tyler, R. W., "Permanence of Learning," *Journal of Higher Education, IV,* April 1933, Table 1, p. 204.

Ullmann, L. P., and Krasner, L., *A Psychological Approach to Abnormal Behavior,* Englewood Cliffs, N.J.: Prentice-Hall Inc., 1969.

Underwood, B. J., "Ten Years of Massed Practice on Distributed Practice," *Psychological Review,* **68** (1961), pp. 229–247.

Wahler, R. G., "Infant Social Development: Some Experimental Analysis of an Infant-Mother Interaction During the First Year of Life,"

Journal of Experimental Child Psychology, **7** (1969), pp. 101–113.

Wallace, W. H., Turner, S. H., and Perkins, C. C., "Preliminary Studies of Human Information Storage," *Signal Corps Project No. 1320,* Institute for Cooperative Research, University of Pennsylvania, 1957.

Wallach, M. A., "Creativity," in Mussen, P. H. (ed.), *Carmichael's Manual of Child Psychology* (3rd ed.), New York: Wiley and Sons, Inc., 1970.

Wallach, M. A., and Wing, C. W., Jr., *The Talented Student: A Validation of the Creativity-Intelligence Distinction,* New York: Holt, Rinehart and Winston, 1969.

Watson, J. B., and Raynor, R., "Conditioned Emotional Reactions," *Journal of Experimental Psychology,* **3** (1920), pp. 1–14.

Webb, W., *Sleep: An Experimental Approach,* New York: MacMillan, 1968.

Wechsler, D., *The Measurement and Appraisal of Adult Intelligence* (4th ed.), Baltimore: Williams and Wilkins, 1958.

Wechsler, H., Grosser, G. H., and Greenblatt, M., "Research Evaluating Anti-Depressant Medications on Hospitalized Mental Patients: a Survey of Published Reports During a 5-year Period," *Journal of*

Nervous and Mental Disease, **141** (1965), pp. 231–239.

Whalen, R. G., "Where Were You the Night of April 23, 1935?" *New York Times Magazine,* December 18, 1949, pp. 18, 25, 27.

Whalen, R., and Edwards, D., "Sexual Reversability in Neonatally Castrated Male Rats," *Journal of Comparative and Physiological Psychology,* **62** (1966), pp. 307–311.

White, B. L., "Fundamental Early Environmental Influences on the Development of Competence," in Meyer, M. E. (ed.), *Third Symposium on Learning: Cognitive Learning.*

White, W. A., *Outline of Psychiatry,* New York: Nervous and Mental Disease Publishing Co., 1932.

Whorf, B. L., "Science and Linguistics," in Newcomb, T. M., and Hartley, E. L., (eds.), *Readings in Social Psychology,* New York: Holt, 1947.

Whorf, B. L., *Language, Thought and Reality,* New York: Wiley and Sons, Inc., 1956.

Wickes, I. G., "Treatment of Persistent Enuresis with the Electric Buzzer," *Archives of Diseases in Childhood,* **33** (1958), pp. 160–164.

Winterbottom, M. R., "The Relation of Childhood Training in Independence to

Achievement Motivation," Unpublished Ph.D. thesis, University of Michigan, 1953. Abstract in Univ. Microfilms, Publication No. 5113.

Wold, C. I., "Characteristics of 26,000 Suicide Prevention Center Patients," *Bulletin of Suicidology,* 6 (1970), pp. 24–28.

Wolf, S., and Wolff, H. G., *Human Gastric Functions,* New York: Oxford University Press, 1947.

Wolff, P. H., "Observations on the Early Development of Smiling," in Ross, B. M. (ed.), *Determinants of Infant Behavior,* Vol. 2, New York: Wiley, 1963.

Wolpe, J., "For Phobia: a Hair of the Hound," *Psychology Today,* 3, 1 (1969), pp. 34–37.

Wyden, B. W., "The Difficult Baby is Born That Way," *New York Times Magazine,* March 21, 1971.

Zelson, C., Rubio, E., and Wasserman, E., "Neonatal Narcotic Addiction: 10 Year Observation," *Pediatrics,* 48 (1971), pp. 178–189.

INDEX

Definitions of terms can be found on the pages indicated by boldface type.

Schultz, H. R., 360
Scott, T. H., 501
Sears, P. S., 438
Sears, R. R., 111, 438, 448
Secondary reinforcement, 101–103, **120**, 151
   token economy, 527–528, **537**
   tokens, 102–103
Seiden, R. H., 599, 600
Self
   ideal, 522, **536**
   phenomenal, 522, **536**
Seligman, M. E. P., 111
Seltzer, A. L., 266
Senility, 504, **537**
Sensation, 292–301
   measuring, 293–294
Sensory
   adaptation, 294, **333**
   deprivation, 242, 258, 501
Sensory-motor period, 368, **380**
Serial-anticipation learning, 159–160, **190**
Set, 215–216, 217, 218, **222**, **333**
   and attention, 307–308
   learning, 184, **189**
Sex determination, 340–341
Sex drive, 237–240
Sexual behavior
   and age, 239–240
   cultural differences in attitudes, 238–239
   Freud's concept of sexuality, 463
Shader, R., 532
Shaffer, L. F., 519
Shaping, 95–98, **120**
   superstitious behavior, 97–98, **120**
Shaw, M. E., 552
Sheffield, F., 574
Sherman, I. C., 278
Sherman, M. C., 278
Shiffrin, R. M., 141
Shirley, M. M., 367
Shlien, J. M., 266
Shneidman, E. S., 598
Shoben, E. J., 487, 519

Short-term memory (STM), 138–140, **146**
Similarity, in perception, 312, 333
Simon, C. W., 19, 20
Singer, J. E., 274
Siqueland, E. R., 363
Skeels, H. M., 404, 405
Skinner, B. F., 93, 205, 229
Skinner box, 93, 94
Sleep
   drive, 234–236
   and hypothalamus, 235
   and learning, 17–22
   measurement of, 20, 61–64
   REM, 63–64, 360
   stages of, 61–63
Smith, A., 44
Snyder, S. H., 585, 590
Snyder, W. U. 521
Social motives, 248–255, **258**
   achievement, 252–254, 257
   approval, 254–255, 257
   dependency, 254, **257**
Social
   psychologist, 11, 12–13, **30**, 542
   psychology, **578**
Socialization, 542–543, **578**
Soloman, R. L., 111
Somatic nervous system, 54, 55, **74**
Sperry, R. W., 43
Spinal cord, 35, 52, **74**
Spiro, M. E., 371
Spitz, R. A., 349
Split-brain, 42–45, **74**
Spontaneous recovery, **120**
   classical conditioning, 84, 85
   operant conditioning, 98–100
SQ3R method, 176–177, **190**
Standardization, 397, **419**
Stanford–Binet test of intelligence, 385–389
   compared to Wechsler tests, 390, 391
Stark, R., 596
Stern, E., 589
Sternbach, R., 237

Stimulus, 9
   and attention, 302–306
   aversive, 108, 109
   complexity, 244
   conditioned, 83–88, 91, 92, 98, **118**
   generalized, 88
   needs, 227, 241–246, **258**
   negative, 88, 90
   neutral, 83–86
   positive, 88, 90
   unconditioned, 83–86, 90–93, 95, 98, **120**
Stimulus generalization, 89, **120**
   classical conditioning, 86–88
   and concept formation, 208
   operant conditioning, 100, 101
   and transfer of training, 182
Stoner, J. A. F., 555
Stranger anxiety, 371, **380**
Stress, 501, 593
   and the autonomic system, 54–56
   general adaptation syndrome, 279–280
   in psychosomatic disorders, 282, 283, 285, 286
   and regression, 449
Structuralis, 9, **30**
Stuttering, 198
Subcortical structures, 48–51, **74**
Suicide, 598–600
Suinn, R. M., 152, 153, 186, 490, 492, 498, 505, 506, 507, 508, 509, 525
Suomi, S. J., 246
Supa, M., 25
Superego, 462, **482**
Superstitious behavior, 97–98, **120**
Suppression, 442, 452
Survey method, 17, 25, **30**
Sutherland, N. S., 127
Swan, T. H., 63
Symbol, 194, **222**
   and thinking, 210–211
Sympathetic branch, 54–56, **74**, 91

ACKNOWLEDGMENTS

The authors wish to thank the copyright owners for permission to reprint the quotations appearing on the following pages of this text:

14–15: from *The Mountain Gorilla*, by G. B. Schaller, © 1963 by the University of Chicago Press.

16, 92, 444, 445, 494, 501: from *Behavior Pathology*, by Norman Cameron and Ann Magaret. Houghton Mifflin Company, 1951. Reprinted by permission of the publishers.

114: from "The Role of Modeling Processes in Personality Develop-ment," by Albert Bandura, in W. W. Hartup and Nancy L. Smothergill, eds., *The Young Child*. Washington: National Association for the Education of Young Children, 1967.

142: from "The Memory Deficit in Bilateral Hippocampal Lesions," by Brenda Milner. *Psychiatric Research Reports*, 11 (1959).

253: from "Business Drive and National Achievement," by D. C. McClelland. *Harvard Business Review*, July-August, 1962.

274: from "Becoming a Marihuana User," by H. S. Becker. *American Journal of Sociology*, 59 (1953).

324–325: from *Outline of Psychiatry*, by W. A. White. New York: Nervous and Mental Disease Publishing Co., 1932. Reprinted by permission of the Smith-Ely Jellife Trust Co.

349, 350: from "Causes of Retardation Among Institutional Children: Iran," by W. Dennis. *Journal of Genetic Psychology*, 96 (1960).

352: from "A Child's Mind is Shaped Before Age 2," copyright Maya Pines, Life Magazine, © 1971 Time Inc.

353: from *Development of A Day Care Center for Young Children*, by J. R. Lally. Syracuse University Children's Center Progress Report, February 1971.

363: from "Prematurity," by A. H. Parmelee, Jr., and L. Liverman, in M. Green and R. J. Haggerty, eds., *Ambulatory Pediatrics*. New York: W. B. Saunders Co., 1968.

370: from *The Origins of Intelligence in Children*, by Jean Piaget. New York: International Universities Press, Inc., 1952.

375–376, 439: from *Early Childhood: Behavior and Learning*, by Catherine Landreth. New York: Alfred A. Knopf, Inc., 1967.

433: from "Richie," copyright Thomas Thompson, Life Magazine, © 1973 Time Inc.

435: from "An Experiment with Young Children," by R. G. Barker, T. Dembo, and K. Lewin, in R. G. Barker et al., eds., *Child Behavior and Development*. Copyright 1943. Used with permission of McGraw-Hill Book Company.

443, 497: from *Modern Clinical Psychiatry*, by A. P. Noyes and L. C. Kolb. Philadelphia: W. B. Saunders Co., 1963.

446–447: from *To Beg I Am Ashamed* by Sheila Cousins, by permission of the publisher, The Vanguard Press, Inc., copyright 1938 by Vanguard Press. Renewed 1965 by Sheila Cousins.

477: from *Abnormal Psychology*, by E. Rosen and I. Gregory. Philadelphia: W. B. Saunders Co., 1965.

487: from "Toward a Concept of the Normal Personality," by E. J. Shoben, Jr. *American Psychologist*, 12 (1957).

488: from Leonard P. Ullman and Leonard Krasner, *A Psychological Approach to Abnormal Behavior*, © 1969. Reprinted by permission of Prentice-Hall, Inc., Englewood Cliffs, New Jersey.

489–490, 492, 498, 499, 505, 506, 507, 508, 509, 525: from *Fundamentals of Behavior Pathology*, by Richard M. Suinn. Copyright 1970, by John Wiley & Sons, Inc. Reprinted by permission.

495: from *The Disorganized Personality*, by G. W. Kisker. Copyright 1964. Used with permission of McGraw-Hill Book Company.

495–496: from I. M. Marks, *Patterns of Meaning in Psychiatric Patients*, Institute of Psychiatry Maudsley Monograph No. 13. London: Oxford University Press, 1965.

500–501: from "Family Dynamics and Origin of Schizophrenia," by S. Fleck. *Psychosomatic Medicine*, 22 (1960).

511–512: from "Immaturity and Crime," by R. S. Banay. *American Journal of Psychiatry*, 100 (1943).

514: from *Textbook of Psychiatry* (9th ed.), by D. Henderson, R. D. Gillespie, and I. R. C. Batchelor. London: Oxford University Press, 1962.

517: from *Theory of Psychoanalytic Technique*, by Karl Menninger, M.D., © 1958 by Basic Books Inc., Publishers, New York.

518–519: from *The Psychology of Adjustment*, by L. F. Shaffer and E. J. Shoben. Boston: Houghton Mifflin Company, 1956. Reprinted by permission of the publishers.

520–521: from *Casebook of Non-Directive Counseling*, by William U. Snyder. Houghton Mifflin Company, 1947. Reprinted by permission of the publishers.

544–545: from "Sex and Temperament," by M. Mead, in *From the South Seas*. New York: Morrow, 1939.

549: from *An Introduction to Social Psychology*, by J. A. Schellenberg. New York: Random House, 1970.

552: from "Communication Networks," by M. E. Shaw, in L. Berkowitz, ed., *Advances in Experimental Social Psychology*. New York: Academic Press, 1964.

560–561: from "Behavioral Study of Obedience," by S. Milgram. *Journal of Abnormal and Social Psychology*, 67 (1963). Copyright 1963 by the American Psychological Association, and reproduced by permission.

564: from "Development of Social Attitudes in Children," by E. L. Horowitz and R. E. Horowitz. *Sociometry*, 1 (1938).

568–569: from *Dark Ghetto: Dilemmas of Social Power*, by K. B. Clark. New York: Harper and Row, 1965.

582–583: from the Preface of *The Politics of Despair*, by Hadley Cantril, copyright 1958, by Basic Books, Inc., Publishers, New York.

589: from *Drugs and Phantasy*, by J. C. Pollard, L. Uhr, and E. Stern. Boston: Little, Brown, & Co., 1965.

594: from "Bystander 'Apathy', " by B. Latané and J. M. Darley. *American Scientist*, 57 (1969).

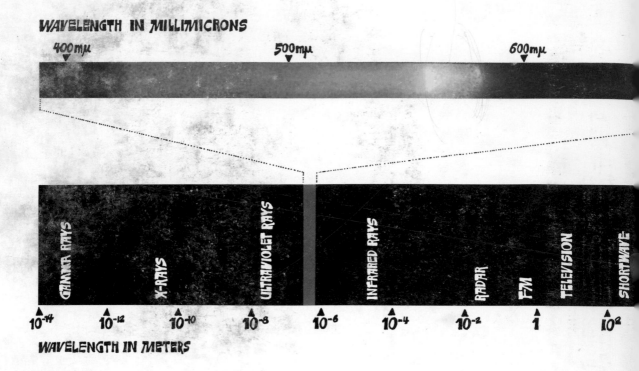

Color Plate I. The Visible Spectrum

The visible spectrum consists of only an infinitesimal portion of the entire electromagnetic spectrum. The range extends from violet to red or from 400 to 700 millimicrons (mμ). A micron is a millionth of a meter. A millimicron is a thousandth of a micron.